T5-AGK-600

ST.
JOSEPH'S
UNIVERSITY
1851
Phil . . Pa.

FOR REFERENCE
Do Not Remove From Library

THE
ANNUAL REGISTER
Vol. 220
WORLD EVENTS IN
1978

ANNUAL REGISTER ADVISORY BOARD

CHAIRMAN AND EDITOR
H. V. HODSON

ASSISTANT EDITOR
BISHAKHA BOSE

CHARLES OSBORNE
Literature Director of the Arts Council of Great Britain
NOMINATED BY
THE ARTS COUNCIL OF GREAT BRITAIN

SIR JOSEPH HUTCHINSON, CMG, ScD, FRS
Drapers' Professor of Agriculture Emeritus, Cambridge
NOMINATED BY
THE BRITISH ASSOCIATION FOR THE ADVANCEMENT OF SCIENCE

M. R. D. FOOT
Formerly Professor of Modern History, University of Manchester
NOMINATED BY
THE ROYAL HISTORICAL SOCIETY

MICHAEL KASER
Fellow of St Antony's College, Oxford
NOMINATED BY
THE ROYAL INSTITUTE OF INTERNATIONAL AFFAIRS

THE LORD ROBBINS, CH, CB
Sometime Professor of Economics at the London School of Economics and Political Science

JAMES BISHOP
Editor, The Illustrated London News

Associated Press

Anti-Shah demonstrators in Teheran, mourning those killed in previous riots in November, display the portrait of their leader Ayatollah Khomeini.

THE
ANNUAL REGISTER

World Events in
1978

Edited by
H. V. HODSON

Assisted by
BISHAKHA BOSE

FIRST EDITED IN 1758
BY EDMUND BURKE

ST. JOSEPH'S UNIVERSITY

ST. JOSEPH'S UNIVERSITY
UNIVERSITY LIBRARY
ST. JOSEPH'S UNIVERSITY 1851 Phil Pa.

0 05907

D
208
.A61
1978

3 9353 00316 1906

ST. MARTIN'S PRESS
NEW YORK
1979

Published in the United States by St. Martin's Press Inc. 1979
© Longman Group Limited 1979
Library of Congress Catalog Card Number 4–17979

PRINTED IN GREAT BRITAIN

CONTENTS

ABBREVIATIONS

AID	Agency for International Development
ASEAN	Association of South-East Asian Nations
AR	Annual Register
CENTO	Central Treaty Organization
CERN	European Organization for Nuclear Research
COMECON	Council for Mutual Economic Assistance
EC	European Community
ECA	Economic Commission for Africa (UN)
ECE	Economic Commission for Europe (UN)
ECOSOC	United Nations Economic and Social Council
ECSC	European Coal and Steel Community
EEC	European Economic Community (Common Market)
EFTA	European Free Trade Association
EMS	European Monetary System
ESCAP	Economic and Social Commission for Asia and the Pacific (UN)
EURATOM	European Atomic Energy Community
FAO	Food and Agriculture Organization
GATT	General Agreement on Tariffs and Trade
GNP	Gross National Product
IAEA	International Atomic Energy Agency
IBRD	International Bank for Reconstruction and Development
ICAO	International Civil Aviation Organization
ICBM	Inter-Continental Ballistic Missile
IDA	International Development Association
IFC	International Finance Corporation
ILO	International Labour Organization
IMF	International Monetary Fund
LAFTA	Latin American Free Trade Association
LDCs	Less Developed Countries
MBFR	Mutual and Balanced Force Reductions
MDCs	More Developed Countries
NATO	North Atlantic Treaty Organization
OAS	Organization of American States
OAU	Organization of African Unity
OECD	Organization for Economic Cooperation and Development
OPEC	Organization of Petroleum Exporting Countries
SALT	Strategic Arms Limitation Talks
TUC	Trades Union Congress
UN	United Nations
UNCTAD	United Nations Conference on Trade and Development
UNDP	United Nations Development Programme
UNESCO	United Nations Educational, Scientific and Cultural Organization
UNFICYP	United Nations Peace-Keeping Force in Cyprus
UNRWA	United Nations Relief and Works Agency
VAT	Value Added Tax
WEU	Western European Union
WHO	World Health Organization

CONTRIBUTORS

Africa, East: Uganda, Tanzania, Kenya
WILLIAM TORDOFF, MA, PH.D
(Professor of Government, University of Manchester)

Africa, North: Algeria, Libya Morocco, Tunisia, Western Sahara
DR ROBIN BIDWELL
(Secretary, Middle East Centre, University of Cambridge)

Africa: French-speaking West and Central Africa, Equatorial Guinea;
O. E. WILTON-MARSHALL
(Writer on African affairs)

Africa: Ethiopia, Somalia, Djibouti
CHRISTOPHER CLAPHAM
(Senior Lecturer in Politics, University of Lancaster)

Africa; former Portuguese territories, Zaïre, Rwanda and Burundi
D. H. JONES, MA
(Senior Lecturer in African History, University of London)

Albania
ANTON LOGORECI, B.SC (ECON)
(Writer and broadcaster on communist affairs)

Arab States of the Middle East: Egypt, Jordan, Syria, Lebanon, Iraq
CHRISTOPHER GANDY
(Formerly UK Diplomatic Service, writer on Middle Eastern affairs)

Saudi Arabia, Yemen and Gulf States
R. M. BURRELL,
(Lecturer in the Contemporary History of the Near and Middle East, School of Oriental and African Studies, University of London)

Australia
GEOFFREY SAWER, BA, LL.M
(Emeritus Professor of Law, Australian National University)

Bangladesh
KEVIN RAFFERTY
(Consultant editor, *Indian Express* group, New Delhi)

Benelux countries
J. D. MCLACHLAN
(Economic analyst and writer specializing in European countries)

Botswana; Lesotho; Swaziland
GERALD SHAW
(Chief Assistant Editor, *The Cape Times*)

Bulgaria
RADA NIKOLAEV
(Head of Bulgarian research section, *Radio Free Europe*)

Canada
BRUCE THORDARSON, BA, MA
(Writer on Canadian affairs)

Caribbean (Commonwealth)
NEVILLE C. DUNCAN, PH.D
(Head, Department of Government and Sociology, University of the West Indies)

China
MICHAEL YAHUDA
(Lecturer in International Relations, London School of Economics and Political Science)

Cyprus
RICHARD SPEAREY
(Editor, *Cyprus Mail*, and writer on Cyprus affairs)

Czechoslovakia
VLADIMIR V. KUSIN, PH.D
(Director, International Information Centre for Soviet and East European Studies, University of Glasgow)

France
MARTIN HARRISON
(Professor of Politics, University of Keele)

Gambia, The
ARNOLD HUGHES, BA
(Lecturer in Political Science, Centre of West African Studies, University of Birmingham)

Germany, West and East
H. N. CROSSLAND
(Bonn correspondent, *The Economist*)

x

Ghana	D. G. AUSTIN
	(Professor of Government, University of Manchester)
Gibraltar	D. G. AUSTIN (see above)
Greece	RICHARD CLOGG, MA
	(King's College, University of London)
Hong Kong	A. S. B. OLVER, MA
	(Specialist in South East Asian affairs)
Hungary	GEORGE SCHÖPFLIN
	(Joint Lecturer in East European Political Institutions at the London School of Economics and the School of Slavonic and East European Studies)
India; Nepal; Afghanistan	PETER LYON, PH.D
	(Reader in International Relations and Secretary, Institute of Commonwealth Studies, University of London)
Iran	KEITH MCLACHLAN, BA, PH.D
	(Senior Lecturer in Geography with reference to the Near and Middle East, School of Oriental and African Studies, University of London)
Ireland, Northern	A. T. Q. STEWART, MA, PH.D
	(Reader in Irish History, Queen's University, Belfast)
Ireland, Republic of	LOUIS MCREDMOND, MA, BL
	(Head of Information in Radio Telefís Eireann, the Irish broadcasting service)
Israel	The Hon. Terence Prittie, MBE, MA
	(Director, Britain and Israel)
Italy	MURIEL GRINDROD, OBE
	(Writer on Italian affairs; formerly Assistant Editor, *The Annual Register*)
Japan	REGINALD CUDLIPP
	(Director, Anglo-Japanese Economic Institute)
Korea	DAVID REES
	(Senior Research Fellow, Institute for the Study of Conflict, London)
Latin America	PETER CALVERT, AM, MA, PH.D
	(Reader in Politics, University of Southampton)
Liberia	ARNOLD HUGHES, BA
	(see The Gambia)
Malagasy	O. E. WILTON-MARSHALL
	(Writer on African affairs)
Malawi	RALPH A. YOUNG
	(Lecturer in Government, University of Manchester)
Malaysia; Singapore; Brunei	MICHAEL LEIFER, BA, PH.D
	(Reader in International Relations, London School of Economics and Political Science)
Malta	D. G. AUSTIN
	(Professor of Government, University of Manchester)
Mongolia	ALAN SANDERS, FIL
	(Far East Regional Editor, British Broadcasting Corporation)
New Zealand	RODERIC ALLEY, PH.D
	(School of Political Science and Public Administration, Victoria University of Wellington)
Nigeria	MARTIN DENT
	(Lecturer, Department of Politics, University of Keele)
Nordic States	T. K. DERRY, OBE, D.PHIL
	(Writer on Nordic history and current affairs)
Pakistan	SALMAN A. ALI
	(Formerly Pakistan Diplomatic Service)
Papua New Guinea	DAVID HEGARTY
	(Senior Lecturer, Department of Political and Administrative Studies, University of Papua New Guinea)

Poland	Z. J. BLAZYNSKI (Writer and broadcaster on Polish and communist affairs)
Portugal	G. A. M. HILLS, BA, D.LIT (Writer and broadcaster on Iberian current affairs and history)
Rhodesia	R. W. BALDOCK, BA, PH.D (Editor-in-chief, Harvester Press; writer on African affairs).
Romania	SYLVIA M. FLORESCU (Specialist on Romanian affairs)
Rwanda and Burundi	D. H. JONES, MA (Senior Lecturer in African History, University of London)
Scandinavian States see Nordic States	
Scotland	PETER GOULDESBROUGH, MA, LL.B (An Assistant Keeper, Scottish Record Office)
Seychelles, BIOT, Mauritius	ROY LEWIS (Journalist and expert on African affairs)
Sierra Leone	ARNOLD HUGHES (see The Gambia)
South-East Asian States (except Malaysia, Singapore, Brunei)	A. S. B. OLVER, MA (Specialist in South-East Asian affairs)
South Africa	GERALD SHAW (Chief Assistant Editor, The Cape Times)
South Pacific	RODERIC ALLEY, PH.D (see New Zealand)
Spain	G. A. M. HILLS (see Portugal)
Sri Lanka	JAMES JUPP, M.SC (ECON), PH.D (Principal Lecturer in Politics, Canberra College of Advanced Education, Australia)
Sudan	AHMED AL-SHAHI, D.PHIL (Lecturer in Social Anthropology, Department of Social Studies, University of Newcastle upon Tyne)
Suriname	NEVILLE C. DUNCAN, PH.D (see Caribbean)
Switzerland	HERMANN BÖSCHENSTEIN, D.PH (Historian and Editor)
Taiwan	BRIAN HOOK (Senior Lecturer in Chinese Studies, University of Leeds)
Turkey	A. J. A. MANGO, BA, PH.D (Orientalist and writer on current affairs in Turkey and the Near East)
United Kingdom	H. V. HODSON, MA (Formerly Editor, The Sunday Times)
USA	JAMES BISHOP (Editor, The Illustrated London News)
USSR	PHILIP HANSON, MA, PH.D (Senior Lecturer, Centre for Russian and East European Studies, University of Birmingham)
Vietnam	A. S. B. OLVER, MA (Specialist in S.E. Asian affairs)
Wales	PETER STEAD (Lecturer in History, University College of Swansea)
Yugoslavia	F. B. SINGLETON, MA (Chairman, Post-Graduate School of Yugoslav Studies, University of Bradford)
Zambia	RALPH A. YOUNG (Lecturer in Government, University of Manchester)

INTERNATIONAL ORGANIZATIONS AND CONFERENCES

African Conferences and Institutions	O. E. WILTON-MARSHALL (Writer on African affairs)
Caribbean Organizations	NEVILLE C. DUNCAN, PH.D (Head, Department of Government and Sociology, University of the West Indies)

Comecon	MICHAEL KASER, MA
	(Reader in Economics, Oxford, and Professorial Fellow of St Antony's College, Oxford)
Commonwealth, The	ALEXANDER MACLEOD
	(Diplomatic correspondent, *The Scotsman*)
Council of Europe	SIR JOHN RODGERS, BT
	(Member, Council of Europe and the Assembly of Western European Union)
Defence Negotiations and Organizations	JOHN C. GARNETT, B.SC(ECON), M.SC(ECON)
	(Department of International Politics, The University College of Wales, Aberystwyth)
European Community	MICHAEL HORNSBY
	(Brussels correspondent, *The Times*)
Nordic Council	T. K. DERRY, OBE, D.PHIL
	(Writer on Nordic history and current affairs)
North Atlantic Assembly	SIR GEOFFREY DE FREITAS, KCMG
	(former President, North Atlantic Assembly)
South-East Asian Conferences and Institutions	A. S. B. OLVER, MA
	(Specialist in S.E. Asian affairs)
United Nations	MARY ALLSEBROOK, BA
	(Writer on international and UN matters)

THE ARTS

Architecture	GEORGE MANSELL, RIBA
	(Architectural writer)
Art	LADY VAIZEY
	(Art Critic, *The Sunday Times*)
Ballet	G. B. L. WILSON, MA
	(Ballet critic of *The Jewish Chronicle*, London, and *Dance News*, New York; author of the *Dictionary of Ballet*)
Cinema	ROGER MANVELL, PH.D, D.LITT, LITT.D (HON)
	(Director, British Film Academy 1947-59; Visiting Fellow, University of Sussex; Visiting Professor of Film. Boston University; author and critic)
Fashion	ANNE PRICE
	(Fashion Editor, *Country Life*)
Literature	DAVID HOLLOWAY
	(Literary Editor, *The Daily Telegraph*)
Music	FRANK GRANVILLE BARKER
	(Music critic and broadcaster)
Opera	RODNEY MILNES
	(Associate Editor, *Opera*)
Television and Radio	RICHARD LAST
	(Television critic, *The Daily Telegraph*)
Theatre	JOHN PETER
	(Literary department, *The Sunday Times*)
New York Theatre	EDWARD G. GREER
	(Assistant Professor, Drama Department, Syracuse University, USA)

ECONOMIC AFFAIRS

International, UK and USA Economic Developments	PETER RIDDELL
	(Economics correspondent, *The Financial Times*)
Economic and Social Data	BEN LOWE
	(Research assistant, *Financial Times* Library)

LAW

International Law	MAURICE MENDELSON, MA, D.PHIL
	(Fellow of St John's College, Cambridge)

European Community Law

Law in the United Kingdom

N. MARCH HUNNINGS, LL.M, PH.D
(Editor, *Common Market Law Reports*)
W. A. MCKEAN, PH.D
(Fellow of St John's College Cambridge)

RELIGION

GEOFFREY PARRINDER, MA, PH.D, DD, D.LITT (HON)
(Emeritus Professor of the Comparative Study of
Religions, University of London)

SCIENCE

Science, Medicine, and Technology
Technology

Environment

JOHN NEWELL, B.SC
(Assistant Editor, Science, Industry and Agriculture,
BBC External Services)
GEOFFREY LEAN
(Editorial Staff, *The Observer*)

SPORT

DOUG GARDNER
(Sports journalist, *United Newspapers*)

PREFACE

SOUTHERN AFRICA, the Middle East and further Asia saw the most important international events of 1978. The Annual Register records the 'internal settlement' and intensification of the guerrilla war in Rhodesia, the controversy over independence for Namibia, the call for sanctions against South Africa and other crucial developments in that area; also the Camp David talks, strife in the Arab world and the frustration of hopes for Middle Eastern peace. In eastern Asia there was double turmoil—the far-reaching waves sent out both domestically and internationally by the new regime in Peking, and the post-Vietnam-war struggle in South-East Asia, where Indo-China became a proving-ground of conflict between the two communist great powers.

It might be thought a shortcoming of the traditional and well-tried structure of the Annual Register, with its sequence of expert articles on different countries and institutions, that major global themes like the dramatic opening of doors between communist China and the rest of the world find no distinct place or comprehensive treatment. For that, however, no apology is needed; for such themes are not peculiar to a calendar year whose events fall to be recorded in these pages but extend often through decades, and those who wish to follow them can find ample material not only in the regional and institutional chapters but also in the documents which enshrine some of their major developments. It is no accident that the Documents section this year includes not only the new Chinese constitution but also the text of the treaties of friendship and co-operation between China and Japan and between the USSR and Vietnam, and the momentous announcement of the opening of full diplomatic relations between the USA and China. The Camp David documents and the terms of the Rhodesian 'internal settlement' can also be found there.

The Government of the People's Republic of China having promulgated a new system of transliteration from Chinese into Western characters, both the new and the old forms of proper names are given in the article on China: e.g. Deng Xiaoping (Teng Hsiao-p'ing). Where Chinese names appear elsewhere, however, the old spelling has been retained for the present volume.

No change has been made this year in the arrangement of the Contents. The Editor welcomes a number of distinguished new contributors.

ACKNOWLEDGEMENTS

The Advisory Board again gratefully acknowledges its debt to the Royal Institute of International Affairs and other institutions for their advice and help with sources, references and the provision of documents, figures and maps. The Board, and the bodies which nominate its members, disclaim responsibility for any opinions expressed or the accuracy of any facts recorded in this volume.

200 years ago

11 May 1778. *The death of Chatham.* The death of the Earl of Chatham, called forth the strongest marks and expressions of grief, with the greatest eulogism on his public virtues, from one side of the House, and was attended with the most exalted and lasting testimonials of public esteem and gratitude, with which departed merit can be honoured, from the whole. This celebrated nobleman (but once more celebrated commoner) who had for several years been a victim to a most excruciating disorder, which reduced him to a state of extreme feebleness with respect to his bodily powers, still retained all that vigour of mind by which in better days he was so much distinguished; and was seized with a fainting fit, the forerunner to his death, some days before in the House of Lords, in the midst of an eager speech which he was making upon American affairs. Thus, he may be said to have died as he lived, in the service of his country.

150 years ago

June 1828. *County Clare election.* Mr O'Connell ... knew that his oratory must be guided by the rules of 'Agitation'; that his rhodomontades must be addressed to the passions. Like his friends, therefore, he did not condescend to speak rationally, but contented himself with talking very wildly about trampled rights—bending necks to masters—bloody bloodhounds—base ministers, and very grandiloquently about the mighty things that he, Daniel O'Connell, would achieve when he got into a parliament in which he could not sit ... The election itself, however, was not attended by any scenes of violence, or any disturbance of the peace; it was conducted with less outrage than not unfrequently disgraces a popular election in England. The Catholic leaders exerted themselves to restrain all attempts at creating disorders ... After a few days polling, Mr Fitzgerald was convinced that he could not continue the contest with any hope of success, and Mr O'Connell was declared to be duly elected.

100 years ago

13 June 1878. *Opening of the Berlin Congress.* The first meeting of the Congress of Berlin was held ... at the Radziwill Palace, the new official residence of Prince Bismarck, and the Foreign Office of Berlin ... Of dinners and interchange of visits the correspondents had more to tell than of the negotiations, and there were graphic accounts to be had of the health and dresses of the different members of the Congress. Prince Gortschakoff was ill and quiet; Count Andrassy well and active. Lord and Lady Odo Russell had a grand reception at the British Embassy, and all the members of the English special mission had a Sunday dinner with the Crown Princes at Potsdam. The British and Austrian Plenipotentiaries conferred with Count Schouvaloff, and the telegrams said the conference was important. A present of strawberry-leaves was sent from high quarters to the Earl of Beaconsfield, supposed to be emblematic of his future; and Prince Bismarck's big dog knocked Prince Gortschakoff down. The flying rumours of the day were busy with small things and with great.

50 years ago

4 November 1928 *Mussolini speaks.* In a rousing speech the Duce reminded his audience that intervention in the war [in 1915] was not forced upon Italy, but was the result of her own free initiative; while the ultimate victory, after intense sacrifice and suffering, was, he declared, 'shiningly' Italian. Amid demonstrations of enthusiasm the crowd answered with a resounding 'Yes' to Signor Mussolini's concluding question, 'If necessary, would you do again tomorrow what you did yesterday?'

ANNUAL REGISTER

FOR THE YEAR 1978

EDITORIAL

THE future of the English language is a matter of no small importance to the Annual Register. These volumes are written in English, they are read and studied by English-speakers all over the world, and their editors and contributors strive to maintain a high standard of English prose. But the matter is of immense concern far beyond our own self-regarding interest, and that concern embraces the spoken as well as the written word.

The English language is neither static nor monolithic. It grows, sheds, changes, and it has different versions—different vocabularies, different turns of phrase, different modes of expression—among the various peoples who speak and write it, and who enlarge and alter it in their own ways. In itself this mobility is to be welcomed, not deplored, but it poses problems, not only in intercommunication but also in recognition and defence of common standards, without which the language would fall apart as a means both of utility and of art.

Dr Robert Burchfield, chief editor of the Oxford English dictionaries, in a paper delivered to the American Library Association in Chicago on 26 June 1978,* expressed his conviction

that the two main forms of English, American English and British English, separated geographically from the beginning and severed politically since 1776, are continuing to move apart, and that existing elements of linguistic dissimilarity between them will intensify as time goes on, notwithstanding the power of the cinema, TV, *Time* magazine and other two-way glueing and fuelling devices.

Dr Burchfield was reported to have said at a subsequent press conference that, given another 200 years, the two forms would have become mutually unintelligible.

If his prediction were to prove true of British English and American English, it would presumably be equally true of British English and Australian or, say, Caribbean English. The consequences would be no less devastating beyond the native English-speaking countries. English has become the pre-eminent language of world-wide politics, diplomacy, commerce and scientific and intellectual interchange. In some countries it is an optional language for parliament, administration and law; in many it is a compulsory subject in secondary schools and an instrument of university education. How are these peoples to fare if there is not one English which they can learn and speak but two—or three or four—'mutually unintelligible' forms in the lands to which they look as the fount

* Reproduced in *Encounter*, October 1978.

of the language? The prospect opened is not a mere bifurcation of English but a Babel within Babel.

For the Annual Register the prognosis is much more than a matter of interesting speculation. Having already been published for 220 years, it can confidently expect to survive for another two centuries, the span of a prediction which if fulfilled could destroy its present world-wide circulation among all those who read and understand a common language, English.

Is the prediction sound? Those who foresee such a separation of several forms of English often draw a parallel with the transformation of Latin, the language of the Roman Empire and the *lingua franca* of Europe in the Dark and Middle Ages, into the half-dozen Romance languages we know today, with their regional variants. But the analogy is weak for two reasons: first, the barbarian invasions not only pushed back the Latin-bearers to their homeland, but also so reduced trade and other communication among the Empire's former territories that for centuries their peoples—though not their educated elites—were largely isolated from each other; and the same is true of the Germanic peoples whose languages, including English, separated from a common stock from the fifth century AD onwards. Secondly, though Latin was the *lingua franca* of those educated elites, by the Middle Ages it was no longer the vernacular tongue of any country, not even of its native Italy. By contrast, there is now a vast web of continuous communication of all sorts among the peoples of the world, and English, the *lingua franca* of their elites, is also the vernacular of over three hundred million of the most advanced and powerful among them. No deduction from ancient examples can apply directly to the fate of English in a world of radio broadcasts, television satellites, pop records, cheap air travel, constant academic, political and business exchanges and an international spate of popular as well as technical or learned literature.

Prophecy was not, indeed, the main theme of Dr Burchfield's Chicago address, which was concerned chiefly with the history of opinion in Britain and North America about the divergence of their languages. His quotations ranged from Dr Johnson, who deplored 'some mixture of the American dialect' in a book he was reviewing, 'a tract of corruption to which every language widely diffused must always be exposed'; through Samuel Webster, who held that 'American English, no longer in his eyes a mere dialect of English, was on a separation course from any variety of English spoken or written in Great Britain'; to T. S. Eliot, American by birth and British by adoption, who a century later believed the opposite. Specific defence of Dr Burchfield's prediction of future divergence awaited an article he wrote in the London *Observer*,* citing a large number of words and phrases drawn from American books or periodicals which he thought, with reason, would be unknown to British readers: 'badmouth', 'boffo', 'schlock', 'gooper', 'living with some turkey in a yurt', and so on.

* 30 July 1978.

One could, conversely, adduce British colloquialisms equally unknown to Americans, such as those derived from the Indian connexion—'dekko', 'cup o' char'—or the products of Cockney rhyming slang—'a butcher's', 'titfer', 'the Sweeney'. Such evidence, however, is far from conclusive. Any sophisticated language acquires at its fringes a swarm of slang words and neologisms. Some are soon adopted into common use in speech and writing; some have a long life in a linguistic underworld which embraces children's language and regional dialects and which used to include those four-letter Anglo-Saxon words never listed in ordinary dictionaries but now openly uttered on the stage and elsewhere; many have a short life and disappear from current use. The last category, *ipso facto*, has no long-term effect in sundering the different national forms of English. Nor has the second category, except in so far as words sometimes emerge from the linguistic underworld into respectable use.

The question at issue therefore boils down to this: of the new words and phrases constantly accruing to colloquial American and British English respectively, are those which neither sink to a linguistic underworld nor vanish from common use in their country of origin so many, and so different between the two forms, that these are diverging at a pace which (if the 200-year prophecy is correct) should be clearly perceptible within a man's lifetime? Only a lexicographer of both kinds of English could give a scientific answer, but a surmise that it would be negative is suggested by the evidence of Webster's Dictionary. Webster was, after all, an early prophet of the 'separation course', and Dr Burchfield claims that between American English and British English 'the outline differences are clearly observable in successive versions of his dictionary' from 1828 onwards. One would be led to expect that Webster would now record, after a century and a half, the vocabulary of a palpably different language from that of the Oxford and other British English dictionaries. But it does not. Nor does it purport to do so. Webster's 'Third New International Dictionary of the English language', the current edition, is offered, in the words of its preface, 'to the English-speaking world'. A random scanning of its pages discloses a vast number of words unfamiliar to ordinarily literate British readers, but equally unfamiliar to their fellows in America, too, being technical, scientific or other little-used terms; it discloses very few indeed that are specifically American and unknown in British English, bar the names of local flora and fauna.

The point is reinforced by the publication in 1978, and the immediate success, of a new dictionary,* designed primarily for the foreign student, which, in the words of its introduction, 'combines the best principles of British and of American lexicography to present to the student a broad description of English as used throughout the world'. This work does indeed distinguish, in a few of its entries, between British English and

* Longman Dictionary of Contemporary English.

American English, either in spelling or in vocabulary or usage. However, the differences in spelling are ancient and familiar and have no bearing on divergence; and, as for the words marked *BrE* or *AmE*, these are almost without exception colloquialisms which according to the compilers (though some would disagree with them) have not yet made the transatlantic crossing. Typical examples under the former head are *clobber* (clothes), *punt* (bet), *scarper*, *zizz*, and under the latter *Bronx cheer*, *derby* (bowler hat), *log-rolling*, *teamster*. Such trivia are no evidence of basic divergence, let alone of its progressive widening. If, indeed, divergence did proceed to real separation, a dictionary like this would presumably develop into a mere code of 'international English', an Anglodesperanto.

Another test is to study 'The American Treasury 1455-1955',* a massive anthology of quotations from American prose and verse, both earnest and comical—extracts from the US Constitution, utterances of the famous and the obscure, advertising slogans, everything. The theory of divergence would suggest that the later the quotation the more likely its including words or passages that need to be translated into British English. There is no sign whatever of such a trend.

If separation, such as it is, has not gone so far in two centuries as to demolish the concept of English as the common language of the British Isles and North America (and of Australasia and the formerly British Caribbean), and as the almost universal medium of scientific and technical information, is the separation likely to accelerate over the next two centuries? The probability seems to be the opposite. For inter-communication in the English-speaking world, both in speech and in writing, is fuller and deeper than ever before. Within a lifetime, films, radio and cheap paperback books have been added to the means of interchange; within half a lifetime, television, international circulation of popular magazines, and cheap air travel. American tourists, few of them rich and many of them young, throng Britain's cities and countryside, and there is a less but rapidly growing traffic the other way; British bookshops and newstands are crammed with American magazines, novels and non-fiction best-sellers. British television series secure vast audiences in the United States, American series appear every day on British screens. All this guarantees that new words and phrases added to the recognized vocabulary on either side of the Atlantic, or new meanings, soon become familiar on the other, and that divergence of written or spoken language is most unlikely to go beyond a point at which breaches of comprehension are still only marginal.

That being so, it is no less important than it ever was to uphold and defend a common standard of good English. The standard will not be unchanging, and it will have regional variations, but it will exist all the same—or ought to exist, if our precious linguistic inheritance is not to be

* Edited by Clifton Fadiman and Charles Van Doren.

squandered. It is threatened less by the bottom tier of literacy, which has never harmed the English of cultivated people, unless they succumb to it out of laziness or a stupid inverted snobbism, than by the middle and upper tiers. By the upper tier because English is habitually tormented by academic or professional experts too idle or too ignorant to ponder the words and constructions they use. Some technical jargon is necessary and proper—new words for new concepts or new objects, linguistic short-cuts for the knowing. But the following sample contains only words known to ordinary people, yet whatever meaning it has is totally hidden from them.

As far as prediction of fertility is concerned Miss Thompson assured us that current practice is . . . moving towards much greater emphasis on decision procedures involving predictive regions in conjunction with users' own risk functions.*

Social scientists, indeed, are more often guilty of needless jargon, obscurity and sheer bad English than physical scientists, who are obliged to be precise and clear in order to communicate their ideas and discoveries; yet social scientists deal in matters much closer to the lives and interests of ordinary people, who look to them for guidance and information, too often in vain. If they were to write more clearly they might think more clearly and have more to say to us that is useful.

In this matter the newspaper and magazine press has a special responsibility; for its products are read by many people who read nothing else or who read much more of them than of more durable literature, and who are apt to follow their example in the use of language. On the whole the standard of journalistic English is reasonably high in Britain, America and other English-speaking communities. Of necessity it must be plain, direct and straightforward. But there are many lapses, sometimes in the misuse of words and phrases or the mindless repetition of clichés, sometimes in slack grammar. There seems, for instance, to be growing use of the conjunction 'with' in a way that defies grammatical analysis, as in 'with the committee's report due tomorrow, the Government is prepared etc'.

Such slovenly constructions are too frequent also in news broadcasts. Like the press in regard to the written word, broadcasting authorities have a special responsibility for upholding standards of spoken English, and in Britain at least they are failing in their duty. Utterances heard on radio and television, even by professional broadcasters, abound in mis-pronunciations and bad grammar. We hear not only the now almost universal *ree*search but also *ree*call, *ree*new, *ree*vive, *ree*deem, *ree*port, *dee*fects, *dee*scend. We hear *dis*tribute, *con*tribute, *com*pel, *com*plete, *con*tinue, *con*tractor, *com*pressed, *dis*pute, *dis*play, *di*rect, *pros*pective, *ann*exing, *sur*veying, with the accent on the first syllable, distri*bute* and contri*bute* with the accent on the last. We hear such howlers as 'less' for 'fewer', 'finally' for 'eventually', 'the choice between X or Y', 'different than', 'equally as good', 'neither . . .

* *News and Notes* of the Royal Statistical Society, May 1978.

or', 'three times as many than before', for which any fifth-form schoolchild would be sharply rebuked. School-teachers who condemn bad spelling but tolerate bad grammar have their priorities wrong.

Apart from demonstrable grammatical errors, faults in spoken English by broadcasters are a matter rather of wrong pronunciation, which presupposes only that there is an ascertainable right one, than of 'bad accents', which presupposes more questionably that one particular accent of the English tongue is good and others are to be condemned. True regional accents—Scottish, for instance, or Irish or West Country—must surely be accepted, indeed cherished, for what they are, just as New England or West Coast or Southern accents are accepted for what they are in the United States. But no anti-elitism can excuse such horrors as the drawing-out of simple vowels into diphthongs or the peculiarly feminine conversion of the short 'a' into a short 'u' (as in 'calling the bunns' or 'hund in hund'

Why do men and women of sufficient education to gain them responsible posts in broadcasting so often commit faults of speech for which, it seems, they have no ear, nor a standard of what is right? We must certainly blame the broadcasting authorities for their complacent indifference. They would not employ, or commission, musicians who played or sang wrong notes; they ought not to employ or commission speakers who utter bad grammar or wrong pronunciations. If this requires, of career broadcasters, as professional a training and practice in speaking as those of musicians in reading scores, so be it. Our inheritance of language and literature is no less than our inheritance of music, and should be treated with equal respect.

A deeper answer to the question may lie in the rapid expansion of secondary and higher education, which has meant an equal, indeed a still greater, expansion of the number of teachers. Children at school are now taking their standard of good spoken English from men and women who themselves have not been taught to speak well nor have had the example of good speaking in their own homes. Thus British English itself is exposed to the same kind of progressive deterioration as is suffered by spoken English in countries where it is not the mother tongue and is taught by people who were taught by others who themselves had it only as a second language imperfectly acquired.

We must not be too superior about all this. We all commit faults of pronunciation and construction of English. But at least we ought to recognize that they are faults, that there is a standard of excellence to which we should strive to adhere, and which should be inculcated in schools, most especially in teacher training colleges, and required of professional communicators. If we do not, the prophets of mutual unintelligibility will be vindicated, and the English language itself, wherever spoken, will lose its elegance and strength.

I HISTORY OF THE UNITED KINGDOM

Chapter 1

A HUNG PARLIAMENT

ON 8 May 1978 the Government were defeated in the House of Commons by eight votes on an Opposition amendment to the Finance Bill reducing the standard rate of income tax by 1p in the £. Some people saw this event as merely a passing incident in a period of minority government which had begun more than a year earlier (see AR 1977, p. 8), a state of affairs which Parliament and the country must continue to tolerate and even enjoy, because it not only slackened the rein of government but also revived the power of Parliament in face of the Executive. Others saw in it, and in the subsequent refusal of Mr Callaghan's Government to resign or seek a general election, a radical revision of the conventions of the British constitution; for here were an Opposition assuming responsibility for fixing the level of revenue while having no responsibility for administering expenditure, and a Government passively accepting a refusal of supply, the classic test of parliamentary support, marginal as that refusal was. The mood of the British people, pleased by any small relief of the tax burden and evincing no clamorous demand for an immediate general election, seemed on the whole not to favour the constitutional purists.

As the parliamentary session wore on, the Government's ability to govern, in terms of being able to count on a majority in the Commons, continued to deteriorate. They lost another seat to the Conservatives at a by-election at Ilford, North, on 2 March, on a swing of 6·9 per cent. Other by elections, at Glasgow, Garscadden, on 13 April, Lambeth Central on 20 April, Epsom and Ewell on 27 April and Wycombe on the same day, made no change in party representation, though in all there was a substantial swing to the right. More interesting was the fate of the smaller parties. At Ilford the Liberal vote slumped from 8,080 to 2,248, only just ahead of the National Front. In the Glasgow by-election, the first in Scotland since the general election, the Scottish National Party virtually held its October 1974 vote on a much smaller poll, but was disappointed not to win the seat as it had confidently hoped to do. At Lambeth the National Front narrowly took third place from the Liberals, but lost its deposit, as also did the Liberals at Lambeth and Wycombe. Compared with October 1974, the Liberal vote fell from 17·3 to 5·3 per cent at Lambeth, at Epsom and Ewell from 26·6 to 12·8 per cent and at Wycombe from 19·3 to 7·4 per cent of those going to the polls.

Disenchantment with the Liberal–Labour pact (see AR 1977, pp. 10-13) was manifestly widespread among former Liberal voters, and infected the party's MPs, though its leader, Mr David Steel, reiterated his claim that the pact had been vindicated by Britain's improved economic performance under the Government which it sustained in office, while preventing further essays in dogmatic socialism. The Young Liberals, meeting in Sheffield in January, called for an end to the pact, their chairman expressing disappointment that in the ten months of its operation nothing concrete or radical had been achieved. However, a special Liberal Assembly, only a week later, carried by over three to one a resolution giving Mr Steel authority to continue the pact until, in consultation with party officers, he should decide to end it. Lord Byers expressed the Liberal dilemma when he said at the Assembly: 'If you want proportional representation you want alliance politics'. The consultations between Ministers and Liberal leaders which were an integral part of the pact now concentrated upon the Budget, the price of Liberal support for the Finance Bill being reported to include fiscal encouragement to profit-sharing schemes, relief of incentive-killing taxation on middle incomes, and additional aid for small businesses. The parliamentary Liberals also showed their teeth when in March they opposed a Bill (supported by both unions and management) reorganizing the nationalized electricity supply, on the grounds that it extended both corporate bureaucracy and ministerial power and patronage. It was obvious, said Mr Steel, that Mr Benn, Secretary of State for Power, regarded the Lib-Lab pact as an unwelcome necessity 'solely to provide lobby fodder for whatever extension of Bennery takes his fancy'. The Bill had to be shelved.

A week before the April Budget, the Liberals published their own fiscal proposals. These included a cut in the standard rate of income tax to 30p in the £, with the object of bringing it down to 20p by 1980; a new low rate should be introduced at the bottom end of the scale, and at the top the maximum rate should be reduced from 83p to 50p in three years. To help pay for all this, standard VAT should go up from 8 to 10 per cent and employers' contributions to national insurance should be raised. Mr Healey, Chancellor of the Exchequer, was reported to have told the Liberals' spokesmen that their proposals ran counter to the Government's anti-inflation strategy, and to have warned them that if the Liberals voted against the Finance Bill there must be an immediate general election.

On 11 April Mr Healey introduced his annual Budget. Its key was a limitation of the net financial stimulus to be given to the economy to £2,500 million in a full year, £2,000 million in 1978-79. Standard income tax would be unchanged at 34p, but personal allowances before tax would be raised, a new band at 25p on the first £750 of taxable income would be introduced, and the threshold of 40p tax would be raised from £6,000 to £7,000. There would be further help for small companies, including a threshold for corporation tax £10,000 higher at £50,000. The only tax heightened was the duty on high-tar cigarettes. Bounties dispensed included free school milk for children between 7 and 11, a rise to £3 a week in child benefit from November and £4 from April 1979, and an increase of retirement pensions in November to £31.20 per week for a couple and £19.50 for a single person. His measures, said the Chancellor, were intended 'to increase the incentive for greater effort and to promote social justice'. He gave credit to the Liberals, in the subsequent debate, for several things in the Budget, including the low-rate band of income tax and the help for small businesses. In his Budget speech Mr Healey also announced that £1,000 million would be repaid to the International Monetary Fund ahead of time, that minimum lending rate (MLR) would be raised forthwith from $6\frac{1}{2}$ to $7\frac{1}{2}$ per cent, and that the British Government would make a $35 million bond issue in New York.

In the House of Commons, next day, Mr Steel expressed the Liberals' disappointment at the failure to cut standard income tax and at the narrowness of the low-rate band. They would table corrective amendments to the Finance Bill. At the end of the Budget debate, however, the Government, with Liberal support, had a majority of 37, and the second reading of the Finance Bill was unopposed.

When the Bill reached Committee the Government faced Liberal amendments cutting 2p in the £ off income tax, raising the threshold for 40p tax by £1,000 and cutting the top rate to 75p, at a total cost of £1,000 million. But it was the Conservatives who made the running. On 8 May a Tory amendment cutting 1p off standard income tax was carried by 312 votes to 304. The joker in the pack on that occasion was the vote of the Ulster Unionists, whose decision to go against the Government, said their spokesman Mr Enoch Powell, was not an economic but a political one, caused by the Government's refusal to remove the injustice to Northern Ireland of having no local authority elections.

The next time the voting balance was held by the Scottish Nationalists. Thanks to them, on 10 May the Government were defeated by a majority of two on another Conservative amendment raising the threshold for 40 per cent tax from £7,000 to £8,000, with consequential effects higher up the scale; but the SNP switched their vote on a further amendment adjusting the top rates to a maximum of 70 per cent, which was defeated by six votes. The combined cost of the two changes carried against the Government was estimated at £445 million. An angry Chancellor gave warning that if he found the limit of £8,500 million on the Public Sector Borrowing Requirement (PSBR) to be threatened the revenue would have to be made good, possibly by increasing company taxation, stamp duty or employers' national insurance surcharge.

When the Prime Minister, at question time, accused the Opposition of 'its usual irresponsibility' in voting to reduce income tax, Mrs Thatcher retorted: 'Then why not put down a Government amendment at the Report stage and treat it as a vote of confidence?'. Mr Callaghan called the suggestion 'very ingenious' and undertook to consider it; but he was not

A*

to be trapped into the risk of having to go to the country willy-nilly before at least the Finance Bill and the Scotland and Wales Bills had reached the statute book.

The Lib-Lab pact had obviously become very shaky. In a speech on 13 May Mr Steel declared that minority government was not merely tolerable but indeed desirable, so long as it was based on a Commons working majority more broadly acceptable than the dogmas of one minority party; but, he added, although the Budget had embodied a number of Liberal-inspired measures, on the crucial issue of tax reform it totally failed to carry out in practice what had been agreed by intent in his exchange of letters with the Prime Minister in July 1977 (see AR 1977, p. 10), namely, 'a shift within the overall level of taxation away from taxes on income'. The blame lay solely with the Chancellor's refusal of reasonable discussion of carefully costed Liberal proposals and 'his failure to enter into the full spirit of the Lib-Lab agreement'.

It came as no surprise, therefore, when on 25 May Mr Steel announced that his party was ending the pact at the close of the current parliamentary session. It had achieved, he said, its main object of providing the political stability needed for economic recovery and a reversal of the upward trend in inflation, but he and his colleagues saw no common long-term basis for continuing it into a third session. In his emollient reply the Prime Minister said his Government were determined to follow the same policies as had brought the country to the existing stage of recovery and to continue the battle against inflation. Although no particular issues were mentioned in the exchange of letters, it was generally understood that besides their disappointment with the Budget the Liberals were disgruntled by the Government's refusal to make any advance towards proportional representation, on which the Liberals were demanding a popular referendum, and by the Cabinet's procrastination over amendment of the Official Secrets Act (see p. 37), on which subject they had put forward detailed liberalizing proposals in March. Their prime motive, however, was undoubtedly the desire to establish their independence in the run-up to a general election which could not be long delayed, and to win back the popular vote which had conspicuously deserted them during the pact's lifetime.

Budgetary finance, meanwhile, was not the only area in which Parliament had grown accustomed to defeating the Government on particular issues which the latter did not choose to regard as matters of confidence, such as the value of the 'green pound' (see pp. 33-4). A number of those defeats affected quite severely the Bills for devolution to Scotland and Wales. On 25 January the Government were beaten three times in Committee on the Scotland Bill. One amendment, moved from their own backbenches and carried by 166 votes to 151, required that a majority 'Yes' vote in the Scottish referendum on the proposals would not be effective unless it represented at least 40 per cent of the registered electorate; another, carried by 168 votes to 142, required that if the 'Yes' vote were less than 40 per cent the Secretary of State must lay an order for repeal of the Act; a third, carried by the huge majority of 204 to 118, would allow the Orkneys and Shetland to opt out of the devolution plan if they expressed that wish in the referendum. This last vote only narrowly escaped being prevented by expiry of the time allotted under the 'guillotine' time-table, when certain Labour members deliberately lingered in the division lobbies; the next day the Leader of the House, Mr Foot, apologized for such 'improper' delay, which the Speaker castigated as 'a grave abuse of our parliamentary proceedings'.

On 14 February the Government were again defeated, by 223 votes to 142, on an amendment requiring that no referendum should be held within three months of general election polling day if Parliament were dissolved. And the next day they had a majority of 55 against them on their attempt to remove the 40 per cent clause, and one of 45 against them on an amendment to reduce the minimum figure to $33\frac{1}{3}$ per cent of the electorate—a convincing sign that the House meant to assert its will. On 22 February the Scotland Bill was given its third reading by 297 votes to 257, most Liberals voting for it; seven Labour MPs voted with the Opposition and two Conservatives with the Government.

The Bill then passed to the House of Lords, which clearly felt unusually free to amend a major Government measure, partly because the guillotine had prevented many of its clauses from being debated in the Lower House, partly because the Commons itself had appeared so unenthusiastic about it. The second reading, however, taken on 15 March, was unopposed, after a debate in which Lord Home, the former Conservative Prime Minister, said that he was in favour of devolution but wanted to introduce proportional representation and to give the Scottish assembly power to raise revenue. When, on 4 April, Lord Kilbrandon, chairman of the Royal Commission on the Constitution which had originally recommended a devolutionary scheme, moved that the assembly be elected by proportional representation, Lord Home said that their lordships had a chance to prevent the importation into the Scottish system of the unhealthy trend whereby a Government supported by a minority of the electorate felt it had a right to impose policies for which the people had not voted. Lord Kilbrandon's amendment was carried by 155 votes to 64. On 9 May the Lords carried by small majorities amendments deleting from the list of devolved subjects the control of aerodromes, forestry and inland waterways, on the argument that all these were satisfactorily managed by United Kingdom authorities and ought to remain so.

In Committee on the Wales Bill the House of Commons rejected by 259 votes to 232 a vital clause empowering the Secretary of State to bring the measure into operation; in this defeat the nationalist parties were taking a tactical revenge for the Government's successful opposition to an amendment obliging the first orders under the Act to be made within 120 days of its receiving the Royal Assent. On the Report stage, however, the Conservatives accepted a restoration of the commencement clause in return for a decision by the Government to accept amendments passed in the House of Lords excising the power of the Commons to override the upper House on certain applications of devolution. By 280 votes to 202 the Commons passed, again contrary to Government wishes, an amendment requiring a 40 per cent affirmative majority in Wales as in Scotland. The Wales Bill had its third reading by 292 votes to 264 on 9 May.

On 6 June the House of Lords carried an amendment to it applying proportional representation. This, however, was rejected on 19 July by 389 to 162 on a free vote by the Commons, which had earlier thrown out the like amendment to the Scotland Bill by 363 votes to 155. Although the majorities were large, the number voting for PR in the former case was the highest ever recorded on this issue. Several Lords amendments to each Bill were accepted by the Government, and on others they were defeated in the Commons, including one disqualifying MPs from membership of the Welsh assembly, another removing forestry from the devolved subjects for Scotland, and (by the hair-breadth margin of 276 votes to 275) a constitutionally crucial one, known as the West Lothian amendment after its indefatigable champion, Mr Tam Dalzell, the Labour MP for that constituency, requiring that if the majority for second reading of any Bill relating only to English affairs was dependent on the votes of MPs from Scotland it must be submitted to a second vote 14 days later. The Opposition on the last occasion was reinforced by half-a-dozen anti-devolutionist Labour MPs and by the Scottish National Party, which acted 'in revenge' for the 40 per cent clause.

In the final debate in the House of Lords, which gave both measures their third readings on 27 July, Earl Ferrers, for the Opposition, made an effective claim for the House's value as a revising chamber. Of the 239 amendments moved there to the Scotland Bill, he said, 96 had been made by the Government to improve their own Bill; on a further 46 the Government had accepted the Lords' contentions. On others they had made substantial concessions, eight they accepted in the Commons after opposing them in the Lords, and on two (forestry and the West Lothian amendment) the Commons had backed the Lords against the Government. If we had a unicameral legislature, said Lord Hailsham, the use of the guillotine would have to be increased, and more Bills would go without free parliamentary debate on them clause by clause. 'I beg MPs and peers to remember that they cannot abolish this House without replacing it unless they destroy the system upon which the freedom of the nation has been founded for 700 years'. The two Bills received the Royal Assent on 31 July. Their operation still depended upon orders by the Secretary of State, and their implementation upon the outcome of the referendums.

The omens meanwhile indicated that the tide of Scottish nationalism was ebbing (see p. 39). At a parliamentary by-election on 31 May in the Hamilton constituency, which the SNP had once held and hoped to win again, the Labour majority over the Nationalists was almost doubled, with a swing of 4·5 per cent, and the Conservatives equally improved their proportionate vote.

Two later by-elections caused by the death of Labour MPs and held on the same day, 13 July, gave the Government some encouragement by comparison with their earlier electoral showing. They held both Moss Side (Manchester) and Penistone with reduced majorities, the swing to the Conservatives being 8·8 per cent in the latter case but only 3·5 per cent in the former. In the English metropolitan district elections on 4 May the Conservatives had a net gain of 60 seats at the expense of all other parties, and won complete control of the metropolitan authorities' national negotiating body; but the variation between different cities and areas baffled any clear deductions.

The signs were pointing to a general election in the autumn, and a pre-election atmosphere prevailed in national politics. On 20 May Mr Steel called on Liberals to prepare for an election that might result in their having a still more powerful role as partners for either a Labour or a Conservative minority Government. If there were another hung Parliament, he said, 'it is difficult to see how either party could refuse a referendum on proportional representation'. The Government narrowly escaped defeat on 14 June on a Tory motion to cut the salary of the Chancellor of the Exchequer. This followed Mr Healey's announcement on 8 June of an economic 'package' designed to check an inordinate increase in the money supply and to restore the planned limit on the public borrowing requirement. It included restrictions on bank credit, an immediate increase of minimum lending rate from 9 to 10 per cent, and a surcharge of $2\frac{1}{2}$ per cent on employers' national insurance contributions. By treating the vote as one of confidence the Government secured the reluctant abstention of the Liberals, despite Mr Steel's castigation of the Chancellor's 'cavalier and bullying' manner, and they scraped home by 287 votes to 282, the minority including both the SNP and the Ulster Unionists.

Mrs Thatcher took no part in that Commons debate, although the Prime Minister wound up for the Government, leaving it to her colleague Sir Geoffrey Howe to make a fierce attack on Government economic policy. On 25 July, however, in a Commons debate on the Government's White Paper on Phase 4 of the pay policy (see pp. 16-17), she entered the fray immediately after Mr Callaghan had turned from his measured defence of the policy to an intense personal attack on her for her 'one-sentence solutions' to the country's problems and her failure, as he alleged, to give the country any clear idea of what her party stood for. Mrs Thatcher did not deign to answer in kind, but instead embarked upon a closely argued critique of Labour's handling of the economy, in a speech which silenced her supporters more than her opponents. It was still more badly received by the press, but her defenders vehemently argued that she had made clear how the battle was joined—between personalities and persuasion, prejudice and reason. The Government secured a majority of 17, with Liberal support. The next day they secured a majority of 15 for the second reading of a Bill, part of the incomes policy, imposing dividend control for a further twelve months (see p. 18); this time they had the support of most of the Scottish Nationalists, who voted less in support of the measure itself than of the Government at the fag end of a divided Parliament.

As if the Liberal Party had not enough handicaps already, it received a further severe wound when on 4 August its former leader, Mr Jeremy Thorpe, MP, was charged along with three others with conspiracy to murder Mr Norman Scott, the man who in face of strenuous denials by Mr Thorpe had claimed an earlier homosexual relationship with him. The alleged co-conspirators included a former deputy treasurer of the Liberal Party, Mr David Holmes, who was a close personal friend of Mr Thorpe's, and two businessmen from South Wales. All were released on bail pending a hearing of the case by a court of first instance on 12 September, a date subsequently twice postponed. Mr Thorpe, who only two days before his arrest had made a telling speech in the Commons debate on Rhodesia which betrayed no sign of his personal anxiety, indicated that there was no question of his resigning his seat and that he intended to fulfil all his political engagements. After meeting him on 5 August the executive committee of his constituency Liberal association in North Devon, in a statement to the press, expressed its full confidence in him and continued:

It has stated its intention of inviting him to stand again as the candidate at the next general election, preferably as an official Liberal, but, if not, as an independent Liberal. Mr Thorpe has indicated his intention of accepting.

This move greatly perturbed Liberal MPs. One of them, Mr Cyril Smith, said on BBC radio on 6 August that the issue was not whether Mr Thorpe should resign, for he must be presumed innocent until proved guilty, but whether in fairness to himself and his party he could fight the next election with a charge of such gravity hanging over him. MPs and prospective candidates, however, could only make the best of a situation which they obviously felt to be acutely embarrassing.

Mr Thorpe's attitude was unchanged when on 1 September the Director of Public Prosecutions stated that he was also accused of inciting Mr David Holmes to murder Norman Scott: indeed it became known that he had been aware from 4 August of this further charge. The resentment of his parliamentary colleagues now focused on his expressed intention of attending the Liberal Assembly, due to open on 12 September. The party's president, Lord Evans of Claughton, urged him to stay away. Nevertheless on 14 September he appeared on the platform for twenty minutes, to a cool reception, and then departed.

The committal proceedings were heard before magistrates at Minehead from 20 November to 13 December. After prosecution evidence Mr Thorpe's solicitor, Sir David Napley, pleaded that there was no case to answer, claiming that the principal witnesses were 'inveterate liars', but all four defendants were committed for trial at the Central Criminal Court. At the request of one of them, full reporting of the proceedings was allowed, and the immense publicity engendered raised in many minds questions, which were widely aired in the press, as to the value, and the potential harm to justice, of committal proceedings amounting to a rehearsal of the prosecution case, without defence witnesses, in advance of the trial proper.

Chapter 2

INCOMES POLICY PHASE 4

THE economic condition of the country improved somewhat in the first half of the year. Unemployment in Great Britain (seasonally adjusted, excluding school-leavers) fell by 60,000 to 1,310,000 (5·6 per cent of the working population) between January and July. The trade balance fluctuated widely from month to month but benefited greatly overall by the flow of North Sea oil. The public's spending power rose faster than prices. By June the rate of inflation, in terms of 12-months rise in the retail price index, had fallen to 7·4 per cent per annum. The Government continued to give control of inflation priority in its economic policies, in face of criticism not only from Labour's left wing but also from a reflationary school of economists.

In those Government policies further wage restraint played a key part. The incomes policy for 1977-78 (see AR 1977, p. 21) was toughly defended, both in the public sector and through pressures upon private employers, and under no major agreement, with the significant exception of the Ford Motor Company (see AR 1977, p. 24), were basic wages increased by more than the prescribed 10 per cent; but, as Sir Geoffrey Howe, a member of the shadow Cabinet, said in the House of Commons, 10 per cent began as a guideline, became a norm, then a target, and finally a platform. To basic wage rises were added productivity bonuses by which no group of workers benefited more than the miners. Their union, which had been demanding a rise of 90 per cent for face-workers (see AR 1977, pp. 22 and 27), coolly accepted a 10 per cent settlement on 8 February, but meanwhile had voted by regions in favour of local productivity schemes— even in Yorkshire, where their left-wing leader, Mr Arthur Scargill, had been the bitterest of all opponents of such arrangements. In consequence some face-workers were reported to be earning as much as the £135 per week which the unions had originally demanded. Nationally, as a result of productivity bargains and the notorious 'wages drift', actual earnings rose by 14 per cent between July 1977 and July 1978, when Phase 3 expired. The threat of wage-inflation was evidently still real.

Government spokesmen made no disguise of their intention to prolong wage restraint beyond Phase 3. Speaking on BBC radio on 1 January, the Prime Minister said that in the coming months the level of wage increases would determine the level of price rises, and that he hoped both would keep to 5 per cent in 1979. This was the first mention of what was to prove a fateful figure. He and the Chancellor of the Exchequer and other Ministers repeated the same theme (though without that explicit numeral) on many occasions. Thus on 21 May Mr Healey told the Union of Post Office workers that there would be runaway inflation unless, on pay policy, the Government and the unions 'came up with an answer which is honest, makes sense and will work for the next twelve months'. The key to keeping down inflation, he said, was to keep down the increase in wage costs. 'Inflation is our major enemy', the Prime Minister told a conference of engineering and shipbuilding unions on 30 June, warning them that the guidelines for 1978-79 would be 'much more modest' than in the current pay year.

This was not at all to the taste of the trade unions. Most of them were staging demands for large rises to be implemented at the earliest wage settlement date after the end of Phase 3. Mr Len Murray, general secretary of the TUC, repeatedly expressed their hostility to rigid pay limits. The TUC chairman, Mr David Basnett was still blunter. Speaking at a conference of his union, the general and municipal workers, on 7 June he declared: 'there will be no agreed norm, no agreed Phase 4, no agreed incomes policy, no acquiescence in direct government intervention in wages. There must be a complete return to voluntary collective bargaining'. The effective word in his negatives was, of course, 'agreed'. Direct government intervention in wages, as employer or provider of money for employment, could hardly be avoided. As the Prime Minister had told another union conference on 1 May, 30 per cent of wage negotiations involved the Government directly or indirectly. Britain, he said, now had an interlocking wage system in private and public employment: 'it is inevitable that the Government—any Government—must have direct discussions with the trade union movement about the future of pay each year'. Inflation, Mr Callaghan added, was still not low enough, and would cost jobs in competition with countries where the rate was lower.

On 21 July the Government issued a White Paper on incomes policy. Pay rises in 1978-79, it pronounced, should be kept within 5 per cent, with some flexibility as between different grades of workers in an industry or enterprise, and with permission for excess payments under self-financing productivity deals and for low-paid workers where the resultant was no more than £44.50 a week. Policemen, firemen and a strictly limited number of other groups of workers could be exceptions to the rule. 'Blacklisting' of firms breaking the limits, that is, denying them government contracts or assistance, would be used to make the policy effective in the private sector. Limitation of company dividends would continue for another twelve months.

Trade union reaction was epitomized in an instant retort from a spokesman of the largest union, the transport and general workers: the 5 per cent guideline was completely unrealistic in terms of correcting anomalies, adjusting differentials and allowing scope for an increase in living standards. Although the TUC continued to back the '12-months rule' barring fresh wage settlements within a year of the last, there was no hope of its otherwise endorsing the Government's policy. A joint Government–TUC statement, 'Into the 80s', issued on 24 July, muffled the issue. 'Free collective bargaining is vital to the trade union function. Side by side with this, particularly in the public sector, agreements made at national level are part of a pattern where the Government is directly or indirectly the employer and takes a view about the outcome of the pay negotiation both as economic manager for the nation and as provider of the "social wage" '. Notional continuance of the 'social contract' (see AR 1974, p. 21) was signalled by adding that 'there must be each year a thorough discussion with the trade union movement so that there is a broad understanding', and by calling for additional spending in order to cut unemployment, with priority for housing, health, education and social services.

Not only in respect of policemen and firemen (see below) had the Government given hostages to fortune by promising increases in Phase 4 much in excess of the general norm; the armed forces, university teachers, doctors and dentists and top-level executives of state industries were others who had been pacified in 1977-78 with pledges of reaching higher pay levels by stages thereafter. On 16 January the firemen returned to work in an uneasy and bitter atmosphere after their two months' strike, a delegate conference at Bridlington four days previously having voted by a large majority to accept the Government's terms (see AR 1977, p. 26), which had been rejected in December but which the Government declined to improve.

Promissory settlements for the police and the armed forces were also hangovers from 1977. The militantly discontented Police Federation (see AR 1977, pp. 22-23) had been appeased by the appointment of an eminent judge to examine the whole question of police pay and conditions. Lord Edmund-Davies's report was published on 17 July. He recommended pay rises averaging 40 per cent, which the Government, in accepting the report as a whole, agreed to adopt in two stages, in September 1978 and 1979.

Lord Edmund-Davies came down against policemen's right to strike, but observed that this required in fairness a means of impartial, equitable settlement of their claims; he recommended that a new negotiating body should be set up to replace the Police Council, which had been boycotted by the Federation for two years, and that it should be charged with updating police pay annually in line with general earnings.

Before 1977 ended, the Government had agreed to accept the recommendations of a review body on armed services' pay, though rises might have to be phased (see AR 1977, p. 26). The review body found that pay of the armed forces had fallen 32 per cent behind that of civilian workers. The Prime Minister announced on 25 April an immediate increase of 13 per cent plus 1 per cent in improved allowances, and promised that full comparability with civilian earnings would be achieved in two further stages by April 1980. Teachers in universities and polytechnics, who were particularly disgruntled with pay restraint because for three years they had lost a basic increase negotiated in 1975 but denied by the standstill of Phase 1, were also promised, on 5 May, that this anomaly would be rectified within two years. On 10 May the Government accepted the recommendation of a review body on pay of doctors and dentists in the National Health Service that they should get 10 per cent more forthwith and a further $18\frac{1}{2}$ per cent within two years. On 23 June the review body on top salaries recommended that chairmen of state industries, judges, high officers of the armed forces and senior civil servants should get an average of 30 per cent more—in one case as much as 70 per cent—to restore comparability. These enhancements also the Government decided to phase. Thus over a wide area of governmental employment pledges had been given of 10 per cent increases or more in 1978-79 against the norm of 5 per cent laid down in the White Paper.

The Tories were caught in two minds about these developments. They could not condemn an anti-inflationary policy root and branch. While they became more and more clearly committed to the principle of collective bargaining free of government regulation, they could not overlook that if they were in office they too would have to take bargaining positions as employers. They were united in denouncing the Government's restrictions on pay of men and women like police and servicemen who risked life and limb for the security of the people. In a Commons debate on forces pay on 22 May, which the Government won by 281 votes to 267, the Opposition front-bench spokesman promised that the Conservatives would restore— at a cost estimated at £250 million—full comparability with civilian earnings in 1979 rather than 1980.

The Tories also found rallying-points in the Government's decision to continue with dividend control and with the blacklisting of firms that did not toe the line on pay. A Bill giving powers for the former purpose was thought at first to run the risk of a Government defeat, but in the event its second reading was carried by a Commons majority of 15 and it was rushed through all its stages before the House rose for the summer recess.

While Labour defended dividend control as an essential balancing factor if workers were to accept wage restraint, Conservatives attacked it as in effect discriminatory, hostile to economic recovery, injurious to the workers themselves through their huge interest in pension and insurance funds, and in principle unbalanced because it applied to capital a legal coercion that was repudiated for labour. Blacklisting was defended by the Government as a necessary sanction for keeping the private sector in step with the public sector on wage limitation. On 7 February they had announced that they were adding clauses to all government contracts requiring compliance with official incomes policy. Breach of the condition would entail termination of fixed-price contracts and forfeiture of cost-plus claims in variable price contracts; the main contractor would be liable for breaches by sub-contractors. This measure was fiercely denounced by the Confederation of British Industry, and Lord Robens, chairman of Vickers, called it 'a terrible miscarriage of justice'. (Later in the year, Lord Robens, a former trade unionist and Labour Minister, who had been a strong-minded chairman of the National Coal Board, announced that he had forsaken the Labour Party for the Conservatives). A Commons motion of censure on blacklisting and the government contracts clause was defeated, however, by 283 votes to 268.

In July the blacklist of firms raising wages beyond the guidelines and so denied the benefit of all government aid was reported to include 57 companies. The first company known to have appeared on it, James Mackie of Belfast (see AR 1977, p. 24), was, however, taken off the list in May, and a month later the firm told its shop stewards that an impending new pay settlement must conform to government policy. The impression was that overall the sanctions in the private sector, however reprehensible, had been effective.

The growing discontent of workers with wage restraint was one cause of the trebling of number of working days lost through industrial action between 1976 and 1977, to just over 10 million in the latter year. The record in 1978 was nearly as bad, the lost days numbering 9·3 million. Among the groups that either struck or applied work-to-rule or similar measures during Phase 3 were school-teachers, electric power workers, hospital electricians, post office engineers (whose prolonged action in the summer on behalf of a 35-hour week had grave effects on telecommunications, before it was appeased by an offer to reduce their weekly hours from 40 to 37½), staff at the Royal Mint, some groups of social workers and various sections of the newspaper press (see Ch. 5). On the other side of the ledger, on 14 July the strikers at the Grunwick factory were obliged to abandon their efforts after a strike which had lasted 591 days and had been such a *cause célèbre* in 1977 (see AR 1977, pp. 28-31). One action which aroused serious anxiety was the 'blacking' of maintenance work on two nuclear submarines, HMS *Revenge* and *Resolution*, at their base on the Clyde at the end of July in a dispute connected with the nation-wide demand of industrial civil servants for more pay. The vulnerability of Britain's Nato commitment to keep at least one Polaris submarine on sea station—and indeed other elements in national defence—to industrial coercive action was nakedly exposed. The Secretary of State for Defence, Mr Frederick Mulley, ordered the work to be done by naval personnel. On 9 August the chief naval officer at the base ordered certain civilian workers to do what they were employed to do and when they refused struck them off the payroll. All the 2,000 workers at the base then went on strike. In talks at high ministerial level the Government made its 'final offer' to the industrial civil servants—consolidation of £8.60 of Phase 1 and Phase 2 increases into basic rates, with corresponding effect on over-time payments, plus 9 per cent of the resultant for Phase 3. The industrial action then gradually ended, but another breach in the strict application of the pay policy had been opened.

The motor industry, as always, suffered from a number of sectional stoppages. On 1 February the chairman of British Leyland, Mr Michael Edwardes, told a meeting of shop stewards and managers from all plants of his rationalization plans, which involved a cut of 12,500 in the work-force. The reaction was remarkably tolerant, though the shop stewards laid down two conditions for their acquiescence, that free collective bargaining should be unhindered, and that there should be no compulsory redundancies or plant closures. The announced closure of the BL plant at Speke, near Liverpool, an area of high unemployment, drew loud cries of protest and threats of strikes, but the generous compensation payments offered to those who lost jobs allayed the hostility and the plant closed peacefully. Chrysler suffered at its Linwood plant in Scotland a particularly damaging strike, which turned a small profit on its British operations in the first quarter of the year into a loss. On 10 August it was announced that the Chrysler management in Detroit had negotiated the sale of its entire interest in the UK to the French car firm of Peugeot–Citroen for $230 million in cash and a 15 per cent interest in the new European group. The British Government, which in the course of its rescue operation (see AR 1975, pp. 35-36) had already sunk £51 million irretrievably into Chrysler, as well as £65 million in loans and guarantees which it might call upon the new group to redeem, was as much taken aback as anybody. Under the terms of that operation it had the power of veto on the sale. Both the Government and the unions launched intensive studies of all the terms and repercussions of the proposed bargain. On 28 September the Secretary of State for Industry announced that the Government had sanctioned its conclusion, although no definite pledges on continued operation or employment had been given. Both Government and unions realized that they had in truth no other option.

The British Steel Corporation faced still graver problems over plant closures than the motor industry. It paid compensation to workers displaced by the March closure of its East Moors plant near Cardiff on a scale rising to £17,500 for a high-paid, long-service worker. At the end of June a letter to employees advancing the proposed closure of its Bilston works from March 1979 to October 1978, and notifying an immediate cut in operations there, drew an unprecedented threat of a national steel strike in August, and the Corporation was obliged to withdraw the letter and engage in further talks with the unions on slimming-down excess capacity. In April BSC forecast a loss of £400 million in 1978. The Secretary of State for Industry, Mr Varley, had told the House of Commons on 22 March that no new steel-making projects would be started until the Corporation's prospects had improved, but that the Government had approved a capital investment programme to improve the quality of operations to a total of £1,000 million in the two years 1978-80.

While BSC was piling up losses, other nationalized industries showed better results. British Rail had an operating surplus of £68 million in 1977. The National Coal Board's profit fell by £10 million to £31·8 million in 1977-78, but that of the Electricity Council rose to £133 million after charging £160 million for replacement of assets. The Post Office was the star performer with a 1977-78 profit of £367 million, to which both the postal service and the highly profitable telecommunications contributed. The PO announced that postal charges would not rise at least until 1979 and that telephone charges would be held at 5 per cent below the actual inflation rate for five years.

Addressing the TUC at its Brighton congress on 5 September, the Prime Minister warned the unions that if they pushed for settlements higher than the 5 per cent norm 'then you will be stepping on the escalator' of inflation 'going up again'. When he insisted that any cuts in the working week would have to be offset against the 5 per cent or any productivity deal he was greeted with cries of 'Shame'. The congress carried overwhelmingly a motion opposing any arbitrary pay limits, and it rejected a motion sponsored by the local government officers' union calling for a new approach to pay based on an economic contract with the Government. Motions were also carried demanding a 35-hour week and an end to the system of cash limits on departmental, local government and nationalized industry expenditure. The bit, it seemed, was between the unions' teeth.

Worse was to come for the Government than rejection of its incomes policy by the TUC. On 2 October the conference of the Labour Party itself, meeting in Blackpool, carried by a majority of over two to one a motion rejecting totally 'any wage restraint by whatever method, including cash limits and specifically the Government's 5 per cent in the coming year', demanding that 'the Government immediately cease intervening in wage negotiations' and instructing the party's national executive 'to organize a campaign in the wider trade union movement against control on wages'. It did so despite powerful pleas not only from Mr Healey but also from Mr Michael Foot, who argued that to leave wages unplanned was a recipe for the destruction not only of this Labour Government but of any Labour Government. Let us, he said, start right now to discuss wages policy between the Government, the party and the unions 'and make sure we do not make the mistake that our forbears made in 1931 when they split to atoms at the critical moment and allowed the Tories in'.

The most effective speech for the Government was made by Mr Sidney Weighell, general secretary of the National Union of Railwaymen, who declared that he did not like the 5 per cent restraint but it was there because the trade union movement had abdicated its responsibilities. 'If you want the call to go out that the new philosophy of the Labour Party is the philosophy of the pig trough and those with the biggest snout get the biggest share, I reject it'. However, the voting result was inevitable because the representatives of most of the biggest unions were mandated to oppose the Government's policy. Mr Alan Fisher of the National Union of Public Employees, moving a motion calling for a national minimum wage of £60 per week, denounced percentage limits as giving least to those who needed it most, and most to those who needed it least. This sentimental view of wage formation can hardly have been shared by the spokesmen of managerial and technical staffs, and of engineering and other skilled workers, who equally denounced the fixed limit, their appetite being for higher differentials for skill and responsibility. Indeed nothing emerged from the critics by way of an alternative ideology of wages.

The Prime Minister in effect invited the trade unions to supply one when he addressed the conference on the following day. At the heart of his speech he insisted that, if in consequence of the conference's decisions inflation started to move up again, then the Government would take offsetting action through monetary and fiscal measures, which would adversely affect employment as well as ability to pay wages. The Government, he said, must control the economy in the interest of full employment and their social ends, and wages could not be left out of that calculation. But instead of sharpening confrontation Mr Callaghan went on to emphasize that incomes policy depended upon support and acquiescence. In this 'we failed this year. We have not got it. So I will look to all of you to make the maximum contribution that lies within your power. You have a job in education to do with your members. . . . I am ready and anxious to take up with the unions the longer-term approach to this problem. . . . We must find a better way to resolve the issue of pay levels. The power of the organized worker in society today demands that we do.' The conference, muffling its previous defiance, gave the Prime Minister a standing ovation.

After a series of subsequent meetings between Ministers and TUC leaders a joint document was at last drawn up, in effect restating their opposed views. The closest it came to compromise between them was in the following clause of proposed TUC guidance to wage negotiators: 'when framing claims unions should consider the impact of their proposals on prices; they should seek stability of the price of the product wherever possible, and in all cases have regard to the impact on the overall price level, recognizing the need to keep inflation from rising'. Even this, however, was too much for the TUC General Council, which on a 14/14 vote declined to accept the document.

Economic Ministers and the TUC economic committee, nevertheless, meeting on 19 December, agreed that such joint sessions should be held regularly at monthly intervals with a view to reaching a consensus on policy towards pay and prices, in both the near and the longer-term future. The Government also agreed to initiate studies of comparative pay in the public and private sectors. Meanwhile, so the Chancellor of the Exchequer emphasized, the 5 per cent pay guideline would stand.

While Labour was in such disarray, the Conservative front on incomes policy had also been publicly broken. At the party conference on 11 October Mr Edward Heath declared: 'If the Government's pay policy has broken down, there is nothing here for gloating. . . . There is a part to play for incomes policy in the economy'. In a television interview on the same day he said 'Free collective bargaining produces massive inflation'. All this was in flat contradiction to the mood of the majority of the delegates and to the hard monetary line of platform speakers like Sir Geoffrey Howe and Sir Keith Joseph. Mrs Thatcher herself, winding up the conference on 13 October, promised that a Conservative Government would restore free wage bargaining, while warning the unions that demanding too much would force companies into liquidation and their members on the dole. By the time Parliament reassembled on 1 November she had obviously decided to play down the differences between herself and Mr Heath and between the Opposition and the Government. In the debate on the Queen's Speech she said: 'Of course in this matter we share the same ends as the Government. . . . I had the impression from a number of things the Prime Minister said that we also agreed on a large number of means as well'. After three phases, a rigid pay policy would not hold and there was no point in arguing about it as if it would; but 'most settlements will have to be within single figures'. In the Opposition's view the target figure should be an average and become a norm only under emergency conditions; and in a television interview on 3 November she characterized her difference from Mr Heath in the same terms—average *versus* norm.

In the same debate the Prime Minister had said that a limit on earnings increases had an important part to play in keeping down inflation and the Government had a responsibility to say what that limit should be.

Monetary and fiscal policies were also important: the counter-inflation policy was a three-legged stool.

Two grave immediate difficulties confronted the Government in pursuing its pay policy in face of union and party hostility. One was the threatened imposition of governmental sanctions upon private businesses that transgressed. The other was the application of the policy to government employees, some of whose unions were among the most demanding.

On both fronts the Government had an immediate issue on its hands. Hospital engineering supervisors were taking 'industrial action' in support of a claim for restoring differentials at a cost of raising their pay by at least 15 per cent. After five weeks, 250 hospitals were closed to non-emergency cases, 9,000 hospital beds were empty and the waiting-list for operations had swollen by 60,000. On 20 October the Secretary of State, Mr David Ennals, made an impassioned appeal to the men involved. 'For God's sake go back to work and stop playing with people's lives', he said. After ACAS had failed to find a solution, the TUC succeeded; a settlement reached on 27 October gave the supervisors a right to participate in 'self-financing' productivity schemes, nominally within the pay guidelines, which it was reckoned would give them an extra 15 per cent within six months. This however, was only a skirmish before the main battle, the lines of which were drawn when unions representing manual workers in government employment, including the NHS and local authorities, more than a million strong, decided to stage a national one-day strike in January after rejecting out of hand, on 12 December, an offer of 5 per cent overall. The unions were demanding *inter alia* a minimum of £60 for a 35-hour week, against an actual minimum of £42.40 for 40 hours, a rise per hour of over 80 per cent. The chairman of the Association of Metropolitan Authorities said on 19 December that there was no question of the big cities settling with their manual workers beyond the 5 per cent norm without Government approval.

In the private sector it was foreseeable that the first big clash on wages policy would happen over the Ford Motor Company, whose wage settlements always came early in the annual round. On 22 September the national negotiating committee of the 13 unions represented at Ford met company representatives who offered a 5 per cent rise in basic pay and discussions on bonuses for productivity. The union negotiators at once denounced this offer as derisory and called for a national walk-out. By the start of the following week, as a result of overwhelming plant ballots, almost all Ford's 57,000 workers were on strike, in clear breach, as the company's chairman emphasized, of their existing agreement, which had still four weeks to run. Nevertheless, within a few days the strike was given official status by the two principal unions bound by the agreement.

Although after less than a fortnight the company abandoned the guidelines in making a new offer, the strike continued for nine weeks, the main cause of dispute being a proposed 'attendance allowance' denied to those who failed to turn up for work on time or at all. When the conditions for this bonus had been diluted, mass meetings voted on 22 November for a return to work. The terms included a 9·75 per cent rise in basic pay, plus the attendance allowance and extra holiday pay estimated to make nearly 17 per cent in all. On 28 November the Government announced that sanctions would be applied against the company; official purchases of Ford cars would be stopped unless no alternative was available, and the breach of pay 'guidelines' would be taken into account in considering discretionary grants. Even to supporters of the 5 per cent policy it seemed ironic that a company which had incurred a wounding strike because of its initial attempt to conform, could well afford to pay the higher wages and was prepared to promise not to increase its prices by more than the 5 per cent norm, should be further heavily penalized while the workers who had forced the breach went scot-free with their 17 per cent booty.

The Opposition demanded a debate on pay sanctions. This was arranged for 7 December but was frustrated by a group of left-wing Labour MPs who ate up most of the time assigned by raising points of order on supplementary estimates which ordinarily went through 'on the nod'. The Government gave up a day on 13 December for the debate, at the end of which it was defeated by 285 votes to 279 on a Tory amendment and by 285 to 283 on its own substantive motion, thanks to the abstention of half-a-dozen Labour left-wingers. The next day the Prime Minister, seeking a vote of confidence, which he won by 300 votes to 290 (see p. 29), said that sanctions in the private sector would be abandoned, and fresh talks opened with the TUC and the CBI. The way was opened to settlements in the private sector beyond the guidelines, often under pressure or threat of industrial action. In the area of nationalized industry, British Leyland manual workers voted by a two-to-one majority on 20 December to accept an offer of 5 per cent plus a three-stage wage-parity scheme calculated to raise the overall rise to 16 per cent, on condition of consent to 6,000 redundancies which were pleaded as justification of the excess on productivity grounds.

Chapter 3

THE NEW SESSION

WHEN Parliament rose on 3 August no one (except perhaps the Prime Minister) knew whether it would meet again before a general election. For six weeks thereafter the expectation grew among the public, the press and most politicians that an election would be held in October. This expectation pervaded not only the Liberal Assembly in September, which approved a policy of working with either main party if the result were another hung Parliament, provided it gave of a cast-iron commitment to electoral reform, but also the annual congress of the TUC. When, on 5 September, Mr Callaghan, addressing the TUC, sang an old Vesta Victoria song 'There was I, waiting at the church' and added 'I have promised nobody that I shall be at the altar in October', it was taken as a joking tease of Margaret Thatcher. In an atmosphere of impending contest the union leaders ardently pledged themselves to work for the return of a Labour Government. Two days later, however, broadcasting on television and radio, instead of announcing an election date Mr Callaghan said: 'We go on because we are doing what is best for Britain. So I shall not be calling for a general election at this time'. Exercising her right of reply next day, Mrs Thatcher scoffed at 'a broken-backed Government that no longer has any authority at home or abroad'.

The political pundits now set about speculating on the motives for what Mr Steel called a 'truly astounding' decision. A successful fight against wage-inflation through the winter, it was supposed, coupled with a generous Budget in the spring, might well revive popular support for Labour. A new electoral register in February would act in its favour. Commons majorities could perhaps be sustained by sops to the regional parties, at least until Scotland and Wales had their referendums on devolution. Not everyone gave the Prime Minister credit for his ostensible motive of persisting with economic policies which he deemed best for the nation until the task was completed. Most commentators felt that he had shirked an election which the latest opinion polls suggested he would lose.

The shadow of an immediate general election having been removed, both the Labour and the Conservative party conferences focused upon incomes policy, on which they aired differences that they might otherwise have concealed or composed (see pp. 21-23). Labour at Blackpool showed signs of a move to the left in its elections to the party's national executive committee, but rejected left-wing motions for the compulsory re-selection of sitting MPs by their constituency parties and for making the whole party, not its parliamentary representatives, the college for electing a leader. It carried motions calling for the nationalization of all agricultural land and reimposition of rates on agricultural land and buildings, and for public ownership of all North Sea oil operations. Mr Tony Benn, accepting the latter policy on behalf of the Government, said: 'In time, the oil companies will be moved from being concessionaires to being contractors'. Detached observers failed to see any ideological or indeed much practical significance in that change, the oil resources themselves having been nationalized under a Conservative Administration in 1964.

Apart from their differences over incomes policy (see p. 23), the Conservatives at Brighton overwhelmingly rejected a motion calling for proportional representation in elections to Westminster, and gave a very rough ride to Mr John Davies, the shadow Foreign Secretary, when he opposed the groundswell of demand that the party should vote against the renewal of sanctions upon Rhodesia (see p. 33). (He shortly afterwards underwent a neurosurgical operation, Mr Francis Pym taking over his shadow portfolio, and later resigned his seat.) Mr William Whitelaw struck the mood of the delegates in a speech on law and order in which he promised, among other things, an early free Commons vote on capital punishment and an amendment of the Children and Young Persons Act, 1969, to restore magistrates' power to commit young offenders to secure custody. Other shadow Ministers pledged the party to make substantial cuts in income tax, to relieve inflationary increments of capital gains tax, to raise the pay of the defence services immediately, to repeal the Community Land Act, to promote further the sale of council houses, to restore the system of direct grant schools by way of an assisted-places scheme, and to do a number of other things dear to Tory hearts.

On race relations and immigration the platform spokesman said the party had to counter the smears and lies put around about its proposals. They started from the proposition that all who were legally settled in this country were in all respects British citizens, equal under the law. But lasting good relations between the different communities required that the numbers entering the country in the future should be finite, accurately defined and under close control. There was a history behind these pronouncements. In a television interview on 30 January Mrs Thatcher said people were afraid that Britain might be 'rather swamped' by people with a different culture. 'We do have to hold out the prospect of an end to immigration, except, of course, for compassionate cases'. If immigration continued at a rate of 40 to 50 thousand a year, her great fear was that good race relations with those already here would be imperilled. She promised not to make immigration a main issue in a general election. Her figures were corrected next day by the Prime Minister: only 28,000 new coloured immigrants were admitted in 1977, and 16,200 already here were granted UK citizenship. A week later Mr Merlyn Rees, the Home Secretary, accused Mrs Thatcher of 'fanning the flames of prejudice' with innuendoes. Immigration was now only 'a trickle'. Addressing Young Conservatives on 12 February Mrs Thatcher declared: 'I do not believe we have any hope of promoting the sort of society we want unless we follow a policy which is clearly designed to work towards an end of immigration as we have seen it in this country in the post-war years'. Campaigning in the Ilford by-election, Mr Healey accused Mrs Thatcher of acting as recruiting officer for the National Front.

On 21 March a Commons Select Committee published a report unanimously recommending stricter controls on immigration, an annual ceiling on admissions from the Indian subcontinent, the setting of a date at which the right of UK passport holders to settle in Britain would cease, save in exceptional circumstances, and sanctions against those who knowingly employed illegal immigrants or over-stayers. Mr Whitelaw described these proposals as a 'framework' for Conservative policy. The Prime Minister, in a non-committal statement on the report, invited Mrs Thatcher to all-party talks on immigration policy, but the Conservative leader declined. In September her party inserted advertisements in newspapers circulating among ethnic minorities, affirming Tory aims of good community relations and claiming that these would be seriously harmed if people already here felt threatened by unlimited new arrivals.

When the new session of Parliament was opened on 1 November the Government had received some encouraging signals as to its electoral standing. A Gallup poll published on 26 October gave Labour a 5½ per cent lead over the Conservatives, after months with the opposite indication. On the same day two by-elections were held, at Pontefract and Castleford, a safe Labour seat, and at Berwick and East Lothian, a seat vacated by the death of a popular Labour member, Mr John Mackintosh (see OBITUARY), which the Tories hoped to win. They failed, the Labour majority being slightly increased; and at Pontefract the swing of 7·85 per cent to the right was no more than could be expected at a by-election in such a constituency. Some Tories, but not their leader, blamed Mr Heath's split with the leadership over incomes policy (see p. 23) for their disappointment. The death of the Conservative MP for Clitheroe on 27 October left the following state of parties in the Commons: Labour and its regular supporters from Scotland and Northern Ireland, 308; Conservatives 281, Liberals 13, SNP 11, Ulster Unionists 10, Plaid Cymru 3, total Opposition 318. The Liberals being no longer with them, the Government clearly had to cultivate one or more of the regional parties.

It was not surprising therefore that the Queen's Speech included not only a promise of referendums on the Scotland and Wales Acts (which the Prime Minister announced would be held on 1 March 1979) but also an increase of Northern Ireland seats from 12 to 17 to make them proportionate to the rest of the country. The Speech anticipated no fewer than 25 Bills, including measures on 'industrial democracy' (see AR 1977, pp. 14-15), compensation to employers working short-week schemes to preserve jobs, increase of National Enterprise Board funds, company law reform, housing, education, nurses' training and regulation, broadcasting, reform of the Official Secrets Act, public lending right and marine pollution, few if any of them likely to unite the Opposition on anti-socialist lines. The debate on the Queen's Speech concentrated largely on incomes policy. It ended with a Government majority of 312 to 300 on a Conservative amendment attacking Labour economic policy. The Welsh nationalists supported the Government and the Ulster Unionists abstained.

Besides all those intended measures, the Government revealed on 21 November a plan to replace motor vehicle licence duty with increased duty on petrol by 1983, with the object both of simplifying administration and of encouraging economy of oil. The first major measure published was the Education Bill, which required parents and teachers to be represented on school governing bodies, and local authorities to meet (wherever possible in point of numbers) the preferences of parents as to the particular schools their children should attend, and enabling authorities to pay means-tested allowances to pupils aged 16 or over who stayed on at school. It was followed by a Bill to increase by £4,250 million the borrowing powers of the NEB and Scottish and Welsh development boards. The Bill to increase the number of Northern Ireland seats received a second reading by 350 votes to 49 on 28 November, figures which expressed the Conservatives' sharing with the Government a desire for friendly relations with the Ulster Unionists.

On 13 December the Government was defeated by 285 votes to 279 on an Opposition amendment hostile to official sanctions against private firms which exceeded the pay guidelines (see p. 25); half-a-dozen left-wing Labour MPs abstained. The next day it tabled a vote of confidence, which it won by 300 votes to 290. The minority included 11 Liberals, 9 Scottish Nationalists and 3 Ulster MPs, but 7 Ulster Unionists abstained and one Liberal and one Welsh Nationalist voted with the Government, which, however, lost the votes of the two Catholic Northern Ireland MPs in protest against the enlargement of Ulster representation at Westminster.

Such was the precarious poise of the Administration when Parliament rose for a month's recess on 15 December. Mr Callaghan's decision not to hold an autumn election, however, appeared so far to have been politically justified. The initiative remained in his hands. Public opinion polls were ambiguous, but gave no great cheer to the Opposition. The economic indicators were, for the time being, quite favourable. Unemployment, after rising in the summer, fell for four successive months to 1,320,700 (seasonally adjusted, excluding school-leavers) in December. Inflation, measured by a year's change in the retail price index, was held to 8·4 per cent in 1978.

Chapter 4

FOREIGN AND COMMONWEALTH AFFAIRS

THE ill-received Berrill report on Britain's overseas representation (see AR 1977, pp. 40-41) was decently buried by a Government White Paper (Cmnd. 7308), published on 3 August, which followed the House of Commons Expenditure Committee, reporting in April, in rejecting all its most controversial recommendations, including the abolition of the British Council and the confinement of BBC external services to communist and Third World countries. A significant stroke of policy was the Foreign

Secretary's announcement at the UN General Assembly on 27 September that the UK would keep up to a thousand troops available for peace-keeping. This had been heralded in a constructive speech on disarmament by the Prime Minister in the same forum on 2 June, in the course of which he said that Vice-President Mondale's 'idea of a permanently earmarked stand-by force is an imaginative one and we should approach it with a view to overcoming the practical problems'.

The predominant parts in Britain's international relations, however, were played by the problem of Rhodesia and differences within the European Community. On Rhodesia the Government's policy remained persistently that of working for a negotiated settlement, based on the Anglo-American proposals published in the previous September (see AR 1977, pp. 39 and 249-50), by way of a conference of all parties to the struggle. Towards the 'internal settlement' reached by Mr Smith and three black leaders on 3 March (see DOCUMENTS) the Foreign Secretary was tepid; though calling it 'very significant' and a start towards majority rule, after Secretary of State Vance had poured cold water on it he insisted that, while parts of it were 'a step in the right direction', a final settlement must stem from a conference including leaders of the Patriotic Front. The failures and delays of the internal settlement as the year wore on seemed to the Government to justify this fabian attitude, but its critics argued that if it had backed the Smith–Muzorewa–Sithole–Chirau regime this could have succeeded in achieving both a cease-fire and approval by the Rhodesian people as a whole, the key condition of bipartisan British policy. Tories accused the Government of being too much under the influence of the United States, and depicted the policy of waiting for an all-round settle-ment as a manifest failure. After the Umtali massacre on 23 June, in which twelve white missionaries and a number of children were slaughtered by guerrillas, Dr Owen spoke of this 'appalling tragedy' and the Prime Minister of its 'barbaric savagery', but they refused the call from the Opposition front bench for 'real support' for the internal settlement. A Tory motion to that effect was defeated in the House of Commons by 171 votes to 165 on 2 August.

Following Rhodesian raids deep into Zambia (see Pt. VII, Ch. 3) Dr Owen announced, after a hurried visit with the Prime Minister to Kano for talks with Dr Kaunda, who was as incensed against Britain for breaches of oil sanctions (see below) as against the Smith regime, that Britain would send Zambia, gratis, a supply of defensive arms, on condition that they were to be used exclusively for national defence. One Tory MP gave vent to his disgust at 'the obscene prospect of British arms defending the training grounds of mass murderers'. Official Opposition hostility was less vehement; in a Commons debate on 8 November Mr Heath again dis-tanced himself from the Conservative leadership by pleading for under-standing of Dr Kaunda's perilous position.

The issue of sanctions against Rhodesia became politically hot, not only because a vote on their renewal must be taken in the new session but also for another reason. Disclosures in the press, and an open feud between the Lonrho company and the two great British oil companies, BP and Shell, in which the former sued the latter for vast damages for injury caused to it by their alleged breaches of UN sanctions against Rhodesia, led to the appointment of Mr T. H. Bingham, QC, assisted by Mr S. M. Gray, to inquire into the whole question of the supply of oil to Rhodesia since UDI. Publication of the Bingham report on 19 September was preceded by the revelation in *The Sunday Times* of 27 August that BP in a letter to the inquiry had admitted protracted breach of sanctions by a South African subsidiary. Sir Harold Wilson, who had headed the Government for much of the relevant time, promptly denied that he knew anything of such sanctions-breaking. He seemed, however, to be contradicted by Lord Thomson of Montifieth, who in a statement on 6 September declared that 'the obvious ineffectiveness of Rhodesia oil sanctions, and the implications this constituted for British oil companies, was discussed frequently by the Ministers concerned before I joined the Cabinet, during my period as Commonwealth Secretary' (1968-69) 'and afterwards'. Mr Jack Jones, retiring secretary of the transport and general workers' union, voiced a common public reaction when he said 'To the eternal shame of our country the world has witnessed the oil sanctions on Rhodesia being brazenly busted wide open by people in authority. . . . There should be no cover-up'.

The Bingham report found that BP and Shell subsidiaries had effectively supplied oil to Rhodesia for most of the period of sanctions. At first this had been done by selling direct to South African firms which exported the product to Rhodesia; then, when the extent of this traffic became known to the companies' headquarters in London and to the British Government, BP and Shell arranged with the (French) Total company to switch orders from suspect customers to Total and sell corresponding quantities of oil to that company. After the ending of this swap arrangement in 1971, oil was supplied direct, mainly to a South African company, Freight Services, by a Shell-BP subsidiary, Shell Moçambique, for onward shipment through Lourenço Marques.

The British Government, Mr Bingham observed, had been anxious to secure the full implementation of oil sanctions from 1965, but had been brought to realize that this could not be, because of breaches by other countries (conspicuously France) and the complete non-cooperation of South Africa, against which an oil embargo was ruled out for wider policy reasons. They were therefore content, in the light of the swap arrangements, to be able to say that no oil was being sent by British-owned companies to Rhodesia, an assurance which was repeated after it had ceased to be true. How far, or how soon, either the top BP and Shell managements in London, or British Ministers, knew of the ending of the swap subterfuge in favour of sales by Shell Moçambique to Freight Services was obscure.

The Government, which had hoped that the Bingham inquiry would satisfy seekers for truth about this unsavoury matter, found quite the opposite. The report was referred to the Director of Public Prosecutions to see whether charges of breaches of the law should be brought, but the press and parliamentarians took the line that this pursuit was unimportant compared with the question of complicity or evasion of the truth by Ministers of successive Administrations both Labour and Conservative. Fortunately for the Government, all these disclosures occurred during the parliamentary recess, and by November reactions had cooled and they could arrange with the Opposition that the debate on the Queen's Speech should be interrupted by a two-day debate on the whole Rhodesian issue, including the Bingham report, policies towards the internal settlement and the Patriotic Front, and arms for Zambia.

In that debate, on 7 and 8 November, Sir Harold Wilson again denied all knowledge of breach of oil sanctions by British companies. A memorandum of a crucial meeting in February 1969 between BP–Shell representatives and Lord Thomson of Montifieth, which revealed the whole situation, never reached his eye, he said. Mr Heath, Prime Minister from 1970 to 1974, also disclaimed any knowledge of the breaches, as did Lord Home in a House of Lords debate on 9 November. Lord Thomson of Montifieth, whose account of events of which he was aware was disputed by none, found it 'deeply disturbing' to hear Sir Harold state that the Foreign and Commonwealth Office record of the February 1969 meeting 'which was sent to him was never seen by him', and he strongly repudiated Sir Harold's suggestion that the reason had been that he and the FCO had not realized the matter's crucial importance. Two peers who had been permanent secretaries of the FCO also hotly rejected Sir Harold's hint that civil servants might have worked to conceal the truth from Ministers.

Introducing the Commons debate, the Foreign Secretary, Dr Owen, had insisted that there had been no cover-up and there would be none. Sir Harold called for a parliamentary inquiry to which all relevant Cabinet papers would be disclosed. The latter course, however, was opposed by Mr Heath as undermining the relations among Cabinet Ministers and between them and their advisers. In the Upper House, Lord Home opposed any further inquiry, declaring that 'no tribunal should be asked to pass judgment on policy decisions'. On 15 December the Prime Minister announced that a commission of inquiry comprising eight MPs or Peers would be set up, with a Lord of Appeal as chairman, subject to the approval of both Houses after the Christmas recess. Its terms of reference would be: 'To consider, following the report of the Bingham inquiry, the part played by those concerned in the development and application of oil sanctions against Rhodesia with a view to determining whether Parliament or Ministers were misled, intentionally or otherwise, and to report'. The commission would sit in private but its report would be published. It would have access to Cabinet and other official papers if the former Prime Ministers concerned agreed, the chairman being empowered to decide which of such papers should be seen by other members.

The sanctions issue muddied the November debate on general Rhodesia policy in both Houses. In the Commons the two most telling interventions were those of Mr Pym, leading for the Opposition, who called upon the Prime Minister personally to bring the Rhodesian leaders together in a Camp-David-like 'summit'—to which Mr Callaghan replied that this was the last card but that if he saw the prospect of success he would not hesitate to play it—and of Mr Enoch Powell, who urged that the House of Commons should stop fooling itself about its influence over events in Rhodesia.

A Conservative amendment expressing the inadequacy of Government policies was rejected by 323 votes to 278. In the vote on renewal of oil sanctions Mr Pym and the Tory leadership had begged their followers to abstain, arguing that unilateral breach of UN sanctions would lose Britain friends all over the world, but no fewer than 114 of the Tory back-benchers rebelled, to give the Government a majority of 320 to 121. Mr John Biggs-Davison, who was among the rebels, promptly resigned his position as a party spokesman on Northern Ireland; Mr Winston Churchill waited to be dismissed by Mrs Thatcher as shadow Minister of Defence. In the House of Lords the Conservative leadership, powerfully expressed by Lord Carrington, Lord Home and Lord Hailsham, was far more successful, and the sanctions order was passed by 165 votes to 65.

On 24 November the Prime Minister told the House of Commons that he was sending Mr Cledwyn Hughes, MP, chairman of the Parliamentary Labour Party and a former Minister respected by all parties, to southern Africa to see whether all the disputants in Rhodesia could be brought to the conference table. This move, to some extent a response to Mr Pym's plea, was cordially welcomed by the Opposition. It was followed on 30 November by the resignation of Field Marshal Lord Carver as resident British commissioner-designate in Rhodesia (see AR 1977, p. 39), his mission being patently out-of-date.

Britain's perennial struggles in the EEC over agriculture and fishing continued unabated. These matters were in the charge of a Minister, Mr John Silkin, whose determination to fight hard for the interests of British consumers, farmers and fishermen was not mitigated by any love of the Common Market in principle. The agricultural dispute focused on the 'green pound', the notional exchange rate which kept British farm prices, converted at the actual market rates, substantially below those ruling in other countries of the Community. On 19 January the Government

B

decided on a 5 per cent devaluation of the 'green pound', but four days later it was defeated on the issue in the House of Commons, which voted by 291 to 281 for a Tory motion raising the figure to $7\frac{1}{2}$ per cent. This brought a confrontation in Brussels between Mr Silkin and his fellow Ministers of Agriculture, who, contrary to all precedent, so he said, accepted the devaluation only in stages and with different terms for various products. Mr Silkin, however, counted it a victory when the Ministers agreed on 11 May to increase CAP support prices by no more than 2·25 per cent, to allow a slower phasing-out of the British butter subsidy, and to permit Britain's milk marketing boards to continue provided the dairy farmers gave evidence of wanting them—which they did almost *nem. con.* in a referendum later in the year.

On fisheries the going for Mr Silkin was even tougher. From the beginning of the year Britain was isolated in the Ministerial Committee in Brussels. At the end of June Mr Silkin declared that new measures to conserve fish stocks in waters around Britain would be imposed whether or not the EEC concurred: the measures were a ban on herring fishing off the west coast of Scotland and continuance of the existing ban in the North Sea. The EEC Fisheries Commissioner said in October that the former ban could not be approved. At a meeting of Ministers in Brussels in September Mr Silkin accused other members of being interested only in keeping British waters open to their fishermen so long as stocks lasted. On 24 November the Ministerial Council broke up in embattled disagreement after its president, Mr Ertl, had said that its British member, who was claiming an exclusive 12-mile zone and preferential rights in a 50-mile zone, was demanding a change in the Treaty of Rome. 'One must pose the question', he said, 'whether Mr Silkin wants the European Community as it is now'.

Indeed it became clear during the year that the British Government wanted far-reaching changes in the policies and practices of the Community. Speaking at a dinner in Brussels on 6 February, the Foreign Secretary said that Britain was not trying to alter the rules of the club that it had joined, but rules could remain while the club changed its character. The Community should realize that Britain's being an island was a fact of geography, not a reprehensible act of anti-Europeanism. It was perfectly justifiable, for instance, for an island nation to have outlooks of its own on fisheries, and with its short, fast-flowing rivers a resistance to harmonized controls based on the pollution problems of the Rhine or the Rhone. For most people in Britain the objective of fully fledged federalism, if a noble goal, was unrealistic, for some mythical. The Rome treaty spoke only of an 'ever closer union among the peoples of Europe'. The Anglo-Saxon tradition of building slowly step by step was more sensible in British eyes than 'attempts to force the Community into a rigid, pre-determined view of what the future should be'. The independent role of the European Commission was a unique characteristic of the EEC, but the Commission should 'change some of its previous practices and attitudes instead of appearing at times to be frozen in the posture of the Commission of the Six'.

The Prime Minister devoted most of his speech at the Lord Mayor's Banquet in Guildhall on 13 November to Britain's financial relations with the Community. Its contribution to the EEC budget was 'clearly out of balance'. The Government could not agree that 'Britain should become the largest net contributor to the EEC', as was threatened by present rules. Mr Callaghan went on to attack the Common Agricultural Policy, which created surpluses of many products and left too little of the Community's resources for regional and industrial aid. Challenged the next day in the House of Commons by Labour irreconcilables who concluded that membership of the Community was against British interests, he said that it would cause a tremendous furore if a major member were to consider withdrawal; and the Foreign Secretary also insisted that withdrawal was out of the question.

It was the proposed European Monetary System (EMS) (see Pt. XI, Ch. 4, and DOCUMENTS) that furnished the latest case of British isolation. After Herr Schmidt and M Giscard d'Estaing had agreed in September upon a joint Franco-German approach to the EMS, British reservations voiced by Mr Healey left him a lonely sceptic in Brussels. A 'Green Paper' on the EMS published on 24 November rehearsed the general and technical arguments for and against, but its tone indicated strong doubts as to the wisdom of Britain's joining, at least initially. Those doubts were shared by many Conservatives, though the official party line was favourable to the system in principle.

At the EEC summit meeting in Brussels over the weekend of 3 December, when Britain was joined by Ireland and Italy in declining to join the exchange rate mechanism of the EMS immediately, Mr Callaghan was reported to have played a reticent role. Observers thought that President Giscard d'Estaing's obdurate refusal to approve an increase of the EEC's regional fund to help poorer countries was as decisive as British doubts in causing the breach between the six and the three. This was confirmed by the later change of mind by Ireland and Italy. Defending his attitude in the House of Commons on 6 December, the Prime Minister said: 'What happened was that national considerations by the nine members prevailed over the attempt to get an international agreement'. When he added that 'Britain was one of those which put its national interest in the forefront' he was loudly cheered by left-wingers opposed to the Community. It had been agreed, said Mr Callaghan, that the UK would be free to join the exchange rate mechanism later if it wished. Meanwhile it would participate in various aspects of the System and in reciprocal consultations on exchange rate policy. He concluded: 'I would hope the EMS will be the precursor to another attempt to get back to more exchange rate stability on an even broader basis, with the dollar and maybe other currencies'. It was a sad day for Europe, observed Mrs Thatcher, and a sad reflection on the performance of the Labour Government that after 4½ years the Prime Minister was content to have Britain openly classified among the poorest and least influential countries in the EEC.

A sense of disillusionment with the Community was widespread in the country and affected many besides the irreconcilable anti-Market minority.

Chapter 5

CRISIS IN THE PRESS

On 30 November Times Newspapers Ltd suspended publication of *The Times* and its several supplements and the *Sunday Times* (which in the course of its long history had never been in the same ownership as *The Times* until the late Lord Thomson of Fleet, who already controlled the Sunday paper, bought *The Times* in 1967). This devastating action, the management claimed, was forced upon them by labour troubles which if not ended would soon permanently destroy both newspapers. As early as 6 May they had warned the unions that suspension would be necessary if disruptions of printing continued: 'the point of irreparable damage is very rapidly being reached'. But no heed was paid. By November *The Times* and *Sunday Times* had lost over 13 million copies through unofficial industrial action, including total non-publication of some issues.

The management were seeking guarantees of an end to unofficial action, the honouring of a reformed disputes procedure and the negotiation of a revised wage structure based on new printing technology and efficient manning levels, coupled with a promise of no compulsory redundancies; in return they offered a prospect of prosperous and secure publications affording higher wages and other benefits to all workers. The problem was complicated by the fact that Times Newspapers had to deal with no fewer than 65 bargaining units ('chapels'), over which the national union leadership could often exert little control. From the complex of issues, however, one stood out—that of direct input to the printing process, under the new technology, by journalists and advertisement staff, as practised, it was claimed, in every other country in the world where the new technology had been introduced. This was bitterly opposed by the union representing the old-style compositors, the National Graphical Association (NGA), whose general secretary, Mr Joe Wade, pronounced at the time of suspension 'There can be no surrender. We fight until we have won'.

The NGA refused to negotiate at all, first under the threat of suspension, then until the notices of termination of employment were withdrawn, but when the management, responding to deep anxieties expressed in an emergency House of Commons debate on 30 November, held up the notices for two weeks it refused to discuss any proposals involving a breach of its members' monopoly of printing input. At the end of the year, although negotiations with several unions were progressing slowly, there was no sign of an end to a suspension which had deprived Britain and the world of the most famous of all newspapers.

The Times group was far from being the only newspaper house to suffer severely from industrial action in 1978. At the end of the year the National Union of Journalists (NUJ) was conducting an official strike against provincial newspapers represented by the Newspaper Society. The *Observer* (which threatened suspension), the *Daily Telegraph*, the *Guardian*, the *Sun* and the *Express* group were among the national newspapers injured by unofficial tactics. Express Newspapers was obliged by the chaotic condition of labour relations in Fleet Street to shelve plans to publish a new London evening paper and a new Sunday paper, but in spite of union opposition at the national level it did successfully launch on 2 November a new Northern daily, the *Star*, printed in Manchester. Its chairman, Mr Victor Matthews, said on 8 June that he might close down the *Daily Express* if there were a big conflict with the unions: without unions to contend with, he could cut the work-force by 40 per cent. There could be no doubt, however, that the future of newspaper production in Britain, or at least in London, hinged upon the battle being waged between Times Newspapers and the unions over industrial discipline and the new technology.

The press was also involved in a number of important legal issues. In May the Commons' Committee of Privileges found the *Guardian* and the *Daily Mail* to be in breach of parliamentary privilege in publishing detailed reports of the proceedings of a Select Committee, but significantly recommended no action. The house organ of the NUJ, along with two left-wing journals, was charged with contempt of court for publishing the name of an intelligence colonel which the judge in a secrets trial had requested to be suppressed, and were modestly fined. Two journalists were among the accused in a remarkable case at the Old Bailey under the Official Secrets Act 1911. After 42 days of trial, during which charges under the graver Section 1 of the Act were dropped on the instruction of the Attorney General, both were found guilty and ordered to pay costs, but were conditionally discharged, their military informant being sentenced to six months' imprisonment suspended for two years. The case, with these light sentences, was widely regarded as another nail in the coffin of a discredited and out-of-date Secrets Act to which the press was unanimously opposed. Express Newspapers successfully sought an injunction to stop the NUJ from instructing its *Express* members to 'black' copy from the Press Association, where a majority of journalists had voted not to stop work as the union leadership had ordered in support of the provincial journalists' strike. The Court of Appeal unanimously upheld the judge's ruling that the instruction was too remote from the original conflict to enjoy the legal protection given by the Trade Disputes Acts to actions in furtherance or contemplation of a trade dispute. The case was important not only for newspapers but also for trade union law in general.

Chapter 6

SOME UNUSUAL HAPPENINGS

THE BISHOP of Truro, speaking in April, described Princess Margaret's holiday in the West Indies with a young man friend as foolish and suggested that she consider withdrawing from public life. The Bishop of Southwark was among those who sprang to her defence: public recognition of her achievements was far more important than censorship of her private life. On 24 May the Princess was granted a decree nisi of divorce from the Earl of Snowdon on the grounds of two years' separation. Lord Snowdon married Mrs Lucy Lindsay-Hogg, a professional colleague, on 15 December.

In March the Royal Society for the Prevention of Accidents urged that the sport, or craze, of skateboarding should be legally banned in public places. Later in the year it was reported that skateboarding accidents had cost the National Health Service £6 million; but the craze had subsided as quickly as it appeared.

By a majority of 6 to 1 the European Court of Human Rights ruled on 25 April that birching of violent offenders in the Isle of Man was 'degrading punishment'.

On Britain's first statutory May Day holiday heavy rain fell, and political demonstrations were drenched. The normal spring bank holiday, four weeks later, was fine and warm.

When Mrs Naomi James (to be made a Dame in the New Year Honours) sailed into Dartmouth on 8 June she became the first woman to sail single-handed round the world. Her voyage, in the course of which her yacht capsized when nearing Cape Horn in a gale, took 272 days.

The Rev. Ian Paisley and another Northern Ireland MP made vocal protest at a Roman Catholic Mass conducted in the Crypt Chapel of the Palace of Westminster on 6 July to mark the quincentenary of the birth of Sir Thomas More, denouncing it as 'blasphemous heresy against the Articles of the national Church'. They then peaceably departed.

On 24 July George Davis, hero of the 'George Davis is Innocent' campaign which had caused the abandonment of a Test cricket match (see AR 1975, p. 423), was sentenced to 15 years' imprisonment for taking part in an armed bank robbery. In 1976 he had been released from a 20-year sentence because of doubts about evidence of identification (see AR 1976, p. 12), and in February 1978 had been acquitted on a stale charge of robbery, but on this occasion, caught *in flagrante delicto*, he pleaded guilty.

On 11 September Mr George Markov, who worked for the Bulgarian section of the BBC's overseas service and Radio Free Europe, died in hospital. His belief that he had been murdered by a stab with a poisoned umbrella ferrule, when he was in a bus queue four days earlier, was vindicated by a post-mortem, which found a tiny metal object in his leg, and by the discovery of an exactly similar object in Mr Vladimir Kostov, another Bulgarian emigré, who had been struck while travelling on the Paris Metro on 24 August. At the inquest on Mr Markov, which returned a verdict of unlawful killing, the poison used was identified as ricin, derived from the seed of the castor oil plant. On 2 October Mr Vladimir Simeonov, yet another anti-communist Bulgarian broadcaster, was found dead in his home, but on medical evidence a verdict of accidental death was returned at the inquest.

Chapter 7

SCOTLAND

In three by-elections Labour held seats in widely-differing constituencies— Glasgow Garscadden in April, Hamilton in May, and Berwick and East Lothian in October (see pp. 7, 13, 28). In elections for regional councils on 2 May Labour and the Conservatives had net gains of 11 and 10 seats respectively and the Scottish National Party a net loss of 8. Labour won overall majorities in Central and Lothian Regions and the Conservatives in Tayside. The Conservatives had won a seat from the SNP in a by-election in Perth and Kinross district in March. In December Lord Kirkhill resigned as a Minister of State at the Scottish Office on his appointment as chairman of the North of Scotland Hydro-Electric Board.

The Scotland Bill received the Royal Assent on 31 July. Of the many amendments to the Bill the most important was that which required that 40 per cent of the Scottish electorate should vote Yes in the forthcoming referendum before Parliament would consider setting up a Scottish Assembly. Orkney and Shetland Islands Councils obtained amendments giving the Secretary of State power to overrule the Assembly in their interests and promising a commission to consider their position after the Assembly had been set up. On 1 November the Prime Minister announced that the referendum would be on 1 March 1979. Mr John Smith, who had piloted the Bill through the Commons, was appointed Secretary of State for Trade on 12 November.

The January unemployment figure for Scotland was 203,629, again the highest since before World War II, and representing a percentage of 9·2 against a UK percentage of 6·5. By December the total had fallen to 171,709, representing 7·8 per cent against a UK figure of 5·7.

A seven-week strike by British Leyland workers at the Bathgate plant ended with a vote on 22 September to return to work, but the company had already announced a decision to cut the investment programme for Bathgate. A similar strike lasted for more than five weeks at the Chrysler UK plant at Linwood in July and August, and in September the Government gave its assent to the takeover of the firm by Peugeot–Citroen (see p. 20). In June Singers announced its decision to close most of its Clydebank factory and in December the unions were still rejecting a revised scheme which would have saved some jobs. Cuts in the British Steel Corporation's investment programme in March caused the shelving of the construction of a major integrated steel plant at Hunterston and the last open-hearth steel furnace at Glengarnock ceased production in December.

In May the Secretary of State confirmed the decision to build a nuclear power station at Torness in East Lothian, but it was to be of the advanced gas-cooled reactor type in accordance with a general Government decision in January. Permission was given in September for the work to begin and led to demonstrations on the site. In March the Secretary of State also gave approval for the construction of the controversial petrochemical scheme at Moss Morran in Fife, but time was given for further objections on safety grounds.

In the North Sea new oilfields were accepted for development and further progress was made in existing fields. In August the Department of Energy gave permission for the development of the Beatrice field near Brora and in December British Petroleum got permission to develop the Magnus field, the deepest and most northerly to date. The Thistle field went on stream in April. A huge platform for the Ninian field was floated out from the West Highland coast in May, and another for the same field towed out from Highland Fabricators' yard at Nigg in June. In July the Nigg yard won the contract for a platform for the Fulmar field and in December the announcement of a government order promised to save threatened jobs at the Marathon yard at Clydebank.

Three Ulster Defence Association men were imprisoned in June for gun-running offences. Two contrasting prison units were in the news. In February it was decided that the sometimes-criticized special unit for dangerous prisoners at Barlinnie Prison in Glasgow should continue, and in December, for the first time for six years, it was decided to send a prisoner to the 'cage' at Porterfield Prison in Inverness.

The dangers faced by deep-sea fishermen were emphasized by the loss of three boats during the year, in February, October and December. The danger to fish stocks led to a ban in June on herring fishing in all western Scottish waters except the Firth of Clyde. In October a proposed large-scale cull of seals in the Orkney Islands by Norwegian marksmen led to protests and was eventually called off in favour of a smaller-scale cull by local men (see Pt. XIII, Ch. 2).

The Government made a second grant, this time of £390,000, to Scottish Opera in February towards the purchase and renovation of the Theatre Royal in Glasgow. In December Mr Alastair Hetherington gave up his position as Controller of BBC Scotland and accepted a minor post because of policy disagreements with the BBC management.

C. M. Grieve (Hugh MacDiarmid), the most notable of modern Scottish poets, died on 9 September at the age of 86 (see OBITUARY). Sadly, two other eminent Scotsmen died at much earlier ages—Councillor Geoff Shaw, convener of Strathclyde regional council, on 28 April aged 51, and Professor John P. Mackintosh, MP (see OBITUARY), on 30 July aged 48.

In the World Cup contest in Argentina the much-publicized Scottish football team won only one of their three games, and that against the most formidable opposition, and failed to qualify for the final stage (see Pt. XVI).

Chapter 8

WALES

THE minority position of the Government allowed the bitterness, the vigour and the ironies of Welsh politics to be fully reflected at Westminster. The debates on the Wales Bill were as troublesome for the Government as had been those on the Scotland Bill and, on occasions, the opposition of some Welsh Labour backbenchers and the voting tactics of opposition parties threatened to make the Bill meaningless. The parliamentary situation changed, however, once the Government had secured a comfortable majority on the third reading. The impending referendum combined with the ending of the Lib-Lab pact to transform the position of the three Plaid Cymru MPs, and in the crucial votes of June, November and December Mr Callaghan was able to count on their support as well as that of at least one Welsh Liberal.

This new relationship between the Government and Plaid Cymru blossomed at the opening of the new parliamentary session. The three Plaid Cymru MPs voted for the Queen's Speech after their representations had led to the inclusion of definite proposals for Wales. One Welsh reporter went so far as to describe it as 'a Welsh speech'; for the Government had announced a £50 million fillip for the Welsh Development Agency, an allocation of £500,000 to cover the cost of bilingual education, a firm commitment to a Welsh-language television channel, and a study of the possibility of compensating dust victims in the North Wales quarries.

Plaid Cymru's willingness to support the Government was essentially facilitated by its desire to ensure that the referendum took place. The

B*

choice of 1 March 1979, St David's Day, was thought to be appropriate, but the delayed announcement of the referendum date ensured that the respective campaigns would be short. Throughout the year a Wales for the Assembly campaign chaired by Mr Elystan Morgan, a former Labour Minister, prepared the ground, but it was only very late in the year that the full line-up of organizations emerged. Plaid Cymru voted to campaign in favour of the Government's proposals, and the joint campaign of the Labour Party in Wales and the Wales TUC revealed that it would be financed by a special grant from the Labour Party. The opposition would be spearheaded by an all-party Say No campaign chaired by a former Conservative Minister, Mr David Gibson-Watt, MP, and a Vote No campaign headed by the six Welsh Labour MPs who remained hostile to their party's policy. The early stages of the contest did not reveal much public enthusiasm; polls appeared to indicate a fairly even division of opinion amongst those intending to vote.

Within Wales, unemployment tended to dominate the debates of most political parties and industrial organizations. Throughout the year there were announcements of further redundancies; in particular, the shutdown of Cardiff's East Moors steelworks, the cessation of steel-making at Ebbw Vale and the closure of the Tri-ang factory at Merthyr highlighted the contraction of manufacturing in Wales. Certainly the size of redundancy payments made to steelworkers and the creation of new jobs through the efforts of Welsh Office agencies such as the Welsh Development Agency and the Manpower Services Commission helped to relieve the gloom, but the continued losses incurred by steel operations in Wales, the failure to carry out modernization at steel plants, and the unemployment total of almost 90,000 combined to make the economic future uncertain.

In 1978 there was a marked intensification of the battle to strengthen the position of the Welsh language. The Welsh Language Council called for a radical £18 million programme to make Wales bilingual, and a much-publicized demonstration at the National Eisteddfod forced British Rail to speed-up the introduction of bilingual station-signs. Above all, Cymdeithas yr Iaith Cymraeg (the Welsh Language Society) concentrated on the demand for the fourth television channel—the present Government commitment being for a Welsh TV service of 20 hours per week by 1982—and even the Archdruid of Wales supported their declared policy of law-breaking to secure this end. Television services were interfered with, but two leaders of the Society were eventually gaoled for six months under the old conspiracy law in a case that led to parliamentary questions about the unrepresentative nature of non-Welsh-speaking juries.

It was a strange period for Welsh rugby; for an era of unprecedented success was followed by three consecutive defeats, the retirement of Gareth Edwards, surely Wales's greatest-ever player, and growing fears over the level of violence creeping into the game (see SPORT).

Chapter 9

NORTHERN IRELAND

PREDICTABLY, in view of the optimism expressed by the Secretary of State, Mr Roy Mason, at the end of 1977, the Provisional IRA made determined efforts to sustain their campaign, and in November they were still capable of launching a major bombing offensive. For much of the year, however, terrorism was at a comparatively low level. Only two persons were killed in January, one UDR man and one civilian. On 8 January Mr Jack Lynch, the Prime Minister of the Irish Republic, in a radio interview reaffirmed his commitment to the unification of Ireland, called upon Britain to withdraw from Northern Ireland and suggested that he might ultimately offer an amnesty to IRA prisoners in the Republic. The call for British withdrawal was repeated a week later by Dr O Fiaich, the Roman Catholic Archbishop of Armagh. Unionists at once accused both men of deliberately boosting IRA morale, and Mr Mason described the statements as 'unhelpful'.

February in fact saw a very sharp upsurge in terrorism, claiming in all 20 lives, the worst incident being the bombing of the La Mon restaurant, south of Belfast, on the evening of 17 February. The terrorists had attached cans of petrol to the bombs, which exploded without warning, creating a fireball which swept through one entire dining-room, killing 12 people and injuring 30. Police took the unusual step of distributing thousands of leaflets with photographs of the charred remains of the victims. Another specially horrifying incident took place on 3 March during the university rag day procession, when gunmen in fancy dress mingled with the students and shot dead a woman civilian searcher and a soldier in Belfast city centre. Throughout the year assassination of off-duty UDR men, police reservists and prison officers continued, in addition to the open attacks on armed soldiers and police.

As the year progressed, the general level of violence gradually declined, and the IRA concentrated on a propaganda campaign for the restoration of 'special category status' to terrorists serving prison sentences. Over 300 IRA prisoners refused to wear prison clothes or obey prison regulations. Naked except for blankets, they fouled their cells with urine and faeces, creating a health hazard for themselves and prison staff, who were at the same time prime targets for IRA murder attempts. The Secretary of State repeatedly made it clear that the Government would not yield on the principle, but the unpleasant conditions in H block of the Maze prison could easily be represented abroad, and especially in the United States, as being created by the authorities, and the propaganda had some success, swelling IRA funds for the renewed operations in the late autumn. On 26 November the deputy governor of the Maze, in charge of H block, was shot dead at his home in North Belfast.

In January the European Court of Human Rights in Strasbourg ruled that interrogation techniques used briefly in August and October 1971 on 14 terrorist suspects, though constituting 'inhuman and degrading treatment', were not torture. In August allegations by Amnesty International of ill-treatment of suspects at Castlereagh RUC detention centre were rejected by the chief constable, Mr Kenneth Newman. Mr Mason promised that an inquiry would re-examine all police practice and procedure. On several occasions during the year he paid tribute to the increasing success of the Royal Ulster Constabulary in bringing the perpetrators of terrorist crimes to justice. In the first six months of 1978, 497 persons were charged with serious offences, including 43 for murder and 55 for attempted murder.

On 17 June a police patrol car was ambushed by the IRA near Crossmaglen. One policeman was found dead, the other had been taken away. Next day in reprisal a Roman Catholic priest, Father Hugh Murphy, was abducted from his home in Ahoghill near Ballymena, his captors vowing to return him in the same condition as the kidnapped policeman; but, after appeals by Protestant church leaders, Father Murphy was released unharmed. The body of Constable Turbitt was not discovered until six weeks later. A post mortem revealed that he had been dying, or was already dead, when he was dragged for hundreds of yards from the scene of the ambush. No trace was found, at the time, of Father Murphy's kidnappers, but in December there was a sensational development when two policemen were arrested and charged with his abduction. One was also charged with the murder of a Roman Catholic shopkeeper in Ahoghill in 1977. Subsequently three other officers were arrested on charges of murder and attempted murder.

In June, also, soldiers shot dead three IRA bombers and an innocent passer-by in an ambush at a post office depot in North Belfast. The use of undercover troops in this way against terrorists was highly effective, but caused controversy because of the risk to innocent civilians. On 11 July at Dunloy in North Antrim soldiers in a similar ambush shot dead a youth who returned to a terrorist arms cache which he had himself discovered and reported to the police.

Although sporadic violence continued to claim lives throughout the summer, there was a perceptible increase in confidence in the community at large, and increasing signs of a return to normal conditions after ten years of the troubles. The city centre of Belfast revived, and security barriers were removed in many provincial towns, prematurely as events were to prove. The police were again able to operate in every part of the country, and in some areas the army was much less in evidence. In September and October army casualties dropped to nil, though one part-time UDR captain was murdered as he attended Newry cattle market on 6 October. Rioting flared again in Derry on two successive weekends, after police allowed a Sinn Fein procession commemorating the tenth anniversary of the first Civil Rights march to pass through the Protestant Waterside district while dispersing a Protestant rally organized by the Rev. Ian Paisley. Forty policemen were injured in clashes, mostly with loyalists.

It was a dull year for politicians. In the absence of any solution to the problem of restoring a form of devolved government for Northern Ireland, continued direct rule found a grudging acceptance from all parties. The Catholic SDLP, however, appearing to abandon hope of a 'power-sharing' settlement, adopted a much more hardline attitude on Irish unity. Its leader, the Westminster MP Mr Gerry Fitt, while continuing to support the Government on most issues, was sharply critical of some aspects of its Northern Ireland policy. The Government's weakened state in the House of Commons inevitably increased the influence of the Ulster Unionist MPs, led by Mr James Molyneaux, and advised on tactics by the redoubtable MP for South Down, Mr Enoch Powell. The Cabinet accepted the recommendation of the Speaker's Conference that Northern Ireland should have five extra seats, a decision bitterly attacked by Mr Fitt.

Meanwhile there were distinct signs that the Opposition was moving cautiously away from the 'bi-partisan' policy on Ulster. On 7 April, Mr Airey Neave, the shadow Secretary for Northern Ireland, declared that power-sharing was no longer 'practical politics' and pledged the support of a future Conservative Government for Official Unionist proposals on upper-tier local administration. In June Mrs Thatcher visited the Province, meeting a wide variety of people in different walks of life, and again gave support to the idea of a regional council structure.

Ulster Unionists had little success in healing the divisions within their own ranks, the Official Unionists remaining at odds with Dr Paisley's Democratic Unionist Party. In March a Ballymena court acquitted Dr Paisley and eight of his supporters on charges of having obstructed the police during the loyalist stoppage in 1977 (see AR 1977, p. 47). A minor political sensation occurred in May when an Alliance Party councillor, Mr David Cooke, was installed as the first non-Unionist Lord Mayor of Belfast, following a bitter disagreement among Unionist councillors.

Despite an ever-worsening level of unemployment, the highest since 1940, there were distinctly encouraging signs for Ulster's economic and industrial recovery, in particular the willingness of some American companies to invest in Northern Ireland. General Motors of Detroit agreed to take over the former Rolls-Royce factory at Dundonald, outside Belfast, to manufacture car seat-belts. After some months of rumour it was announced in August that the De Lorean Motor Company was to build an assembly plant at Twinbrook, a suburb of West Belfast, to produce sports cars for the American market. Mr John De Lorean had previously been unable to secure sufficient financial backing for his project in the United States, Puerto Rico and the Irish Republic. Public elation at the news that Ulster was to have its first car industry was tempered by doubts about the technical feasibility of the project, the high costs of transport to the US, the competitiveness of the American market, and the fact that the plant was to be sited in a strongly Republican area. When it was revealed that of the £65 million required £56 million was to be supplied by the Government, the wisdom of the investment was openly questioned. In October the Harland and Wolff shipyards received a £30 million order to build ferries for the British Rail Dover–France route. At the European Off-Shore Petroleum Exhibition in London it was announced that Ulster's indirect industrial earnings from off-shore oil had exceeded £50 million in 1977. In November the Government announced that it would spend £1 million on a project to revive coal-mining at Coalisland in Co. Tyrone.

November saw a return to preoccupation with the troubles. Industrial action by prison officers demanding an increase in their danger allowance (a separate dispute from the national one) caused serious problems, but the claim was quickly settled. While it lasted, an Order in Council was signed by the Queen to change the law requiring remand prisoners to appear in court. This evoked a protest from some sections of the legal profession, and Mr Mason's blunt remarks in the House of Commons, that only those defending IRA prisoners had objected, caused a further outcry. On 7 November the RUC, acting apparently on firm information, began an intensive search for the body of the West German consul Herr Nieder-mayer who was kidnapped in 1973 (see AR 1973, p. 60). Nothing was found, and after some days the search was called off.

On the night of 14 November IRA car-bombs exploded simultaneously in Omagh, Dungannon, Enniskillen, Derry and Belfast. It was soon clear that this marked the beginning of the IRA's winter offensive, and that the autumn lull had been used by them to regroup and stockpile explosives and weapons. The further bombing of 14 towns on 1 December raised the question of restoring the security barriers, though traders in general were opposed to them. December also saw, for a few brief hours, the spread of the bombing to cities elsewhere in the United Kingdom, bringing momentarily something of the atmosphere experienced in Northern Ireland over the last decade. Shortly before Christmas three Grenadier Guardsmen were machine-gunned to death in Crossmaglen before crowds of shoppers. The reasons for the continued exposure of uniformed soldiers to gunmen in this border town remained obscure to the man in the street. A vicious spate of letter bombs in the Christmas post injured the wives of four prison officers. The IRA declared that there would be no Christmas truce.

At the end of the year, however, the attention of most people in the Province was not on terrorism but on the severe weather. On 28 December, after three days of heavy rain, several rivers burst their banks, causing serious flooding. The rainfall for December was the heaviest on record.

II THE AMERICAS AND THE CARIBBEAN

Chapter 1

THE UNITED STATES OF AMERICA

FOR most Americans 1978 proved to be an uneasy and in some ways a baffling year. The uncertainty derived partly from overseas distrust of the dollar, which, for long a source of pride and a symbol of national self-confidence, was for most of this year in steady and, on occasion, precipitous decline; partly from the fear of inflation and official confusion about how best to deal with it; and partly from the frustrations accompanying the acceptance of limitations on the ability of the United States to influence events in other parts of the world. The American way of life seemed to be changing, and though as a nation America had always welcomed the new there was unusual doubt that this time the change would necessarily be for the better. The passing of an Energy Bill, though much feebler in content than that proposed by President Carter, was a significant recognition by a reluctant Congress that the old profligate ways could not continue much longer, and the adoption of a massive support operation for the dollar, which began to recover some lost ground in the last months of the year, and of a programme of national austerity designed to ward off inflation without braking the economy into recession, indicated that by the end of 1978 Mr Carter's Administration had made up its mind what to do.

For much of the year there was doubt. It was a common criticism of the President in the first half of 1978, when his popularity dropped farther and faster than that of any of his predecessors since opinion polls began (on 30 June only 38 per cent of Americans approved of his conduct of the presidency, compared with 51 per cent six months earlier), that he was ineffective. Mr James Reston, of the *New York Times*, commented that the 'main charge against him is not that he doesn't listen to anybody, but that he listens to everybody and cannot make up his mind—or maybe that he makes it up too often.' What was lacking, his critics maintained, was leadership, and that at a time when a bemused nation badly needed to be led. It was even suggested in Washington that Mr Carter might turn out to be a one-term President. But most Presidents halfway through their first term have found themselves in something of a slump, and by the end of 1978 Mr Carter seemed to have recovered his ground. The turning-point came with some notable achievements in foreign affairs—the signing of the Panama Canal Treaty, his dramatic initiative in inviting President Sadat of Egypt and Prime Minister Begin of Israel to a meeting at Camp David, and his winning of Congressional approval for the resumption of arms supplies to Turkey—and at home with the passage in the last hours of the

95th Congress of the Energy Bill, the tax-cuts Bill and some, though by no means all, of his reform proposals. And at the end of the year he surprised the nation, and the Congress which he had failed to consult, by announcing that the USA was to establish diplomatic relations with China on the first day of the new year. It was not a bad record, and if Mr Carter thought, as he told the American press, that he had been 'overly cautious and even timid' during his first two years of office, there could be no doubt that his Administration was in a far stronger position at the end of 1978 than it had been at the beginning.

HOME AFFAIRS. When Mr Carter came before a joint session of the two Houses of Congress to deliver his first State of the Union address on 19 January, one year after taking office, he was faced with the fact that during that year he had failed to get much of his legislative proposals through the Congress. His approach at the start of 1978 was consequently conservative and decidedly low-key. He declared that the state of the union was sound, 'militarily, politically, economically and in spirit', he reminded his audience that the American people were confident, hard-working, decent and compassionate, and would so remain, and he pointed out that 'for the first time in a generation we are not haunted by a major international crisis or by domestic turmoil, and we now have a rare and priceless opportunity to address the persistent problems which burden us as a nation and which became quietly and steadily worse over the years.'

The programme he presented for taking advantage of this opportunity was qualified by warnings on the limitations of government. 'We need to realize that there is a limit to the role and the function of government', he said. 'Government cannot solve all our problems, set all our goals, or define our vision. Government cannot eliminate poverty, provide a bountiful economy, reduce inflation, save our cities, cure illiteracy, provide energy or mandate goodness. Only a true partnership between government and the people can ever hope to reach these goals. Those of us who govern can sometimes inspire. And we can identify needs and marshal resources. But we cannot be the managers of everything and everybody.' The President evidently did not feel that this was the time for inspiration or exhortation, preferring to try to define his priorities. And the first of these, he said, was the resolution of the energy crisis.

The President's programme for gradually reducing the annual growth rate in US energy demand had been presented to Congress in April 1977 (see AR 1977, pp. 53-55) and there it had stayed. Mr Carter said he recognized that it was not easy for the Congress to act, but the fact remained that on energy legislation 'we have failed the American people'. The country was spending $120 million every day of the year on importing oil. This slowed economic growth, lowered the value of the dollar overseas and aggravated unemployment and inflation at home. The fact was that almost five years after the oil embargo of 1973 had dramatized the problem the US still did not have an energy programme. 'Not much longer can we tolerate this stalemate', warned the President. 'It undermines our national interest both at home and abroad. We must succeed, and I believe we will.' In the event the Energy Bill did not finally receive Congressional approval until 15 October, and then only after a last-minute filibuster in the Senate had been abandoned because Senators wanted to wind up the session so that they could return to their constituencies to campaign for mid-term elections. And the legislation fell far short of the proposals the Administration had put forward 18 months earlier.

The President had hoped for a package that would reduce American oil imports from the current 9 million barrels a day to some $4\frac{1}{2}$ million barrels a day by 1985. The most optimistic calculations of the result of the complex compromise measures passed by Congress were that they might save some 2,300,000 barrels a day by 1985. Plans for increased petrol taxes did not get through, though 'gas-guzzling' cars doing less than 15 miles to the gallon and made from 1980 onwards would be subject to some additional taxes, but there would be no rebates to those who bought gas-saving cars. Proposed taxes on crude oil and on utility and industrial use of oil and natural gas were rejected, but some tax credits were agreed for home insulation and for solar or wind-powered heating equipment. Specific regulations to force industry and utilities to switch from oil to coal were watered down to a requirement that new utilities and new industrial plant should use fuel other than oil or gas, but there were many exemptions. A new system of price controls for natural gas was introduced which would allow a gradual increase of prices, expanded availability of substantial existing reserves, and elimination of most price controls by 1985.

In practical terms this was the Administration's most significant achievement in the Bill; for it was estimated that it would cut oil imports by about 1,400,000 barrels a day by 1985, though some experts argued that the new control system, which involved 17 main categories of natural gas, would prove unworkable and perhaps even lead to a reduction of output. The failure to deal with oil prices, which Mr Carter had at one time called the centrepiece of his energy programme, and the dilution of many other measures might reduce its effectiveness, and probably made further energy legislation inevitable; but this did not lessen the Bill's historical importance, which lay in the fact that it represented, in the words of the *Washington Post*, 'a turning-point in the way that Americans think about fuel and energy'.

In political terms the passage of the Energy Bill was an undoubted success for the President. He had staked his reputation, and that of his young Administration, upon it, and there had been times during its 18 months passage through Congress when it seemed that no legislation would emerge. In the end the much-amended version was passed by a vote of 60-17 in the Senate and by 281-168 in the House of Representatives in their final sessions. The 95th Congress also completed work, in a last marathon session, on a flurry of other Bills, including the important tax-cut Bill (see Economy, below). This gave the President a rather more satisfactory legislative record than he had anticipated earlier in the year, when he had been bitterly critical of Congress's failure to act on his programme and had appealed to the people to support him by writing letters of protest to their Congressmen, and when, on 4 October, he vetoed a public works appropriation Bill for $10,200 million on the grounds that it contained too many unnecessary and inflationary items of a pre-election 'pork-barrel' nature.

In its last hours on 15 October Congress passed two of the President's main reform Bills—those for reforming the civil service and for the de-regulation of the airlines. During his election campaign Mr Carter had undertaken to reform the civil service, and the new law would enable him to carry out his promise to make the American bureaucracy less rigid and to remove some of the incompetents who had for so long found refuge within it. The Act for the de-regulation of the airlines provided for the closure of the Civil Aeronautics Board by 1985, by which time government regulation of air fares would have ceased. The Act would allow increasing competition among domestic airlines and, it was presumed, lower fares. Congress also passed a Bill for the reduction of airport noise, though refusing to allocate funds for it, and finally agreed to a modified version of the Humphrey–Hawkins full-employment Bill which had originally been designed to commit the nation to reducing unemployment to 4 per cent in 1983, but which in its final version was so hedged about with qualifications and restrictions that it stood no chance of achieving this goal. Among the measures which Congress failed to act upon, or which were killed outright, were those on tax reform, welfare reform, the setting-up of a national health service, the reform of the electoral college and the financing of Congressional elections.

The reluctance of Congress to go along with many of the President's reforming proposals suggested that they believed the dominant mood of the country to be conservative. Their political percipience was confirmed by the results of the mid-term elections, held on 7 November. The Republicans made small gains in both Houses and won six governorships from the Democrats. In the Senate the Republicans made a net gain of three seats, winning eight and losing five, and in the House of Repre-sentatives they made a net gain of 12. The Democrats remained in firm control of both Houses, ending up with 59 seats in the Senate compared with the Republicans' 41, and with 276 seats in the new House compared with the Republicans' 159, but there were some notable losses among liberal Democrats, including Senator Dick Clark of Iowa, an expert on African affairs and one of the President's staunchest supporters in the

Senate, and Senator Thomas McIntyre of Maine, a member of the Armed Services Committee.

In the contest for governorships, of which 36 were up for election, the Republicans won nine from the Democrats and lost three, to bring their total to 18 out of 50. Republican victories included the states of Minnesota, Pennsylvania and Texas, and they successfully held on to Michigan and Ohio, both of which they feared they might lose. Though the overall result was far from being a disaster for the Democrats (mid-term elections usually being bad for any President's party), it was not regarded with any enthusiasm by Mr Carter, since in its composition the new Congress seemed likely to prove even more troublesome to work with than the last.

An aspect of the voting which was watched with anxiety by administrators throughout the country was the possible spread of the Californian taxpayers' revolt. This had originated on 6 June when voters in California decided in a referendum on the primary election ballot to cut their property taxes to 1 per cent of assessed values. Their vote, by nearly two-to-one, in favour of what was known as 'proposition 13' meant that property taxes in the state were cut by an average of 57 per cent, and that local authorities lost $7,000 million of taxation a year. The revolt against property taxes was initiated by Mr Howard Jarvis, a 75-year-old Californian, following a reassessment of home values by the state and a resultant big increase in property taxes, and proposition 13 became the dominant topic in the state primary elections. When the result of the vote became known Mr Jarvis declared that it was the greatest victory ever achieved by the people of California, and added: 'Tonight we know how our forefathers felt when they dumped tea in the Boston harbour and paved the way to the revolution.'

The state governor, Mr Jerry Brown, who had strongly opposed the proposition, said after the vote that it was clear that people wanted the spirit of frugality to spread across California, and he proposed to carry out the will of the people 'in a sensitive, humane and straightforward way'. This proved none too easy to achieve. Most local authorities had to make extensive cuts in their services, laying off employees, reducing planned wage increases, cutting education budgets and increasing direct charges to the public for transport and other services. Mr Brown announced that more than $300,000 would be cut from the state budget for the next fiscal year.

The California experience was closely and sympathetically observed in other states in the union, and proposals similar to proposition 13 were included in the ballots in a number of states in the November elections, but voters elsewhere were reluctant to repeat the experiment—perhaps because the full implications of the California decision had still to be learnt. Only in Missouri and Idaho were substantial positive votes recorded for the reduction of property taxes. In other states the idea was rejected or received indecisive verdicts, and other proposals for limiting public expenditure in some way produced mixed responses. Nonetheless the warning of the California revolt was clear: that there was a limit to the amount of taxation a free society could tolerate, and once that limit was crossed the resistance movement it inspired was difficult to control. The campaigning for the mid-term elections indicated that American politicians were not ignoring the warning.

As in previous years the plight of American cities, particularly in the ghetto areas that lay close to the heart of many of them, again stirred the conscience of the United States in 1978. Two years earlier, when on the campaign trail, Mr Carter had promised the mayors that if he became President they would have 'a friend, an ally and a partner in the White House'. On 27 March President Carter announced a programme designed to give effect to that pledge. His package included loans and business incentives to firms investing in distressed areas and hiring people who had been unemployed for a long time, a $1,000 million 'soft' public works employment programme for refurbishing public buildings, parks and neighbourhoods, some direct aid for cities, a small amount for housing, and a relaxing of the Clean Air Act to allow cities to attract new industries.

On analysis the programme, in spite of its attempt at comprehensiveness, or perhaps because of it, was seen to be stronger in encouragement than it was in practical assistance. Spending for state and local government was already at a high level, and the Administration evidently decided that it could not offer much in the way of direct aid without aggravating the budget deficit and boosting inflation. Those who had been campaigning for massive urban assistance were disappointed with the President's proposals; others noted that a presidential commitment to a specific urban policy was a new development in American politics, and one to which Congressmen, only about a third of whom represented urban constituencies, were likely to respond with particular caution. In previous years Congress had certainly shown little enthusiasm for rescuing New York, the most obvious example of an American city in trouble.

That city again teetered on the edge of bankruptcy in 1978. The short-term loans from federal sources that had averted bankruptcy in 1975 (see AR 1975, pp. 65-67) were due to come to an end in the middle of the year, and although the city had made some drastic cuts in its expenditure since that year it was still not in a position to balance its books when the loans ran out. So the city's mayor, Mr Edward Koch, went to Washington in June to ask Congress for further federal assistance to keep New York solvent. Appearing before the Senate banking committee the mayor said that unless Congress provided long-term guarantees for some $2,000 million worth of New York City bonds his city would lurch from crisis to crisis, and its 'physical plant, its infrastructure, will continue to deteriorate and economic development will be stifled'. The Senators were not impressed. 'We run the risk of turning New York into a guarantee junkie', said Senator William Proxmire, the chairman of the committee. In the end Congress concluded that the problems posed by a bankrupt New York were likely to be greater than those incurred by bailing the city out, and on 9 August Mr Carter was able to spend a happy day visiting New York during the course of which he signed, on the steps of City Hall and at a desk once used by George Washington, the authority for a new $1,650 million federal loan guarantee for the city.

The New York newspapers ran into difficulties during the year. A new daily paper called *The Trib*, launched with considerable fanfare on 9 January, closed down on 5 April after losing some $5 million during its three-months life. On 10 August the three remaining daily newspapers stopped publication when their printers went on strike following the introduction of new electronic printing processes and the imposition of new manning rules which reduced the number of printers employed. One of the three newspapers, the *New York Post*, resumed publication on 5 October, having broken off joint negotiations to make its own deal with the print unions. The other two, the *New York Times* and the *Daily News*, did not appear on the streets again until 6 November. It was estimated that the 88-day strike cost the newspapers some $150 million in lost advertising and sales revenue, while employees lost $60 million in wages.

A reporter from the *New York Times*, Mr Myron Farber, was sent to prison in August to serve an indefinite sentence imposed by a New Jersey Court for contempt of court in failing to hand over his confidential notes to a judge in a murder trial. The newspaper was fined $5,000 a day until the notes were handed over. An appeal to the New Jersey State Supreme Court on behalf of the newspaper and its reporter failed, but Mr Farber was released after serving 27 days in jail pending an appeal to the Supreme Court in Washington, and the newspaper's payment of the fines was also suspended. On 10 October Farber was returned to jail, but he was released again on 24 October when the accused man in the murder trial was found 'not guilty'. The *New York Times* had by then paid $285,000 in fines and nearly $1 million in legal fees. The appeal to the Supreme Court was continued, mainly because the newspaper regarded the reporter's right to protect his sources of information as an issue of principle, protected by the First Amendment. In an editorial on the subject the newspaper asked the questions: 'If we betrayed one informant's trust, who could trust us again? If we honoured a court's right to pry in our unpublished notes, who could publish anything again from a confidential source without having to risk the source's safety or their own?' The Supreme Court had not delivered its judgment when the year ended.

A strike of coal miners which had begun in the last month of 1977 continued to trouble the country in the early months of 1978. The President intervened on 15 February, when he made an urgent plea to representatives of the industry to begin talks to bring the strike to an end, and won the support of Congressional leaders in both Houses to do whatever he felt necessary to end it. The implication was that he would invoke the Taft–Hartley Act, which would have ordered the 160,000 miners back to work for a 'cooling-off' period while negotiations continued. But some miners had declared that they would not go back to work even if the Taft–Hartley Act was invoked, and it was not until coal supplies had been reduced to a critically low level, and tens of thousands of workers in other industries had been laid off, that the President finally used the Act to order the miners back to work. The miners defied the order and did not go back to work until 27 March, when their leaders had finally agreed the terms of a new three-year contract.

A new director of the Federal Bureau of Investigation took office during the year. Mr William Webster, a former Federal Appeals Court judge in St Louis, succeeded Mr Clarence Kelley, who retired in February. Mr Webster, a 53-year-old Republican, was the President's second choice for the post; the first, Mr Frank Johnson, withdrew for health reasons. A former acting director of the FBI, Mr Patrick Gray, was indicted by a federal grand jury in April, accused of conspiring to violate civil rights by using illegal surveillance methods in 1972 and 1973.

In space in 1978 the American concern was with the planet Venus. A total of six spacecraft were involved, four of them having been carried in one of two larger craft launched on the 220-million-mile journey to the planet from Cape Canaveral in Florida in August. They all arrived at Venus early in December, four of them landing on the surface. The 'space bus' acted as a scientific measuring device, and the sixth spacecraft went into orbit round the planet at a height of between 90 and 41,000 miles. By the end of the year much information had been transmitted back to Earth, including what seemed to some American scientists to be convincing evidence that the primeval Venusian atmosphere was different from Earth's, a conclusion which in turn suggested that Earth and Venus had different origins.

A good deal closer to home, three Americans completed the first crossing of the Atlantic by balloon in August. Setting off from Maine, they landed in France, about 60 miles from Paris, 137 hours and six minutes later, succeeding where at least 18 previous attempts had failed.

FOREIGN AFFAIRS. In terms of time and energy the deep-rooted problems of the Middle East proved to be the greatest foreign preoccupation for the USA during 1978, though a remarkable amount of advice, exhortation, influence and inspiration had not achieved much discernible progress by the end of the year. President Carter himself took a hand in affairs early on when, on 3 and 4 January, he briefly visited Saudi Arabia and Egypt. The Americans were anxious to try to persuade the Arabs to relax their insistence that an independent Palestine state should be an essential part of a Middle East settlement, but the message the President received from both the Saudi Arabians and the Egyptians was that there could be no agreement unless the right to self-determination by the Palestinian Arabs was included. Mr Carter appeared to have accepted the point when, after a cordial 90-minute meeting with President Sadat of Egypt during a stop-over in Aswan, he listed to his Egyptian audience the fundamental principles which he said must be observed before a just and comprehensive peace could be achieved. 'First', he said, 'true peace must be based on normal relations among the parties to the peace. Peace means more than just an end to the belligerency. Second, there must be withdrawal by Israel from territories occupied in 1967 and agreement on secure and recognized borders for all parties in the context of normal and peaceful relations in accordance with United Nations Resolutions 242 and 338. Third, there must be a resolution of the Palestinian problem in all its aspects. The solution of the problem must recognize the legitimate rights of the Palestinian people and enable the Palestinians to participate in the determination of their own future.'

On his return home the President emphasized, in his State of the Union address, that the US would continue to contribute its good offices to maintain the momentum of negotiations, and to keep open the lines of communication among the Middle East leaders. 'This is a precious opportunity for the historic settlement of a long-standing conflict', he said, 'an opportunity which may not come again in our lifetime. Our role has been difficult—and sometimes thankless and controversial—but it has been constructive and necessary and it will continue.' The Administration kept up the pressure on the Middle East leaders. Secretary of State Cyrus Vance went to Cairo on 20 January following the abrupt withdrawal of the Egyptian delegation from the Jerusalem talks, but failed to find a formula to persuade the Egyptians to return. A week later President Sadat visited the USA at Mr Carter's invitation to 'review progress', but the meetings failed to break the deadlock, even though it was revealed that Mr Carter had sent three messages of protest to Mr Begin, the Israeli Prime Minister, during January about the new Jewish settlements in occupied Sinai and the West Bank—one of the main issues of contention in the breakdown of negotiations.

On 14 February Mr Carter tried a new initiative by proposing to send 60 F15 fighters to Saudia Arabia, 50 F5E fighters to Egypt, and 75 F16 fighter bombers and 15 F15 fighters to Israel to add to the 25 already promised. It was the first time the USA had offered arms to Egypt since the 1950s, and the proposal was met with dismay by Israel and a good deal of opposition in the US Congress, but the President was gambling that the offer of arms would be sufficient to keep the peace talks alive. Though he won Congressional approval for the arms deal, after adding another 20 F15s for Israel, the move did not lead to further progress on the peace negotiations.

Mr Begin came to Washington in March for what proved to be a series of difficult meetings. He was put under great pressure to make substantial new concessions to Egypt in order to save the peace talks, but he refused to do so. The result was a severe deterioration of American-Israeli relations, and as Mr Begin left Washington the two sides were unable even to agree on a joint statement. Mr Vance announced that Israel had rejected three fundamental points: that UN resolution 242 be accepted, that the Sinai settlements be abandoned, and that the West Bank be given a degree of self-determination. For their part the Israelis believed that the Americans were withdrawing their support, and were indeed so suspicious of American diplomacy that they believed the US was plotting to have Mr Begin removed as Prime Minister—a suggestion denied by Mr Vance.

The wreckage took some time to clear. Mr Carter some weeks later reassured Mr Begin that America's commitment to Israel was complete and eternal, in spite of their occasional differences, and at the beginning of July he sent the Vice-President, Mr Walter Mondale, on a goodwill visit for the celebrations of Israel's thirtieth anniversary. Finally he made the imaginative gesture of inviting Mr Begin and President Sadat to open-ended meetings at Camp David, his presidential retreat in Maryland. The two leaders arrived on 5 September and talked sometimes with each other, sometimes with Mr Carter individually, and more frequently with their own staffs, until 17 September, when they emerged into the glare of the Washington television lights to sign two documents which seemed to take a jump towards peace.

The first was called 'The Framework of Peace in the Middle East' and the second 'Framework for the Conclusion of a Peace Treaty between Egypt and Israel' (see DOCUMENTS). Between them the two agreements dealt with the four major aspects of the peace process as envisaged by the US. The first of these was the recognition of Israel as a normal and permanent Middle Eastern state, and in the second document, on the peace treaty, Egypt committed itself to normal relations with Israel. The second element of peace was security for all parties. This was covered in both documents, which included provisions for demilitarized zones in Sinai and for the stationing of UN forces on both sides of the frontiers between Egypt and Israel. The third element was the delineation of frontiers, in which respect Israel conceded the ultimate return of the whole of Sinai, but the question of its West Bank frontiers was left open. However, Israel undertook not to develop existing Jewish settlements on the West Bank and not to create any new ones while negotiations were going on. The final element was the future of the Palestinians, and on this question Israel accepted the American-Arab condition that the Palestinians must take part in the determination of their own future. The agreements laid down that the peace treaty between Israel and Egypt should be signed within three months.

In spite of Mr Carter's undoubted personal triumph in persuading the two leaders to come to Camp David, and in prevailing upon them to stay there until an agreement had been forged, there were some obvious limitations to the agreements as published. One was the unresolved question of the West Bank. Another was the interpretation of the clause allowing Palestinians participation in the determination of their own future. A third, and the one which was to create the most immediate difficulties, was the question whether President Sadat would be supported by some other Arab nations in negotiations on the framework for peace in the Middle East, or whether he would be left on his own to finalize a bilateral treaty with Israel—a step he had said he would never take. To try to overcome this anticipated danger Mr Cyrus Vance set off at once for Jordan and Saudi Arabia in the hope of persuading King Hussein and King Khalid to agree to take part in the negotiations.

Mr Vance returned from the Middle East without any commitment from the Jordanians or the Saudi Arabians to participate in the peace negotiations, but he was able to draw some comfort from the fact that neither had he received any positive refusal. But the revelation in October by Israel that it proposed to extend its settlements in the occupied West Bank dampened even Mr Vance's optimism, and drew a formal expression of concern from the State Department. 'We regard the reported decision taken by the Israeli Government to "thicken" some of the settlements on the West Bank as a very serious matter and are deeply disturbed by it', the statement said. 'We have already communicated with Prime Minister Begin and will refrain from any further comment until we receive his response.' The response was not satisfactory, and as the deadline of 17 December approached it seemed unlikely that a treaty could be got ready in time. President Carter warned that failure to reach agreement by the deadline would have 'far-reaching adverse effects', and Mr Vance was again dispatched to Egypt and Israel to try to overcome the continuing disputes. He failed, and when the year ended no peace treaty had been signed. Though Mr Carter said he would continue to pursue peace tenaciously, the US for the time being abandoned its mediating role. In reply to a question about the possibility of another Middle East summit Mr Carter said: 'I've got other pressing international problems.'

Within hours of expressing his frustration at the failure to reach agreement in the Middle East the President was able to announce that the United States would establish diplomatic relations with the People's Republic of China on 1 January 1979. A joint communique issued in Washington and Peking (see DOCUMENTS) said the US recognized the Government of the People's Republic as the sole legal Government of China, which meant that diplomatic relations with Taiwan would be broken off, though cultural, commercial and other contacts would be maintained and the American defence treaty would run for another year, after which it could be legally terminated. In a televised address to the nation Mr Carter said that the US and China would exchange ambassadors and establish embassies in Washington and Peking in March, and that before then the Chinese Deputy Premier, Teng Hsiao-p'ing, would visit the USA. It would be the first visit of a senior Chinese communist leader since the end of the Chinese civil war in 1949, when diplomatic relations were broken off following the communist victory and the fleeing of the Nationalists to Taiwan. In addition to the joint communique the US also issued a unilateral statement declaring that it expected that the Taiwan issue 'will be settled peacefully by the Chinese themselves'.

The news was not universally well received within the USA. The Republican Senator Barry Goldwater denounced it as 'a cowardly act' and said that it 'stabbed in the back the nation of Taiwan'. Other Republicans made similar comments, and two Democrats on the Senate Foreign Relations Committee questioned whether the President had fulfilled the legal requirement for 'prior consultation' with Congress before altering the status of American relations with Taiwan. In Taiwan itself there were some violent demonstrations against a US delegation visiting Taipei to try to ensure the maintenance of trade, cultural and other ties.

Closer links with China carried clear risks for the United States of a consequent worsening of relations with the Soviet Union, and the opportunity for the Soviet leaders to indicate their feelings was conveniently to hand in the form of the strategic arms limitation talks (SALT II), which the US had confidently expected to complete by the end of the year. So confident, in fact, was the State Department that preparations were being made in October for a visit by President Brezhnev to Washington early in 1979 when it was expected that the new treaty would be ready for signature. Mr Vance visited Moscow at the end of the month, but again left without a final agreement in his briefcase. He was confident, he said, that agreement was close, and when he left to meet Mr Andrei Gromyko, the Soviet Foreign Minister, in Geneva in December he said he did not think the US agreement with China, which had just been announced, would stand in the way of a SALT II agreement. But when he got to Geneva Mr Vance was met with a number of new proposals which effectively wrecked the chance of any agreement being reached before the end of the year, and no visit by Mr Brezhnev was arranged.

Much though the US wanted an agreement, it was not prepared to make more than a limited number of concessions to achieve it, and this attitude was a fair reflection of the Carter Administration's firmer policy towards the Soviet Union, slowly developed in response to the Russian arms build-up, increasing Russian and Cuban involvement in Africa, and continuing abuse of human rights. The President defined American policy towards Russia most clearly in an address at the Annapolis Naval Academy on 8 June, when he made it clear that, although America wanted detente, it could not be detente at any price. There must be conciliation also on the other side. 'The Soviet Union can choose either confrontation or co-operation', he said. 'The United States is adequately prepared to meet either choice.' America must be willing to explore avenues of cooperation, he said, but to the Soviet Union detente seemed to mean 'a continuing aggressive struggle for political advantage and increased influence, in a variety of ways. The Soviet Union apparently sees military power and military assistance as the best means of expanding their influence abroad. Obviously, areas of instability provide a tempting target for their efforts, and all too often they seem ready to exploit any such opportunity.' He thought the Soviet military build-up over the past 15 years was excessive, far beyond any legitimate requirement for the defence of themselves or their allies.

On this occasion, as on others during the year, Mr Carter warned Russia and Cuba about their continuing involvement in Africa, which should be allowed to remain a continent free of the dominance of outside powers. This concern led the US to work closely with the British Government in efforts to resolve the Rhodesia crisis. Mr Cyrus Vance and Dr David Owen, the British Foreign Secretary, tried on several occasions to call a conference of all interested parties, including representatives of the Patriotic Front, but though they won the agreement of Mr Ian Smith, the Rhodesian Prime Minister, and his colleagues in the transitional Government when they came to Washington in October they failed to persuade members of the Patriotic Front to take part. The State Department originally decided against issuing Mr Smith a visa when he was first invited to put his case to members of Congress and to the American people, on the grounds that he was leader of an illegal regime, but changed its mind because it believed that the visit could 'contribute to the process of achieving a settlement of the Rhodesian conflict to which the Administration remains entirely committed'. When in Washington Mr Smith argued strongly that the reason for the failure of the cease-fire in Rhodesia was the fact that the American and British Governments were supporting the Patriotic Front instead of supporting the internal settlement, but he failed to convince the State Department that the latter could bring a lasting and peaceful settlement to Rhodesia.

In a written message to Congress delivered at the same time as his State of the Union address, President Carter wrote of the difficulty created by the spiralling increase in the trade in conventional arms, which both increased the likelihood in conflict and diverted resources from other human needs. He promised that America would begin to cut back on its arms sales 'in recognition of the fact that, as the world's principal seller, we have a duty to take the first step'. America's responsibility to its allies, and to the security of Nato, was sometimes in conflict with this aim, as it had been in the case of the Middle East, and as it was to be with Turkey. The US had imposed an embargo on military aid to Turkey in 1975, following its invasion of Cyprus in the previous year, but in April the President asked Congress to end the arms embargo and to approve $225 million in military aid to that country. The request met with strong opposition in Congress, and was voted down in the Senate Foreign Relations Committee on 12 May after it had been narrowly approved in the House of Representatives. However, the Administration did not give up the struggle, and on 25 July the Senate voted, by 57 to 42, in favour of a compromise that allowed the resumption of arms supplies provided the President could report progress towards a solution of the dispute between Greece and Turkey over Cyprus, and the embargo was formally lifted when the President signed an International Security Assistance Bill on 25 September.

Unconventional arms also caused the President some problems in 1978. After much hesitation he announced in April that he had decided to postpone production of the neutron bomb, or 'weapons with enhanced radiation effects' as they were officially called, which meant weapons with warheads with minimal blast but lethal radiation impact on people. The decision was generally welcomed, both in America and among its allies, though Mr Harold Brown, the Defense Secretary, had some explaining to do, for he had spent the early months of the year trying to persuade the British and German Governments to accept the weapon as the most effective way of improving the defence of Western Europe. The President was quick to rebuff Mr Brezhnev when the Russian leader suggested that his country would not produce the neutron bomb if America agreed to do the same. The Russians had no use for the weapon, Mr Carter said, for it was designed for use against massive and overwhelming tank forces in the central European area. The Soviet Union had expanded its tank forces much more than had Nato, and the neutron bomb was designed to neutralize that inequality.

Later in the year Mr Carter, apparently persuaded of the need for the US to modernize its stock of tactical nuclear weapons, ordered the production of a new generation of tactical warheads which could be adapted for use as neutron bombs. The 'neutron' components were likely to be stored in the USA, but they would provide an option for Nato to counter an attack on Western Europe by deploying neutron weapons. It was emphasized in Washington that the President's decision to proceed with production of tactical warheads that could be converted did not mean that a decision had been taken to go ahead with neutron weapons.

In 1977 President Carter had signed an agreement with the President of Panama by which the United States gave to Panama full control of the canal and the Canal Zone by the year 2000. The agreement comprised two treaties—one covering the operation of the canal and its defence until 1999, the second guaranteeing its permanent neutrality (see AR 1977, p. 65). In 1978 President Carter had to secure the ratification of the treaties by Congress. In the Senate a two-thirds majority was required, and on 16 March the second of the treaties, guaranteeing the neutrality of the waterway, was given that majority by a margin of only one vote, and then only after two modifications had been made—one spelling out American rights to continue to defend the canal if its neutrality was threatened, and the other giving priority to American ships in time of war. On 18 April the Senate voted to ratify the first treaty, dealing with the operation of the canal until 1999, again by one vote more than the required two-thirds majority, but with an amendment to the effect that formal ratification would be postponed until enabling legislation regarding some sections of the treaties had been passed in the US, or until 31 March 1979, whichever was sooner. It appeared that there might be some resistance to this enabling legislation, particularly in the House of Representatives, but in spite of this Mr Carter went to Panama on 16 June to exchange documents of ratification with the Panamanian leader, Brigadier-General Omar Terrijos Herrera.

The gradual collapse of the Shah's regime in Iran took the US by surprise, and it was unable to provide any practical assistance against the violent opposition that challenged the rule of one of America's stauncher allies. In December the US air force helped evacuate American families from the country, and by the end of the year the State Department was resigned to having to accommodate itself to a change of government which it hoped would quickly gain sufficient command of the situation to enable the flow of oil to be resumed.

A small, little-known American religious sect called the People's Temple created grisly headlines throughout the world in November when more than 900 of its followers died, most by suicide, in their commune in a remote jungle area of Guyana, in South America. The Guyana group of the People's Temple, most of whom came originally from the poor areas of San Francisco, was led by the Rev. Jim Jones, a 47-year-old white man who moved his sect to Guyana when complaints began to be made about the rigorous methods used to impose discipline on his followers. Similar complaints began to be made after the group had moved to Guyana, and in November Congressman Leo Ryan, a Democrat from South San Francisco, set off with a small party of pressmen and others to Jonestown, where the sect had its Guyana headquarters, to investigate. When he was about to board his aircraft for the return journey he was shot dead, together with four other Americans. In the camp itself more than 900 followers of the sect, including children, were then persuaded to drink cyanide found mixed with a fruit drink in a tin tub, and those who tried to escape were shot down by the camp's armed guards. Mr Jones was one of those found shot dead. The bodies were flown back to the USA for burial.

ECONOMIC AFFAIRS. At home the state of the economy proved to be the major anxiety throughout the year. Though the President was able to claim in his State of the Union address that 1977 had been a good year for the USA, with unemployment at the lowest it had been since 1974, good growth in business profits and investment and, after taxes and inflation, 'a healthy increase in workers' wages', there were fears that inflation was beginning to take grip and uncertainty about the Administration's policies for dealing with it, an uncertainty shared overseas, as the rapid decline in the value of the dollar was showing. Mr Carter declared that his economic policy was based on four principles:

First, the economy must keep on expanding to produce the new jobs and better income which our people need. The fruits of growth must be widely shared; more jobs must be made available to those who have been by-passed until now; and the tax system must be made fairer and simpler.

Second, private business and not the Government must lead the expansion.

Third, we must lower the rate of inflation and keep it down. Inflation slows down economic growth, and it is most cruel to the poor and to the elderly and others who live on fixed incomes.

Fourth, we must contribute to the strength of the world economy.

On 22 January the President announced his package of tax cuts and tax reform measures, and on the following day his Budget for the fiscal year beginning on 1 October. His tax proposals involved a total of $34,900 million in tax cuts and $10,400 million in additional levies, resulting in a net tax reduction of $24,500 million. Changes in the tax system, which were mostly planned to become effective on 1 October, were designed to make it more progressive and to benefit principally the middle and lower income earners, the net personal tax cuts amounting to $16,700 million. Corporate tax was to be reduced from 48 to 45 per cent, and greater reductions were proposed for small companies with low profit levels. Corporate tax cuts totalled $6,000 million, with a further $2,400 million coming from improved investment credits. Among the measures for reform were sharp reductions in business entertainment and travel deductions (including those claimed by executives for theatre tickets, club membership subscriptions, first-class air fares, yachts and hunting lodges), and the elimination of tax subsidies for domestic international sales corporations and tax deferrals for American companies which invested overseas.

In his Budget the President proposed federal expenditure of $500,200 million, which would result in a deficit of $60,600 million, slightly less than that of the current year. With the planned tax cuts there would be an increase in the budget of 8 per cent, of which 6 per cent was inflation, and a small reduction, from 22·6 to 22 per cent, in the proportion of the national income spent by the Government. More would be spent on welfare, scientific research, health, education and defence, though the defence budget was $8,000 million below that projected by the previous Administration. A total of $7,700 million was assigned for foreign aid, including military assistance. In presenting the Budget Mr Carter emphasized that he was aiming to follow a fiscal policy that provided for a continuing recovery from the 1974-75 recession, bearing in mind the fact that resources were limited and 'the need for careful and prudent management of the taxpayers' resources'.

The President's tax proposals, though popular in the country at large, were strongly opposed in Congress and by a number of influential economists, largely because of their inflationary aspects. Mr William Miller, the new chairman of the Federal Reserve Board, called for a reduction in the 'degree of stimulus' in the face of rising inflation, and on 11 April the President responded to the growing pressure by announcing that he proposed to take the lead in breaking the wage and price spiral by granting no pay rise in 1978 to himself or his senior colleagues, and by limiting white-collar federal employees to rises of 5·5 per cent. He sent letters to all state governors and to the mayors of the largest cities urging them to follow his example, and he appointed Mr Robert Strauss, his special trade representative, to take on additional duties as a special adviser on inflation. On 12 May he bowed further to the demands of the Federal Reserve Board, and to a series of alarming economic indicators suggesting a rate of inflation of more than 10 per cent, by agreeing to reduce his proposed tax cuts to $20,000 million and to delay their implementation until the first day of 1979. After blatantly electioneering moves in the Senate to increase the level of tax cuts to $30,000 million, and threats in the House of Representatives to reduce them to $16,500 million, Congress finally, on 15 October, passed a Bill which set the level of tax cuts at $18,500 million. But the President's plans for reforming the tax structure were not included.

Meanwhile the value of the dollar continued to decline. In August the President declared that he was deeply concerned about it, though he expressed his confidence in its underlying strength (provided Congress acted on his proposed energy legislation). In September he addressed the opening meetings of the World Bank and the International Monetary Fund, promising to maintain a sound dollar and revealing that further anti-inflationary measures were on the way. A 12-point 'national export programme' was unveiled in Washington on 26 September, designed primarily to strengthen the dollar by reducing the balance of payments deficit through the expansion of exports. The new programme comprised a series of measures to encourage American manufacturers to pay more attention to export markets, together with an increase in the allocation of funds for the US Export–Import Bank.

Another and more detailed anti-inflation programme was introduced on 24 October, when Mr Carter declared that he was setting the country on a course of national austerity. He hoped that the programme would boost sagging business confidence, stabilize the dollar in world markets, and lead to cuts in the high level of interest rates (the banks had just raised their prime lending rates to $10\frac{1}{4}$ per cent).

The central feature of the programme was an appeal to limit wage increases, including fringe benefits, to 7 per cent. Unions negotiating three-year contracts would be allowed to obtain slightly higher first-year rises provided that the average increases for the three-year period were not more than 7 per cent. As an inducement to accept this limit the Government proposed a 'real wage insurance' under which workers would receive tax rebates if inflation in the following year exceeded 7 per cent. Individual firms would be expected to keep price increases in the coming year to one-half of one percentage point below their average annual rate of increase during 1976-77. In that year prices rose by 6·2 per cent, compared with the average rate in the current year of 8 per cent. So far as was possible government purchases would be restricted to companies abiding by this standard of price increases, but it was made clear by Mr Robert Strauss that there would be no resort to mandatory wage and price controls which, he said, simply did not work. For its part, the Government undertook to cut public spending and to reduce the number of people employed in government jobs.

Following the introduction of these anti-inflation measures the Administration at the beginning of November set up a massive new support operation for the dollar. Credit was further tightened, and a total of $30,000 million was mobilized, half of it coming from borrowing facilities with the central banks of West Germany, Japan and Switzerland, $10,000 million from the sale of American government bonds, and $5,000 million through the International Monetary Fund. In addition the USA doubled the size of its monthly sales of gold from the reserves. These had begun in May, when 750,000 ounces had been sold. The introduction of these measures marked the end of the Administration's opposition to tighter domestic monetary policies, and also indicated its support for the Federal Reserve Board's efforts to restrain the growth of the nation's money supply. The Administration's previous reluctance to act was based on the fear of recession, but Mr Michael Blumenthal, the Secretary of the Treasury, said that he did not think that recession would follow from the tighter monetary conditions now being imposed. Certainly the new support programme achieved its immediate aim. On the Wall Street stock exchange, prices of American shares rose by record amounts, and on the currency market there was what one dealer described as a 'dollar buying stampede'. In the previous twelve months the dollar had declined by 25 per cent against the Deutschemark, and by more against the Swiss franc. By the end of 1978 it had recovered about one-third of these losses.

The end of the year also saw a higher rate of growth in the economy than had been expected, the gross national product in the last quarter increasing at an annual rate of 6·1 per cent in real terms, which brought the 1978 rise in output to 3·9 per cent, after removing the inflation factor. The major contributor to the last quarter's progress was consumer spending, much of it on borrowed money, which brought with it a quickening of the inflation rate. For the last quarter the rate of price increases, after declining in the third quarter from the double-figure level of the second, rose to 8·5 per cent, which brought an increase for the year as a whole of 7·5 per cent. This left Americans facing the new year with inflation, in their own graphic phrase, as Public Enemy No. 1.

Chapter 2

CANADA

ECONOMIC and political uncertainty continued to dominate developments in Canada during 1978. In April, the third anniversary of the federal Government's imposition of price and income controls, the twelve-month inflation rate stood at 8·8 per cent. During the phasing-out of controls, which continued during the remainder of the year, consumer prices rose at a similar rate. The unemployment rate also remained above 8 per cent throughout the year. In January, the total number of unemployed rose to 991,000.

The precipitous drop in the value of the Canadian dollar, which had begun in 1977, continued throughout the year. From a level of approximately 90 cents US in January, the dollar dropped another 5 cents in spite of energetic counter-measures by the Government. In February the Minister of Finance, Mr Jean Chrétien, announced that the Government was borrowing $200 million from a special $1,500 million stand-by credit which it had arranged with Canadian banks to protect the value of the dollar. In March Canada borrowed US$750 million in New York and arranged stand-by foreign credit of another US$2,500 million. In April Mr Chrétien announced an additional foreign borrowing of US$725 million from a major West German bank. As well, the Bank of Canada increased its lending rate on six separate occasions during the year in an attempt to moderate downward pressure on the dollar by keeping Canadian interest rates in line with those in the United States.

Labour unrest, while not as severe as in previous years, showed signs of reappearing following the removal of wage and price controls. After a last-minute avoidance of a pilots' strike in August, a strike of ground-service workers resulted in a ten-day shutdown of Air Canada. Rotating strikes by inside postal workers led Parliament to pass back-to-work

c

legislation in October. The postal workers, who were urged by their leadership to ignore the legislation, finally returned to work only when the Postmaster General announced that any worker who did not return by 26 October would be considered to have abandoned his job and would be fired. Also indicative of increasing labour unrest was the decision of the Canadian Labour Congress to withdraw its representation from the Economic Council of Canada, which had been requested by the Government to monitor wage and price increases. The Congress also announced its intention to participate actively in the next election campaign on behalf of the New Democratic Party (NDP).

The need to stimulate the private sector, which was advocated throughout the year both by the Liberal and Progressive Conservative (PC) parties, was formally recommended in a Royal Commission report released on 15 May. The Royal Commission on Corporate Concentration, which had been established in 1975, recommended a gradual elimination of corporate income taxes and an immediate end to the capital gains tax which had been introduced in 1972. The report also said that it saw no serious threat to competition in Canada arising from merger activities by major corporations, and recommended against any significant further tightening of rules against foreign investment. While it advocated more competition in the banking industry, the Commission concluded that no radical changes in the laws governing corporate activity were necessary to protect the public interest.

Conferences of federal and provincial First Ministers were held in February and November in an attempt to bring about a more coordinated response to the economic difficulties facing the country. The first conference agreed upon thirteen capital projects which should receive priority attention, ranging from natural gas pipelines in the East to grain facilities in the West. At the November session, the Prime Minister and provincial Premiers spent much of their time in an unsuccessful attempt to reach agreement on a federal proposal to postpone a planned increase of $1 a barrel in the price of domestic oil. Although they agreed on general principles required for economic development, the Ministers made little progress toward the formation of an industrial strategy. At both conferences the Quebec Premier, Mr René Lévesque, complained that federal policies were infringing on areas of provincial jurisdiction.

In two Budget speeches during the year, the Minister of Finance attempted to stimulate economic growth without encouraging inflation or adding to the growing federal deficit. On 10 April Mr Chrétien announced a six-month reduction in retail sales taxes, which led to a prolonged dispute with the Government of Quebec over the most appropriate way of reimbursing that province for lost revenue. On 16 November the Minister decreased federal sales taxes on manufactured goods and announced a slight reduction in personal income taxes. Mr Chrétien said that the

Government's $2,500 million reduction in expenditures had enabled it to make these tax reductions, but admitted that they would cause the 1978 deficit to climb to $12,100 million.

Almost as significant as the two formal Budget speeches was the Prime Minister's nationally-televised address on 1 August, following his return from the July summit meeting of Western leaders in Bonn. Mr Trudeau said that significant cuts in federal spending would shortly be made, and that the Government would take a tough line with public service unions in future wage negotiations. The Prime Minister announced that the Government had decided to convert the Post Office into a Crown Corporation in an attempt to give management more flexibility in dealing with labour problems. The federal Government's specific expenditure reductions, announced two weeks later, included a freezing of the country's foreign aid budget, reductions in proposed defence expenditures, elimination of bonuses paid to federal employees required to work in both English and French, the closing of four diplomatic missions abroad, and a reduction of 5,000 public service jobs.

These new economic measures were widely interpreted as preparation for a federal election campaign, which was expected to be called in the traditional manner during the fourth year of the Government's mandate. On 11 May, following publication of an opinion poll which indicated that the Liberals and Progressive Conservatives each had 41 per cent of the decided vote, the Prime Minister announced that no election would be held in the spring or summer. Mr Trudeau denied rumours that his leadership was being questioned within the Liberal Party. In September Mr Trudeau announced that he would lead his Government into a general election in the spring of 1979. The Prime Minister said he would concentrate his attention on the autumn session of Parliament and on fifteen by-elections scheduled for October to fill vacancies in Parliament.

The by-election results, which saw the Progressive Conservative Party (PC) win ten of the fifteen seats, were widely interpreted as an expression of anti-Government feeling throughout the country. Particularly noteworthy was the PC victory in five previously Liberal constituencies in Ontario, the most populous province. By November, public opinion polls indicated that the PCs had moved ahead of the Liberals in popularity for the first time since January 1977, holding 42 per cent of the decided vote compared with 37 per cent for the Liberals and 17 per cent for the New Democratic Party.

In a major restructuring of the Cabinet in November, the Prime Minister announced the disbanding of the Urban Affairs Ministry and the creation of a Board of Economic Development Ministers to be headed by Mr Robert Andras, who had been President of the Treasury Board. Appointed as new members of the Cabinet were Mr Pierre de Bané, Minister of Supply and Services, Mr John Reid, Minister of State for

Federal–Provincial Relations, and Mr Martin O'Connell, Minister of Labour.

At the provincial level, events in Quebec continued to occupy the attention of Canadians. One of the most significant developments was the election on 15 April of Mr Claude Ryan as the new leader of the provincial Liberal Party. Mr Ryan, former editor of the Montreal newspaper *Le Devoir*, said that his party would devote its efforts toward winning the referendum on independence, expected for 1979, as well as the subsequent provincial election, and would then engage in discussions with Ottawa on restructuring the Canadian federation. While Mr Ryan's election was regarded as a significant strengthening of the federalist forces in Quebec, other developments were not. The decision of the Sun Life Assurance Company to move its head office from Montreal to Toronto as a result of new provincial language legislation was widely criticized by both the federal and Quebec Governments. In January the Prime Minister urged English-speaking Quebecers not to abandon the fight against separatism by leaving the province. Mr Trudeau challenged the Quebec Government to set an early date for the promised referendum and to indicate a percentage figure that it would accept as a decisive win or loss.

The Quebec Government, for its part, released during the year a series of 'black books' designed to demonstrate the extent to which the province had suffered from federal interference in such areas of provincial jurisdiction as housing policy. The federal Government responded with its own analysis of the extent to which Quebec gained from joint federal–provincial programmes, and released studies which indicated the economic losses that Quebec would suffer in the event of separation from Canada. A somewhat more neutral study, released on 10 November by the Economic Council of Canada, said that independence would cost the province 21,500 jobs, less than 1 per cent of its present employment, but that taxes would rise by 19·8 per cent if an independent Quebec attempted to maintain the present level of government services.

The strategy of the Quebec Government appeared to be to play down the extent of separation envisaged. On 7 March the Minister of Intergovernmental Affairs, Mr Claude Morin, stated that an independent Quebec would examine the possibility of a joint defence pact with Canada and would participate in Western military alliances such as Nato and NORAD. In October the Premier, Mr Lévesque, made a formal statement on his Government's goal of 'sovereignty-association', which his critics claimed was still designed to mean all things to all people. He said that sovereignty and association would have to be negotiated with the federal Government without a break and concurrently, once the provincial Government had received such a mandate in a referendum; an independent Quebec would share a common currency with Canada and there would be no customs barriers between the two. While the federal Government remained adamant in its refusal to contemplate such negotiations, the Conservative leader, Mr Joe Clark, indicated that a Government under his leadership might conceivably do so. The continued uncertainty of the situation was reflected in public opinion polls which indicated that, while the Quebec Liberal Party had moved ahead of the Parti Québécois in voter popularity, a majority of Quebecers nevertheless remained satisfied with both their federal and provincial Governments.

The federal Government proceeded during the year with the introduction of legislation which it claimed would bring about the kind of renewed federalism desired by a majority of Quebecers. Bills were introduced to enable the federal Government to call its own referendum on matters concerning national unity, to ensure all Canadians the right to trials in the official language of their choice, and to revise the Constitution by increasing the role of the provinces in a revised Senate and Supreme Court and including language guarantees in a charter of human rights. While the Quebec Premier refused to enter into any constitutional discussions, other provincial Premiers said at a joint meeting in August that economic matters and revised federal–provincial power-sharing arrangements were of greater importance than the constitutional changes proposed by the Prime Minister. By year-end only the legislation dealing with language rights during trials had been passed by Parliament.

Elections dominated developments in four other provinces during the year. The only change of Government occurred in Nova Scotia, where Mr John Buchanan's Conservatives ousted the Liberals after eight years in office. In New Brunswick the Conservative Government was re-elected for a third consecutive time, but with a vastly reduced majority of only two seats over the Liberals. In Prince Edward Island Premier Alex Campbell led his Liberal Party to a narrow victory over the Conservatives, but stunned observers five months later by announcing his resignation from politics. Mr Campbell, who was subsequently appointed by the federal Government to the bench, was replaced as Premier by Mr Bennett Campbell. In Saskatchewan the New Democratic Party retained its one remaining provincial stronghold with a convincing victory over the Conservatives.

On the international scene, the improving state of Canadian–American relations was highlighted by visits to Canada by the US Vice-President and the Secretary of State. The two countries reached agreement on plans to change a US convention tax which had harmed the Canadian tourist industry, on a new water quality agreement for the Great Lakes, on an end to competing incentives to attract auto manufacturing plants, and on environmental safeguards attached to proposals to renew construction of the Garrison Diversion Project in North Dakota.

Relations with the Soviet Union, on the other hand, were marked by friction. The crash of a Soviet nuclear-powered satellite in the Northwest

Territories led to a Canadian protest about the lack of advance warning of the crash and a request that the Soviet Union pay for the approximately $10 million clean-up operation. This controversy was followed by the announcement on 9 February that the Government was expelling thirteen Soviet officials for attempting to recruit a Royal Canadian Mounted Police officer to supply information on Canada's security service.

Nuclear proliferation continued to be a major theme of Canada's foreign policy throughout the year. In January Canada signed a new safeguards agreement with Japan which specified that Canada must give its consent before Japan could reprocess Canadian uranium imported for non-military use. During the same month Canada signed an agreement with the European Economic Community which ended the embargo on shipments of uranium that Canada had imposed in 1977 because of unsatisfactory safeguards. The agreement provided that no material supplied by Canada could be used for nuclear weapons or for any other explosive device. During an unusual appearance at the UN General Assembly on 26 May, Prime Minister Trudeau told the special session on disarmament that Canada was in the process of ending the nuclear capability of its fighter aircraft assigned to North American defence. The Prime Minister went on to propose a comprehensive test ban on peaceful as well as military nuclear explosions, a halt to testing of missiles and aircraft designed to carry nuclear weapons, an agreement to stop all production of fissionable material for weapons, and an accord on limiting and reducing military spending on new nuclear weapons systems

Chapter 3

LATIN AMERICA

ARGENTINA—BOLIVIA—BRAZIL—CHILE—COLOMBIA—ECUADOR—
PARAGUAY—PERU—URUGUAY—VENEZUELA—CUBA—THE DOMINICAN
REPUBLIC AND HAITI—CENTRAL AMERICA AND PANAMA—MEXICO

ARGENTINA

FROM the beginning of the year a rapid escalation took place in the dispute with Chile over the award to Chile of the Beagle Channel Islands, at the entrance to the Straits of Magellan (see AR 1977, p. 78). Chile having already accepted the award, the deadline for Argentina to indicate its views was 2 February, but it was generally expected that the Government would refuse to accept. These expectations gained colour when both countries recalled their ambassadors for consultation and took measures to assume a war footing. On 11 January a fleet of 23 ships sailed from

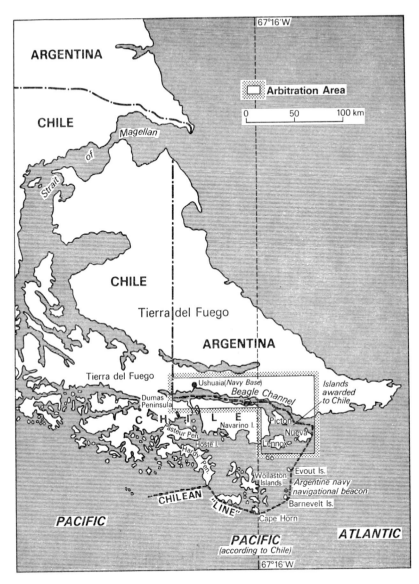

The Times

THE BEAGLE CHANNEL DISPUTE

The map illustrates the award of the Arbitration Court of five international judges, under the presidency of Sir Gerald Fitzmaurice (UK), in the dispute between Argentina and Chile, which brought them close to war in 1978, heightened as it was by the implication of sovereignty over the tiny islands to the extreme east and south for claims to exclusive economic zones extending 200 miles from national shores.

Buenos Aires for Antarctic waters, and was already on station when on 25 January the Foreign Minister, Admiral Oscar Montes, informed the British chargé d'affaires and the Chilean ambassador that his Government did not recognize the outcome of the arbitration.

After hurried negotiations, President Jorge Videla met President Pinochet of Chile at Puerto Montt on 20 February, and the two Presidents agreed jointly to set up a bilateral commission to produce an agreed solution. The commission commenced work on 1 March, but was hampered by the insistence of President Pinochet on making belligerent statements; one in particular, by raising the issue of the extension by the award of Chile's maritime zone into the Atlantic, raised exceptional anger in Argentina, since it contradicted the principle of the 1881 Treaty between the two countries that the Atlantic would be regarded exclusively as an Argentine sphere of influence. Talks were renewed at intervals but by September it was clear that no progress was being made. During the seventh session in October, with the new deadline of 2 November almost upon them, the Government called up reservists who had left the forces in the previous five years, and expectation of a more flexible attitude following the retirement in September of Admiral Emilio Massera, commander of the navy, seemed to be incorrect. On 28 October the Foreign Minister, Admiral Montes, resigned, and the Minister of Defence, Air Vice Marshal José María Klix, took over the Foreign Affairs portfolio *ad interim*. As troops concentrated in the south, Argentine aircraft flew over the disputed islands, and Chilean aircraft entered Argentine airspace, the two countries seemed to be on the verge of war, if only a limited one. But on 22 December, encouraged by the United States Government, both agreed to accept the visit of a special envoy from the Vatican to seek a mediated settlement.

At home, despite a rate of inflation which had been 168 per cent in 1977, the early months of the year had seen an improvement in the economy. A contract was awarded for a gas pipeline across the Straits of Magellan, highlighting the economic importance of the region, and in March the state petroleum monopoly YPF announced the first strike of oil on the South Atlantic continental shelf in the Gulf of San Jorge. The shooting in the street of Dr Miguel Tobias Padillah, Under Secretary for the Coordination of the Economy, by terrorists on 11 April, whilst he was in the middle of important negotiations, was a reminder, however, of the fragile state of public order, and at the beginning of August an explosion destroyed the flat of Vice Admiral Armando Lambruschini, commander-in-chief designate of the navy, and killed his daughter.

On the other hand the Government raised the restrictions on the press, and released some 3,064 prisoners between February and June, and it was estimated that in fact only 200 guerrillas were still active, out of the thousands formerly so. On 31 July General Jorge Videla retired from the army, and the Government became technically a civilian one. He remained as President for a three-year term, and was succeeded as commander of the army by General Roberto Viola. A further sign of liberalization was evident in November when a two-day rail strike, formally illegal, won its participants exemption from the military ban on free collective bargaining.

Above all, however, it was for Argentina the year of 'El Mundial', the World Cup, when its team played host to the finest football teams of the globe and, in a climax of nationalist fervour, headed them all. Its success, notwithstanding critics abroad, silenced the voices of those at home who had considered that the country could ill afford the heavy expenditure incurred.

BOLIVIA

Since President Hugo Banzer Suárez had declared on 1 December 1977 his intention not to seek election to the Presidency that he had held since seizing power in August 1971 (see AR 1971, p. 83), the armed forces in Santa Cruz adopted General Juan Pereda Asbún, his nominee, as candidate for the Presidency on 18 December and confirmed General Banzer in the revived post of commander-in-chief of the army. On 14 January General Pereda resigned a six-week tenure of the post of commander of the air force to devote himself to his campaign, to which a new significance was given by a general amnesty, conceded four days later in the face of mass demonstrations and a hunger strike by the wives and children of miners. Church mediation had been vital in securing the concession, which was followed later in the month by the recognition of the Bolivian Workers Federation (COB) as a legal organization. On 14 February the last batch of political prisoners was released.

Having failed to gain the support of any significant faction of the two principal political parties, General Pereda was backed in his campaign by a new organization, the People's Nationalist Union (UNP). His main rival, it became clear, was ex-President Hernán Siles Zuazo, candidate of the Democratic and Popular Unity Front (FUDP), formed at the beginning of April from his own faction of the National Revolutionary Movement (MNR-I) and several other groups including the (pro-Soviet) Communist Party and the supporters of former President Torres.

Despite a number of incidents of intimidation and reports of attempted coups, polling day on 9 July was relatively peaceful. Then, to no one's great surprise, early returns showed General Pereda leading by two votes to one for Dr Siles Zuazo. The latter, having claimed he was the victim of fraud—a claim in which he was supported by the other candidates, including ultimately General Pereda himself—began a hunger strike.

On 20 July the Central Electoral Board annulled the elections. That night, in a rising of air force and civilian elements in Santa Cruz, General

c*

Pereda called for the resignation of the President. At first General Banzer seemed disposed to resist, imposing a state of siege, but when the next day General Pereda threatened to bombard the presidential palace if he did not leave it General Banzer handed over power to the triumvirate of military commanders, who appointed General Pereda to the vacancy thus created.

On 25 July President Pereda appointed a new Cabinet, after which he promised reforms and fresh elections. Some of the promises were subsequently kept: the state of emergency was lifted, the radio stations seized at the time of the coup were returned, and troops in the mining areas were ordered to behave better, though not, as promised, withdrawn. But on 6 August the President announced that 1979, being the centenary of the loss of the seacoast, was not a propitious time for elections, which would be held in 1980. This announcement was greeted with great hostility from opposition elements, the principal of whom were still in hiding, and the appointment of ex-President Banzer as ambassador to Argentina, from which he returned to Bolivia temporarily when President Videla visited Yacuiba in October, was regarded as proof that the coup had his connivance.

In face of official bans, a mass rally and demonstrations were called for 24 November. However, in the early hours of that morning the Pereda Government was itself overthrown by a new military coup, led by the commander of the army, General David Padilla Aranvibia, whom Pereda himself had appointed, and backed by younger, left-wing officers who had entered the service since 1952—the so-called 'Villaroel Lodge'.

The new Government, which received the early if cautious support of the COB, was entirely military in composition except for Sr Raúl Botelho, the Foreign Minister. It included Colonel Raúl López Layton (Interior) and Colonel Gary Prado Salmon (Planning and Coordination), who had jointly attempted to overthrow President Banzer in 1974 (see AR 1974, p. 99). Colonel López Layton lost no time in indicating that ex-President Banzer would not be welcome to return. New elections were called for 1 July 1979, but the other intentions of the new Government, with its evident left-wing complexion, remained uncertain at the year's end.

BRAZIL

The year opened with the announcement by President Ernesto Geisel that he had selected General João Batista de Oliveira Figueiredo to be the Presidential candidate of the ruling Aliança Renovadora Nacional (Arena) and hence, effectively, the new President for six years from March 1979. The General, who was 60 on 15 January, was born in Rio de Janeiro but brought up in Alegrete, Rio Grande do Sul, whence at the age of 10 he had gone to military academy in Porto Alêgre. After a distinguished career as a cavalry and staff officer he had, for the past 25 years, served as an intelligence officer, and for the past eight years held Cabinet-level rank as head of the national intelligence service. Personally austere and a tee-totaller, he was unknown to most Brazilians, some of whom took comfort, however, from the fact that he was son of the General Euclydes Figueiredo who in 1932 had led an unsuccessful democratic revolt against the Government of President Vargas.

For the first time since 1964 the nomination was made by the incumbent President without consultation with senior army leaders, and it provoked the immediate resignation of the head of the President's military household, General Hugo Andrade de Abreu, whose charges that officers uncomfortably close to the nominee were tainted with 'pay-offs' from large companies doing business in Brazil found an echo in an alliance of other military figures with Arena's most prominent civilian politician, Senator Magelhães Pinto, which briefly appeared to threaten the nomination's unanimity. After, however, the party's convention had ratified it, events took a new turn when on 23 August retired General Euler Bentes Monteiro, aged 61, agreed to accept the nomination of Brazil's only other legal political party, the Brazilian Democratic Movement (MDB).

This move, which broke the long tradition of army unity, received the support of General Abreu, who was put under arrest for 20 days during the time of the election. This was effected by the indirect choice of an Electoral College meeting in Brasília. On 15 October the College chose General Figueiredo by 355 votes to 226; a demonstration outside the Congressional palace by some 200 students, itself a possible portent of change, dispersed peacefully before police arrived.

At the municipal elections held on 15 November, during the course of which a public opinion poll disclosed that General Figueiredo had the support of only 7 per cent of those interviewed, Arena again lost heavily in the principal urban areas of Rio de Janeiro and São Paulo, and the MDB did well, despite an almost total prohibition on MDB publicity under the rules arranged in 1977 (see AR 1977, p. 77). In the Congressional elections held concurrently, with only one-third of the Senate at stake, Arena won 15 of the 20 Senate seats and 231 of the 420 seats in the Chamber of Deputies. At the end of November it was announced that the restrictions on the formation of new parties would be lifted with effect from 1 January, and some relaxation of the emergency legislation was expected.

Abroad, in an important diplomatic initiative in January, President Geisel visited Mexico and extended his contacts further afield in Latin America. The Mexicans were disappointed that the draught of Brazilian tankers would not allow Brazil to buy oil from them, but in a final communique they supported the Brazilian desire for the peaceful development of atomic energy. In March the President paid a state visit to West

Germany and received the Prince of Wales in Brasilia. And in October President Giscard d'Estaing of France paid a state visit to Brazil to mark the importance attached by France to closer relations between the two countries. Investment in Brazil continued despite the great size of the external debt, which continued to rise at the rate of 20 per cent per annum, while inflation, which had fallen below 39 per cent in 1977 according to official figures, continued to be unacceptably high by most standards.

CHILE

In the referendum held on 4 January President Pinochet scored a considerable personal gain over his political opponents both within and without the Government by obtaining the support of 75 per cent of the voters for his rejection of United Nations criticism of his Government. 4,173,547 voted 'yes' to 1,130,185 'no', with 238,849 votes void, and the President lost no time in communicating the result to Dr Waldheim. Despite the rejection by Argentina of the Beagle Channel Islands award (see above, p. 71), early in March the state of siege was replaced by the milder state of emergency, restoring the right of habeas corpus suspended since 1973, and removing some of the President's arbitrary powers of exile, expulsion or deprivation of citizenship. The 2.00 to 5.30 a.m. curfew continued for a time, but was abolished later in the year.

This followed the demotion of the Foreign Minister, Admiral José Toribio Merino, in a Government reshuffle, and was itself followed by indications that the increasing dominance of the Government by the President was viewed with varying degrees of hostility in the other services. The rivalry thus engendered came to a head in the swift and surprising events of 24 July, when the other three members of the military Junta deposed the fourth, General Gustavo Leigh, commander of the air force. He was placed on the retired list together with eight other of the 21 air force generals, ten more choosing retired status voluntarily. No move occurred within the air force in opposition either to the removal of General Leigh or to the appointment of General Fernando Matthei Aubel in his place, both of which were attributed to General Leigh's public criticism of the extreme slowness with which the Junta had been moving towards the restoration of constitutional government.

COLOMBIA

At the Congressional elections held on 26 February, votes cast for the slate pledged to presidential pre-candidate Julio Cesar Turbay Ayala exceeded those for his Liberal rival, ex-President Carlos Lleras Restrepo, by half a million votes, and Señor Turbay Ayala thus became the official candidate of the Liberal Party at the convention held on 17 March. The composition of the new Congress was: in the Senate, 62 Liberals, 49 Conservatives, and one for the coalition of the National Opposition Union, the National Popular Alliance and the Independent Liberal Movement (UNO–ANAPO–MIL); in the House, 109 Liberals, 86 Conservatives, 4 UNO–ANAPO–MIL.

At the presidential elections held on 4 June, Señor Turbay Ayala defeated his only serious opponent, Señor Belisario Betancur, of the Conservative Party, by 2,506,228 votes to 2,358,644, following a recount. Four other candidates divided the balance of 3 per cent of the votes cast. Turn-out was 38 per cent of the 12 millions eligible to vote. Señor Turbay Ayala, aged 62, formerly ambassador in Washington, took office for a four-year term on 7 August. An early departure of the new Government was the establishment of diplomatic relations with Algeria, Nigeria, Morocco, Iraq and Vietnam.

However, at home its main problem was the visible and serious deterioration in public order. Unrest had begun following a 12 per cent increase in transport fares on 8 May, and had rapidly assumed serious proportions, a student being killed in riots at the National University on 30 May. Once started, the disturbances proved hard to control, and intermittent bombings and kidnappings punctuated the rest of the year. And, although the elections had shown a spectacular drop in the support for the populist ANAPO since 1974, they continued to demonstrate the widespread political apathy towards the two traditional political parties.

ECUADOR

The adoption of the new Constitution at a referendum held on 15 January marked the end of the first stage of the return of the country to civilian rule. In a flurry of activity some old political alignments reappeared and new alliances were formed, but in a relatively stable economic situation no one candidate of the several presenting themselves was able to gain overwhelming support. In the first round of the elections on 16 July, the leader in the poll, Jaime Roldos Aguilera of the Rally of Popular Forces (CFP), obtained only 30 per cent of the votes cast, or 425,000, to 310,000 for Sixto Durán Ballen, former mayor of Quito, representing the Frente Nacional Constitucionalista (FNC). A second round of the elections was, therefore, to be held between the two leaders.

In the meantime the military Government that continued to hold office extended its powers of arrest and trial through the Military Security Law, while other legislation favoured the development of large-scale agriculture. As silence continued on the date for the second round of the elections, it was widely assumed that conservative pressure for their abandonment would in the end prevail. However, on 6 December the President, Admiral Alfredo Poveda Burbano, reiterated the intention of the armed forces to return to civilian rule, authorized the release of the results of the first round, and set the date for the second round as 8 April 1979. This followed the shooting in Guayaquil of the candidate who came fourth, Abdon Calderon Muñoz, who subsequently died of his wounds. Economically it was a good year, with a spectacular increase in industrial production leading an otherwise still sluggish economy.

PARAGUAY

In a year in which many Latin American elections had surprise results, those held in Paraguay on 12 February did not. General Alfredo Stroessner was re-elected as President for his sixth successive five-year term by 890,361 votes (89·6 per cent) to 103,186 (10·4 per cent) for the two opposition candidates, Sr Germán Acosta Caballero of the Liberal Radical Party (PLR) and Sr Fulvio Celauro of the Liberal Party (PL). Nineteen trade union leaders arrested at Yparacai on 28 December 1977, accused of associating with a left-wing guerrilla group, were released the day before the election, at which voting was compulsory. On 1 July the Eighth General Assembly of the Foreign Ministers of the Organization of American States called on Paraguay to lift the state of siege which the Government of President Stroessner had renewed every ninety days since 1954.

PERU

For Peru it was a year of austerity, opening with the announcement on 13 January by General Alcíbades Saénz Barsallo of new measures of economic restraint. Inflation in 1977 had been 32·4 per cent. On the retirement on 31 January of General Guillermo Arbalú Galliani, he was succeeded as Prime Minister by General Oscar Molina Pallochia, and a Government reshuffle followed. President Morales Bermúdez also retired, but remained in office as President, thus civilianizing the Government. On 12 May General Saénz was dismissed as Minister of Economy and Finance and replaced by a civilian, Sr Javier Silva Ruete, who introduced a new austerity package three days later, raising prices and further devaluing the sol, which fell during the year by some 50 per cent. Inflation for the year rose again, it was estimated, to 70 per cent. Not surprisingly, the new measures touched off violent disturbances, despite prior precautions, and on 20 May a state of emergency was proclaimed in Lima. In a two-day general strike on 22 and 23 May, 25 persons died in the fighting, and the Government deported ten left-wing candidates for the Constituent Assembly and detained thirty more.

Elections for the Assembly, which was to prepare the way for the return to civilian rule, were scheduled for 4 June, but postponed to 18 June on account of the disturbances. Meanwhile the Government lifted the state of emergency but retained a ban on some public meetings and had all radio and television speeches subjected to censorship. The results of the election were interesting as the first test of public opinion since 1963. The Alianza Popular Revolucionaria Americana (APRA), led by 83-year-old Víctor Raúl Haya de la Torre, won 37 seats. The Christian Popular Party (PPC), of Dr Luis Bedoya Reyes, with 25 seats, came second. On the left the main grouping was the trotskyist Popular Front of Workers, Peasants and Students (FOCEP), with 12 seats, twice as many as either the Revolutionary Socialists (PSR) with 6 or the (pro-Soviet) Communist Party (PC-Unidad) also with 6. Also represented were the Popular Democratic Unity (UDP), 4, the Peasants and Workers Front, 4, and the Christian Democrats (PCD), the Odriistas (UNO) and the Pradistas (MDP), 2 seats each. Sr Haya was elected President of the Assembly when it began to meet on 28 July.

In the meantime there were signs that the Government had already taken note that, despite the wide variety of left-wing views, the weight of moderate opinion was heavily in the majority. In mid-July a new amnesty was decreed, and seven newspapers returned from public ownership to private hands, though not to those of their former owners, who could take only a 25 per cent share. The strict job security legislation decreed by President Velasco in 1970 was also amended, but conflict with 40,000 miners over pay and rehiring demands showed that a conservative policy was likely to be no easier than a radical one.

URUGUAY

Uruguay remained an exception to the general move back towards civilian rule in Latin America. While approximately 12 per cent of the population had emigrated since 1973, some 2,600 prisoners were still in custody, and more than a thousand former public figures were deprived of political rights for a period of fifteen years, military control of the country remained absolute. The appointment of a new commander-in-chief of the army, General Gregorio Alvarez, in February, gave hope in some quarters of a new political initiative, but it appeared that the military had been all too successful in eliminating possible political office-holders. Having stated that they would accept only members of the traditional political parties, they were rebuffed in the search for a civilian presidential candidate by Sr Adolfo Tejera, former Nationalist (Blanco) Minister of the Interior, who refused to collaborate unless basic civic freedoms were restored.

Pressure for such a restoration from the United States was made manifest when under the initiative of that country the Organization of American States refused to hold its annual meeting of Foreign Ministers in Uruguay. Then, following the publication of a report by Amnesty International which stated that torture was still being practised, the chief of the intelligence service, General Amauri Prantl, was placed under house arrest on 26 June, while at the beginning of July, in what was generally seen as a victory for moderate opinion within the armed forces, the Foreign Minister, Sr Alejandro Rovira, who had been one of the most ultramontane apologists for the regime and an advocate of a 'South Atlantic' alliance, resigned, and was replaced by Sr Adolfo Folle Martínez. At the end of December, ex-President Jorge Pacheco was nominated ambassador to Switzerland.

Inflation, which had been 42 per cent in 1977, continued at about the same level, resulting in a fall of some 40 per cent in average real wages over the two years, with no prospect of relief.

VENEZUELA

The economy continued in a healthy state, with the inflation rate for 1977 held to 8·5 per cent and a generally satisfactory rate of growth: 8 per cent in manufacturing industry. A sharp dip in oil production and exports, owing to sluggish demand, in January and February resulted in a reduction in the budget estimates for the coming year to take account of the fall in revenue, but by June production had recovered from an average 1·75 million barrels a day to 2·04 million barrels. Oil production in 1977 had already fallen by a further 0·76 per cent on the previous year, a level which, however, exceeded that intended for reasons of conservation. The previous fourteen operating companies were merged into four: Lagovén, Maravén, Menevén and CVP-Llanovén, covering the principal regions of the country. Another rationalization was the signature of an agreement with Cuba, Spain and the USSR by which Venezuela would supply Cuba with 10,000 barrels of petroleum a day in exchange for the USSR sending the same amount direct to Spain, thus saving on transport costs. The situation in agriculture, however, was less satisfactory, because of damage to crops by heavy rains early in the year.

Politically the presidential campaign, which opened formally on 1 April, dominated the year, though the visit of President Carter on 28 and 29 March was regarded by all as a sign of the crucial importance attached to Venezuela by the United States. At the elections on 3 December victory went to Sr Luis Herrera Campins of the Social Christian Party (COPEI) with some 46 per cent of the vote to 41 per cent for Sr Luis Piñerúa Ordaz of Acción Democrática (AD). Two other candidates, José Vicente Rangel and Diego Arria Salcetti, obtained 7 and 3 per cent respectively.

CUBA

Abroad, Cuban forces continued to be deeply engaged in Africa, an announcement by the Ethiopian head of state at Addis Ababa on 2 March being the first public admission that they had been used in the front line in the Ogaden. Further information released in *Granma* in a special edition on 14 March revealed that they had begun to arrive during December 1977. They had made their first appearance at the battlefront on 22 January, when they had helped check the Somali attack 500 metres from the strategic road from Harar to Diredawa. United States sources estimated there were as many as 12,000 of them, including pilots, tank crews, artillery and armoured infantry brigades. Cuban advisers continued to be active in Southern Africa, and a tour of African states by President Fidel Castro, between 11 and 20 September, was evidence of the continuing significance of the continent in Cuban foreign policy. Distinguished foreign visitors to Cuba included the Ethiopian head of state, Lieut.-Colonel Haile Mariam Mengistu, the Presidents of the Congo and São Tome and Principe, and the Prime Minister of Spain, Señor Adolfo Súarez. But the most spectacular visit was that of 18,500 delegates to the Eleventh World Festival of Youth between 28 July and 4 August.

Negotiations with the representatives of exile groups for the release of the 3,600 political prisoners held by the Cuban Government resulted in the release just before Christmas of the first batch of 400, and President Castro stated that all except 'those guilty of serious crimes' would be released by the end of the year. Those exiles who wished would also be allowed to return to Cuba.

At the National People's Power Assembly in Havana on 28-30 December it was reported that the sugar harvest had been 7·3 million tons, and a new penal code was approved which included new penalties for motorists driving under the influence of alcoholic beverages.

THE DOMINICAN REPUBLIC AND HAITI

The elections in the DOMINICAN REPUBLIC on 16 May witnessed an event with few parallels in its history when the electors rejected President Joaquín Balaguer, who had held office since July 1966 and was seeking a fourth term of office, in favour of his opponent, Sr Silvestre Antonio Guzmán Fernández, of the Partido Revolucionario Dominicano (PRD). At 4 a.m. on the following day, on the orders of the commander of the national police, Major-General Neit Nivar Seijas, troops occupied the headquarters of the National Election Board and halted the count. For two days the situation hung in the balance while through the medium of paid advertisements in the press the major national and professional associations expressed their opposition to military intervention. Then early in the morning of 19 May President Balaguer conceded defeat in a national television broadcast, the votes cast, as recorded by the Board on 8 July, being 716,358 for Balaguer and 868,496 for Guzmán.

The allocation of four disputed seats in the Senate to President Balaguer's Partido Reformista (PR), however, gave them a blocking majority of 16 seats to 11 for the PRD, the seats in the Chamber being 42 to 49 respectively. President Guzmán took office for a four-year term on 16 August, one of the first tasks of the new Congress being to pass a general Amnesty Bill and with it to legalize the Communist Party.

In HAITI an easier political atmosphere prevailed following the visit to the country of ambassador Andrew Young on 15 August and the release of 104 political prisoners on 22 September 1977, the anniversary of the Duvalier regime.

CENTRAL AMERICA AND PANAMA

The murder on 10 January in Managua, NICARAGUA, as he was on the way to work, of Sr Pedro Joaquín Chamorro Cardenal, a leading Conservative and as editor of *La Prensa* the most serious political opponent of President Anastasio Somoza Debayle, touched off a series of events which rocked the regime to its foundations. Fierce demands for the President's resignation culminated in a two-week general strike beginning on 23 January, and at the municipal elections on 5 February, held despite the disturbances, only 20 per cent of the population voted. Not surprisingly the result was a clean sweep for the ruling National Liberal Party (PLN). Between 26 February and 1 March, despite the promise of reforms, fighting flared up in Masaya, León and Leton, and 21 died as the National Guard were brought in to quell the disturbances. Between April and August a united Opposition Front (FAO) was formed. The bishops, who early in January had criticized the Government in a joint pastoral letter, called on the President to resign at their conference in early August, but the request was ignored.

All this was accompanied by threats and intermittent incidents by the guerrilla Sandinist National Liberation Front (FSLN). Then on 22 August, in a coup spectacular even by Latin American standards, the FSLN commando 'Rigoberto López Pérez', under the command of a 22-year-old woman, stormed the National Palace in Managua and took prisoner José Antonio Mora Rostrán, the Minister of the Interior, a majority of the Deputies and several officials, including José Somoza Abrego, the President's nephew. Sr Luis Pallais Debayle, cousin of the President and Vice-President of the Chamber of Deputies, together with Sres Mora and

Somoza, were held as hostages for the guerrilla demands, and were freed when they were fulfilled and the guerrillas had landed safely in Panama and Venezuela.

In September guerrillas seized control of León and parts of Managua, but were dislodged after massive assaults by the National Guard, with hundreds of casualties; fighting was also reported from Masaya, Chinandega, Grenada and Esteli. On 25 September the Government accepted international mediation. At the year's end, as fighting continued in the north, it appeared that, although the FAO had disintegrated under the strain of negotiations and the Government might have won some respite, its long continuance could no longer be assured at such a cost.

Because of President Somoza's complaints that the guerrillas were receiving aid from COSTA RICA, that country found it necessary to appeal for international support under the Inter-American Treaty of Guarantees. Domestically, attention focused on the presidential election, in which victory went to Sr Rodrigo Carazo Odio, a businessman aged 51, who as candidate of the opposition Unity coalition gained 418,642 votes to 363,158 for Luis Alberto Monge, the candidate of the ruling National Liberation Party (PLN) and 22,744 for Sr Rodrigo Gutiérrez Sáenz of the 'Pueblo Unido'. The new President, a Social Christian who was pledged neither to leave the country during his term nor to live in the presidential residence, took office on 8 May, faced with the problem of a divided Congress in which Unidad held only 27 seats to 25 for the PLN, 3 for Pueblo Unido and one each for the Frente Popular and the Cartago Farm Union. As a former professor of economics he made his major target corruption in government.

Presidential elections in GUATEMALA on 5 March were dominated by army pressure, and followed the assassination of a prominent trade union leader, Victor Manuel Paniagua, and an attempt on the life of the secretary of the Christian Democrats, Vinicio Cerezo. On 6 March counting of the votes was suspended in a barrage of charges and countercharges of fraud and intimidation from, in particular, ex-President Enrique Peralta Azurdia, running as candidate of the Movement of National Liberation (MLN). On a recount, Congress declared that General Peralta had come second, with 211,696 votes, to the Government candidate, General Romeo Lucas Garcia, of the Broad Front coalition of the Revolutionary Party and the Party of the Democratic Left (PR–PID). General Ricardo Peralta Méndez, of the Christian Democrats (PDC), was third with 156,730 votes. In a series of disturbances following the elections a plot was uncovered to assassinate the Minister of Defence, General Otto Spiegler Noriega, but the new President duly took office on 1 July, subsequently naming Lic. Donaldo Alvarez Ruiz to the Ministry of Interior and Ing. Rafael Castillo

Váldez to that of Foreign Affairs. Negotiations with the British Government over the future of Belize were thereafter resumed.

In EL SALVADOR, amid general apathy, the ruling Party of National Conciliation (PCN) maintained its control at legislative and city council elections in mid-March. Strikes and demonstrations being prohibited and a virtual state of emergency in force, the elections were boycotted by the opposition. In late November Mr Frits Schuitema, Philips' general manager in the country, was kidnapped and held for 36 days by the guerrilla organization Armed Forces of National Resistance (FARN). He was released unharmed when Dutch overseas radio broadcast the guerrilla manifesto to El Salvador, but at the year's end, despite the mediation of the Archbishop of San Salvador, there was still no news of Mr Ian Massie and Mr Michael Chatterton, British executives of the Bank of London and South America, who had been kidnapped on 30 November and for whom a similar ransom had been demanded.

In HONDURAS, President Juan Alberto Melgar Castro's Government was subject to accusations of wasteful expenditure, while senior army officials were reported to be engaged in the drug traffic. On 8 August the President, himself regarded as of the right wing, was deposed in a coup led by three right-wing generals, General Policarpo Paz Garcia, commander of the armed forces, General Domingo Alvarez Cruz, commander of the air force, and Lieut.-General Amílcar Celaya, commander of the national police. Free elections were promised in 1980.

For PANAMA it was a memorable year, when the two treaties signed on 7 September 1977 with the United States on the future of the Canal were ratified by the US Senate (see p. 61). On 16 June President Carter visited Panama in person for the formal exchange of the Panama Canal Treaty documents, and was welcomed at the airport by General Omar Torrijos and thousands of cheering schoolchildren. In August the first elections since 1972 were held for the National Assembly, which in October chose as the new President Aristides Royo, a 39-year-old lawyer, thus completing the return to civilian rule announced by General Torrijos in September 1977.

MEXICO

For Mexicans the year was dominated by the growing realization that new oil discoveries in the Isthmus region were on a scale far exceeding expectations and that even on the normally conservative government estimates Mexico, with its traditionally cautious oil depletion policy, could face the economic future with exceptional confidence. The agreement engineered in 1977 by President López Portillo between the labour sector and management to restrain wage demands to 10 per cent, had, however, been more drastic than anticipated in restraining wages, while prices of essential foodstuffs for Mexico's rapidly growing population continued to rise. After confrontation between the Government and electrical workers in Chihuahua on 8 February the hydroelectric plants concerned were closed down. It was only the first of a series of strikes which indicated that unrest continued despite the ominous number of unemployed and under-employed, estimated at anything between eleven and eighteen millions.

At the end of August the President declared his intention to eradicate the problem of *latifundismo* from the country by stamping out the practice of holding land illegally in excess of the permitted maxima. At the same time he decreed the expropriation of 30,000 hectares in the states of San Luis Potosí, Hidalgo and Veracruz. In October, however, the peasants of Oaxaca, who had in the previous months banded themselves together in an Association for Self-Defence for Peasants, occupied lands near Tuxtepec, but relinquished them after seven days when, backed by 200 armed men, the chief of police, Adolfo Ferrer Lateón, promised them that their grievances would be dealt with at once by the President in person. In December the explosion of a gas pipeline under a village in Tabasco, which killed 52 people, was an uncomfortable reminder of the high price paid for technological progress and the sometimes alarmingly low standards of safety and cleanliness tolerated in the pursuit of it.

Chapter 4

THE CARIBBEAN

JAMAICA—GUYANA—TRINIDAD AND TOBAGO—BARBADOS—GRENADA—
ST LUCIA—ANTIGUA—ST VINCENT—MONTSERRAT—BELIZE—
ST KITTS-NEVIS—DOMINICA—THE BAHAMAS—SURINAME

JAMAICA

THIS was another year of agony as the political leaders struggled to avoid financial collapse and internal disorder. They kept their wickets intact but the runs came very slowly. They had sought all kinds of assistance from a number of countries along a wide political spectrum. Since 1970, according to a UN Development Programme report, Jamaica had received over J$350 million in various kinds of assistance from a variety of international sources. During the first six months of 1978 it had secured agreements for over J$500 million to be expended over the next few years. Of this sum

J$240 million was approved by the IMF under rigid terms which included an initial devaluation of the Jamaican dollar by 15 per cent plus 1 to 1½ per cent over a 12-month period. All told, when all the aids, loans, trading, technical and other cooperative pacts and export earnings were taken into account, Jamaica had almost a thousand million dollars in foreign exchange with which to pay for its imports during the year.

This advantage allowed Jamaica to increase the quota of goods from the Caribbean Common Market (Caricom) region to J$25 million in the first half of 1978 and J$20 million in the second half, an action which helped to resuscitate the regional integration movement. It also enabled Jamaica to import much-needed capital goods as well as to relieve some of the severe shortages of important consumption items.

The tourist industry had a good year and there were signs of even greater recovery on the way. Earnings from bauxite and alumina (on which Jamaica depended to provide 65 to 70 per cent of foreign exchange earnings) picked up considerably.

The residents of the parishes of Kingston and St Andrew breathed a sigh of relief when a 'truce' was called in Western Kingston among warring factions. It gave the hope that the violence which secured for Jamaica a very bad news coverage in 1977 and had harmed the tourist industry was easing.

Between the two major political parties it was still a case of 'confrontation' politics. The opposition Jamaica Labour Party (JLP) refused to participate in local government elections and contested none of the by-elections during the year. It claimed it was protesting against the fraudulent electoral system. It also refused to nominate any replacements for the eight opposition Senators who had resigned en bloc. Since then there developed some measure of accord on the question of electoral reform.

GUYANA

Against the background of a G$235 million balance of payments deficit, a 26 per cent decline in the value of exports, a 3 per cent drop in calcined bauxite production, and external debts totalling G$700 million in 1977, the Guyana Government moved to tackle the problems through its 1978 budgetary provisions. There was a G$643 million budget and a four-year capital development programme of G$128 million. Major emphasis was laid on drainage and irrigation projects to bring a quarter of a million acres into productive use.

The difficulties also obliged Guyana to seek IMF assistance, and it received G$19·5 million in standby credit and G$27·3 million for compensatory financing facility for export shortfall. Negotiations were still continuing for further assistance. Like Jamaica it received sizeable loans and lines of credit from a wide range of countries. Apart from the usual international sources, substantial assistance came from East Germany and North Korea.

The most startling event of the year was the slaying of a United States Congressman and some of his entourage who were investigating a religious commune of US origin in Guyana, and the mass suicide/murder of over 900 of its members there (see p. 61 and RELIGION). This commune was virtually 'a state within a state' in Guyana.

Perhaps the most important event was a Referendum (Amendment to the Constitution) Bill which was passed in the Guyana Parliament, and which the population was asked to accept or reject. It received the support of 97·4 per cent of the electorate. The effect of this was that Article 73 of the constitution was amended to permit the most deeply entrenched constitutional clauses to be changed by a two-thirds majority instead of a straight majority of the electorate. The Guyana Parliament then transformed itself into a Constituent Assembly to prepare a new constitution and prolonged its life for this purpose by fifteen months. All this occurred under severe charges of electoral fraud and fascism made by opposition parties and groups.

Administratively there was a process of rationalization. The state or its agencies controlled all imports, and a State Planning Commission was established to monitor the performance of various organs in achieving financial and economic targets.

TRINIDAD AND TOBAGO

Having substantial foreign reserves, which stood at TT$3,486 million approximately, the Government through its TT$3,000 million budget made a serious attempt to establish a modern-day welfare state in which the needs of the family were treated as paramount. Mainly through private placement of bonds in Switzerland, Japan and the Federal Republic of Germany it sought to realize a loan of TT$250 million, out of TT$500 million needed in the Budget, to assist in the development of energy-based industries and for development projects. The main beneficiary was a massive industrial estate at Point Lisas, to include an iron and steel plant, fertilizer plant and light industries, which was expected to provide 3,000 permanent jobs. A liquefied natural gas plant, with 51 per cent government participation, costing TT$4,000 million became the main motor in the diversification of the economy to include heavy and light industries.

Serious doubts remained about the capacity of the public administrative system to implement these welfare and developmental programmes. Continuous complaints abound about the poor state of the telephone system, electricity supplies, roads, water, and the air and seaports. Some improvements in the two airports were forthcoming with Canadian aid.

In spite of high oil revenues, that industry as well as the economy in general was in doubtful shape. The sugar industry was in trouble, there were significant decreases in agricultural production, especially in sugar, coffee, copra, broilers, milk and vegetables. Unemployment was 12·2 per cent of the work-force. There were shortages in essential foodstuffs, housing shortages and exorbitant land prices. This outlook was relieved by the news of massive discoveries of natural gas and new oil resources, and the announcement of a large and varied package of incentives for the agricultural industry.

Politically the opposition party was embroiled in a leadership struggle, there were two resignations from the ruling party, and legislation was passed to declare vacant the seat of a representative who resigns or is expelled from his party.

BARBADOS

Barbados was kept on a tight economic rein. It ended the year with a surplus on the balance of payments accounts, had a record-breaking number of tourists and a new oil find, and increased exports in the manufacturing sector. Very high losses continued in the sugar industry and the actual tonnage of sugar was 15 per cent less than the previous year.

The Barbados National Bank began operations in March, and work was well under way on the new airport terminal and an extension to the deepwater harbour. The US Government decided to close down a naval facility in the island after refusing to meet the Barbados Government's demands. A number of public commissions reported; the most important, the Duffus Commission, found no corruption by the previous Government. A threatened invasion of Barbados by mercenaries was apparently scotched by public revelation of the plot.

GRENADA

The year started with the Government's rejection of the recommendations of the Public Service Review Commission. However, an agreement on salary increases was reached in February. The Grenada Mental, Manual and Intellectual Workers Union, led by Prime Minister Eric Gairy, withdrew from the Trade Union Congress and set up a rival umbrella organization.

The EC$75 million Budget came under severe opposition criticism. The infrequency of parliamentary sittings, the failure to present the estimates by the required date and the absence of an Auditor General's report for the past six years were among the many charges made against the Government. In addition, the close association with Chile, the passage of sixteen tax measures without any debate and with limited notice, and the complaints by growers and workers about the small size of bonuses paid out for their cocoa, nutmeg and bananas made this a very active year for opposition forces.

ST LUCIA

St Lucia saw itself as the Caribbean's 'newest industrial frontier'. The previous year saw the announcement of the EC$135 million Hess project. This year there was the announcement of an EC$125 million tourist and agricultural project by an American corporation. Industry continued to boom, it was another excellent year for tourism, and an important and easy-to-develop power resource, geothermal energy, was found to be commercially viable and extensive.

The Budget involved no additional taxes and the entire current expenditure, as well as 20 per cent of the capital budget, was financed out of local revenues.

Independence from Britain for this Associated State was set for 22 February 1979, prior to the general elections.

ANTIGUA

Premier Vere Bird turned his attention to the question of independence from Britain in November 1979. Adverse international attention was drawn by the alleged use by the Space Research Corporation (SRC) of Antigua as a transhipment port for arms bound for South Africa. The Premier called for a central bank for member states of the Eastern Caribbean Currency Authority (ECCA) on the ECCA or Caricom level.

There were plans for the reintroduction of the sugar industry on a small scale and a foreign firm, Aramco Incorporated, took over a controlling interest (80 per cent) in a small oil refinery there.

ST VINCENT

The 'Unity Movement' between the St Vincent Labour Party and the People's Political Party (PPP) was terminated with the dismissal of Mr Ebenezer Joshua (PPP leader) as Minister of Trade and Agriculture. Premier Milton Cato announced a EC$1 million surplus on current account—the first time this had occurred in several decades.

There were over two hundred tax-haven organizations registered in St Vincent, revenue had increased by nearly 80 per cent during the last four years, and a box plant and flour mill started production.

Independence and general elections were anticipated for 1979.

MONTSERRAT

The most important event was the stunning victory of the three-year-old People's Liberation Movement (PLM) led by the former Agriculture Minister, Mr John Osborne, over the Progressive Democratic Party (PDP), the party of the former Chief Minister, Mr Austin Bramble. This was preceded by a period of labour disturbances sparked off by civil service discontent over salary increases, and by the refusal of the British Government to permit salary increases to be paid out of the 1977 budgetary surplus or the accumulated profits of the government savings bank.

BELIZE

Once again Belize was preoccupied with trying to reach 'a secure independence with the preservation of all its territory'. Premier George Price revealed that a plan had been put to him informally to cede 1,000 square miles of territory, including a sea-front, to Guatemala. Support for a multinational defence guarantee and for early independence came from six independent Commonwealth Caribbean states. According to the Mexican State Petroleum Company (Pemex) a large petroleum zone included the port of Belize.

ST KITTS-NEVIS

The year saw the death of former Premier Sir Robert Bradshaw (see OBITUARY) after more than thirty years of unbroken political supremacy. The new Premier, Mr Paul Southwell, moved to secure independence by November 1979, appealed to Anguilla to reunite, and offered a substantial measure of autonomy to Nevis as an inducement not to secede.

The Government lost the court battle over its possession of the Island's sugar estates. Sugar production was good.

DOMINICA

The dominating event occurred on 3 November, when Dominica became the latest independent state in the Commonwealth Caribbean. Prime

Minister Patrick John claimed that it would pursue 'New Socialism'. There would be emphasis upon cooperative development and joint-venture exercises in a mixed economy with public, private and cooperative sectors. Britain's parting gift was a grant of £5 million, a £5 million interest-free loan, and several years of special financial assistance.

THE BAHAMAS

Prime Minister Pindling promised full employment by October 1980, the current rate of unemployment being estimated at 25 per cent. The basis of this optimism was the increase of over 26 per cent in tourist arrivals to the territory. The tourist industry was expected to earn well in excess of the US$500 million it earned in 1977.

In the US$253·3 million Budget, special emphasis was placed on education and health.

SURINAME

Suriname (the spelling adopted in official documents and the local press in English) entered the Treaty of Tlatelolco which aimed at banning nuclear weapons from the region. Treaties of cooperation were entered into with Brazil, and it joined the Amazon treaty of cooperation between Bolivia, Brazil, Colombia, Ecuador, Guyana, Peru and Venezuela. Prime Minister Henck Arron also took the opportunity, at the signing of the Amazon treaty, to resolve some of the differences between Suriname and Guyana, especially the fishing dispute, and was able to allay some fears about claims to Guyana's territory.

Suriname joined the Sistema Economico Latino Americano (SELA), the International Monetary Fund (IMF) and the World Bank, and stated its intention to join the group of non-aligned countries in accordance with its declared principles in foreign relations. Diplomatic ties were established with East Germany, a resident mission was established in Trinidad and Tobago as part of a diplomatic and trading thrust into the Caribbean region, and important treaties were concluded with Venezuela for economic, scientific, technical and cultural cooperation. One aspect of the economic agreement was a provision for close cooperation in the field of bauxite mining and processing. Suriname moved to protect its offshore resources with a 10 June proclamation of the Act of 14 April 1978 which provided for the extension of Suriname's territorial sea to twelve miles and established an adjacent 200-mile economic zone.

A number of big economic projects were either inaugurated or continued in 1978. Among these were the US$60 million drainage and irrigation project for the district of Nickerie, designed to bring 50,000 hectares of land under rice cultivation; continued work on the West Suriname railroad, for which the Government secured a NF.50 million loan from the Algemene Bank Nederland for its completion; and a palm oil refinery, inaugurated on 10 June, in which the state of Suriname and Handels Vereniging Amsterdam each had 28 per cent of the shares, the rest being held by the Nederlanse Participatiemaatschappij voor Suriname. Additionally, there were projects involving a saw mill, a large harbour, expansion of the bauxite industry and a hydro-electric station.

Most of these were linked with the multiennial economic development programme and with the continued confrontation with the Netherlands Government over the alleged wasting of the sizeable development aid given to Suriname at independence. Dr Michael Cambridge, Minister of Development, charged that 'the Netherlands should not continue to impose rules that impeded Suriname's freedom of action'. He argued that the problems between Suriname and the Dutch Government centred on who should dictate where the machinery for the projects should be purchased and who should be the contractors for the projects.

An EEC report on Suriname noted the heavy dependence on Dutch aid and stated that up to 1990 the Dutch would supply US$1,400 million in aid, equivalent to nearly half the cost of Suriname's ten-year development programme.

On the political front the coalition Government's majority (see AR 1977, p. 93) was reduced to one when two parliamentarians from the Indonesian Party (KTPI) joined the opposition.

III THE USSR AND EASTERN EUROPE

Chapter 1

THE USSR

THROUGHOUT 1978 the Soviet Government maintained, in almost all matters, a stance indicative either of defiance or of arthritis—possibly of both. The only changes in the Politburo were such as to raise its average age. The leadership's dominant concern appeared to be with the state of the Soviet economy, but no significant changes of economic organization were made. If the US Administration's barrage of criticism and threats of economic pressure had any effects on the treatment of Soviet dissidents, such effects were hard to discern. A series of harsh sentences in the summer suggested, indeed, that the Soviet authorities might even have been stung into demonstrating as forcefully as possible their determination to conduct their own internal affairs in their own way.

In foreign affairs, China's courting of Romania and Yugoslavia was an affront to which the Kremlin responded sharply, so that relations with Bucharest deteriorated during the year. On the other hand, the Soviet Union also made some useful, if unspectacular, gains, cementing relations with Ethiopia and with the new regime in Kabul and welcoming Vietnam into the Council of Mutual Economic Assistance.

DOMESTIC AFFAIRS.—*Government and Society.* There were some unexpected changes during the year in the composition of the country's top leadership group, the Politburo. On 17 July Fedor Kulakov, who at sixty was one of the Politburo's youngest members, died; despite the handicap of responsibility for agriculture, he had been seen by some observers as a possible successor to Brezhnev, at least in the long run. The fact that in June he had been made head of the Soviet delegation to the XI Congress of the Yugoslav League of Communists had strengthened this view. On 27 November another relatively young Politburo member, Kirill Mazurov, resigned. The official announcement described this resignation as being 'at his own request' and in connexion with health problems; this, however, is a standard formula and could have covered a variety of circumstances.

On the same date, 27 November, the promotion to Politburo membership of Konstantin Chernyenko was announced. At 66, he was older than the man he replaced, though somewhat younger than most of the other Politburo members. A Party apparatus man, with more than twenty years of Central Committee work behind him, he was widely regarded as a Brezhnev protégé, and had only shortly before (in 1977) been promoted to candidate-membership of the Politburo.

All these changes were watched with special interest because of the continued poor health of the Party General Secretary and President of the USSR, Mr Leonid Brezhnev. A history of heart trouble was acknowledged publicly for the first time in November when the second volume of his memoirs, containing references to two heart attacks in the 1950s, came out. Despite probable continued heart trouble and other ailments (rumoured to include emphysema and, in some versions, leukaemia), he travelled extensively in 1978. He visited Siberia and the Soviet Far East in March and April, Bonn in May and the Transcaucasus in September. It was noted, however, that the Bonn trip had had to be postponed, apparently for health reasons, and he appeared in poor shape to those who saw him at close range in West Germany. It was also noted that his journey to Baku in September was made, at some inconvenience to his schedule of meetings in Moscow, by train instead of by air.

Efforts by foreign observers to identify an emerging successor or to detect more general signs of change in the political hierarchy were highly speculative, however. The two plenary meetings of the Party Central Committee on 3-4 July and 27 November were mainly devoted to agricultural problems and to general economic problems, respectively. In the course of the year there were public reprimands or demotions for a number of middle-level Party officials, but these did not appear to derive from inter-factional strife. Mr Brezhnev's public statements on domestic affairs concentrated heavily on economic problems. His speech at the November Central Committee plenum (see below) treated several of these problems as urgent and was notable for its extensive criticism of top-level state administrators, that is to say, of Ministers in charge of branches of the economy. The speech was unusual in stressing the frequent failure of the top Party leadership to get its wishes in economic policy implemented: Mr Brezhnev came close to implying that the Politburo was unable to control economic policy.

During the year the USSR's constituent republics adopted new constitutions in line with the new USSR constitution adopted in 1977 (see AR 1977, pp. 94-95 and 482-497). In only one case did any difficulties associated with these changes become public. In Georgia the initial draft of the new constitution failed to reaffirm that Georgian was the republic's official language. It was reliably—though not officially—reported that substantial demonstrations resulted. On 14 April the Georgian First Party Secretary was reported to have assured a large demonstration in Tbilisi that the old language clause would, after all, be retained in the new constitution, and this assurance was implemented. It was also conjectured by some observers that the transfer of the Estonian First Party Secretary, Ivan Kebin, to an honorific state post was connected with some similar confrontation over 'minority' issues in Estonia's new constitution.

The problematic nature of high political office in the USSR was illustrated by the life-story of Mr Anastas Mikoyan, who died on 21 October at the age of 82 (see OBITUARY). He was not the last surviving Old Bolshevik who had worked with Lenin before the Revolution. He was, however, the only one to retain high office through the Stalin and Khrushchev eras and into the Brezhnev era; his retirement in the 1960s might even have been voluntary.

The Economy. Preliminary official figures showed (Soviet-definition) national income utilized growing by about 4 per cent in 1978. This was somewhat up on 1977 (3·5 per cent) but well below the annual average target growth rate for 1976-80 (4·7) and previous growth rates (e.g., annual averages of 5·1 in 1971-75 and 7·1 in 1966-70). In terms of Western-definition real GNP, growth in 1978 was probably of the order of $3\frac{1}{2}$ per cent. The annual plan for 1979, announced at the end of November, set a target increase of 4·3 per cent in Soviet-style national income, only very slightly up on the 1978 outcome. In short, it became still clearer that in the 1970s the USSR had entered an era of slower growth and was unlikely in the near future to resume the high growth rates of earlier periods.

Several short-term economic problems were nonetheless eased during the year. The record grain harvest of 235 million tonnes reduced grain import requirements for 1978-79 and thus reduced the severity of hard-currency balance-of-payments difficulties. It was equivalent to about 897 kg per head of the end-year population—not far short of the metric tonne per head of population which was regarded by the planners as the long-run desideratum. The harvest improvements helped to support the continued growth of the livestock sector, so that hopes of some improvement in meat and dairy-produce supplies could still be sustained.

The energy sector, moreover, failed to fulfil the bleak predictions made for it in 1977 by the US Central Intelligence Agency (see AR 1977, p. 97). Crude petroleum output, which the CIA saw as the key problem area, expanded and was approximately on target. Only in coal, among primary fuels, was there a clear shortfall.

The third area of short-term improvement was the hard-currency balance of payments. (This, the balance on transactions mainly, but not entirely, with the developed West, is of special importance for the USSR's capacity to import such key items as grain and advanced machinery.) Figures published during the year showed that the hard-currency trade deficit had been cut, as expected, to around $3,000 million in 1977 (see AR 1977, p. 98). Developments in 1978 suggested that it would again be contained within modest levels—levels at which net invisible earnings, gold sales and arms sales might even generate a small current-account surplus. The Soviet policymakers continued, however, to hold new orders for Western machinery down to a level much below that of 1976, in order to restrict or reduce the hard-currency debt burden. This was done despite the continued readiness of Western banks and governments to extend more credit to Moscow. Nowhere was the pronounced conservatism of the present Soviet leadership more vividly demonstrated.

The leadership's economic worries concerned the medium term. This was made clear by President Brezhnev's speech to the November plenum. The prospect of much slower growth of the labour force led him to stress once more the inadequate rate of introduction of new technology in Soviet production. This was compounded, in his account, by bottlenecks in supplies of steel and fuel and in transport, and by construction delays. He complained that numerous decrees by the Party leadership on these matters were not implemented, and he laid the blame for this, in an unusually sweeping way, principally on the branch ministries. The only remedies he proposed were some commissions of investigation and a strengthening of the powers of USSR Gosplan, the State Planning Committee. Such an increase in central authority was the opposite of what was advocated, however guardedly, by several Soviet economists during the year: a devolution of some decision-making authority from branch ministries down to enterprises and associations.

Dissent and emigration. After the Belgrade review of the Helsinki Final Act ended in March, the Soviet authorities moved briskly to deal with a number of prominent members of Helsinki monitoring groups and other dissidents. Most of the sentences were for several years' imprisonment, to be followed by a period of internal exile. Among those sentenced were Yurii Orlov (18 May), Vladimir Slepak (21 June), Viktoras Petkus (12 July), Aleksandr Ginzburg (13 July), Anatoly Shcharansky (14 July) and Aleksandr Podrabinek (15 August). There were numerous other sentences. In November the outside world learnt that action had been stepped up against those Crimean Tatars who had filtered back illegally to the region from which this national group had been expelled *en masse* during World War II. A number of Armenian nationalists were arrested in connexion with the 1977 Moscow Metro explosion (see AR 1977, p. 99) and several of the 'unofficial trade unionists' (see AR 1977, p. 100) were also arrested during the year.

Several observers interpreted these actions as a determined effort by the Soviet authorities to demonstrate to the outside world that they were not susceptible to pressures on 'human rights' issues. This was not, however, demonstrated beyond all reasonable doubt. Pressures about, and contacts with, Soviet Jewish 'refuseniks' by visiting US politicians (*e.g.*, by a group of Congressmen in March and by Senator Edward Kennedy in September) probably contributed to the increase in exit visas issued during the year. Two refuseniks of long standing, on whom Western campaigns had focused, were among those allowed to leave. They were Veniamin Levich and Boris Katz. Nor was it clear that the threatened use of economic leverage by the United States Administration in July over human rights matters was without effect; at all events, repressions of dissidents did not continue in the autumn and winter at the rate observed in the summer.

Nevertheless, 1978 was on balance a harsh year for the various un-official 'opposition' groups, whether they were concerned with religious freedom, the position of national minorities or civil rights generally.

Arts and Sciences. The events in the world of arts in the USSR which attracted attention outside the country tended, as usual, to be those which contained elements of political controversy. One of the more interesting scandals concerned a production of Tchaikovsky's opera, *The Queen of Spades.* On 31 March the Soviet Ministry of Culture confirmed that it had barred Yurii Lyubimov from staging his reportedly *avant garde* production of this opera at the Paris Opéra. This followed an attack in *Pravda* on 11 March by the Bolshoi conductor, Algis Zhuraitis, which described the production as 'a calculated act of destruction of a Russian cultural monument'. A reply by Lyubimov and his collaborators, Gennadii Rozhdestvenskii and Alfred Schnitke, was not printed by *Pravda* but appeared in *Le Monde* in April. It included the sly observation that the defender of national monuments, Zhuraitis, had himself introduced maraccas into a work by Borodin, in concerts given in Japan.

Behind this curious episode, it appeared, lay a long history of con-troversial productions by Lyubimov at the Taganka theatre in Moscow; the use of his name at the 1977 Venice Biennale in connexion with dissent, and an interview he had given to *L'Humanité*. One outcome was that the Paris Opéra withdrew from planned joint Franco-Soviet projects for 1982 and 1983.

One subsequent development may have been prompted in part by a desire on the part of the Soviet authorities to restore Parisian faith in the moderation of Soviet cultural controls. Ilya Glazunov, a painter of religious and old-Russia themes, was permitted a one-man exhibition in Moscow in the summer. It attracted large crowds and some unofficial controversy. He visited Paris as a member of the Soviet delegation to Unesco and received an official invitation to paint a fresco at the Organiza-tion's headquarters as a gift from the Soviet Government.

Developments such as this cast some doubt on the notion that a new cultural freeze was under way with the appointment early in the year of a reputed neo-Stalinist, Yevgenii Chekharin, as a deputy Minister of Culture. At all events, this did not prevent the poet Rimma Kazakova from pub-lishing in *Literaturnaya gazeta* in September a remarkably uninhibited attack on official poetry-publishing policies favouring little-known—and, she implied, generally untalented—authors from the provinces and from various national minorities at the expense of poets whose work people wanted to read. Nor did it prevent the holding in Tallinn in November of a

D

festival of early and *avant garde* music at which Soviet electronic composers got a rare public hearing and works by Stockhausen and Cage were performed in public in the USSR for the first time.

Conspicuous events in the world of science and technology included two successive manned space flights that broke space endurance records. The first, completed on 16 March, beat the existing American record and showed that the Russians could dock two capsules simultaneously at a space station and that they could keep an orbiting space station supplied for very long periods of time. The second flight ended on 2 November when Aleksandr Ivanchenkov and Vladimir Kovalenok returned to earth after four and a half months in space—a new record.

While the Soviet, unlike the US, space programme continued with manned space flights, it was by no means confined to them. The Russians, like the Americans, launched a space probe to Venus. The Soviet Venus 12 spacecraft was launched on 14 September; on 21 December a module detached from it landed on Venus and transmitted information back to earth for 110 minutes.

The development of the Soviet Union's supersonic passenger plane, the Tu-144 (see AR 1977, pp. 100-1), received a major setback. Its introduction into commercial service (between Moscow and Alma-Ata) had been on a limited scale and had been accompanied by reports of various problems. Flights were suspended after early June and it was eventually learnt that there had been a crash.

FOREIGN POLICY.—*Relations with other socialist countries.* Moscow seemed, during the year, to be contending almost continuously with Peking, and on a number of different fronts. The Sino-Soviet border itself remained the most sensitive area of all. On his visit to the Soviet Far East President Brezhnev was accompanied by his Defence Minister, Marshal Dmitrii Ustinov, and made morale-boosting speeches to troops close to the border. These somewhat provocative actions were matched by military exercises near the frontier. Border talks between the two countries were nonetheless resumed on 4 May, but their start was promptly followed by a border clash on 9 May.

The Chinese continued to exert pressure on the Soviet Government, sometimes in unexpected places. Chairman Hua Kuo-feng's visits in August to Yugoslavia and Romania were seen in Moscow—no doubt correctly—as an attempt to weaken Soviet positions in Europe. The Soviet leadership stopped short of open criticism of Romania at the time but attempted, in Warsaw Pact negotiations and at a meeting in December of Party ideologists in Sofia, to secure from all its Warsaw Pact allies a public condemnation of the Peking regime, an increase in defence spending, tied implicitly to the 'Chinese threat', and the placing of all Warsaw Pact troops under a unified command. In a Romanian Independence Day speech on 1 December, President Ceauşescu reaffirmed Romanian political and military sovereignty. At the subsequent Sofia meeting Romania, backed by Eurocommunists, declined to condemn Peking.

Meanwhile, by concluding in August a treaty with Japan including an anti-hegemony clause aimed at the USSR (see DOCUMENTS), Peking did its best to sour Moscow's relations with Tokyo. Similarly, the phrasing of the documents exchanged in the US 'normalization' of relations with China in December (see DOCUMENTS) also drew Soviet criticism, in a telegram from Brezhnev to President Carter, whose full text was released by Tass on 21 December.

Moscow was not, however, totally without assistance in Asia in putting some pressure on China in return. Vietnam's links with the USSR were ostentatiously strengthened during the year, first by its admission in the summer into CMEA and, secondly, by the signing on 3 November of an economic treaty and a treaty of friendship and cooperation with the Soviet Union (see DOCUMENTS). And the April coup in Afghanistan brought a strongly pro-Soviet Government to power in Kabul. Soviet military and civilian advisers in the country were reported to have increased sharply in numbers, and *Pravda* on 6 December reported the signing of a treaty of friendship, good neighbourliness and cooperation with Afghanistan. China responded by developing its own neighbourly relations with Afghan tribes rebelling against the new regime of President Taraki.

Relations with the non-communist world. The first half of the year was marked by considerable contention and suspicion between Moscow and Washington. If exchanges were a shade less antagonistic in the latter part of the year, this was because some of the contentious issues died down somewhat, not because any mutually acceptable resolution of them was reached. The main source of contention at the start of the year was Soviet activity in Africa. The massive Soviet airlift of arms to Ethiopia (see AR 1977, pp. 102 and 214), together with reports of Soviet involvement in the invasion of the Shaba province of Congo, attracted criticism and rather vague public warnings directed at Moscow from the US Administration.

Meanwhile the Soviet Union was on the defensive over human rights at the Belgrade review and on the offensive in a major propaganda exercise against US production and Nato deployment of neutron warheads. Both campaigns appeared to achieve some success, since the final communique from the Belgrade review made none of the points on human rights which Western states had tried to insert, and on 7 April President Carter announced that production of neutron warheads would be postponed for the time being, in the hope of a corresponding moderation in Soviet behaviour. The sequels, however, entailed no gain for Soviet foreign policy. The harsh sentencing of dissidents in the summer drew strong international criticism. The US Administration initiated a review of potentially important sales of oil industry equipment to the USSR, with the threat of vetoing deals if Soviet 'human rights' behaviour did not improve. And in October the go-ahead for neutron warhead production was given after all.

None of these developments aided Soviet–US negotiations on a SALT-II agreement (see Pt. XI, Ch. 3) or on other matters. Several rounds of talks between Secretary of State Vance and Mr Andrei Gromyko were followed by assurances that progress towards a SALT-II agreement was being made, but negotiating gaps remained at the end of the year and the long awaited Brezhnev–Carter summit, to be marked by the signing of SALT-II, had still not materialized.

The Soviet leaders, if they needed any consolation for this, probably found it in Middle Eastern developments. The Camp David 'settlement' (see pp. 171, 176 and DOCUMENTS) allowed the Soviet Union to improve its standing with the 'rejectionist' Arab states and the PLO: in a speech of 5 October, President Brezhnev pledged Soviet support for the hard-line Arab governments. The signature of a non-aggression pledge with Turkey on 23 June was a useful bit of troublemaking for the Western alliance, and later in the year internal disorder in both Turkey and Iran rounded things off nicely.

Chapter 2

THE GERMAN DEMOCRATIC REPUBLIC—POLAND—CZECHOSLOVAKIA—
HUNGARY—ROMANIA—BULGARIA—YUGOSLAVIA—ALBANIA—MONGOLIA

THE GERMAN DEMOCRATIC REPUBLIC

THERE were strong denials in East Berlin of reports by West German intelligence sources that a small number of East German specialists collaborated with Cubans and Russians in planning the invasion of the Shaba province of Zaïre in May. However, evidence was building up of an increasing East German involvement in the trouble spots of Africa. According to unconfirmed reports, at least 1,000 East German army specialists were serving as instructors or advisers in Africa, and considerable quantities of East German equipment, arms and ammunition were being supplied to African countries.

Quite apart from evidence gathered by the intelligence authorities, the cat was let at least partly out of the bag during a well publicized tour of Africa by the East German Defence Minister, General Heinz Hoffmann. In Ethiopia, Colonel Mengistu thanked the East Germans for their support. 'Progressive comrades from the Soviet Union, Cuba, South Yemen and

East Germany', he said, 'are fighting at our side'. It was well known that the East Germans had been reorganizing the police force in the People's Republic of Yemen, and that they were helping to secure internal security in Ethiopia. Moreover, the Rhodesians claimed that they had come across crates of ammunition stamped with the East German flag.

East Germany was finding it more and more difficult to finance urgently needed Western imports. Normally these were financed by compensation deals—goods for goods. But East Germany had a heavy trade deficit with its fellow Comecon countries, and was desperately trying to close the gap by increasing its exports to them. This was stretching its productive capacity beyond the limit, and meant that East Germany had to pay cash for many imports from the West. Economic growth, set at 4·3 per cent for 1979, was slowing down, but not alarmingly.

Under a long-term traffic agreement signed in East Berlin on 16 November, East Germany could look forward to a tidy DM7,100 million over the next 11 years from its capitalist neighbour in the West. Some DM1,200 million of this money was earmarked to cover two-thirds of the total cost of a new motorway between West Berlin and Hamburg across East Germany. The motorway was to be completed by 1983, and would cut the four-hour journey by half. East Germany was also to get DM690 million for improvements to existing motorways and for reopening the Teltow Canal in West Berlin and dredging and widening two others. From 1979 there was to be a rise in the annual lump sum paid by the West German Government for the use of the motorway between West Germany and West Berlin by Western travellers from DM455 million to DM525 million. Between 1970 and 1977, these transit payments earned East Germany a total of DM1,700 million.

The West Germans were already paying out huge sums in interest-free trade credits to East Germany. All in all, West Germany's contacts with East Germany between 1970 and 1977 cost West Germany DM11,300 million in hard cash.

Possibly encouraged by President Carter's stand on human rights and by developments in other countries of the Soviet bloc, East German dissidents increasingly showed their disaffection with the regime. In January, the West German magazine, *Der Spiegel*, began publishing a manifesto ostensibly written by dissident officials of the East German Communist Party. The party leadership dismissed the document as a bad joke, got up by West German intelligence with the connivance of West German correspondents in East Berlin. Some West German politicians and observers, on the other hand, considered that the document was genuine, and represented the tip of an iceberg of dissatisfaction.

The authors of the manifesto introduced themselves as democratic and humanistic thinking socialists, and appealed to like-minded comrades in West Germany and West Berlin to join them. Their aims were not confined to East Germany alone, but rather at bringing about the reunification of Germany as a nation in which Social Democrats, Socialists and Democratic Communists would outnumber 'conservative forces'. They would have Nato forces withdrawn from Western Europe, West Germany would leave Nato, East Germany the Warsaw Pact, and a reunified Germany, its neutrality guaranteed by the United Nations, would be totally disarmed.

Herr Rudolf Bahro, a former Communist Party official turned dissident, was sentenced to eight years' imprisonment in June on charges of spying for the West. He was the author of the book, 'The Alternative', which was published in the West in 1977. It strongly criticized the East German regime, and was thought to be the real reason for Herr Bahro's arrest and imprisonment. In a letter sent to West Germany in October, he said that during his secret trial he made no admission of guilt. He reiterated that he remained in favour of East Germany's staying non-capitalist, nor was he hostile to the Soviet Union. What he wanted was a new structure, built on the existing foundations.

POLAND

'History has smiled on the Poles but there is no room for triumphalism', a Warsaw intellectual wrote after Cardinal Wojtyla of Cracow became John Paul II on 16 October, the first-ever Polish Pope. In Poland's climate of political frustration and economic recession Mr Gierek's team responded with expedients designed to avoid trouble, procrastinating in the hope that new investments would at last be coming on stream.

The planned economic targets for 1977 were not achieved, while those for 1979 had to be reduced. Poland's Western debts rose to $14,000 million despite a slight improvement in the trade deficit and the switch of imports from West to East. Imports of Western grain amounted to 9 million tons worth $1,000 million in the agricultural year 1977-78, and further hard currency was spent in Western markets to supplement oil shortages which the Soviet Union was unable to cover. Progressing inflation eroded some improvements in living standards. Chronic shortages of meat, housing and consumer goods persisted and too much money was still chasing too few goods.

At the Party national conference in January, five study commissions (see AR 1976, p. 111) produced no solutions. Basic food subsidies continued but prices were allowed to slide gradually upwards. In March the Central Committee plenum increased investments in agriculture. Prices paid by the state to farmers were raised, but supplies did not improve. In May Gierek criticized economic managers for granting excessive wage increases and warned workers that there might be wage reductions if productivity did not improve. In November he predicted further economic difficulties and tough austerity measures in the coming years. Gierek blamed Western recession and discrimination for Poland's trade and supply shortages, and called for an expansion of economic coordination with Moscow. This was agreed upon during his two meetings with Brezhnev in April and August. It was admitted, however, that the leadership, internally divided, was over-ambitious and slow in adapting to change.

The opposition movement expanded, thus further challenging the state's monopoly both in information and in education (see AR 1977, p. 107). The dissident Students' Solidarity Committee, represented in all university cities, initiated so-called 'flying academic courses' in private homes to offset 'socialist'-biased curricula in state universities (thus recalling symbolically a similar venture under Tzarist rule in Poland). In January 65 scholars and intellectuals publicly formed an unofficial Educational Courses Society to strengthen the venture. The Church encouraged this in a pastoral letter in March. The Independent Team for Scientific Cooperation grouped together young scientists pledged to undertake 'independent research' in various fields. In some industrial cities committees of free trade unions sprang up. A quarter of a million private farmers refused to pay pension contributions (see AR 1977, p. 106) that were deemed too high, organized strikes in milk deliveries and formed a Peasants' Self-Defence Committee. They also complained of being bypassed in policy decisions. This Gierek promised to correct. Even some former Party leaders, in a letter to Gierek, spoke of a crisis of conscience and called for liberal reforms. The Polish Writers Union condemned censorship (7 April) and elected to its board four dissenters. Party spokesmen promised to create a kind of appeals tribunal for censorship grievances.

Dissent now extended into virtually every segment of society. The leadership, faced with pressure for pluralism and participation, reacted with a mixture of harassment and grudging tolerance. Towards the end of the year an unofficial discussion forum appeared, consisting of Party and non-Party members, including dissenters. The ideas for reform were presented to the Party, which unsuccessfully insisted on maintaining its 'leading' role. On the 60th anniversary of Polish independence (proclaimed 11 November 1918) Gierek, while omitting some crucial historical facts, appealed for 'patriotic unity of hearts, thoughts and actions'. The Episcopate replied with a pastoral letter demanding that 'conditions must be created in which people can fully feel themselves masters of their fatherland'. Following a Mass in Warsaw attended by thousands, speakers appealed for respect for human rights and for truth concerning Poland's history. The authorities did not intervene.

Official negotiations between Church and State were resumed but no significant results appeared. The Government tried to obtain the Church's cooperation at minimal cost to itself, although Primate Wyszynski was now being described as 'an eminent Polish patriot'. The Episcopate, in outspoken statements, demanded respect for human rights, full access to the media (including transmissions of the Mass), an extension of the independent Catholic press, the creation of an independent Catholic youth organization, and education based on national, Christian traditions. They condemned censorship, discrimination against believers and the imposition of a 'godless ideology'. The cornerstone of any normalization must be the recognition of the Church's legal status (6 January), for which the Government was 'not yet ready', as Archbishop Poggi, the itinerant Papal Nuncio, reported after visiting Poland. The Primate's 'historic' visit to West Germany (20 September) was seen by the Episcopate as evidence that genuine progress 'along the road to rapprochement' was feasible.

The election of Cardinal Wojtyla to the Papacy, described as the most important event in a thousand years of Polish Christianity, was greeted by the people with an euphoric elation and produced a massive infusion of confidence tainted with political realism. After some hesitation the authorities had to join in the general jubilation. Passports were issued almost immediately to over a thousand pilgrims who travelled to Rome by special planes. But four dissenting intellectuals, Cardinal Wojtyla's friends, were refused exit visas. The head of state, Henryk Jablonski, led the official delegation to the installation ceremony. For the first time the whole inauguration Mass was transmitted live by Polish television at the request of Church authorities. All over the country the people crowded before TV sets, leaving streets deserted. After the transmission millions went to churches in an extraordinary demonstration of religious fervour.

After a grudging coverage on the day of the election the media later did their best in the existing circumstances. Censors ordered that press headlines, except in Catholic papers, should be inconspicuous and that photographs should not exceed two columns in width. They also deleted some passages from the Pope's Christmas message to his Cracow archdiocese.

According to the Episcopate's communique, 'the Polish people received a prize for their faith and live religiousness'. In the message of congratulations Polish Communist leaders combined a note of cautious optimism with evident national pride. In his reply the new Pope pledged to continue what he called the spirit of dialogue between Church and State. He received Chairman Jablonski in a private audience and in another message to Warsaw in November expressed his conviction that the Church's work, 'consistent with the principles of freedom of religion, would continue to develop in Poland'.

Cardinal Wojtyla's election enhanced still further the Church's role in public affairs in Poland. 'We feel that we can walk a little straighter', a student said in Warsaw. Wojtyla was already missed by many as the foremost champion of human rights and of the Church's mission, and as one of the most accessible, simple, open-minded and friendly of churchmen. One of his last acts was to make available five churches in Cracow for full-time academic courses supplementing state education. A student girl remarked in Cracow: 'we gained a Pope but lost a father'.

While Polish leaders continued their contacts mostly with capitalist countries (receiving among others President Giscard d'Estaing in Warsaw), the question being asked was: would John Paul II come to Poland in May 1979, as Cardinal Wyszynski had suggested after his return from Rome.

CZECHOSLOVAKIA

The Czechoslovak leaders continued to play with vehemence the role of the most unoriginal followers of Soviet foreign policy. Long tracts were constantly being published on the noxious qualities of the Chinese leadership and of the Eurocommunists, sometimes even surpassing in tone similar Soviet pronouncements, and the Moscow line was heeded on all the other issues, such as the Ethiopia–Somalia war, the Vietnam–Cambodia conflict and the attempted Egypt–Israel settlement. International pomp and circumstance were chiefly served by Mr Brezhnev's visit in May–June and by the space flight of Czechoslovak captain Vladimír Remek in March in a Soviet launch. Of the other top-level communist visitors, Edward Gierek came twice, and the Mongolian leader Tsedenbal made a ceremonious appearance in June. The Ethiopian leader Haile-Maryam received conspicuous publicity when visiting in November. Most of the travelling on the Czechoslovak side was done by Vasil Bilak, who copiously attended ideological conferences abroad, and by the Prime Minister, Lubomír Štrougal, mainly on economic business. Gustáv Husák, the President and Party general secretary, went twice to the Soviet Union. His only other sortie abroad, a brief visit to West Germany in April, long delayed, was formal and cool.

There was, in fact, speculation throughout the year that Husák would lose his party post as a prelude to a shift in favour of the more flexible, technocratically minded faction led by Štrougal. When Husák underwent an eye surgery in September, rumours were particularly rife, but he was back in circulation very soon. The only personnel change in high quarters that actually took place was the departure of Čestmír Lovětínský from the party secretariat to the embassy in Moscow (March–April) and his replacement by Josef Haman, an economist. Haman, who also bore the title of Central Committee secretary, had been a close associate of Husák, whose faction in the leadership he obviously strengthened.

The two Central Committee meetings in March and December (plus a gala session in February to celebrate thirty years of undivided communist rule) were singularly lack-lustre and barren. Both were devoted to

D*

questions of the economy but failed to produce more than exhortations to better work, criticism, self-criticism and frugality. The party membership, which stood at 1,473,112 on 1 January 1978, would be screened again in 1979 when old party cards would be exchanged for new ones. One-third of all present members had been admitted since the great purge of 1970. Impassive members, those who maintained erroneous views and those guilty of disciplinary infractions would be weeded out next year, so the leaders announced in December.

There was much to cause worry in the economic field, even though the public enjoyed adequate supplies of basic items and shortages seemed no worse than could be tolerated with a little grumbling and somewhat more bribery. The plan was not being fulfilled in the production of exportable merchandise, in deliveries for new industrial capacity and in reducing production costs. The internal market was still very much a seller's affair, with no great say for the consumer either as an individual or as a manufacturer. Coal extraction turned out to be a bottleneck, not only because machinery for surface mining was late in delivery and full of defects, but presumably also because the targets had been set too high in an effort to relieve pressure on costly imports of oil. Despite extensive overtime working by the miners and advancing ecological devastation due to ruthless open-cast mining, the energy situation remained taut and power cuts had to be effected. Towards the end of the year the annual industrial output looked like being in excess of plan, but only in overall indicators. An assortment of agricultural, building and investment goals would not be met. In foreign trade Czechoslovakia continued to be cautious in buying on Western markets, but still looked set for a deficit in her foreign trade balance. A directive to decrease importation still further was issued.

A timid experiment in new planning and management forms, designed to improve enterprise efficiency and quality of production, was started in 150 manufacturing, nine trading and 21 research organizations. The Federal Minister of Finance, Leopold Lér, appeared to be the moving spirit behind the three-year experiment, which by the end of 1978 was said to be doing well. This was the first official reformist attempt since the Prague Spring and not all the Party luminaries seemed to be looking kindly on it. The experiment centred on a higher measure of independence for enterprise associations and more effective stimulation of economic activities that mattered most, such as attainment of a desirable product mix, quality and exportable goods. Only after three years would it be decided whether the new principles should be applied throughout the country's economy.

Four important anniversaries were commemorated. A spate of salubrious articles, speeches and meetings greeted the thirtieth anniversary of the communist takeover in 1948, but the ceremonial highlight in February somehow failed to live up to expectation, perhaps because no foreign leaders turned up. Forty years since the Munich *diktat* in 1938 elicited only a relatively sparse and predictable response. There may have been an intention to play down the sixtieth anniversary of the birth of 'bourgeois' Czechoslovakia in 1918, but in the end fear of causing offence to the public forced the official propaganda-makers to take note. They did so by emphasizing the crucial impact of the Russian October Revolution on the dismemberment of Austria–Hungary and radicalization of the Czechoslovak masses. Echoes of the tenth anniversary of the Prague Spring and its suppression by Soviet tanks found expression in a number of restatements of the official line, unchanged since 1969. The reforms of 1968 were still viewed as attempted counter-revolution which the Warsaw Pact troops, rendering Czechoslovakia 'fraternal assistance', rightly crushed.

Human rights activists and other oppositionists kept up their critical barrage against the regime's violations of its own constitution and international commitments. The Charter 77 movement continued to publish clandestinely documentary evidence of the misbehaviour of the authorities and, towards the end of the year, issued its first 'discussion paper'. This went beyond challenging the Government's human rights record to expose the ecological dangers deriving from the hasty but clumsy efforts to produce nuclear energy. One of the main initiatives by the Chartists led to the establishment of direct contact with Polish dissidents; two joint meetings were held and a third one was prevented by the police. As the ranks of the Chartists widened and diversified (leading to disputations between 'moderate' and 'integral' oppositionists), so the repressive action grew in scope and intensity. Arrests, detentions, trials, forced expatriation and even physical violence against the protesters were the order of the day, giving birth in April to a new instrument of opposition, the Committee for the Defence of Unjustly Persecuted Citizens. Cultural *samizdat* activities continued; for the first time a writer was arrested and detained for letting his friends read the manuscript of a new novel of his.

A series of successful and foiled hijackings of airliners took place between May and August, leading to swift trials and heavy sentences. There were also a few cases of espionage before the courts but the official stories which were made public looked distinctly suspect. Several foreign newsmen were harassed, detained, interrogated and expelled, invariably because they sought contact with critics of the regime. Prague is probably the East European capital worst covered by the Western press, with the exception of Tirana.

The 1977 agreement with the Vatican was put into practice in that František Cardinal Tomášek received government clearance to be enthroned as Archbishop of Prague (in March), and diocesan boundaries were adjusted to conform to Czechoslovak state borders. No great improvement appeared to have been made in the other pressing Church questions, such as appointment of new bishops and parish priests. The election of a Polish pope received meagre coverage.

The overall impression was that of a system simmering with tension and unresolved problems but successfully managing to delay taking the lid off.

HUNGARY

The dominant theme in Hungarian politics, and one which became the source of mounting concern during the year, was the state of the economy. The relative optimism and confidence with which the tenth anniversary of the introduction of the New Economic Mechanism was greeted gave way to more sombre prognoses. The problems lay in the spheres both of foreign trade and of domestic production. As to the former, because of Hungary's heavy dependence on its foreign trade the world economic crisis of 1973 and the subsequent worsening of the terms of trade—the steady rise of raw material prices—were serious blows to the country's position. The effect was exacerbated by the over-optimistic assessment made by economic policy-makers, who expected that the crisis would blow over rapidly and that world prices would stabilize again, and who failed, in consequence, to make adequate provision for cushioning the impact and improving productivity. In the years after 1973, there were continuing over-investment and uneconomic stockpiling, and insufficient attention was paid to quality. Hence too many weak enterprises producing goods expensively were able to survive, insulated as they were by central subventions from the rigours of the market.

To overcome these problems, economic planners undertook a far-reaching campaign to restore the economic equilibrium. Its most important aspect was to be a return to real pricing, and throughout the autumn public opinion was prepared for price rises. The budget figures for 1979, discussed at the December session of the National Assembly and of the Central Committee, told their own story. National income was to grow by only 3 to 4 per cent (as against 4 to 4·5 per cent in 1978), real wages to increase by 1 per cent (1978, 2·8 to 3 per cent), while consumer prices would increase by 4·7 to 4·9 per cent. This would clearly mean an actual deterioration in living standards, for the first time in over a decade, given the practice of hidden price rises not directly reflected in the statistics.

Clearly there was a considerable element of political risk in this strategy. The steady rise in living standards had become one of the main pillars in the relationship between the regime and the population, and any change in this was likely to impair the country's political stability. The legitimacy of the Party was dependent on the kind of economic performance that would produce prosperity, and any setbacks could result in disaffection that could not be controlled by coercive measures. The leadership was not unaware of these risks and tried to minimize their likely impact by preparing public opinion for the necessity of price rises, by instructing the trade unions to improve the quality of information they were to transmit upwards about the popular mood, and by making concessions in one important economic field, namely housing. Housing was to be the one exception from the general belt-tightening. A Central Committee session in October unveiled a new plan for 1975-90, under which 1·2 million new dwellings would be built. The Government itself would build only 30 per cent of these; the rest would be financed by private venture, while the Government would make available loan finance, materials and equipment.

In foreign policy, there were few important developments. The Hungarian Communist Party's line on Eurocommunism (see AR 1977, p. 112) was cautiously reiterated on a number of occasions, stress being placed on the right of each party to develop policies in line with domestic conditions. Relations with Romania continued to be uneasy, and concern about the fate of the Hungarian minority in Transylvania found ever greater public expression. At the turn of the year, Gyula Illyés, Hungary's most talented poet, published a long article in which he accused Romania (though not by name) of having subjected its Hungarian minority to a policy of apartheid. A Romanian reply to this, which dismissed Illyés as an outmoded irredentist, was firmly rebutted. Polemics also continued in a more indirect fashion, over the so-called Daco-Roman continuity theory, which asserted that Transylvania had been an area of continued Romanian settlement since the Roman period. The Romanians insisted on its validity, whereas the Hungarians denied this, arguing that the Romanians did not begin to settle there until the mediaeval period. In parallel with questioning the treatment of the Hungarian minority in Romania, the Hungarian state placed ever greater emphasis on the very favourable treatment accorded to the small non-Hungarian minorities in Hungary.

There was one significant political change in the leadership. At an expanded plenum of the Central Committee, Béla Biszku, for many years regarded as János Kádár's second-in-command and possible successor, was dropped from his post of Central Committee Secretary in charge of cadres. Although Biszku remained on the Politburo, his political career was seen as over; the reason for his dismissal was thought to have been over-ambition and impatience.

Two items of domestic legislation were of some importance. A law on internal trade was passed by the National Assembly in its spring session, and in the autumn the Presidential Council issued new regulations on foreign travel to replace those issued in 1970 (see AR 1970, p. 129). Existing practice was to remain little changed, but the Ministry of Interior would be less restrictive in that there were now only three mandatory grounds for refusing an application. At the same time, while Austrian citizens could enter Hungary without visas from January 1979, there would be no substantive relaxation for Hungarians.

The opposition continued functioning in a rather cautious fashion. A few older dissident intellectuals accepted the offer of passports and emigrated, the younger generation of dissidents pursued their policy of trying to break the Government's monopoly of information by *samizdat*. One important *samizdat* document which reached the West in the summer provided details of the number of those tried on political grounds, around 250 to 300 a year, according to official figures. Almost all of these were workers or peasants who were given relatively short sentences for 'incitement' or for abuse of the Soviet Union or of the communist system. The official response to opposition activities was muted—about half-a-dozen younger intellectuals were sacked from their jobs but were given other opportunities to make a living.

ROMANIA

In 1978 President Ceauşescu actively pursued his policy of greater independence from Soviet control. He visited China and five other countries in the Far East and paid official visits to the United States and Britain, where he was given the highest honours, and to Yugoslavia. In August he was host to China's Chairman and Premier Hua Kuo-feng on an official visit that was angrily criticized by the Soviet press.

On 22-23 November Ceauşescu attended a Warsaw Pact summit meeting in Moscow, where he signed a Common Statement advocating detente, disarmament, security and peace in Europe and the world. He refused, however, to agree to a last-minute Soviet request that member countries increase military expenditure by an undisclosed percentage in order to strengthen their joint defences. He was apparently the only one to refuse the request.

On his return to Bucharest he addressed separate meetings of workers, peasants, intellectuals, the armed forces and youth organizations, giving the following reasons for his refusal: (1) any increase in military expenditure was contrary to the efforts being made by the socialist countries to reduce military tension in Europe and to the very principles laid down in the Common Statement signed in Moscow: (2) there was no evidence that Nato posed any immediate danger to the Warsaw Pact countries; (3) increased military spending would seriously jeopardize Romania's economic development and the drive to improve living standards. He declared that, as the Warsaw Pact was purely defensive, Romania would never participate in an attack on another country, but would honour its obligations as a Warsaw Pact member in case of imperialist aggression against a fellow member. He laid great stress on the proviso that Romania's armed forces would fight only under exclusively Romanian command, stating that no Romanian military unit nor a single Romanian soldier would ever take orders from abroad.

This attitude was endorsed by the Party Central Committee (CC) and the Grand National Assembly at a solemn session of the latter held on 1 December to commemorate the 60th anniversary of the union of Transylvania with Romania.

On 19 December the CC decided to increase the monthly allowance for each Romanian child by 10 lei. This would amount to an annual expenditure of 500 million lei, to be covered by a corresponding reduction in the military budget, 'which in any case was substantially higher than in 1978'. This step was clearly intended as a defiant gesture to the Warsaw Pact countries.

At a meeting of central party and state organizations held on 3 August, Ceauşescu pointed out that a tendency to interfere in the internal affairs of certain Communist Parties was still apparent, that the principle of the economic independence of the socialist countries, endorsed by the 1976 East Berlin Conference of European Communist Parties, was not being respected, and that the argument in favour of economic isolation from capitalist countries could only have a negative influence on the socio-economic development of the socialist countries. Speaking of the 'extremely serious' situation in Africa, he condemned all foreign military intervention in African countries—a veiled reference to Soviet and Cuban participation in the fighting in Angola and Ethiopia.

Apart from political considerations, there could be little doubt that the decisive reason underlying Ceauşescu's refusal to increase defence costs was the unsatisfactory economic situation. At a CC meeting on 6 July, the President admitted the existence of serious shortcomings in practically all fields of industrial production: coal, oil, rolled steel, cement, chemical products, mechanical engineering, as well as in agricultural production for export. He stated that export was the overriding problem, as it alone made possible the importation of the equipment, raw materials and fuel required for the multilateral development of the Romanian economy. He attributed these shortcomings to inefficient use of equipment and miscalculated distribution of manpower; in every industrial unit there were 4 to 5 auxiliary and office employees to every manual worker.

Ceauşescu's critical and negative attitude towards the Soviet Union raised the question whether this tenacious policy might not endanger not only his own position but even the territorial integrity of Romania. Apparently President Carter took this possibility into account when he sent Mr Blumenthal, Secretary of the Treasury, to Bucharest in December, with a message of support for the Romanian President. Mr Blumenthal told reporters in Bucharest that the reason for his visit was to reaffirm to the Romanian people and President Ceauşescu the importance attached by the United States to Romania's independence and to Romano-American friendship.

Meanwhile the rigorous internal regime imposed by the Party con-tinued unabated. A report published by Amnesty International stated that harassment and persecution of political dissidents in Romania had been stepped up. Coercive methods included internment in psychiatric hospitals and short periods of detention, during which prisoners were maltreated by the security police.

In July General Pacepa, Deputy Minister of the Interior, led a Romanian delegation to Cologne to negotiate with VFW-Fokker for a licence to manufacture West German passenger planes in Romania. On 28 July General Pacepa disappeared from his hotel and the West German police later informed the Romanian Embassy in Bonn that he had asked the United States for political asylum and was no longer in West Germany. Apparently he had been the senior security officer responsible for Ceauşescu's safety, and his defection gave rise to widespread dismissals of officials and diplomats. Interior Minister Coman, Health Minister Nicolescu and Minister of Tourism (formerly Deputy Interior Minister) Doicaru were dismissed forthwith, as well as twelve security generals and senior officers, some of whom were arrested. In September twelve Romanian ambassadors, including the Romanian ambassador in Wash-ington and the head of the Romanian mission to the United Nations, were recalled. On 30 August, the 30th anniversary of the setting-up of the security police, Ceauşescu sent a message stating that even in the socialist countries there were still some decomposed, *déclassés* elements ready to betray their country for a handful of silver, and he called on the security police to show more responsibility and greater vigilance in their activity. There was no mention in the press of the decorations and promotions customarily given on such occasions.

BULGARIA

The year 1978, as assessed by Bulgarian media, was marked by two events: the 100th anniversary of the liberation from Turkish domination on 3 March, and the National Party Conference, held on 20 and 21 April.

In the life of the Bulgarian Communist Party (BCP) an exchange of party membership cards began, to be completed in 1980. Official state-ments repeatedly denied that the exchange would mean a purge, adding, however, that it would help the party to rid itself of persons who had proved unworthy of membership. Each BCP member (817,000 at the beginning of 1978) would be subjected to assessment by his party organiza-tion, which would decide whether to renew his party card, to refuse it, or to reconsider his case some months later.

No major changes in the BCP hierarchy occurred in 1978. In July Central Committee (CC) secretary Ivan Pramov was released from this post which he had held since 1962, and two new CC secretaries were elected, Stoyan Mihailov and Todor Bozhinov.

The National Party Conference, devoted to 'improvement of organization of labour and planning', took no spectacular decisions. It sanctioned, however, overall application of organization of labour by brigades. A new system of wages, decided upon at the beginning of 1977, proved to be rather complicated and controversial and its introduction had repeatedly to be postponed. Only 12 economic organizations and enterprises received official authorization to apply it from 1 November 1978 and another 23 from 1 January 1979. It was claimed that the system would bring an overall increase of wages: everybody would be paid only for the work he actually did, and various methods of measuring each individual's performance had been tested.

The country's administrative structure was thoroughly reorganized. At the beginning of the year the 27 districts were divided into 252 'systems of inhabited places', intended to develop as socio-economic, territorial-structural and cultural entities. In December, however, their number was increased to 283 and they were made administrative entities with the status of municipalities. This meant a sharp reduction in number and increase in size of the municipalities, which previously numbered about 1,400. All towns and villages with more than 100 inhabitants within a municipality would have mayors, an office abolished after the communist takeover. The new administrative structure was coupled with a reorganization of the management structure of agro-industrial complexes.

For Bulgarian agriculture 1978 was a bad year because of heavy, widespread hailstorms, but part of the losses were compensated by second crops. Economic plans, according to preliminary data, were unfulfilled in almost all economic sectors. Instead of an annual plan, for the first time a plan for two years, 1979 and 1980, was approved in December.

In November Bulgaria and the Soviet Union inaugurated their new joint ferry line Varna-Ilichevsk, the biggest in the world and important because more than half of Bulgaria's foreign trade is with the USSR.

Some protest demonstrations against the communist Government were unofficially reported during the first half of 1978, among them a 'Declaration 78' said to have been circulated in Sofia, calling for observance of human rights. The extent and impact of these manifestations were difficult to assess; they were not known to have had any repercussions.

The cultural scene was dominated by a speech by First Party Secretary Todor Zhivkov, addressing young writers on 2 December 1977, published only on 3 February 1978. The speech dealt with a number of political subjects and contained the first official comment on whether or not there are dissidents in Bulgaria. Subsequent numerous comments on the importance of the speech centred on Zhivkov's expression of the party's care for young writers and on his call for observance of the party line. In December the Politburo issued a decision on encouraging young talent in literature and the arts.

The State Council issued in May a document designed to encourage the process of substituting new 'socialist holidays and rites' for all religious occasions and ceremonies.

In December Bulgaria hosted a four-day theoretical conference of 73 communist and workers' parties, aimed at defending marxism-leninism and 'real socialism' and at condemning China. Although several important parties were absent and those participating were far from unanimous, the USSR and its allies attributed great importance to the conference.

The standing Bulgarian-Yugoslav controversy over Macedonia flared up with new vehemence in connexion with Bulgaria's celebration of its 100th liberation anniversary, because of the inevitable references to the San Stefano treaty under which Macedonia had been given to Bulgaria. The dispute reached a culmination after a speech made by Zhivkov in Blagoevgrad (Pirin Macedonia) on 15 June, which was treated by Bulgarian propaganda as a declaration of the country's 'principled, peaceful foreign policy', especially in the Balkans.

Zhivkov paid official visits to Japan in March, to Austria in September, and to Nigeria, Angola, Mozambique, Ethiopia, and South Yemen in October.

YUGOSLAVIA

Although the Eleventh Congress of the League of Communists (LCY), held in Belgrade on 21-23 June, was officially promoted as the major political event of the year, there was little to excite comment in the resolutions that were passed unanimously by the 2,300 delegates. It was an occasion for stocktaking and for surveying the progress of Yugoslav society since the much more significant Tenth Congress (see AR 1974, pp. 144-45). The optimistic claims that the system of self-management was an instrument for 'the overcoming of every form of wage-labour relations and exploitation' and also a key factor in the growth of output had to be set against the open admission by President Tito and other speakers that Yugoslavia faced serious economic and social problems. The official report referred, for example, to the fact that 'infant mortality is still one of the highest in Europe', and that inequalities in levels of development between the republics remained an intractable problem. Changes were made in the organization of the LCY which were intended to improve its effectiveness in moulding Yugoslav society. Great importance was attached to the 'cadres policy', which ensured that key posts were held by people whose political reliability could be vouched for by the LCY.

In his final address the President urged his comrades to improve the level of communist education, and he expressed pleasure that, since the Tenth Congress, 700,000 young people had joined the League, the total membership of which stood at 1,629,082. He also took the opportunity to reaffirm, in the presence of hundreds of foreign observers and fraternal delegates, Yugoslavia's determination to maintain its independent, non-aligned foreign policy. Behind the enthusiasm with which the delegates greeted the man who held the offices of Life President of the LCY and of the Yugoslav Republic was the unspoken thought that this might be the last Congress at which he was likely to play a leading part. Despite his 86 years, he showed no inclination to rest on his laurels; for he declared that he 'would be happy to work for another 50 years'.

Throughout the year Tito continued to play an active role in public affairs, receiving foreign visitors—among whom were Chairman Hua Kuo-feng, President Ceauşescu, Colonel Mengistu Haile-Maryam and Prince Charles—and touring the country to address meetings in all the constituent republics. His own travels abroad were limited to a visit to the USA and Britain. A projected journey to Moscow was cancelled because of the hostile Soviet reaction to the visit of Chairman Hua Kuo-feng. Chairman Hua's visit was in return for Tito's visit to China in 1977 (see AR 1977, p. 118). During the year there were several exchanges of party, governmental, cultural and sporting groups between the two countries. The choice of Macedonia as the venue for a speech in which the Chinese leader endorsed Yugoslavia's foreign policy was intended as a warning to the Bulgarians and their Soviet allies. The Bulgarians used the occasion of the centenary of the Treaty of San Stefano, by which Tsarist Russia offered Bulgaria most of Macedonia, to issue provocative statements about the national identity of the Macedonians.

The Albanians, no longer China's friend in Europe, were also displeased by Chairman Hua's visit. Although Enver Hoxha issued attacks on Yugoslav foreign policy, on the treatment of Albanians in Kosovo, and on the 'bourgeois capitalism' and 'bureaucratic despotism' displayed in Edvard Kardelj's defence of self-management, these ideological disputes did not disrupt the steady growth of trade and cultural exchanges between the two countries.

Relations with Romania remained close. However, the defiant stand of President Ceauşescu at the Warsaw Pact meeting in November was greeted with some caution, as the Yugoslavs feared that an open breach between Romania and the USSR might lead to Soviet intervention, which would have unpleasant consequences for the security of the Balkans.

Relations with the Federal Republic of Germany were strained by a dispute over the extradition of alleged terrorists. The Bonn Government refused a Yugoslav request for the repatriation of Croat exiles, some of whom had already served sentences for acts of violence against Yugoslav citizens in Germany. In November the Belgrade district court rejected a German request to extradite four suspected members of the Baader–Meinhof gang who had been detained by the Yugoslav police.

Economic problems gave cause for concern. In his frank address to the 8th Congress of Trade Unions on 21 November President Tito spoke of rising inflation and unemployment, low productivity, wasteful investments and a chronic balance of payments deficit. He also warned that the selfishness of the richer republics in failing to ease the problems of the underdeveloped areas was a potential threat to the unity of the federation. The main culprits were identified as members of the 'techno-bureaucratic monopoly' who had been allowed to misuse the system of workers' self-management for their own ends.

Inflation rose to over 15 per cent, official unemployment figures touched a record 750,000 (14 per cent of the public sector work force) and the balance of payments deficit for the first nine months, although 14 per cent below that of the same period of 1977, still reached the enormous figure of $4,300 million.

Attempts to obtain better terms of trade with EEC countries bore little fruit. An agreement was reached on 14 November with the European Investment Bank for a credit of $30 million to assist in the construction of a European-standard motorway following the line of the existing Brotherhood Unity Highway.

Elections for the Federal and Republican Assemblies were held in May on lists of delegates approved by the Socialist Alliance. The new collective Presidency chose the Albanian-speaking Communist from Kosovo, Fadilj Hodža, as its Vice-President, and proposed the renewal of Veselin Djuranović's term as Premier. The Croat Josip Vrhovec replaced the Serb Miloš Minić as Foreign Secretary.

In December Dr Bakarić, the veteran Croatian leader, and President Tito both warned that severe measures would be taken against dissenters who were attempting to use the Helsinki Final Act on human rights as a cover for subversive activities. Both named the former leader Milovan Djilas as an important figure involved in meetings with other dissidents. Dr Bakarić alleged that 'there was a struggle for freedom of speech for such anti-communist figures as Mihajlo Mihajlov' (see AR 1977, p. 119), 'a struggle to establish some kind of parliamentary rule in the country'.

ALBANIA

The deterioration in Albania's relations with China, which had become evident during the previous year, reached its climax in 1978. During the early part of the year, the Albanian leaders and press continued to criticize the theory of the Three Worlds (see AR 1977, p. 120) and other Chinese policies. China was also accused of having had a hand in the border clashes between Vietnam and Cambodia.

These prolonged and rather obscure recriminations came to a head in the summer. On 7 July the Chinese Government sent a Note to Albania in which it announced the cessation of all economic and military aid as well as the withdrawal of Chinese experts from the country. According to the Note, this drastic step was being taken because the Albanian side, to suit its own domestic and external purposes, had maligned China's aid programme, had tried to sabotage economic and military cooperation between the two countries, and in general had pursued policies detrimental to its ally.

In support of its case against Albania, the Chinese Government cited a number of incidents, involving Chinese and Albanians, which, it alleged, had occurred in various industrial and military establishments in Albania. In addition, the Chinese made public, for the first time, specific details of the economic and military aid they had given Albania during nearly a quarter of a century. The total aid came to 10,000 million yen. This sum was used to build 142 industrial projects, of which 91 had been completed, 23 were under construction, 17 had been surveyed and designed. China had also provided Albania with large quantities of arms and military supplies, steel products and grain; had sent there some 6,000 experts, and had trained several thousand Albanians.

The Albanian Government replied to the Chinese Note on 29 July. It maintained that Albania had by that time made use of about 70 per cent of the promised Chinese aid, which was said to have been somewhat smaller than the figure mentioned by Peking. The reply listed a series of complaints against the former ally: most industrial projects built with Chinese aid had suffered delays of from one to six years; a ferro-chrome factory had not been built at all; Chinese experts had either destroyed or removed the blueprints of several industrial concerns with which they had been associated; the Chinese side had tried to give the impression that its economic aid had practically kept Albania alive, whereas this aid had been only an auxiliary factor in the country's industrial development; the public disclosure of China's military assistance to Albania constituted a betrayal of military secrets.

The Albanian Note denied China's claim that it never interfered in the internal affairs of other countries. It alleged that whenever Albania had disagreed with the many sudden shifts in Chinese policies it was subjected to economic pressure from Peking. There had been several ideological and political differences between the two Governments. In 1968, when an Albanian delegation headed by Beqir Balluku, then Minister of Defence, went to China to seek military aid, Chou En-lai told the delegation that as Albania was not in a position to defend itself, no matter what military supplies it received from China, its best course of action was to conclude a military alliance with Yugoslavia and Romania. This suggestion, repeated in 1975, was rejected by Albania on both occasions. The Albanian Government had also objected to President Nixon's visit to China in 1972, to the assumption of power by Hua Kuo-feng and Teng Hsiao-p'ing in 1976, and to China's friendship with Yugoslavia. These objections had been disregarded, as had Albania's proposals for holding a meeting at which differences between the two countries could be discussed.

The end of the close friendship between China and Albania was finally sealed in August when Chairman Hua Kuo-feng paid official visits to Bucharest and Belgrade but not Tirana. His visit to Yugoslavia in particular was seen by Enver Hoxha, the Albanian Communist Party leader, as a clear indication that China was no longer guided by the basic principles of marxist-leninist ideology.

After the shock of suddenly losing the protection of a powerful ally which had been the only source of valuable economic and military aid for several years, the Albanian leadership fell back on the old policy of exhorting people to increase production in every possible field and to rely more than ever on their own efforts and on national resources. The Government announced at the end of the year that it would do its utmost to promote and expand trade with Yugoslavia, Greece, Italy, France, the smaller countries of Western Europe and the Scandinavian states.

MONGOLIA

The December 1977 plenum of the Mongolian People's Revolutionary Party (MPRP) Central Committee was described as an event of 'important programmatic significance' for having placed at the centre of public attention the matter of 'sharply raising Party and State cadres' responsibility and discipline'. Addressing the plenum, Yumjaagiyn Tsedenbal, the MPRP's First Secretary and President of the Republic (MPR), expressed concern about the poor state of animal husbandry after the disasters of the past two years, and called for greater care for the cooperatives' herds and public property in general. A Central Committee resolution published in April 1978 re-emphasized this point, saying: 'Everybody must from an early age become scrupulously economical, sparing and thrifty, and with a sharp eye protect at every step every grain of socialist property and respect labour reverently.' A passage from Tsedenbal's speech was also turned into a slogan: 'We must keep pure and guard as something sacred, first, public property, and, second, honest labour—the source of socialist property.'

Several leading figures fell foul of this drive. The most prominent dismissals were those of two deputy Ministers of Culture (May), for 'unparty-like and irresponsible' behaviour, grave offences against Party and State discipline, and failure to protect Party unity. The chairman of the central council of the Physical Culture and Sports Association, who was also the chairman of the Mongolian Olympic Committee, lost his job (July), after a Central Committee decision on 'unpartylike and irresponsible leadership' of the council.

New regulations were brought in which obliged people who had settled in towns without permission to return to the countryside. Inter-city travellers were no longer issued with air, train or bus tickets unless they had an official pass or travel permit. Tsedenbal said at the December plenum that population movements should be regulated, to improve the exploitation of labour resources and ensure that people settled down to work.

In an attempt to trim private livestock holdings down to regulation size, a Party CC resolution in April gave details of the maximum numbers that members of cooperatives and also town dwellers could keep, saying that in some cases the officially permitted figures had been exceeded by 300 per cent or more. This had led to the neglect of the collective herds. Livestock (including pigs and poultry) in excess of the regulation numbers were made subject to compulsory sale to the Government.

After the heavy livestock losses of the previous two years, in 1978 animal husbandry took a turn for the better, the number of animals surviving from birth exceeding 9·2 million—2 million more than in 1977. An overall total of about 24·5 million head was planned for the year. The 1978 targets set for crop-growing were, for grain 547,000 metric tons, potatoes 64,000 metric tons, vegetables 31,000 metric tons, and hay 1,113,000 metric tons, but initial harvest reports indicated that some of these figures were not met: grain output fell short by 170,000 metric tons.

The most significant event in the country's economic life was the official entry into operation of the first stage of the joint Mongolian–Soviet copper and molybdenum mining and concentrating combine at Erdenet. The combine, designed to mine 16-20 million metric tons of ore a year, at full capacity would supply the Soviet metallurgical industry with several hundred thousand metric tons of concentrate annually. Erdenet, one of the biggest such enterprises in the world, was by far the largest industrial project ever built in Mongolia. Its estimated output would double the value of Mongolia's exports in four or five years' time.

The combine, together with a railway, roads, power lines, housing and services for a town of 35,000, a carpet factory and dairy farm, was built in four years with the help of thousands of Soviet workers and soldiers. Paying tribute to them at the opening ceremony in Erdenet on 14 December 1978, Tsedenbal said that Erdenet demonstrated the 'mighty strength of the close alliance and fraternity of the Mongolian and Soviet peoples in the struggle to build a new society'. Erdenet represented a highly successful 'new integrational form of cooperation' which would lead eventually to the 'internationalization of the economic life of nations'.

Mongolia's relations with China remained at a low ebb. An MPR Government Note, presented to the Chinese Government in April, described a Chinese demand, made in a Note to the Soviet ambassador in Peking, that the Soviet Union withdraw its troops from the MPR as a 'new crude act of interference' in Mongolian internal affairs. The Mongolian Note said that the Chinese demand had been made without reference to the MPR Government, and could be seen only as an 'attempt to ignore the MPR as an independent state': Soviet military units had been stationed in the MPR at the request of the MPR Government, because of the Chinese leaders' 'concentration of a huge number of Chinese troops, construction of military objectives, holding of army exercises and organization of anti-MPR sabotage in areas directly adjacent to the MPR's state frontier'.

In May, Tsedenbal inspected a unit of the Soviet armed forces 'temporarily stationed on the territory of the MPR at the request of the Mongolian Government', accompanied by the whole MPRP Politburo, the Minister of Defence and the Minister of Public Security (responsible for border defence). Addressing the troops, Tsedenbal spoke of a 'direct threat to the freedom and independence' of Mongolia resulting from the aggressive policy of the 'Maoists'.

Mongolia's relations with Japan blew warm, then cool. The Mongolian authorities accepted a Japanese offer to build in Ulan Bator the world's most productive cashmere and camel hair factory, the first big project in Mongolia by a non-communist country. As soon as the Sino-Japanese treaty (see DOCUMENTS) had been signed, however, the Japanese ambassador was called to the MPR Foreign Ministry to receive a *Note verbale*. The MPR considered that the treaty's inclusion of an 'anti-hegemony' clause amounted to connivance by Japan at the 'great-power chauvinist actions of the Chinese leaders against the MPR and other peace-loving states'. The people of Asia including the Mongolians had still not forgotten their bitter suffering in the past at the hands of Japanese militarism. 'We are unsure whether Japan, having made one concession to Peking, will not make another, under pressure from abroad and at home.'

IV WESTERN, CENTRAL AND SOUTHERN EUROPE

Chapter 1

FRANCE—THE FEDERAL REPUBLIC OF GERMANY—ITALY—BELGIUM—
THE NETHERLANDS—LUXEMBOURG—REPUBLIC OF IRELAND

FRANCE

THIS was a year in which harsh realities in the uphill struggle for economic recovery were drowned by constant political squabbling—as much between nominal allies as with declared enemies.

Much of this politicking was to be expected, as the protracted campaign for the March parliamentary elections at last reached its climax. In the closing weeks the breakdown of the left-wing alliance became even more evident, as Socialists and Communists accused each other of betraying the Common Programme. M Georges Marchais, the Communist general-secretary, even threatened to refuse the customary second-ballot solidarity of the left unless his party polled strongly in the first round. Relations were little warmer in the Government camp. The Gaullist leader, M Jacques Chirac, was openly critical of the 'majority's' programme unveiled by the Prime Minister, M Raymond Barre, at Blois. Costed at 22,000 million francs annually (£2,500 million)—less than a third of the left-wing programme—its 110 proposals 'to promote freedom and justice' would, it was claimed, end the traditional divide between left and right, safeguard the Fifth Republic, promote economic recovery, create greater freedom and participation, and benefit the under-privileged. Throughout the closing weeks rivalry sharpened between M Chirac's Rassemblement pour la République (RPR) and the President's supporters, hastily grouped under the new banner of the Union pour la Démocratie Française (UDF).

For much of the campaign the President remained prudently aloof. However, he found occasion to urge the voters to 'vote the right way', and to warn them that, should the left succeed, they could not look to him to block the implementation of the Common Programme. In the event the difficulties of governing with a conservative President and a socialist Government were avoided. Although the left-wing parties had a narrow lead on the first ballot—when the turnout was 83·37 per cent—imperfect voting discipline on the left and a surge of support for the Government at the second ballot meant that the ruling coalition finally won 290 of the 491 seats. This was a net loss of only 10 compared with 1973. The detailed results were:

	Votes (first ballot)		Seats	
	1973†	1978	1973†	1978
Extreme Left	778,195	954,661	3	1
Communists	5,085,108	5,870,340	73	86
Socialists + Left Radicals	4,559,241	6,964,449	101	113
RPR (Gaullists)	5,684,396	6,451,454	185	153
UDF (Giscardians)	5,519,933*	6,122,180	106	137
Other Government	784,735	684,985	14	1
Environmentalists	—	612,100	—	—
Others	671,505	793,276	8	—
			491	490

* 1973 = Independent Republicans, Reformists and CDP.
† The 1973 figures do not precisely accord with those given in AR 1973, p. 144, because of changes in classification.

Politically the country emerged cut neatly in four. The Communists had actually increased their vote—only to be outstripped by the Socialists for the first time since 1936. Yet this was not enough to end the twenty-year ascendancy of the centre-right. The ruling coalition's success, while partly due to the divisions of the left, also owed much to M Chirac's tireless campaign and the President's political judgment. Politically M Giscard d'Estaing was considered the great victor of the campaign. He immediately asked M Barre to form a new Government.

There was little change in the political balance of the new Government of 38 (four of them women), and there were few new faces. The vast Finance Ministry was split into two departments, Economy and Budget, and there were new full ministries of Environment and Quality of Life, and Commerce and Crafts. (In minor reshuffles in the autumn Mme Monique Pelletier was to be promoted as Minister for the Feminine Condition, and M Jean François-Poncet replaced M Louis de Guiringaud as Foreign Minister.)

President Giscard d'Estaing had hoped to 'open out' political life and establish a more relaxed relationship with the Opposition. But he reckoned without M Chirac's anger at receiving so few of the fruits of victory. This was fanned when Parliament reassembled, and M Chirac's candidate for the presidency of the Assembly, the veteran Edgar Faure, was defeated by M Jacques Chaban-Delmas. M Chaban-Delmas, who had earlier been passed over by the RPR, was widely taken to be the President's candidate. Although M Barre's policy statement to the new Assembly was comfortably approved by 260 votes to 197, the RPR gave notice that its support could not be taken for granted. M Chirac's relations with the President steadily deteriorated until, in December, he virtually accused M Giscard d'Estaing of being an agent of a foreign power in European policy (see p. 125). Despite the virulence of his criticism, M Chirac made it clear that he would not overthrow M Barre's Government. Nevertheless the Government's legislative programme was in for a rough ride. Although not all the RPR shared M Chirac's erratic acrimony, he had most of his party well in hand.

Meanwhile defeat cast the left into more embittered turmoil. M Robert Fabre, the Radical leader, declared that the Union of the Left was dead, and shortly afterwards accepted a commission to investigate unemployment for the President. Communists and Socialists were locked in mutual recrimination. But each had internal problems too. The Communist leadership's attempt to throw all the blame for defeat upon the Socialists provoked an exceptionally noisy public row. The leadership was forced to give ground and join a debate that it had initially refused. Morale and membership slumped. They would recover in time, but it seemed unlikely that the leadership's hold would ever be quite the same again.

Responsibility for defeat was less controversial among the Socialists, but M François Mitterrand was seen by some as an ageing three-times loser. Amid much ideological skirmishing younger men were staking their claim to supplant him as the party's standard-bearer in the 1981 presidential campaign. The resulting rifts were deep and acrimonious. Even so the Socialists did well in a series of autumn by-elections, winning two seats. But such occasional victories were one thing; finding a winning leader, policies and alliances for 1981 would be altogether a more formidable proposition.

Meanwhile M Barre was trying to stand apart from feuding within the Government coalition, and to press forward with his declared priorities of economic recovery, greater social justice, and improved relations between the state and the citizen. Concern for the last two aims was reflected in a series of modest social measures during the autumn session and proposals for local government reform published in December. But the economy remained the central concern. Freed from the threat from the left, the new Government immediately increased public service tariffs by 10 to 20 per cent in order to reduce subsidies, which had risen to 30,000 million francs (£3,300 million) annually. M Barre also promised to restore price freedom, to take a tough line on industrial 'lame ducks' and to peg real wages— which had remained remarkably buoyant through the recession.

In September M Giscard d'Estaing announced removal of price controls from manufactured goods—the first time bread had been decontrolled in 175 years. In December rents on nearly four million privately-owned houses and flats were freed from January 1979. The Budget brought little cheer. Taxes were raised on petrol, alcohol, tobacco and vehicle licences, but estimated receipts of 445,885 million francs (up 15·2 per cent) were still 15,000 million (£1,800 million) short of expenditure, although this would halve the 1977-78 deficit. In December sharp increases in employees' social security contributions were announced, to meet a projected deficit of 17,000 million francs (£1,900 million). The increased burden was to fall most heavily on the better paid.

The continuing high level of unemployment also led the Government to introduce urgent measures to reform the system of benefits. The social security and employment benefit changes angered the unions. However, their protests remained largely vocal. Indeed, the election and high unemployment contributed to relative industrial peace. The most widely felt dispute had only a minor economic impact. This was the air traffic controllers' go-slow, which disrupted summer holiday flights for much of Western Europe.

It was a record year for bankruptcies, and many major companies got into serious difficulties, notably in shipbuilding, tanning and machine tools. The Marcel Boussac textile empire collapsed during the year. While the Government generally stuck to its liberal policies, not all lame ducks could be allowed to perish. The Government stepped in to help the giant steel corporations Usinor and Sacilor and the smaller Chiers-Chatillon group by converting their huge debts into a majority state holding at a cost of 10,000 million francs. Officially this was a temporary measure. In fact it amounted to back-door nationalization. It also meant the pruning of excess capacity with the loss of thousands more jobs in Lorraine.

But it was not all gloom. Peugeot–Citroen's takeover of Chrysler's European operations (see p. 20) was seen as proof that France could hold its own with the major Japanese and American companies. And the officially-backed technology transfer between the American Motorola Corporation and Thomson–CSF gave hope that France might overcome her backwardness in the integrated circuits industry. Advanced technology, however, also brought problems. The wrecking of the supertanker Amoco Cadiz on the Brittany coast in the spring, France's gravest pollution accident, proved a minor economic disaster for the region's tourist industry. And in December a nation-wide power blackout emphasized that delays in the nuclear power programme due to technical troubles and ecological opposition had left France with a power deficit.

M Barre's economic programme had mixed fortunes. Inflation was contained within single figures at 9·5 per cent—though this was much worse than forecast. GNP rose by 3·5 per cent—also less than hoped. Unemployment fell from its worst level to 1,300,000 in December (5·7 per cent). This was over 140,000 up on a year earlier, and stubbornly resistant to government job creation programmes. On the other hand, real incomes rose slightly and the trade balance improved from an 11,000 million francs (£1,200 million) deficit in 1977 to a small surplus. But despite the austerity of the Barre plan France had again done less well than its major competitors, and the public remained at best sceptical about his chances of success.

Foreign affairs. Africa was much to the fore of France's diplomatic preoccupations. Visiting the Ivory Coast in January, President Giscard d'Estaing declared that France stood ready to help any black state facing an external threat, though it had no wish to be the continent's gendarme; Africa was for the Africans. He believed that France was the only Western power with both a policy and the will to act in Africa. French troops continued their help to Mauritania against the Polisario guerillas. In April, 500 paratroopers and legionnaires were dispatched to Chad, and in May the rapid French intervention at Kolwezi made a deep impression on African leaders assembled in Paris for the Franco-African summit. (The operation also showed that France's limited professional intervention force was stretched to the limit.)

These African initiatives and the decision to contribute 1,000 men to the UN peacekeeping operation in Lebanon roused domestic criticism over both their manner and their substance. Despite the success at Kolwezi, doubt persisted over the desirability of rallying to the support of corrupt or tyrannical regimes. M de Guiringaud ran into sharp criticism of French interventionism when he visited Nigeria in March. However, Kenyan President arap Moi's choice of France for his first foreign visit was seen as a sign that the efforts to court anglophone Africa were at last bearing fruit. A September visit by President Ratsiraka of Malagasy improved a strained relationship. An even more striking reconciliation was sealed by M Giscard d'Estaing's visit to Guinea in December, ending the hostility stemming from President Sekou Touré's explosive *Non!* to de Gaulle in 1958. Although Africa policy was sometimes hard to reconcile with Arab policy, there was some relaxation of relations with Algeria and Libya, strained by the Sahara conflict and the Chad rebellion respectively.

The President's most notable international initiative of the year came in his speech to the United Nations General Assembly in May. His series of disarmament proposals, distinguishing between areas covered by nuclear deterrents and those not, included the winding-up of the Geneva disarmament negotiations—which France had boycotted—the calling of a conference of the Helsinki participants in 1979, an international agency to control observation satellites, and progress towards regional arms limitations agreements. However, international reaction was cool.

M Giscard d'Estaing's European policy was domestically far more controversial. Tensions between the President and the Gaullists crystallized around European elections. M Michel Debré warned that direct elections would spell a slide into greater supranationalism, while M Chirac attacked the *'parti de l'étranger'* which would subject and degrade France into 'a vassal in an empire of merchants'. These attacks were made despite M Giscard d'Estaing's refusal of any increase in the powers of the European Parliamentary Assembly short of a general move towards a European confederation. The Gaullists' opposition went to the extreme of voting with the Communists against legislation implementing an EEC directive on the harmonization of VAT. They again joined with the Opposition to reject Community financial aid for the European elections. It was probably no coincidence that as the year closed France was taking a tough line on trade talks and postponing operation of the European Monetary System, which the President had done so much to promote in alliance with Chancellor Schmidt (see p. 132). The split within the governing coalition was casting its shadow over French behaviour at Brussels, and would clearly continue to do so.

Defence. Defence was another sensitive area on both sides of the political divide. In January the Socialists somewhat hesitantly followed the Communists in accepting nuclear weapons, though protesting that abolition was still their long-term aim, and half-promising a referendum on the issue. But after some twenty years of controversy it seemed that all the major parties now accepted French nuclear forces. Further underground tests were conducted in the Pacific to develop miniaturized warheads. Plans were also announced for developing cruise missiles. However, reports that France had the neutron bomb were denied. In May it was decided to equip the strategic submarine force with M20 missiles capable of delivering a one megaton payload over more than 3,000 km, and in September the President announced the construction of a sixth nuclear submarine. The Gaullists, who had campaigned long and hard for this, were jubilant. *Inflexible* would have M4 MIRV missiles with ranges of around 4,000 km, and would enter service in 1985. With Nato's decision to proceed with the AWACS system (see Pt. XI, Ch. 3), France decided to develop its own independent airborne early warning system, paying special attention to its exposed Mediterranean flank. While this insistence on independent forces stood very much in the tradition of Gaullist defence doctrine, here, as with the change in the Socialist line, it was clear that the Government's policy reflected a much broader consensus on France's place in the world.

THE FEDERAL REPUBLIC OF GERMANY

INTERNAL AFFAIRS. The Federal Government's efforts to stimulate the economy met with considerable success. By the end of the year the Government had fulfilled its promise, made at the summit meeting of the leading industrial nations in Bonn in July, to reflate by a further 1 per cent of gnp. It accomplished this by pumping some DM13,000 million into the economy, mostly by reducing income tax and by granting tax concessions to industry. Real growth of gnp for the year was estimated at 3·5 per cent, inflation was well below 3 per cent and, although unemployment remained stubbornly high at around 900,000, there were signs of a modest improvement. In spite of the persistent weakness of the dollar, exports to the United States increased by 15 per cent in the first eight months, and there was also an encouraging growth of trade with European countries. The West German motor industry was booming, the stock markets had a good year, and the public, responding to the mood of cautious optimism, was saving less and spending more.

However, a deterioration of labour relations, which were traditionally rather good in Germany, added another hazard to the forecasting of economic trends. For nearly four weeks in March and April IG Metall, the engineering union, brought out some 85,000 of its members in south-west Germany in support of a pay claim which was eventually settled with an increase of 5·5 per cent. The employers retaliated by locking out 145,000 workers in the affected plants. At about the same time the printing workers' union, IG Druck und Papier, called a strike of 2,200 workers after talks had broken down over the introduction of new technology. The employers' answer was to lock out 32,000 workers in 500 printing firms. Subsequently, both unions started litigation in the labour courts to try to have lock-outs declared illegal.

The Constitution does not expressly mention lock-outs or strikes. It states that the 'right to form associations to safeguard and improve working conditions shall be guaranteed to everyone and to all professions. Agreements which seek to hinder this right shall be null and void; measures directed to this end shall be illegal.' Both sides of industry had always recognized this article as the constitutional definition of the right to strike, but the unions argued that it was inadmissible to read into those words the right of lock-out. It was expected that their case would ultimately be taken to the Federal Constitutional Court.

In November the first strike in the West German steel industry for 50 years began in North-Rhine Westphalia. IG Metall initially brought out 37,000 of its members working in ten plants which are major suppliers of tin-plate to the car industry, and several weeks later, after negotiations had failed to produce a settlement, called a further 20,000 workers out on strike. Again there was a lock-out, originally limited to 29,000 workers. The dispute was not so much about pay or holidays as about job security. The labour force of some 200,000 was decreasing at the alarming rate of about 1,000 a month, and the union demanded, as the best solution, the phased introduction of the 35-hour week, plus a 'modest' increase in pay of 5 per cent. The employers said that, far from saving jobs, the 35-hour week would cause a drastic rationalization and a still more rapid reduction of the work-force. It would be tantamount, they said, to an increase of pay of around 20 per cent, which an industry that had its last good year in 1974 obviously could not afford.

The old idea of industrial partnership which had stood the country in good stead for so many years appeared to have been abandoned. The unions were still smarting under the decision of the employers' federation to challenge the new law on industrial co-partnership in the Federal Constitutional Court, and for this reason were refusing to take part in those periodic meetings of the 'concerted action committee'—a get-together with the Chancellor, employers' and Federal Bank representatives—which used to yield an amazing degree of consensus. But probably the main reason why the unions had changed their attitude was that the leadership appeared to have lost control over the rank and file. Politicians began to talk of the dangers of importing the 'English malady'.

On the political front, the popularity of the Federal Chancellor, Herr Helmut Schmidt, was never higher. He was given most of the credit for maintaining a high degree of economic stability, and was widely respected at home for his role as an international statesman.

Nonetheless, his coalition Government of the Social Democratic Party (SPD) and the Free Democratic Party (FDP) did not always look safe in the saddle. In the Länder elections in Hamburg and Lower Saxony in June the FDP failed to clear the 5 per cent hurdle, the proportion of votes necessary to secure parliamentary seats. They polled 4·8 per cent in Hamburg, where they were in coalition with the Social Democrats, and 4·2 per cent in Lower Saxony, where for the previous 18 months they had been in a Government led by the Christian Democratic Union (CDU). The Free Democrats suffered, more so than the two larger parties, from the intervention of groups of ecologists, standing for the first time in state elections. These groups, which were supported by many young people, polled 3·9 per cent in Lower Saxony (18 per cent in the constituency where a nuclear fuel reprocessing plant was planned) and 4·5 per cent in Hamburg.

However, the Free Democrats rallied. In the Länder elections in Hesse and Bavaria in October they managed comfortably to retain their parliamentary representation, polling 6·6 per cent and 5·9 per cent respectively. This was a tense time for the Federal Government. A change of power in Hesse, ending 33 years of Social Democrat rule, would have increased the Christian Democrat Opposition's majority in the Bundesrat, the Upper House of the Federal Parliament, to two-thirds, placing all Government legislation at the mercy of the Christian Democrats. Most people thought that the Free Democrats' survival would indicate that the Federal Government was likely to stay the course without undue trouble until the next federal election in 1980.

Mr Schmidt's Government, however, lived more dangerously than its parliamentary majority of eleven would suggest. It was saved from defeat in an important division on 14 December only after the four Free Democrat Ministers, who comprised a quarter of the Cabinet, threatened to resign unless a group of rebels in their party gave up their plan to vote against the Government. The issue was nuclear energy, and concerned specifically the future of the fast breeder reactor under construction with Dutch and Belgian participation on the Lower Rhine at Kalkar.

Construction of this prototype, the first reactor of its kind in West Germany, was started in 1971. Ecologists had been fighting the project in the courts since 1973. The case was finally taken to the Federal Constitutional Court, which decided on 8 December that the project did not involve a violation of the Basic Law. The Court said that when Parliament, back in 1959, gave its blessing to the development of nuclear energy, it clearly envisaged that fast breeder reactors would be part of the programme. Further, the authorities had taken the necessary steps to identify the risks early, and to eliminate them.

Parliament was faced on 14 December with a motion to give the go-ahead to the construction of the third stage of the Kalkar power station. Until the eleventh hour six Free Democrat MPs said they would vote No. This would have meant defeat for the Government because the Christian Democrats in opposition had also decided to reject the motion. The Opposition did not object to nuclear energy, or indeed to the Kalkar project: it wanted to speed things up. It also relished the sight of the Government parties feverishly trying to whip up a majority.

The Free Democrat dissidents were on firm ground. At their party conference in November, the FDP approved a left-wing resolution that there should be a moratorium of several years on the construction of Kalkar. Indeed, it was only the threat of resignation by the Economics Minister, Count Otto Lambsdorff, that prevented the conference calling for a complete stop to the atomic energy programme. The six rebels were faced in December with the threatened resignation not only of the Economics Minister but also of the Foreign Minister, Herr Hans-Dietrich Genscher, the Minister of Agriculture, Herr Josef Ertl, the Interior Minister, Herr Gerhart Baum, and the leader of the party in the Bundestag, Herr Wolfgang Mischnick. In the event, the rebels abstained. The Government carried the day by 230 votes to 225.

It was not as if Kalkar, which was to cost at least DM2,400 million, was going to start fast breeding tomorrow. A fourth and fifth building stage had still to be approved. And the Government still had to appoint a commission of inquiry to examine whether the plant, once completed, could safely be put into operation. West Germany had 14 nuclear power stations in use, producing 3·3 per cent of the country's primary energy requirements and 10·8 per cent of its electricity. Another ten were being built, and three more were held up by the courts. Estimates of future nuclear energy output could be no more than guesswork.

There was continued discussion about the long-term strategy of the Christian Democratic Union and its Bavarian sister party, the Christian Social Union (CSU), which had been in opposition in the Federal Parliament since 1969. So long as the Free Democrats stayed allied to the Social

E

Democrats there seemed little hope of a change of power at federal level. Even Herr Helmut Kohl, the chairman of the Christian Democratic Union, appeared to have abandoned hope of coaxing the Free Democrats from Herr Schmidt's embrace. The alternative, it was argued, would be to form a fourth party, or rather to extend the operations of the Christian Social Union, led by Herr Franz-Josef Strauss, beyond the borders of Bavaria. The theorists, most of whom belonged to the CSU, calculated that the CDU, fighting its own battle and therefore less susceptible to Bavarian influence, would attract Free Democrats and rightish Social Democrats. Herr Strauss's party, fielding candidates federally, would offer a political home for anybody right of the CDU. Then, assuming they had an absolute majority, the two parties would form a coalition. Herr Strauss and Herr Kohl, whose relationship remained brittle, agreed to defer discussion of this and other plans until the spring of 1979. In the meantime, Herr Strauss was settling down in his new role as Prime Minister of Bavaria. Before his election to this office after the Bavarian state election in October he made it clear that he had no intention of becoming less active in federal politics.

After five and a half years as Minister of Defence, Herr Georg Leber (SPD) resigned in February after disclosures that three alleged spies in his department had betrayed to East Germany secret information of 'unprecedented value' to a potential enemy. It emerged during the long investigation into this case that Herr Leber had been told only part of the story—but still enough, one might have thought, for him to ask some searching questions. He had not asked them, and when the tale was finally told he excused his ignorance by saying that he could not be expected to read who-dun-its from morning till night.

Under his supervision, the defensive capability of the Bundeswehr and its reputation at home and abroad had continued to grow, but in the months preceding his resignation it had seemed that he no longer had his large and bewilderingly complex department in hand. It was not merely that he was kept in the dark about spying. In December 1977 the Federal Constitutional Court set aside the decision, for which Herr Leber bore the political responsibility, to stop questioning the sincerity of conscientious objectors. This had led to a big increase in the number of young men applying for other forms of service. Moreover, several young officers who were dismissed the service in 1977 after anti-semitic incidents at the Bundeswehr University in Munich were subsequently reinstated by courts of appeal. Herr Leber was replaced as Defence Minister by Herr Hans Apel, the former Minister of Finance.

There was also a change at the Interior Ministry. Herr Werner Maihofer (FDP) resigned as Minister in June over a major bungle by the security authorities in the hunt for terrorists. A tip-off about the possible whereabouts of Herr Hanns-Martin Schleyer, the employers' leader who was kidnapped and later murdered by terrorists in 1977, had been lost in the bureaucratic thicket of the federal criminal investigation department. Herr Maihofer shouldered the responsibility after an inquiry.

The new Minister, Herr Baum, who was formerly Herr Maihofer's deputy, said in September that terrorist groups, far from being subdued by massive police operations and a hunt in which the whole country had been urged to take part, were attracting new recruits. Some young people were dropping out of their bourgeois lives, going underground and joining the terrorists; many others, while not prepared to become frontline activists, were providing valuable logistic assistance. Germany had been spared terrorist attacks since the Schleyer kidnapping, but police came across evidence in September that something big was being planned. The operation was probably postponed, if not abandoned, as the result of the death on 6 September of one of the most wanted terrorists, Willy Peter Stoll, who was shot by police in a restaurant in Düsseldorf when he tried to pull a gun on them, and by the discovery of two flats used as terrorists' headquarters.

Stoll's death reduced to 14 the number of known and most-wanted terrorists who were still free. The German Government tried in vain to obtain the extradition of four others who were in prison in Yugoslavia (see p. 115). After some neat detective work by the German authorities, the four alleged terrorists—all on Germany's most-wanted list—were arrested by Yugoslav police in Zagreb at the beginning of May. The German Government immediately applied for their extradition. But the Yugoslav Government was looking for a deal—the extradition of eight Yugoslav (mostly Croatian) exiles, living in Germany. These were rounded up by the German police, but seven of them on appeal to the German courts won verdicts that the evidence supplied by the Yugoslavs was not strong enough to warrant extradition. The eighth man, Stjepan Bilandzic, the one the Yugoslav Government wanted most of all, could be extradited, a Cologne court ruled. In fact, he was not sent back to Yugoslavia. The Government decided against his extradition. The Yugoslavs retaliated by setting free the four German alleged terrorists and allowing them to travel to a country of their choice.

The West German Federal Parliament was called from the summer recess in August to lift immunity from a Social Democrat MP, Herr Uwe Holtz, chairman of the development aid committee, who was suspected of espionage. He and Herr Joachim Broudré-Gröger, the personal assistant of Herr Egon Bahr, general secretary of the SDP, had been accused of spying by a Romanian defector, General Ion Pacepa. They were both cleared without charges being brought.

After a six-month struggle for political survival, Herr Hans Filbinger, Prime Minister of Baden-Württemberg, resigned in August. During the war he was a naval judge, and his handling of two cases against German sailors in 1945 prompted the playwright Rolf Hochhuth to comment that Herr Filbinger had been 'a terrible jurist'—so much so that 'it must be assumed he is a free man only because those who knew him kept their silence'. Herr Filbinger, who fought a libel action against Herr Hochhuth and lost, was subsequently disclosed to have passed death sentences on three naval deserters in 1945, and had condemned another sailor to death in 1943 for looting. He had also presided at a court martial held in a British prisoner of war camp in Norway after the war when a young German sailor was sentenced to six months' detention for calling a superior a Nazi swine.

FOREIGN AFFAIRS. It was a year in which West Germany's growing international political importance was clearly demonstrated. The days when the Federal Republic was regarded as an economic giant but a political dwarf were over. West Germany played a significant role in the United Nations, and in attempts by the West to reach a peaceful solution to the problems of Southern Africa and the Middle East. But Herr Schmidt was at pains to stress that Germany would use its diplomatic weight only in concert with its Western allies.

The mid-July Bonn meeting of the heads of government of the seven leading nations of the capitalistic world attracted much publicity and aroused many hopes. In the event, it produced a batch of undertakings or promises—some of them, like West Germany's, specific, others, like those of the United States and Britain, vague. Precisely what the meeting had achieved in the long term, whether it had eased the solution of the world's economic problems, could be answered only when the heads of government met again in 1979.

The Bonn summit was preceded by a conference of the heads of government of the Nine in Bremen. There the EEC decided to press ahead with attempts to find a way of bringing about a closer integration of their currency systems. The aim was to create a greater coordination of economic policy inside the Community and, at the same time, to form a currency block whose very existence would help to reduce currency speculation and its harmful effects on world trade. This was the prelude to the creation of the European Monetary System (see Pt. XI, Ch. 4 and Pt. XVII, Ch. 1), a process in which the German Chancellor played a leading part.

President Carter's talks in Bonn with Herr Schmidt helped improve their somewhat uneasy personal relationship. Ever since President Carter took office relations between Bonn and Washington had been delicate. There were differences about the President's stand on human rights, about the transfer by Germany of the entire nuclear fuel cycle to Brazil and about American charges that West Germany had not done enough to stimulate its economy and thereby to assist world recovery. Finally, there was President Carter's deferment of a decision to produce the neutron bomb. This caused the biggest shock of all, and prompted Herr Strauss, a former

Minister of Defence, to comment that for the first time since the war an American President had 'openly knuckled under to a Russian Czar'. With 20 Soviet armoured divisions stationed in East Germany, the West Germans were naturally sensitive to the slightest suspicion that the Americans might be weakening in their resolve to defend Western Europe. President Carter did his best to allay these suspicions.

Just before the July summit, President Carter visited West Berlin and renewed the United States' pledge to defend the city. 'Was immer sei', he said, 'Berlin bleibt frei' (Whatever happens, Berlin will stay free). He said he believed that since the Four Power Berlin Agreement was signed in 1971 there had been a great improvement in the Berlin situation. But he did not think that anything could hide the deprivation of human rights as exemplified by the Berlin Wall. 'This is the first time in history', he added, 'that a wall was built not to protect one's nation from foreign aggressors, but to protect one's own people from the right to escape.'

The highest-ranking Chinese politician ever to visit West Germany, Fang Ji, a member of the Politburo, had talks in Bonn in October and made a tour of industrial concerns and research centres. China placed orders for mining equipment worth DM8,000 million with German firms, and many more contracts were being planned.

The Soviet leader, Mr Leonid Brezhnev, visited Bonn in May, and German sources said that Soviet–West German relations had developed beyond the point where only bilateral problems were discussed. The two statesmen talked about the wider issues of disarmament, the Middle East and Africa. It was Mr Brezhnev's second visit to Bonn, the first being in 1973. The Russians were most anxious that West Germany should not establish too close a relationship with China.

ITALY

Early in January the Communist, Socialist and Republican parties intensified their pressure for an emergency Government of the democratic parties, including the Communists, to deal with the pressing problems of inflation and increasing terrorism. The single-party Christian Democrat Government, formed in July 1976 under Giulio Andreotti, had hitherto survived through the abstention from parliamentary opposition of the Communists and the four other democratic parties. On 16 January the Communists, Socialists and Republicans withdrew their support and the Government therefore resigned. President Giovanni Leone at once called on Signor Andreotti to form a new Government.

The subsequent negotiations dragged on for 54 days against a background of economic difficulties, student revolt and extremist violence. On 12 January the US State Department issued a statement that 'the USA did not favour Communist participation in West European Governments and would like to see Communist influence reduced'. But neither the Christian Democrats nor the Communists were in a position to pay much heed to this admonition. Both sides were under pressure within their own parties. Right-wing Christian Democrats were standing out against any closer links with the Communists, while die-hard Communists contested the line adopted by their party leader, Enrico Berlinguer, who aimed, not at a take-over of power, but at his long-term goal of a 'historic compromise' between Communists and Christian Democrats, tempered for the present by an increasingly effective Communist role in the governmental set-up and in policy-making. Neither side wished to face the alternative of a general election, and indeed both Andreotti and Berlinguer were acutely aware of the need to put up a united front against inflation and terrorism.

By early March the Communists had gradually whittled down their demands for a place in the Government and were instead prepared to accept agreement on a precise programme with limited objectives, put forward by Andreotti. The programme included stiffer measures for economic austerity and for dealing with crime and political extremism; and it was specifically stated that no change would be made in foreign policy, including Italy's continued adherence to Nato and the EEC. The programme pact meant that the Communists would now vote officially for the Government and have a more definite say in policy-making and even in the formation of the Government. It secured agreement on 8 March from five of the six parties concerned; only the Liberals objected and went into opposition.

The Christian Democrat party chairman, Aldo Moro, had played an important mediating role in the negotiations for this agreement, and it was partly on his advice that the Cabinet announced by Andreotti on 11 March played safe and differed little from its predecessor. It was in fact still a single-party Christian Democrat Government, in which the main change was at the Treasury Ministry, where the ex-Finance Minister, Filippo Maria Pandolfi, moved up to replace Gaetano Stammati, who went to Public Works.

Extremist violence formed a sinister background to these negotiations. Student clashes with the police occurred in Rome and Florence universities. On 14 February in Rome members of the extreme-left Red Brigade shot dead Judge Riccardo Palma, who had been making arrangements in Turin for the resumption of the twice-postponed trial there of 15 Red Brigade leaders, including the group's founder, Renato Curcio, and of 33 smaller fry. When the trial reopened on 9 March, one of the accused threatened revolution and further violence—which followed next day when a former special-branch police official was shot dead.

But worse was to come. On the morning of 16 March Aldo Moro was kidnapped from his car in a Rome street and his five bodyguards were shot dead. The Red Brigades at once claimed responsibility for the attack, and two days later they issued a message saying that Moro was being held in a 'people's prison' and would be tried by a 'people's tribunal': his abduction was only the beginning of an offensive to 'carry the battle to the heart of the State'.

Parliament was summoned at once and that same afternoon gave the new Government a massive vote of confidence. An emergency plan was drawn up, and some 50,000 police embarked on an intensive but unavailing search for the kidnappers, thought to number about a dozen including a woman.

Throughout the 53 days of Moro's captivity the Red Brigades issued a stream of messages vilifying and threatening Moro and demanding the release, first, of 'all communist prisoners' and later, on 24 April, of 13 leading comrades on trial in Turin in exchange for Moro's release. On 5 May a message said the sentence of death passed on Moro by a 'people's court' would be carried out. His body was found in a stolen car in Rome on the morning of 9 May, following a telephone call to the police. He had been shot in the chest 11 times.

Aldo Moro, aged 62, the leading figure in the Christian Democrat Party and its chairman, had been at the centre of the Italian political scene for the past 30 years (see OBITUARY). He had been several times Prime Minister, author of the centre-left coalition of 1963-76, and the guiding mediator in 1977-78 in bringing about the collaboration between Christian Democrats and Communists. It was that last action that made him an especial target for the Red Brigades, who regarded the Communists' association with a Christian Democrat Government as a betrayal of the leftists' cause. But in their eyes Moro was the personification of all the shortcomings of the Christian Democrats and the bourgeois state over the past 30 years.

Throughout the long-drawn-out tension of his captivity the Government consistently refused to negotiate with the terrorists despite appeals for his release from Moro's family and from the Pope himself, and in the face of letters which Moro was induced or forced to write under duress to Christian Democrat leaders. The parties supporting the Government were virtually united in this stand, although the Socialists at one point adopted a somewhat individual attitude in urging clemency. But in fact the terrorists' efforts to shatter Christian Democrat–Communist collaboration had the opposite effect, for cooperation between the parties became even closer than Moro himself could have envisaged. On the day of his death Berlinguer spoke of him as 'this great democratic leader' who had been 'slaughtered by an organization of criminal terrorists'.

After Moro's death the inevitable recriminations began concerning the inefficiency of the police in failing to track down the terrorists and their place of concealment. In debates in Parliament police inadequacy was admitted, but on 16 May the Government secured a massive vote of confidence and sterner measures against terrorism were passed. The respected Minister of the Interior, Francesco Cossiga, however, felt he should resign. His successor, Virginio Rognone, took office on 13 June.

After several finds of hideouts and arms caches by the police in April and May it was thought that the 'Rome-Sud' group of the Red Brigades might have been neutralized and their operational headquarters transferred to the north. This theory was borne out when in September and early October the newly-formed anti-terrorist squad of 50 hand-picked men under the carabiniere General Carlo Alberto Dalla Chiesa achieved successes which had eluded the regular police. On 13 September Corrado Alunni, believed to be the successor of the Red Brigades' imprisoned leader Renato Curcio, was arrested in a Milan flat where arms, explosives and false passports were found; and in a series of raids in Milan on 1 and 2 October the special police discovered Red Brigade hideouts, captured nine terrorists and found not only extensive arms caches but also files including an entire historical archive of the Red Brigade movement, more letters written by Moro in captivity and tape-recordings of his 'trial'. This material was sent to Rome for investigation. The original intention was to keep the contents secret for reasons of security, but excerpts were leaked (probably by the Red Brigades) and in the face of public demand it was decided on 17 October to publish a summarized version of the dossier. It revealed little that was not already known.

After a lull during the summer terrorist activity revived. On 11 and 12 October a leading magistrate in Rome and a criminologist in Naples were shot dead, and on 8 November the Frosinone public prosecutor and his driver and bodyguard were killed. Two policemen guarding the Turin prison were killed on 15 December, and later in December there were a number of petrol-bomb attacks on industrial establishments in the Veneto. The aim seemed to be to choose scattered targets and spread panic. During the year 35 people were killed in political violence, 25 of them by the Red Brigades, and there were over 35 victims of kneecapping attacks.

Local elections involving about a tenth of the electorate, held on 14 May and thus within a week of the Moro tragedy, provided a vote of solidarity for the Christian Democrats, who secured 42·5 per cent of the total, whereas the Communists lost ground. Regional elections held in the Trentino and Alto Adige provinces on 21 November brought a warning to both Christian Democrats and Communists, who lost ground to parties of local appeal, and in particular, in the mainly German-speaking Alto Adige, to the Südtiroler Volkspartei. A nationwide referendum held on 11-12 June rejected the demand of the small but vociferous Radical Party for the abrogation of two laws, one, of 1975, to deal with growing violence (now in any case superseded by the sterner measures taken after Moro's death), and the other, of 1974, concerning the financing of political parties from public funds.

In mid-June President Leone was forced to resign in the face of allegations concerning fiscal misconduct and his possible involvement in the Lockheed bribery scandal. He was in any case within six months of the end of his term of office. Ironically, the most favoured candidate to succeed him in December would have been Aldo Moro. Instead, on 8 July the electoral body chose for the first time a Socialist President, Alessandro Pertini, aged 81 but still active in politics, who had had a fine record in wartime Resistance and had been president of the Chamber of Deputies in 1968-76.

On 31 October Signor Andreotti announced details of the three-year (1979-81) economic stabilization plan which had been worked out by Treasury Minister Pandolfi. It called for reduction in the large public sector deficit (which had come under strong criticism from a visiting IMF team in June), a near-halt in wage increases and increased mobility in the labour force. Both southerners and the trade unions regarded its provisions for the south as inadequate, and some 30,000 Calabrians demonstrated in Rome in support of their case. Unemployment was still running at over $1\frac{1}{2}$ million. But the balance of payments was in surplus—a remarkable improvement—and foreign exchange reserves rose to over $9,000 million.

Inflation, though reduced to around 12 per cent, was still a good deal higher than in the other EEC countries, and this consideration caused Italy to bargain for the best possible terms if she were to join the European Monetary System. At the Brussels summit meeting on 4 December Andreotti asked for a week's pause for consultations at home—the Communists and Socialists being against entry. But on 11 December, following pressure from President Giscard d'Estaing and Chancellor Schmidt, he announced that Italy would join.

Signor Andreotti visited the USA (28 May-3 June) and received praise from President Carter for the fight Italy was putting up against inflation and terrorism. He also went to Spain (5-6 September) and promised support for Spain's entry into EEC. The Communist leader Enrico Berlinguer visited Paris, Moscow and Belgrade (4-11 October). In Moscow, to which he had been invited, he saw Brezhnev and appeared to have secured approval for his policy of 'historic compromise' provided that an open breach between the Soviet and Italian Communist Parties was avoided. The Chinese Foreign Minister Huang Hua visited Italy (5-10 October) and saw Andreotti and President Pertini, and the Foreign Trade Minister Renato Ossola had trade talks in China at the end of October. Trade was also discussed when Signor Andreotti made a brief tour (15-20 October) to Libya, Egypt, Jordan and Iraq.

E*

BELGIUM

Although in January it seemed at one point as if the devolution plan along federal lines agreed in 1977 might be about to collapse, the problems were seemingly resolved. However, these difficulties could, with the benefit of hindsight, be seen as foreshadowing the collapse of what had appeared only a short time before to be a comprehensive and long-term federal solution that would satisfy the separate aspirations of the French-speaking and Flemish-speaking communities. In effect, the Walloon elements in Mr Tindemans's coalition Government claimed to have detected a plot between the Prime Minister and his own Flemish wing of the Social Christian Party, involving the collaboration of the Flemish nationalist Volksunie Party, to delay implementation of some crucial concessions to French-speaking residents in the technically Flemish communes surrounding Brussels. Thus, Belgium's central socio-political problem entered yet another phase of labyrinthine complications that by the end of the year would bring the resignation of the Government and a full-scale resumption of inter-communal wrangling, absorbing the authorities' attention and energy and, by impeding the formulation of coherent policies, exacerbating Belgium's economic difficulties.

Nevertheless, the country appeared to go further down the road towards a federal constitution in early March when the Prime Minister obtained parliamentary approval for the basic texts which were to prepare the way for a change from a unitary state to three autonomous regions (Wallonia, Flanders and Brussels), despite differences of interpretation concerning the content of the Egmont agreement (see AR 1977, pp. 139-40), on which the devolution plan was based. However, large parts of the constitution remained to be re-written (and, in any case, only the next National Assembly, after general elections, could have enacted the legislation bringing the new federal system into being). A public opinion poll taken at the time showed that more than half of the respondents did not believe that a solution to the intercommunal problem had been found.

The Government also found itself in difficulties over its handling of the economy when the Prime Minister attempted to push through an 'anti-crisis plan' designed to curb expansion in public spending, which had generated a budget deficit so dangerously large as to limit severely the Government's ability to deal with the many problems besetting the economy. In particular, job creation by means of higher state investment was not practicable on a scale large enough to mitigate Belgium's massive unemployment (the highest since 1945). Resistance to Mr Tindemans's proposals from the Socialists, who were key members of the coalition, produced his resignation. This, however, was viewed by the King as a tactical move and was not accepted. A compromise solution was then agreed by the coalition parties and the Tindemans Administration continued in office. However, it was evident to all that only a superficial harmony had been restored, and that the so-called anti-crisis plan amounted to very little beyond a means of appeasing the competing economic interests of the parties in the coalition in order to prolong its life.

The economy was in a prolonged emergence from recession, with the main business indicators—industrial production, investment, personal consumption and exports—showing only an uncertain trend towards recovery. In these circumstances, the absence of a clear-cut government strategy and the lack of a consensus between government, employers and the unions, combined with Belgium's very high export and import ratios (each equivalent to over 50 per cent of the gross national product), made the economy more than usually a straw in the wind of developments elsewhere (mainly in West Germany and France).

In the end, and with seeming historical inevitability, it was differences between the two language communities, rather than the economic problems, that brought the resignation of the Government. Notwithstanding apparent prior agreement on the devolution plan, centrifugal forces reasserted themselves, and the Flemish wing of the Social Christian Party, the senior member of the coalition, repudiated the concessions made earlier to the Walloons. The result was that Mr Tindemans tendered the resignation of his Government on 11 October. It soon became clear that general elections were inevitable, and these were called for 17 December by the caretaker Government, almost identical in composition with its predecessor, formed by Mr Vanden Boeynants, head of the French-speaking wing of the Social Christian Party.

The general elections produced no material changes in the strengths of the main political parties, and as the year closed no basis had been found for forming a new Government.

THE NETHERLANDS

The new Centre-Liberal Government of Mr Andries Van Agt, with a majority of only two in the Lower House, turned out to be less fragile than expected. In a declaration of economic policy on 16 January, Mr Van Agt stated that his Government, unlike its predecessor, intended to encourage private industry by means of investment and export incentives; pay restraint and price controls would also be maintained. Balancing these measures was a planned extension of the programme for increasing worker participation in industry, involving an expanded role for works councils and supervisory councils, with strengthened employee representation.

Given the coalition's slender parliamentary majority, the provincial elections, held on 29 March, assumed a national as well as purely local importance. The outcome was clearly going to provide a measure of the strong polarization that had developed between the centre-right Government parties and the Labour Party plus its satellites. The result was a victory for the forces supporting Mr Van Agt.

This was reinforced at the municipal elections held on 31 May. The results showed a shift of voters towards the centre compared with the provincial elections. Mr Van Agt's Centre Party increased its poll strongly by Dutch standards, though his Coalition partners, the Liberals, lost ground. The Socialists held on to their previous share of the municipal vote, but took only 30·7 per cent of the poll in May compared with 36·5 per cent at the March provincial elections.

A further episode of political violence, involving the seizure of hostages by the South Moluccan separatists resident in Holland, demonstrated the persistence of this serious problem, which came to be generally regarded as insoluble. The South Moluccans maintained their adamant refusal to become socially integrated with the Dutch population. The influx of citizens of the Netherlands Antilles in advance of the probable independence of the islands created fears of further racial problems resulting from the presence in the Netherlands of 10 per cent of the Antilles population.

Economic problems remained severe during the first half of the year. Industrial production was virtually static, investment by industry at a low ebb, and only personal consumption continued to grow, notwithstanding the high level of unemployment. The one achievement was bringing down the rate of inflation, as expressed by the retail price index, to under 5 per cent annually by mid-year, with a prospect of no more than 4·5 per cent inflation for 1978 as a whole.

The Prime Minister chose curbs on the rise in public spending and an incomes policy as the main weapons with which to prevent any resurgence of inflation. The intention was to allow a small—0·5 per cent—annual rate of increase in the purchasing power of lower-paid workers, stability (*i.e.* zero real increase) for the middle band of salaries, and a reduction of 3 per cent per annum in the purchasing power of higher incomes. Public employees, who traditionally enjoyed higher than average pay rises, were to be obliged to accept less than their equivalents in the private sector. Predictably, civil servants found this difficult to accept and staged a one-day strike (illegal for state employees under Dutch law) on 23 June.

To general surprise, the 1979 Budget, announced on 19 September, showed a record deficit and a massive (highly inflationary) borrowing requirement. Nevertheless, the expenditure increase was within the Government's target rate, and represented 'austerity' compared with the previous years. The opposition parties objected vociferously, claiming that heavier expenditure was necessary in order to create more jobs.

Despite the relative severity of the coalition Government's economic policies, especially those concerning wages restraint, Mr Van Agt's Christian Democratic Party succeeded in retaining its popularity in the public opinion polls to the end of the year. However, it appeared evident that this support rested as much on the public's unwillingness to face the prospect of another nine-month-long government crisis of the kind that preceded the formation of the Van Agt coalition as on positive faith in the latter's capability to deal with the nation's severe economic problems.

LUXEMBOURG

For Luxembourg 1978 was a quiet year politically, and the main pre-occupation of the Government was the serious difficulties affecting the economy. Initially, the crisis in the steel industry overlaid everything else and accounted for the greater part of unemployment—though this latter problem was mitigated by the ease with which the Grand Duchy's location permitted its residents to obtain employment in adjacent countries. By March, however, it was apparent that the performance of the steel industry, though still unimpressive, was nevertheless improving. Inflation came further under control during the year and was running at only about 3 per cent per annum by December. In an effort to aid diversification of the economy, the authorities introduced additional fiscal incentives for foreign companies to locate in Luxembourg.

REPUBLIC OF IRELAND

The February Budget completed the implementation of promises made in the election manifesto which had secured the return to office of a Fianna Fail Government in 1977 (see AR 1977, p. 143). Taxation relief added a further impulse to the economic boom already under way, and the Finance Minister, Mr George Colley, predicted a substantial reduction in unemployment. Job creation fell short of expectations owing to a rapid expansion of consumer spending, an unprecedented 30 per cent increase in house prices and trade union demands for pay rises exceeding the levels permitted under the National Wage Agreement. The resultant pressure on credit facilities, mortgage rates and investment potential undermined the Government's hopes for an improvement in national prosperity, and the year ended with an inflation rate of $8\frac{1}{2}$ per cent for the twelve months instead of the 6 per cent or less which had seemed likely in the aftermath of the Budget. A credit squeeze introduced in November was designed to channel resources away from spending to productive enterprises.

The need to curb public expenditure and to restrain wage rises became the dominant tone of Government pronouncements both in a Green Paper on the economy and in statements by the Taoiseach, Mr Jack Lynch, and the Minister for Economic Planning, Dr Martin O'Donoghue. The trade unions, noting the incentives given to industry and the 20 per cent increase in farm incomes, were less than responsive. Strikes disrupted the telephone and telex services, the national airline, cement and petrol supplies, broadcasting and motor assembly. A number of employers, profiting from the boom, preferred to settle on productivity bases essentially outside the terms of the National Agreement for the sake of industrial peace. This in turn confirmed the suspicion of the trade unions that direct bargaining would benefit them better than the long-established system of annual Agreements. In November the Irish Congress of Trade Unions voted not to enter into discussions on a new Agreement. By now both Government and trade unions had reverted to traditional basic positions which seemed to signal a return to official restraint in the teeth of worker militancy. The closing weeks of the year, however, brought a totally new factor into the situation when Ireland joined the European Monetary System.

Entry to the EMS had been foreseen since midsummer. Given satisfactory support arrangements from the EEC, both the Government and the Fine Gael opposition party strongly favoured entry. While public understanding of the implications was certainly limited, the move attracted tangible popular approval. Some at least of the country's economic difficulties stemmed from the parity link of the Irish pound with sterling. Mortgate rates, bank interest charges and the earnings from Irish trade with the Continent were all affected by British industrial difficulties and even by the political needs of the British Government. After five years of beneficial EEC membership, the Irish public could see little reason why their agriculture-based economy should be buffeted by the quite different problems of the United Kingdom. Dependence on trade with Britain, while still considerable, had been much reduced and expressions of concern on that score were discounted. An EEC survey had recently revealed that commitment to the Common Market was stronger among the Irish than among the population of any other country in the Nine. These elements combined to ensure little resistance to the Government's pursuit of EMS membership, which was generally presented as 'the break with sterling'.

In the event, entry to the EMS proved cumbersome. The goodwill towards the Irish case voiced to Mr Colley and Mr Lynch in the course of exploratory visits to Bonn, Paris and other capitals failed to produce the £650 million in grants over five years which the Government had said would be needed by Ireland. The December summit offered less than £300 million based on loans, which Mr Lynch said he could not recommend to his Government. Following the Taoiseach's return from Brussels, confusion and controversy arose over the precise details of the offer. Intensive diplomatic activity during the next ten days resulted in an enhanced offer, mainly through the agency of Chancellor Schmidt, and on

15 December the Government announced that Ireland would join the EMS on the 2¼ per cent narrow band of permitted currency fluctuation rather than on the 6 per cent band chosen by Italy, whose decision to enter had also been delayed. The Central Bank of Ireland immediately announced a number of exchange controls to prevent the flow of 'hot money' into or out of the country and to encourage the repatriation of Irish funds held abroad. By the end of the year, with the launch of the EMS postponed, the official exchange rate with sterling remained at parity.

The Government came under strong criticism from the Opposition and the newspapers for alleged mishandling of the EMS entry, and the Labour Party doubted that even the revised offer was adequate. The trade unions sought further protection for firms engaged in trade with the United Kingdom and warned that the discipline required to survive within the EMS must not be imposed at the expense of workers' pay. The Irish measures, on the other hand, were apparently welcomed in Whitehall, where the steps taken had spared the Treasury the trouble of extending its own exchange controls. This was one of the happier episodes in Anglo-Irish relations, which, in the earlier part of the year, had been no more than tepid.

Mr Lynch and his Minister for Foreign Affairs, Mr Michael O'Kennedy, became embroiled during the spring in a controversy with the Northern Ireland Secretary, Mr Roy Mason, over the extent to which Northern violence originated in the Republic, and the argument continued sporadically until 5 May, when Mr Mason came to Dublin and publicly acknowledged the extent of cooperation on cross-border security. Little progress was made on policy regarding Northern Ireland, and the impression grew in the Republic that no initiative was to be expected from the United Kingdom as long as the Ulster Unionists had to be placated by a British Government which lacked a parliamentary majority.

A new cultural awareness was evident in the upsurge of popular resentment against the decision to build city offices for Dublin on the Wood Quay site, where impressive remains had been found of the original Viking settlement. The Irish theatre suffered a tragic loss with the death of the veteran actor, author and designer Micheál MacLiammóir (see OBITUARY). In music, the New Ireland Chamber Orchestra enjoyed a remarkably successful tour in the United States. The national broadcasting service, RTE, opened its second television channel in November. An old debate revived before Christmas with the introduction of a Bill by the Health Minister, Mr Charles Haughey, to legalize the sale of contraceptives on a doctor's prescription. Another unresolved dispute concerned the involvement of religious orders in education. Queen Margrethe of Denmark came on a state visit to Ireland in May and President Patrick Hillery paid state visits to India and Luxembourg.

Chapter 2

DENMARK—ICELAND—NORWAY—SWEDEN—FINLAND—AUSTRIA—
SWITZERLAND

DENMARK

IN internal politics the event of the year was Mr Anker Jørgensen's success in forming the first-ever coalition between his own Social Democratic Party and Venstre—the century-old, often conservative party of the more substantial farmers. Announced on 30 August after three weeks of intensive negotiations, the arrangement involved a Cabinet of record size, in which the Prime Minister's party held 14 seats and Venstre seven. It had 88 supporters among the 179 members of the Folketing, so that the help of one of the two Greenland representatives and of one single-member party in the centre was enough to achieve a majority. The trade unions, however, strongly resented action taken in defiance of their wishes by a leader who had risen originally from their own ranks. One ingenious device for holding the coalition together was the pairing of each Venstre Minister with one of his other colleagues, in order that he might be informed of current business in departments under Social Democratic control in advance of a conclave of the Venstre section of the Cabinet, to be held every Friday at 7 a.m.

By the end of the year a series of drastic economies, including the raising of VAT from 18 to 20 per cent, had reduced the deficit in the balance of payments from 10,000 million kroner to 7,000 million, but unemployment had mounted to 8 per cent of the work-force. One project to be further delayed was the long-contemplated bridge from Zealand to Fünen (see AR 1973, p. 173), linking Copenhagen with the continent, about which the Danish minority in Schleswig-Holstein protested to the EEC Commission in Brussels. Mr Jørgensen also informed the Swedes that the concomitant plan for bridging and/or tunnelling the Sound could not be executed until after construction of the Great Belt bridge.

On 29 November Queen Margrethe countersigned a Bill which, if approved by a plebiscite of the Greenlanders in January 1979, would give the island a system of internal self-government on the model of the Faeroes, subject to special arrangements for joint exploitation of mineral resources. The Queen hoped that 'the future cooperation within the Danish realm might be loyal and fruitful'. One of the many possible hindrances was adumbrated by a grant from the EEC of 70 million kroner towards the expenses of Danish air control over Greenland waters forming part of the Community sea: the Greenlanders had recorded a majority of 70 per cent against inclusion in the Community (see AR 1972, p. 156).

Mr Mogens Glistrup, the leader of the Progressives (see AR 1975, p. 149), still figured in the headlines. In January he acted as second vice-president of the Folketing. Next month his protracted trial in the Copenhagen city court ended in a conviction which was to cost him rather more than five million kroner. The prosecution deemed this to be misplaced leniency and appealed, but by the end of the year their resourceful opponent had made his own appeal, addressed to the Human Rights Tribunal at Strasburg and Commission in New York, with copy to Amnesty International.

ICELAND

In May the local government elections registered 12 per cent gains by the Opposition, the right-wing Independence Party losing control of the capital after more than half a century, while the general election on 25 June showed the largest turnover of votes since the second Icelandic Republic was established in 1944. The results of the general election were as follows (previous representation in brackets):

Independence Party	20 (25)
Progressives (Agrarians)	12 (17)
Social Democrats	14 (5)
People's Alliance (including Communists)	14 (11)
Left Liberals	0 (2)

Nevertheless the Independence Party remained the largest in a legislature where 32 seats were the minimum support needed to give the Cabinet control over both Divisions. The President of the Republic attempted various combinations of parties, including one which was to be headed by Mr Lúdvik Jósefsson, the chairman of the virtually communist People's Alliance. When this failed, he claimed that the reason was that 'the Social Democrats accepted instructions to deny him the premiership from those in power in Norway, Washington and Brussels' (*Nordisk Kontakt*, 23 October). The upshot was the formation on 1 September of a Cabinet under Mr Olofur Jóhannesson (Progressive), with two colleagues from his own party, three Social Democrats and three from the People's Alliance; only the Premier had previous ministerial experience. A condition of the coalition was postponement of the contentious issue of the Keflavik base (which the People's Alliance wanted to close) by referring it to an all-party parliamentary commission.

The Icelandic krone was devalued by a further 15 per cent on 6 September, and on 30 November the Government carried stringent economy measures through the Allting, with a view to checking the inflationary consequences of a 14 per cent wage increase which was due to take place next day. The new Prime Minister hoped to lower the rate of inflation below 30 per cent per annum by the end of 1979. As regards external relations, he announced that the main lines of foreign policy would not be changed without the approval of all three Government parties. The opposition of the People's Alliance to membership of Nato and to the presence of American troops on the island was, however, stated in the Government programme, which also promised a thorough review of security problems, including defence against terrorists as well as the larger issues of safeguarding the national interests in peace or war.

The ex-Prime Minister, Mr G. Hallgrimsson, was among the eight members of the Independence Party who laid three proposals before the Allting concerning maritime rights. One called for a closer examination of the continental shelf. Another proposed friendly negotiations with Norway regarding claims which the latter might base upon its possession of Jan Mayen. The third demanded uncompromising opposition to the British possession of Rokkur, alias Rockall.

NORWAY

The krone was devalued on 10 February by 8 per cent, whilst remaining in the 'currency snake', but towards the end of the year Norway opted out of the EEC's new proposals for regulating the exchanges, partly for fear of being drawn into the Community—which had the support of less than one in five of those questioned in a recent opinion poll—but chiefly with a view to maintaining an exchange level which would help its exports to Sweden and Britain and its shipping transactions in American dollars. The all-overshadowing problem was how to restore the competitiveness of Norwegian exports, which had priced themselves out of the market by the high wages and heavy social burdens imposed on industry. In July the latter were further increased by the bringing into force of a measure allowing a worker to be absent for up to three days on as many as six occasions in a year on account of indisposition without forfeiting any pay or producing any medical certificate.

The most important of the Government's attempts to stem the economic crisis was a sixteen-month freeze on prices and wages, imposed in September, whilst its primary aim of preventing mass unemployment was pursued by putting public money into some of the many concerns which threatened to close down. It was also able to paint a rosy picture of the benefits which would accrue to the Norwegian economy in the long run through acceptance of the Swedes' offer of Norwegian participation in their hitherto abundantly successful Volvo enterprise (see p. 148). But the last months of the year brought further bad news—the full development of the Statfjord oilfield was likely to exceed the original estimate of cost by 3,100 million kroner; Statoil (see AR 1975, p. 151) expected its deficit in 1979 to amount to 400 million kroner; and the Tandberg electronics business crashed in a bankruptcy of record dimensions. The last event had the biggest impact on public opinion, both because the work-force could not be absorbed elsewhere and because it was as recently as January that Tandberg had been 'rescued' by the Ministry of Industry at a cost equal to £6 per head of population.

The bourgeois opposition found the Government's policies inadequate to the situation abroad as well as at home, voting 61 to 65 against ratification of the temporary compromise over control of the Barents Sea fisheries (see AR 1977, p. 148). Unexplained anchorings of Russian vessels in Norwegian territorial waters caused further uneasiness in the public mind, whilst the many uncertainties surrounding the situation on Svalbard were highlighted when a Russian military aircraft crashed on Hopen Island (29 August) and the Russians formally contested the right of the Norwegian authorities to read the (coded) contents of the flight recorder. The Foreign Minister warned the Storting to be 'mentally and practically prepared for new episodes' in what was now a sensitive area, advice which consorted ill with the action of his Defence colleague (Mr R. Hansen) in publicly castigating the commander-in-chief, Nato North (General Sir Peter Whiteley), for remarking in an interview with a Norwegian newspaper that he wished the Storting would elect to spend more on defence appropriations.

SWEDEN

Subject to ratification after the next election, the Riksdag voted on 20 April to change the law against female succession so that the infant daughter of the reigning sovereign should become Heir Apparent. In politics, however, the succession became much less clear when Mr T. Fälldin, after threatening to resign the premiership for personal reasons, finally threw in his hand on 5 October because the other coalition parties would not accept the Centre Party's demand for a plebiscite on its proposal to halt nuclear power developments (see AR 1976, p. 153). Mr Ola Ullsten, who had become Liberal leader on the resignation of Mr P. Ahlmark earlier in the year, made the future prospects of the bourgeois parties as a whole very problematic by declining to share power with the Conservatives and by taking office with the support of 39 Liberal votes in a legislature of 349 members. This was possible because the Social Democrats, who were the *tertius gaudens* in the strife between bourgeois parties, could veto any other proposed combination. In such a situation it was perhaps a happy coincidence that in the previous month every Swedish household had been presented with a 32-page pamphlet in four colours on the history, functioning and personnel of the Riksdag.

In December the new Prime Minister agreed with his Norwegian counterpart on the terms of a big business deal with Norway, first announced on 22 May, when it was welcomed by every Swedish party except the Communists. Norway was to pay 75 million kroner for a 40 per cent share in Volvo, which would find work for 3,000 to 5,000 hands in Norway, and Sweden was to gain access to North Sea oil development. The managing director of Volvo, Mr P. G. Gyllenhammar, had originated the project after the failure of the Wallenberg interests in their attempt to merge Volvo with Saab (see AR 1977, p. 149) and the repulse of his own plans to gain financial support for expansion from the Government. Though the details were open to criticism, it was widely hoped that this might be the beginning of a mutually advantageous and far-reaching cooperation between Nordic neighbour states.

FINLAND

A record number of 260 of the 300 members of the electoral college were chosen to support President Kekkonen, who entered upon his fifth term of office on 1 March, when he repeated his original pledge to follow the foreign policy of his predecessor, Mr J. K. Paasikivi, the author of the pact with Russia. In an address in Stockholm on 8 May he renewed the plea he had made in 1963 for an atom-free zone in northern Europe, pointing out that infringements of neutral air space were to be feared most in the event of limited nuclear warfare. In October the Minister of Defence explicitly denied a Dutch newspaper report that his Russian colleague had made repeated proposals for joint military manoeuvres.

A devaluation of the Finnish mark to the same extent as, and in direct reply to, that of the Norwegian krone (see p. 146) caused dissension in Mr Kalevi Sorsa's coalition Cabinet, which nevertheless survived the year with only minor changes in its composition. But the grave economic problems seemed insoluble pending the next year's election, partly because the Government represented so many divergent political outlooks (see AR 1977, p. 151) and partly because of the constitutional requirement that any basic economic reform must be accepted by a qualified majority of the legislature.

The acuteness of the divisions, not only in the Edskunta but also within a single party, was clearly shown when the sixtieth Communist Party Congress on 4 June was attended by representatives from 23 other states, and 25,000 supporters marched through the centre of Helsinki. Although a greeting from President Brezhnev contained a plea for party solidarity in Finland, only formal unity was preserved. Except for the capital itself, the industrialized southern and eastern regions were represented by the minority which opposed the majority's participation in the Government, the proportion of 215 to 278 among the delegates reappearing as 6 to 9 and 21 to 29 in the political and enlarged central committees of the Party.

AUSTRIA

For ordinary Austrians, it was a prosperous and uneventful year, with a touch of drama in July when Austria's borders were blockaded by heavy lorry drivers from Austria, Italy and West Germany, protesting against the imposition of a new Austrian 'transit tax' on heavy vehicles. For the ruling Socialist Party (SPÖ), however, 1978 brought unexpected political set-backs, and at the end of the year its chances of retaining an absolute majority in the 1979 elections looked slim. It had already lost a potential coalition partner in February when the Freedom Party (FPÖ) designated the right-wing mayor of Graz, Dr Alexander Götz, as party leader from September in succession to Herr Friedrich Peter, a tacit supporter of the SPÖ.

The first cloud on the SPÖ's horizon was the financial scandal which developed during the summer over the private business interests of Dr Hannes Androsch, the young and hitherto very successful Finance Minister, Vice-Chancellor and deputy party chairman. During his eight years at the Finance Ministry, his tax consultancy firm had allegedly become one of the largest in Austria. Dr Androsch's determination to resign rather than give it up led to a well-publicized dispute with his former patron, the Federal Chancellor Dr Bruno Kreisky. It was not until mid-December that he agreed to conform to the rules governing compatibility of public function and private business by resigning his majority holding in the firm to a trustee.

The provincial elections on 8 October in Vienna and Styria brought a further setback. The popular and competent mayor of Vienna, Herr Leopold Gratz, widely tipped as a possible successor to Dr Kreisky, failed to dispel widespread dissatisfaction with the city government among Socialist voters, and the SPÖ lost four seats to the opposition People's Party (ÖVP), although retaining its large absolute majority with 57 per cent of the vote. In Styria the ÖVP lost a seat not to the Socialists but to the FPÖ.

Socialist defections, this time on a national issue, also contributed to the Government's narrow defeat, by 50·5 per cent, in Austria's first referendum, held on 5 November to decide whether Austria's first nuclear power station, at Zwentendorf, should be put into action. Those in favour argued that nuclear power was the only solution for Austria's dwindling energy resources and soaring import bills: those against, that no arrangements had been made for disposal of nuclear waste, nor any contingency plans for a possible future disaster. Dr Kreisky had previously indicated that he regarded the country's approval of his energy policy as a personal vote of confidence, but this hint of resignation was quickly forgotten. On 6 November the SPÖ reconfirmed Dr Kreisky as party leader, and conferred new powers of decision on him. His importance to the SPÖ was demonstrated by an opinion poll carried out in December, which showed 57 per cent preferring him to the ÖVP leader, Dr Josef Taus, who was put first by only 23 per cent. The same poll indicated that the SPÖ could still hope to poll about 49 per cent of the vote at a national election.

On the economic front, the Government was in a fairly strong position, having achieved a substantial and unexpected improvement in the balance of payments by October. Exports, now benefiting from wider EEC markets and price reductions, rose by approximately 7·5 per cent over 1977, and receipts from tourism also improved. The reorientation of economic policy in October 1977 (see AR 1977, p. 152) had slowed down growth without a corresponding rise in unemployment, and positive measures to promote investment were taken in April. The increase in real GNP for 1978 dropped to an estimated 1·5 per cent, but domestic inflation was also down from 5·5 to about 3·6 per cent. The 1979 budget aimed at consolidating these gains and achieving further modest expansion, although with a deficit comparable to that of 1978 (estimated at A.Sch.50,000 million). Control of government indebtedness therefore remained a problem for the future, and increased consumption and higher imports arising from tax reliefs proposed for 1 January could also compromise the Government's economic strategy.

There were no major foreign policy initiatives during 1978 and Austrian efforts were directed overwhelmingly towards increasing trade and strengthening economic cooperation with Eastern Europe. Austria's visible trade deficit with the Soviet Union had risen sharply (to A.Sch.3,800 million in 1977), and trade with Eastern Europe, while still in surplus, also threatened to decline. Apart from state visits, paid by President Zhivkov of Bulgaria in September and by President Rudolf Kirchschläger to Romania in November, there were numerous official and ministerial exchanges in which Dr Kreisky took a prominent part.

SWITZERLAND

Since 1960 the Swiss Federal Council had been composed on the basis of the so-called 'magic formula': two Socialists, two Christian Democrats, two Liberal-Radicals, one People's (farmers') Party. This system operated fairly well, though the Socialists launched various initiatives against the recommendations of the Federal Government. But in 1978 the left-wing tendency to oppose the Government's measures became strongly marked. In defiance of the Socialist President, Willy Ritschard, his party supported the constitutional initiative against nuclear power stations, to be the subject of a referendum at the end of February 1979.

The most important step taken by the parliamentary Socialist Party, however, was rejection of the draft for the financial equilibrium of the federal state. The Government as well as the three non-socialist parties were determined to stop the deficit-spending, but the fourth partner of the 'magic formula', demanding heavier taxes on the flourishing Swiss banks, voted against the advice of the Government. Accordingly the referendum on the new system of reduced Value Added Tax, probably to be held in May 1979, would once more underline the division between the socialist and the 'bourgeois' camps. Whether the present kind of coalition could continue indefinitely depended on the issue of the federal elections at the end of October 1979.

The high value of the Swiss franc increased the difficulties of the export industries, particularly textiles and watchmaking. Nevertheless, the economic situation as a whole, with the lowest inflation rate in Europe, only 0·3 per cent unemployment (not counting 625,000 foreign workers who had little chance of regaining lost employment, and nearly 300,000 of whom had already returned to their native countries), no strikes at all, a good agricultural year and satisfying results in the tourist industry, could hardly explain the political unrest. Its most significant signs were the endless constitutional initiatives: in 1978 the Swiss were called four times to the polls to decide on 13 issues by referendum.

On 26 February the initiative to reduce the competence of Parliament to build new highways in favour of a popular referendum was rejected by 1,100,000 votes to 700,000. The left-wing initiative to lower the age for old-age pensions was defeated by 1,450,000 votes to 380,000, whilst a new legal basis for the pensions scheme was accepted by 1,200,000 votes to 625,000, as well as a new constitutional article enabling the Government to intervene in times of economic crisis or exaggerated boom, approved by 1,200,000 votes to 542,000. In these two matters, contested by a small right-wing opposition, the majority in Parliament won clear victories.

After nearly thirty years of struggle by the movement for an independent 'Canton of Jura' an overwhelming majority of 1,300,000 votes against 282,000 accepted the creation of a 23rd Swiss canton, composed of the northern Jura districts of the present Canton of Berne. But the three southern French-speaking districts of the Jura opposed the partition of the Berne Canton, to which the whole Jura had belonged since the Congress of Vienna in 1815.

Two very lively referendums were held on 28 May and 3 December 1978. The proposal to introduce European summer time was rejected by 964,000 votes to 886,000, Parliament's draft for the legitimization of abortion was again rejected by 1,230,000 votes to 560,000, the popular constitutional initiative to prohibit any motorized traffic on twelve Sundays each year was rejected by 1,200,000 votes to 680,000, and, last, federal subsidies for the cantonal universities were refused by 1,000,000 votes to 792,000. In order to ease the situation of the overcrowded universities the Canton of Lucerne intended to found a new high school in Lucerne, but this the electors refused, thus clearly demonstrating their bias against academic and intellectual circles.

On the other hand, a modern law to promote professional education was accepted by 902,000 votes to 707,000, though the trade unions opposed it as inadequate for industrial workers. In view of the over-production of milk Parliament ordered limited quotas for each dairy farmer; this scheme was adopted by 1,100,000 votes to 502,000, mostly left-wing farmers. Finally a federal law for the protection of animals was contested only by the movement against scientific experiments and was adopted by the huge majority of 1,340,000 votes to 300,000. The creation of a federal police force to fight terrorism, however, was defeated by an 'unholy union' of strong cantonalists, insisting that the police were a matter for the cantons and not for the federal state, and left-wing groups opposed to any stronger police forces. The adverse vote was 920,000 against 723,000. In this case the Socialists again opposed a draft supported by their representatives in the federal Government.

At the end of the year Parliament unanimously elected the Christian Democrat Hans Huerlimann as President and the French-speaking Liberal-Radical Georges-André Chevallaz as Vice-President of the Swiss Confederation. It was a typically Swiss demonstration of goodwill on the eve of Christmas, but nobody could overlook the deepening of the gulf between the Socialists and the three other partners in the Government. No change could be expected before the elections, and what might happen later would depend partly on whether the economic situation caused a certain unrest in a spoilt nation used to full employment and steadily increasing wealth.

Chapter 3

SPAIN—PORTUGAL—MALTA—GIBRALTAR—GREECE—CYPRUS—TURKEY

SPAIN

WHEN the draft of the Constitution (which had been leaked to the press in November 1977) was put before Congress, the lower House of the Cortes, in January, no fewer than 1,133 amendments were tabled to it. The eight-man commission responsible modified the grammar and syntax as suggested in some of those amendments, and handed over the work of further revision to a new inter-party parliamentary commission of 36 selected in April. On 24 May, after some weeks with little progress, a majority in the commission agreed to seek the highest factor of agreement on principles, and to exclude from the text details which would be more properly determinable in separate legislation. They achieved such a degree of consensus that when the rewritten draft was presented to the House all but 187 amendments were withdrawn.

Discussion of those amendments and voting on them and on the text clause by clause was carried out during three weeks in July. That sovereignty resides in the people and that Spain should be a multiparty democracy was approved almost unanimously. A proposal from a Catalan leftist that it should be a republic was supported by only 8 votes, three cast in error by monarchists. That Spain should be a parliamentary monarchy was approved by 196 (including the 20 Communists) to 9, the Socialists abstaining on the grounds that they could not vote positively for monarchy 'our of loyalty to their historic past'. In due course they did so, however, in establishing the King as head of state, and giving him powers similar to those of the British Crown though more closely defined. There were overwhelming majorities for the articles making the Government answerable to the Cortes, limiting the maximum life of the Cortes to four years, continuing proportional representation and reducing the voting age to 18.

One of the features of this Constitution was the extent of its recognition of human rights and freedoms. Apart from guaranteeing freedom of speech and its diffusion, of assembly, association and movement, it declared inviolable the privacy of the individual and the family. Everyone, it stated, had the right to life and physical and moral integrity; therefore it abolished the death penalty and forced labour, and outlawed all torture and degradation. Even a convicted criminal in prison had a right to learn a trade, to earn a living, to receive social security benefits and to exercise his political rights. Parents would have the right to determine the religious and moral education of their children and would therefore have a say in the management of schools. Private schools would be allowed. Private property was declared a right of individuals or communities. An ombudsman was to be appointed to protect the individual from bureaucratic abuse.

Most, but not all, the articles on human rights and freedoms were approved by the House with little opposition. Thus the abolition of the death penalty had only one vote against it (that of a Basque of extreme left views who opposed almost every clause), while the 15 members of the right-wing Alianza Popular (AP) abstained. AP alone voted against an article opening the door to civil divorce. The Socialists and Communists abstained from voting on the article authorizing not only strikes but also lockouts. There were only three abstentions and no vote against the clauses which guaranteed the ideological and religious liberty of individuals and communities and freedom of (public) worship, and protected the individual from being forced to declare his ideology, religion or beliefs. However, the Socialists moved for the deletion of the specific reference to the Catholic Church in the clause which read; 'There will be no state religion; however, public authorities will bear in mind the religious beliefs of Spanish society and will accordingly cooperate with the Catholic and other churches.' Their amendment was defeated by the joint vote of the Communists, the ruling Centre Democratic Union (UCD) and AP.

The Congress approved the text overall on 21 July and passed it to the Senate. The Senate also approved it, on 5 October, with some minor alterations which the Congress readily accepted. It was formally voted upon by both Houses on 31 October. The vote in the Senate was 226 for, 5 against, and 8 abstentions; in the Congress 325 for, 6 against, and 14 abstentions. In both Houses the votes against came from the outer ends of the political spectrum, including some AP; members of the Basque Nationalist Party (PNV) accounted for most of the abstentions; AP 'moderates' and diehard Republicans accounted for the others.

Throughout all the discussions back to 1977 there had been a major difficulty: how to reconcile the large percentage of Spaniards (mostly but not entirely of the right) who equated state and nation with the considerable percentage of Basques, Catalans and others anxious to recover the autonomy they had lost in the eighteenth and nineteenth centuries. By July a formula had been evolved which satisfied all but 33 Congressmen, mostly AP on the one hand, and PNV on the other: Article 2 affirmed 'the indissoluble unity of the Spanish nation, the common and indivisible motherland of all Spaniards', but recognized and guaranteed 'the right to autonomy of the nationalities and regions of which it (was) composed'. Other articles expanding that principle offered those 'nationalities and regions' far greater autonomy than that which the Republic had granted to Catalonia and Euzkadi (the Basque Provinces). Euzkadi already had its General Council, authorized under royal decree-laws of 30 December (see AR 1977, p. 159). The Basques, however, could not accept wording which implied that their new autonomy would be a concession of the Spanish state and that the restoration of their ancient 'fueros' ('liberties') was circumscribed 'within the framework' of this Constitution. They were a people, they claimed, with rights antedating the Spanish state. Furthermore, acceptance of that wording would leave Euzkadi at the mercy of the central power: 'he who has the right to give has the right to take away'.

The UCD held talks with the PNV right up to October to find a formula which would satisfy the Basques yet not provoke violent reaction from the right. Not only the *ultras* outside Parliament but the AP within it were already referring to the Constitution as 'the instrument for the dismemberment of Spain' and 'an encouragement to civil disorder'.

Between January and July some 50 persons had been assassinated by extremists of the left and right. The victims included an ex-mayor of

Barcelona and his wife in January and the director of prisons in March. The ETA were now openly committed to the establishment through violence of a marxist Euzkadi. They sabotaged industrial plants and levied from terrified industrialists and businessmen a 'revolutionary tax'. Policemen still remained the ETA's favourite target. The object was obvious: to provoke the Civil Guard and *Policía Armada* either into revolt against the Government which had amnestied ETA militants and no longer countenanced torture in the interrogation of suspects, or into indiscriminate violence against the public.

They came close to success in July. On 8 July ETA killed a magistrate. The following day in the bull-ring at Pamplona an *Armada* platoon fired at youths chanting ETA slogans, killing two and wounding several. Three and four days later another platoon assaulted civilians and wrecked shops in Eguía and Rentería near the Franco-Spanish frontier. On 21 July, the very day of the approval of the Constitution by the Congress, ETA assassinated in Madrid a general and a lieutenant-colonel. The joint chiefs of staff had to issue a statement which was in effect a warning to discourage an army revolt. By October the year's total of policemen killed by the ETA had reached 20. Over the weekend of 15 October several hundred policemen in Bilbao refused to obey orders.

On 24 October the PNV's president declared that Euzkadi was 'beginning to smell like Ulster'. Terrorism had not helped the Basque cause. No non-Basque party had supported the last compromise amendments which the PNV had proposed before the Senate passed the draft Constitution.

The Constitution, having been approved by the Cortes, had now to be put to referendum. This was fixed for 6 December. The PNV recommended abstention for the Basques. The extreme right and left campaigned for its rejection. AP was divided. The major parties, UCD, Socialist and Communist, urged a massive 'yes' vote. The Catholic hierarchy as a body urged everyone to vote as he saw fit. The Archbishop of Toledo, however, issued a pastoral in which he drew attention to ambiguities in the text which perturbed him.

To counteract *ultra* propaganda linking terrorism with democracy and the Constitution, the Socialists and Communists, seconded by the UCD, organized mass demonstrations of protest against terrorism in Madrid and 80 other towns on 10 November. The ETA killed another two Civil Guards the following day and on 16 November a Supreme Court judge in Madrid. That evening the arrest was ordered of a Civil Guard lieutenant-colonel, Tejero Molina, and a *Policía Armada* captain alleged to be involved in a plot with other army officers to kidnap the Premier and other Cabinet Ministers on the following day, after the King had left on a state visit to Mexico. On the evening of 17 November, in Cartagena, General Juan Atarés Peña, who had been GOC of the Civil Guard in the Basque and adjoining provinces until March, publicly insulted the Vice-Premier and Minister of Defence, General Gutiérrez Mellado, and was arrested. Tejero had been removed from command of the Civil Guard in Guipuzcoa towards the end of July.

The two incidents were said to have no connexion. The Tejero plot appeared to be poorly devised but perhaps well timed, for on that day the chiefs of staff of the three services and the commanders of the armoured, mechanized and parachute brigades quartered round Madrid, of whose loyalty to the King and Government there was little doubt, were all due to be in Ceuta or the Canaries; and again on 17 November *ultras* wearing military-type party uniforms and travelling in several thousand motorcars were to begin concentrating in Madrid to attend a rally on Sunday 19 November in commemoration of the third anniversary of Franco's death. At a press conference on the eve, their leader, Blas Piñar, spoke of the situation in Spain as one in which a military rising would be 'morally justifiable'. When on 22 November General Gutiérrez gave the lower House a brief account of the plot, he received a standing ovation from all its members except those of the AP.

The army cooperated with the police to prevent incidents on the day of the referendum. It was a day of inclement weather in Madrid and most of Spain. The turnout nationwide was 68 per cent, of whom 87 per cent expressed assent to the Constitution and under 8 per cent disapproval. The percentage of voters and of the 'yes' vote would have been higher but for those in Euzkadi, where only 45 per cent of the electorate voted and the 'no' vote was almost 24 per cent. The Government and constituent Cortes were not unduly dissatisfied with the results.

On 27 December the King signed the Constitution as 'head of state and symbol of the nation', in the presence of both Houses of the Cortes. Outside the building units of the armed forces acclaimed their approval.

The wage restraints agreed upon in 1977 had their desired effects. Unemployment was kept at 6 per cent of the labour force. The inflation rate fell from 29 to 17 per cent. There was a 3 per cent increase in the gross domestic product. Neither the Socialists nor the Communists pressed the Government too hard over the only partial fulfilment of its promises in the Moncloa pacts (see AR 1977, p. 159). Discussion on a new pact began at the end of the year.

There were two major political developments. The small Popular Socialist Party merged with the Socialist Workers Party (PSOE). The Spanish Communist Party (PCE) held its IXth Congress in April. It dropped 'leninist' from the definition of itself and emphasized its independence from all other Communist Parties.

PORTUGAL

Dr Soares resigned as Premier after his defeat in the Assembly (see AR 1977, p. 162). President Eanes then prevailed upon him to attempt a coalition. After unsatisfactory talks with the communist PCP and social democrat PSD, Soares gave the centre democrat CDS three ministerial posts. In presenting the new Government's programme to the Assembly on 2 February he declared that this was not the time to build socialism: the urgent tasks were economic recovery and administrative reform. In order not to damage productivity there would be a halt to nationalization; to curb the inflation rate (almost 30 per cent per annum) wage increases during the year would be limited to 20 per cent (except in special cases) and taxation would be heavier. Imports would be curtailed. The combined vote of the PSP's 102 members and the CDS's 41 gave Soares an easy majority over the PSD's 73 and PCP's 40.

Increases of between 25 and 50 per cent in the charges for gas, water, electricity and public transport were authorized on 1 April in order to reduce government subsidy. A rise of 22 per cent was authorized in food prices. Serious social unrest was avoided by increasing unemployment pay and authorizing a rise of 26 per cent in the minimum wage of industrial workers (to the equivalent of $126 monthly) and one of 31 per cent in the pay of agricultural workers (to the equivalent of $102 monthly). The communist-controlled labour organization Intersindical accepted the 20 per cent limit on other wages when the Government imposed heavier sales and income taxes.

Those measures, a further devaluation of the escudo and an undertaking to reduce the balance of payments deficit to $1,000 million per annum by March 1979 persuaded the IMF in May to allow Portugal a new standby arrangement to the value of $70 million. The United States then released $200 million of the $300 million medium-term loan passed in June 1977 (see AR 1977, p. 161), and Portugal's precarious economy was again shored up.

On 28 January the PSD elected a new leader, Antonio Sousa Franco, in place of Dr Sa Carneiro whose strong criticism of Eanes and Soares over many months had displeased many in the party. In March Carneiro called for a revision of the articles in the Constitution which committed Portugal to socialism and instituted the military Council of the Revolution as 'the guarantor of the fulfilment of the Constitution'. In doing so he incurred the anger of the remaining leftist officers in the Council, who accused him of seeking to oust Eanes from the presidency. On 3 April Carneiro did indeed call for new parliamentary elections: a PSD victory at those, he said, would be proof that the country was dissatisfied with the President and the Constitution. Three days later the Government moved a two-part motion in the Assembly. The first part, which condemned attacks against the President, was approved almost unanimously, but most PSD members abstained from voting on the second part, which expressed support for Eanes. This was interpreted by Sr Franco as contrary to a decision at the party congress that the PSD should oppose the PSP–CDS Government 'firmly but only selectively'. He resigned.

On 15 April the Deputy Premier arrived in the Azores without first consulting the PSD-dominated regional authorities. He was assaulted by members of the Azores Liberation Front and refugees from the former Portuguese African territories. The Lisbon Government sent riot police to the Azores, and accused the PSD of complicity with the Liberation Front, whose leader, Jose de Almeida, had earlier declared that if Lisbon refused to negotiate the complete independence of the islands it could expect an armed rising. Thereafter all hopes faded of cooperation in Portugal between the Socialists and Social Democrats. Carneiro regained the leadership of the PSD in July.

There had been little evidence of a real effort to improve the national economy. The trade deficit for the first six months of 1978 had risen to 64,600 million escudos as against 48,000 million for the corresponding period of 1977. The CDS had agreed to support Soares on the understanding that the smallholders of the Alentejo would get their lands back according to the law passed in 1977. The Socialist Minister of Agriculture had found excuses not to enforce the law, and there had indeed been new seizures of land. The CDS warned Soares that the Minister was endangering the coalition and on 23 July the three CDS Cabinet Ministers resigned. Under the Constitution Eanes had to dismiss Soares, and Portugal was without a Government for the second time within a year. This time no party was prepared to accept the leader of any other as Premier. In late August the President persuaded a wealthy industrialist of 'socialist views', Alfredo Nobre da Costa, to form a Government of 'technocrats'. The Council of the Revolution approved, but its programme and therefore da Costa's premiership were not endorsed by the Assembly.

In November Professor Carlos Mota Pinto formed another Cabinet of 'technocrats', somewhat less to the left than da Costa's. It received the constitutionally necessary approval of the Council of the Revolution. It duly presented its programme: rigid adherence to Portugal's promises to the IMF to stabilize the economy, and enforcement of the law to return the smallholdings in the Alentejo to their pre-revolution owners. On 12 December, at the end of a five-day debate, the PCP moved the rejection of the programme. Supported by five Socialists who in February had formed a separate party entitled 'Workers Brotherhood', they obtained 45 votes. They were opposed by 109 votes from the Social and the Centre Democrats, while Soares's PSP abstained. So Pinto survived into the new year.

MALTA

Much of the year was spent in the familiar pursuit of greater political control at home and new allies abroad. The intended withdrawal of British forces in March 1979 meant a future loss of M£28 million a year. Neither Italy nor France nor Algeria would meet Mr Mintoff's hopes of further subsidy. The only obvious source of supply was Libya, and on 15 December the Qadafi Government approved the document sanctioned by its local Popular Committees in November when Mintoff made one of his many visits to north Africa. The document provided for financial help over five years, increased investment in Maltese industries, additional employment for Maltese workers in Libya, and wider opportunities for Libyans to study in Malta. Other negotiations between the two countries included the establishment (18 July) of a joint Air Mediterranean Company for light aircraft maintenance and related facilities in Malta.

On a wider front Mintoff and fellow Ministers visited Yugoslavia in April to discuss with Tito's Government the concept of a neutral Mediterranean and joint economic development; Dr Cassar (Minister of Justice and Parliamentary Affairs) represented Malta at the five-day meeting of non-aligned countries in Belgrade (26-31 July). Such visits were part of the general move of the Malta Labour Government towards a non-aligned neutrality, a policy opposed by Dr Fenech Adami and the Nationalist Party, which argued both at home and in meetings with European leaders that neutrality with Libya would mean not independence but a poor exchange of patrons.

A running quarrel between the Government and the BBC and newspapers in Britain—over articles in the *Guardian* in February and over the broadcasting of news about Malta—led to the temporary ban in July and August on the entry of British journalists and on the local UK Forces Radio.

The most notable feature of domestic policy was the widening of the dispute between the Medical Association of Malta (MAM) (see AR 1977, p. 162) into a major clash between the Government and the University of Malta. The Education (Amendment) Act 1978, effective from 1 August, promoted the Malta College of Arts, Science and Technology (MCAST) to the status of a second university alongside the existing university in its new buildings at Msida, and transferred all subjects but law, theology and humanities to the new institution, at which courses—including medicine, architecture and engineering—were to be based on student–workers selected by employers and trade unions. The change came under attack not only from the political opposition but also from students uncertain of their future, from faculty staff who faced dismissal, and from the Director of the London School of Economics, Ralf Dahrendorf, and the Vice-

Chancellor of the University of Salford, John Horlock, both of whom resigned from the Malta Higher Education Commission. Dr Walwyn James of Newcastle Polytechnic was appointed Rector of the new university, but the position of both institutions was still far from clear at the end of the year.

Party conflict diminished in 1978 after the violence of the previous year. But those who criticized the Labour Government were quickly muzzled. They included Attard Kingswell, former general secretary of the General Workers Union, who tried to oppose the amalgamation of the GWU and the Labour Party: he was suspended from office by 23 votes to 12 after Mintoff had talked to union council members in the Auberge de Castille. Legislation was also introduced on 1 November which restricted the use of the words 'Malta' and 'Nation'. Numerous organizations, including newspapers, were obliged to change their name: for example, from *Malta News* to *News* and from *Times of Malta* to *The Times*. Parties, however, obtained exemption. There was a general tightening of control by the Government in this intensely argumentative society in which politics are pervasive and economic divisions embitter party disputes.

GIBRALTAR

For the first time since June 1969, there appeared grounds for mild hope that some amelioration of the long-standing dispute between Gibraltar and Spain could be achieved. First, there were tripartite meetings, beginning on 9 April and continuing throughout the year, not only between London and Madrid, but with the participation also of Sir Joshua Hassan and Mr Maurice Xiberras as 'Gibraltarians'—a request by Hassan and a concession by Spain of some importance. Agreement was reached on the establishment of three working parties to consider telecommunications, a direct ferry link, and pensions for Spanish workers formerly employed in Gibraltar.

Secondly, telephone links (though not telex) were allowed to remain open throughout the year between Spain and Gibraltar after the usual Christmas period of concession. Thirdly, the new Spanish Constitution approved on 31 October contained strong regional provisions (Arts. 143-58) by which local autonomy was guaranteed, including the use of regional flags. Fourthly, there was the movement by Spain towards EEC and Nato membership, raising the possibility of an internationally agreed status of either autonomy or of joint Anglo-Spanish sovereignty.

Against such trends, however, there remained formidable difficulties, some of long standing, some new. Because of the dispute, there was still strong resentment (except perhaps among the small Gibraltar Autonomy Party) towards Spain. There was also continued reliance on external aid from Britain. Parity of wages and salaries with the UK was now accepted, and a three-year development programme formulated by the Minister for Overseas Development, Mrs Judith Hart, and Gibraltarian Ministers in April envisaged aid expenditure of £28 million over 1978-80, in addition to local purchases by British forces based on the Rock. Average earnings were now at £43 a week including overtime (£31.75 basic wage for a 40-hour week plus a £2 productivity bonus), and under the parity agreement they were likely to rise sharply. Protests against the agreement were voiced by Mr Wilfred Garcia, president of the chamber of commerce, expressing in particular the fears of hoteliers.

But, whatever the financial outcome, few Gibraltarians were likely to look kindly on their attachment (however autonomously) to the very poor Andalusia region of Spain. There was also the renewed if sporadic violence within Spain as a whole. Against such obstacles the tripartite talks could easily be seen as closer to cosmetics than to the heart of the matter; yet perhaps the two might be related in the long term.

GREECE

The most important developments in Greece during 1978 concerned foreign affairs. When the US State Department announced in April that President Carter intended to ask the Congress to lift the partial embargo on the supply of arms to Turkey that had been imposed in 1975, the acting Foreign Minister, Evangelos Averoff, described the move as being 'neither right nor fair'. Nonetheless the Senate (by a majority of 57 to 42 on 25 July) and the House of Representatives (by a majority of 208 to 205 on 1 August) voted to lift the embargo upon the President's certifying, *inter alia*, that 'the Government of Turkey is acting in good faith to achieve a just and peaceful settlement of the Cyprus problem'. Although this decision clearly occasioned disquiet in Government circles, official reaction in Athens was relatively restrained, in contrast to the vociferous protests of the Leader of the Opposition, Andreas Papandreou. In a bid to mend fences the US Deputy Secretary of State, Warren Christopher, visited Athens in October. Among the subjects discussed was Greece's desire to negotiate a special relationship with Nato, whereby the country's armed forces would remain under national command during peacetime but would be integrated with those of Nato in the event of East–West conflict.

Disappointment over the decision to lift the arms embargo was, however, balanced by a significant breakthrough on 21 December in the negotiations for Greek entry into the EEC. Prime Minister Karamanlis' concern with what he considered to be their slow pace was reflected in three visits to European capitals during the course of the year: to London, Brussels, Paris and Bonn in January; to Copenhagen, Luxembourg, The

F

Hague and Rome in March; to Rome, Paris and Dublin in October. That the negotiations were meeting difficulties was made plain by the President of the European Commission, Mr Roy Jenkins, in the course of a visit to Athens at the end of September. The December agreement reflected a compromise between the Greek and Community positions. A five-year post-entry transition period was agreed for Greek agricultural products, with the exception of tomato paste and peaches for which the period was to be seven years. A transition period, also of seven years, was adopted before Greek workers would have the right to seek employment elsewhere in the Community. In the light of this agreement, 1 January 1981 looked a realistic date for Greek entry, somewhat later than the date sought by Karamanlis, but three years earlier than the date envisaged in Greece's 1962 Treaty of Association.

The other significant development in Greece's external relations was the meeting in Montreux on 10 and 11 March between Karamanlis and the Turkish Prime Minister, Bülent Ecevit, the first such meeting between the two leaders. Little was accomplished in practical terms but a climate of mutual confidence was said to have been established. Moreover, it was agreed that this encounter should be followed by meetings between the secretaries-general of the Greek and Turkish Foreign Ministries, Byron Theodoropoulos and Şükrü Elekdağ. Two such meetings took place in July and September. After the first, Theodoropoulos described the talks as 'very constructive and encouraging for the future'. Little concrete progress was made, however, and in other bilateral talks at the level of experts no developments were recorded in the disputes between the two countries over flight control and the delimitation of their continental shelves in the Aegean.

On 19 December the International Court of Justice at The Hague declared itself incompetent to pronounce on the question of the Aegean continental shelf (see INTERNATIONAL LAW). On 24 May, however, Greece and Italy reached agreement over the delimitation of their respective continental shelves in the Ionian sea. During a visit to the United States at the end of May and beginning of June to attend the Nato summit in Washington and to address the UN General Assembly, Karamanlis repeated his offer of a non-aggression treaty with Turkey. The Turkish Prime Minister's response was, however, guarded. In furtherance of Karamanlis' policy of developing good relations with Greece's Balkan neighbours, the Prime Minister visited Bulgaria on 6 and 7 July, while on 28 March a weekly flight between Athens and Tirana was inaugurated. Some days previously the Albanian leader, Enver Hoxha, had encouraged the Greek minority in his country to maintain its language and culture.

On the domestic front Karamanlis suffered something of a setback in the municipal elections, the first round of which was held on 15 October. Although the Government had carefully refrained from endorsing particular candidates, the opposition parties showed no such hesitation and opposition-backed candidates secured control of such major cities as Thessaloniki, Patras, Volos, Larissa and Heraklion, while Ioannina and Kavala returned independents. The biggest upset occurred in Athens, where George Plytas, who had resigned as Minister of Culture to contest the mayoral election, was defeated by Dimitris Beis, who enjoyed the support of all the opposition parties.

In May a major Cabinet reshuffle took place. In what was termed an 'opening to the centre', Constantine Mitsotakis, of the small New Liberal Party, became Minister of Coordination, and Athanasios Kanellopoulos, a former Union of the Democratic Centre deputy, became Minister of Finance. Some weeks earlier Ioannis Zigdis, chairman of the provisional steering committee of the Union of the Democratic Centre set up following the party's disastrous showing in the November 1977 elections, expelled the leadership of the party's youth organization together with five deputies. These included John Pesmazoglou and Virginia Tsouderou.

Important laws were enacted during the course of the year to check widespread tax evasion, to counter terrorism and to reform higher education. At the end of April, after prolonged student disturbances and a strike by junior teaching staff, the Government announced that all university assistants with doctorates and three years' service would receive tenure. Student elections in January confirmed the dominance of the various groupings of the left.

On 21 June Thessaloniki, Greece's second city, was struck by an earthquake registering 6·5 on the Richter scale. Casualties included over fifty killed, almost all from one collapsed apartment block, and there was extensive material damage, which was particularly marked in the older buildings and antiquities of the city. Continuing small tremors led to a mass exodus from the city which lasted for many weeks. Fears that the next full moon would bring with it another major earthquake prompted Karamanlis to pay a special visit of reassurance to the city.

In February the Minister of Social Services, Dr S. Doxiades, announced that the ban on the burning of 'mazut' fuel oil had reduced the sulphur content in the atmosphere of Athens by 50 per cent, to the advantage of the marbles of the Parthenon. On 18 August Professor Manolis Andronikos announced the discovery of a second royal grave in the same tumulus where, during the previous year, he had excavated what some scholars believe to be the tomb of King Philip II of Macedon.

CYPRUS

The island remained divided between the Greek-Cypriot south and the self-proclaimed Turkish Federated State of Cyprus (TFSC) in the north,

The intercommunal talks remained suspended but the year closed with a diplomatic initiative by the United States aimed at breaking the deadlock.

Following the release of what became known as the 'American Plan', Foreign Minister Nicos Rolandis flew to New York on 14 December to see UN Secretary-General Dr Kurt Waldheim, through whom the Cyprus Government insisted any settlement attempts must be channelled. On his return Mr Rolandis said it would probably be known by mid-February whether the deadlock could be broken.

The Turkish-Cypriot leader, Mr Rauf Denktash, reserved judgment on the plan until the new 'Cabinet' and 'Legislative Assembly' in the TFSC had had time to consider it. The plan envisaged a bi-communal state of two constituent regions but with a federal government. The Greek-Cypriot side was split over the plan, the socialist EDEK Party rejecting it as 'partitionist', the communist AKEL Party opposing it 'as a matter of principle' and the majority Democratic Party of President Spyros Kyprianou reserving comment. The right-of-centre Democratic Rally Party supported the plan as a basis for negotiation.

The only direct political contact between the two sides had come on 14 January when Dr Waldheim visited Cyprus and persuaded President Kyprianou and Mr Dentash to lunch together. Dr Waldheim was assured that the Turkish side would present fresh proposals soon and he spoke of a 'turning-point' in the conflict. An outline of Turkish proposals was presented in April but they were immediately rejected by President Kyprianou, who said that to accept them would be suicide. The Turks offered to withdraw from six points along the ceasefire line and called for a seven-year freeze on any constitutional proposals.

The most dramatic event of the year was the shooting at the Nicosia Hilton on 18 February of Yusuf Siba'i, editor of the Cairo newspaper *Al-Ahram* and a friend of President Sadat, by two Palestinians. After the shooting the gunmen, Samir Mohammed Khadar and Hussein Ahmet al Ali, seized eleven hostages and commandeered a plane, but no country would offer them refuge and the plane returned to Larnaca Airport. While negotiations were going on for the release of the hostages a plane-load of Egyptian commandos, sent from Cairo, tried to storm the hostage plane, but the attack was foiled by the Cyprus National Guard, who opened fire. Fifteen Egyptians were killed. As a result Egypt, a longtime ally of Cyprus, severed diplomatic relations. The two Palestinians surrendered and were later convicted of murder and sentenced to be hanged, but President Kyprianou commuted the sentence to life imprisonment.

Spyros Kyprianou was elected unopposed as President for a full five-year term on 26 January, having held the post in a caretaker capacity since the death of Archbishop Makarios the previous August.

A few weeks later the right-wing underground movement EOKA-B, responsible for the militant campaign against Makarios leading to the coup in 1974, announced that it had voluntarily disbanded. This was in response to appeals for unity from President Kyprianou. The group admitted that it had been wrong and that the coup had precipitated the Turkish invasion.

The biggest diplomatic setback in the eyes of the Cyprus Government was the lifting of the US arms embargo against Turkey, which was approved by Congress in August. Congress had made the decision conditional on progress towards a Cyprus settlement but the Carter Administration argued that the embargo was harmful to US security interests, to Nato and US relations with Turkey, a Nato ally, and that to lift the embargo would encourage Turkey to move towards a settlement. President Kyprianou expressed bitter indignation at the move, claiming it would make the Turkish side more intransigent.

The Greek-Cypriot negotiator at the intercommunal talks, Mr Tassos Papadopoulos, was sacked by President Kyprianou on 17 July following a speech implying that the talks were being abandoned. The Government declared that it supported talks if there was a chance of constructive progress.

Mr Denktash proposed on 20 July that Varosha, formerly the prosperous Greek-Cypriot part of Famagusta but now a ghost town sealed by Turkish troops, be placed under an 'interim administration', allowing the progressive resettlement of 35,000 Greek-Cypriot refugees to start as talks resumed. The idea was dismissed by the Greek side as a ploy to encourage Congress to lift the arms embargo. The Government presented a counter-proposal that the Turks withdraw from Varosha and the town be placed under UN control.

In his annual report to the General Assembly on 13 September Dr Waldheim described the past year as 'highly frustrating' for peace efforts in Cyprus and appealed for a change of attitude by the parties. Cyprus came before the Assembly again on 3 October when the Turkish Foreign Minister, Mr Gunduz Okcun, said the problem was ripe for resolution on the guidelines agreed between Mr Denktash and Archbishop Makarios back in February 1977 (see AR 1977, p. 167). President Kyprianou told the Assembly it was time for the UN to consider enforcement measures against Turkey. The Assembly passed a resolution demanding the immediate withdrawal of all foreign troops and urgent resumption of intercommunal talks. It recommended the Security Council to examine the implementation of previous UN resolutions and consider adopting appropriate measures—in effect, sanctions. The Security Council, however, agreed on a much watered-down resolution, urging the communities to resume negotiations and setting 30 May 1979 as the deadline for a progress report by Dr Waldheim. It fell short of mentioning sanctions, such action being strongly resisted by the United States.

The economy, which had shown tremendous growth since 1974, began to show signs of strain. In the first nine months imports (C£207·2 million) were more than double the value of exports (C£94·7 million), leaving a trade gap of C£112·2 million, primarily the result of increased consumer spending. A shortage of skilled labour hampered expansion, and industrialists and Ministers began to stress the need for a change of course away from traditional labour-intensive industries (essential in 1974 with the huge influx of refugees) to capital-intensive industries concentrating on exports. The ordinary and development Budgets for 1978 allowed for expenditure of C£118 million and the policy was aimed at a more restrained growth rate to avoid 'over-heating'.

On 27 November seven 'Ministers' of the Turkish-Cypriot administration resigned and others followed, resulting in the resignation of 'Prime Minister' Osman Orek. The crisis was caused by a plan to grant rights to a Panamanian-based multinational company to conduct tourism operations in the north. A new 'Cabinet' under Mr Mustafa Cagatay was sworn in on 12 December.

The only constructive cooperation between the two communities during the year was over an integrated sewerage scheme for Nicosia financed by the World Bank. Agreement on its implementation was reached following a number of meetings between the Mayor of Nicosia, Mr Lellos Demetriades, and his Turkish-Cypriot counterpart, Mr Akinci, on neutral ground controlled by UNFICYP (United Nations Force in Cyprus).

The year closed with intensive efforts by Dr Waldheim through his special representative, Mr Reinaldo Galindo Pohl, to find a basis for reopening the intercommunal talks, armed with the American Plan and his own suggestions. In response President Kyprianou announced that the Greek side was ready for talks without conditions but he warned that he would not tolerate protracted or barren negotiations.

TURKEY

Turkey at last acquired a stable Government, but this brought no relief to the country's troubles, notably in the economy and in public order. Following the defeat in Parliament and resignation of the right-wing Nationalist Front coalition under Mr Süleyman Demirel on 31 December 1977 (see AR 1977, p. 171), Mr Bülent Ecevit, leader of the left-of-centre Republican People's Party (RPP), formed a new Administration, based on his own party but including independent politicians who had resigned from Mr Demirel's Justice Party. The small liberal Republican Reliance Party (RRP) also took part in the Government, although the party's leader, Professor Turhan Feyzioglu, later resigned his portfolio as Deputy Prime Minister. The programme of the new Administration was approved by the National Assembly on 17 January by 229 votes to 218, and the Government majority, though small, held firm until the end of the year.

Replying to the vote of confidence, Mr Ecevit stated that his Government's main duty was to ensure peace in the country. In 1977 (according to official data given by the new Minister of the Interior, Mr Irfan Özaydinli, on 24 January), 262 people had been killed and over 2,700 injured in over 1,200 incidents. The new Government repeatedly declared its intention to re-establish order without recourse to extraordinary measures. This policy did not work. In addition to increased killings in the vendetta between rightist and leftist gangs, there were murders of prominent personalities (including two university professors) and bloody riots in eastern Turkey, where the minority Shiites, who supported Mr Ecevit by and large, clashed with the Sunnis.

In Malatya, riots broke out on 18 April, after the mayor, who was an ethnic Kurd, and three of his relatives had been killed by a letter bomb. In Sivas, a curfew had to be imposed when nine people were killed in Sunni–Shiite clashes on 3 September. In November, left-wing organizations which normally supported the Government came out against Mr Ecevit's proposal to tighten security legislation. Finally, in three days of riots, 23 to 25 December, again between Sunnis and Shiites, 104 people were killed in the city of Kahramanmaraş (known as Maraş until recently, when the title 'kahraman'—heroic—was added to commemorate the expulsion of the French occupation forces in 1920, and thus to retaliate against the erection in Marseilles of a monument to the victims of Armenian massacres).

The Government then proclaimed martial law in 13 of the country's 67 provinces, including the two main metropolitan centres of Ankara and Istanbul. Universities, which were disrupted throughout the year, closed their doors once again. The proclamation of martial law was endorsed almost unanimously by the Assembly on 26 December. The Minister of the Interior, who had stated that both the right and the left had been to blame (while Government supporters put the onus on the extreme right-wing Nationalist Action Party of Colonel Alpaslan Türkes), resigned, but the Government survived a no-confidence motion tabled by Mr Demirel. By the end of the year the toll of victims exceeded 800.

In the economy, 1977 had closed with a record trade deficit of $4,000 million and a current payments deficit of $3,400 million. In February, the new Government introduced a stabilization programme aimed at alleviating inflation and the shortage of foreign exchange. On 1 March, the Turkish lira was devalued by 23 per cent against the dollar. In April, the programme was supported by the IMF, which agreed to give Turkey access to drawings totalling $450 million, subject to periodic reviews. These led to disagreements which were not resolved by the end of the year. In May, members of the Turkish consortium of the OECD agreed to postpone repayments of government or government-guaranteed loans, thus providing the Turkish balance of payments with relief totalling $1,200 million over the next two years. Simultaneously, international banks began negotiations on the consolidation of short-term debts amounting to $2,500 million. However, Turkey could obtain less than $1,000 million in fresh trade credits, and this led to a drastic curtailment of imports.

While the balance of payments thus appeared improved, shortages developed, industry was forced to work at levels well below its capacity (an estimate of 50 per cent capacity utilization was given by government sources), and unemployment increased—to an estimated 20 per cent, although the rate must be qualified because of the agricultural basis of the Turkish economy. Price rises accelerated and exceeded an annual rate of 50 per cent, partly because the Government was forced to raise substantially the price of state-produced goods. The December increase in oil prices was estimated to cost Turkey an additional $200 million, and the annual bill for imported oil would approach the total revenue from exports.

The need to obtain aid dominated the conduct of foreign policy. At the beginning of the year exchanges with the West were aimed at securing the lifting of the US arms embargo, imposed after the Turkish landings in Cyprus in 1974. In spite of visits to Ankara by US Secretary of State Cyrus Vance in January, and of Deputy Secretary Warren Christopher in March, progress was slow. On 18 May Turkey decided not to participate in the Nato programme to increase defence expenditure. However, relations with the West improved after Congress voted to lift the embargo in August. Following the signature of the foreign aid law by President Carter in September, Turkey announced on 4 October that two of the US defence installations in the country, which had been closed in retaliation against the embargo, would be reopened immediately. Negotiations also started on a new US–Turkish defence cooperation agreement, with Turkey putting forward substantial financial demands. These negotiations were still in progress at the end of the year. Turkey's demands for aid also dominated negotiations with the EEC in October and the visit of Nato secretary general Joseph Luns to Ankara in November.

In an effort to improve relations with Greece, Mr Ecevit secured a meeting with the Greek Prime Minister, Mr Constantine Karamanlis, at Montreux on 10 and 11 March. The two Prime Ministers' decision to seek a peaceful solution to the problems between the two countries prevented a deterioration of relations, but subsequent meetings between the secretaries general of the two Foreign Ministries, and meetings between other senior diplomats on the Aegean continental shelf and the control of air traffic over the Aegean, produced no concrete results. The decision of the International Court of Justice at The Hague on 20 December that it had no jurisdiction in the proceedings concerning the Aegean continental shelf gave satisfaction to Turkey, which prepared to continue discussing the matter bilaterally with Greece, as recommended by the Security Council.

On Cyprus, Turkey participated through its constitutional adviser Professor Mümtaz Soysal in the preparation of the Turkish Cypriot proposals which were officially presented to the UN Secretary General, Mr Kurt Waldheim, in Vienna on 13 April, only to be rejected by the Greek Cypriots. On 20 July Mr Ecevit seconded a further offer by the Turkish Cypriot leader, Mr Rauf Denktash, to allow 35,000 Greeks back into the Varosha area of Famagusta (see p. 165).

Relations with the USSR, with other communist and with some Arab countries developed. The Soviet chief of the general staff, Marshal N. V. Ogarkov, visited Turkey between 25 and 29 April, and Mr Ecevit was in the Soviet Union between 21 and 27 June. As well as signing a political document on friendly relations, he concluded a number of agreements, one of which provided that the USSR would supply Turkey with 3 million tons of oil annually. Soviet warships paid a first official visit to Istanbul in November. A political document on cooperation was also signed with Romania when the Romanian Prime Minister visited Ankara on 27 April.

The campaign by Armenian terrorists against Turkish diplomats abroad continued with the murder on 3 June of the wife of the Turkish ambassador in Madrid, Mme Necla Kuneralp.

F*

V THE MIDDLE EAST AND NORTH AFRICA

Chapter 1

ISRAEL

ISRAEL'S Government and people were preoccupied during the whole of 1978 with the prospects for a Middle East peace. President Sadat's sensational visit to Jerusalem on 19 November 1977, and the return visit of Israel's Prime Minister, Mr Menachem Begin, to Ismailia on 25 December (see AR 1977, pp. 173 and 179) raised hopes very high. On 10 and 11 January Egyptian delegates arrived in Israel, and Israeli delegates in Cairo, for talks respectively on the political and military aspects of a peace agreement. Detailed political talks lasted, in fact, only a few days and were broken off by President Sadat on 19 January. His main reason was that Israel would not readily agree to proposals for withdrawal from areas occupied in the 1967 war and for full self-determination to be given to the Palestinian Arabs. On 23 January, however, the Egyptian Government made it clear that the political talks were only 'frozen', not abandoned.

The military talks continued intermittently until 26 July, when Egypt asked the Israeli delegation to leave Cairo. These talks had, however, been at least partly successful, and a measure of agreement had been reached on the modalities of an Israeli withdrawal from Sinai, and on future military arrangements for the peninsula.

Between 19 January and the end of July all sorts of efforts were made to restart the political peace talks. This entailed exhausting 'shuttle diplomacy', in which American, Israeli and Egyptian Ministers and diplomats moved between Washington, Jerusalem and Cairo. In addition, Sadat had meetings with both Ezer Weizman, Israel's Minister of Defence, and the Israeli Labour Opposition leader, Shimon Peres, in Austria. These exchanges made plain that Egypt would continue to insist on the return of all Arab territories occupied in 1967, while Israel wanted a territorial settlement based on negotiation and compromise.

Two Israeli leaders suggested constructive moves: Foreign Minister Moshe Dayan offered unilaterally-granted self-rule for the occupied West Bank and Gaza Strip, while Defence Minister Weizman proposed the formation of a 'national Government of peace' in Israel which could offer material concessions in advance of a peace treaty. On his side, Sadat proposed the return of the West Bank to Jordan, and of the Gaza Strip to Egypt, pending discussion of the future of the Palestinian Arabs.

A major effort to restart negotiations failed, when the Foreign Ministers of Israel and Egypt met at Leeds Castle in Kent on 18 July. A proposal to hand over the Sinai town of El Arish to Egypt, as a goodwill gesture, was turned down by Israel. More hopeful was a statement on 24 July in the Knesset (Parliament) by Mr Dayan that the status of the administered territories could be renegotiated five years after an Israeli-Egyptian agreement. Sadat once again rejected territorial compromise, but President Carter was sufficiently encouraged by the Leeds Castle conference to invite both Sadat and Begin to talks in Camp David. The invitation was made on 8 August and the talks began on 5 September.

They were unexpectedly successful and by 18 September the frameworks had been agreed for two peace treaties, one between Israel and Egypt and the other on the shape of an overall Middle East settlement (see DOCUMENTS). The former was relatively straightforward, and provided for full Israeli withdrawal from Sinai, for the partial demilitarization of the peninsula, and for a future United Nations peace-keeping role. The outcome of this agreement was to be the establishment of full diplomatic and economic relations between the two countries and free movement between them of goods and people.

The other agreement was more complex and imprecise. It included phased Israeli withdrawal from the West Bank and Gaza, the establishment of an 'autonomous' Palestinian entity, the temporary retention of an Israeli military presence, and the final determination of the status of these territories after a transitional period of five years. Machinery would be established for negotiation and for periodic review of developments in these territories, bringing in representatives of Jordan and of the Palestinians. Israel's Knesset on 27 September approved the Camp David agreements by 85 votes to 19. They were popularly acclaimed in Egypt, and a dramatic diplomatic breakthrough seemed to have taken place. The Nobel peace prize was awarded jointly to Sadat and Begin on 27 October (Begin, but not Sadat, went to Oslo to receive it in December).

But the Camp David agreements were rejected by other Arab states and by the Palestine Liberation Organization (PLO), claiming to represent the Palestinian Arabs. King Hussein of Jordan refused to be drawn into peace talks. These setbacks were followed in November and December by a series of new demands by Sadat, after further talks between the Israeli and Egyptian Foreign Ministers in October had disclosed growing differences. He called for prior acceptance of the principle of full Palestinian self-determination, and of total Israeli withdrawal from territories occupied in 1967. On 15 November he demanded the return of Gaza to Egypt as a prior condition for the signing of a peace treaty. He called for a revision of military arrangements in Sinai after five years, for the postponement of diplomatic relations until the West Bank and Gaza had been granted autonomy, for a timetable for the holding of elections in these territories and the setting-up of a civilian administration, and for admission of Egypt's right to take part in a future Arab war against Israel.

In addition, he wanted an Egyptian police force to take control of the Gaza Strip.

Israel pointed out that all these demands were new, and were not covered by the Camp David agreements. They constituted a close 'linkage' between the two agreements, which was not provided for at Camp David. Whereas the Cabinet had accepted the bilateral agreement on 25 October, it rejected linkage with the second agreement. It had been hoped, at Camp David, to have the bilateral agreement signed by mid-December, but peace talks were still deadlocked at the end of 1978. A by-product was a worsening of US-Israeli relations; in Israel's view, undue American pressure had been applied against the Begin Government, and American statements that the whole of the West Bank must be evacuated were ill-timed. Israel was additionally concerned by American determination to go ahead with sales of advanced aircraft to both Egypt and Saudi Arabia.

Israel, on its side, came under criticism for reinforcing existing Israeli settlements on the West Bank. This was announced on 31 October. Earlier, on 26 February, the Cabinet stated that there would be no new decisions on settlements, and the Government continued to evict 'illegal' settlers who attempted to seize Arab lands. Israel's settlements policy may have contributed to increased hostility and unrest on the West Bank; during 1978 there were a great many demonstrations and a number of terrorist actions. There were several bomb explosions in Jerusalem, in which several people were killed and upwards of 100 wounded. A major terrorist attack was carried out by the PLO on 11 March, resulting in 37 deaths and the wounding of dozens of people just outside Tel Aviv. The intruders, all of whom were killed or captured, had been landed from the sea.

Israel was, at long last, temporarily drawn into the three-years'-old civil war in Lebanon. Increasing terrorist activity in southern Lebanon led Israel to mount an organized military offensive which began on 14 March. By 19 March Israeli forces were occupying all Lebanon south of the Litani river, with the exception of the port of Tyre. A massive exodus of Lebanese Moslems took place, while PLO forces numbering about 8,000 were driven out of the area. Israel lost only 18 dead in the military operations, and claimed to have killed at least 300 terrorists. The UN Security Council condemned Israel for causing civilian casualties, and demanded the immediate withdrawal of Israeli forces. Israel proclaimed a ceasefire on 21 March, facilitated the gradual occupation by UN forces which began on 23 March, and carried out a phased withdrawal which was completed early in June. Lebanese Christians stayed in their homes, cooperated fully with the Israelis and established their own local militia—with Israeli help— in a 'buffer zone' four to five miles wide along Israel's northern border.

Renewed PLO terrorist activity in southern Lebanon brought Israeli air-strikes in August and October against PLO bases. Those in August were partly motivated by the PLO attack on an El Al airlines bus in

London on 20 August. An air hostess was killed and three of the crew were wounded. On a happier note, Israel continued its 'good fence' policy on the Lebanese border, and by the end of 1978 had given nearly 3,000 Lebanese wounded and a thousand Lebanese expectant mothers treatment in Israeli hospitals.

The Begin Government had its domestic political troubles. On 23 August the Democratic Movement for Change, a coalition partner, split; 5 of its 15 Knesset members left the party, but its leader, Yigal Yadin, remained Deputy Prime Minister. There were several rallies of the peace-hungry 'Peace Movement', but also a number of demonstrations by 'hard-liners' against the Government. One Minister left the Government, as well as the Prime Minister's adviser on information, Shmuel Katz. A new President, Yitzhak Navon, was elected, however, without real opposition, and the mayor of Jerusalem, Teddy Kollek, retained office by an overwhelming majority.

Israel experienced a desperately difficult year economically. Inflation was almost 50 per cent, the Israeli currency dropped in value, and there was an unending series of strikes—of seamen, journalists, port and postal workers, government employees and even magistrates and judges. Sales of Jaffa oranges were temporarily disrupted by reports in West Germany, Holland and Britain that they had been poisoned.

Other events included the death of former Prime Minister Mrs Golda Meir on 8 December (see OBITUARY), the celebration of Israel's 30th year of independence and of Jerusalem's 11th anniversary of reunification on 10 May and 4 June respectively, and the decision of the broadcasting authority in June to introduce colour television.

Israel was once again under criticism by international bodies, including the UN General Assembly, Unesco and the World Health Organization, and the possibility of carrying out an arms embargo against Israel was discussed in the UN. More positive were Pope Paul VI's statement on 12 January that the Vatican no longer wanted a 'separate' status for Jerusalem, and the report of the Select Committee of the House of Lords on 31 August, urging firm British Government action to curb the workings of the Arab trade boycott in Britain.

Chapter 2

THE ARAB WORLD—EGYPT—JORDAN—SYRIA—LEBANON—IRAQ

THE ARAB WORLD

OF the Arabs in 1978 it might be said, as Jane Austen did of the Bennetts, that had they 'made an agreement to expose themselves as much as they could . . . it would have been impossible for them to play their parts with more spirit or finer success'. While President Sadat of Egypt laboured for peace without dishonour, most of the rest, united only in denouncing him, fought each other in wars civil (Lebanon), guerrilla (Algeria/Morocco), subversive (the Yemens, Syria/Iraq) or plain gangster (Iraq/PLO). The cooler heads could achieve little against this chaos, which they were often financing (Saudi payments in 1977 to Fatah, the PLO's main component, were $34 million) and which was symbolized by inter-Palestinian feuds. Even when united against Camp David, it was not clear what the Arabs could or would do to frustrate it.

President Sadat's negotiations, which at the end of 1978 were stranded on Israel's insistence on a separate peace with Egypt and refusal to budge from the West Bank, and most of the inter-Arab conflicts, are recorded elsewhere (see pp. 170–2, 175–7).

The Arab world divided into three—the hardliners directing their energies more against Sadat than against Israel; Egypt, supported by Sudan and Morocco; and the uncommitted remainder (the Arabian oil states and Jordan). The Arab League, still based in Cairo, was ineffective, its meetings being cut by hardliners and intensive Sudanese efforts failing to produce reconciliation. No Arab summit meeting could be held except the Baghdad conference in November which excluded the most influential Arab country and put the League into suspense. The mandate of the Arab Deterrent Force in Lebanon was, however, prolonged.

The hardliners, too, were divided. Five of them (Syria, Algeria, Libya, South Yemen and the PLO) met in Algiers from 2-4 February to anathematize Sadat's 'capitulationism'. Iraq boycotted this front even when, reassembled in Damascus (20-23 September) after Camp David, it threatened to sever economic relations with Egypt and subvert its government, besides advocating a Soviet alliance. Soon, however, the repercussions of Camp David had reconciled Iraq with Syria and drawn the moderate states to November's Baghdad conference (2-6 November).

Its decisions, less drastic than expected or recommended at Damascus, condemned Camp David, but endorsed, as Sadat had done at Jerusalem in 1977, the realistic objective of recovering Arab territory captured in 1967, thus implicitly conceding Israel's right to its pre-1967 frontiers. Nor did they mention a boycott of Egypt or a fighting fund (to support Syria, Jordan and the PLO), though the press reported agreements on these topics. Another decision taken but missing from the communique (presumably because Sudan and others did not accept it) was that the League should, for the time being, not meet in Cairo. This relative moderation reflected Saudi influence. On 4 November the conference sent Sadat a delegation under the Lebanese President, inviting him to repudiate Camp David and promising Arab aid should he do so: but Sadat would not see them.

At the hardline meetings the Palestinians demanded close alignment with the USSR, which the hardline leaders visited assiduously. This lacked appeal for the conservatives in the Gulf, and even President Qadafi of Libya, who also attacked the Palestinians for their refusal to bury hatchets, seemed suspicious. Syria appeared dissatisfied with Soviet arms supplies and Iraq had its own disagreements with the Soviet Union.

Of all the Arabs the Palestinians cut the sorriest figure. Personal rivalries inside this fragmented movement were aggravated by the patronage of particular groups by individual governments, Iraq's being the most divisive. Its protege, Abu Nidal, started an exchange of murders with the PLO in London (4 January), Paris, Kuwait, Pakistan and elsewhere. In Lebanon, Iraqi- and Syrian-supported groups clashed lethally and the PLO failed to reconcile its duty to its Lebanese host with its itch for terrorism against Israel. Later, at the Baghdad summit, Iraq had its first dialogue with the PLO for years and according to reports began to muzzle, possibly even to sack, Abu Nidal, though Baghdad radio continued to broadcast anti-PLO material, including a reported Fatah attack on Iraq-supported Palestinians in Lebanon. Even Fatah, the largest single Palestinian group, was often divided against itself, while also competing with minor factions. The movement as a whole achieved only explosions and press conferences, the reinforcement of Israeli intransigence and a large contribution to the ruin of Lebanon.

The most dreaded Palestinian terrorist, Waddei Haddad, who arranged the mass hijacks of September 1970, and probably that which ended at Mogadishu in 1977 (see AR 1977, p. 131), died in East Berlin on 28 March.

EGYPT

Egypt's negotiations with Israel isolated it from the Arabs but linked it closer to the USA. The apparent breakthrough at Camp David in September remained words on paper. Impetus towards political freedom slackened but external finances improved. The peace negotiations were slow, intricate, sometimes acrimonious. President Anwar Sadat was determined to repel Arab accusations of treason without forfeiting US sympathy. He deepened American involvement and commitment to Egypt.

On 4 January, in Aswan, President Carter recognized the Palestinians' right to participate in determining their own future; and on 12 January he condemned all Israeli settlements in occupied territory. On 18 January Begin's jingoistic speech provoked Sadat to withdraw his delegation from the Jerusalem talks. As the US laboured to revive them, Secretary Vance and his staff were often on shuttle duty. While visiting America in February, Sadat pressed the US Government to become a full partner in negotiations. Israel marked gains nevertheless: President Carter repeatedly opposed an independent Palestinian state, and Sadat on 10 May met a traditional Israeli thesis by advocating instead the West Bank's provisional return to Jordan, whose participation in Egyptian plans thus became important. Egypt secured one great objective: on 15 May the Senate, defying Israeli protests, agreed to the supply of military aircraft.

As the Begin Government continued to make statements reflecting determination to stay indefinitely in the West Bank, Sadat showed increasing impatience, threatening to denounce the current Sinai disengagement agreement and even to resume fighting (6 June). On 20 June Secretary Vance told Congressmen that, as Israel showed no flexibility, Egypt should revive the negotiations by presenting its own plan. This emerged on 5 July: after a five-year transitional period, with Jordan and Egypt administering the West Bank and Gaza respectively, the Palestinians should determine their own future. Israel took only four days to reject this: but, accepting a US proposal, met the Egyptians at Leeds Castle in Kent on 18 July, without result.

Carter now invited Sadat and Begin to Camp David on 5 September. After days of apparent deadlock, two important papers (see DOCUMENTS) were signed on 17 September. The first, a 'Framework of Peace' provided for a five-year transitional period, during which occupied Palestine would come under an autonomous authority set up by Egyptian-Jordanian-Israeli negotiation (with Palestinian representation); some Israeli forces would withdraw, the rest would be confined to 'specified locations'. These arrangements implied active Jordanian participation, or at least support, which seemed unlikely. Meanwhile negotiations should decide the final status of occupied Palestine and draft an Israel–Jordan peace treaty. The second paper concerned an Egyptian-Israeli peace treaty, to be signed by 17 December, requiring Israeli withdrawal to the 1967 Sinai frontier, a largely demilitarized Sinai with UN forces on the border and at Sharm al Shaikh, a highway from Egypt to Aqaba, normal diplomatic and commercial relations and Israeli passage through the Suez Canal.

Letters attached to these agreements dealt with Israeli constitutional processes, the status of East Jerusalem and other matters. Subsidiary agreements were reported (US finance for new Israeli defences, re-equipping Egypt's airforce and replacing Arab aid if cut off) but not published.

For the Arabs all this held disadvantages: first, no deadline for beginning negotiations on the autonomous area; second, no explicit Israeli commitment ever to withdraw from it; third, no firm provision for Israeli withdrawal from occupied Syria.

Camp David, like UN Security Council resolution 242 (see AR 1973, p. 524), had been left vague and incomplete enough to secure signature. However, given the now close American involvement in the negotiations, US views were of vital importance and they became clearer in a document given to King Hussein on 16 October and Carter's press conference of 9 November: Camp David had pre-supposed a comprehensive settlement

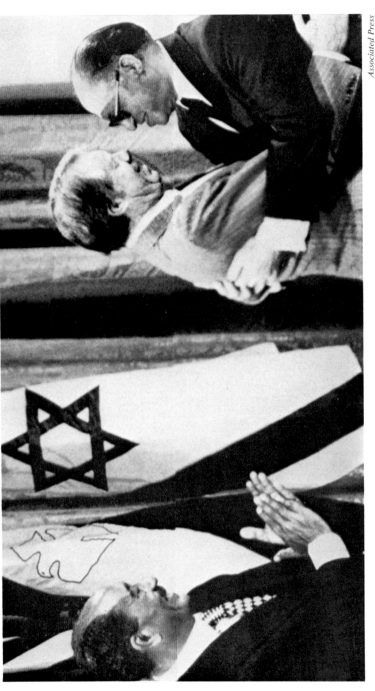

Associated Press

Israel's Prime Minister Menachem Begin and US President Jimmy Carter embrace to the applause of Egypt's President Anwar Sadat as agreement at Camp David is announced on 17 September 1978.

Associated Press

The perils of the Vietnamese 'boat people' are vividly illustrated by this picture of refugees on a sinking boat beached on the Malaysian coast on 4 December 1978.

Press Association

A thrilling Anglo-American finish to the 1978 Derby Stakes: Shirley Heights, ridden by Greville Starkey, wins by a head from Hawaiian Sound, ridden by the American jockey Willie Shoemaker.

Associated Press

Devastating floods and a political come-back by Mrs Indira Gandhi were outstanding events of 1978 in India; here Mrs Gandhi is seen on a tour of flooded areas in September.

for all the occupied territories, not just an isolated Egyptian-Israeli treaty: the US wanted the final status of the West Bank and Gaza settled in Israeli-Arab negotiations based on UN resolution 242 (in its US interpretation, *i.e.* withdrawal by Israel on all fronts) and rejected Israel's claim to exclude east Jerusalem from any negotiations.

The evacuation of Israeli civilian settlements from Sinai passed the Knesset on 28 September, despite emotional opposition. Next came the negotiation of the bilateral treaty. Talks began in Washington on 12 October. On 20 October the US had to present its own draft, which both delegations seemingly accepted on 22 October. Next day Egypt said it must be referred back (henceforward, to US irritation, both Governments often rejected what their delegates had accepted), while Begin and Moshe Dayan, to secure Cabinet approval, on 26 October reasserted Israel's unshakeable right to establish settlements in occupied territory without 'dreaming' of removing a single one. This 'deeply disturbed' Carter: Camp David, he held, precluded any new settlements before the autonomous area's establishment and allowed them thereafter only by negotiation. He had to plead with Sadat to continue talking.

The negotiations' failure seemed likely from this moment (thereby discrediting the Nobel committee who had on 27 October prematurely awarded Sadat and Begin the peace prize), especially after the Baghdad proceedings in November (see p. 174) had threatened Sadat with losing Saudi aid. Israel repeatedly declared its readiness to sign the bilateral treaty as presented, but its statement of 26 October had undermined Camp David's assumption of a comprehensive peace. For its part Egypt refused to subordinate its previous Arab commitments to the Israeli treaty and now wanted the exchange of ambassadors linked to the establishment of the autonomous area, to fix a time-table now for elections to the latter, to recover Egypt's pre-1967 position in Gaza without delay and to have the Sinai defence arrangements reviewed after four years.

Carter vainly warned against missing the 17 December deadline. Returning to Cairo on 10 December Vance drafted with the Egyptians an exchange of letters to cover Sadat's points but Israel rejected it, accusing the US of favouring Egypt. Vance tried to break the deadlock by assembling Egyptians and Israelis in Brussels at Christmas, but without clear result. Israel halted the withdrawal of military material from Sinai.

Throughout 1978 Sadat gave priority to peace, keeping close to the US who 'held 99·9 per cent of the cards' and whose money would be essential should the Arab oil states desert him. These states had not yet announced reductions in their aid, but in November 'temporary Saudi financial difficulties' were reportedly delaying the delivery of US aircraft to Egypt, and an Egyptian parliamentary statement on 5 December that 'some Arab states had suspended their aid this year as a result of misunderstandings' tended to confirm this indication. Presumably it was these suspensions which had led the Cairo media on 14 November to attack Kuwait and the other oil states.

Sudan and Morocco remained predictably friendly, and in December Morocco was reported mediating between Egypt and Saudi Arabia. Less was heard of the quarrel with Libya. Egypt's isolation from Arab militancy was not accompanied by much hostile terrorism (despite threats to Sadat from a so-called Arab Peoples' Conference in Damascus and Baghdad) except for the murder by Palestinian gunmen of Sadat's friend Yusuf Siba'i (see p. 164) when Egyptian over-reaction and miscalculation were tragically displayed. Egypt over-reacted again in December by breaking with Bulgaria whose embassy had used force to evict Egyptian tenants.

Despite Foreign Minister Muhammad Ibrahim Kamil's resignation rather than sign the Camp David agreements, Sadat's pursuit of peace and defiance of Arab nationalism was not generally unpopular in Egypt, nor did the economic riots of January 1977 recur. Sadat remained hyper-sensitive to criticism. In May he attacked the recently-formed New Wafd Party and indeed all the opposition and on 21 May, in a referendum on the suppression of 'alien ideologies and corrupt reaction', won a 97 per cent 'yes' on a reportedly low poll. Legislation followed against parliamentary and press opposition. The New Wafd and the leftist United Peoples' Party suspended or disbanded themselves; 131 people with 'reactionary' or 'subversive' pasts were banned from politics and journalism. Egyptian journalists, including some working abroad, were investigated. Opposition papers ceased to appear regularly.

The experienced and respected Abdul Munim Qaisuni finally resigned his economic overlordship on 2 May. Sadat's own National Democratic Party (NDP) emerged on 6 August, led by a Copt: it seemed just the heir to the former Arab Socialist Party, most of whose members hurried to join it. On 4 October Mamduh Salim and his Government gave way to Mustafa Khalil, an American-trained engineer who had opposed Nasser's pro-Soviet policies. The new Cabinet included many new but few young faces. Some saw it as a peace-time Government, putting Egyptian interests first. The previous Minister of War and hero of 1973, General Gamassi, and his chief of staff were dropped. On 21 December Sadat proclaimed for 1979 a sweeping decentralization of initiative to provincial governors.

As for the economy, in June the IBRD could say in Paris that Egypt was out of its short-term foreign exchange crisis, having cleared all commercial arrears, largely thanks to Gulf, US and IMF aid and to inflows from emigrants' remittances ($1,800 million), net oil receipts ($700 million), Canal tolls ($550 million) and tourism ($400 million). But inflation remained a problem (25 to 40 per cent, depending on social class) as did growing dependence on imported food and Cairo's decrepit infrastructure.

The question-marks for 1979 were the future of the peace negotiations and of the Saudi and other Gulf subsidies, which might be affected by the

Iranian collapse: and, if these were answered satisfactorily, whether peace would really reduce armed forces, government expenditure and inflation.

JORDAN

By dividing the US and Egypt further from other Arab states and making the West Bank a crucial issue, 1978 intensified King Hussein's dilemma between anxiety for Arab unity, including his links with Syria, and his sympathy for his US benefactors and their peace-making. Finding President Sadat's negotiations (see EGYPT) unlikely to produce a comprehensive, durable peace, he refused the part they allotted to him: but, unlike other Arabs, was courteous to both sides and burned no bridges.

On 1 January in Teheran, President Carter tried to persuade him into the negotiations, but Prime Minister Begin's flat refusal to withdraw from the West Bank or allow a Palestinian state made it easier for Hussein to refuse the invitation, while praising Sadat for unmasking Israeli intransigence. Even this irritated Syria. Hussein also feared that accepting US/Egyptian invitations would provoke accusations of abandoning the Rabat decision of 1974 (that only the PLO could speak for the Palestinians). On 13 February he was reported to have assured the PLO leader, Yassir Arafat, of his view that the Palestinians must determine their own future, but on 8 March *Le Monde* reported that extremist Palestinian opposition had stopped Arafat from pursuing the reconciliation. Hussein's flexibility did not extend to readmitting armed Palestinians into Jordan.

He kept contact with both Egypt and its critics and on 3 April Amman radio reported Jordan's proposal for a summit conference to reconcile Sadat with them and face Israel united. On 24 July, after the unsuccessful Egyptian-Israeli talks at Leeds Castle, Hussein spoke to a US official of preferring a renewed Geneva conference to bilateral talks.

Hussein refused to attend Camp David, restating his position on 2 September: any settlement must include Israeli withdrawal from all occupied territories and self-determination for the Palestinians. The Camp David agreements falling short of this, Hussein rejected them. This was followed by pained US reference to the possible (*sc.* financial) effect on US–Jordan relations. Hussein welcomed the Iraqi President's invitation to November's Arab summit in Baghdad (see p. 164) and himself attended it. The US made a further attempt to persuade Hussein by sending Senator Byrd on 4 December with a message from President Carter: but, while expressing a desire to maintain a dialogue with the US, he again declined to join the negotiations.

Jordan's partnership with Syria continued, not much affected by their different views: and relations with Libya, renewed in 1976 after six years' break, became warmer. Prime Minister Mudar Badran visited Libya in

April, securing a Libyan loan for fertilizer projects. On 22 September President Qadafi unexpectedly paid his first visit to Jordan to persuade Hussein to join the anti-Sadat front in Damascus. He was accompanied by Arafat who had not been in Jordan since the battles of 1970. Visits by PLO delegations followed in late November and mid-December. Jordan was equally firm in loyalty to the 1974 Rabat decision and in its resolve not to have PLO forces back. Propaganda from Baghdad insinuated that the delegation had promised not to attack Israel from Jordan.

The King was active as ever. Besides marrying on 15 June his fourth wife, Miss Liza Halaby, of a Lebanese-American family (turning Muslim, she became Queen Nur), he visited the UK, Spain, Austria, Norway, Italy, Yugoslavia and Iran, besides plying between the Arab states.

The chief internal development was the inauguration on 24 April of a 60-member National Consultative Assembly (NCC) appointed by royal decree. The previous, elected, parliament, with many Palestinian members, dissolved in 1974 to comply with the Rabat decision, had not been replaced. The NCC included three serving and various former Cabinet Ministers (and three women) but fewer Palestinians than before. Hussein indicated that the nominated NCC would last only until elections became possible.

Jordan's economy still flourished, gross domestic product having risen by 19·4 per cent in 1977. A 1977 visible deficit of $216 million became a payments surplus of $210 million through increasing remittances ($500 million) from 300,000 Jordanians working abroad. Central bank reserves reached $752 million in January 1978 and might soon exceed $1,000 million. The 1978 Budget deficit was estimated at less than 5 per cent of revenue and could easily be covered from foreign loans. More than half the revenue came from foreign aid. Security expenditure exceeded 25 per cent of the total, but investment and capital expenditure took up to 42 per cent. This prosperity reflected Beirut's decline. Aqaba was active in transit trade: a stock exchange opened: and tourism was 50 per cent above 1976 and still increasing.

Foreign exchange financed much development, particularly of Jordan's phosphate and potash, a fertilizer plant going up near Aqaba and one to produce potash from the Dead Sea being planned to open in 1982. Other developments were in hotels, airports, roads and water supplies, for which the UK lent $7 million.

There were some shadows. Rapid development was accelerating inflation (34 per cent at October 1977) though Badran claimed in June 1978 that it had fallen below 30 per cent. Agriculture remained weak and much wheat was imported. Emigration meant labour shortages, especially of qualified staff, and measures were taken against it; and some of the visible deficit, which was on the increase, represented conspicuous consumption by returned emigrants, whose flashy style contrasted disagreeably with rural poverty.

SYRIA

Resentment at President Sadat's peace negotiations dominated Syria's foreign policy, eventually suspending the long quarrel with Iraq and strengthening ties with Moscow. There was no sign of stability in Lebanon, especially after the Israeli invasion in March, and Syrian troops had to stay there, clashing violently with Maronite militias and burdening Syrian finances.

On 23 January the Foreign Minister, Abdul Halim Khaddam, said that Sadat's capitulation had made rearmament first priority, and Soviet weapons flowed in: others were imported from France. President Hafiz al Asad went to Moscow himself on 20 February, after another meeting in Algiers of the anti-Sadat states, which, however, Iraq could not be persuaded to join.

The Lebanese imbroglio worsened. Syrian forces faced aggressive Christian elements of the Lebanese army: Syrian-Maronite hostility deepened, particularly after Israel invaded Lebanon in March and openly supported the Maronite militias. Asad eschewed provocative measures and reportedly opposed activity south of the Litani river by Syrian or Palestinian forces. On 17 April the Defence Minister, justifying Syrian restraint, said that Israel had sought to lure Syria into a disastrous battle: on 24 May the Information Minister warned the PLO not to help Israel by attacking UN forces. Syrian propaganda, however, supported the PLO. Hostility to Maronite collaboration with Israel intensified after the massacre in June of the Franjiehs (see p. 184): like the 1976 massacre of pro-Syrian Palestinians, this was a personal outrage to Asad, a Franjieh family friend, and sharpened attacks on the Maronite militias in Beirut.

In September, Camp David's threat of a separate Egyptian peace with Israel, which would leave Syria alone, except for Jordan, to face the enemy, produced a sudden reconciliation with Iraq. Anti-Iraqi propaganda ceased, presidential messages were exchanged, Khaddam accepted Iraq's invitation to an Arab summit, Syria reopened its frontier with Iraq and Asad visited Baghdad, for the first time for many years, on 24 October. A charter of Syrian-Iraqi cooperation was signed (see p. 185): this sudden rapprochement, with its talk of 'constitutional unity', ironically recalled that with Egypt less than two years before. At the Baghdad summit in November Asad demanded, unsuccessfully, a total boycott of Egypt.

Indignation over Camp David reinforced the warmer relations with the USSR, which Asad revisited on 5 October to coordinate anti-Camp David strategy and discuss Syrian rearmament. On the latter point, Syria appeared dissatisfied with Soviet offers, in November curtailing a military visit to Moscow. This disappointment was perhaps also related to Syria's refusal to sign an Iraqi-style treaty with the USSR or give it base facilities.

Syria kept in touch also with the West, even with the USA despite Congressional opposition to the modest aid for Syria. Asad visited West Germany, Syria's biggest trade partner, in September and a week later saw Secretary Vance for several hours, advocating a comprehensive settlement based on UN resolution 242: here Syria differed from the other hardline states.

The planned Syrian-Jordanian integration continued, though Jordan's attitude to Sadat was much milder than Syria's. The year saw fewer high-level visits, though King Hussein went to Damascus in July and the Jordanian-Syrian higher committee had a routine meeting.

Foreign preoccupations reduced attention to internal affairs. On 8 February Asad was elected President for another seven years, the referendum claiming a 97 per cent turn-out and a 99·6 per cent 'yes'. A new Prime Minister, Muhammad Ali Halabi, a lawyer and parliamentarian, was appointed on 27 March: his Government included two communists. Policy seemed unchanged. Murders of Alawites continued, including a kinsman of Asad's.

The economy suffered from the expense of garrisoning Lebanon (about $3·6 million per diem). Syria's forces, now over 200,000, were costing 10 per cent of gnp and 24 per cent of the budget. In January the Government raised its employees' pay (extra cost over $160 million) and the same sum went on subsidizing prices. No wonder inflation was around 30 per cent. The Government found one interesting source of revenue: Syrians in the Gulf could buy themselves off conscription with $5,000 paid to the treasury.

However, 1978 was better economically than its predecessors. The oil states, which had cut their payments in disapproval of Syrian intervention in Lebanon, increased them: one report said that Saudi Arabia had in June sent $167 million as 'a reward for moderation'. The reconciliation with Iraq might soon replace the $600 million lost by the 1976 closure of the Kirkuk pipeline, Syrian oil output was up to 10 million tons per annum, and the final stage of the Euphrates dam was opened on 18 March, promising greatly increased water and also electric power. Unfortunately unexpected soil conditions would apparently impair irrigation and the Euphrates might not suffice to keep the dam full.

LEBANON

No cure was found for the lack of effective government or for disorder in the south. Both were aggravated by Israeli intervention, inter-Maronite feuding and clumsy Syrian handling of the Beirut militias. The resulting conflicts were bloody, destructive and unceasing and the unhealing division of Beirut not only bred violence but paralyzed economic life.

Even in January, Beirut being still full of uncollected weapons, the Arab Deterrent Force (ADF) could not suppress the inter-zonal fighting. Initially it collaborated with the Lebanese army, but apparent partisanship by Christian officers soon led to clashes between Syrian and Lebanese troops. Henceforward ex-President Camille Shamoun and his National Liberal Party (NLP) consistently opposed the ADF.

In the south the Christian militias, under Major Sa'ad Haddad and dependent on Israel, fought Palestinians and leftists. UN observers reported frequent crossing of the frontier by Israelis. A Palestinian terrorist attack on 11 March was followed on 15 March by Israeli invasion of Lebanon up to the Litani river. Israeli-supported Maronite militias massacred Muslim villagers and over 1,100 other Lebanese and Palestinians died in the fighting. The UN Security Council's resolution 425 of 16 March demanded Israeli withdrawal and instituted the UN Interim Force in Lebanon (UNIFIL), whose first units arrived on 22 March. Their task was arduous. Israeli forces, though ostensibly ceasing fire on 21 March, stayed in Lebanon till 11 June, handing over to Haddad's militias, which they continued to support in order to perpetuate Maronite control and prevent Palestinian reoccupation. Neither Maronites nor Palestinians cooperated properly with UNIFIL.

The Israeli invasion set 200,000 villagers fleeing northwards and by renewing Maronite opposition to the Palestinian presence created a new ministerial crisis. The Muslim Prime Minister, Salim al Hoss, presented the resignation of his non-political Cabinet, partly to facilitate political government (which proved impossible) and partly bowing to accusations that he had not curbed ADF intervention in Beirut. There was no alternative Prime Minister and Hoss carried on till formally reinstated on 15 May. A parliamentary declaration of 27 April had advocated implementation of UN resolution 425, the abolition of private armies, stopping Palestinian and non-Palestinian armed action in Lebanon and rebuilding the Lebanese army. This, though passed overwhelmingly through Parliament, met opposition from the left wing, the Palestinians and the Maronite supporters of ex-President Suleiman Franjieh. Besides, to succeed it needed a determined use of government force, but the Government still had virtually none, since the Maronites, accustomed to occupy most military commands, resisted the necessary non-sectarian restructuring of the army. This subject even divided Ministers against each other. Lebanon still therefore depended on the ADF, whose difficulties were now aggravated by a flare-up of extra violence.

Inter-Maronite quarrels, due often to the intransigence and ambition of Shamoun, had long impaired national unity. Now to bloodshed between Falangists and Shamounists were added other clashes. Franjieh had angered other Maronites by his Syrian links, by rejecting partition, a non-Arab foreign alignment and connivance with Israel, and by holding the northern town of Zghorta as a blatant family fief. On 23 May his men broke with them and bloody hostilities began. After several Falangist and Shamounist deaths a mass attack on Franjieh's family on 13 June left thirty dead, including women and children. Franjieh warned Falangists to leave Zghorta or abandon the Falange and their weapons. Many did but on 28 June over 20 were murdered.

From early July the ADF was more often drawn into the Beirut battle. The massacre of his friend Franjieh's family had enraged President Asad of Syria. There was constant inter-zonal fighting, the ADF reacting with shelling to Maronite sniping. This intensified Maronite opposition to the renewal of the ADF's mandate, which the Government, to Shamoun's disgust, eventually asked the Arab League for on 27 September and got a month later.

South Lebanon remained tumultuous. Israel, to assist Haddad and the Maronite militias in Beirut, periodically flew fighters over the city and shelled Lebanon from the sea, ostensibly as anti-PLO reprisals. The Lebanese troops sent to garrison the south remained pinned down by Maronite and probably Israeli fire-power.

Politics were equally confused. Government initiatives to promote decentralization (anathema to the left, chicken feed to the right), strengthen the army and introduce political government met both left- and right-wing opposition.

External forces—France, the US and the UN Security Council—vainly tried their hand. Eventually President Elias Sarkis organized a conference of governments manning or financing the ADF from 15-17 October. Its final communique called for restoring effective central government, disarming private militias, recruiting a non-sectarian army and punishing collaboration with Israel. This partly recalled the parliamentary declaration of 24 May but, insufficiently reflecting Maronite views, remained ineffective. Despite an attempt to replace Syrian by other ADF units in sensitive areas, fighting in Beirut continued: the Israelis snapped their fingers at government attempts to outlaw Haddad, whom they continued to support: and army reform still stuck on sectarian jealousies, especially those connected with the President's powers as commander-in-chief. The few signs of reconciliation made no headway. The President's 21 November broadcast summed up grimly: 'Lebanon is disintegrating before our very eyes'.

IRAQ

Iraq stayed isolated and hostile, especially to Syria and the PLO, until Camp David (see pp. 174, 176–7) produced reconciliation and a Baghdad summit. There were more anti-Kurdish operations and a ruthless reaction to communist proselytization in the army. Big development projects involved many contracts with capitalist countries.

In January Iraq refused Algerian and Libyan pleas to join the anti-Sadat conference in Algiers, calling vainly for a meeting in Baghdad to form a purely rejectionist front (no recognition of, or negotiation with, Israel).

A bloody Iraqi-PLO feud arose from Iraq's harbouring of the Palestinian gangster Abu Nidal (already condemned to death by the PLO) whose men were accused of murdering PLO representatives in London and elsewhere. Violent reprisals followed against Iraqis in various capitals. Iraq also continued organizing subversion against Syria and quarrelled with Libya, which supported the PLO.

This all changed in the autumn after Camp David, which soon brought a reconciliation with Syria. After exchanging presidential messages, President Asad of Syria visited Baghdad—for the first time in five years— from 24-26 October and signed with President Ahmad Hasan al Bakr a 'National Charter for Joint Action', condemning imperialism, zionism and Egyptian 'treason' and establishing a joint higher political organization with military, economic and other committees. Communications were re-opened and discussions started on sharing Euphrates water and re-activating oil pipelines closed in 1976. In early November Baghdad organized an outwardly harmonious summit and there was a reconciliation, not quite whole-hearted, with the PLO (see p. 175).

An outrage unconnected with inter-Arab feuds was the murder in London on 9 July of a former Iraqi Prime Minister, which led the UK to expel eleven Iraqi agents and Iraq seriously to threaten UK exports.

The Ba'ath was ruthless with communists and Kurds, despite their nominal participation in government. On 7 June the Revolutionary Command Council (RCC) admitted that 21 Iraqi communists had been shot in May for forming cells in the army: a communist coup was even suspected. This and Iraqi loyalty to Eritrea against Soviet-backed Ethiopia cooled Soviet-Iraqi relations. Iraq had long bought non-military items mostly from capitalist countries and seemed now to be trying to reduce dependence on Soviet arms. In June the French Defence Minister discussed arms sales in Baghdad: the commander-in-chief of the French air force came in October. On 12 December, when Saddam Hussein, the Vice-President and RCC strong man, revisited Moscow, Iraq was reported dissatisfied with Soviet arms supplies.

Deportations and depopulation of the Turkish and Persian frontiers to prevent gun-running provoked continued Kurdish unrest. In July Turkish newspapers reported incendiary bombings of frontier villages. Kurdish resistance suffered from feuding between partisans of Mustafa Barzani and those led from Syria by Jallal Talabani.

Though often on bombing terms with other Arabs, Iraq remained friendly with Iran: many visits were exchanged and on 6 October Iraq obliged Iran by expelling the Shia firebrand Khomeini. Nor was there much open friction with Saudi Arabia: though Iraq still opposed a Gulf security pact, it was reported to be cooperating with Iran and Saudi Arabia to ensure freedom of Gulf navigation.

As shown by the executions of communists, internal security, especially fear of anti-Ba'ath activity in the armed forces, preoccupied the regime. On 6 July an RCC decree forbade, on pain of death, retired soldiers or policemen from working for non-Ba'ath parties. On 6 June Saddam Hussein warned against religious, presumably Shia, opposition (the Ba'ath being mainly Sunni). But on the 14 July anniversary 260 political prisoners were officially reported released.

If Mr Hyde often ran diplomacy and security, Dr Jekyll kept his place at economics. In May the Government claimed to have given $2,200 million in 1977 to developing countries. Most government wages rose 50 per cent in January and a social security scheme was reported in May to give old-age pensions to 500,000 peasants. Impressive development and housing projects involved extensive cooperation with capitalist countries, especially Japan. Revolutionary anniversaries were celebrated with mass inaugurations of projects. Of the total budget, 37 per cent was for investment and by comparison with 1977 this had increased more than current expenditure. Oil exports were running at about 2·1 million barrels a day and were expected to match 1976 and 1977; and although the Oil Minister on 1 March advocated reducing dependence on oil he anticipated increased exploration. More Kirkuk production would, it was forecast, enable Iraq to meet increased Soviet demand. A Soviet-equipped oilfield near Basra, promising an extra 2·5 million tons per annum, opened on 7 April. In OPEC Iraq continued to be much less accommodating than Saudi Arabia, this time with more success.

In January Iraq cut off oil supplies to Turkey, which owed arrears of $300 million, but resumed them in September after an agreement, signed in August, to liquidate the arrears by accepting Turkish exports.

Chapter 3

SAUDI ARABIA—YEMEN ARAB REPUBLIC—PEOPLE'S DEMOCRATIC REPUBLIC
OF YEMEN—KUWAIT—BAHREIN—QATAR—UNITED ARAB EMIRATES—OMAN

SAUDI ARABIA

ALTHOUGH 1978 appeared to be tranquil and was characterized by continuing prosperity, there was a distinct and growing feeling of insecurity among some members of the ruling dynasty. King Khalid's health continued to give rise to some concern, but the heart operation performed on him in the USA in October was judged to have been successful. Crown Prince Fahd was still regarded as the certain successor to the King but there appeared to be little agreement as to who would be the next Crown Prince. The most serious doubts, however, arose from foreign rather than from domestic affairs. President Sadat's continued search for an agreement with Israel caused wide dissension within the Arab world and Saudi Arabia had little reason to welcome any development likely to increase the influence of the more radical opponents of Israel. The Lebanese civil war continued its bloody course with no lasting solution in sight, while across the Persian Gulf the ostensible stability of the Shah's regime crumbled rapidly in the face of massive public opposition and civil unrest.

A traditional tenet in the foreign policy of Saudi Arabia—opposition to the spread of communism—took on even greater significance in the light of the pro-Russian coup in Afghanistan in late April, the increased involvement of the USSR in the Red Sea area and the violent coups on Saudi Arabia's southern frontiers in the Yemen Arab Republic and the People's Democratic Republic of Yemen in June. In the face of this apparently inexorable increase in the regional influence of the USSR, Riyadh looked for evidence of counter-activity by the USA and was alarmed by the apparent lack of response from Washington. It was noteworthy that the French military action in Zaïre received strong public support from Saudi Arabia. The unwillingness, or the inability, of President Carter to offer effective assistance to his avowed ally the Shah began to raise doubts in some Saudi minds about the value of the much-vaunted special relationship with the USA.

The feeling of insecurity was increased by the realization that, despite its enormous wealth, Saudi Arabia had fewer effective diplomatic or political weapons at its disposal than might be thought. Riyadh rejected the proposed Camp David agreements and was believed to have warned President Sadat that if he were to sign a separate agreement with Israel then subsidies from Saudi Arabia would be reduced and could even be terminated; but the Egyptian leader calculated that other nations, particularly the USA, would be prepared to give financial assistance to his country if there was a real prospect of peace with Israel. The massive size of the Soviet effort in supplying military equipment and other assistance to Ethiopia meant that Riyadh was left without an effective means of strengthening the opponents of that Government unless Washington was prepared to back such a policy. Events in the PDRY showed that Saudi attempts to buy political compliance with financial subsidies were by no means assured of automatic success.

Relations with the USA were improved, albeit briefly, in May by the Senate's confirmation of President Carter's decision to sell 60 F-15 aircraft to Saudi Arabia at a cost of $2,400 million; but it was realized that it would be at least three years before the aircraft were delivered and Saudi pilots had received the necessary degree of training. In June Saudi Arabia was able to prevent any increase in oil prices by OPEC, and while the Government regretted the decline in the value of the US dollar it continued to resist any moves away from the exclusive use of that currency for the pricing of oil.

Oil production fell in the early months of the year but it increased sharply at the end of the year as Iranian supplies diminished rapidly. The Government's intention remained that of maintaining an average daily production of some 8·5 million barrels over the year as a whole, and more efforts were made to increase to about one-third of the total the proportion of heavy oil exported. Income from petroleum was believed to exceed $115 million per day, and monetary reserves continued to rise at a rate in excess of $1,000 million per month. In August Saudi Arabia finally secured the seat on the board of the IMF which it had sought. The number of directors was increased to 21 so that no country lost its previous board membership.

Internal economic developments proceeded at a somewhat slower pace than in the past, as it was realized that some of the projects which had been begun were expensive and were unlikely to prove competitive or profitable. A desire to retain Islamic values and an awareness of the potential dangers of continuing to increase the size of the expatriate labour force were also factors in the fresh evaluation of development plans. A re-emphasis of religious values was seen in the imposition of traditional punishments for crimes such as breaking the ban on the sale and consumption of alcohol, and in the decision to restrict employment opportunities for both native and expatriate women. Hopes continued to be expressed that minerals other than oil might be discovered in commercial quantities, but there were few signs of activity apart from the opening of an incline to investigate possible gold deposits at Mahd adh Dhabab, some 200 miles north-west of Jeddah.

One of the most significant developments occurred at the very end of the year when it was reported that the USSR had recently approached Riyadh with a view to establishing diplomatic relations and to making purchases of Saudi Arabian oil.

YEMEN ARAB REPUBLIC

Political life continued to be violent in 1978 with attempted coups in May and October and the assassination of President Ahmad al Ghashmi in June. Since coming to power in October 1977 after the assassination of his predecessor (see AR 1977, p. 192) al Ghashmi had sought to maintain the loyalty of the armed forces by improving the conditions of military service, while at the same time he had strengthened relations with Saudi Arabia. In return for following the wish of Riyadh to eschew any attempt at unification with the marxist regime of the People's Democratic Republic of Yemen the President had secured considerable financial subsidies from Saudi Arabia.

In February it was announced that a Constituent People's Assembly was to be formed with 99 members, and it was envisaged that elections for the People's Assembly, which had been in suspense since 1974, would be held before the end of the year. Such hopes were dashed as more traditional ways of politics reasserted themselves. The first open signs of discontent emerged in May when it was reported that Major Abdullah Abdul Alim, the commander of the paratroop brigade, had led an insurrection among the troops stationed near the important southern town of Taiz. Major Alim had been a colleague of al Ghashmi and was a member of the three-man Presidential Council which had been created in October 1977. After this unsuccessful coup he was believed to have fled to the PDRY.

It was from there that the next violent intervention in the politics of the YAR was planned. On 24 June an emissary from the regime in Aden entered al Ghashmi's office carrying a briefcase; when this was opened it exploded, killing both the President and the envoy. It was believed that the President of the PDRY, Salim Rubai Ali, who was himself executed two days later after a bloody coup in Aden (see p. 191), did not know of the plan to kill al Ghashmi. According to informed observers the plot was more likely to have been the work of the powerful secretary general of the National Liberation Front in the PDRY, Abdul Fattah Ismail. The reason for the latter's hostility to al Ghashmi lay in the close ties which had developed between the YAR and Saudi Arabia. Immediately after the assassination in Sana a four-man Provisional Presidential Council was created under the chairmanship of Abdul Karim al Arashi, the Speaker of the Constituent Assembly, and diplomatic relations were broken with the PDRY. Saudi Arabia was quick to condemn the murder and it promised to provide any assistance necessary to preserve the stability and integrity of the YAR.

Saudi Arabia and the YAR sought an emergency session of the League of Arab States to condemn the PDRY regime and the meeting opened in Cairo on 1 July. After two days of debate a resolution was passed calling on members of the League to freeze political relations with the PDRY, to suspend economic and cultural cooperation and to cancel any technical assistance extended to Aden. This was the first time that the Arab League had imposed sanctions on one of its members. It was later suggested that the decision might have had the unwitting effect of making the regime in Aden even more pro-marxist in its policies and of deepening its dependence on the USSR and the communist bloc. A demand by the YAR for the expulsion of the PDRY from the Arab League could not be met, for such a resolution would have required the consent of all the other members of that organization and five of them—Iraq, Syria, Algeria, Libya and the representative of the PLO—were not unintentionally absent from the Cairo meeting.

On 17 July it was announced that the new President of the YAR was to be Lieut.-Colonel Ali Abdullah Saleh and that al Arashi would be the Vice President. The new head of state, a member of the powerful Hashid tribe from the north, had played an important part in the coup which had brought Colonel Ibrahim al Hamdi to power in June 1974. It was widely believed that the new President would continue al Ghashmi's policy of maintaining very close relations with Saudi Arabia and of opposing any rapprochement with the PDRY.

In September seven men alleged to have taken part in the May coup attempt were executed, others having been sentenced to death in absentia. On 15 October there was another attempted coup in the capital city, but this was frustrated by units of the tank corps and air force which remained loyal to the President. The YAR Foreign Minister, Abdullah al Asnag, later indicated that the PDRY regime had again been responsible for the planning of the coup, and other informed observers believed that Iraqi and Russian agents might also have been involved. Trials of alleged participants were held and twelve of those found guilty were executed in early November. These executions gave rise to a brief protest demonstration by Arab students at the YAR embassy in Moscow.

The domestic economy remained weak throughout 1978. The absence of a million or so Yemeni men working abroad—chiefly in Saudi Arabia— meant that children still constituted an important element of the labour force and the minimum legal age for employment remained at only ten years. Exports continued to consist largely of cotton and coffee and they showed little increase in volume or value. Imports, however, went on rising rapidly and some estimates put their value at over 60 times those of exports. With such an adverse balance of trade, and with domestic inflation continuing at a high level, subsidies from Saudi Arabia and remittances from citizens working abroad played an ever more important part in sustaining the domestic economy.

PEOPLE'S DEMOCRATIC REPUBLIC OF YEMEN

The year was characterized by the development of even closer relations with the USSR and by a renewal of political violence. The expulsion of Russian experts from Somalia in November 1977 (see AR 1977, p. 214) was followed by the transfer of a Soviet dry dock from Berbera to Aden, and in February the Prime Minister of the PDRY, Mr Ali Nasir Muhammad, visited Moscow for talks with Mr Brezhnev and Mr Kosygin. Discussions were concerned chiefly with events in the Horn of Africa and the two countries expressed support for the Ethiopian Government in its struggle against both Somalia and the Eritrean separatist groups.

The PDRY became an increasingly important staging-post for the shipment of Soviet military supplies to Ethiopia. Russian aircraft refuelled at Khormaksar airport near Aden and oil products from the refinery at Little Aden were supplied to Ethiopia. It was also reported that troops from the PDRY had been sent to fight alongside the Ethiopian army in its Eritrean campaign. Some military equipment previously supplied to the PDRY by the USSR was also transferred to Ethiopia. Russian military advisers were believed to have arrived in greater numbers during the year. The German Democratic Republic continued to provide training for the police force, while more Cuban instructors were believed to have joined the paramilitary forces.

Internal political unrest came to a head on 26 June when, after fierce fighting in Aden, the President of the PDRY, Salim Rubai Ali, was overthrown. He was tried summarily together with two other members of the National Liberation Front, Mr Jassem Saleh and Mr Ali Salem al Awar, and all three were executed by firing squad the same day. It was reported that Cuban pilots had been engaged in attacks against the presidential palace and that vessels of the Russian navy had shelled targets in Aden and settlements on the Hadhramaut coast. Estimates of casualties caused by these actions ranged as high as 6,000 killed or wounded, but the official report said that 40 people had been killed and about 115 injured. Some members of the army and air force loyal to the President were reported to have sought refuge in the Yemen Arab Republic and there were a series of border clashes with the YAR and Saudi Arabia for some weeks after the coup.

That violent upheaval followed only two days after the assassination of the President of the YAR (see above, p. 189) and it was widely believed that the two events were linked. According to the new regime in Aden the executed President had tried to replace the collective leadership of the country by a more personal type of rule and this had been resisted by the popular militias. Informed sources tended to discount this explanation and suggested instead that the powerful secretary general of the National Liberation Front, Abdul Fattah Ismail, had staged the coup in order to prevent the President from seeking better relations with the YAR and with Saudi Arabia. Salim Rubai Ali was reported to have been opposed to Russian use of facilities in the PDRY for sending military aid to Ethiopia and to have wished to reduce dependence on the communist bloc. The former President had also shown signs of wishing to improve relations with Somalia and of seeking financial assistance from Arab oil producing states to help rebuild the very weak and depressed economy of the PDRY. Abdul Fattah Ismail, on the other hand, wished to strengthen the PDRY's links with the USSR.

After the coup a major purge took place within the National Liberation Front and a five-man Presidential Council was created under the chairmanship of Ali Nasir Muhammad. The other members were Abdul Fattah Ismail, who retained the influential position of secretary general of the NLF, Muhammad Saleh Mutea, the Foreign Minister, Lieut.-Colonel Ali Ahmad Nasir al Antar, the Minister of Defence, and Ali Abdul Razzaq Badib, the Minister of Culture and Tourism. The new regime was widely regarded as being more receptive to the wishes of the USSR and this caused alarm in several neighbouring countries, particularly in Saudi Arabia. In October it was announced that a new political party was to be formed which would replace the NLF and other groups and that it would be known as the Yemen Socialist Party. The only discernible difference of opinion between the new regime and the USSR occurred over the question of Israel. The PDRY, together with the other so-called 'rejection front' states, continued to express total opposition to any settlement with Israel, even one negotiated under the auspices of the Geneva conference of which the USSR was co-chairman.

KUWAIT

The year began with a 40-day period of mourning for the late ruler, Sheikh Sabah al Salim al Sabah, who had died on the last day of 1977 (see AR 1977, OBITUARY, p. 514). His successor was Sheikh Jabir al Ahmad al Jabir al Sabah, and an announcement on 31 January named Sheikh Saad al Abdullah al Salim al Sabah as Crown Prince and Heir Apparent. Sheikh Saad had previously held simultaneously the posts of Minister of Defence and Minister of the Interior. He became Prime Minister in the new 19-member Cabinet formed after the period of mourning had ended, with few changes in personnel or responsibility.

The year was relatively quiet politically and the National Assembly remained in suspension. Kuwait condemned the proposed Camp David agreements and continued to express considerable reservations about President Sadat's peace initiative. It insisted on the need for a restoration of the rights of the Palestinian people—a view which was doubtless influenced by the size of the Palestinian community in Kuwait. On 15 June Mr Ali Yasin, the head of the PLO in Kuwait, was murdered at his home. It was widely believed that he had been killed by a member of an extremist guerrilla group, and the al Fatah organization accused Iraq of harbouring those responsible.

The Government continued to emphasize consolidation rather than expansion as the theme of economic policy and it stressed that any future growth would have to be gradual and carefully controlled. While this message was seen as soundly-based there were doubts about the degree to which such a policy could be implemented. It was observed that there already existed a very large foreign labour force within Kuwait and that any serious and sustained contraction of economic activity would cause unemployment, which in turn could lead to political unrest.

In the early months of the year, when there was a glut of oil supplies, Kuwait experienced some difficulty in selling its oil. The fact that all of the oil produced was of the heavy variety made the position even more difficult and for a time the price was reduced by ten US cents per barrel. A more serious cause for concern was the long-term decline in the value of the US dollar, and it was calculated that Kuwait was losing at least one million dollars per day in revenue because of this factor. Several spokesmen expressed the wish to see the price of oil expressed in terms of a basket of currencies instead of US dollars. Kuwait welcomed the scheme for increases in the price of oil announced at the end of the year. Contracts were signed for the expansion of the oil loading facilities at Mina al Ahmadi; these included provision of a berth which could handle tankers of up to 500,000 tons deadweight. Plans were also announced for the modernization of the oil refinery at Mina al Ahmadi.

BAHREIN

The domestic political scene remained tranquil in 1978, with no sustained demand for the reconvention of the National Assembly, which had been suspended in August 1975. On 28 January new exchange rates were introduced, as in Qatar and the United Arab Emirates, based on IMF Special Drawing Rights; as a result the Bahreini dinar was revalued by approximately 2 per cent against the US dollar.

Oil production and throughput at the refinery both declined, but domestic consumption rose, leaving less oil available for export. The Budget, which was announced in March, forecast that government expenditures would remain constant in real terms; the shortfall in oil income would be compensated by increased revenues from taxes and fees on the banking sector, which continued to expand. The Government gave renewed emphasis to the service sector and showed continued reluctance to embark on further large-scale industrial and construction projects. The sole exception was the announcement that a contract had been signed for the building of a gas gathering and liquefaction plant. The performance of the large dry dock which had been opened in 1977 (see AR 1977, p. 196) was less than encouraging; for expatriate labour costs were very high and it was found difficult to secure an even flow of repair work.

G

QATAR

The year was a quiet one for Qatar with no noteworthy political developments. On 28 January new exchange rates were introduced, as in Bahrein and the United Arab Emirates, calculated on the basis of IMF Special Drawing Rights. The effect was to increase the value of the Qatari riyal by about 1·8 per cent against the US dollar. In contrast with several of its neighbours Qatar's oil production was greater than in 1977 and the policy of industrial expansion was continued. Plans were announced to increase the capacity of the existing petrochemical industry by the construction of a new polyethylene plant. The capacity of the cement industry was also to be enlarged. A Japanese firm was awarded a large contract for the reconstruction of the natural gas liquefaction plant at Umm Said which had been destroyed by fire in 1977 (see AR 1977, p. 197). It was hoped that this new plant would be ready for operation by the end of 1980.

UNITED ARAB EMIRATES

This was a somewhat uneasy year in the United Arab Emirates, with increased signs of strain between the two most important members of the Federation, Abu Dhabi and Dubai, the renewed outbreak of minor but troublesome border disputes between the UAE and Oman and between Dubai and Sharjah, a general and notable slackening in economic activity (particularly in the construction industry and the property sector), and a growing and widespread sense of apprehension about the fate of the Shah and the political future of Iran.

The first signs of tension between Abu Dhabi and Dubai were seen in early February over the decision to implement plans which were reported to have been already agreed for the unification of the armed forces of the member states of the Federation. Dubai claimed that it had not been consulted over the appointment of the son of Sheikh Zaid, the ruler of Abu Dhabi, as commander-in-chief of the unified forces. The fact that Sheikh Zaid was absent abroad when the decision was announced deepened suspicions in Dubai about his motives. Later in the year there were widespread rumours that Dubai was about to secede from the Federation, but these were officially denied. It was reported that Great Britain, Saudi Arabia and Iran had all made offers to mediate between Abu Dhabi and Dubai, but relations between the two states remained somewhat strained throughout the rest of the year, and further moves towards the unification of military and civilian activities under federal control went into abeyance.

There continued to be a notable lack of overall economic planning at the federal level and the projected National Planning Board was not instituted. The boom years which had followed the massive oil price increases of 1973 were seen to be at an end and the property and construction sectors remained depressed. The effects of this were most noticeable in Sharjah and were least in evidence in Dubai. In mid-December the federal Government announced its intention of taking over all the real estate and industrial loans which had been made by the commercial banks, but no further details were announced. The initial reaction in local financial circles was to welcome the decision to take over the housing and property loans but reluctance was expressed at the possibility of losing opportunities to provide industrial finance.

Several of the industrial projects already in operation, including the dry dock and ship repair yard in Dubai, were reported to be making losses. Some projects collapsed during the year, notably the fishmeal processing venture in Ras al Khaimah. That state suffered a further blow when offshore drilling again failed to find oil in commercial quantities. An earlier and erroneous report that drilling had been successful gave rise to claims by Oman that the suggested oilfield lay in its territory and not in that of Ras al Khaimah. Exploration drilling off Umm al Qaiwain also caused disappointment when it failed to find natural gas in commercial quantities. Dubai went ahead with its previously announced plans to create a massive industrial zone at Jebel Ali, and the expansion of the already huge port continued; but it became clear during the year that the UAE was over-supplied with such facilities. This cast doubt on the viability of plans to construct a new harbour at Fujairah.

Oil production fell overall in the first six months of the year but Dubai again proved to be exceptional and experienced an increase in output. Abu Dhabi announced plans in July to construct a new liquefaction plant to process gas from onshore wells at a total cost of approximately US$1,600 million. On 28 January the UAE, in common with Bahrein and Qatar, announced new exchange rates based on IMF Special Drawing Rights. This meant a revaluation of the UAE dirham by approximately 0·5 per cent against the US dollar.

OMAN

The year was a quiet one in domestic politics. Minor Cabinet changes were announced in June when a new Ministry of Posts, Telegraphs and Telephones was created. The Ministry of Communications, which had previously handled those matters, retained responsibility for roads, ports and civil aviation. Oman remained a country without railways. The fact that the Sultan still did not have an heir continued to cause some disquiet about the future of the dynasty.

The upheavals in the Yemen Arab Republic and the People's Democratic Republic of Yemen (see pp. 188-92) were viewed with considerable alarm in Muscat, and Oman was quick to condemn the regime in Aden for the assassination of President Ahmad al Ghashmi in Sana. The Sultan repeatedly criticized the USSR for seeking to expand its influence by military means in the Horn of Africa. The announcement on 26 May that diplomatic relations were to be established with China, and the subsequent and much-publicized visit by the Minister of State for Foreign Affairs, Qais Abdul Munim Zawawi, to Peking, were seen as signs that Oman was endeavouring to widen its circle of support against the USSR. Oman continued to commend the Egyptian peace initiative.

There were fears of renewed guerrilla activity after five British engineers were killed in an ambush on 1 June near Taqa on the Dhofar coast. Two other engineers escaped with their lives in this attack. There were occasional reports of rifle-fire attacks against military helicopters flying over the Dhofar mountains but generally speaking security remained good in this once troubled province.

The domestic economy continued to cause concern, as oil production remained in decline. There were hopes that new oil discoveries made in Dhofar during the year would help to offset decreases in production in other fields, but it was estimated that this relief would not be available until equipment had been installed and that this would take at least two years.

Experts from the IMF who visited Oman criticized the persistent reliance on grants to cover budget deficits and they urged that considerable attention should be given to schemes which would increase domestic revenues from the non-oil sector of the economy.

Chapter 4

SUDAN—LIBYA—TUNISIA—WESTERN SAHARA—ALGERIA—MOROCCO

SUDAN

As a result of the national reconciliation which began in 1979, President Nimairi appointed some members of the traditional political parties to the Politbureau and the Central Committee of the Sudan Socialist Union (SSU). Prominent among these were al-Sasiq al-Mahdi, Hassan al-Turabi (leader of the Muslim Brothers) and Ahmed al-Mirghani (the brother of the leader of the Khatmiyya). The national reconciliation was further supported by the return of the Rev. Philip Abbas Ghaboush, the president of the United Sudanese National Liberation Front, and Elia Duang, former secretary of the Patriotic Front for the Liberation of Southern Sudan. The President freed from detention 29 members of the Communist Party. Sharif al-Hindi, a prominent leader of the National Front (composed of traditional parties), continued to live in exile despite an agreement with the Government in which he agreed to return to the Sudan and to dissolve the National Front. He claimed that the promises of the agreement had not been implemented and he continued to oppose the regime.

The reconciliation ran into further trouble when al-Sadiq al-Mahdi, who supported the supremancy of the SSU and regional autonomy for the South, resigned from the Politbureau but later withdrew his resignation. The reasons reported for his resignation were the slow pace of the national reconciliation and the Sudan's continued support of Egypt over the Camp David agreement, which might alienate the Sudan from other Arab countries.

Three events attracted publicity. First, the Khartoum International Fair, in which 100 firms from 30 countries participated, was opened in January. Secondly, heavy rain in July affected the Gezira scheme and approximately half a million people were made homeless and $1\frac{1}{2}$ million acres of crops were submerged. The President appealed for international help and a number of Arab countries rendered assistance in kind or cash. Thirdly, the Sudan played host to the fifteenth summit conference of the Organization of African Unity in which 30 heads of state and four heads of government participated (see Pt. XI, Ch. 6). President Nimairi as present chairman warned against foreign intervention in Africa lest the continent should become an arena of confrontation among the super-powers.

In his capacity as chairman of the Arab League's Solidarity Committee the President visited a number of Arab countries to attempt a reconciliation, particularly between Egypt and other Arab countries opposed to President Sadat's peace initiative. Sudan's relations with Libya improved and an agreement was reached for the resumption of diplomatic relations after a break of two years. Diplomatic relations with Russia were also resumed. Ethiopia agreed to normalize relations with the Sudan but military operations by the Ethiopian Government against the Eritreans resulted in an additional influx of thousands of refugees to the Sudan.

Elections for the third People's National Assembly (comprising 304 members) were held and some followers of the traditional political parties were elected. Elections to the People's Regional Assembly (comprising 110 members) were also held and were followed by certain changes in the Executive. Joseph Lagu, the former Anyanya leader, was appointed president of the Southern Region High Executive Council in place of Abel Alier, who was defeated in the election but retained his position as Vice-President of the Republic.

President Nimairi carried out a reshuffle of his Government and dismissed some senior members of the SSU. He removed the Defence Minister, whose portfolio he resumed himself, and the Energy Minister. Seven new Ministers, a new prosecutor-general and a new chief of staff of armed forces were appointed. It was reported that 17 high-ranking officers were dismissed from the army because of their criticism of the policies of the regime. The army was supplied with weapons by Western countries after the Sudan discontinued its reliance on Russian military equipment. West Germany supplied army helicopters, the United States delivered six Hercules C-130 military transport aircraft and agreed to the sale of 12 fighter planes, and France agreed to supply the Sudan with 14 Mirage aircraft.

Arab oil-producing countries continued their financial investment in the Sudan. The Arab Fund for Social and Economic Development declared it would invest $3,500 million over ten years to develop food production. The Kuwait Fund for Arab Economic Development made a loan of $17½ million for railway development projects. The British Ministry of Overseas Development would make available £14 million over three years to finance development projects. France agreed to provide privileged credits to the amount of $21 million. Also, the French oil company, Total, sold 75 per cent of its holding to the Sudan Government. West Germany agreed to make a grant of $38½ million to finance rural electrification and transport projects. Japan promised to lend the Sudan $21 million for water supply projects. The International Development Association, a World Bank affiliate, agreed to provide a total of $76 million to finance mechanized farming, agricultural research in Western Sudan, port expansion and livestock marketing.

The policy of rapid and diverse economic development continued to be pursued. Saudi Arabia agreed to give $8 million to finance a micro-wave telecommunication link between Port Sudan and Saudi Arabia. A cotton spinning mill was to be set up at Port Sudan at a cost of $27 million, and the International Finance Corporation would provide a loan of $6½ million for a cotton mill at Wad Medani. Three steel silos, for storing cereals, would be built in the Southern Region at a cost of Fr. 20 million financed by loans from private banks and companies. The Sudanese-Egyptian joint technical committee on transport agreed to implement the project to link Egypt's railways with Sudan.

Despite local and international investment the rate of inflation was rising and there was an acute shortage of basic commodities. A conservative estimate put Sudan's foreign debt at $1,000 million and there was delay in paying interest on loans or repaying loans. Under pressure from the IMF and Saudi Arabia the Government devalued the Sudanese pound by 20 per cent. In consequence, the IMF approved credits of $62.8 million to help Sudan's balance of payments. To meet current difficulties, the Saudi Arabian Monetary Fund loaned $7.2 million, and a grant of £15 million was given by Britain. Also the Netherlands cancelled Sudan's repayment of loans amounting to $18.6 million and Britain converted its foreign aid and loans to the Sudan into grants and cancelled interest payments due.

In view of petrol shortages, the Jedda-based Islamic Development Bank granted the Sudan $10 million for the purchase of refined petroleum. The Sudan concluded an agreement with Egypt whereby Sudan would supply 50,000 bales of cotton in exchange for 140,000 tons of crude oil from Egypt. Reports about the discovery of large quantities of oil in southern Kordofan and the Southern Region were not clear as to the amount found and the viability of extracting oil.

LIBYA

During the year Colonel Qadafi elaborated his doctrine of a third way between capitalism and communism and enforced it upon a populace long accustomed to apathetic acceptance of the whims of its ruler. In February he published the second volume of his *Green Book*, which, he claimed, 'not only solves the problems of material production but also prescribes the comprehensive solution of the problems of human society'. He preached that food, drink, clothing and transport should be free, for no man could have liberty if someone else controlled his essential needs: no man should exploit another or own more than his basic requirements, even if earned through his own skill or industry. No one should own land although all might use it.

In pursuance of these doctrines Qadafi in September 'abolished' workers and everyone became a 'partner in production'. The people were instructed 'to march now and take over their establishments . . . (and) . . . crush with their feet and forever the slavery of wages'. Within a month 58 factories had been taken over by their employees and at the end of the year all private importing firms had been replaced by worker cooperatives. A further development was the declaration in December that money would be abolished in 1979. December was indeed a busy month for Qadafi but he found time to salute the spread of his ideals to Australia and Curaçoa, to propose a change in the Islamic calendar which, he said, should date from the death of the Prophet rather than from his flight to Medina, to enunciate a new slogan 'Power, wealth and arms in the hands of the people' and, for the first time for more than a year, to resign all his offices, although he promised that he would continue to devote all his attention to the revolution and 'to guard the authority of the people'.

Even before these measures there were rumours of conspiracies against Qadafi, and religious leaders questioned whether his socialist measures were consonant with Islam. The business community was naturally thrown into panic: trades like barber and cafe-owner were declared parasitic, hotel-keepers found that their lodgers now owned the rooms in which they stayed, and one shop in three in Tripoli closed. In May conscription for three years in the army or four in the other services was ordained for all aged between 18 and 35 and this caused still further gloom.

Economically it was a good year; for, thanks to a unilateral rise in prices, oil revenues increased although the deliberate policy of prolonging stocks caused less to be exported. Attention was paid to the creation of other industries and a contract for a $515 million chemical complex was awarded to a German company. There was particular stress on agriculture, with the aim of self-sufficiency in food, and this sector received the largest share of the development budget announced in January. There were great improvements in communications; the docks at Tripoli were enlarged and a new airport opened there in September, although the old habit of seizure of all printed material by the customs was maintained. A hindrance to development was the fact that already one-third of the labour force was foreign.

There was the usual large increase in the armed forces and the most modern MiG 25s were shown on the Revolution Day parade. Qadafi hoped, moreover, to have within two years the largest navy in the Mediterranean after those of France and Italy.

Reaction to President Sadat's peace initiative dominated Qadafi's policy in the Arab world. In January he offered Egypt 'hundreds of tanks' for use against Israel and in May he declared his willingness to unite the armed forces of the two countries. Receiving no response, Qadafi organized in October a 'trial' of Sadat for treason to the Arab nation: few journalists bothered to attend the proceedings in Tripoli. Qadafi made a prolonged effort to woo Jordan into the rejectionist front by means of money. Syria, previously attacked for its policy in Lebanon, was also courted, and relations with the Sudan, broken in 1976, were restored in February.

Qadafi's dream of a united North Africa continued to make contradictory his policy towards his western neighbours. In January there were rumours that he had had a hand in stirring up the labour unrest in Tunisia, but in March he agreed to settle the dispute about territorial limits in the Gulf of Gabes (see AR 1977, p. 203) and to exchange commercial delegations. In May, however, he refused to receive the Tunisian Prime Minister, who was in Tripoli for a summit meeting. He vacillated also with regard to Algeria and the Sahara; for in April, to the annoyance of his neighbour, he invited Ould Daddah of Mauritania and talked of a negotiated settlement. In June he declared that force was the only solution and hinted that he would support Polisario, but in September he returned to his call for negotiations. Despite his calls for Maghreb unity, relations with Algeria had more than a hint of rivalry for influence, particularly in Tunisia, Niger and Chad.

Throughout the year Qadafi consistently advocated that Africa should settle its own problems, and he reduced his support for those dependent upon foreign bayonets, even those of his friends. He gave aid to Niger, Mozambique and Swapo in a bid to lessen their reliance upon outside aid. This policy was extended to Malta, although a startled Mintoff found that he had to put his case for financial help to a General People's Congress, which recommended that Malta should accept Islam, Arabic and popular committees. Relations with Chad were broken in February when the Government of General Malloum complained to the UN Security Council about Libyan interference. They were soon restored and in March Qadafi apparently secured a triumph by helping to negotiate a peace settlement between the Government and the rebels, but in September Qadafi's former client, now Prime Minister of Chad, accused the Libyans of planning to annex half of his country.

Although the US took one-third of Libya's oil exports, the two Governments regarded each other with suspicion. America refused to export spare parts for Libyan aircraft, while Qadafi proclaimed that the US was the main terrorist power. In June he toured all the Russian satellites except Romania and in October hinted that he might join the Warsaw Pact. Rumours spoke of a Russian airbase at Kufra in the Libyan desert and of the possible supply of atomic weapons. France, which supported the Chad Government, was a target for the Colonel's abuse, being accused of military and economic colonialism and assailed with demands that it should liberate all the islands that it occupied (the same was said of Britain).

The Libyan Government showed itself anxious to disprove the old charge that it was the friend of all terrorists; the IRA was disavowed, the Moro kidnapping condemned and the murderers of the Egyptian journalist Siba'i denied entry. Nothing came of what could have been the most exciting foreign story of the year: in March Qadafi hinted that he might go to Pakistan and personally liberate Mr Bhutto from his death-cell.

TUNISIA

Until very recently Tunisia had given the impression of a peaceful country developing steadily under wise and stable leadership. Bourguiba had led the state since independence in 1957, and since 1970 there had been no change of a Prime Minister who appeared to eschew politics in favour of economic progress. Clearly there was some regionalism and some nepotism, and the bureaucracy of the single Destour Party (PSD) had ossified, but these did not appear matters of great importance. Underneath the surface there were, however, severe tensions: a revival of Islam, particularly among the young, led girl students to return to the veil and youths to attack bars and places of entertainment, while on the other extreme there was the clandestine marxist People's Unity Movement (MUP) associated with the exiled Ahmed ben Salah. As recorded last year (see AR 1977, pp. 204-5), all the movements of discontent came together under the banner of the trade union movement (UGTT) and its forceful

G*

leader Habib Achour, forming what the Prime Minister, Hedi Nouira, was to call 'an amalgam of unnatural alliances'.

In December 1977 Nouira decided to end a series of unofficial strikes by a show-down and dismissed his more liberal Minister of the Interior, Taha Belkhodja, an advocate of conciliation and of a more open society. Five more Ministers thereupon resigned, and there were by now far more politicians of importance outside the Government than within its ranks. Their number was further increased when on 10 January Achour resigned from the party Politbureau.

The first days of 1978 saw strikes by the phosphate workers and then on the railways. The UGTT then claimed that its local offices had been attacked and its representatives assaulted by members of the PSD militia and that in Sousse these elements had been assisted by the police: it therefore severed all relations with the Government and with the Destour Party and called for a general strike for 26 January. The situation quickly got out of hand, the demonstrators were joined by masses of unemployed teenagers, avid for loot, and Tunis was plunged into chaos as the security forces strongly reacted. According to official figures 51 people were killed (unofficially the number was put at 200), 346 were wounded (of whom 181 were from the security forces) and 1,187 arrested, including ten of the thirteen members of the UGTT executive and nineteen less important officials. The former Minister Ahmed Mestiri demanded an enquiry into government brutality, which had 'made an unbridgeable chasm' between itself and the people, and claimed that the riots had been provoked by the Party to provide an excuse to get rid of Achour. For Nouira there had been 'a premeditated plan' to plunge the country into chaos, while for yet others the cause had been a plot by young SPD militants to oust Nouira.

The first obvious effect was that the UGTT, deprived of its militants, humbled itself before the Government. In March, as a measure to remove the young unemployed from the streets, workless youths were conscripted into a civil force and kept in camps. An underground marxist newspaper appeared, but for the next few months the achievements of the Tunisian football team in the World Cup made politics of secondary importance. In June, however, Mestiri applied for a permit to form a Social Democratic Party: this was not forthcoming and Nouira appeared to have missed an opportunity of allowing a 'respectable' opposition.

More than half of those arrested in January were quickly released, but a series of trials started in July. In Sfax sentences of up to thirty months were given, while in Sousse 101 local UGTT officials were indicted for the possession of arms. Allegations of torture were made and officially denied. After a fortnight the Court ruled that the charge was not criminal but a matter of state security and was therefore beyond its competence: such a refusal to convict despite strong government pressure was rare outside the Western world and reflected credit upon the Tunisian judiciary.

In September the State Security Court sat to try Achour and his 29 lieutenants. Expectations of a spectacular trial were dashed: Achour, who had been close to the inner circle of government for twenty years, had threatened to reveal all the murky secrets of his former colleagues but in the end kept silence. The substance of the case was never discussed and nothing was said of Achour's real offence, which had been to try to change the system by intrigues with outsiders rather than by pressure from within. The defendants were mostly mute and, despite the prosecution's demand for death sentences, six were acquitted, eight were given suspended sentences while others were to be imprisoned for between six months and ten years. Achour, who received the heaviest term, was probably saved by the Government's desire not to create a martyr and by discreet pressure from the Western powers and from the ICFTU, of which he was a vice-president.

Naturally these labour troubles discouraged the foreign investment that was vital for development, although the Saudis made a loan to finance irrigation and some oil companies continued to prospect off-shore. Preoccupation with internal problems meant that there were no events in foreign policy worthy of record, apart from a successful visit to Washington by Nouira in November.

WESTERN SAHARA

In the early part of the year there were several strikes by French aircraft against Polisario raiding parties and it became clear that the Saharans would never be allowed to win their war. Their ability to do so anyway was questioned when the anniversary parade of the armed forces in May could muster only six cavalrymen, 25 camelmen and 350 infantry amidst growing rumours that the Algerians were becoming irritated at the intransigence of their proteges.

The situation was apparently transformed by the overthrow of the Mauritanian President on 10 July, whereupon Polisario proclaimed a cease-fire in the southern area. Against Morocco it continued its activities, claiming a series of dramatic military successes probably unequalled since Napoleon. In November it announced that the casualties inflicted in the past twelve months had been 6,794 killed, 5,379 wounded and 322 prisoners, while material destroyed was said to have included ten aircraft, 801 vehicles and 36 locomotives. Communiques told of spectacular raids deep into Morocco but these were not noticed by visitors in the areas concerned. In fact the main successes were the kidnapping of eight Spanish fishermen in April and the massacre of a further eight in October: the first group were released in October in return for some sort of recognition of Polisario.

A proposal in August for a 'mini-state' of that part of the former

Spanish Sahara which had been incorporated in Mauritania was quickly scotched by King Hassan. He offered, however, to take some Polisario leaders into his Cabinet.

Events took a dangerous turn on 27 August when for the first time since February 1976 a clash occurred between Moroccan and Algerian regular troops in which 12 Moroccans were killed some 70 km within their own borders. Further fighting took place at the end of September, when for the first time tanks were involved. Each side accused the other of preparing for war, but the disappearance from the scene of President Boumédienne damped things down and threw doubt over the whole future of Polisario.

ALGERIA

The death of a dictator must be the most important event in any year's history of a country and few dictators were more absolute than had been Houari Boumédienne, who died on 27 December (see OBITUARY). He had concentrated nearly all powers in his own hands, combining the Presidency of the Republic with that of the Revolutionary Council and of the Council of Ministers; he was also Minister of Defence and chief of the general staff and controlled civil service and religious affairs. He had emphasized his lofty pre-eminence by refusing to fill the posts of Vice-President and Prime Minister, and official action was paralysed from the time that he became ill in September. The Council of Ministers never met, the sole party had already been stripped of all initiative and the trade union movement existed merely to re-echo his orders. October he spent incommunicado in a Moscow hospital and a few days after his return in mid-November he went into an Algiers hospital from which he never emerged. Sixty-two specialists (surely some sort of record) were summoned to his bedside from places as diverse as Japan and Cuba.

Early in the year a surprising relationship became obvious. Algeria, aspiring to lead the Third World, differed from the USA on most issues of foreign policy, but the economic links between the two countries developed into what was almost a special link. It was calculated that the American stake in the country had become worth $10,000 million. America took 56 per cent of the oil that Algeria exported and 28 per cent of the liquid gas. It was building a gas plant at Arzew for $240 million, a plant for road-making equipment for $100 million, and a factory for colour television sets, and was administering a complex of technical colleges, while there were 2,500 Algerian students in the US. Some veteran socialists wailed that Algeria was selling its soul to the capitalists for economic progress.

Otherwise, from the development point of view, 1978 was a blank year between Plans. There were indications that some big prestige projects would be dropped and more stress put upon agriculture. While it ought to be self-sufficient, Algeria needed to import $700 million worth of food, mostly from France. This led to a serious imbalance of trade that soured relations, for the former imperial power preferred to take its oil from Saudi Arabia. There were also several angry attacks on French policy in Africa, but a visit by the Foreign Minister, Abdel Aziz Bouteflika, to Paris in August led to amicable statements on both sides.

In the Arab world Algeria devoted its energies to opposing Sadat's peace initiative and Boumédienne made several attempts to heal the rift between Syria and Iraq. Tension with Morocco over the Sahara continued and was exacerbated in December when Rabat was accused of dropping three tons of arms to its agents within Algeria. With its habitual churlishness Algeria refused to allow a Moroccan delegation to attend the funeral of Boumédienne.

MOROCCO

For Morocco 1978 was a difficult year, as inflation raged at twenty per cent and living standards fell, weakening the unity around the throne which had been so evident since the start of the Saharan question. In April miners, teachers and students amongst others went on strike and in May there were complaints of police brutality when airline employees came out. Morocco had had one of the most persistent failures of any developing country in achieving a balance between exports and imports, and nearly a quarter of the value of all exports was required merely to service the foreign debt. A series of bad harvests, three years of war in the south and generous efforts to develop the new Saharan provinces added to financial difficulties.

In June the King announced a series of austerity measures, raising taxes, devaluing the dirham and cutting imports by 20 per cent: luxury goods, such as washing machines and beer, were prohibited, licences had to be obtained for other articles and no relief was promised before 1981. The 1973-77 Plan, which had been based on the expectation that the price of phosphates would continue to rise, was replaced by a transitional plan, postponing major projects like the steel works at Nador and relying on savings and the investment of local rather than external funds. In October there were further cuts and the King warned of a growing suffering among the poor which was causing a gulf and upsetting social justice. However, things began to look brighter with announcements that oil had been found and that there was a hope of developing uranium from phosphates.

The exceptional economic relationship that grew between Algeria and the USA despite political incompatibility was exactly paralleled between

Morocco and Russia. In March the two Governments signed what Hassan II called 'the contract of the century', by which Moscow would make a loan of $9,000 million over twenty-five years, being repaid by the product of the enormous phosphate mine to be exploited with the money. The Russians were also to build housing for the workers and a railway to take out the phosphates to a newly-created port. Trading relations were already close with Russia, which took one-third of Morocco's citrus crop and supplied a quarter of Morocco's oil, and became yet more important with the signature in December of a fishing agreement which gave Russia rights along the entire Moroccan coast: Moscow thus implicitly recognized the disputed Sahara as part of Morocco. It was noticeable that Moscow refrained from comment on the Sahara or on Morocco's action in sending troops to Zaïre to combat left-wing forces there.

Conversely there was little trade with America, for the US had its own phosphates and its exports were too expensive. Washington's decision in April to delay answering a request for $200 million worth of arms was regarded as unfriendly in Rabat. In September Kenitra, the last US base in Africa, was closed, rendered obsolete by satellite intelligence and bases in Spain. At the end of November the King made his frequently postponed visit to America and this led to renewed cordiality.

Relations with Spain suffered as a result of what Rabat regarded as an increasingly equivocal attitude towards the Saharan problem. In October a speech by the Foreign Minister Boucetta, in which he spoke of the enclaves of Ceuta and Melilla, led to the cancellation of a proposed visit by King Juan Carlos. With France close friendship continued and again the two countries collaborated in moving Moroccan troops to Zaïre.

There was little political activity during the year apart from a meeting in October of 4,000 delegates of political independents in Casablanca. The independents, who dominated Parliament, were mostly loyal King's men and they decided to form a political party (RNI) 'to inject enthusiasm into the masses'. Very many of them were technocrats without any local power base, and the long-established Istiqlal sneered that they were 'a trunk without roots which would be blown down at the first storm'.

VI EQUATORIAL AFRICA

Chapter 1

ETHIOPIA

FOR Mengistu Haile-Maryam's Government, 1978 was a year of victories both against the Somalis in the south-east and against the Eritrean guerrilla movements in the north, though these were achieved through massive Soviet and Cuban intervention and at an appalling cost in human suffering. The Government's 'red terror' campaign against suspected domestic opponents, started in November 1977, continued until June, but was at its most intense from December 1977 to February, during which period about five thousand young people were executed and thirty thousand detained. Amnesty International reported the systematic torture of detainees. The campaign appeared to have succeeded in its aim of eradicating the marxist Ethiopian People's Revolutionary Party (EPRP). The Government reported nine attempts on Mengistu's life during the ten months to June, in one of which he was slightly wounded.

While Mengistu retained control throughout the year, divisions within the ruling council (Derg) were reported, both from those who feared over-reliance on the Soviet Union and from those who, with tacit Soviet support, wished to replace the military regime with a Communist Party Government. A crisis erupted in May when the Cuban embassy secretly brought into Ethiopia the exiled vice-president of one such party, Meison, which was supported especially by the trade unions; he was expelled, the Cuban ambassador also left, and the union leadership was purged. A further wave of arrests in the armed forces and political movements took place in October.

In south-east Ethiopia Somali guerrillas, who had occupied the whole Ogaden region in 1977, penetrated the city of Harar in January but were forced to withdraw. The Ethiopian forces made local counter-attacks in late January, and the Somali position became increasingly critical during February, as Soviet arms shipments and Cuban combat troops arrived in Ethiopia. The Somali Government failed in its appeals for arms to Western states, which, led by the United States, refused to supply them so long as Somalia occupied the territory of another African state; some Arab states, including Egypt and Saudi Arabia, supplied Somalia with financial aid and limited quantities of arms. On 12 February Somalia publicly committed troops to the Ogaden war, where fighting had until then ostensibly been conducted by guerrillas of the Western Somalia Liberation Front (WSLF).

The expected Ethiopian offensive opened on 4 March, with an attack led by a Cuban armoured brigade and some 10,000 Cuban troops on the Somali-held town of Jigjiga, which fell after two days' fighting. The Ethiopians then rapidly reoccupied the other main centres in the Ogaden, and on 9 March Somalia announced the withdrawal of its regular forces from the area. Ethiopia abided by an earlier undertaking not to invade Somalia itself. WSLF guerrillas continued fighting at greatly reduced intensity for the rest of the year, briefly capturing the town of Gode in June and attacking the recently reopened Djibouti–Addis Ababa railway line in July; the Ethiopians retaliated with air attacks on Somali frontier towns. Attacks on government troops and installations elsewhere in southern Ethiopia, including Arusi and Sidamo provinces, were claimed by two further guerrilla groups, the Oromo Liberation Front and the Somali Abbo Liberation Front.

After recapturing the Ogaden, the Ethiopians were able to turn their attention to Eritrea, where they held only four towns at the start of the year. The two main guerrilla movements, the Eritrean Liberation Front (ELF) and Eritrean People's Liberation Front (EPLF), formed a common command in April, but differences between the movements continued, and the third and smallest, the Saudi-backed People's Liberation Forces led by Osman Saleh Sabbe, was excluded. There were divisions also on the Ethiopian side, since the Cubans, who had earlier supported the Eritreans, refused to allow their troops to become directly involved, though a Cuban brigade was stationed in Asmara. However, the Soviet Union gave unqualified support to Ethiopia, and helped to plan and direct the operation; Russian specialists, especially pilots, appear to have been heavily involved in the fighting, using napalm and possibly also cluster bombs.

The first Ethiopian attempts to break the siege of the capital, Asmara, in mid-May were unsuccessful. A further series of coordinated attacks in July and August captured several centres in western Eritrea and raised the siege of Asmara. Keren, the last large town in guerrilla hands, fell in November after earlier attacks had been beaten off, and in the same month government forces reopened the road from Asmara to the port of Massawa. By the end of the year the situation was much as it had been two years previously, with the government holding the towns and guerrillas operating throughout the countryside, but both sides had suffered very heavy losses; in August, Ethiopia announced that thirteen thousand of her troops had been killed and thirty-three thousand wounded during the war.

In the adjoining province of Tigre, fighting took place in the first half of the year between rival anti-government groups, with the Tigre People's Liberation Front, allied to the EPLF, coming out on top. Clashes with government forces later in the year reflected the government's reoccupation of areas which it had earlier abandoned. The most conservative of the anti-government movements, the Ethiopian Democratic Union led by noblemen prominent in the Haile-Selassie regime, suffered from leadership divisions and appeared to have collapsed as an effective force.

The fighting led to an influx of refugees, totalling probably over a million, into the Somali Republic, Djibouti and the Sudan, placing enormous strains on food and medical supplies and the resources of the host governments. In addition, the worst desert locust swarms for several years were reported, their numbers being increased both by rainfall in the breeding areas and by the difficulties in spraying in the war zones.

As the above account suggests, relations with Cuba and the Soviet Union were very close, while those with the West were strained. President Castro visited Ethiopia in September, and in November Mengistu Haile-Maryam visited the USSR, with which he concluded a treaty of friendship and cooperation. An Ethiopian delegation attended the Comecon summit, and suggested that Ethiopia might join the organization. However, Western powers were careful not to strain relations with Ethiopia to breaking-point, and Ethiopian relations with Kenya remained close and friendly in the face of a common Somali threat. In November an important Ethiopian delegation visited France for talks on economic assistance, especially to the Djibouti–Addis Ababa railway.

SOMALIA

In a traumatic year, which saw military defeat and the collapse of hopes of Somali unification, President Siyad Barre staved off an attempted military coup and remained in power. The withdrawal of the Somali army from the Ogaden in the face of overwhelming Ethiopian military superiority (see p. 208) provoked a crisis in the army; arrests and executions of army officers were reported, and the units concerned were kept away from Mogadishu. The President's increasing reliance on members of his own Marehan clan, emphasized by a Government reshuffle on 1 April, was a further source of resentment. The expected coup, led by two officers noted for their Soviet sympathies, erupted prematurely in Mogadishu on 9 April, and was crushed by units loyal to the Government. Seventy-four officers were tried for complicity, of whom twenty-one were released, thirty-six imprisoned, and seventeen, including an air force colonel, publicly executed on 26 October. Several opponents of the regime, including a former ambassador and an army colonel, defected to Kenya. A massive influx of refugees, especially in the north, severely strained food and medical resources.

Despite domestic insecurity, President Siyad undertook an exhausting round of foreign visits, including China, the United States, Britain, France and West Germany, in search of desperately needed military, economic and humanitarian aid. An agreement on economic and technical cooperation was signed with China in April, and in August Deputy Premier Mrs Chen opened the Burao–Belet Uen road built with Chinese aid. West Germany provided substantial development aid, and the United States offered defensive weapons, but only on condition that Somalia renounce the dearly-held claim to national unification.

DJIBOUTI

The embryo republic survived a particularly difficult second year of independence. Internally, the division between Afars and Issas came to a head in early January with the resignation of five Afar Ministers, led by Premier Ahmed Dini Ahmed, in protest at the elimination of Afars from key posts after independence. A list of Afar demands was presented to the Issa President, Hassan Gouled, and a new Cabinet led by another Afar, Abdallah Mohamed Kalil, was installed in 6 February. The Ethiopian victory over Somalia made it additionally necessary to reconcile the Afars, who looked to Ethiopia for protection against the Somali-supported Issas. It led also to an influx of some 25,000 refugees from the March fighting. In April Djibouti established diplomatic relations with the Soviet Union, and in May the Ethiopian leader Mengistu Haile-Maryam claimed that Somalia was massing forces for an attack on the Republic. The opening of the railway to Addis Ababa in June offered some relief to Djibouti's shattered economy.

KENYA

The death of President Jomo Kenyatta on 22 August (see OBITUARY) marked the end of an era. He had given political stability to a multiracial, private-enterprise society. But he also bequeathed glaring social inequality, corruption in high places, mounting pressure on the land from a rapidly increasing population, a serious problem of urban unemployment, and a rising crime rate. The immediate problem, however, was to elect a new President, since Mr Kenyatta was a 'colossus without an heir'. Intense jockeying for position was predicted between two factions, one led by Mr Daniel arap Moi, the Vice-President since 1967, who, though himself a Kalenjin, had the backing of two powerful Kikuyu Ministers—Charles Njonjo, the Attorney-General, and Mwai Kibaki, Minister of Finance and Economic Planning—and the other led by Dr Njoroge Mungai, a former Foreign Minister who was favoured by key members of the Kenyatta family and entourage.

In the event, the vested interests of the powerful middle-class ensured a peaceful succession, though an alleged plot to assassinate Mr Moi, who became Acting President upon Mr Kenyatta's death, was still being investigated at the end of the year. On 6 October Mr Moi was unanimously adopted by a special delegates' conference of the ruling Kenya African National Union (KANU) as the party's president and its sole candidate for the national Presidency; he was declared elected unopposed on 10 October. The new President was 54, married with two children, a former head teacher, and Chief Scout of Kenya with strong interests in youth welfare and education, besides being an astute politician and a farmer with business interests.

President Moi appointed Mwai Kibaki as national Vice-President. At the end of October Mr Kibaki was elected party vice-president at the first national conference of KANU to be held for 12 years. He retained his Finance portfolio, but a separate Ministry of Economic Planning was created under Dr Robert Ouko. Home Affairs was also constituted into a separate Ministry—hitherto it had come under the Vice-President's office. Mbiyu Koinange, formerly Minister of State in the President's office, became Minister of Natural Resources (effectively a demotion), but a major Cabinet reshuffle was left until after the 1979 general election.

President Moi pledged that he and his Government would continue his predecessor's policies. He earned popularity not only by condemning smuggling, land-grabbing, corruption and indiscipline, but also by initiating remedial action. He changed some permanent secretaries, ambassadors and police chiefs—Bernard Hinga, the Commissioner of Police, ostensibly resigned—and re-established joint command of the army, navy and air services under Lieut.-General Mulinge. In December, to mark the fifteenth anniversary of independence, he ordered the release of all political detainees, including Professor Ngugi Wa Thiongo, head of the University of Nairobi literature department and a leading novelist and playwright, and four former MPs; university students demonstrated in support of the President's action. In December, too, he announced the start of a five-year crash course to combat adult illiteracy and an undertaking by employers to increase the wage-earning work-force by 10 per cent.

No agreement having yet been reached on the equitable distribution of the considerable assets of the East African Community and its corporations, the recently established national services continued to prosper. Within a year of commencing operations on 31 January 1977, Kenya Airways had captured 85 per cent of the market once enjoyed by East African Airways. Kenyan aircraft were not allowed to over-fly Tanzania, and international airlines, as distinct from charter flights, could not operate direct services between the two countries. Kenya Railways were still running to and from Uganda (not Tanzania), but trains were subject to border delays and operational problems: in February the movement of goods trains was temporarily halted because of outstanding Ugandan debts. The exchange of diplomatic representatives between the two countries announced in March, seemed likely to ease such problems: there was no separate diplomatic representation under the Community. Though each former partner state was operating its own posts and telecommunications service, mails were still exchanged between them; the jointly-owned earth satellite station near Nairobi was now serving Kenya alone, and the other members were building their own stations. The Kenya Ports Authority was running the port of Mombasa. In November three Lake Victoria steamers were handed over to Tanzania; the latter, however, still refused to reopen the border, and Kenya continued to cultivate alternative markets in the Middle East.

The main road to Uganda was open, a road link with Sudan was planned, and a new road was completed between Nairobi and Addis Ababa, bringing the prospect of increased trade with Ethiopia. The Government feared that the fighting in Ethiopia's Ogaden region might spill over Kenya's borders and that a victorious Somalia would renew her claims to parts of the North-East Province; it therefore strongly opposed the supply of arms to Somalia. However, the impounding in February of an Egyptian arms-carrying jet aircraft backfired when Egypt seized two Kenyan airliners at Cairo airport; the planes were exchanged. Further military aid was negotiated with the American Government, in view of the substantial military build-up in neighbouring states. The visit in November of a high-level delegation, led by President Moi, to France, Belgium and Britain reflected Kenya's wish to strengthen its relationship with the EEC countries individually or collectively.

In March the Upper Tana reservoir scheme—the biggest single development project ever initiated in Kenya—was officially started, with finance provided mainly by Britain, West Germany and the EEC. Anti-poaching efforts were stepped up and a ban on trade in animal skins and other game trophies took effect in March. Mr Bruce McKenzie, for many years Minister of Agriculture in the post-independence Government, was killed in May when his aircraft exploded on a return flight from Kampala; the Uganda Government was asked to investigate, but the incident went unexplained. A major invasion of desert locusts threatened northern Kenya, as well as Tanzania, Uganda and Sudan, at the end of the year.

TANZANIA

The Government remained committed to socialist goals, but responded pragmatically to sluggish performance in the state industrial sector and in the production of export cash crops; it accepted the need for individual incentives on the farm and in the factories. No one was allowed to leave his village without permission—some farmers were reported to be drifting away. Small-scale private enterprise was selectively encouraged and import licences were granted more freely. State-run industries were expected to operate profitably, and the Government closed one loss-making, state-run transport company, after returning public butcheries to the private sector in 1977. The reliance on foreign aid remained substantial, but Lonrho's assets were nationalized in June and compensation was being negotiated.

On 5 March over 350 students of the University of Dar es Salaam and two other institutions were expelled for unlawfully demonstrating against salary increases and fringe benefits awarded to Ministers, other MPs and party officials; they wanted such increases to go to workers and peasants. At the end of May the bulk of the students (including one of the President's sons) were conditionally pardoned; 19 others were to be allowed to resume their studies in July 1979, but the 21 ringleaders were barred for five years from all institutions of higher learning, both within and outside Tanzania.

In June, in the wake of the invasion of Zaïre's Shaba province, President Nyerere condemned Western attempts to create a pan-African security force, but defended the role of the Soviet Union and Cuba in Africa. He drew a distinction between legitimate African governments and those which had lost popular support. In November, as chairman of the 'front-line' Presidents, he told Mr Cledwyn Hughes, the British Prime Minister's envoy, that there was no prospect of an all-party conference on Rhodesia without a prior commitment by the Government in Salisbury to implement the Anglo-American proposals. He regretted Zambia's decision in October to reopen its border with Rhodesia and to use Rhodesia Railways again, though the hold-up of essential Zambian imports caused by severe congestion at the port of Dar es Salaam and the shortage of locomotives and wagons on the Tanzania–Zambia Railway (Tazara) had contributed to that decision. The Tanzania railway corporation contracted to buy new equipment from Britain and West Germany.

In October regular forces of the Ugandan army occupied some 700 square miles of Tanzania territory on the north-west border, north of the Kagera river. Bukoba was bombed, the Kagera sugar factory was badly damaged, and widespread incidents of pillage, murder and rape were reported, causing over 30,000 people to flee their homes. Troops were moved from all over the country to the war zone, petrol tankers were commandeered, and Kenya was vainly requested to stop supplying oil to Uganda. Spurning offers of mediation made by Kenya and other states, President Nyerere said in a radio broadcast: 'We did not want to fight him' (Amin), 'but now we are going to fight until this snake is out of our house'. Following OAU intervention, President Amin withdrew his forces in the latter half of November and claimed that some 10,000 Tanzanian troops had penetrated into Uganda, but this Tanzania denied. The Government was convinced that a new invasion was imminent and prepared for protracted warfare; this, together with the higher cost of petroleum products, was damaging to the economy. Increases in the prices of beer, spirits, soft drinks and textiles were announced in mid-November to pay for the war effort.

Existing anti-poaching patrols were supplemented by 200 heavily-armed rangers who, after completing their training in January, were stationed throughout the country. In February more than 7,000 prisoners and detainees were released in an amnesty to mark the first anniversary of the establishment of *Chama cha Mapundizi* (see AR 1977, p. 217). Some 200 people died as the result of a cholera outbreak.

UGANDA

President Amin announced that 1978 would be a year of reconciliation and that a human rights commission was to be established in Uganda, under the Ministry of Justice. However, in October an Amnesty International publication put the death toll since 1971 at not less than 300,000. Mr Raphael Sebugwawo-Amooti, a leading judge and chairman of the Industrial Court, was shot dead outside Kampala in March—officially by 'highway robbers', but allegedly by the security forces.

In March, too, serious differences within the military elite were reported to have surfaced at a Cabinet meeting; Brigadier Moses Ali, the Minister of Finance, lost his post some months later. In a separate incident Major-General Mustafa Adrisi, Vice-President and Minister of Defence, was injured in a 'road accident'. After many months in a Cairo hospital, he eventually returned to Uganda but in December was stripped of the Defence portfolio. The President accused some top officers and Ministers of stealing public funds and blamed them for mass killings (of which he claimed to be innocent). He undertook a major reorganization of government and the security forces; the Ministry of Finance and the Ministry of Planning and Economic Development were merged. He himself assumed the portfolio of Information and Foreign Affairs, which needed 'a lot of diplomacy and a cool head', and took personal control of the police and prisons: their senior officers were, he said, guilty of corruption, drunkenness and jealousy, and some were removed. Civilians were ordered to surrender their firearms because of the sharp increase in highway robbery and other crimes. The President also replaced Major-General Isaac Lumago as chief of defence staff; the latter's successor, Major-General Gowon, was himself suspended in December, allegedly for opposing President Amin's plan for a second invasion of Tanzania. In December, too, Lieut.-Colonel Jarouk Minawa, a Kakwa and director of the dreaded State Research Bureau, was made Minister for Internal Affairs. There were reports of fresh internecine killings in the armed forces.

The economy, which had benefited from the high coffee price in 1976-77, was adversely affected by the American Congressional decision in July to cut off virtually all trade with Uganda, whose Government 'engages in the international crime of genocide'. Since alternative markets could probably be found, the drop in price was more damaging. Foreign exchange difficulties caused a delay in paying for fuel supplies and petrol shortages resulted, the oil companies having insisted on advance payment. Smuggling was rampant, while the Government sought to check widespread black-marketeering by fixing the prices of everyday commodities at a level similar to that prevailing on the black market.

In October Uganda claimed to have been twice invaded by Cuban-backed Tanzanian forces, though this was denied by Tanzania. These charges were possibly meant to conceal serious army discontent, and also provided a pretext for the invasion of Tanzania. President Amin publicly welcomed offers of mediation by Kenya, Libya (which was reported to have flown troops and military equipment to Uganda) and the Organization of African Unity. Tanzanian troops found the bodies of over 100 Ugandan soldiers, killed other than in fighting between the two armies. The situation along the border remained tense.

Chapter 2

GHANA—NIGERIA—SIERRA LEONE—THE GAMBIA—LIBERIA

GHANA

GENERAL IGNATIUS KUTU ACHEAMPONG was deposed on 5 July by the chief of the defence staff, Lieut.-General F. W. K. Akuffo, in the army barracks at Burma camp near Accra. Always ready to let hope triumph over experience, Ghanaians welcomed the change, since it was difficult to see how anything that altered the existing situation could be other than an improvement—whether on an inflation rate of 150 per cent, or on the introduction of a 'Union Government' which no one could understand except as the prolongation of Acheampong's personal rule.

The enforced removal of the head of state followed the referendum on Union Government in March when the electorate were asked to vote 'Yes' or 'No' to the proposals. The results were very uncertain. According to Acheampong, there had been 'a massive acceptance': for, 1,100,000 (56 per cent); against, 880,000 (46 per cent). The figures were in themselves suspicious, and made more so by the sudden flight across the border of Mr Justice Abban, the Electoral Commissioner, during the night (31 March) when returns were being counted. He later declared that he had been driven from his office by armed soldiers, and that carbon copies of the true figures showed a very different count: for, 1,399,330; against, 1,600,294. On 5 April, detention orders were issued against first 17, then 35, leading figures, including Adamua Bossman, president of the Ghana Bar

Association; the former head of state, General Afrifa; and Nana Akufo-Addo, a barrister and son of the former President. Then, in July, Acheampong himself was placed under close house arrest. 'Union Government' was over before it had begun.

Akuffo—an Akwapim, aged 41, Sandhurst-trained—served with the United Nations Emergency Force in the former Congo in 1962, became commanding officer of the air force training school and parachute battalion, and then chief of the defence staff. The coup within the coup was bloodless and limited. That only Acheampong of the Supreme Military Council (SMC) was removed was a difficulty which became pronounced by the end of 1978, since, if Acheampong had become wrong and corrupt, was it really the case that all those around him had been honest and right? Meanwhile, Akuffo assumed the office of head of state and Chairman of the SMC but vested executive power collectively in all seven members of the Council. Yet on 6 November Akuffo had to invoke 'all the measures which go with a declaration of a state of emergency' because of widespread strikes, including a total shutdown of water and electricity supplies in Accra (3-4 November), following a 58 per cent devaluation of the cedi and a harsh deflationary budget.

On 12 November a new draft constitution was presented to the SMC by Dr Thomas Aboagye Mensah, chairman of the Constitutional Commission. It proposed reforms under six main headings: an executive President and Vice-President plus Ministers drawn from outside Parliament; a Parliament of 140 members; an independent judiciary; a council of state to link the separated powers of the executive and legislature; a lowering of the voting age from 21 to 18; and the denial to government of any power to recognize or withhold recognition from chiefs. Akuffo's broadcast statement of 6 July had declared that the SMC would 'hand over power to a transitional national government on 1 July 1979' on the basis of free elections, but 'without the operation of political parties'. The interim Government should last for four years, and there should be 'no institutional representation of the armed forces or the police force'. On 17 November district council elections were held, and a Constituent Assembly was expected to end its discussions by 31 March 1979: but by the end of the year there was growing uncertainty not only about the time-table but also about the direction of reform.

Nowhere was that more evident than in the economy. True, there were mitigating features. In August, the UK Government renewed its export credit guarantee backing for some £10 million of credit to cover essential imports, and there was hope of further EEC support. Oil began to come on stream in October from the small Bunsu Field in shallow waters some ten miles off the coast, sixty miles from Accra. Production at 1·7 million barrels a year (compare Nigeria's 2 million barrels a day) was expected to meet about 20 per cent of domestic consumption. It was good-quality light oil, but total resources were put at only 6·5 million barrels. The budgetary deficit for the year was in the region of 800 million cedis, plus a further 100 million cedis to meet the supplementary cost-of-living payments of between 10 and 15 per cent for lower-paid workers.

Cocoa prices doubled, from 40 to 80 cedis per 30 kg bag, but at world prices of £1,800 a tonne, or 325 cedis per bag, it still meant that the farmer was receiving only about a quarter of the export price. When, too, the SMC itself talked of 15 cedis as the price of a square meal and the basic urban daily wage was only 4 cedis, the economic horizon was dark. Smuggling, black market, currency deals, price-fixing (or *Kalabule*)—all the necessary pursuits of needy men—continued under Akuffo as under Acheampong. Such was the price of the huge rise in the money supply during the two years prior to July 1978, when (as the *Bank of Ghana Bulletin* noted) it 'increased by 1 billion cedis at a period when neither agriculture nor industry showed any marked increases in output'.

In August Dr K. A. Busia, former Prime Minister (1969-71) and leader of the Progress Party, died in exile at his home near Oxford (see OBITUARY). A state funeral was accorded the former academic and politician by the SMC in September.

There was one bright illumination of the year: the periodical, *The Legon Observer*, reappeared—intelligent, informed, combative.

NIGERIA

In the history of Nigeria 1978 will be known as the 'year of the Constitution'. At the beginning of the year, the elected Constituent Assembly, having held its open session in 1977, went into 'committee stage' and began to discuss the Constitution clause by clause, in secret. The basic outlines of the Draft Constitution were agreed, and resembled those of the US Constitution, but with the addition of far greater detail, and of several independent commissions to insulate vital areas of government from political control. The choice of an Executive Presidency, as opposed to the old parliamentary and Prime Ministerial model, took place only after heated discussion. The more symbolic issue of the 'Sharia controversy', over the precise form of the Federal Appeal Court to hear Muslim personal law cases on appeal from the state Sharia Courts of Appeal, nearly wrecked the Assembly. All 95 of the Muslim members of the Assembly walked out in protest at the 'cavalier manner' in which they alleged the issue was being handled by the chairman. After two weeks of quiet reconciling activity by senior Nigerians of good will on both sides, and after specific warnings and appeals from General Obasanjo, the head of state, and M. D. Yusufu, the inspector general of police, the Muslim members returned, the dangers of religious polarization were averted and the

Assembly went on to complete its consideration of the draft constitution. The Supreme Military Council in turn added several important amendments of its own and promulgated the Constitution in Decree No. 25 of 21 September. The Constitution runs to 279 sections and 6 schedules.

Political parties were then permitted to form and campaign in preparation for the five elections, for which 47 million voters had been registered, to federal and state legislatures and to state governorships and the Federal Presidency due to be held in 1979 to choose the government for the return to civilian rule on 1 October. Thirty parties were formed almost at once, but the Federal Electoral Commission, charged not only with running elections but also with ensuring that political parties observe the code of conduct laid down in the Constitution and in the Commission's decrees, soon reduced the number to five.

The party with the most chance of success appeared to be the National Party of Nigeria, which held a successful nominating convention and chose as its presidential candidate Alhaji Shehu Shagari, a former Northern People's Congress (NPC) Minister and later Federal Commissioner for Finance under General Gowon. Shagari, a somewhat quiet man, has a good reputation for probity and administrative ability. The party's programme is a pragmatic one of national unity, rural development, economic liberalization, encouragement to foreign investment and emphasis upon administrative continuity. The Unity Party of Nigeria, formed to support the candidature of Chief Awolowo (formerly Premier of the Western Region, leader of federal Opposition, and later, under Gowon, Federal Commissioner for Finance), is well organized and active and has put forward radical and more or less socialist policies. It is, however, weak in the North. The People's Party split at its nominating convention into the Great People's Party, whose candidate is Alhaji Waziri Ibrahim, a former NPC Minister, and the People's Party, whose candidate is Dr Azikiwe, the former President, a veteran nationalist leader now 74 years old. The most left wing of the five parties is the People's Redemption Party, whose candidate is Alhaji Aminu Kano, former leader of the Northern Element's Progressive Union (the radical opposition in the old North) and later a Commissioner under Gowon. Thus all the presidential candidates are old hands.

So far, under the close scrutiny of the military Government, which wisely called a meeting of all political leaders to agree on the 'rules of the game', the party competition has been good-humoured and constructive, a remarkable contrast with the bitter politics of the First Republic from 1960 to 1966.

Although it had only a year of office to run before the total surrender of power to civilians, the military Government took strong action in many fields. In foreign affairs it was host to an ECOWAS meeting of West African states, it received President Carter on an important state visit, and it provided the meeting ground in Kano for an emergency discussion between President Kaunda and Mr Callaghan (see p. 30). An important trade fair was also held in Lagos. In African affairs Nigeria continued to support continental solidarity and firm resistance to minority white Governments. General Dan Jumaa was sent to exercise good offices between Uganda and Tanzania in an attempt to stop the fighting. Nigeria also helped President Sekou Touré to come back from his position of diplomatic isolation and extremism into the community of West African states. In the conflict over Zimbabwe, Nigeria maintained firm support for the Patriotic Front, but also entered the practical field of peacemaking by sponsoring, together with President Kaunda, a secret meeting between Mr Smith and Mr Nkomo, attended by the former Nigerian Commissioner for Foreign Affairs, Brigadier Garba.

At home the military Government issued a number of decrees intended to correct abuses in the political system. The intention was admirable but sometimes the actions were too sweeping and too authoritarian and provoked a good deal of opposition. The Land Decree codified the position as it existed in the North, and vested control of all land in the state governments; it also limited to $1\frac{1}{2}$ hectares the amount of under-developed urban land that any one person can hold. It left intact, however, large and lucrative property development holdings in the rapidly growing towns. Strikes and wage increases were forbidden and dividends limited to 30 per cent; the feverish entrepreneurial boom encouraged by oil wealth and the indigenization decrees had not been matched, however, by any effective moves towards social equality, and meanwhile inflation had continued at a rate of some 30 per cent per annum.

The Nigerian economy was very severely affected by the fall in demand for oil in the middle of the year, which resulted in a reduction in sales from 2 million barrels per day to under $1\frac{1}{2}$ million, though in the last quarter demand recovered and daily production rose to 2·3 million barrels. During the slump General Obasanjo told the nation that Nigeria was still one of the poorest nations in the world, and that he would have to cut government expenditure and ban the import of non-essential goods. Federal allocations to states were cut by up to 50 per cent. The universities were also severely affected and the National Universities Commission responded by announcing a 200 per cent increase in board and lodging fees for students. The summary way in which this was done and the intemperate haste with which the Nigerian Union of Students launched public protest marches produced a situation of confrontation, in which police and army opened fire in several universities and killed some 12 students and others. This provoked strong criticism from the press. However, the Government managed to weather the storm, and held a judicial commission of enquiry, after which two Vice-Chancellors were dismissed, including Nigeria's most distinguished historian, Professor Ajayi.

Despite the opening of a second refinery at Warri and the commissioning of a third at Kaduna there was a severe shortage of petrol at the end of the year. The military Government banned the importation of sixty different sorts of goods, many of them in common use, and also insisted on the prior inspection for quality, by Inspection Services Ltd of Geneva, of all goods sent to Nigeria. The country suffered severe shortages of goods, and home-produced foodstuffs rose in price even faster than imported goods. Exports of groundnuts and palm oil, once a thriving trade, sank to nothing and even the cocoa crop was down to two-thirds of its level in 1970. Meanwhile the cost of completing the ambitious projects of the five-year development plan mounted and Nigeria had to negotiate loans of about £1,500 million with banking consortia.

The Government made strenuous efforts to improve the efficiency of the public service and especially of the nationalized industries, but there was some evidence that the morale of the higher echelons of the public service had declined since the wholesale purges of 1975. The railway performed so inefficiently that the Government had to contract out its entire management for three years to Rail India Technical and Economic Services Ltd.

While the sincerity of General Obasanjo in preparing Nigeria for a return to civilian rule was appreciated, the year saw mounting criticism in the press and elsewhere of the authoritarian style of military government by blanket decrees interfering with individual liberties, and a determination to enjoy a more open and less interfering style under civilian rule.

Two distinguished Nigerian chiefs, Akenjua II, the Oba of Benin, and Orcivirigh Gondo Aluor, the Tor Tiv, died in 1978.

SIERRA LEONE

Following a controversial national referendum held on 5-12 June, Sierra Leone was declared a one-party state on the Tanzanian model. The role of Prime Minister was replaced with that of two Vice-Presidents, and President Stevens assumed full executive powers. Some credence was lent to opposition charges of electoral irregularities by the unusual results in two provinces; the 'yes' vote outnumbered the total electorate and not a single negative vote was recorded in the north. The official returns gave the Government 2,152,454 votes and the opposition only 63,132 votes, largely in the Eastern Province.

President Stevens explained his volte-face on the issue of one-party rule (he had led opposition to it in the mid-sixties) by claiming that it was the wish of the vast majority of the population and the prevailing practice elsewhere in the world. In order to attempt a reconciliation with the remaining elements of the now disbanded Sierra Leone People's Party, political detainees were released and the size of the Cabinet greatly increased to make room for all sections of society. In December, when illness forced First Vice-President Koroma to resign, C. A. Kamara-Taylor, the Second Vice-President, moved up and his vacated post was given to a former opposition leader.

Political changes did little to affect the now familiar economic difficulties affecting Sierra Leone. Dwindling mineral production, diamond smuggling, an inability to boost agricultural production and financial mismanagement by public officials led the Finance Minister to describe the situation as 'not encouraging' in his Budget speech. Economic decline was partly masked by buoyant world prices, better industrial performance and IMF assistance. A range of loans and rescheduled foreign debts enabled the Government to continue with its development programme. EEC backing for a hydro-electric complex on the Mano River was obtained in conjunction with Liberia. Two unusual departures were the break with sterling and the decision to join Air Afrique, hitherto confined to French-speaking African states.

THE GAMBIA

During 1978 the Government had to contend not only with the serious effects of the previous year's drought but also with continued opposition from the National Convention Party (NCP) and divisions within its own ranks. In June the NCP held on to the Bakau seat in a by-election caused by the death of its sitting member, an event which caused consternation in Government ranks. The resignation of A. B. N'Jie, the Vice-President in charge of the Government during the by-election, was widely attributed to this reversal rather than to advancing years. A number of other changes within the Government took place in August as well. Assan Camara gave up the Finance Ministry to return to the Vice-Presidency and his post was given to M. C. Cham, the Minister of Economic Planning. The Interior Minister was dismissed and the influential Yaya Ceesay, the Agriculture Minister, was first demoted and then relieved of his Government position. The full effects of these changes and the divisions underlying them remained to be seen. On the positive side the Independent United Party member for Banjul South defected to the Government, giving the ruling People's Progressive Party 30 seats in Parliament to the five of the NCP.

The gravity of the economic setbacks caused by drought was reflected in a one-third fall in groundnut exports and a commensurate decline in food production, gross national product and private sector employment. Greatly increased food imports resulted in a significant trade deficit, though prevailing high prices for groundnuts and generous international assistance with drought relief helped restore the balance. The anticipated budgetary deficit would be made good by increased taxation and the use of reserves. Development projects, though not up to Plan expectations, showed improvement on previous years and were directed towards drought alleviation, principally improved road and water supply facilities. Modest gains were made in the manufacturing sector with the opening of the Banjul breweries and increased production at the Basse cotton ginnery. Tourism had a disappointing season in 1977-78, despite the publicity generated by the 'Roots' phenomenon. Recession in Sweden, which furnished most of The Gambia's foreign tourists, was mainly to blame for this. The 1978-79 season got off to a good start, facilities at Yundum Airport having been improved and several new operators entering the field.

Relations with Senegal remained excellent and the existing bilateral arrangement was superseded by a Gambia River Basin Development Organization (OMVG). There were hopes of an early start to long-standing plans for river control. As President of the Sahelian region anti-drought organization (CILSS) President Jawara spent much of the summer touring Western capitals to obtain long-term assistance for the affected countries. He also attended the ECOWAS summit at Lagos and sided with Mauritania in the Western Sahara dispute.

LIBERIA

Continuing evidence of President Tolbert's determination to combat maladministration was provided in May and August when five Cabinet Ministers and the director of police were dismissed for corruption and lack of 'dynamism'. Two unexpected events were the death of Mckinley De Shield, general-secretary of the governing True Whig Party, and the rather premature announcement by the President that he did not intend seeking re-election in 1984. In March President Tolbert presided over an historic reconciliation in Monrovia between President Sekou Touré of Guinea and his ancient political foes, Presidents Houphouet-Boigny of Ivory Coast and Senghor of Senegal. An enthusiastic reception was given President Carter when he made a brief stop-over in the Liberian capital after his visit to Nigeria. The heads of state of Nigeria and Guinea Bissau also paid official visits to Liberia, and Tolbert himself made a number of foreign visits, the most important being to Peking. The pattern both of economic assistance and of diplomatic excursions reflected Liberia's desire to maintain ties with old friends and establish new ones with countries of widely different political persuasions.

The economy continued to suffer from the effects of world depression, including a fall in demand for iron ore, the country's principal export. The plight of the American dollar also adversely affected Liberia. The trade deficit was more than made up by improved tax collection and foreign aid, the latter being intended principally for infrastructural improvements and the modernization of agriculture.

Chapter 3

SENEGAL—MAURITANIA—MALI—GUINEA—IVORY COAST—UPPER VOLTA—
TOGO—BENIN—NIGER—COMORO STATE—EQUATORIAL GUINEA—CHAD—
CAMEROON—GABON—CONGO—CENTRAL AFRICAN EMPIRE

SENEGAL

SENEGAL's political year centred on the presidential, parliamentary and municipal elections which took place on the same day, 26 February. The event was an important step in the direction of President Leopold Sedar Senghor's efforts to build a multi-party democracy, although the President's own position, or that of his party, the *Parti Socialiste* (PS), was never seriously in doubt. Of an electorate of 1,550,487 voters, 37·05 per cent abstained. Of those voting, 82·03 per cent cast their ballot for President Senghor, and 17·12 per cent for the only other candidate, Maître Abdoulaye Wade, leader of the *Parti Democratique Senégalais* (PDS), the first person ever to stand against Senghor in a presidential election. The percentages were approximately the same in the elections for the National Assembly, where the PS gained 83 seats and the PDS 17. The third party permitted under the recently amended constitution to take part, the marxist-leninist *Parti Africain de l'Indépendance* (PAI), obtained only 0·32 per cent of the vote. The high level of abstentions was at least partly attributable to the fact that the three permitted parties did not in fact represent all sectors of opinion, and notably that the supporters of Cheikh Anta Diop's *Rassemblement Nationale Democratique* (RND) were not allowed to express their electoral preference.

Because of allegations of irregularities and alleged unfair use of the official media, the PDS legal opposition boycotted the first session of the National Assembly. The liberal attitude of the regime towards media freedom, however, permitted a flourishing of small, relatively free and often very critical opposition papers attached to different groups. In the latter part of the year there was also an attempt to coordinate some of the smaller opposition groups within the *Coordination de l'Opposition Senégalaise Unie* (COSU) around the former Premier Mamadou Dia. The RND and the PDS, however, were not among them.

The ruling party also had its difficulties when in September the long-standing rivalry between Premier Abdou Diouf and Foreign Minister Babacar Ba culminated in the dismissal of the latter, who also resigned from his party posts. This was seen as strengthening the position of the Premier, the official successor to Senghor—who, however, announced unequivocally that he was going to stay in office as President until 1983.

The political effervescence accompanied a difficult economic year, due to the drought and poor groundnut harvests of the previous year. Plentiful and evenly distributed rains fell, however, in 1978, so the prospects for the groundnut harvest were good, and an economic upturn was likely.

MAURITANIA

The military coup of 10 July which bloodlessly overthrew President Moktar Ould Daddah was the key event of the year and marked a watershed in Mauritania's post-independence history. The author of the coup, who became the Chairman of the new Military Committee for National Recovery (CMRN), was Colonel Moustapha Ould Salek, who had been made chief of staff of the armed forces only in February. He soon made clear that one of the main reasons for the coup was unhappiness on the part of the military with the war which had been waged against the Algerian-based Polisario Front guerrillas fighting for the independence of the former Spanish Sahara. The Committee also, however, described the Ould Daddah Government as 'corrupt, anti-national and unpopular' and suspended the constitution and dissolved Parliament. There were, furthermore, reports that some civilian elements had been disturbed by an anti-corruption drive organized by President Ould Daddah in the few weeks before his overthrow.

The immediate effect of the coup on the military situation was an announcement by Polisario of a unilateral ceasefire on their Mauritanian front, which was followed by the opening of discreet diplomatic contacts. By the end of the year these had shown little visible sign of progress. A suggestion that they had been broken off was denied by both parties, but it was clear that the options for Mauritania were limited, in view of the continuation of the guerrilla war against Morocco and the presence of a substantial number of Moroccan troops on Mauritanian soil, brought in at the invitation of President Ould Daddah. Morocco would take a dim view of any sign of weakening on the part of Mauritania, and even if the Mauritanians accepted an independent Sahraoui state in the Mauritanian part of the territory such a move would be strongly contested by Morocco. The Mauritanians did not forget that their independence in 1960 was strongly contested by Morocco, which claimed the former French territory as part of 'Greater Morocco'. At the end of the year there were still 8,000 Moroccan troops in Mauritania. Thus it was not surprising that the French military assistance to Mauritania was still considered important. In the first part of the year French Jaguars, based in Dakar, were used on a number of occasions in support of the Mauritanian army's operations against guerrillas.

MALI

A turning-point in the destinies of Mali's military Government (which celebrated its tenth anniversary in power in November) came on 28 February, when three of its most powerful figures were arrested and accused of high treason and plotting to kill the head of state, Colonel Moussa Traore. Those arrested were Lieut.-Colonel Kissima Doukara, Minister of Defence, the Interior and Security; Lieut.-Colonel Tiercoro Bagayoko, director-general of the security services; and Lieut.-Colonel Karim Dembele, Minister of Transport and Public Works. Subsequently a fourth member of the ruling *Comité Militaire de Libération Nationale* (CMLN), the Foreign Minister, Colonel Charles Semba Sissoko, was arrested on his return from overseas, also accused of complicity in the plot, according to which he would have become the new head of state.

The arrest was the occasion of considerable public jubilation and street demonstrations of support for the head of state, who, it was said, had at last had the courage to take action against the most unpopular members of his Government. Doukara was accused in particular of having used his position as chairman of the National Commission to Aid Drought Victims to embezzle funds intended for combating drought, and Bagayoko was widely feared because of his repressive and arbitrary use of the security services. The four, as well as other alleged accomplices, were publicly tried in October, and Doukara and Bagayoko were sentenced to death, while Dembele received 20 and Sissoko 5 years' hard labour. At the end of the year they were still waiting to hear their appeals. Most commentators agreed that the arrests marked the opportunity for the President to make a new start, and to take advantage of the reinforced popular respect he now enjoyed to move in the direction of civilian rule, which he had long been promising. By the end of the year doubts were beginning to surface again that he was really going to be able to deliver, or that he was going to respond to the popular desire for the elimination of corruption, which was one of the main charges against the arrested officers.

GUINEA

The year saw the twentieth anniversary of the Guinean Republic, as well as a major turning-point in the country's history, with what appeared to be a definitive reconciliation with its neighbours in West Africa, and a swing in foreign relations towards better relations with the West. This culminated in the successful official visit of the French President Giscard d'Estaing in December, finally burying the hatchet of the quarrel that had begun when General de Gaulle had cut all ties with Guinea after the

H

massive 'No' vote in the 1958 referendum, which had led to Guinea's independence.

The reconciliation with the neighbours, notably the Presidents of Senegal and Ivory Coast, took place in the Liberian capital of Monrovia, in the presence of a number of other West African leaders, and marked a major contribution to peace in the West African area. The poor relations of Guinea with Senegal and the Ivory Coast and the constant accusations of plots and planned mercenary invasions had caused all attempted reconciliations in the past to be stillborn. This time, however, the basis was laid for real change, and President Sekou Touré's commitment not to ask for the return of Guinean opposition elements marked a major change of policy on his part. He also seemed to have acquired a new confidence which permitted him to travel extensively outside Guinea, not just to his im-mediate neighbours, but also to a number of Middle Eastern countries, and to the OAU summit in Khartoum, the first time he had been to the OAU since the mid-1960s. This new confidence came in part from the improved financial condition of Guinea, as the foreign exchange deriving from major increases in the export of bauxite and alumina began to flow in, but he also seemed now satisfied with the assurances received from the French and other Western powers that there would be no covert attempts to destabilize the Guinean regime, as had undeniably taken place in the past—notably the Conakry invasion of November 1970. The major architect of the reconciliation was the French ambassador in Conakry, André Lewin, formerly a special envoy of the UN Secretary-General, but the World Bank president Robert McNamara and EEC development commissioner Claude Cheysson also played their parts.

The only question-mark remained the human rights situation in Guinea; as to the large number of distinguished political prisoners in Guinea there was no certainty whether they were dead or alive. Before President Giscard's visit it was claimed authoritatively, for example, that former OAU secretary general Diallo Telli had been killed after his arrest in 1977, and no proof was offered to contradict the claim.

IVORY COAST

The year ended on a remarkably sour note in what had been one of the most stable and economically successful of independent African countries. President Félix Houphouet-Boigny denounced the authors of anti-French tracts which had been distributed by a 'handful of Ivorian extremists' having links with French intellectuals. Referring to a growth of banditry in Abidjan, the capital, including attacks on French citizens, he said that no one should count on him to be a passive witness to disorder.

This was a major public admission of a malaise that had existed for some time, relating in part to criticisms of corruption and bureaucracy in the ruling party, the *Parti Democratique de la Côte d'Ivoire* (PDCI), which went back to the big Government reshuffle of 1977, but also to the new uncertainties surrounding the economy. Although the growth record had been remarkable, there were increasing worries that there had been over-heating of the economy, leading to a too rapid growth in debts, which, combined with an unexpected decline in coffee production (plus the expected decline in world prices for both coffee and cocoa) had obliged the Government to put the brakes on. (The crop prospects for 1978-79 improved, however.) Fears were also expressed in Ivory Coast that the French reconciliation with Guinea would lead to a diminution of French interest in Ivory Coast because of Guinea's great economic potential.

UPPER VOLTA

A new phase in Voltaic politics opened with a new return to civilian rule undertaken voluntarily by the military, who had held the reins of power since the military coup of 1966. The previous return had been partial, as army officers still held key ministries, and had lasted only from 1971 to 1974. The head of the army, General Sangoule Lamizana, had also re-mained as President. This time, the return to civilian rule was more com-plete, the army completely withdrawing from political life, except for President Lamizana himself, who was one of the candidates in the presiden-tial election.

In parliamentary elections at the end of April, the *Union Democratique Voltaique* (UDV), which had commanded the majority of seats in all previous assemblies since independence (1960-66, 1971-74), remained the leading political party, with 28 out of 57 seats, although its previous position of total domination had been reduced by the presence of the *Union Nationale pour la Défence de la Democratie* (UNDD), grouping supporters of the country's first President, Maurice Yameogo, who was forbidden to take part in active politics. They obtained 13 seats, and the left-wing *Union Progressiste Voltaique* (UPV) of Joseph Ki-Zerbo obtained nine. The constitution provided that only the first three parties past the post should continue to exist, so all other parties than those three were disbanded. In November the leader of the parliamentary opposition, Dr Ki-Zerbo, resigned from political life.

In presidential elections in May, President Lamizana was elected for a five-year term. Having failed to qualify with an absolute majority in the first round, in the second round he obtained 711,736 votes against 552,619 cast for Macaire Ouedraogo, the UNDD candidate. Both presidential and parliamentary elections were notable for the large number of abstentions.

The 40 per cent of the electorate who did not vote for the legislature rose to 57 per cent in the second round of the presidential election.

One of the UDV leaders, Dr Joseph Conombo, a member of Upper Volta's political 'old guard', was appointed Prime Minister, at the head of an all-civilian Government. Major economic problems continued to face the country.

TOGO

A campaign against corruption began in Togo, where there was a big government purge in November, accompanied by a major session of the ruling party, the *Rassemblement Populaire Togolaise* (RPT), to discuss the question. Proceedings were expected against several sacked Ministers. At the same time more details were disclosed of a bizarre 'mercenaries' plot' first revealed in 1977 (see AR 1977, p. 231). This involved a number of British soldiers of fortune allegedly working for members of Lomé's Brazilian community, including the sons of the first President of Togo, Sylvanus Olympio, assassinated in 1963. Latest revelations also included members of the Togolese military, including a lieutenant-colonel.

BENIN

The remarkable continuity that military government had given to what, prior to 1972, was one of the most unstable countries in independent Africa continued in 1978, preparations being made, within the framework of a marxist-leninist People's Republic, for representative institutions and elections. In spite of the vitriolic row between Benin and Gabon (a delayed fall-out from the 'mercenaries' invasion of 16 January 1977), which led to large-scale expulsions from Gabon of Benin citizens, mainly traders, and also damaged relations with France, a reconciliation with France was carried out by the end of the year, resulting in the dispatch of a new French ambassador to Benin.

NIGER

A quiet year politically was more notable for the increasingly optimistic forecasts for a basically very disadvantaged economy because of higher revenues from uranium production, due to the quadrupling of uranium prices since the energy crisis of 1973 and the simultaneous expansion of production in Niger. Between 1975 and 1978 government royalties would have risen from 4,000 million CFA francs to an estimated 12,000 million.

Niger's uranium output in 1977 reached a record figure of 2,000 tonnes, making it the world's fifth largest producer. In 1978 production started at a new mine at Akouta, of whose output Japan was to import more than 40 per cent in the next 20 years. Hitherto France had taken much of Niger's uranium output.

COMORO STATE

The erratic and arbitrary rule of President Ali Soilih came to an end on the night of 13-14 May with a coup d'etat which, it subsequently emerged, had been directed by the notorious French mercenary (veteran of the Congo and Biafra), Bob Denard. President Soilih, who had offended traditional Islamic leaders with some of his socialist policies, as well as having disrupted the administration by sacking civil servants and replacing them with members of the youth movement, was killed a few days later.

The politico-military directory under two co-Presidents, Ahmed Abdallah and Mohammed Ahmed, was replaced after a constitutional referendum in October (approved by 99·31 per cent of voters) by a federal constitution. Abdallah, who had been the first Prime Minister after independence but had been dethroned in a coup, became President and Salim Ben Ali became Prime Minister. Denard, who had taken the name Moustapha Madhjou, and had briefly held the post of head of security, was prevailed upon to leave the islands in September because of the hostile international reaction to his presence. The Comoro delegation had, for example, been refused a seat at the OAU conference in Khartoum. Relations with France, virtually broken off under the Soilih regime, were resumed, and there was a possibility that a dialogue about the island of Mayotte, which had voted to remain French, might be resumed.

EQUATORIAL GUINEA

The sombre state of the former Spanish Guinea, now independent for ten years, continued to receive only occasional international attention, compared to the publicity given to marginally less atrocious regimes. The latest report on conditions there, published by the International Commission of Jurists in December, stated that ten of the twelve Cabinet Ministers appointed at independence in 1968 were now dead, two-thirds of the Independence Assembly had disappeared, and one-quarter of the 400,000 population were now living outside the country. Those who remained were subject to forced labour and other brutalities, while 'the economy is a shambles and the infrastructure, both human and physical, is now devastated'.

CHAD

In the first half of the year, abortive peace attempts between the Government of President Félix Malloum and the rebel Frolinat (*Front Nationale pour la Libération du Tchad*) were followed by a serious deterioration in Malloum's military situation, and in April the French military presence in Chad was reinforced by troops from an armoured regiment of the Foreign Legion. By June, it was estimated that 1,500 French troops were once again stationed in Chad, although the French base at Ndjamena had been closed in 1976. Some 300 of the troops wore Chad army uniforms. The rest consisted of two regiments and two squadrons, which were reinforced at the end of April by ten Jaguars and other support aircraft.

A truce organized at the end of March at the Libyan town of Sebha broke down amid accusations of mutual violations. Malloum's Government suspected that Libya, which strongly backed Frolinat, was using the cease-fire to strengthen the rebels' positions. Frolinat, in March, set up a Revolutionary Council incorporating other groups at Faya-Largeau, a major centre in Northern Chad now under Frolinat control. By May there were indications that Frolinat troops were moving into large areas of central Chad and might soon be within striking distance of the capital.

A major battle at Ati in central Chad, 320 miles from Ndjamena, in which French troops were heavily involved seemed to hold off the threat, and in the second part of the year events in Chad were dominated by the surprise return of Hissène Habré to head a Government in Ndjamena. Habré, a rebel leader who achieved notoriety as the man who kept hostage for three years the French anthropologist Françoise Claustre at a hideaway in the Tibesti mountains, and who left Tibesti after differences with the local Frolinat leader, Goukouni Oueddai, had seemed for some time to be playing an increasingly lone game. He set up a Government of largely unknown figures, many of whom were from northern Chad, but by the end of the year it was still uncertain whether his presence in Ndjamena was having any noticeable effect on the loyalties of the rebel-held areas, since the Libyans had put most of their resources into backing Goukouni. Malloum, in any case, still retained control of the Chad army, with Habré's own men conducting their own freelance military operations. Relations between Habré and Malloum were also extremely tense.

CAMEROON

In May elections were held for the list of the ruling party, the *Union Nationale Camérounaise* (UNC), for the National Assembly. Of 3,663,358 registered voters, 3,615,463 used their vote, and 99·98 per cent voted for the list presented. The sweeping nature of the result was above all an indication of the control exercised by the Government of President Ahidjo, which still had an extensive security apparatus, allowing few outlets for democratic expression.

Economically the emphasis was on the beginning of offshore oil production, which had now reached 800,000 tonnes, and was expected to reach 5 million tonnes in the early 1980s. Work also started on the construction of a second oil refinery at Victoria in the English-speaking area, the existing refinery being at Douala.

GABON

After the 'years of the fat cow', 1978 was the year in which Gabon really began to count the cost of imprudent expenditure during the oil boom. President Bongo said in August 'Gabon has entered into a period of economic slow-down. Rigorous finance, austerity and prudence are the law by which we must live for at least the next three years.' The middle-future prospect was not encouraging, since few new oil discoveries had been made, and existing reserves might last only another seven or eight years. The principal concern must be to find resources for the costly prestige project, the Trans-Gabonese railway, of which only one-third had been completed, and whose costs were inflating all the time.

President Bongo surrendered his chairmanship of the OAU with an unedifying row with President Kerekou of Benin, which he followed by the expulsion of several hundred Benin citizens, who had held a predominant position in the retail trade. Earlier in the year he had also faced his first serious bout of student unrest, which led to the closure of the University of Libreville.

CONGO

Early in the year, the trial of 42 persons alleged to have assassinated President Ngouabi in March 1977 took place in Brazzaville before a special revolutionary court. Ten of them were subsequently executed. Shortly after the sentences were passed and carried out, the leader of the commandos said to have carried out the assassination, Captain Barthelémy Kikadidi, the only one to have escaped, was tracked down and killed.

In August, President Joachim Yhombi-Opango announced the uncovering of a plot to overthrow his Government involving foreign mercenaries and combat aircraft. They had planned to stage a coup during the celebrations of the 15th anniversary of the Congolese revolution in 1963 when the Abbé Fulbert Youlou, the country's first President, was overthrown. President Yhombi announced the cancellation of the celebrations, as well as the arrest of prominent figures, including former National Assembly President Dieudonné Miakasissa and former army commander Felix Mouzabakani, as well as some close associates of the late Abbé, and an 'advance party' of mercenaries, including a Frenchman and a Ghanaian.

CENTRAL AFRICAN EMPIRE

The Emperor Bokassa I celebrated his first anniversary as Emperor in December, having shortly before stripped his eldest son, Prince George, of his title for making defamatory remarks about his father. Prince George, who had been Minister of State in charge of National Defence since the confrontation in 1977, was arrested and expelled from the country.

Relations with France, which in the past had known their ups and downs, continued to improve—an indication of the excellent relations enjoyed between President Giscard d'Estaing and the Emperor. The Empire contributed 300 troops to the French-sponsored intervention force in Zaïre, and there were reports of reinforced military cooperation between France and the Empire.

The Emperor's taste for reorganizations did not appear to have diminished. In May he reshuffled the military leadership, giving the army the task of 'monitoring the public services to discover and put an end to the causes of their poor operation', and in July he sacked the Government of Prime Minister Ange Patasse and appointed a new one with several new faces under Henri Maidou.

VII CENTRAL AND SOUTHERN AFRICA

Chapter 1

THE REPUBLIC OF ZAÏRE—RWANDA AND BURUNDI—GUINEA-BISSAU AND
CAPE VERDE—SÃO TOME AND PRINCIPE—MOZAMBIQUE—ANGOLA

THE REPUBLIC OF ZAÏRE

THE event of the year brought an uncovenanted new lease of life to the
discredited regime of President Mobutu. It began with reports of widespread unrest and brutal repression, notably of a massacre of civilians at
Idiofa in Bandundu province. The most immediate dangers sprang from
the critical state of the economy—the country's international indebtedness
amounted to some $2-3,000 million—and the military insecurity arising
from very strained relations with Angola. Despite a soothing New Year
message to the Angolan President and 'encouraging talks between the two
countries' in January, President Mobutu continued his clandestine support
for the Angolan dissident movements, and Angola responded in kind, with
support for the guerrillas of Colonel Mbumba's Congolese National
Liberation Front (FNLC). The situation was further aggravated by the
spate of rumours which had arisen over the lease of an experimental rocket
range in Shaba province to a West German firm, Orbital Transports and
Rockets, apparently for the development of observation satellites, which
was blown up into a project for a Franco-German military base. (In
November the firm announced that it proposed to place its operations
under UN surveillance.)

The President began the year with a tour of Europe and the Middle
East in search of foreign aid. His return in February was followed by the
discovery of an allegedly impending coup, in which the Libyan ambassador
together with American and Belgian diplomats was said to implicated.
There were many arrests, including a number of senior army officers, and
a military tribunal passed 19 sentences of death. The execution on 17 March
of nine officers and four civilians ignored international appeals for
clemency and brought a rebuke from M Simonet, the Belgian Foreign
Minister.

At the same time there were reports from the south-west of renewed
guerrilla activities by the FLNC and of hostile troop concentrations across
the Angolan border. These culminated in the second week of May in a
seemingly well-prepared re-enactment of the previous year's invasion of
Shaba province (see AR 1977, p. 236), this time by a rebel force, variously
estimated at 2,000 to 4,000, with the more or less open participation of
Angola, Cuba and East Germany and the backing of the Soviet Union.
On 13 May the rebels again occupied Kolwezi, the key centre of Zaïre's

H*

vital copper-mining industry. The demoralized Zaïrean army was manifestly unable to offer any effective resistance and President Mobutu again appealed for aid to Belgium, France, Morocco, the United States and China. Immediate international concern was for the safety of the 3,000 European technicians and their families (mostly Belgian and French), trapped in the war zone and threatened by the indiscipline of the rebels. The US declined to commit combat troops. The Belgian Government also decided to confine its intervention to a defensive action to cover the evacuation of white civilians. Its evident lack of enthusiasm for going to the rescue of President Mobutu's threatened regime contrasted with the positive French attitude of support for Zaïre, and caused some tension between the two Governments and lack of liaison in their military operations.

On 18 May several thousand Belgian troops were airlifted (with American logistic support) to Kamina, about 125 miles north of Kolwezi. On the following day, a parachute drop by 400 men of the French Foreign Legion cleared the town of rebels, but failed to achieve the intended surprise or to prevent the massacre of more than 100 Europeans. In the next three days, some 2,000 more were airlifted to safety. There was a general exodus of European families from the province at the end of May. The rebels had now retreated into Angola, but the threat remained and, as the French and Belgian troops were gradually withdrawn in June, they were replaced by a 2,300-strong Pan-African Defence Force, the result of another French initiative, mainly Moroccan but with token contributions from Senegal, Gabon, Togo, the Central African Empire and Ivory Coast. The most immediate task of this force was the protection of the hapless civilian population from the vengeance of the Zaïrean troops, who had started an orgy of killing and looting. Belgium, France and Morocco undertook to provide instructors for training a new Zaïrean army. Chinese support was expressed by the visits in June of the Foreign Minister Huang Hua and of a strong military delegation.

Besides the inevitable recriminations between the great powers to which it gave rise, the rebellion had deeply divided opinion in the OAU (see Pt. XI, Ch. 6) and damaged Zaïre's relations with a number of countries. President Mobutu recalled his ambassadors from the Soviet Union, Libya and Algeria, but a breach with Zambia (whose territory had been crossed by the rebels) was averted by a meeting between the two Presidents on 6 June. President Mobutu had also been angered by Belgium's equivocal attitude and by the freedom accorded in Brussels to the activities of a plethora of Zaïrean opposition groups, but following a partial clampdown by Belgium the central committee of the ruling party, the Revolutionary People's Movement (MPR), decided on 6 July against a breach of diplomatic relations. Matters were further smoothed over when M Simonet visited Kinshasa at the beginning of August.

The alarms of May also raised a serious question-mark over the prospects for an international aid package for the ruined Zaïrean economy which IMF officials had been working for months to get together. In the event, the discussions scheduled for Brussels in June did take place, and the ten nations involved—France, Belgium, West Germany, Britain, the US, Japan, Italy, Canada, Holland and Iran—together with the World Bank, agreed upon a $60 million programme of emergency aid to Shaba. There was, however, a clear disposition to make the implementation of the long-term rescue operation conditional upon effective reform and substantial concessions to the internal opposition. Meeting again in November, this consortium expressed satisfaction at such recent developments as the 20 per cent devaluation of the Zaïrean currency, but once again applied pressure by taking no firm decisions on the long-term plan.

President Mobutu, while angrily rebutting foreign criticism, nevertheless proclaimed a new crack-down on corruption, and on 21 June granted a general amnesty to all refugees and exiles willing to return. This was extended to political prisoners on 10 July, and the former Foreign Minister, Mr Nguza Karl 1 Bond, imprisoned for treason in 1977 (see AR 1977, p. 237) was also released on 14 July.

A further response to these external pressures, much more important for future security, was the unexpected rapprochement with Angola. Thanks to the mediation of President Opango of Congo, delegations from the two countries held talks in Brazzaville on 15-17 July, at which agreement was reached on the mutual repatriation of refugees (who numbered several hundred thousand), the reopening of the Benguela railway, and the setting-up of an OAU commission, to be composed of Sudan, Nigeria, Cameroon and Rwanda, to check on any military development on the Angola–Zaïre frontier. There was understood to be a further implicit agreement that both sides should abandon their encouragement of the other's dissidents. Further negotiations, including a secret meeting between Presidents Mobutu and Neto, led to the announcement on 30 July that the two countries had decided to exchange ambassadors. President Neto, who was accompanied by several of his Ministers, was warmly received when he visited Kinshasa on 19-21 August. Progress was then reported on an agreement for close cooperation which was signed when President Mobutu, in his turn, visited Luanda on 15-16 October.

Shaba, meanwhile, remained quiet. More than 30,000 refugees had returned from Angola and Zambia by the close of the year and an end to martial law was promised for January 1979. The physical damage to the mining installations had not been very severe and some copper production was resumed in June. There was, however, a 50 per cent cut-back on contracted export deliveries to the end of 1978, and it was impossible to assess the long-term consequences of the flight of so many indispensable technicians. The Benguela railway, linking the mineral wealth of the province to the Angolan port of Lobito, was officially reopened, after a three-year closure, on 4 November, but its operations continued to be seriously impeded by acts of sabotage by the Angolan rebels.

The celebration in November of the thirteenth anniversary of Zaïre's second republic was attended by Mr Moose, US deputy Secretary of State for African Affairs and Mr McHenry, US deputy ambassador to the UN. Great interest across the country was aroused in November by the broadcasting, for the first time, of parliamentary debates, in which members were allowed to question Ministers on a wide range of topics.

In the same month it was announced in Brussels that four of the opposition groups (not including the FNLC) had come together to form the Organization for the Liberation of Congo-Kinshasa (OCL), under the leadership of one of President Mobutu's former Ministers, Mr Mbeka Makosso.

RWANDA AND BURUNDI

President Habyalimana of Rwanda visited Peking in June. The country began the return to constitutional legality after five years of military rule. The draft of a new one-party constitution was approved by the central committee of the ruling National Revolutionary Development Movement in October, and by a referendum in December, held simultaneously with the election which confirmed the President in office.

Burundi agreed to compensate Tanzania for frontier violations in 1973 (see AR 1973, p. 281) and in May plans were announced for closer co-operation between both countries and Tanzania, especially in the fields of transport. A Cuban embassy was opened in Burundi in May.

President Bagaza of Burundi reshuffled his Cabinet in October, the key ministries remaining in the hands of military officers.

Both countries suffered from a serious epidemic of cholera, which broke out in June, and received emergency aid from Belgium and other Western countries.

GUINEA-BISSAU AND CAPE VERDE

Both countries had begun to follow a more clearly non-aligned foreign policy. The state visit to Lisbon in January by President Cabral of Guinea-Bissau initiated an improved relationship with Portugal, which enabled Bissau to mediate successfully between Angola and the former metropolis in June. Both countries, too, had been hard hit by drought and depended heavily upon rice and other food shipments from the United States and Britain.

In April President Cabral and President Pereira of Cape Verde both participated in the Lagos summit conference of Ecowas.

Mr Mendes, the Chief Commissioner (*i.e.* Prime Minister) of Guinea-Bissau, was killed in a road accident in July. He was succeeded *pro-tem* by Mr Teixera, the Interior Minister, and definitively in September by Mr Vieira, the former Minister of Defence, who had been a prominent leader throughout the struggle for independence. The new Government announced in October showed few changes of personnel.

In November, Bissau government forces captured a group of armed rebels, said to have infiltrated from Senegal.

Cuba continued to provide scholarships and other technical assistance, but more substantial aid came from the United States, West Germany, Norway, Sweden, Brazil, Saudi Arabia and Kuwait. France was planning to open embassies in both countries.

SÃO TOME AND PRINCIPE

There was an alarm in February of an impending invasion by mercenaries, but nothing came of it. The country was drawing closer to the francophone African states and was represented at their Paris summit in May. President Pinto da Costa visited Tripoli in April and signed a treaty of technical cooperation with Libya. A loan of $8 million from the African Development Bank was earmarked for the renewal of cocoa plantations.

MOZAMBIQUE

Having the most active of the Zimbabwe guerrilla movements, Mr Mugabe's Zimbabwe African National Union (ZANU), based upon its territory, Mozambique continued to be embroiled, as the most committed of the 'front-line' states, in the deteriorating situation in Rhodesia. Talks in Maputo from 7 to 9 January between President Machel and Field Marshal Lord Carver, the British commissioner-designate for Rhodesia, and the UN representative Major-General Prem Chand achieved a large measure of agreement on the Anglo-American proposals for a settlement, but this relatively conciliatory stance proved unavailing upon the subsequent breakdown of the Malta talks (see p. 246). The President condemned the 'internal settlement', and in February Mozambique became a member of the new military committee set up by the military committee of OAU. ZANU stepped up its military operations, and Rhodesia, while claiming to have 'no quarrel' with the Government of Mozambique, responded with a succession of raids on guerrilla camps inside that country. These culminated on 30-31 July in a large-scale assault, with heavy air support, which penetrated a hundred miles beyond the border and was claimed to have 'neutralized' ten of the camps.

Meanwhile the economic situation looked desperate, production nowhere attaining pre-independence levels, reserves dwindling to vanishing-point and the trade deficit reaching $280 million. A further cruel blow was the ending in April of the very lucrative arrangement which permitted Mozambique to sell on the open market the gold earned by its workers in South Africa.

Major Government changes in April, which brought the governor of the bank into the Ministerial Council, seemed designed to give priority to the task of economic reconstruction. At the same time four of the ten provincial governors were dismissed, to 'reinforce the defence of public order'. The collectivization of agriculture was creating problems and the Minister responsible was dismissed for corruption in August. In the same month the People's Assembly approved a new constitution and ratified laws to reform banking and local government and to nationalize the Moatize coal mines.

An agreement for technical and economic cooperation with Libya was ratified in April, and President Machel obtained similar treaties from his visit to North Korea and China in May. A treaty of friendship with Angola was signed by Presidents Neto and Machel in Maputo on 19 September. The two leaders took this enthusiastic occasion to reaffirm their total support for the Zimbabwean Patriotic Front and their determination to build their societies on marxist-leninist principles. There was a further minor reshuffle of the Government in October. The Cuban Foreign Minister, Mr Malmiera, visited Maputo in November.

ANGOLA

The abortive left-wing coup of the previous May (see AR 1977, p. 243) had been followed by a drastic purge of the ruling party, the Popular Movement for the Liberation of Angola (MPLA), but in the opening months of the year the opposition guerrilla movements continued to represent a real threat to the stability of President Neto's Government. A diplomatic initiative in Kinshasa in January failed to persuade President Mobutu of Zaïre to withdraw his support from the Front for the National Liberation of Angola (FNLA) and the National Union for the Total Independence of Angola (Unita). Little credibility could be accorded to the FNLA claims of new successes in the north, but the situation was more dangerous in the south, where the Unita forces of Dr Savimbi were successfully tying down perhaps as many as 19,000 Cuban troops. In spite of government attempts to win over the population by the extension of medical and educational services, Unita appeared to enjoy widespread support among the Ovimbundu people, the largest tribal group in the country. It was also receiving regular aid, from beyond the frontier, from South Africa and Zaïre. Angola complained in January of many violations of its frontier. The military position was further complicated by the guerrilla war against the South Africans in Namibia being waged from Angolan soil by the South-West African Peoples' Organization (Swapo) with the assistance of Angola and Cuba, and the continued presence on the Zaïrean border of the 'Katangese' rebels who had invaded Shaba province in March 1977 (see AR 1977, p. 236).

In February there were reports of heavy fighting in the south, in which South African troops were reported to be involved. In March the Government opened a major offensive against Unita in the south-eastern province of Cuando-Cubango, in which the civilian population was said to have suffered heavily. East German as well as Cuban military elements participated in these operations, and the East German Defence Minister, Major-General Hoffman, visited Luanda at the beginning of May, at the head of a strong military delegation. A strong South African raid on 4 May against Swapo bases deep in Angola was condemned by the UN Security Council and evoked a concerted protest to Pretoria from its five Western members. Then came the renewed 'Katangese' invasion of Shaba (see pp. 233–4), with which, of course, Angola unconvincingly denied its involvement.

The ensuing flurry of diplomatic activity was accompanied by a marked shift in Angola's foreign policy towards conciliation with the West. The first Angolan ambassador to Lisbon took up his appointment at the beginning of June, and on 26 June, after three days of surprisingly cordial talks in Guinea-Bissau, Presidents Neto of Angola and Eanes of Portugal concluded a three-year treaty of cooperation, promising a return to the close economic ties of the past. It was agreed to set up a joint committee to deal with outstanding financial differences arising out of Angola's nationalization of Portuguese assets. Angola released a number of Portuguese prisoners, while Portugal endorsed the stand taken by the lusophone African states on the conflicts of Southern Africa.

Already on 20 June Secretary of State Vance had said that the US should seek improved relations with Angola 'to improve the prospect for reconciliation between Angola and Zaïre as well as for achieving a peaceful settlement in Namibia', and the offer of this olive branch was quickly followed up by a visit to Luanda by Mr McHenry, the US deputy ambassador to the UN. Responding on Angola's past, Mr Jorge, the Foreign Minister, said on 15 July that his Government planned to diversify its relations with all other countries in accordance with its policy of non-alignment. In August, the President himself declared that 'we are prepared to establish diplomatic relations with the US', but the Americans 'will have to take us as we are'. He was not prepared, that is to say, to pay for improved relations with the US by any reduction of the Cuban military and advisory presence in Angola.

There was the beginning of a thaw too in relations with France, but the most important contribution to a relaxation of tension in the region was the reconciliation with Zaïre, which was sealed by President Neto's official visit to Kinshasa on 19 August (see p. 235). In all this, the greatest gain for Angola was the prospect of the withdrawal of all external support for FNLA and Unita. For the former the end seemed to be in sight, and when President Mobuto visited Luanda in October he claimed that its forces in Zaïre had already been largely disarmed. The last remaining threat came from continued South African aid for Unita, and its removal would clearly have to wait upon an international resolution of the problem of Namibia.

In September the President held talks with President Opango of Congo in the Cabinda enclave and signed a cooperation agreement. During this visit, Dr Neto announced a forthcoming amnesty for hundreds of political prisoners associated with FNLA, the National Liberation Front of the Cabinda Enclave (FLEC), and dissident groups within the MPLA. To complete 'the plan for national harmony' he called for the return of Angola emigrants living in Portugal and elsewhere in Africa.

A renewed offensive, in alliance with Swapo, was launched against Unita in October, but the guerrillas, though hard pressed, seemed far from defeat. They were held responsible for the two bombs which exploded in the municipal market in Huambo on 10 November, killing 40 people and injuring 121.

On 7 November Major Carreira, the Defence Minister, ordered general mobilization in anticipation of a major airborne attack from South Africa which the Government was said to be expecting. Indeed the President asserted that South Africa was already waging an undeclared war against Angola by the aid it was giving to Unita. On 14 November the UN Special Committee on Apartheid appealed to all governments to help Angola to repel South African aggression. South Africa hotly rejected these charges, describing them as a propaganda smokescreen for a projected communist aggression against itself, and pointing to the recent arrival of a battalion of East German paratroops in southern Angola. On 21 November the US deputy Secretary of State for African Affairs, Mr Richard Moose, arrived in Luanda with the strongest American delegation ever to have visited Angola, and it was speculated that the US was seeking a compromise settlement between the Government and Unita.

The first British ambassador was appointed in September and presented his credentials in November. In that month, France, too, proposed to raise its diplomatic representation to ambassadorial level. The country was visited in December by the Presidents of Bulgaria and Liberia and by US Senator McGovern.

In such a troubled year there was inevitably small sign of economic recovery. Production nowhere regained the levels of 1973, and the country remained heavily dependent on its revenues from the off-shore operations of the Gulf Oil Company. Dr Neto had proclaimed 1978 the year of agriculture, but little was achieved in the face of peasant discontent with socialization. Besides its heavy military commitment, Cuba supplied several hundred secondary school teachers and more than 2,000 scholarships for training in Cuba. The Catholic radio station was nationalized in January, and the Jehovah's Witnesses were banned in March.

Chapter 2

ZAMBIA—MALAWI—RHODESIA—BOTSWANA—LESOTHO—SWAZILAND

ZAMBIA

ZAMBIA endured a bleak year. Economic problems escalated. Impending national elections had an unsettling influence politically, in face of popular discontent over the Government's performance. Armed conflict in Southern Africa spilled over three borders, most seriously that with Rhodesia. Though the economic crisis was easing toward the year's end, future prospects remained uncertain. At the December elections, Dr Kenneth Kaunda, Zambia's President since independence, won impressive support and a fourth term, but no basic issues were resolved.

Zambia's vital copper industry suffered multiple blows from depressed market prices, mounting production costs and shortages of essential materials, spares and skilled staff; transportation bottlenecks created a serious copper export backlog. Both state-owned mining companies again made losses, requiring substantial loans to maintain operations. The balance of payments continued in deficit, and foreign exchange reserves were exhausted; by April import payment arrears reached 15 months. Consumers experienced frequent shortages of basic domestic commodities.

Following an austere January Budget, a tough stabilization programme was negotiated with the International Monetary Fund. In return for a short-term US$390 million loan, Zambia promised further cuts in government expenditure, reduced public indebtedness and a progressive shortening of delays in import payments. The mines were to improve profitability and restrain borrowings. The kwacha was devalued by 10 per cent.

Despite the IMF package, Zambia's aid requirements remained substantial. In May, an appeal for an additional US$400 million brought a massive loan offer from unidentified Arab sources—an offer later rejected because there were 'strings attached'. In late June the World Bank assembled 20 countries and international agencies in Paris to consider a possible rescue operation. A subsequent attempt to organize a sizeable loan through commercial banks had disappointing results.

Unless the mining industry regained profitability, such aid efforts appeared a problematic palliative; by the year's end, per-capita foreign indebtedness was the heaviest in Africa. The emergency measures also brought political problems. A harsh election-year Budget risked a popular backlash. Mine industry layoffs, favoured by management, were resisted by a Government concerned about potential electoral consequences. Further public spending cutbacks might undermine Zambia's defence capabilities and diplomatic posture in an unsettled Southern African arena. Loan offers reportedly brought external pressures on Zambia to moderate its stand over Rhodesia.

Transportation difficulties caused persisting disruption, weighing heavily in the failure to meet IMF targets for reducing import arrears. The Chinese-built Tanzam railway, opened in 1975, carried under half its planned capacity because of management and operational problems; departing Chinese technicians were recalled. Dar es Salaam (Tanzania) now handled 90 per cent of Zambia's trade, but port facilities were overburdened.

On 6 October, Zambia unexpectedly reopened its southerly trade link through Rhodesia. When the border was closed in January 1973 in defiance of Rhodesian threats over Zambia's support for black nationalist guerrillas, this link represented Zambia's principal external trade route; its loss entailed enormous economic sacrifice in developing alternative communications arteries. Ostensibly the policy's reversal was necessary to increase copper exports and permit vital fertilizer imports before the November planting season. But the Government also faced heavy pressure to relax its stand, both domestically and from the IMF.

While Zambia claimed that the decision involved neither reopening the entire border nor actual trade with Rhodesia, its close allies in Southern African affairs, Tanzania and Mozambique, were dismayed. Zambia's initiative would boost Government morale in Salisbury and decrease Rhodesia's diplomatic isolation. It further strained the fragile unity among the 'front-line' African states. Dependence on Rhodesian and South African cooperation might require moderating Zambia's support for the armed liberation struggle in Southern Africa. It would certainly inhibit black guerrilla strikes against Rhodesia's railways; Joshua Nkomo, leader of the Zambia-based ZAPU wing of the Patriotic Front, promised that his forces would respect Zambia's decision (though the Mozambique-based ZANU wing said theirs would not). Zambia's insistence on maintaining the link after the fertilizer's arrival raised uncertainty regarding the Tanzam railway, jointly owned with Tanzania.

Zambia's economic difficulties thus interacted closely with its foreign and security problems. When Angola-based rebels used remote Zambian roads to launch a bloody invasion of Zaïre's Shaba province in May, Zaïre accused Zambia of complicity, expelling hundreds of Zambian citizens from Shaba. Zambia subsequently urged reconciliation between Zaïre and Angola, hoping partly to secure agreement to reopen the Benguela railway, which carried nearly half Zambia's trade until it was closed by the Angolan civil war in August 1975. Though officially reopened in November, harassment by guerrillas opposing Angola's marxist regime rendered this route unusable.

Over Rhodesia, Zambia initially maintained a low profile, having already withdrawn support from the Anglo-American plan for a constitutional settlement. By March, after the signing of the 'internal settlement' in Rhodesia and two major Rhodesian strikes against ZAPU camps in Zambia, diplomatic pressures were resumed. The 'internal settlement' was denounced; against the possibility that it might gain Western recognition, Zambia warned that this would escalate armed conflict, forcing Zambia to seek Soviet and Cuban assistance.

Zambia also revived its backing for the Anglo-American scheme involving a British-controlled transitional administration, a UN security presence, and elections before independence. Yet a separate strategy was apparent, for Mr Ian Smith twice secretly visited Zambia in August to meet Mr Nkomo. The meetings revived fears that, with Western encouragement, Nkomo might be enticed to join the 'internal settlement', jeopardizing the guerrilla struggle; the meeting of Patriotic Front leaders and 'front line' state Presidents in early September was stormy.

The downing by ZAPU guerrillas of a Rhodesia Airways Viscount on 3 September sealed this initiative's fate. The Bingham report, published on 19 September, confirmed participation by British oil companies in breaking UN sanctions, thus providing ammunition for Zambia's £4,000 million court claim against 17 Western oil firms for damages due to alleged sanctions violations. Revelations that sanctions-busting had involved official complicity deeply angered President Kaunda, bringing a meeting with the British Prime Minister and Foreign Secretary in Kano, Nigeria, on 22-23 September; discussions were reported to have centred on renewed British commitment over Rhodesia and further aid for Zambia.

Some two weeks after Zambia reopened the 'southern route', Rhodesian forces made a massive foray, striking 12 ZAPU camps, several deep inside Zambia and one near Lusaka. Hundreds died. Further strikes occurred near Lusaka on 2 November and Kabwe on 22 December. Besides mollifying white Rhodesian opinion, the raids apparently sought to forestall a ZAPU offensive and deadlock Anglo-American attempts to mount a settlement conference. With relatively few guerrillas committed inside Rhodesia, ZAPU's vulnerability was exposed; so also was Zambia's weakness, leaving the army divided about its role. Britain promptly donated 100 tons of 'defensive' military equipment.

The attacks worsened race relations. On 7 November, following allegations in government-controlled newspapers of expatriate 'fifth columnists' assisting Rhodesian raiders, angry mobs molested Europeans on Lusaka's main boulevard. ZAPU guerrillas also began harassing white commercial farmers in areas adjoining guerrilla camps, provoking demands that the camps be removed; these the Government rejected.

On 20 November Zambia announced that it would divert funds from development programmes to arms purchases. Following the December elections, President Kaunda warned that Zambia might seek Soviet arms, and declared his disillusionment with the Anglo-American settlement proposals; only war would settle Rhodesia's future.

National elections took place on 12 December in an inauspicious setting of economic dislocation and escalating conflict with Rhodesia. The credibility of the sole legal United National Independence Party (UNIP) having been damaged by reduced popular support at local party elections in 1977, it seemed, after the poor turnout at Zambia's first one-party elections in 1973, that public discontent might prevent President Kaunda's gaining the absolute majority required for election.

While only one presidential candidate would face the national electorate, several contestants might vie before UNIP's quinquennial General Conference for this privilege. By August President Kaunda had three challengers, most notably Simon Kapwepwe; once Zambia's Vice-President, Kapwepwe abandoned UNIP in 1971 to form a rival party. Formerly considered radical, Kapwepwe's platform was conservative, and included reopening the Rhodesian border. In September the General Conference passed constitutional amendments effectively disqualifying Kapwepwe; the other contestants showed limited support.

In the event President Kaunda won comfortably. Though the 'no' vote increased, he still won eight of every ten votes on a 67 per cent turnout. In the National Assembly elections, at least 24 sitting MPs lost, including ten serving or former Ministers.

MALAWI

President Kamuzu Banda continued his efforts at liberalization. On 29 June, Malawi's electorate voted for the first time since 1961, the election bringing to power the sole legal Malawi Congress Party. Since 1961 Banda had handpicked parliamentarians from party-prepared lists; he now chose alternative candidates for popular judgment. Forty constituencies went unopposed, many candidates being eliminated by an English proficiency test, not required since 1964. In 47 contested seats, 31 incumbent MPs lost, including two Cabinet Ministers.

Prohibited since 1973, Western journalists were readmitted, and Banda gave his first press conference in ten years. In August they were again banned.

Economic expansion continued. After the resumption of recruitment for South African mines in 1977, Malawian migrants there appeared to be stabilizing at around 20,000.

RHODESIA

For Rhodesia 1978 was a year of dramatic change and considerable tragedy. In January the minority Rhodesian Front Government of Mr Ian Smith held firm political control, but within two months an internal constitutional settlement had been reached and black Ministers shared Cabinet portfolios with white. By the end of the year almost all racially discriminatory legislation had been abolished and a new majority rule constitution framed. Behind political change lay the intensifying guerrilla war, which killed 5,500 Rhodesians of all races during the year. Almost the entire country was placed under martial law and in December the vulnerability of the capital itself was demonstrated when guerrillas blew up a major fuel-storage complex only six miles from the centre of Salisbury.

Talks to reach an internal settlement of differences over the transition from white to black rule had begun in November 1977 following Mr Smith's announcement of his Government's acceptance of the principle of majority rule. Discussions were resumed in the new year, the African participants being Bishop Abel Muzorewa, leader of the United African National Council (UANC), the Reverend Ndabaningi Sithole, head of a wing of the African National Council (ANC-Sithole), and Senator Chief Jeremiah Chirau, senior member of the moderate Zimbabwe United People's Organization (ZUPO), who together claimed to represent 85 per cent of black Rhodesians. After ten weeks of difficult negotiations, which threatened to break down at several points on the issue of white parliamentary representation, a compromise was reached on an independence constitution. Further talks resolved the question of the shape of the transitional government, and an agreement on independence under black rule by 31 December 1978 was signed in Salisbury on 3 March. The agreement outlined the central features of an independence constitution and provided for the establishment of an interim government to enact it (for text, see DOCUMENTS).

Outside Rhodesia the Salisbury agreement was widely condemned as illegal and unacceptable. It was rejected by the 'front-line' African states, by the Organization of African Unity and, on 14 March, by the United Nations Security Council, the major Western powers abstaining in the vote. Chief among the opposition was the Patriotic Front, an uneasy alliance of the two Rhodesian nationalist movements in exile, the

Zimbabwe African People's Union (ZAPU), led by Mr Joshua Nkomo, and the avowedly marxist Zimbabwe African National Union (ZANU), led by Mr Robert Mugabe. Both men boycotted the Salisbury talks. They attended instead a meeting in Malta on 30-31 January to discuss with Dr David Owen, the British Foreign and Commonwealth Secretary, and Mr Andrew Young, the United States permanent representative at the UN, the Anglo-American plan for peace in Rhodesia (see AR 1977, pp. 249-50) which remained, in theory, an alternative option.

Of the internal settlement Mr Nkomo said 'we are not going to allow it', and the Patriotic Front appeared to have the resources to do so. At its disposal it had a substantial guerrilla force, comprising the Zimbabwe People's Revolutionary Army (ZIPRA), controlled from Zambia by Mr Nkomo, and the Zimbabwe African National Liberation Army (ZANLA), controlled from Mozambique by Mr Mugabe. The Patriotic Front was armed and financed predominantly by China and Eastern Europe, although during 1978 Mr Nkomo obtained additional aid from Cuba. In a controversial move, too, in August the World Council of Churches authorized a grant of £42,500 to the Patriotic Front for humanitarian purposes, the Salvation Army suspending its membership of the Council in protest (see RELIGION).

During March and April the new Rhodesian Administration was established and began to outline its policies. On 21 March Mr Smith ceased to be Prime Minister and joined Bishop Muzorewa, Chief Chirau and Mr Sithole as a member of the country's Executive Council. Two weeks later an 18-member Ministerial Council was constituted, with one black and one white Minister holding responsibility over each of nine portfolios. The existing Parliament was to be retained throughout the transitional period, however, and the Joint Operations Centre, the supreme war council, remained wholly in white hands.

The new Government took immediate steps to lighten the political atmosphere. A constitutional commission was charged with drafting the details of the independence constitution and the ban on the operations of both ZANU and ZAPU was revoked. Political detainees were released, a promise given to dissolve the 'protected villages' and an amnesty offered to guerrillas wishing to return to Rhodesia. In July a committee was formed to consider ways of removing racially discriminatory legislation.

By mid-year, however, the interim Government was showing few signs of real progress. The artificial structure of the Ministerial Council was reflected in tension and disputes; Mr Byron Hove (UANC), the co-Minister of Justice, Law and Order, was dismissed only a month after his appointment for criticizing the racial exclusiveness of the police force. The Executive Council's lack of credibility threatened Bishop Muzorewa's position within his party. Movement towards dismantling racial discrimination was disappointingly slow. Legislative provisions announced on 8 August eliminated the superficial manifestations of segregation, and further amendments made public on 10 October were said to abolish discrimination in respect of land tenure, housing, education and medical facilities. In substance the changes replaced access to privilege by virtue of colour with access by virtue of wealth which, in the circumstances of Rhodesia, amounted to much the same thing. More serious was the Government's failure to secure the two major improvements on which its reputation most depended. It failed to win international recognition and the end of sanctions, and it failed to secure a cease-fire. Indeed eight emissaries of Mr Sithole and Bishop Muzorewa, dispatched into country areas in June to promulgate the amnesty, were themselves killed by guerrillas.

The success of the internal settlement was not aided by the continued commitment of the British and US Governments to the Anglo-American package. Both Governments held that any settlement which excluded the Patriotic Front could not be taken as acceptable to the people of Rhodesia as a whole. At the beginning of April President Carter announced plans to convene an all-party conference on Rhodesia. Later that month Mr Cyrus Vance, the US Secretary of State, and Dr Owen met Mr Mugabe and Mr Nkomo in Dar-es-Salaam for preliminary discussions on a new conference and on the role of a UN supervisory force during a future transitional period. The meeting was also attended by Field Marshal Lord Carver, resident commissioner-designate for Rhodesia, and by the designate head of the UN 'presence', Major-General Prem Chand. On 16 and 17 April Mr Owen and Mr Vance held further exploratory talks with the South African Foreign Minister in Pretoria and with the Rhodesian Executive Council in Salisbury. Between April and July Mr John Graham, a deputy under-secretary at the British Foreign and Commonwealth Office, and Mr Stephen Low, the American ambassador to Zambia, made repeated visits to political leaders inside and outside Rhodesia in an attempt to prepare for an all-party conference. The Rhodesian Executive Council opposed the attempts, however, Mr Smith anticipating a repetition of the Geneva stalemate (see AR 1977, p. 248) and the African leaders declaring the internal settlement 'final and unalterable'.

The worsening effects of the guerrilla war, however, forced a reconsideration of this rigid position. By mid-August both Mr Sithole and Chief Chirau had declared themselves ready for all-party talks, while Mr Smith conceded that the interim Government was in 'a tight corner'. The idea of accommodating Mr Nkomo in the Executive Council, previously mooted by Dr Owen (17 March), by the South African Prime Minister, Mr Vorster (27 May) and by Mr John Davies, the British Conservative front-bench spokesman on foreign and Commonwealth affairs (9 July), proved prophetic at the end of August. After a fortnight of vigorous denials from both sides, it emerged that Mr Smith and Mr Nkomo had met in secret in Lusaka on 14 August. Mr Smith was reported to have invited the ZAPU leader to return to a position of power in Rhodesia. Mr Nkomo, despite alleged intermittent rivalry between ZAPU and ZANU, refused to abandon his Patriotic Front colleague, Mr Mugabe.

The revelation, deeply damaging to both parties, put paid to further hopes of an all-party conference, and an incident in the war a few days later made rapprochement between the Smith and Nkomo factions virtually unthinkable. On 3 September ZIPRA forces, using a Russian-made Sam-7 heat-seeking missile, shot down an Air Rhodesia Viscount on a domestic flight from Kariba to Salisbury. Thirty-eight passengers and crew died in the explosion, and 10 of the 18 survivors were massacred by guerrillas where the plane fell, 50 miles west of Karoi. ZAPU claimed the aircraft had been engaged on military operations. The tragedy strongly alienated white opinion in Rhodesia. Mr Smith's consequent promise of 'more action, less talk' culminated, on 9 October, in a devastating retaliatory air attack on ZIPRA transit camps 12 miles from the Zambian capital of Lusaka. At least 300 died; Rhodesian sources claimed 1,500 casualties.

Having failed to woo Mr Nkomo, Mr Smith returned to the defence of the internal settlement. On 6 October he travelled to the United States as guest of the 'American Security Council', a conservative organization led by Senator Samuel Hayakawa of California. The visit was a major exercise in public relations, during which Mr Smith and Mr Sithole toured extensively for 20 days 'explaining' the internal agreement. The US Government, which had initially declined to grant the Rhodesians entry visas, took little obvious interest. Mr Vance received Mr Smith for discussions, but President Carter made it clear he saw no reason to do so.

During the year the guerrilla war reached new levels of ferocity and horror. By July an estimated 6,000 to 10,000 guerrillas were operating within the country, while incursions on three fronts—the borders with Mozambique, Zambia and Botswana—left the security forces fully extended. The war absorbed 15 per cent of Rhodesia's gross national product, or £500,000 a day. All white males below the age of 50 were mobilized, either in the regular army or in the reserve, and on 17 September the Executive Council announced unpopular plans to conscript blacks in addition to the existing large African volunteer force. Although martial law had been proclaimed over most rural districts, some localities were plainly in guerrilla control. In these areas rural life was seriously disrupted. Taxes were left unpaid, local councils ceased to function, schools and missions were forced to close and agricultural production was disturbed. The contraction of veterinary services in tribal trust land resulted in the loss through disease of half a million cattle, valued at £30 million. In November Mr Smith conceded that, if his Government was not losing the war, it was no longer in a position to win it.

Guerrilla attacks continued to concentrate on 'soft targets', missions, schools and isolated white-owned farms. During June 19 missionaries were killed in various parts of the country. The savage murder on 23 June of twelve Britons at the Elim Pentecostal Church mission station near Umtali captured the attention of the world's press. The identity of the murderers was not conclusively proven, insurgents and security forces each accusing the other. Guerrilla groups also extended their strikes deeper within the country and closer to urban centres. Umtali was shelled on 8 September and the presence of guerrillas near Salisbury was shown by attacks on outlying houses and by the fuel-storage depot bombing in December. A new feature was the appearance of 'private armies', factional groups of renegade guerrillas and deserters, responsible for random violence and intimidation of rival supporters. These represented an ominous threat to future stability and order.

Pre-emptive strikes by the security forces on guerrilla base-camps inside neighbouring territories continued, without conspicuously stemming the influx. In February Rhodesian commandoes attacked a ZIPRA base inside Zambia, killing guerrillas and at least eight Zambian troops. In the same month a security patrol pursued guerrillas inside the Botswana border, causing the death of several Botswana soldiers. Between 19 and 24 September a major strike was launched against ZANLA camps in Mozambique, including the base at Chimoio, the scene of a similar attack in 1977 (see AR 1977, p. 251). With much of Rhodesia an operational zone, villagers and tribesmen became unwitting victims of the guerrilla war. On 16 May, for example, 50 curfew-breakers from the Gutu area were killed in crossfire between Rhodesian forces and ZANLA guerrillas. Since 1965 over 2,600 black civilians had been killed in the war, compared to fewer than 350 whites.

The high cost of the war left Rhodesia with a constricted economy and a budget deficit of £100 million. The dollar was devalued by 8 per cent on 3 April in an attempt to improve the unfavourable balance of payments. Inflation fell to 7·7 per cent, however, while mineral and agricultural production showed an increase in value, though not in volume, on the 1977 figures. The economy stood to benefit from the reopening of the border with Zambia at the Victoria Falls. A critical shortage of fertilizer and other commodities had compelled President Kaunda to revoke the closure of 1973. Rhodesia attracted fewer tourists than in the previous year, and the emigration of 13,700 whites indicated a disintegration of white morale. Indeed the cohesion of the white community and the traditional sanctity of the Rhodesian Front were both under attack. On the left, businessmen openly criticized the Administration's ineptitude and, on the right, Mr Smith himself was termed a traitor at a public meeting in December.

In Britain it was revealed in September that the Southern African subsidiaries of two multinational petroleum companies, British Petroleum and Shell, had been involved since UDI in 1965 in an arrangement with the French company Total to supply Rhodesia with oil in contravention of British and UN sanctions legislation. The report of an enquiry conducted by Mr Thomas Bingham QC and published on 19 September raised questions about the role and complicity of successive British Prime Ministers and their Cabinets (see pp. 31-32). The Rhodesian sanctions order was nonetheless renewed in the House of Commons for the fourteenth year, despite the dissentient votes of a large body of Conservative MPs (see p. 33).

Politically the year ended on a pessimistic note. Mr Cledwyn Hughes, sent to Africa in November by Mr Callaghan, the British Prime Minister, to attempt to revive the option of all-party talks, found that the sides were too far apart for constructive discussion. Within Rhodesia Mr Rollo Mayman, co-Minister for Internal Affairs and a founder member of the Rhodesian Front, resigned from the Cabinet on 27 December, claiming that the country's best course would be to surrender itself to British jurisdiction. Mr Smith confirmed that the 31 December deadline for the attainment of majority-rule government could not be met. On 22 December he introduced a draft constitution for the proposed new state of Zimbabwe Rhodesia. Plans were announced to submit the constitution—in which substantial guarantees for whites were to be entrenched for ten years after independence—to a referendum of the European electorate on 30 January 1979, and to hold national elections on 20 April.

BOTSWANA

Botswana, like Lesotho and Swaziland, continued to accommodate substantial numbers of refugees from South Africa. But the Botswana Government reaffirmed that it would not allow its territory to be used as a springboard for attacks on targets in the Republic. Botswana would continue to provide an open door to refugees, it was stated, but would refuse passage to armed insurgents, as it had done since becoming independent in 1966.

An upsurge of student activism in Gaberones led to clashes between students and police. It appeared that the opposition Botswana National Front, which favoured lending support to the South African liberation movements, was gaining ground among students at the University College of Botswana. The influx of refugees from Rhodesia and South Africa was said to have had a marked effect on the political climate in the country.

There were further reports during the year of skirmishes between Rhodesian and Botswana troops on the Botswana–Rhodesia border. Speaking on the 12th anniversary of Botswana's independence, the President, Sir Seretse Khama, said what was happening in Rhodesia was bound to happen in South Africa, if Pretoria continued to frustrate the implementation of the Waldheim report on Namibia (see p. 256).

LESOTHO

A United Nations commission visited Lesotho in June in terms of a Security Council decision to keep the economic situation in the kingdom under constant review. The commission also visited Swaziland and Botswana, reviewing the UN's economic assistance programmes for these countries. In October, it was announced that Lesotho would build an international airport at a cost of R25 million. Earlier, Lesotho had entered into an agreement with Mozambique for the opening of an air service between the two countries.

Lesotho's relations with the South African Government continued on a somewhat uneasy footing. A visit by a Cuban delegation to Lesotho caused concern in Pretoria that Lesotho might be about to enter into diplomatic relations with Cuba. The South African Minister of Foreign Affairs, Mr R. F. ('Pik') Botha, said that, while his country did not interfere in the affairs of its neighbours, there was reason to hope that Lesotho would not do that.

At the UN General Assembly, Lesotho's Foreign Minister, Mr Charles Molapo, said that his country's willingness to meet the obligations of Security Council resolutions concerning South Africa should be matched by a willingness in the international community to assist his land-locked country. Lesotho, he said, was harbouring more than 700 refugee children from South Africa.

SWAZILAND

The Government of Swaziland, in a statement in December, denied that guerrillas of the African National Congress (ANC) had established bases in the country for the purpose of infiltration into South Africa: Swaziland had an obligation under the UN refugee convention to grant asylum to people fleeing their countries for political reasons, but, contrary to false newspaper reports, had never pledged secret support for terroristic activities against South Africa. During the year, some members of both the ANC and its rival nationalist organization, the Pan African Congress, were detained by the Swaziland authorities, and some South African newspapers spoke of a clamp-down on the activities of the South African liberation movements in the territory.

In August, Dr Ambrose Zwane, leader of the opposition National Liberatory Congress Party, escaped from detention and, it was rumoured, fled across the border to Mozambique. Dr Zwane's party was banned by King Sobhuza II in 1973 and Dr Zwane himself had served four 60-day periods in detention.

In October, Royal Swazi Airways launched a weekly air service to Zambia. The airline was already flying to Johannesburg, Durban, Malagasy, Mauritius and Blantyre, Malawi.

Chapter 3

THE REPUBLIC OF SOUTH AFRICA AND NAMIBIA

IN 1978 the National Party Government of South Africa was rocked by the most serious political scandal in the country's history. Details came to light of the misuse of secret propaganda funds operated by the Department of Information, and the scandal led to the resignation of the Minister of Information, Dr Connie Mulder, and tarnished Nationalist Afrikanerdom's traditional image of unswerving rectitude in financial administration.

At the same time, Mr John Vorster, Prime Minister since Dr Verwoerd's assassination in 1966, stepped down from the premiership on the grounds of ill-health, precipitating a bitter leadership struggle in the Afrikaner Nationalist movement. The battle was won by the Minister of Defence, Mr P. W. Botha, a member of the so-called 'verligte' (enlightened) wing of the Government in racial policies but, in the past, somewhat hawkish in military and diplomatic policy. The Information scandal, and Mr Botha's actions to contain it, created severe internal tensions in the Afrikaner Nationalist establishment and threatened to split the National Party. It remained to be seen whether Mr Botha would be able to maintain party discipline and unity as effectively as had Mr Vorster.

As 1978 ended, appeals to Afrikaner solidarity were effectively rallying the ranks. Major differences, however, persisted within the National Party. The upheaval in white politics overshadowed developments on the inter-racial front, which was relatively peaceful after the traumatic years of 1976 and 1977 when the Soweto demonstrations and their violent suppression by the authorities attracted world-wide attention.

On the external front, the dominant concern was the continuing negotiation with the West and the United Nations over the future of Namibia (South West Africa). Here, South Africa, still administering the territory in spite of UN resolutions demanding its withdrawal, managed to fend off the threat of UN sanctions and to keep open the door for an internationally recognized settlement which, it was hoped, could be reached in the course of 1979, creating an independent Namibia. Throughout the year, a low-intensity guerrilla war continued in the northern sections of the territory, where insurgents of the South West African

Peoples' Organization (Swapo) operated from bases in neighbouring Angola and Zambia, and where South African security forces mounted counter-insurgency operations, including retaliatory raids across the border. South Africans were watching the deteriorating situation in Rhodesia with anxiety, but there was no likelihood of South African military intervention across the Limpopo, although the possibility remained of a limited rescue operation to evacuate beleaguered Rhodesian whites if the need should arise.

The Information scandal first broke into the open when the Auditor-General, Mr F. G. Barrie, reported to Parliament that unauthorized expenditure had been undertaken by the Department of Information. The full dimensions of the scandal did not become clear until after Parliament had risen and there was a series of shock disclosures in the South African press, notably in the *Sunday Express*, and an announcement by a Supreme Court judge, Mr Justice Mostert, that evidence had been given to him of large-scale misappropriation of public funds and of 'corruption in the wider sense of the word'. Against the express wishes of the new Prime Minister, Mr Botha, who believed that disclosure was premature, Judge Mostert made public the transcript of evidence given before him by a millionaire business man, Mr Louis Luyt, and others. Judge Mostert, who was sitting as a one-man commission of inquiry into exchange control contraventions, was dismissed from the commission by Mr Botha and it was wound up. Amid Opposition charges that he was engaging in a cover-up, Mr Botha appointed a new judicial commission of inquiry, under the chairmanship of Mr Justice Erasmus, to examine the allegations made before Mr Justice Mostert.

The Erasmus commission sat in secret but its report, which was quickly forthcoming, penetrated to the core of the matter. The truth of the Mostert revelations was confirmed, notably that Mr Luyt had acted as a front for the Department of Information, secretly employing public funds in an unsuccessful attempt to take over the powerful anti-Nationalist SAAN group of newspapers. It was also confirmed that, subsequently, about R30 million of public funds had been spent on the establishment of a pro-Government English-language daily newspaper, the *Citizen*, operating in direct competition with the liberal *Rand Daily Mail*. Judge Erasmus also found that there was evidence pointing to criminal activity and that the secret funds had been used to buy seaside flats in South Africa and properties in Cannes, in the South of France, and in Miami, Florida.

At an early stage, the Secretary for Information, Dr Eschel Rhoodie, and his brother, Dr Denys Rhoodie, had been prematurely retired from the Department of Information. After the publication of the Erasmus report, their passports were ordered to be confiscated. But Dr Eschel Rhoodie had gone abroad and there was no indication that he would return to South Africa. The Erasmus report was scathing in its references to the retired head of the Bureau for State Security, General Hendrik Van den Bergh, and referred to evidence that General Van den Bergh had attempted to cover up the scandal in Dr Mulder's interests at the time of the succession struggle following Mr Vorster's resignation. Meanwhile, the disclosures had led to the resignation from the Cabinet of Dr Mulder, the Minister responsible for the whole operation.

Dr Mulder's resignation, under pressure, angered the conservative wing of the National Party, some of whose members believed that Dr Mulder, along with General Van den Bergh and the Rhoodies, was being made a scapegoat. Many Nationalists felt, it appeared, that there was nothing wrong in using public funds to finance a pro-Government newspaper, which could help create a more favourable picture of the country. It was felt that Dr Mulder had acted with the best motives and in the national interest and was being unfairly victimized. Feelings against the Cape-based Botha camp, which favoured full exposure of the scandal, were running high in the Transvaal when the head committee of the National Party in that province met to elect a successor to Dr Mulder as Transvaal leader. Dr Mulder declared in a public statement that his conscience was clear. As a gesture of support to him, the Transvaal party rejected candidates favoured by Mr Botha and elected instead a hardline ideologist, Dr A. P. Treurnicht.

The election was a slap in the face for the new Premier, who had pointedly overlooked Dr Treurnicht in appointing two 'verligtes', Dr Piet Koornhof and Mr Punt Janson, to ministerial posts in the key Department of Plural Affairs, which is responsible for the administration of legislation affecting blacks, urban and rural. The appointment of the relatively liberal Dr Koornhof was seen as a clear signal that Mr Botha intended to steer the party in a reformist direction. But the hostile gesture of the powerful Transvaal party suggested that he would find difficulty in 1979 in leading the National Party away from traditionalist, hardline attitudes.

Mr Botha was committed to introduce a new constitution, giving a greater political say to Coloured (mixed blood) and Indian South Africans, and was also under pressure from 'verligtes' to improve the political and economic lot of the urban blacks. But the conservative element in the party was expected to inhibit Mr Botha's freedom of action. In similar circumstances, Mr Vorster had always opted to shelve reform for the sake of maintaining Afrikaner unity. As 1979 began it was not yet clear whether Mr Botha was any more prepared than Mr Vorster had been to risk a split in the Nationalist movement and consequent dilution of Afrikaner Nationalist control of the country.

Meanwhile, the National Party and the prestige of its leaders, including Mr Vorster and Mr Botha, had been seriously harmed by the scandal. Opinion polls suggested that the party would lose some seats, particularly in English-speaking areas, as a result. Although the Erasmus Commission cleared both Mr Vorster and Mr Botha of any stain on their personal integrity, Opposition politicians argued that Mr Vorster, in particular, should bear the political responsibility, as it had been his personal decision which had created the secret funds, authorizing a radical departure from the traditional parliamentary control of public expenditure. In his new position as State President, however, Mr Vorster was constitutionally above the political battle and took no part in the ensuing controversy.

The Information scandal distracted public attention from the continuing negotiations over Namibia, which came close to breaking-point once or twice, with the threat of UN sanctions in the offing. In February, the ambassadors of the Western Five, as they became known (Britain, the United States, France, West Germany and Canada) delivered proposals for an internationally agreed settlement to the South African Minister of Foreign Affairs, Mr R. F. ('Pik') Botha. Eventually, in April, Mr Vorster announced in Parliament that South Africa had accepted the proposals, which called for a cease-fire, UN-supervised elections and a phased withdrawal of South African forces from the territory. Meanwhile the Western Five were exerting diplomatic pressures to secure Swapo acceptance of the proposals and were on the point of success when a South African raid over the Angola border, aimed at destroying Swapo guerrilla bases, took place amid considerable loss of life, including civilians, at a village known as Cassinga. In response, Swapo broke off discussions. Swapo guerrilla activity in Namibia continued throughout the year and there were a number of instances of urban terrorism, including the assassination of anti-Swapo political leaders such as the president of the Democratic Turnhalle Alliance, Mr Clemens Kapuuo, and bomb outrages in Windhoek and Swakopmund.

Meanwhile Western diplomatic endeavours to secure a peaceful settlement were intensified, and behind the scenes, it appeared, the support of the so-called front-line Presidents, including President Neto of Angola and President Kaunda of Zambia, was secured. In June, President Nyerere of Tanzania made his own contribution towards a Namibian settlement by releasing Mr Andreas Shipanga, a Swapo dissident, from detention. Mr Shipanga returned to the territory to found an independent political grouping known as the Swapo Democrats. Eventually, in July, it was announced that Swapo had accepted the proposals of the Western Five, presumably under strong pressure from the front-line Presidents.

On 27 July the Security Council of the United Nations approved the Western plan and resolved that it should be put into operation with the immediate dispatch of a special emissary of the Secretary-General, Dr Waldheim, to Windhoek. On 1 August, South Africa indicated its willingness to receive the special representative—Dr M. Ahtisaari—who arrived in Windhoek on 6 August and remained in the territory until 22 August, holding discussions with the Administrator-General of the territory, Mr

Justice M. T. Steyn, and drawing up a programme for implementation of the Western plan. On 24 August ten South African soldiers died in a Swapo rocket attack on Katima Mulilo and South African forces carried out a reprisal raid into Zambia. On 30 August the details of the UN programme for carrying out the Western plan were disclosed in a report to the Security Council by Dr Waldheim which called for a UN task force of 7,500 troops. It was to be the biggest UN operation of its kind since the Congo in the 1960s. However, on 31 August, the South African Minister of Foreign Affairs made it known that his Government objected to the size of the UN force and to other aspects of the Waldheim report, including Dr Waldheim's abandonment of the agreed date for elections and Namibian independence by 31 December 1978. Mr 'Pik' Botha flew to New York and handed over a 20-page letter to the Secretary-General, setting out his Government's objections.

On 20 September, Mr Vorster, who had been ill, called a press conference, and made two shock announcements—that he intended to step down from office, and that South Africa would proceed forthwith with its own internal elections in Namibia. Mr Vorster said he was not closing the door to further negotiations to achieve internationally recognized independence in Namibia. But there were fears that South Africa would go it alone with a so-called 'internal solution' and that the guerrilla war would be intensified.

In a last-minute attempt to salvage the Namibian peace plan, the Foreign Ministers of the Western Five flew to Pretoria on 16 October. During the discussions, the US Secretary of State, Mr Cyrus Vance, and the new South African Premier, Mr P. W. Botha, were said to have established a good personal rapport. One immediate result was a cessation of anti-Western and anti-American rhetoric by South African politicians. Eventually, it was announced that South Africa and Mr Ahtisaari would resume discussions on the implementation on the Waldheim report. While the Western powers would take no cognizance of the proposed internal elections, South Africa said it would do all in its power to persuade a newly-elected constituent assembly to cooperate in the holding of a second, UN-sponsored election. At the same time South Africa indicated that South African troops would be withdrawn from Namibia only when a complete and comprehensive cessation of hostilities had been established. South Africa insisted on the setting of a firm date for the UN-sponsored election, which was to be adhered to whether or not violence had ceased and, hence, whether or not South African troops had been withdrawn.

In December, the internal elections, which were boycotted by Swapo and the Namibian National Front, produced a landslide victory for the moderate, multi-racial Democratic Tuurnhalle Alliance (DTA), which immediately signified its willingness to cooperate in the holding of a UN-sponsored election, provided that the terms and conditions were acceptable.

In the internal elections, on an 80·3 per cent poll, the DTA won 41 out of 50 seats in the constituent assembly. The election was denounced as a sham by Swapo spokesmen in Windhoek.

After further exchanges of views between the South African Government and the Secretary General, it was disclosed that Dr Waldheim had signified his agreement with Pretoria's insistence on a complete cessation of hostilities in advance of the implementation of the UN proposals. In a letter to the South African Government, the Secretary General stated that the parties in the dispute had informed him of their willingness to undertake a comprehensive ceasefire. Dr Waldheim said he would propose a procedure for the start of the ceasefire at the appropriate time. Dr Waldheim felt the UN-sponsored election should be held not later than 30 September 1979. The Waldheim letter was welcomed by the South African Minister of Foreign Affairs as 'positive and constructive', and it was agreed that Mr Ahtisaari should return forthwith to Pretoria and Namibia for final talks on the deployment of UN personnel in the territory.

On the black political front, a significant development in 1978 was the cementing of the 'Black Alliance' between Chief Gatsha Buthelezi's Inkatha movement, a powerful Natal-based organization originating in the Zulu community, and the Labour Party, the strongest political grouping in the Coloured (mixed race) community. The alliance was committed to a policy of negotiation. Discussions continued during the year between the Labour Party and the Nationalist Government about Mr P. W. Botha's new constitutional plan aimed at extending greater political rights to the Coloured and Indian communities. The Labour Party insisted throughout, however, that it would not participate in a constitutional reform that did not extend political rights to the urban African masses.

According to Nationalist policy, blacks are excluded from a political say in the central government and are restricted to franchise rights in the tribal homelands in the rural areas, the so-called Bantustans, of which the Transkei, under Chief Kaiser Matanzima, and Bophutatswana, led by Chief Lucas Mangope, had already attained 'sovereign independence'. It seemed plain, however, that continued insistence on exclusion of the urban black millions from franchise rights in the central government would shipwreck plans for constitutional reform in 1979. While the 'black consciousness' political movements associated with the late Mr Steve Biko remained under prohibition, and many black consciousness leaders were banned or detained, a large section of the politically articulate African youth remained entirely outside the political process.

Politically-motivated violence continued during 1978, although sporadic and on a lower level than in the previous two years. The chief of the South African security police, Brigadier C. F. Zietsman, said that an estimated 4,000 black South Africans were receiving guerrilla training in Angola, Libya and Tanzania, many of them young Soweto schoolboys who had left the country in 1976 and could be expected to return, equipped with arms and explosives. In March, two bomb blasts rocked the central area of the coastal city of Port Elizabeth, leaving two people dead and three injured. In November, a guerrilla band entered the Northern Transvaal, apparently from Botswana, and a policeman was shot and injured in an ambush on a remote farm in the Louis Trichardt district. In the previous month, two guerrillas were shot dead in a clash near the Botswana border in the newly-independent tribal homeland of Bophutatswana.

The security police were active throughout the year in detaining political suspects and enforcing banning orders. In September, according to the Department of Justice, 78 people were in detention under the Terrorism Act, which provides for detention and interrogation in solitary confinement and incommunicado. There were a number of instances during the year of counter-violence, presumably by vigilante right-wing groups, directed against militant opponents of the Nationalist regime, the most notable of which was the murder of Dr Richard Turner, a banned left-wing intellectual, who was shot dead on his own doorstep by an unknown killer.

VIII SOUTH ASIA AND INDIAN OCEAN

Chapter 1

IRAN—AFGHANISTAN

IRAN

THE Iranian regime was overtaken during 1978 by a growing clamour of opposition of a scale and violence sufficient to shake the Shah's Government to its foundations and to put its entire future in question. In the early part of the year the main area of opposition was the universities, where demonstrations against the regime gathered in strength and were not put down by the authorities. On 7 to 9 January there was rioting in the important religious centre of Qom, when a call was made in public by the religious leaders in support of the Shah's most bitter opponent, Ayatollah Khomeini. Some 60 deaths resulted from the events in Qom, which set in motion a regular sequence of mourning for those killed by the authorities, rioting, repression and mourning again on a predictable 40-day cycle. Severe riots flared in Tabriz on 18 February, in Yazd on 14 March and in Tabriz on 9 April, eventually culminating in general street riots in Teheran and a strike in the bazaar on 7 May. A signal of the nationwide nature of opposition to the Shah was made on 17 June, which was widely observed as a national day of mourning. While it seemed that the tide of violence was receding in mid-year, outbreaks of bloody rioting at Meshhed on 22 July and a general clash between the security forces and mosque-goers on 30 July kept up the momentum of instability.

By August, the regime began to make concessions to public opinion in the hope of dividing the moderates from the extremists of right and left wings. Dr Amouzegar resigned on 6 August after exactly one year in office and Mr Sharif-Emami was appointed Premier. Although close to some of the religious establishment, Sharif-Emami was also associated with the regime and his appointment did little to placate the opposition, which, by this time, was almost entirely led and organized by the Muslim leaders supporting Khomeini. The new Prime Minister had to impose military rule in Esfahan on 12 August, and the opposition groups grew in strength as the regime haltingly made concession after concession and allowed the economy to fall further into recession. Terrorist involvement in a cinema fire at Abadan, in which some 430 persons died, tended to rebound against the regime, while the arrest in August of the former Prime Minister, Mr Amir Abbas Hovaida, on charges of corruption merely served to confirm allegations of massive corruption at the highest levels of the administration.

General and violent rioting in Teheran during the period 1 to 5

November led to the collapse of the Sharif-Emami Government. On 6 November military government was introduced led by General Azhari, the chief of staff. Martial law was declared throughout all major cities. The new Government promised to end corruption, to punish those who had offended against the public interest in the past, and to take greater cognizance of Muslim sentiments.

The major test for the military Government came during the Shi'i month of mourning, Muharram, when the religious leaders were traditionally at their peak of influence on the Muslim community and when the launch of a *jihad* or holy war against the Shah had been threatened. On 10 and 11 December, the height of the '*Ashura* feast, demonstrations were planned in Teheran. Although serious confrontation was expected, the army withdrew from the scene and the marches passed off peacefully, an estimated one million persons taking part on each of the two days. Under appreciable pressure from the United States to return to civilian government, the Shah spent much of his time attempting to bring the more moderate opposition groups into government and to abandon martial law. For the most part, leaders of the small and poorly supported political parties were unable to bring adequate backing to establish a Government and were averse to accepting leadership without major concessions from the Shah on the question of the constitution. For their part, the religious leadership remained adamant that they would not deal with the Shah at all and would use their power with the population to bring about calm only when Ayatollah Khomeini had returned from his 15-year exile and the Shah had gone.

Economic effects of the political strife were considerable. Sporadic strikes in the public services and industrial sectors early in the year later became orchestrated into a widespread and systematic sabotage of the economy. Two of the most damaging areas of industrial unrest were in the banking sector, where a combination of a withdrawal of labour and the physical destruction of banks by demonstrators effectively brought the banking system to a halt, and in the oilfields. A first strike of oil workers took place in November and was never entirely ended before a second phase of strikes began in December, virtually bringing oil production to less than one million barrels per day and often to less than the domestic demand within Iran. Exports, disrupted in November, ceased by late December. Meanwhile, many of the non-Iranians in the oil industry withdrew from the country, and indeed the exodus of foreign staff reduced ability in most sectors to produce at normal levels even when power supplies and raw materials were available. As the breakdown in services and law and order intensified towards the end of 1978, many Iranians in the entrepreneurial and professional classes left the country and further reduced available skilled manpower.

As the stability of the regime became increasingly open to doubt, US-

Soviet rivalry in the area increased. Both powers supported the Shah openly in the earlier part of the year but took up more ambivalent stances as his position deteriorated. The British Foreign Secretary, Dr Owen, expressed overt public support for the Shah during the year, but many states, including Japan, were quick to review their plans for future investments in Iran.

By the year end, the Iranian financial position was much undermined by falling oil exports, the flight of money overseas and continuing domestic price inflation. Foreign borrowing also became difficult and in December a group of foreign banks refused a major loan under negotiation with Iran. Imports ran at very high levels during the first half of 1978 but fell seriously during the fourth quarter of the year. Business confidence deteriorated sharply as the traditional bazaars closed in protest against the regime and as government spending on development dwindled. By the end of 1978 the economy was in great disarray and firmly sinking into recession.

AFGHANISTAN

In Afghanistan intense personal rivalries and severe food supply difficulties combusted with the strains inherent in efforts to modernize a mostly barren and very mountainous Islamic state, whose people are at times riven by ferociously combative tribalism, to precipitate another coup in Kabul in late April. The leading coup-makers were mostly the former accomplices of Mohammad Daud, who had himself come to power by means of a coup in 1973 and then had out-manoeuvred many of his former associates in a series of actual or simulated counter-coups to maintain his regime, until his eventual deposition and murder in April (see OBITUARY). During his five years of sternly imposed rule Daud had repressed right-wing Islamic groups such as the Muslim League. Meanwhile, Afghanistan's Communist Party split into two factions, the pro-Soviet Parcham and the more neutral Khalq. The latter, led by Nur Muhammad Taraki, was unwilling to accept Soviet advice that it should support Daud.

Daud had increasingly alienated various important elements in Afghan political life, either because his economic policy was insufficiently radical or because of his efforts to improve relations with Iran and the USA and to shelve ethnically-based irredentist claims to Pathan or Baluchi territory in Pakistan. Eventually repressive measures against radicals caused the Khalq and Parcham to reunite and Afghan politics rapidly polarized. On 27 April a relatively small group of educated middle-class officers, with some civilian support, formed a Military Revolutionary Council (MRC), stormed the presidential palace and government buildings, killed Daud and many of his supporters, and proclaimed a 'Republican Revolutionary

Council' (RRC) from which in effect the Government of the new 'Democratic Republic' of Afghanistan would be principally chosen.

Taraki was made President of the RRC and Prime Minister. A Government composed mostly of members of the Khalq and Parcham was formed, with Colonel Abdul Khadir, a leading member of the MRC, as Defence Minister. Afghanistan's leading Soviet-trained air force officers and some of the more technically competent army leaders affirmed strong support for the new regime. In his first broadcast Taraki denied that the regime was either communist or a satellite of the Soviet Union. He sought to allay the fears and secure the support of tribal and Muslim opinion.

The Democratic Republic was proclaimed on 30 April and recognized that day by the USSR, then on 1 May by India, Cuba and Bulgaria, and soon afterwards by Pakistan, the USA, China and many others. On 7 May Taraki said that relations with foreign countries would be influenced by how much economic assistance they provided. A few days later five economic agreements were signed with the Russians, including provision for oil and gas exploration. Taraki also expressed a wish to improve relations with Iran and with China, and even with Pakistan—ironically enough he made this last point whilst also reaffirming support for Afghani irredentism in the lands of the Pathan and Baluch. Non-alignment was still said to be a main *leitmotif* of foreign policy. During the rest of the year there were sporadic reports of factionalism and tribal skirmishes and localized expressions of disquiet and dissent throughout the country. Anxiety was expressed in Iran, Pakistan, China and a number of other countries regarding the pro-Soviet proclivities of the new regime in Kabul.

Perhaps in an attempt to allay some foreign criticism Mr Hafizullah Amin, Vice-Premier and Foreign Minister of Afghanistan, while in Havana in the first week of June to attend the bureau meeting of the non-aligned countries, gave an account of recent developments in his country. He said the revolution started on 27 April but preparations began on 16 April. The new ruling party, the People's Democratic Party, was established more than 30 years ago, Mr Amin said. It was a party of the working class and peasants. In recent times the party acquired deep influence in the military. 'The whole air force was for the People's Democratic Party, so that we could have accomplished our revolution one or two years before, but we wanted to stage the revolution at an appropriate time, without making heavy sacrifices.'

Chapter 2

INDIA—PAKISTAN—BANGLADESH—SRI LANKA—NEPAL

INDIA

THROUGHOUT 1978 India's foreign relations were relatively smooth and without any clearly adverse repercussions either domestically or externally. By contrast its domestic politics were markedly acrimonious, factitious and at times violent. There was no dramatic change during the year comparable with the electoral avalanche of March 1977, which had swept out Mrs Gandhi's Government and had brought in Mr Morarji Desai to be Prime Minister in a Janata (thinly disguised coalition) Government in New Delhi. Instead 1978 provided much evidence of factionalism and disarray within Janata and also saw the unmistakable beginnings of Mrs Gandhi's political recovery.

Consonant with the Janata Government's professed intention to practise a foreign policy of equal friendship with all and of 'genuine' non-alignment, a very considerable number of official visitors and delegations came to India and many missions went abroad. In foreign policy matters India's leaders (most notably the Foreign Minister, Mr Atal Bihari Vajpayee, a principal figure from the strong Jana Sangh contingent within Janata) throughout the year managed well the strenuous and at times difficult feat of staying on good terms with tried friends, particularly the Soviet Union and such fellow non-aligned stalwarts as Egypt and Yugoslavia, whilst gradually and circumspectly improving relations with former foes, such as the United States, Pakistan and even China.

First President Carter and then Mr Callaghan made official visits to India in early January. The Shah of Iran and later the Prime Minister of Vietnam visited in February. Mutually congratulatory joint communiques were published at the end of each of these various bilateral discussions.

Both Mr Carter and Mr Callaghan in turn discussed with Mr Desai, *inter alia*, the problem of nuclear proliferation. After their visits, however, Mr Desai publicly restated India's objections to signing the nuclear proliferation treaty and said that his country would not accept 'full scope' inspection, meaning IAEA inspection of all a country's nuclear facilities, wherever it got them from, unless and until the USA and USSR agreed to halt all nuclear explosions and started reducing their nuclear production and stockpiles as an essential prelude to the eventual elimination of all nuclear arms. More specifically, Mr Vajpayee said in the Lok Sabha on 18 April that India would have to be ready for a 'contingency' should the USA fail to supply enriched uranium for the Tarapur plant. The next day the Prime Minister told Parliament that the country would become self-reliant in the production of heavy water within two years, the requirement for India's atomic plants being about 250 to 300 tonnes a year.

In foreign policy matters generally there was cautious low-key continuance and confirmation of policies begun by Janata in the previous year, or of policies in effect inherited and accepted from the previous Government. A slowly unfolding detente with Pakistan was being worked out painstakingly, virtually issue by issue, such as the resumption of consular and trade relations. The Salah dam project was signed as a joint venture in April after eight years of intermittent and often stalemated negotiations. Some issues in Indo-Pakistan relations remained in effect non-negotiable, notably Kashmir, for reasons of local domestic politics as well as the more general political and security concerns of the two countries. Communal clashes, especially reports of violence by Hindus against Muslims in India, such as occurred in both north and even in south India (where Muslim minorities are usually relatively smaller than in the north) in 1978, could quickly agitate and inhibit the completion of any constructive business in Indo-Pakistan relations.

A detente with China was sought by the Indian Government even more gingerly than with Pakistan. Mr Vajpayee's planned visit to Peking in October was postponed because of his illness; but he had been to Moscow just beforehand, as if to convince the Russian leaders that any improvement in Sino-Indian relations would not be purchased at the price of a deterioration in Indo-Soviet links, whose multifaceted quality was amply demonstrated by the variety, size and frequency of missions of one kind or another journeying between the two countries.

In several respects 1978 was a good year for India's economy. The (June) 1977-78 grain harvest of 126 million metric tonnes was a record, and domestic demand and investment began to pick up after several years of sluggishness. The stock market index rose to 40 per cent above its 1977 low point. Industrial growth shot up to 9 per cent in the first half of the fiscal year; the wholesale price index was lower at the end of 1978 than it was a year before. Rising domestic demand cut exportable surpluses and the trade gap approached US$1,800 million by the end of 1978. This gap was bridged, however, and turned into a surplus by aid and remittances from Indians abroad. Foreign exchange reserves had continued to edge upwards towards US$7,000 million by the end of the year.

Some of the year's economic achievements were, however, in part legacies from the immediately preceding years of Mrs Gandhi's Government. One of the Janata Government's most serious shortcomings was its apparent inability to bring down unemployment. Despite the promise entirely to eradicate unemployment within a decade the number of people actually registered with employment exchanges had increased by 18 per cent between the time Janata came to power in March 1977 and the end of 1978. This figure alone indicated that the economy was not as healthy overall as other statistics suggested.

India's overall economic growth in 1977-78 was expected to average

5 per cent, and a draft of the sixth Five-Year Plan (1979-84) released on 21 March set an annual average growth target of 4·7 per cent.

On 24 May the Reserve Bank of India upvalued the rupee by 2·54 per cent relative to the pound sterling. On 10 August the rupee was devalued by 1·30 per cent against the pound. In an age of floating exchange rates a revision in the rupee–sterling rate became due whenever the pound sterling—India's intervention currency—appreciated or depreciated in terms of an agreed basket of currencies by more than 2·5 per cent.

Meeting in Paris in June the Aid-India Consortium pledged that a sizeable part of its aid for 1978-79 would consist of project assistance. Out of the US$2,431 million of aid pledged in Paris, $1,133 million were to be bilateral aid, with precise contributions on a country-by-country basis, depending on subsequent negotiations with each member of the Consortium: $1,250 million were to come from IBRD and IDA and $48 million from the EEC.

On 26 August India and the USA signed three agreements for development assistance worth $60 million to India. These grants were announced as being intended to support collaborative research and development activities falling within the priority areas identified by the Indo-US Joint Commission and its sub-commissions. The loans were made repayable over forty years, including an initial ten-year grace period after which interest would run at 3 per cent. The signing of these agreements marked the resumption of US development assistance to India, suspended in 1971.

In November an agreement was reached between India and the EEC whereby they would jointly undertake construction of industrial and other projects in third countries. Indian construction and consultancy companies and those of EEC member-countries would meet in Brussels early in 1979 to discuss details of collaboration arrangements.

The Janata Party, which became the governing party of India after the general election of March 1977, was a hastily contrived coalition of different interests animated by a common opposition to Mrs Gandhi. Throughout 1978, however, Mrs Gandhi's faction of the former governing Congress Party scored spotty successes in by-elections and was recognized as the official Opposition in the Lok Sabha on 12 April. The ever-moving Indian political mosaic became even more complicated during the year, especially within some states. In West Bengal, for instance, the local Communist Party (marxist) consolidated its position in village and district elections.

Kashmir, too, confirmed its reputation for factionalism and highly personalized volatile local politics when in October the Chief Minister, Sheikh Abdullah, abruptly dismissed his deputy, and colleague for forty-five years, Mirza Afzal Beg, from his Cabinet and his party, the National Conference. Reciprocal accusations of family nepotism and of harbouring

1*

dynastic ambitions, cries of which carried echoes elsewhere in India, lay at the root of this breach.

India's principal political limelight was, however, cast on Janata's chequered performance in office and the rampant internal dissension within the party, both at the centre and in some states. After considerable intra-party debate it was decided in early August that the 'annual' elections of the Janata parliamentary party would be postponed until the following 1 May. Mr Desai took a strong stand that the elections should be held as scheduled; at first, eleven members of the parliamentary party executive favoured holding the elections, while ten were against. Later three of them switched their votes, changing the former narrow majority into a minority. Elements from the erstwhile BLD (Charan Singh's group of well-to-do agriculturalists, mostly from India's north-west grain-producing states), the Socialists and the Jana Sangh (Hindi-speaking nationalists) combined together to frustrate their Prime Minister's wishes. The former Jana Sangh, in votes and seats the largest single previous party component within Janata, was deeply divided on this issue. Dr Subramanian Swamy, otherwise not known for his support for Mr Desai, was as vehemently in favour of holding the elections as Mr Vajpayee was opposed. The Union Petroleum Minister, Mr H. N. Bahuguna, was reported to have canvassed for a postponement among the members of the executive.

Despite earlier denials that she was interested in returning to Parliament, after her defeat in the general election, Mrs Gandhi carefully chose to stand as a candidate in a by-election in the Chikmagalur constituency in the southern state of Karnataka, where local support for her was strong. In early November she was duly elected and then made her political re-entry into the Indian Parliament, after a brief visit to Britain.

Throughout most of the year, however, the one-man Shah Commission appointed to investigate charges of misconduct under Mrs Gandhi's former Government continued its work and issued reports condemnatory of various acts performed by Mrs Gandhi and her associates while in office. Mrs Gandhi herself refused to testify under oath and questioned both the procedures of the Commission and its right to compel a Prime Minister to account for her official acts. She was cited for contempt.

In mid-December the Lok Sabha (Lower House) voted 279-138 (with 37 abstentions) in favour of a motion that Mrs Gandhi be expelled from Parliament and gaoled for breach of privilege and contempt of the legislature and stripped of her parliamentary seat. On 19 December Mrs Gandhi was arrested and taken from Parliament to Delhi's Tihar jail. Within the next week more than 50,000 protesters were arrested, over 15,000 of them in the northern state of Uttar Pradesh, Mrs Gandhi's former political base. Similar numbers were imprisoned in Tamil Nadu and Maharashtra states, the two southern states where her supporters command electoral majorities. In Lucknow two men skyjacked an Indian

Airlines Boeing 737, in a vain attempt to get Mrs Gandhi released, and were themselves remanded in custody. Mrs Gandhi was released one week later, as Parliament prorogued, because her committal to prison had been set to last out the current session of Parliament. She said that she would be a candidate at Chikmagalur when a new by-election was held. Some neutral observers surmised that the rising tide of violence in India could mean that Mrs Gandhi would attract support from the middle classes and all those longing for a return to order and discipline.

In a statement in Parliament on 22 December to explain his 'resignation' five months earlier Mr Charan Singh accused the Prime Minister of treating him as his servant in a letter demanding the Home Minister's resignation for openly criticizing the Government and for violating the principle of Cabinet solidarity. Mr Singh also accused Mr Desai of taking revenge on him for demanding an inquiry into allegations against Mr Kanti Desai, the Prime Minister's son, and of dismissing Mr Raj Narain, the former Health Minister, merely for suggesting the names of two people for posts.

The dispute between Mr Desai and his former Home Minister had been festering within the Janata Government at least since the spring of 1978, when Mr Singh began complaining publicly that Mr Desai was not urging swift and severe treatment of Mrs Gandhi, and perhaps went back to the very formation of the Government when Mr Desai and not Mr Singh became Prime Minister. The dispute erupted more prominently into the open when Mr Desai met President Carter in Washington in June. During their Prime Minister's absence Mr Singh and Mr Narain issued a series of statements sharply criticizing Mr Desai's Government. They contended that the Cabinet consisted of a 'group of corrupt, impotent Ministers'. They also demanded the establishment of special courts to try Mrs Gandhi and those of her associates who had introduced and implemented the 'Emergency' period of martial law.

Nearly a million peasants from all over northern India gathered in New Delhi during the weekend of 23-24 December, ostensibly to demand their rights and to pay homage to their leader, Mr Charan Singh, on his 77th birthday. The rally, which according to some press reports was the biggest ever in Delhi, had two main purposes: to demand from the Janata Government a better deal for peasants, and to demonstrate political support for Mr Singh. The rally was even bigger than that which assembled in December 1971 to hear Mrs Gandhi's victory speech after the war with Pakistan out of which an independent Bangladesh emerged. The enormous size of the crowd lent credence to Mr Singh's claim that he is the only political leader in India who can attract as large a gathering as Mrs Gandhi—at least in northern India.

Quite an array of prominent politicians joined Mr Singh on the dais. The Chief Ministers of Uttar Pradesh, Bihar, Harayana and Punjab, a

Union Cabinet Minister, three of the four general secretaries of the Janata Party and several members of Parliament thereby openly demonstrated support for Mr Singh and, at least by inference, criticism of the way he had been treated by Mr Morarji Desai. A ten-thousand-strong contingent of Akali (Sikh) warriors brandished swords and shouted anti-Morarji slogans. Perhaps the most politically intriguing gesture came from Mrs Gandhi, who sent Mr Singh a bouquet of flowers from her prison cell. Undoubtedly this gesture added spice to speculation, which was already rife, about Mrs Gandhi's alleged overtures to form political alliances either with Mr Singh and his supporters and/or with Mr Y. B. Chavan and Congress (Official) elements.

The patent disarray of Mr Desai's Government was further revealed when Mr L. K. Advani, the Minister for Information, resigned from the Cabinet on 26 December. This followed deadlock in the Rajya Sabha (upper House of Parliament), of which he was the leader, on the issue of charges of corruption against Mr Kanti Desai, the Prime Minister's son. Mr Advani withdrew his resignation a little later when the Cabinet agreed that a group of Ministers should examine the whole case afresh.

PAKISTAN

General Mohammad Zia ul Haq, Chief Martial Law Administrator, faced three major tasks as Pakistan entered 1978: first, to create suitable conditions for holding elections in preparation for the orderly transfer of power to the elected representatives of the people; second, to assure the aid-giving countries friendly to Pakistan, and the Muslim countries of the Middle East, that his Administration intended to restore democracy; third, to take effective measures to reactivate the ailing economy. Initially he had promised to hold elections within 90 days of taking over the Government on 5 July 1977. Subsequently, however, the elections were postponed because of the 'polarization still existing' among the various political parties. 'My efforts for holding the elections in 90 days were not realistic', he said, 'because I was not fully aware of what the inside contained. It was necessary to ensure before the elections that there would be no instability and negation of the object for which the 5 July operation was carried out.'

Following the postponement of elections General Zia ul Haq proposed to form, with the participation of the major political parties, an interim national Government which would function and share power and responsibility with the military. However, not all the major political parties agreed to participate in a national Government and the plan was dropped. But by July he was able to form a federal Cabinet comprising 17 Ministers and 5 Ministers of State belonging mainly to the Muslim League. 'We have laid a brick for the holding of elections in the country', he said.

In August the Pakistan National Alliance (PNA) parties decided to join the national Cabinet with General Zia ul Haq continuing as the Chief Executive. Air Marshal M. Asghar Khan of Tehrik Istiqlal and Mr Sherbaz Khan Mazari of the National Democratic Party declined to follow the PNA and demanded instead the holding of elections without further delay. But the parties in the national Cabinet did not favour an election before all the cases of alleged corruption with which former public representatives had been charged had been disposed off by the special courts. Besides, disunity in the ranks of the PNA and the break-up of the Muslim League into two factions created some problems not only for the PNA, of which the League was a constituent member, but also for the national Cabinet in which the party's representatives held several portfolios. A prematurely timed election, it was feared, might generate an abrasive political atmosphere. A late autumn election in 1979 was considered more possible, but no date was announced.

On 16 September President Fazal Elahi Chaudhry, having completed his normal five-year term under the Constitution, relinquished his office at his own request, and the Chief Martial Law Administrator, General Zia ul Haq, assumed the office of President of Pakistan until the election of a new President under the Constitution.

Meanwhile, in a unanimous judgment delivered on 18 March, a full bench of the Lahore High Court held the former Prime Minister, Mr Zulfiqar Ali Bhutto, and four other accused guilty in the murder case of Nawab Mohammad Ahmed Khan and sentenced all five to death. Mr Bhutto and the other four accused appealed to the Supreme Court against the High Court's verdict. After a hearing lasting seven months, said to have been the longest in the judicial history of Pakistan, the Supreme Court on 23 December declared the hearing closed and reserved its judgment.

Foreign relations presented a mixed picture. Relations with the Muslim countries of the Middle East were seen to have come closer during 1978. General Zia ul Haq's visits to King Khaled of Saudi Arabia, the Emir of Kuwait and the Shahenshah of Iran served to promote better mutual understanding. Following his talks with King Khaled in Riyadh in April, agreement was reached on expanded cooperation, and General Zia ul Haq declared himself satisfied with Saudi support for his policies.

Following the visit of the Indian Foreign Minister, Mr A. B. Vajpayee, to Islamabad in February, it seemed that relations between the two countries might improve. But this hope was short-lived. Commenting on a Pakistani statement on the subject of self-determination for the people of Kashmir, Mr Vajpayee told the lower House of the Indian Parliament on 6 December that in raising this question the Pakistanis were 'playing with fire'. They should not forget, he went on, that Pakistan's eastern wing was now Bangladesh and the consequences of any adventure by it would not be good. Not surprisingly his remarks caused resentment in non-government political circles in Pakistan.

In the first week of March President Daoud of Afghanistan paid a visit to Pakistan, returning General Zia ul Haq's earlier visit to Kabul. Before returning home, he told newsmen that 'a new chapter of goodwill and understanding had opened with the renewal of talks between Pakistan and Afghanistan'. But this promising climate of Pakistan-Afghan accommodation was dissipated in less than two months when President Daoud's Government was overthrown by a communist-led revolution in Kabul on 27 April (see p. 261). There were so many imponderables in the new situation that Islamabad, after recognizing the new regime, decided to adopt a wait-and-see attitude towards Kabul.

The year saw the successful completion of the Karakoram highway linking Pakistan and China. Built with Chinese technical assistance, it was regarded as a triumph of engineering and a symbol of practical friendship. China's Vice-Premier, Teng Hsiao-p'ing, came specially for the inauguration of the 500-mile highway by General Zia ul Haq on 1 June.

Washington's opposition to Pakistan's plan for acquiring a nuclear reprocessing plant from France led to cutbacks in American aid, except for the supply of concessionary wheat. The sale of arms to Pakistan remained in suspense, and Washington's reluctance to support Islamabad's request for rescheduling its debts was seen as linked partly to political reasons. These US moves led Islamabad to undertake a re-examination of the purposes of its membership of Cento, and to participate as an observer in the non-aligned conference of Foreign Ministers held in Belgrade in July.

The decline in the economy, evident during the past few years, was arrested and the private sector was given a wide range of incentives to encourage its participation in development and investment. The aim, as stated in the Five Year Plan, was to increase the private sector's stake in industry from 26 per cent to nearly 50 per cent.

In its survey of the national economy the report of the State Bank of Pakistan for the year 1977-78 stated that 'the overall performance of the economy during 1977-78 showed a marked improvement compared to the preceding year'. The overall balance of payments recorded notable improvement, mainly on account of a sharp rise in home remittances (estimated at $100 million per month) by some 1,200,000 Pakistanis working abroad. The agricultural sector had a mixed performance. While cotton production rose sharply by more than 30 per cent, wheat production declined by an estimated 6·7 per cent, and the fall could eventually turn out to be much larger.

However, the State Bank cautioned that the improvement in the overall performance of the economy during 1977-78 was largely in the nature of a recovery of the ground lost in 1976-77. The report underlined the fact that the improvement in the balance of payments during 1977-78 was mainly due to two factors: a sharp rise in home remittances by Pakistanis working abroad, and re-emergence of raw cotton as a major export item after its almost complete disappearance during 1976-77. Neither of these two factors, the Bank warned, represented a basic improvement in the exporting capacity of the country. Besides, the burden of foreign debt servicing was progressively mounting and the situation did not warrant any complacency.

BANGLADESH

Bangladesh continued its slow march back to democracy in 1978; its economy made steady progress, the national figures showing growth of 8 per cent and food production reaching record figures.

Major-General Ziaur Rahman had become President in April 1977. He offered himself for election in June 1978 by popular vote and won a massive 4 to 1 majority over General M. A. G. Osmany, commander-in-chief of the Bangladesh forces during the 1971 liberation war and a former Minister in Sheikh Mujibur Rahman's Government. Then President Zia set the machine in motion for parliamentary elections in late 1978 or early 1979. After hesitating for some time the President committed himself to a political role by forming and becoming president of the Bangladesh Nationalist Party.

Tricky negotiations continued until the end of the year to persuade the other political parties to contest the elections. At first it looked as if there would be a mass boycott, as fifteen parties declared that the terms of the elections were unfair. Though the opposition could not agree on a common platform they had four basic demands: that martial law be dropped; that President Zia should retire from the army; that political prisoners should be released; and that a parliamentary and not a presidential form of government should be adopted.

Both sides, however, had too much to gain from elections. President Zia wanted to put the full 'democratic' stamp of legitimacy on his rule. The other parties wanted a chance to make their voice heard and to get closer to the spoils of power. Concessions were made on both sides; President Zia released large numbers of prisoners, lifted the martial law restrictions that would limit the freedom of the politicians, and promised that the elections would be free and fair and Parliament sovereign. The opposition parties wanted more time, so Zia postponed the elections until mid-February 1979 and most of the opposition, including all the important parties, decided to contest them.

This activity reflected the growing confidence of President Zia, who also worked hard to expand Bangladesh's international links and to try to remove the impression that the country was a hopeless 'basket case'. He visited Japan, South East Asia, Yugoslavia, Romania, the United Arab Emirates and North Korea, and British Prime Minister James Callaghan and Chinese Vice-Premier Li Hsien-nien were among visitors to Dacca. There was tension with neighbouring Burma when more than 200,000 Muslim Rohingya refugees fled to Bangladesh. After protracted talks an agreement was made between Dacca and Rangoon and at the end of 1978 a slow trickle of refugees began returning to Burma.

Efforts in the foreign policy field were crowned late in the year when Bangladesh won the second Asian seat on the United Nations Security Council against the opposition of Japan. Tokyo's predictions had been that Japan would get the seat on the first ballot with a large majority, but after two ballots Bangladesh held a slight but growing lead and Japan withdrew.

Economically, the Bangladesh national accounts also showed improvements, growth of GNP being 8 per cent in the 1977-78 fiscal year, compared with 1·7 per cent the year before. Food production improved and was expected to reach 13·5 million tons in 1978-79, a substantial amount of wheat being produced in addition to the traditional more costly and less nutritious rice. Migration of workers to the oil-rich Middle East was also beginning to boost the balance of payments through remittances worth more than $100 million a year.

Nevertheless, the masses of Bangladesh were cut off from prospects of hope. Official land surveys conducted in late 1977 revealed that almost half of the population effectively had no land and that landlessness was increasing through distress sales at a rate two to three times as fast as that of the overall population. As there was industrial employment for only 6 per cent of the workers and unemployment was estimated at about 40 per cent, the prospects for the masses looked grim indeed.

Other studies also showed alarming trends. Competition for scarce land was becoming fiercer because senior army officers, policemen and bureaucrats were looking for land. In addition, academic research suggested that President Zia's attempts to encourage village 'self-help' schemes were making the rich rural barons better able to help themselves and were having little impact on the poor. Since the big landowners were prominent in the major political parties there were fears that the return of 'democracy' would make the Bangladesh masses' plight worse.

SRI LANKA

In 1978 Sri Lanka adopted a new constitution which marked the first major step away from the Westminster parliamentary system and towards a presidential system since independence had been granted thirty years before. Presidential powers had already been given to Mr J. R. Jayawardene (see AR 1977, p. 272) and from 4 February he was replaced as Prime Minister by Ranasinghe Premadasa, a former organizer and trade union official for the United National Party (UNP) and the first lower-caste Premier in the country's history.

The new presidential Constitution was eventually adopted by 137 votes to seven on 9 August after the major opposition parties had walked out of the National State Assembly. It reversed or altered many features of the Sri Lanka Constitution of 1972 adopted by the previous Government of Mrs Bandaranaike (see AR 1972, p. 286). The President would have power to appoint and dismiss Ministers, including non-Cabinet Ministers appointed to deal with district problems. As with the French Fifth Republic, the Prime Minister would be expected to command an Assembly majority but the President would have power to dismiss the Parliament under certain conditions without then having to stand for office again himself. Proportional representation was to be introduced, avoiding the landslides now common in general elections (see AR 1977, p. 271) but also making it unlikely that any party would gain the two-thirds majority necessary to replace or amend the Constitution. The President was empowered to call for a referendum, the independence of the judiciary was to be protected and there would be a parliamentary commissioner on the 'ombudsman' model. Fundamental rights were to be justiciable before the Supreme Court, non-justiciable rights and duties were enumerated, and the country was renamed the Democratic Socialist Republic of Sri Lanka.

Despite this change of name the UNP Government continued with measures designed to encourage private investment, to reduce the level of public welfare and subsidy and to reverse many of the policies of its predecessor. The Budget of 18 November gave a five-year tax holiday to small firms, freed 75,000 public servants from income tax for the coming year and liberalized estate duty for home-owners. A Tax Amnesty Bill was passed unanimously at the same time and a National Development Bank set up. The Minister of Finance, Ronnie de Mel, described these measures as 'the last chance for the private sector to reform itself'. As promised during the general election of 1977 (see AR 1977, p. 271) the Government set up a public authority in the greater Colombo area to manage a free trade zone close to Katunayake airport and designed to attract foreign investment from India and elsewhere. On a visit to India in October J. R. Jayawardene met President Sanjiva Reddy and Prime Minister Morarji Desai, reached an agreement to increase trade and claimed that there was considerable Indian interest in the free trade zone.

Throughout the year a special presidential commission investigated the actions of the previous Government and particularly allegations of malpractice against Mrs Bandaranaike and some of her relatives. The main allegation was that the former Prime Minister had violated the Land Reform Act (see AR 1976, p. 272). Mrs Bandaranaike appealed successfully to the Court of Appeal to stop the enquiry, a decision which was, however, overturned by subsequent legislation. Members of the Janatha Vimukthi Peramuna (JVP) also appeared before the commission to give their account of the insurrectionary events of 1971 (see AR 1971, pp. 282-84). In a reversal of the previous Government's position the former Governor-General Sir Oliver Goonetilleke was pardoned and returned to the island on 18 November (see AR 1975, p. 265 and 1976, p. 273, and OBITUARY).

Two major disasters struck Sri Lanka during November. On 15 November a plane full of Indonesian pilgrims crashed at Katunayake, killing 201 passengers. This was the second major disaster involving pilgrims in recent years (see AR 1974, p. 299). The safety of the airport was questioned by international pilots' organizations, the President ordered an official inquiry and a team from Indonesia also conducted investigations. At the end of November the east coast was struck by a cyclone, at least one thousand died in Eastern Province, the town of Batticaloa was destroyed and emergency laws were invoked on 30 November. The cyclone was followed by severe flooding.

The domestic political situation remained fairly calm, although there were student strikes in January over changes to the examination system. The University of Sri Lanka was reorganized into five campuses and the controversial system of weighting admissions introduced by the previous Government was amended. It was announced on 18 November that the capital would be moved to Kotte, the pre-colonial capital in the suburbs of Colombo, and that a new parliament house would be built there.

NEPAL

Throughout the year Nepalese leaders sought to stay on mutually acceptable terms with both India and China, a difficult feat even at the best of times now that Nepal's geographical and diplomatic isolation had become much less than it was before the 1950s, and especially when Sino-Indian relations had made this frontier sector of the Himalayas a zone of sporadically expressed rivalry rather than mere separation. Whether or not to maintain a marked inclination either towards India or towards China was an actual or potential source of discussion and controversy within Nepal's small political elite, much as it had been in 1977.

In April Nepal's Prime Minister, Mr Kirtinidhi Bista, visited New Delhi, in effect returning the visit made by Mr Desai to Kathmandu the previous December. In October Nepal's Premier went to Peking, the second such major visit to China from Nepal in recent years. Peking expressed support for the King of Nepal's proposal for a South Asian 'zone of peace', an idea for which Indian leaders showed no enthusiasm. New local 'nationalisms' in Nepal, and in Bhutan, were ending the political passivity which was once a basic precondition of their 'buffer state' status.

Chapter 3

SEYCHELLES—MAURITIUS—BRITISH INDIAN OCEAN TERRITORY—
MALAGASY

SEYCHELLES

THE Seychelles continued its policy of combining a hardline marxist dictatorship with an up-market tourist trade in 1978. The coup which installed Mr Albert Réné in power and swept away democracy in 1977 did not deter the tourists, whose numbers, the Government claimed, increased. Plans were made to add 500 'tourist beds' in luxury hotels with a target of 78,000 visitors by 1980 at a cost of $24 million in additional facilities, including a training school for Seychellois hotel workers. Token moves were made to attract proletarian tourists at cheaper rates, and 'island lodges' were projected in beauty spots.

A conference of Indian Ocean island communist parties and opposition groups was staged and resounding resolutions passed against the imperialist world from which the tourists came. In May, upon the return of Mr Réné from an instructional tour in North Korea, a plot by ex-President Mancham's supporters was announced, along with discoveries of caches of arms (which were not shown to the press), and 21 persons were charged with conspiring to bring about an armed invasion. Mr Jaques Houdoul alleged that Kenya was implicated and was encouraging M 'Bob' Denard to repeat in Seychelles his feat of overturning the leftist regime in the Comoros (see p. 229). Kenya denied it, and in London Mr Mancham scouted the charge as a complete fabrication, claiming that the regime's excesses, and those of Mr Réné's Tanzanian bodyguard of 'advisers', had raised his own prestige in the island to a spectacular height.

The scare enabled Mr Réné to continue ruling by presidential decree and to reject calls for an election that he would lose; and some foreigners, including the Belgian honorary consul, were deported. In June private medical practice was made illegal and a land distribution scheme to end 'feudalism' was proclaimed but not implemented on any scale.

In August all the suspected traitors were quietly released, the emergency was called off, and it was announced that Russian demands for a naval base had been rejected. Mr Réné inconspicuously visited London to confer with Mrs Hart, Minister of Overseas Development, partly about the flight of capital. The need for British aid was stressed, and Mr Réné undertook not to impose exchange control. Burmah Oil Company continued to prospect for oil, South African Airways continued to fly tourists in, and Mr Réné declared that the US tracking station was not military and remained welcome. His Government declared a 200-mile limit which covered an immense area of ocean and said that henceforth it would not tolerate unrestricted fishing in the area by Russia, Korea or Japan.

MAURITIUS

In Mauritius the anticipated retirement of the veteran Labour Party leader and Prime Minister Sir Seewoosagur Ramgoolam did not take place after all, following the successful celebration in March of the tenth independence anniversary. Sir Seewoosagur had been expected to hand over to Sir V. Ringadoo or Sir S. Bulell, but it became clear as the year wore on that Sir Seewoosagur intended to hold on until opportunity presented itself for an election that the Labour Party could win outright, ending its uncomfortable position of holding office only with the support of the right-wing Parti Mauricien Social-Democrat, led (from outside the House) by Sir Seewoosagur's old rival-cum-ally M Gaetan Duval. The Movement Mauricien Militant (MMM) remained within one seat of a majority, but proved powerless to exploit its parliamentary strength.

Both main parties, in fact, suffered divisions during the year. A faction of the Labour Party led by Mr H. Boodhoo complained that the Government was out of touch and even moribund, arguing that the MMM was outflanking them with public opinion. The MMM, however, spoke with two voices. On the one hand it promoted a militant image in the countryside, and several of its members went to gaol for their activities in the protests over the raising of bus fares and demands for a cheap nationalized transport service. The MMM control of key municipalities, however, led to no constructive work, and considerable disillusion. The left wing's greatest success was its promotion of the port strike, which led to losses of trade and investment and even the closure of existing firms in the industrial zone.

Such strangulation was not appreciated by everyone when it entailed losses of jobs and lower wages. The Hindu majority, as well as the Creole minority, being mainly, if not wholly, bourgeois in mentality, both M Béranger, the MMM secretary general, and M de Lestrac, its chairman, began to make reassuring reformist noises after returning from the Seychelles conference, announcing that no coup or invasion was in prospect, that in Mauritius the only way to take power was through the ballot box, and that thereafter fundamental change would be gradual—even including the phasing-out of South African tourism.

It was a good year for tourism, but otherwise the economy suffered. The port strike accelerated the inflationary rise of 10 per cent in prices, and, as the boom in sugar ended, the problem of renegotiating Mauritius' favourable quotas and prices with the EEC in 1980 cast a shadow. Since these quotas were largely due to Sir Seewoosagur's foresight, there was some reason in his retention of power at a delicate moment when a balance of forces had to be watched, and it seemed to provide the best hope of stability until a new electoral verdict could be obtained.

BRITISH INDIAN OCEAN TERRITORY

Indian Ocean security remained a preoccupation of the islands as well as the littoral states in a year that saw the introduction of 200-mile fishing zones and the withering away of the negotiations between Russia and the United States on force levels, which had seemed to make progress in 1977. The Seychelles conference (see p. 275) demanded that the superpowers dismantle all naval bases, while Mauritius showed its displeasure at OAU proposals that Réunion should become an independent state, thus destabilizing its own area. However, the United States indicated that the arming of Diego Garcia would not go beyond the level envisaged in 1975, while Soviet naval forces were scaled down after the Americans had sent in a large task force including the carrier *Enterprise*, and it seemed that for the present the policy of 'matching prudence' was being observed by the superpowers.

MALAGASY

An official visit to France by President Didier Ratsiraka in September marked a formal reconciliation that fell within the general framework of France's attempts to establish good relations with the radical regimes of French-speaking Africa (see also pp. 225–6, 228). Relations had been difficult since the fall of the pro-French Philibert Tsiranana in 1972. Discussions centred on economic cooperation, and included consideration of compensation for nationalized French assets. It was significant that the detente occurred in spite of Malagasy criticism of French involvement in the May coup in the Comoro Islands (see p. 229).

In May the Ratsiraka regime was shaken by riots and school strikes, mainly related to student demands on the conduct of examinations. About 150 arrests were made and the Prime Minister, David Rakotoarijaona, linked the riots to subversive activities in the Comoros and the Seychelles.

IX SOUTH-EAST AND EAST ASIA

Chapter 1

MALAYSIA AND BRUNEI—SINGAPORE—HONG KONG—BURMA—THAILAND—
INDONESIA—PHILIPPINES—VIETNAM—CAMBODIA (KAMPUCHEA)—LAOS

MALAYSIA AND BRUNEI

PRIME MINISTER Datuk Hussein Onn led the Barisan Nasional (National Front) ruling coalition to a decisive victory in general elections for the federal parliament and ten state assemblies which were held from 8 July. Of the 154 seats in the federal parliament, the Barisan Nasional secured 131. The opposition Democratic Action Party (DAP) secured 16 seats (including one in Sabah), Party Islam (PAS) secured five seats, while the new Sarawak People's Organization (SAPO) secured one seat. An independent candidate was elected in the state of Sabah. The Barisan Nasional was victorious in all the state assembly elections; voting did not take place in the states of Kelantan, Sarawak and Sabah. Of the 276 state assembly seats, the Barisan Nasional secured 240.

Elections for the state assembly of Kelantan had been held earlier in March following its dissolution and the imposition of emergency rule in the preceding November (see AR 1977, p. 277). The contest between the United Malays National Organization (UMNO) and Party Islam (PAS) resulted in a decisive victory for UMNO, which was a major consideration in the holding of general elections a year earlier than necessary under the constitution.

Datuk Hussein Onn was confirmed as president of UMNO at the party's annual assembly in September, despite a challenge from a former publicity officer, Suleiman Palestin. Dato Seri Dr Mahathir Mohamed, the Deputy Prime Minister, was returned unopposed as deputy president of UMNO. In the contested elections for the three posts of vice-president, the successful candidates were Tengku Razaleigh Hamzah (Minister of Finance), Datuk Musa Hitam (Minister of Education) and Abdul Ghafar Baba.

In August, four Moslem Malays, who were desecrating a Hindu temple in Kerling, North of Kuala Lumpur, were killed by temple guards. The Malays were members of a fundamentalist group, itself a part of a wider Dakwah (missionary) movement which had gained adherents among young educated Moslems. Governmental concern at the course of Islamic fundamentalism was expressed by the Deputy Prime Minister, Dr Mahathir, when he denounced religious extremism on the eve of the UMNO annual assembly.

Additional evidence of communal tension was indicated in the demand by Chinese guilds and educational groups for a Merdeka (Freedom) University which would provide instruction in the Chinese medium. This more symbolic than practical assertion of Chinese cultural identity, in the face of a national educational policy which favoured the Malays, was firmly repulsed by Datuk Musa Hitam, the Minister of Education, in his address to the UMNO annual assembly in September. An attempt in October by the sponsors of the Merdeka University to hold a mass meeting was banned by the Government on the ground that it posed a danger to public order and security. Strong Chinese feeling on the issue contributed to the victory of the DAP in a by-election in December for the Penang state assembly.

In March, the King of Malaysia rejected an appeal for a pardon by the former Chief Minister of Selangor, Datuk Harun Idris, who had been convicted on corruption and forgery charges. He began a six-year prison sentence amid the prospect of a clash between his political supporters and the police. In November, Lim Kit Siang, opposition leader in the federal parliament and secretary-general of the Democratic Action Party, was convicted in the High Court in Kuala Lumpur on five charges under the Official Secrets Act concerning the purchase of Swedish fast patrol boats for the Royal Malaysian Navy; Mr Lim was fined the equivalent of £3,300 with the alternative of 41 months in prison.

In April, Malaysian and Thai security forces resumed joint operations against the insurgent Malayan Communist Party in the Betong region to the north of their common border. In December, communist insurgents mounted an attack on a police station at Beranang just 28 miles from the capital, Kuala Lumpur. In the attack, the first of its kind to occur in the state of Selangor for three years, the insurgents seized fourteen firearms.

In October, Pham Van Dong, the Vietnamese Prime Minister, paid a visit to Malaysia as part of a tour of the countries of the Association of South-East Asian Nations (ASEAN). In Kuala Lumpur, Pham Van Dong admitted that his country had trained Malaysian communist guerrillas in the past. He promised that such training would not be resumed and committed his Government to refrain from interference in Malaysian internal affairs. In November, Teng Hsiao-p'ing, the Chinese Deputy Prime Minister, visited Malaysia in an exercise in competitive diplomacy with Vietnam. He maintained that the Communist Party of China would continue to support the banned Malayan Communist Party without prejudice to intergovernmental ties between China and Malaysia.

In November, the appearance off the west coast of peninsular Malaysia of the freighter *Hai Hong* carrying some 2,500 refugees from Vietnam drew international attention to the problems which the Malaysian Government faced in coping with a major exodus from Vietnam. Many more refugees had landed in small boats on the east coast of the peninsula. By the end of the year, approximately 50,000 refugees were in temporary camps on offshore islands, despite the official policy of the Malaysian Government in declaring the refugees illegal immigrants.

In June the Sultan of BRUNEI, Sir Hassanal Bolkiah, and his father, Sir Omar Ali Saifuddin, held discussions in London with Lord Goronwy-Roberts, Minister of State at the Foreign and Commonwealth Office. It was agreed that the Sultan and a representative of the British Government would sign a new treaty under which the state of Brunei would assume full international responsibility as a sovereign and independent state at the end of 1983. The relevant documents, which were initialled in London in September, provided for the retention of a batallion of Gurkhas in Brunei until, at least, the end of 1983.

SINGAPORE

The Government committed itself to a social policy of bilingualism. Its object was to ensure the effective use of English as the working language of the Republic and at the same time to encourage members of the racial communities to acquire fluency in their respective vernaculars. A major feature of this policy was the revision of the role of the Chinese-medium Nanyang University. From July, English was introduced as the medium of instruction, while its first-year students commenced parallel courses with those of the English-medium University of Singapore.

At the beginning of the academic year, the Government suspended the requirement for university entrants to possess a suitability certificate. This requirement had been introduced in 1964 in an attempt to prevent communists from infiltrating institutions of higher education. In November, Said Zahari, a former newspaper editor, and Dr Lim Hock Siew, a founder member of the ruling People's Action Party, were released from detention and exiled to off-shore islands after having been imprisoned without trial since 1963.

In September, Prime Minister Lee Kuan Yew indicated that he might retire in ten years' time when a second-generation leadership would be ready to assume responsibility for high office. During both the visit of Vietnam's Prime Minister, Pham Van Dong, in October and that of China's Deputy Prime Minister, Teng Hsiao-p'ing, in November, Lee Kuan Yew left his guests in no doubt that their expressions of good intent would be judged in the light of their Governments' conduct. In this respect, he engaged in caustic comment following the conclusion of a treaty of friendship and cooperation between Vietnam and the Soviet Union in November (see p. 286 and DOCUMENTS).

HONG KONG

Chinese encouragement, low interest rates and good trade growth, despite growing protectionism in Western Europe and elsewhere, stimulated the economy. Peking welcomed joint ventures in China and extended its investments in Hong Kong. Air flights and hovercraft services to Canton started and through passenger train services were planned. The railway carried 1·9 million tons of freight from China and made progress with double-tracking the line to the border. Total exports increased by 20 per cent to nearly £6,000 million and imports by 29 per cent to £7,000 million. Incoming tourists increased by 17 per cent to over 2 million.

The High Island reservoir, made from an arm of the sea with dams able to hold water up to 200 feet above sea level, almost doubled storage capacity. More water from China, another new town (at Junk Bay), road links to Lantao Island, expanded medical services, better secondary school standards and compulsory education up to 15 by 1980 were planned, as were part-time university degree courses and higher levels of work in both the Polytechnic and the technical institutes. Pressure on services was expected if many more Chinese and Vietnamese seeking better living conditions arrived; 250,000 Chinese had already come in over five years. In 1978, the birth rate fell further to 1·75 per cent, but nearly 100,000 immigrants and low and steadily declining infant and general mortality rates produced a population increase of 3·4 per cent to 4,720,000.

Half government expenditure went on education, housing, health and social welfare, and another quarter on services, such as roads and water supply. For 1978-79, allocations rose by a quarter, the electricity companies had large capital programmes and private building of factories, offices and flats ran at high levels, as did the greatly expanded programme of government housing and new town development and work on the tube railway. Buoyant exports and domestic spending, and labour shortages, also tended to overheat the economy. Average real industrial wages had in September risen by 9·5 per cent over 12 months to around £30 a week. By the winter money supply was up by 30 per cent and retail prices by 8 per cent over 12 months. Interest rates were then increased, and money supply growth halved, in order to check inflation.

BURMA

Voting took place in January for 464 People's Congress seats and some 175,000 seats in state, division, township and village councils. Only Burma Socialist Programme Party candidates were eligible, but they had to win 60 per cent of votes cast to secure election. On 7 March U Ne Win was re-elected President. Guerrillas from the Burma Communist Party and minority races were again active in the north and east, but during August repeated calls for unity suggested dissension within the BCP. Teng Hsiao-p'ing visited Burma in January and the new Burmese Foreign Minister visited China in September, but there was no sign that the Chinese intended to cease supporting the BCP. The Thai Prime Minister arrived on 10 May to discuss, *inter alia*, smuggling of opium and consumer goods across the border.

During April six men were found guilty on charges which included working for the secession of Arakan, while Arakanese Muslims, who thought themselves threatened by Burmese troops, crossed into Bangladesh in large numbers; the Burmese claimed merely to be looking for illegal immigrants. A visit by the Foreign Minister to Dacca on 13 April failed to resolve the problem and by August over 200,000 people, including many young children, had fled. On 9 July the Government agreed with Bangladesh to take these Muslims back and to demarcation of the land boundary. The first few refugees returned to Arakan on 31 August, but the rest were still afraid to move and on 7 October it was agreed to ease, simplify and accelerate procedures for repatriation. By late October only 500 had returned, but movement then increased and by December the flow had virtually reached the target of 2,000 every three days.

There were again official complaints of inefficiency and malpractice in distribution and transport, and suggestions that these failings reached to the level of Minister. Steps were taken to revive offshore oil exploration, to open a copper mine and to improve telecommunications and railway rolling-stock. Despite renewed flooding, which had contributed to a poor harvest in 1977-78, an improved rice crop was officially forecast for 1978-79. Reduced tonnage of rice available for export turned the external trade balance from surplus into deficit and a further deterioration was expected in 1978-79.

THAILAND

The policies followed by the new Prime Minister, General Kriangsak Chamanand, of accommodation with neighbouring countries, of national reconciliation and, in the economic field, of more even distribution of the benefits of growth, made some progress. The authorities took steps to restrain Burmese rebels operating from Thai bases and to improve co-operation with Malaysian forces in the south. The Communist Party of Thailand made little headway. The Foreign Minister visited Cambodia in January and reaction to attacks on Thai villages along the Cambodian border was restrained. Peking also urged restraint on the Cambodian regime and a Khmer Vice-Premier visited Bangkok in July. He spoke of 'misunderstandings' and discussed the exchange of ambassadors. Preparations were then made to open a Thai embassy in Phnom Penh and border incidents declined.

The Vietnamese and Laotian Foreign Ministers visited Bangkok in January and March, followed in July by a Vietnamese Vice-Premier, who commended Thailand's 'friendly attitude towards its neighbours', and a Laotian deputy Minister of Trade, who spoke of 'sincere and enthusiastic consultations'. The Mekong Committee was revived and there were discussions with Hanoi on trade and, with little result, on the earlier Vietnamese refugees in Thailand. There were, however, further incidents along the Laotian border which in December caused General Kriangsak to postpone a visit to Vientiane. In September the Vietnamese Prime Minister visited Bangkok. The Thais were glad to exchange undertakings not to support subversion, while reserving judgment on Vietnam's real intentions, but treated proposals for other agreements with caution. The Chinese senior Vice-Premier was unable in Bangkok in November to give a similar undertaking, but was, nevertheless, regarded as having a more reassuring attitude to Thailand.

A constitution to replace the 1976 and 1977 arrangements had its final reading on 18 December. It was intended to be more democratic, without endangering political stability. It was passed by 300 votes to nine, but was criticized from both right and left, the Democrat Party describing it as totalitarian. Late revisions reduced the influence of the National Policy Council, composed mainly of senior military men, and possibly of organized parties, and strengthened that of the Prime Minister. Parliament was to have a 298-seat elected lower house and a 224-seat appointed upper house. These were to vote together on important issues such as budgets and election of Premiers. The Premier was given the right to impose martial law, and Ministers need not be members of either house. Kriangsak, who appeared to consolidate his political position, announced on 20 December that he would not be a candidate in elections due in 1979. A Bill, introduced on the initiative of the King, exculpated those on both sides involved in the events at Thammasat University in October 1976, including 18 on trial on treason and other charges and others who had joined the communist guerrillas.

The 1977 trade deficit of over US$1,050 million and a reduced 1977-78 rice harvest led to measures to cut imports by reduced credit and higher tariffs on luxuries, to stimulate exports by easier credit, and to increase remittances from Thais abroad. Heavier monsoon rains seemed likely, despite flooding, to increase agricultural output, especially in the northeast. The baht went from a fixed parity with the US dollar to a moving daily rate related to a basket of currencies. The Budget proposed to limit the deficit, while allowing for increased defence spending. Growth of money supply and inflation eased, while economic growth and foreign exchange reserves improved and private investment revived.

INDONESIA

The political excitement stimulated, especially amongst some student groups, by parliamentary elections and the prospect of presidential and vice-presidential elections was firmly deflated by the regime before the Congress met on 11 March. Within the Congress the Muslim Party, PPP, voted against the renewal of the President's special powers and walked out of the debate on state ideology because of proposals to give mysticism a formal religious status. The PPP nevertheless supported the nominations of President Suharto for re-election and of Dr Adam Malik to become Vice-President in succession to Sultan Hamengku Buwono, who had declined to stand again. Suharto and Malik were elected unanimously on 22 and 23 March.

Nearly half the members of the new Cabinet were military men, while the technocrats maintained their influence and PPP ceased to be represented. In October Suharto became chairman of the advisory board of the Government party, Golkar, which was given a more civilian appearance. Admiral Sudomo, who succeeded Suharto as commander of the Security and Order Command, Kopkamtib, and Malik, who was also to oversee efforts to stimulate development, were made responsible for acting against corruption.

Policy was to be centred around acceleration of economic growth, wider and more even distribution of its benefits and more honest and effective administration. Action against corruption was expected not to be retrospective, but to deal harshly with further misdemeanours. The new Defence Minister insisted on a 'clean and moderate' style of living for officers and greater attention to the welfare of the rank and file and to relations between the forces and civilians, while Malik sought administrative changes which would impede corruption. The anti-corruption campaign was not expected to touch the very highest circles, but the national police chief was replaced and his deputy and a dozen other police generals were tried for misappropriating state funds.

The chief political concern was with Muslim movements. Greater formal recognition for mysticism and a campaign to rehabilitate the reputation of President Sukarno were designed to provide alternatives to Muslim fundamentalism, while publicity was given to the more unattractively violent Muslim extremist movements, such as Aceh Merdeka and Komando Jihad. Steps taken to appease devout Muslim opinion included limitations on proselytization by missionary groups. There were minor incidents in Aceh and West Irian, where the defence ministry sought not to alienate the indigenous people. In East Timor considerable success was achieved in mopping up Fretelin remnants.

Diplomatic relations were re-established with Cambodia in August, but not with China. The military remained intensely suspicious of Peking's policies towards Overseas Chinese and communist dissidents and cautious about restoration of direct trade with China. It was feared that stagnant or reduced exports would lead to balance of payments problems. On 16 November the rupiah was devalued by a third against the US dollar and a 'managed float' was introduced to inhibit imports and stimulate non-oil exports and local manufacturing; it was recognized that this might also revive inflation. There was a better rice harvest and the minimum procurement price was raised by 13 per cent to stimulate production.

PHILIPPINES

On 17 January President Marcos announced that elections for an Interim National Assembly would be held in April. Martial law conditions were eased slightly but a system of party list voting was adopted. The Liberal Party insisted that without a free press and adequate time for campaigning elections would be a 'farce'. On 1 February, after discussion with the Nacionalista Party, Marcos announced a New Society Front under which Government candidates would stand. There were some opposition candidates and in Manila and the Visayas these presented an effective challenge. In Manila the Laban grouping, covering both Liberal and left-wing candidates, was headed from detention by Benigno Aquino.

Aquino succeeded in making a television appearance, to answer charges made against him on television, and in addressing a press conference, both with evident effect. Laban rallies attracted greater support than the Government front and action was taken to prevent them from continuing to reach the electorate and to ensure additional votes for the New Society Front's Manila list, headed by Mrs Marcos. Laban succeeded, however, in organizing a striking eve-of-poll 'noise demonstration' on 6 April in protest against election rigging and there was disbelief of Government claims to have won all 21 Manila seats. In the central Visayas, resignation of an electoral commission official in protest against ballot rigging induced the commission to award seats to all thirteen candidates from a regionalist opposition list.

On 12 June Marcos became Prime Minister as well as President. He made it plain to Parliament that progress towards a more democratic system would be cautious; foreign campaigns in favour of human rights were subsequently denounced as 'moral imperialism'. More political prisoners were, however, released and sedition charges against priests and nuns were dropped. The press became more adventurous, and in November an ombudsman was appointed and Marcos announced that investigations had started into the extent of corruption in government.

Guerrilla activity by the Muslim MNLF and the Maoist NPA revived, especially late in the year in the Sulu Islands and Basilan, while MNLF guerrillas made an incursion into Palawan, off which there were further oil strikes. The Filipinos reinforced their presence in the potentially oil-rich Spratly group of islets and shoals west of Palawan, as did the Vietnamese. The two countries agreed to negotiate on problems which might arise over the Spratlys, to which Peking and Taipei also laid claim.

Negotiations on future arrangements for American bases reached agreement in principle. Economic and trade agreements were concluded early in the year with Vietnam, Japan and China. There was concern over the sluggish growth of exports and a weakening of the balance of payments. In October it was decided to cut government expenditure, especially on defence and large capital-intensive public works. Greater priority was proposed for rural developments, including feeder roads and small irrigation schemes, and less for large industrial projects, but little was done to tackle the high population growth rate.

VIETNAM

Hanoi's foreign and political policies led it into increasing economic difficulties. A dry season offensive into eastern Cambodia had proved disappointing, partly because of mishandling by the Vietnamese army of its overwhelming superiority in numbers, tanks, artillery and air support in face of Cambodian tactics, which allowed armoured columns to push ahead and then harrassed them in the flanks and rear. The army also had problems with the supply and maintenance of heavy equipment and with morale, not least amongst South Vietnamese reluctant to fight Hanoi's wars. There were complaints of 'the limited understanding displayed by the southern people . . . of the task of strengthening national defence' and of 'pacifist thoughts', and calls for 'ironlike discipline'. Preparations, delayed by unusually heavy floods in the autumn, were nevertheless made for a renewed assault to permit installation of a subservient Cambodian regime.

To neutralize Chinese support for Cambodia, Hanoi had to abandon the policy of playing off Peking against Moscow and openly entered the Russian camp. In June Vietnam was admitted to the Soviet bloc's Council for Mutual Economic Aid, or Comecon, and on 3 November signed a treaty with the USSR (see DOCUMENTS) committing the parties to consultation with a view to eliminating any attack or threat of attack, to ideological solidarity and to political, economic, social and technical cooperation, including the coordination of national economic plans. The treaty was stated not to override other rights and obligations and not to be directed against any third country, but was clearly designed to give Vietnam Soviet protection against China.

Pressure was increasingly exerted on the large and economically important Chinese minority. In April Peking publicly expressed concern at the flood of Chinese fleeing to China. These were mostly peasants from districts along the border with China, together with dockers, miners, factory workers and fishermen from the coastal and industrial areas of North Vietnam; an exodus of traders, technicians and professional men from South Vietnam also began. Despite talks in August, polemics and frontier incidents increased steadily and troops were massed along the common border. Meanwhile visits by Ministers, including the Prime Minister, were mounted to persuade Vietnam's neighbours of its peaceful intentions. The Prime Minister undertook to 'strictly respect' others' independence, sovereignty, territorial integrity and political systems and to refrain from use of force, interference in internal affairs or subversion. These assurances were received with caution and subsequently devalued by Vietnamese conduct towards Cambodia.

In March a UN official suggested that Vietnam would need some US$800 million of aid in 1978 and $920 million in 1979. Vietnamese policy, however, ensured that most of this would have to come, if at all, from the Soviet bloc, which seemed more concerned to provide military supplies. Moreover, the drain of manpower into military operations, the loss of Chinese skilled workers and technicians and another inadequate harvest, due mainly to lack of inputs and incentives, caused further economic difficulties. There was some extension of cultivation and irrigation, although the 'new economic zone' programme went more slowly than planned, and some factory production was restored, despite shortages of fuel, raw materials and equipment. Complaints of administrative incompetence, bribery and corruption continued, however, and attempts in the spring to destroy 'capitalist trade' and in November to force the southern peasants into greater collectivization seemed likely to retard economic revival.

CAMBODIA (KAMPUCHEA)

A large-scale Vietnamese incursion into eastern Cambodia which had begun in 1977 was frustrated by successful harrassing tactics, but smaller-scale raids across the border by both sides continued. On 5 February Hanoi demanded a cease-fire and guarantees in terms rejected by Phnom Penh, which insisted that several attempts had been made without success to reach agreement with Vietnam on frontier problems and mutual relations. In May it was claimed that another attempted Vietnamese coup had been foiled and by June the Vietnamese were openly broadcasting harsh accounts of the regime's conduct towards its own people and calls for its overthrow. Thereafter large Vietnamese armoured, infantry and air forces were assembled in South Vietnam and southern Laos and efforts were made to wear down Khmer Rouge forces and to establish a Khmer group under Vietnamese direction within Cambodia. In December the Premier, Pol Pot, indicated that if the Vietnamese launched a massive offensive empty cities would fall into their hands and the Khmer Rouge would resort to protracted guerrilla warfare.

On 3 December the Vietnamese announced the establishment of a 'Kampuchean National United Front for National Salvation' which was at once warmly welcomed by the USSR. This body, which was said to be led by Khmer Rouge defectors, issued an eleven-point programme which offered freedom of residence, movement, association and religion, a more normal money and wage system and less extreme working conditions. These were calculated to meet the basic complaints made by Cambodians about government policy, although perhaps not to offset their deep antipathy to the Vietnamese. The Chinese, who expressed support for the regime in terms suggesting that this might be moral and material rather than military, were thought to have urged similar changes in internal policy, a more conciliatory external policy and formation of a united front to exploit Prince Sihanouk's influence. That this was still thought considerable was suggested when he was allowed to reappear in the autumn and send a message of congratulation on the Communist Party's anniversary.

LAOS

There was a steady flow of refugees across the Mekong into Thailand, including many Lao with sorely needed skills and training and some officials. On 30 April eight men were sentenced to death and 41 to lengthy imprisonment for trying to overthrow the regime, while an editorial in August appealed for 'internal unity and unity among nationalities'. The refugees included Meo and other minorities. The Meo remained under assault by Vietnamese and local forces, their villages falling under heavy aerial and artillery bombardment. The authorities claimed in November to have 'wiped out' all major Meo strongholds, but there were subsequent references to Meo resistance and to rebellion elsewhere in northern Laos, including the old communist province of Phong Saly. In the southern provinces resistance was primarily Lao with some Pathet Lao support. The depleted population of towns such as Pakse were under night-time curfew, supplies had to be brought in under day-time convoy and such security as there was depended on Vietnamese troops.

The economic situation deteriorated further. Floods in the Mekong valley and lack of enthusiasm on the part of both lowland Lao peasants and hill tribes for collectivization and socialist planning led to an admission in August that 'difficulties and starvation' would be 'even worse' than in 1977, when Laos had been given grain either by the UN, using funds contributed by Western countries, or by China. To increase export earnings and food and other imports, the regime relaxed attempts to control private trade and sought to reopen and expand trade with Thailand. Officials discussed navigation on the Mekong in January, the Foreign Minister visited Bangkok in March, being assured that Thai territory would not be used for activities against Laos, and on 31 May the Thai Foreign Minister arrived in Vientiane to sign a trade and transit agreement. Supplies thereafter improved, while completion of the second phase of the Nam Ngum hydro-electric project in November permitted increased sales of electricity to Thailand. Apart from Thailand, however, the exclusion of influences other than those of the Soviet bloc continued. Diplomatic and cultural relations with France were in effect broken and China was accused of carrying out or planning subversion in Laos.

Chapter 2

CHINA—TAIWAN—JAPAN—SOUTH KOREA—NORTH KOREA

CHINA

THE year was marked by a dramatic acceleration of the drive for modernization and attempts to return to institutional regularity after the hiatus of the previous fifteen or more years. Externally, as a bitter conflict erupted with Vietnam, China moved out of its relatively isolationist position to become more actively and globally engaged. The long-awaited treaty of peace and friendship was signed with Japan and the new foreign policy was crowned at the end of the year with the announcement of the normalization of relations with the United States.

Internal Developments. The Second Plenary Session of the 11th Central Committee of the Communist Party of China (CPC) was held in Peking on 18-23 February. Its tasks were to complete preparations for the Fifth National People's Congress (NPC—described officially as 'the highest organ of state power', but generally regarded by foreign observers as China's rubber-stamp parliament) and the Fifth National Committee of the Chinese People's Political Consultative Conference (CPPCC—described officially as 'an organization of the Chinese people's revolutionary united front', that is, the platform from which the CPC appeals to intellectuals, former bourgeois groups, the Kuomintang and overseas Chinese). The Plenary Session discussed and approved the draft documents and appointments submitted by the Political Bureau which were subsequently adopted by the NPC and CPPCC respectively.

The CPPCC, which had not been convened since before the Cultural

K

Revolution, met from 24 February to 8 March. Deng Xiaoping (Teng Hsiao-p'ing)* was elected Chairman; 22 vice-chairmen and a 243-member standing committee of the National Committee were also elected. A new constitution was adopted, as was the main resolution calling on people from all circles to carry out the chief policies and tasks laid out by the Party and state organs. In his speech Deng recounted the damage done to the cause of national unity by the suppression of this united front body by the 'gang of four', and emphasized the role of the CPPCC in 'democratic consultations on state affairs'.

The Fifth NPC opened in Peking on 26 February with a total of 3,456 deputies in attendance. A further 1,803 from the CPC, the State Council, the People's Liberation Army (PLA) and the CPPCC attended as observers. In his capacity as Premier of the State Council, Hua Guofeng (Hua Kuo-feng) delivered a three-and-a-half-hour report on the work of the Government. This report outlined the events since the last NPC of 1975 and mapped out the main programmes for modernization and for developing further the new political order. Premier Hua claimed that as a result of the measures adopted since the fall of the 'gang of four' the national situation had improved in all respects and that the Chinese people had more than made good the losses sustained between 1974 and 1976. As examples of the losses caused by the 'interference and sabotage' of the 'gang' the report cited a shortfall of 100,000 million yuan in the value of industrial output, and losses of 28 million tons of steel and 40,000 million yuan in state revenue. Many factories were idle, agricultural production had been affected, corruption and disorder had been widespread. Rapid modernization was regarded as essential if the national humiliation of the hundred years or more following the opium war of 1840 was not to be repeated.

To this end the report outlined some of the main points of the state economic plan (unpublished), to be realized by 1985 as part of the larger programme for transforming China into a powerful modern socialist country by the year 2000. The targets, regarded by foreign observers as very ambitious, call for the annual production by 1985 of 400 million tons of grain (the 1978 output was 295) and 60 million tons of steel (1978 output was 31). In each of the eight years from 1978 to 1985, the value of agricultural output is planned to increase by 4·5 per cent and of industrial output by over 10 per cent. The plan also calls for the achievement of 85 per cent mechanization of the major processes of farm work. It envisages the expansion of light industry so as to attain 'a considerable increase in per capita consumption'. It details the construction of an advanced heavy industry and the build-up of transportation and communication networks.

---

* Chinese names are written in the new official spelling with the old transliteration in brackets (see Preface, p. xv).

Twelve large commodity grain bases are envisaged, while in industry the state plans to build 120 large-scale projects, including ten iron and steel complexes, nine non-ferrous metal complexes, eight coal mines, ten oil and gas fields, 30 power stations, six new trunk railways and five key harbours. The report announced that foreign trade would expand greatly.

The report also called for the development of science, education and culture commensurate with the needs of modernization. It noted that the scientific and technical gap between Chinese and advanced-world levels had widened in recent years. The report announced plans for what amounted to a shock programme in education by establishing 'key' universities and schools. Another section of the report was devoted to measures for strengthening and regularizing the state security organs, restoring the legal institutions and developing popular democracy. One aspect of these measures was limiting revolutionary committees to being organs of local government, thus leaving production and education units to the charge of factory directors, school principals and the like under the leadership of Communist Party committees. The report also outlined policies designed to encourage cordial relations with national minorities and overseas Chinese and win over their support.

The new Constitution adopted by the NPC (see DOCUMENTS) sought to strengthen and specify clearly the roles of the organs of state power while simultaneously restoring the legal institutions (abandoned during the Cultural Revolution) and itemizing the civil democratic rights of citizens. In short, it was designed to establish a socialist legal democratic order which would limit the arbitrary powers of officials and facilitate the drive for modernization.

The Fifth NPC closed on 5 March, having adopted the Constitution and approved the report on the work of the Government. Ye Jianying (Yeh Chien-ying) was appointed chairman of the standing committee of the NPC, which made him technically head of state. The NPC also made the following appointments: Hua Guofeng, Premier of the State Council; Jiang Hua (Chiang Hua), President of the Supreme People's Court; Huang Huojing (Huang Huo-ching), Chief Procurator of the Supreme People's Procurate; and, upon the Premier's recommendation, the following 13 Vice-Premiers of the State Council (an asterisk denotes a new appointment): Deng Xiaoping (Teng Hsiao-p'ing), Li Xiannian (Li Hsien-nien), *Xu Xiangjian (Hsu Hsiang-chien), Ji Dengkui (Chi Teng-K'uei), You Qiuli (Yu Ch'iu-li), Chen Xilian (Ch'en Hsi-lieu), *Geng Biao (Keng Piao), Chen Yonggui (Ch'en Yung-kuei), *Fang Yi, Wang Zhen (Wang Chen), Gu Mu (Ku Mu), *Kang Shien (K'ang Shih-en) and *Chen Mu hua (Ch'en Mu-hua). It appointed Guo Moruo (Kuo Mo-jo) as president of the Academy of Sciences and Hu Qiaomu (Hu Ch'iao-mu) as president of the Academy of Social Sciences. It further appointed 37 Ministers (eight more than in the previous Administration).

China's new eight-year plan for the rapid and vigorous expansion of science was announced and discussed at the National Science Conference held in Peking from 18 to 31 March.

A measure of the determination of China's leaders to realize their ambitious modernization targets was the pace of change throughout the year. One by one the impediments left over from the Mao era were abandoned. In foreign trade, for example, practically all the injunctions against accepting foreign loans, foreign investment in China, joint development projects and the like were abandoned. Meanwhile Ministers contracted to purchase plants and projects on a gigantic scale involving tens of billions of dollars. In agriculture Mao's favourite agricultural model, Da Zhai (Ta Chai), was scaled down in national significance as new patterns of remuneration were adopted.

Indeed Mao himself was reduced in scale. A major speech of his in January 1962 which admitted to serious errors was published officially for the first time on 1 July. In October a 1949 speech of Zhou Enlai (Chou En-lai) was published in which, while praising Mao as a great man, he warned against regarding him as a demigod. By the end of the year Marshal Peng Dehuai (P'eng Teh-huai), who had been personally purged by Mao in 1959, was posthumously rehabilitated, as were some of the prominent leaders who were purged with Mao's approval at the early stages of the Cultural Revolution.

The senior Vice-Premier, Deng Xiaoping, increasingly emerged as the driving force behind the new policies. In November a working conference of the CPC Central Committee began a secret session to review the economic and political developments of the year. Deng's position was further enhanced by the decision to revise the official view of the Tien An Men incident of 5 April 1976 (see AR 1976, p. 292, and 1977, p. 290). It was now described as 'completely revolutionary'. The CPC Central Committee decision against Deng was rescinded. At the same time this reversal of the verdicts embarrassed those Party leaders who had been involved in what was now designated as the wrong side of the incident. It also raised new doubts about the legitimacy of Hua Guofeng's succession. It was hardly coincidental that shortly after the new announcement Deng told a foreign journalist that he could have become Premier but had decided against it.

As the Party working conference began, a remarkable new wall-poster campaign started up in the centre of Peking in which demands were made for a more genuine democracy and legality, redress of grievances against arbitrary officialdom and the removal of certain unpopular leaders. Whether or not this movement had started spontaneously it soon acquired degrees of spontaneity in a way never before seen in the history of the People's Republic. Moreover, many of the existing barriers to communication with foreigners broke down as eager young Chinese enquired of

Westerners about democracy and legality in their countries. Various discussion groups were formed and such was the level of interest in the movement and the broadness of the issues raised that Deng Xiaoping, who alone had the necessary prestige, made it clear that while the wall-poster movement should not be suppressed the interests of unity and stability required the young people concerned to scale down their activities and their demands for change. By the middle of December a lot of the heat of the campaign died down. Nevertheless some posters continued to be put up.

The Party working conference prepared the way for the third plenary session of the CPC Central Committee, which was held between 18 and 22 December. The communique issued at the end of the session declared the end of the two-year campaign against Lin Biao (Lin Piao) and the 'gang of four' and decided 'to shift the emphasis of our Party's work and the attention of the people of the whole country to socialist modernization'. Evidently the slow pace of advance in agriculture was giving rise for concern and it was decided that the 'whole Party should concentrate its main energy and efforts on advancing agriculture as fast as possible'. The session also reopened some of the major political issues going back as far as 1959 and rehabilitated many previously disgraced senior leaders. Mao Tsetung Thought was reaffirmed but only in line with Deng's favourite dictum that 'practice is the sole criterion for testing truth' and subject to the injunction to 'develop it under the new historical conditions'. Attention was also paid to the need to 'improve the practice of democratic centralism'.

The following new appointments were made. Chen Yun (Ch'en Yun), who had been demoted from one of the highest positions in the Party in the late 1950s for his opposition to Mao's Great Leap Forward, was now elected as the sixth Vice-Chairman of the Party and given precedence over Wang Dongxing (Wang Tung-hsing). He was also made a member of the standing committee of the Political Bureau and nominated head of the newly-created 100-member Central Commission for Inspecting Discipline. Deng Yingchao (Teng Ying-ch'ao), Hu Yaobang (Hu Yao-pang) and Wang Zhen (Wang Chen) were added to the Political Bureau.

External Relations. In January and February Peking's media carried both Kampuchean (Cambodian) and Vietnamese accounts of their armed conflict and it seemed possible that Peking might mediate between them even though its sympathies lay with Kampuchea. But in April the hitherto concealed conflict between Vietnam and China was made public in a series of increasingly vitriolic mutual exchanges which initially centred on the question of ethnic Chinese in Vietnam. By July 160,000 had fled to China and the Chinese closed the border. By this stage it had become clear that the refugee question was secondary, while strategic, traditional and historical rivalries were primary. China claimed that Vietnam sought dominance over the whole of Indo-China and that it had tied itself to the Soviet hegemonistic aims in the area. In short, the Chinese claimed that Vietnam had become an 'Asian Cuba'. In July the Chinese announced the ending of all aid to Vietnam and Deng claimed that over the years China had extended US$10,000 million worth of aid to the ungrateful Vietnamese, much of it free and at great cost to China's own domestic needs. Vietnam in turn accused China of 'great power chauvinism' and of seeking to undermine Vietnam's efforts to build the economy. China's fears of Soviet encirclement were enhanced by the close association between Vietnam and the Soviet Union, particularly as symbolized in July by Vietnam's accession to membership of Comecon. In November Vietnam signed a treaty of friendship with the Soviet Union (see p. 286 and DOCUMENTS).

The Sino-Vietnamese conflict centred on the war between the Pol Pot regime in Kampuchea and Vietnam. Despite reservations about the character of the Pol Pot regime, China backed it against Vietnam, and, especially after the Soviet-Vietnam treaty, the Chinese warned of an impending dry-season offensive to conquer Kampuchea. They denounced the Kampuchean National United Front for National Salvation (see p. 288) as a Vietnamese puppet. The Vietnamese invasion of Kampuchea duly began on 25 December. Although border incidents took place between Vietnam and China with increasing frequency and intensity, and despite substantial Chinese troop movements to the neighbouring provinces, the Chinese leaders took no steps to divert Vietnamese forces from the Kampuchean invasion to the Chinese border.

The Sino-Vietnamese conflict led to a flurry of diplomatic efforts by both sides in South-East Asia to win over support to their respective positions. Deng Xiaoping, following closely on the heels of Vietnamese leaders, visited Thailand, Malaysia and Singapore in November. Although he refused to follow their lead and declare the end of China's support to communist insurgencies in the area, his visits were regarded as successful, at least on the Vietnam issue.

China's new outgoing diplomacy, inspired by the drive for modernization and the need to counter the Soviet threat, had begun much earlier in the year. Besides continuing to receive a wide range of world leaders and delegations of all kinds, China's senior leaders themselves began once again to visit other countries and take various diplomatic initiatives. In March the senior Vice-Premier Li Xiannian (Li Hsien-nien) visited the Philippines and Bangladesh, and Deng visited Burma and Nepal. In May Chairman Hua himself travelled to North Korea, and as if to challenge the Soviet Union in its own backyard he visited Romania, Yugoslavia and Iran in August. Five of China's other Vice-Premiers and the Foreign Minister visited more than twenty other countries, ranging from the Middle East and Africa to Western Europe and the Caribbean. Trade and scientific technology exchange agreements were signed with many countries.

More Chinese delegations at all levels and interests visited Western countries than in any previous year. Furthermore, despite vigorous and threatening Soviet protests, the Chinese also obtained agreement in principle for the sale of advanced weapons (in limited numbers and of a 'defensive' character) by Britain and France. Relations with Albania, by contrast, declined to a new low with the announcement in July of the ending of all Chinese aid (see p. 117).

China's major foreign policy triumphs of the year, however, concerned relations with Japan and the United States. In February a private barter trade agreement worth US$10,000 million each way by 1985 was signed with Japan, according to which Chinese oil and coal would be exchanged for Japanese steel and advanced technology plants. But the major breakthrough occurred in July with the signing of a Sino-Japanese peace and friendship treaty which included the so-called 'anti-hegemony clause' (see DOCUMENTS). The wording of the treaty involved concessions by both sides, so that the Japanese were later able to claim that they could still follow their policy of 'equi-distance' with all other countries. From a Chinese perspective this was a triumphant breach of the Soviet effort of encirclement and a big rebuff to Soviet attempts to obstruct the agreement by warning Japan of its possible dire consequences. In the event, however, these did not materialize. Deng Xiaoping then made a highly popular and successful visit to Japan in October.

The strategic significance of the new relationship with Japan was enhanced by the agreement with the United States on 18 December to normalize relations (see DOCUMENTS). Here, too, there were concessions by both sides. Although the United States acceded to China's three principles for normalization (*i.e.* ending official diplomatic relations with the regime on Taiwan, withdrawal of all American troops from the island and the abrogation of the mutual defence treaty) without obtaining public assurance that reunification would be attempted by only peaceful means, the United States was able to insist on its right to continue to sell arms to Taiwan and to maintain all its other treaties (some of them governmental) with Taiwan. It was common to both sides that America's economic relations with the island would continue. Immediately upon publication of the agreement, China's leaders began to make all kinds of overtures to Taiwan for reunification (the term 'liberation' having been dropped), based on granting extensive autonomy. But all were rejected. Nevertheless from the perspective of Peking the Sino-American move was plainly the culmination of the new foreign policy. Henceforth China would have access to the world's power-house of advanced technology, while in strategic terms the new relationship was of significance both globally and regionally.

TAIWAN

Until the sudden if not unexpected joint communique of 16 December (see pp. 58, 295 and DOCUMENTS) concerning the establishment of diplomatic relations between the People's Republic of China (PRC) and the USA, the main focus of attention in 1978 had been changes in the composition of Taiwan's leadership, developments in the economy and measures to ensure continued growth and stability. As a result of the communique, the mainstay of Taiwan's already anomalous international position was to be removed, and the year ended as contingency plans laid in the period following the Nixon visit to China (see AR 1972, pp. 305-9) were to be put to the test. The communique announced that the PRC and the USA would establish diplomatic relations on 1 January 1979, thus precipitating the closure of the US embassy in Taipei, but that the people of the USA would maintain cultural, commercial and other unofficial relations with the people of Taiwan. The US-Taiwan mutual defence treaty was being terminated in accordance with its provisions (reports indicated that it would continue until the end of 1979) and remaining US military personnel would be withdrawn within four months. The PRC Government's statement reiterated its stand on Taiwan's being part of China and, significantly, referred to bringing the province back to the embrace of the motherland and reunifying the country, rather than effecting reunification by liberating Taiwan. In this context, contrary to the PRC's wishes, the US would continue selectively to sell a limited amount of arms to Taiwan for defensive purposes.

The Taiwanese reaction was epitomized in statements by President Chiang Ching-kuo in which he complained of broken promises damaging to the USA's credibility and a failure by the USA to uphold justice. Measures taken included placing the military on the alert, urgent top-level meetings to avert economic repercussions and to meet the developing situation, postponement of the parliamentary election scheduled for 23 December and an increase in military expenditure. Personal reactions by leaders included the resignation of the Foreign Minister, Shen Chang-huan, who was replaced by the secretary general to the President, Y. S. Tsiang, and the attempted resignation of the Premier, Sun Yun-hsuan. Popular indignation was expressed as crowds gathered at US establishments in Taipei, but after minor incidents it was clear that the Taiwan authorities were keen to draw a line between protest and violence, the media seeking to present the decision as the work of a small minority of US politicians whose action should not affect the friendship between the peoples of Taiwan and the USA.

The communique and its repercussions inevitably overshadowed earlier political events and economic developments which might well prove to be of equal significance in determining Taiwan's future. Changes in the leadership included the election of Premier Chiang Ching-kuo (Chiang Kai-shek's son) as President in succession to Yen Chia-kan, who, as Vice-President, had succeeded Chiang Kai-shek on his death; the election of the Taiwan provincial governor, Shieh Tung-min, as Vice-President; the appointment of the Minister of Economic Affairs, Sun Yun-hsuan, as Premier, of Taipei's mayor Lin Yang-kang as governor of Taiwan, and of minister of state Lee Teng-hui as mayor of Taipei; and the appointment of several new members of the Cabinet. These changes marked the beginning of a second-generation government in Taiwan, noteworthy for the unprecedented choice of a native Taiwanese Vice-President and moves towards further Taiwanization, albeit under the auspices of the ruling Kuomintang.

Economic statistics provided further evidence of underlying strength and stability. Two-way trade totalled US$23,727 million, an increase of $5,856 million over 1977. Exports amounted to $12,705 million, an increase of $3,344 million. Imports totalled $11,022 million, an increase of $2,511 million. Of 1978 exports 89·1 per cent were industrial products, while agricultural and industrial raw materials constituted 68·5 per cent and capital goods 24·7 per cent of the imports. The USA remained Taiwan's biggest export market, accounting for 39·4 per cent of the total, Japan being second and Hong Kong third with 12·5 and 6·8 per cent respectively. Taiwan's main suppliers were Japan, the USA and Kuwait. Taiwan's competitiveness in foreign markets was spurred by the fall in the value of the US dollar, to which the local currency was pegged. So marked was the effect in the first six months of the year, when exports increased sharply and the trade surplus reached US$674 million, while such symptoms of inflation appeared as a 30 per cent increase in the money supply, a 7 per cent rise in consumer prices, and wage increases at an annual rate of nearly 15 per cent, that the Government had to announce a 5·26 per cent currency revaluation on 11 July. In future, flexible rules would govern the exchange rate, which, for the time being, was set at NT$36 to the US dollar.

Against this background, there were further signs of Taiwan's enterprises moving up-market both organizationally and technologically. They included the creation of big trading companies such as Pan Overseas and Collins, patterned after Japanese and South Korean models, and investments to reduce dependence on imports, such as projects to improve shipbuilding capacity by producing diesel engines under licence, to establish an alloy steel mill with a capacity of 50,000 metric tons of stainless steel, to increase power capacity with an additional thermal power plant having a capacity of 4·7 million kw, to expand the facilities at the Kaohsiung oil refinery, to build new reservoirs and to extend oil and gas exploration. These projects represented large investments and would complement the modernization programme referred to in Premier Sun Yun-suan's report to the Legislative Yuan on 22 September 1978 as the twelve major

K*

construction projects, most of which concerned the infrastructure of the economy, such as communications, power capacity, new towns and steel production; these were planned to follow on the previous ten major construction projects (see AR 1974, p. 322). Taiwan's economic progress was further boosted by foreign and Overseas Chinese investment of US$213 million, an increase of 30 per cent over 1977, including Overseas Chinese capital amounting to US$76 million; investments by US and Japanese interests dominated the total from foreign sources. Tourism also increased, over a million and a quarter visitors justifying investments aimed at modernizing and expanding hotel facilities.

Taiwan's international relations were temporarily eclipsed by the Sino-US communique, but a significant feature was an invaluable link in the Middle East, notably with Saudi Arabia, where important construction projects were being undertaken by Taiwanese enterprises. At the same time formal diplomatic links remained with some 21 states, mainly in Africa, Central and South America; and, as an indication of how Taiwan had, so far, thwarted diplomatic isolation by substituting economic links, the Chinese External Trade Development Council reported that it had sent 232 missions to promote exports in eight years, mounted 21 exhibitions and participated in 96 expositions.

JAPAN

Mr Masayoshi Ohira, Japan's Prime Minister, provided two sensations as a somewhat pedestrian 1978 drew to a close. The first was that he became the nation's chief executive at all; the second was that he nearly ceased to be so after only eleven days in office, at the hand of a would-be assassin.

Mr Ohira, 100 per cent a Japanese despite the Irish ring to his name, was about to step into his car after inspecting his official residence for the first time. Darting forward from a group of bodyguards and newsmen accredited to Prime Ministerial business, a knife-wielding, self-styled rightist threw himself at Mr Ohira, shouting 'You damned fool'. The Premier staggered backwards as bodyguards pinned the attacker against the car. Blood spilled in the porchway came not from pale-faced Mr Ohira but from a bodyguard and, after a short rest, the Prime Minister went on his way unharmed.

Perhaps it was as well that the attack came so early in his new career—it would doubtless prolong his active life, because the reprimands handed out after the incident would ensure a redoubling of precautions. He was the fourth post-war Japanese Premier to have escaped assassination. Incredibly, the 21-year-old student concerned had climbed over an insufficiently protected three-metre fence at 3.30 a.m. and had availed himself of the hospitality of the newsmen's club, just inside the official residence, all day from 10 a.m. till 5 p.m. when he struck his blow. He told a reporter who questioned his identity that he represented the (non-existent) *Toyo Shimpo*, and later informed the police that he had no intention of killing Mr Ohira. He had only wanted to stab him 'as a protest against the degenerate Liberal Democratic Party'.

It was Mr Ohira's unexpected election to the presidency of the LDP, Japan's long-reigning party, that gave him the Premiership automatically. But there was never any thought of his turning upon his assailant with an 'Et tu, Brute?' because Japanese politicians content themselves with an internecine war of words and wangles, not dire deeds. In fact, Mr Takeo Fukuda, deposed as party president and Prime Minister by Mr Ohira after 713 days in power, gave his assurances of 'harmonious party operation' within hours of the succession—and bequeathed Mr Ohira his headaches about economic growth, industrial restructuring, rising unemployment and yen appreciation. The Premiership had gone to Mr Fukuda as a welcome Christmas present in 1976; it had been taken away shortly before Christmas 1978 with scarcely a presentiment on his part. But his long experience of politics should have taught him that former Japanese Premiers, like old soldiers, never die; indeed, they hardly fade away. Two of them had a hand in his undoing—Mr Takeo Miki, Premier 1974-76, who exacted a promise of party reform from Mr Fukuda as the price of stepping down in his favour; and Mr Kakuei Tanaka, Premier 1972-74, who felt obliged to resign the job and was currently a defendant in the Lockheed payoff trial, but who still commanded one of the strongest followings in the LDP.

Mr Miki's legacy was the holding of the first-ever selection of a party president by election, formerly the purview of party elders dutifully endorsed by rank and file. This time the choice was to be made via a primary in which $1\frac{1}{2}$ million party members and associates, most of them new recruits, could cast their votes—for Mr Fukuda, the incumbent Prime Minister; Mr Ohira, LDP secretary-general and thus influential party manager seeing most of the game; the ambitious Mr Yasuhiro Nakasone, LDP executive council chairman; or Mr Toshio Komoto, a Miki man then Minister of International Trade and Industry.

LDP factions, once declared dissolved, came rapidly to life again as the campaign got under way—especially the Tanaka faction, in support of Ohira (the men were old friends and Ohira had been Tanaka's Foreign Minister and Finance Minister in different Cabinets). Nakasone and Komoto were never reckoned to have much of a chance, and Fukuda was seen as the obvious winner. Instead of putting up a stiff fight to retain the presidency, Mr Fukuda seemed lulled into over-confidence and complacency by the cheering messages of the opinion polls—or else preoccupied with a last-ditch stand to honour the '7 per cent economic growth' pledge which had heartened his foreign colleagues at the Bonn summit in July.

He was destined to lose the election and Japan the 7 per cent target. There were 1,525 electoral points at stake in the primary. Fukuda forecast he would win by more than 100; instead he lost to Ohira by 110 (Ohira 748, Fukuda 638, Nakasone 93, Komoto 46). By the rules of the game, Fukuda could then have had a straight re-run with Ohira but he saved himself from further possible humiliation and withdrew. Ironically, the day he bowed out saw publication of the latest *Jiji Press* poll giving his Cabinet its highest-ever popularity rating of 34·8 per cent against its detractors' 32·5 per cent. But the clock had already struck midnight for the political Cinderellas.

Likewise had the bell tolled for the 7 per cent. While Mr Ohira was still wearing his victory smile, an economic messenger at the gates informed him that 7 per cent would be impossible to achieve. It was a fact of life which everybody but Mr Fukuda (and probably even he) was already acknowledging, but with Japan under new management it was easier to break the news, and the Prime Minister did so at his first press conference.

Soon the new Cabinet was talking of 6 per cent, give or take a decimal point. It was indeed a new Government, because only Foreign Minister Sunao Sonoda stood up to be counted after the Fukuda heads fell with their chief's. Japanese Prime Ministers have to master the art of picking Cabinets according to the strength of the factions supporting their power base. Twelve of the 20 Ministers were faces new to Cabinet, which was somewhat unusual in a country where the game of political musical chairs enables most backbenchers to taste the fruits of office at some period of their careers, if only for a few months at a time. There did not seem to be that number still 'unblooded'. Perhaps 'new faces' needed qualifying, though: eight of the twelve were aged 65 and over. Mr Ohira himself was 68, comparatively junior to 73-year-old Mr Fukuda.

Mr Ohira revealed his practised political hand by retaining Mr Sonoda, who, having wrought a treaty of peace and friendship with China (see DOCUMENTS), could now turn his attention to bettering relations with the Soviet Union. The men of Moscow had turned rather sour over what they regarded as an anti-Russian tinge to the Japan–China pact—'the contracting parties declare that neither of them should seek hegemony in the Asia-Pacific region and in any other region and that each is opposed to efforts by any other country or group of countries to establish such hegemony'. This phrase was surely a masterpiece of Oriental compromise, when China would just as soon have mentioned Russia by name and Japan was anxious to display her new-found 'all-directional peace diplomacy'—meaning that the nation wanted to be friends with everybody.

Mr Sonoda would be fortified in his approaches to the Soviet Union, which also wanted a pact with Japan, by a further clause saying that 'the present (Japan–China) treaty shall not affect the position of either contracting party regarding its relations with third countries', but how would he overcome Moscow's blank refusal first to discuss the return of four islands off Hokkaido seized as booty in the last days of World War II? 'The demand for the islands' return is tantamount to releasing the devil of war', so visiting Japanese socialists were told in Moscow by a Soviet Politburo member.

The pact with China came six years after normalization of diplomatic relations and appeared to be in the balance even mid-way through 1978. However, it was obviously as much to the liking of China as of Japan, and when Vice-Chairman and Vice-Premier Teng Hsiao-p'ing became the first Chinese leader to visit Japan since the founding of the People's Republic of China in 1949 the scene was set for a new era in relations between the two countries. Mr Teng told Emperor Hirohito that China attached great importance to Sino-Japanese relations in the future rather than in the past, to which His Majesty replied that there had been unfortunate events for a while but they were things of the past.

Mr Teng even showed understanding of Japan's 'basic position, including a build-up of its self-defence capability, as well as the top priority given to the security arrangements with the USA'—and neither he, nor any other Chinese, would have said that a few years before. And the Chinese leader's attitude to the potentially worrying Senkaku islands issue contrasted strongly with Russia's Hokkaido islands stance. Peking claimed rights to the uninhabited Senkakus, south-west of the Japanese prefecture of Okinawa, in 1971. For one thing, oil was presumed to lie in the vicinity. An April 1978 invasion of the islands by Chinese fishing boats, some armed, had Japan jumpy. Mr Teng carried a bit further Chinese assurances to Mr Sonoda that they would never allow a recurrence of this incident: he told newsmen in Tokyo that the territorial problem involving the Senkakus could be 'shelved for even ten years, to let it be solved by the next generation'.

But man could not live by treaties alone. Mr Teng took a look at Japanese industry and liked what he saw. He sought Japan's help in catching up with the Western nations by the end of the century. 'We have much to learn from Japan', he said, 'in such fields as technology, science and finance.' He spoke, too, about doubling and then doubling again the $20,000 million worth of two-way business planned in the Sino-Japanese trade arrangement. Japanese industrialists liked what they heard—here was a country actually seeking Japan's technical help and trade. Japan's rivals elsewhere had continued to complain about its exports without sympathizing over the problems presented by a soaring yen (from 237 to the dollar in January to 175 in October, when President Carter at last took effective steps to stop the dollar drop, and ending the year around 195). In any case, Mr Fukuda's promise at Bonn of 'moderation in Japan's exports'—by which he meant volume, which was controllable, and not value, which was subject to the extraneous force of exchange fluctuations—was in part fulfilled. Even Japan's imports rose by 12 per cent during the year, to spare some of its blushes. The yen advance had some compensations by way of cheaper raw materials.

It was a bit perturbing to Mr Ohira to learn of President Carter's regret at the ditching of Mr Fukuda's 7 per cent so soon after the President had spent twenty minutes on the hot-line congratulating him on achieving the Premiership and looking forward to continuing good relations, but he recovered in time to coin a motto for his new Administration: 'Credibility and Consensus'. Japanese Governments, no less than Japanese companies, needed a slogan. Political pundits searched their thesauruses for words to describe the new chief executive: less flamboyant than Fukuda; not skilled in self-expression; a man with a soft touch and reserved manner; prudent in decision, quick in action; 'prefers dialogue to unproductive confrontation'; sleepy-eyed; slow of speech, somnolent, soporific.

'Witty' was the verdict of one writer, recalling that Mr Ohira had once said 'I'm a poor speaker but people tell me I have a sweet face—in a way.' The Japanese people knew they had a seasoned and capable administrator at their head—like Fukuda he was once a Ministry of Finance man—and they could not fault the idea of consensus, especially if allied to credibility. An early test of consensus would be the public's view of a proposed variant of Value Added Tax—Japanese as a nation are averse to taxes. Possibly equally important for Mr Ohira, the Japanese business community liked the sound of promised 'small government', which in the Japanese context meant less intervention in the private sector. A Japanese Premier without business support is foredoomed.

It would be two years at least before Mr Ohira might be destined to share the fate of Takeo Fukuda (to be remembered only because 'he' failed twice to achieve a growth target and to stop the payments surplus soaring, even though he cut the consumer price increase from 10 per cent to three or four per annum). Meanwhile, there was the Tokyo summit to stage in mid-1979, putting Japan on level-pegging with the previous hosts, Britain, France, USA and West Germany.

SOUTH KOREA

Throughout 1978, the South Korean economy continued to expand, the main emphasis being on industrial growth combined with an export-led trade drive. Overall production increased by 12·5 per cent, while the per capita gross national product (GNP) reached US$1,240. Despite world-wide protectionist trends, South Korea's exports earned US$12,700 million, and its foreign exchange holdings rose to US$4,900 million at the end of 1978. The cargo-handling capacity of Pusan, South Korea's chief port, was doubled to 14 million tons per annum; another notable infrastructure project, South Korea's first nuclear power plant, was opened on 20 July.

Apart from the economy, problems of defence and national security predominated on the national scene. Although the slow withdrawal of US troops proceeded in line with President Carter's decision of January 1977, US-South Korean relations improved during the year. In February the American Defence Secretary, Mr Harold Brown, stated in Congressional testimony that the US would carry out its 1953 treaty obligations towards Seoul, that advanced military equipment was being transferred to South Korea, and that an extra squadron of twelve USAF F4D Phantoms was being deployed to the country. These aircraft arrived at Taegu air force base in November. After Mr Brown had conferred with his South Korean counterpart, Ro Jae-hyun, at San Diego, California, at the end of July, a joint communique reaffirmed that South Korea would remain under the US nuclear umbrella, and that the US would provide 'prompt and effective' aid to South Korea in case of armed attack.

Along the 155-mile Demilitarized Zone (DMZ) separating North and South Korea, tension remained high. On 27 October, the UN Command at Panmunjom announced that a large North Korean tunnel underneath the DMZ had been discovered. The tunnel was designed to emerge 4 km south of Panmunjom itself, with only the Imjim river and a 25-mile drive separating the North Koreans from the South's capital of Seoul. A UN Command spokesman considered that the tunnel was built for invasion rather than infiltration, and that its size, 2 metres square, meant that thousands of North Korean troops per hour could have passed into the South. Two other tunnels had been discovered during 1974-75 along the DMZ; experts considered that the DMZ area was probably 'catacombed' with other North Korean tunnelling projects. North Korea, meanwhile, denied all knowledge of the Panmunjom tunnel, and averred that it was a fabrication of the 'US imperialists'.

On 6 July, the South Korean President, Park Chung Hee, was re-elected by an overwhelming majority in the electoral college for a further six-year term of office under the provisions of the 1972 Yushin ('Reform') Constitution.

During the year, President Park's regime adopted a more relaxed attitude towards the dissidents of its internal opposition imprisoned under Emergency Decree 9 of 1975. Dissidents were released from gaol on several occasions, a process which culminated in a sweeping amnesty announced on 26 December. This included the regime's leading opponent, Kim Dae Jung, and over a hundred other political dissidents. These developments defused to a large degree the human rights issue in South Korea.

NORTH KOREA

North Korea's economic difficulties continued during 1978, the country's foreign indebtedness being estimated at about US$2,000 million. In his Budget speech to the Supreme People's Assembly in April, the Finance Minister, Kim Kyong-ryon, stated that the Budget was drafted on the basis of 'total mobilization' for the North Korean Seven Year Plan (1978-84), which the Assembly had approved in the previous December. The speech revealed only the basic proportions of the Budget: 58·5 per cent for the economy, 23·6 per cent for social welfare, 16 per cent for the military and defence sector, and 1·9 per cent for other purposes.

The Chinese Communist Party leader and Premier, Hua Kuo-feng, visited North Korea from 5 to 10 May. No communique was issued, but Chairman Hua expressed support for what he described as North Korea's 'peaceful' programme for Korean reunification. Despite his non-committal speeches, it was generally believed that Chairman Hua's visit was connected with North Korea's indebtedness to China over grain and petroleum supplies. Significantly, after Hua's visit the North Korean press attacked 'dominationism', Pyongyang's code-word for the USSR. The net result of the much-publicized visit indicated, therefore, that Pyongyang had at least partly abandoned its neutrality in the Sino-Soviet schism, and was tilting towards Peking.

Speaking on 9 September, the 30th anniversary of the founding of the North Korean state, the Party leader and President, Kim Il Sung, reiterated the need for North Korea's 'three revolutions' in the fields of ideology, industrial technology and national culture. There was little change, mean-while, in Kim Il Sung's position on the perennial question of Korean reunification. He stressed the need for a withdrawal of all US forces from South Korea and the establishment of a pro-Communist, pro-Pyongyang regime in Seoul. Only in this way could peaceful Korean reunification come about. Given these terms, the prospects for Korean reunification at the close of 1978 were as remote as ever.

X AUSTRALASIA AND SOUTH PACIFIC

Chapter 1

AUSTRALIA—PAPUA NEW GUINEA

AUSTRALIA

THE federal coalition Government of the Liberal and National Country Parties under Prime Minister Malcolm Fraser maintained its decisive political ascendancy in the Parliament at Canberra, although public opinion polls suggested that its electoral support was declining and at state levels the Australian Labor Party (ALP) improved its position.

In May, the people of New South Wales approved by referendum an amendment to the state constitution which changed the Legislative Council (upper House) from an indirectly elected body (which it had been since 1933) to one directly elected by adult (over 18) suffrage in a single constituency of the whole state, voting by a modified Hare–Clark system of proportional representation, elections for a third of the House to coincide with those for the Legislative Assembly (lower House) and members to hold office for a maximum of nine years. Mr Neville Wran, who had established a strong personal ascendancy as ALP Premier of the state, governing with a majority of one in the lower House and a minority in the upper, procured a general election on 7 October, including the first election for the Council under the new system. The ALP swept the poll, obtaining majorities of 27 in the Assembly and of 3 in the Council. The leader of the Liberal Party lost his seat.

There were feuds and leadership disputes in the Queensland and Victorian branches of the Liberal Party, but in Queensland the National Country Party Premier, Mr Bjelke Petersen, retained a strong personal position, as did the Western Australian Liberal Premier, Sir Charles Court. Mr Fraser reshuffled the federal Cabinet and Ministry three times, and a senior Minister, Senator R. Withers, was compelled to resign because of adverse comment on his conduct in a judicial report about the circumstances of an electoral redistribution in 1977; the circumstances were minor in character, and the somewhat harsh attitude of Mr Fraser towards Senator Withers, who had played a major part in his accession to power, and his generally aloof style of leadership, caused some backbench muttering.

The Fraser Government continued its 'new federalism' policy, designed to increase the autonomy and capacity for policy initiatives of the state governments. The federal monopoly of income tax was modified by legislation permitting the states to impose additional tax, to be collected by the federal officials under federal assessment law, or to provide their taxpayers with rebates from the federally-imposed rates, paid for by subtraction from federal grants to the rebating state. The ALP-governed states (New South Wales, South Australia and Tasmania) immediately announced that they would not use this legislation, since ALP standing policy required the retention of the federal income tax monopoly, established by ALP Governments in 1942-50. The Liberal-Country-governed states (Queensland, Victoria and Western Australia) showed no enthusiasm about the proposals, and no state budget in 1978 made any provision for using them.

All states, however, supported and used a modification of the system for raising loans for public purposes, which had been in force since 1927 under agreements given constitutional standing by s. 105A, added to the Commonwealth of Australia Constitution Act by amendment in 1928. The agreements vested the power to raise and distribute public loan raisings in a Loan Council representing the Commonwealth (federal) and six state governments, in which the states had a voting majority but the Commonwealth dominated proceedings because of its paramount banking and commerce powers. The states were now given leave to put up programmes of borrowings for state developmental purposes, subject to broad federal guidelines and Loan Council approval, which each state could raise on its own initiative and security. The 1978 programmes totalled A$1,767 million.

The Northern Territory, whose self-governing powers had been developed by all federal Governments since 1973, entered on the nearest approach to state-like autonomy that it could reach without becoming an additional state. It now possessed a single-chamber parliament (Assembly), elected by adult suffrage, and a Westminster-style parliamentary Executive of Ministers chosen from the majority party in the Assembly and formally acting through advice to an Administrator, equivalent to a state Governor, appointed by the federal Governor-General. Since 1976, departments of the federal government had by stages been absorbed into or transferred their powers to departments of the Northern Territory government administered by its Ministers—known until 1 July 1978 as 'Executive Members of the Assembly'. On that date, they became 'Ministers', and further substantial functions were handed over by the federal authorities. Some transfers remained to be made, particularly in relation to judicial affairs and the administration of lands vested in the Aboriginal people, numbering about a half of the Territory's population of 100,000. The Territory Government was invited to participate in the gatherings of federal and state Ministers known as 'Premiers' Conferences', and to apply for federal grants through the Commonwealth Grants Commission.

The Fraser Government also conducted a plebiscite in the Australian Capital Territory to see whether the 200,000 inhabitants of that area wished to adopt a state-like autonomous system of government; nearly

70 per cent of the voters answered 'No', preferring the existing system of substantially federal administration with an advisory elective Assembly.

The Fraser Government continued to concentrate its economic policy on the reduction of the rate of inflation and budget-balancing, and resisted calls from the ALP opposition, and from some of its own supporters at both federal and state levels, for measures to alleviate continued unemployment which might be reflationary in effect. The 1977–78 accounts showed a higher deficit than desired—A$3,331 million, exceeding the estimate by $1,100 million—because reductions in the public service and other economies were offset by declining revenues. Nevertheless, the inflation-reduction programme was strikingly successful; in January, the price level was rising at a rate in excess of 9 per cent per annum, but by December the rate was below 8 per cent and the decline was expected to continue.

Some discontent with the deflationary policy was spreading, however, because it had not yet been accompanied by any obvious improvement in business conditions and employment. Company profits improved a little on average, but there were great differences between different branches of industry and commerce. The motor car industry continued to show signs of serious structural maladjustment. General Motors—Holdens, the premier Australian manufacturer, made its first loss since 1948, and the Chrysler company stumbled from difficulty to difficulty. Broken Hill Proprietary Co., the Australian steel giant, made a substantial profit, but mainly from its share in Bass Strait petroleum; the steel operation barely paid its way.

The external balance of payments was in deficit on current account, but was amply maintained by government borrowings and inflow of private capital, and the climate of capital-attracting development was well maintained by fresh oil finds in the Bass Strait (Victoria), Roma (Queensland) and Cooper Basin (South Australia) fields, coal finds in New South Wales and Queensland, and a substantial diamond find (the first Australian discovery of commercial importance) in Western Australia. The rural industries had a fair year, with substantial harvests and clips selling at reasonably firm prices; beef in particular recovered somewhat. Employment, however, remained sluggish; there was dispute about the extent and causes of unemployment, exacerbated by multiplicity and mutual disagreement of official as well as unofficial statistical records, but on the most optimistic (and probably reliable) official series, that of the federal Bureau of Statistics, the unemployment rate through the year ranged around 6.2 per cent of the work force (full and part time).

The federal Budget, opened on 15 August, was nevertheless determinedly deflationary, though still aiming at a small deficit (A$2,813 million). Personal income tax rates were increased by 1·5 per cent and a number of concessions abolished. Some indirect taxes were increased, notably on petrol, tobacco and alcohol. Further reductions in the public service and statutory authorities were required. The federal commitment to public health expenditure was reduced by finally abolishing the already much modified Medibank system for paying hospital and medical accounts which had been introduced by the Whitlam ALP Government in 1974–75, and with it any compulsion to carry health insurance or an equivalent payment to government. The 'indexation' of pensions to the over-70s was made subject to a means test, and there were other economies in welfare payments, some of which had to be modified because of backbench objections in parliament. The oldest federal aid to families, established in 1912—a cash payment to mothers on birth of a baby, without means test—was abolished. The sole substantial fiscal aid to employment was a reduction in the sales tax on motor vehicles.

There were a few strikes in demonstration against the Budget, and employees of the Australian Broadcasting Commission (which had been required to make considerable cuts in staff and programmes) imposed a blackout on parliamentary broadcasts. Business circles were also dissatisfied, and not much mollified by a decision to cut down considerably the powers of the federal Prices Justification Tribunal—a step which enraged trade union leaders.

During the year, several thousand square kilometers of tribal lands in the Northern Territory and South Australia were handed over to representatives of the Aboriginals by the federal and South Australian Governments. The Queensland Government was opposed to this policy, and obstructed its execution in tribal areas of western Queensland; the Fraser Government was not prepared to test its constitutional powers in the matter, and a compromise settlement with the Queensland Government resulted in the lands being leased to the local Aboriginals for fifty years, with provision for renewal. The policy of providing 'homelands' for Aboriginals was complicated by the existence, in many of the relevant areas, of valuable mineral deposits, in particular uranium and alumina, and one of the reasons for resistance to the federal programme in Queensland and Western Australia was the wish of the state Governments to retain power to compel the Aboriginal organizations to grant mineral leases; most of those organizations were in fact willing to negotiate with mining companies, but some were not. The federal legislation also reserved power to Canberra to require exploitation of mineral resources in the public interest, but federal policy favoured giving effect to Aboriginal views on the matter.

The question of uranium exploitation raised special difficulties, because of a powerful nation-wide movement, having no connexion with Aboriginal interests, to prevent the mining, treatment and export of fissile material. The Fraser Government strongly favoured the exploitation of uranium and commenced negotiations with possible purchaser countries in order to secure terms which the Government considered would provide adequate guarantees that the material would be used only for peaceful purposes and that waste products would be disposed of safely. The official policy of the ALP and of the Australian Council of Trade Unions was to allow extraction and export only to the extent of the few firm contracts already made, and in the case of the ACTU even this concession was qualified by requirements of satisfaction as to safety of handling and disposal of wastes. The ALP was prepared in principle to reconsider the matter in the light of new techniques and safeguards ensuring peaceful use, but it became apparent during the year that a majority of trade unions, in particular the communist-led transport unions, were committed to blocking by any means available the exploitation of uranium deposits and had substantial support from conservation and environment-preservation movements.

Notwithstanding those influences, the Northern Land Council of Northern Territory Aboriginals agreed to the commencement of uranium extraction at the Ranger deposits in territory controlled by them, and confirmed the decision after opponents from the outside used their influence with Aboriginal minorities to procure a reconsideration. It seemed unlikely that the wish of Aboriginals to derive some profit from the deposits of uranium in their territories would have any influence with the interests determined to prevent exploitation, but since it would take at least two years for the yellowcake to be produced in saleable form a showdown on the issue was postponed.

In January, the federal Government extended legal recognition to the absorption of Timor into Indonesia. In November, agreement was reached with Papua New Guinea on the 'boundary' between the two countries in the Torres Straits. Australia retained sovereignty over the islands in the Strait, so avoiding a possible constitutional clash with Queensland in whose territory the islands were situated; no specific boundary drawing was attempted in the high seas, but lines were laid down to mark off areas of sea-bed resources and local fisheries; large-scale commercial fisheries were to be shared, and in specified areas it was agreed that no mining or drilling would be permitted for ten years.

Throughout the year, the arrival of 'boat people' refugees from Vietnam and Cambodia, mainly Chinese, created problems of settlement and caused acute differences of opinion among Australians. The federal Government committed the country to receiving 32,000 by the end of 1979, of whom nearly 20,000 had arrived by December. Selection teams were sent to the transit camps in Malaysia and Thailand, and coastguard arrangements along the northern coasts were reorganized in the hope of discouraging 'queue-jumping'. A conference of heads of (British) Commonwealth Governments of the East and South-East Asian and Australasian region was held at Sydney in February, as part of the Fraser Government's policy of building up the non-communist Governments of the region. Its chief result was a bomb explosion by persons still unknown at year's end, possibly meant only as a demonstration, in which a garbage collector was killed, and a consequential urgent investigation and reorganization of Australia's anti-terrorist forces after a report by Sir Robert Mark, former chief of Scotland Yard.

PAPUA NEW GUINEA

Concern over the economic and political direction of the country provided the context for an intensely political year. The climax arrived in November when the seven-year-old Pangu-PPP (Peoples' Progress Party) coalition Government split up. Pangu, led by Prime Minister Somare, retained power in coalition with the former opposition United Party. The catalyst for the split was the Prime Minister's proposal, in March, to introduce a stringent 'Leadership Code' by which national leaders would divest themselves of all private business interests. Mr Somare and his advisers had become concerned at increasing corruption, at the apparent neglect of the Government's development objectives, and at the emergence of a *comprador* pattern of elite behaviour. The PPP, essentially a *petit bourgeois* party and more explicit in its commitment to free enterprise than Pangu, opposed the Code largely on the grounds of its impracticability. In August the PPP voted with the Opposition to block the introduction of the Code. Partly in retaliation, Somare reshuffled his Cabinet, effectively demoting PPP Ministers, who then withdrew from the Government. The new coalition held a parliamentary majority of ten and, apart from the elevation of some more radical Ministers, it foreshadowed little substantial change in policy.

The political year saw the rejuvenation of the parliamentary opposition under the leadership of the highlands politician Iambakey Okuk. Okuk led an aggressive, if somewhat confused, attack on Government policy and performance and outlined an alternative strategy. Maintaining that the Government's planning and redistributive strategies had impeded growth, he argued the case for increased foreign investment, joint ventures, urban industrialization and the encouragement of national capitalists. His inappropriate description of the Government as 'socialist' and his criticism of decentralization cost him some support and credibility. As well, his parliamentary base and his aspiration for a united highlands bloc was eroded somewhat by the switch of the United Party.

The major structural change since independence, that of political and administrative decentralization to the provinces, proceeded rapidly, but also became the source of some dissent. The politicization objective was amply demonstrated throughout the year by increased local-level political activity, but many administrative problems remained, including manpower shortages and adequate financial controls. MPs from all sides expressed concern at the extravagant emoluments and conditions which provincial leaders had granted themselves.

The major foreign policy issue continued to be PNG's relations with Indonesia, which hinge on the existence and operation of the West Papuan Freedom Movement (OPM) along the border with Irian Jaya. PNG took a tougher stand against the movement by mounting a border patrol coincidental with an Indonesian military offensive against the guerrillas in June. Late in the year, two OPM leaders were captured in PNG territory and subsequently gaoled. This stand, together with the general foreign policy of 'universalism', attracted criticism from MPs and student groups, and a revision, particularly of the latter policy, seemed likely in the new year.

Chapter 2

NEW ZEALAND

THE return to office of Robert Muldoon's National Government with a substantially reduced majority was the dominant event of 1978 in New Zealand. In a November poll, National won 50 of the new Parliament's 92 seats, its Labour opposition 41, the remaining seat being captured by the Social Credit Political League. With 40 per cent of the vote, Labour in fact polled more votes than did National (39 per cent), and Social Credit, with 16 per cent, claimed its paltry representation to be a manifest injustice of the country's first-past-the-post electoral system. Allied as this claim was to wider charges of maladministration, particularly in the enrolment of voters, matters of electoral conduct and representation were promised a review in 1979.

The slump in the Government's support was widely attributed to its failure to realize earlier pledges of economic rectification and more disciplined, less chaotic industrial relations. As well, voters registered a clear discontent with Prime Minster Muldoon's overbearing, abrasive, heavily centralized style of leadership. His subsequent attempts to blame the news media for the Government's electoral reverses lacked that credibility which he had earlier claimed would be a key election issue. Somewhat generalized promises about 'taking New Zealand into the 1980s' aside, the incumbent party did little to convey or seek fresh guidelines for what it was attempting to achieve in office.

The outcome saw Labour leader Bill Rowling consolidate his personal support and his party's standing as credible alternatives. Prominent themes voiced through Labour's election campaign were tax reforms designed to ease existing burdens upon single-income families, regional development assistance proposals, and a return to a more moderate, effective style of international diplomacy.

Yet, in a year of campaigning, the major political parties did little to illuminate how they might tackle substantial problems such as stagnant productivity, increased indebtedness through external borrowing, or worsening unemployment. Disillusioned, many voters accordingly turned to Social Credit, though still uncertain as to the nature of its abstruse monetary ideologies, an issue bypassed by its articulate and personable leader Bruce Beetham. That so many former National Party voters switched to Social Credit was one of the major surprises of the election.

On the economic front, Mr Muldoon's partially revitalized, post-election Administration faced a host of stubborn problems: a balance of payments deficit still exceeding $400 million; an internal deficit, before borrowing, of some $1,500 million; unacceptable unemployment levels exceeding 50,000; a net loss of 30,000 permanent, long-term migrants; worsening internal production costs, charges and inefficiencies; an annual inflation rate still at 11 per cent; and poor levels of investment throughout New Zealand's key agricultural sector. Indeed, the year seemed yet another of failure to boost exports, expand productivity, rationalize key services such as transport or the construction industry, and curb public spending.

Nevertheless, purchasing power was injected into the economy through public service salary increases, tax cuts, and a mildly expansionary Budget. Hopes for any spending-led recovery faded in the final quarter, however. As a country living essentially beyond its means, New Zealand entered 1979 with a likely devaluation and further domestic belt-tightening well in prospect.

Economic considerations also dominated foreign relations. In March, Foreign Minister Talboys made an extensive tour of Australia where, after strenuous advocacy, it was agreed each Government, when determining support for local industries, would 'take into account' the situation and prospects for the industries concerned in the other country. Nevertheless, the ailing trade agreement between the two countries (NAFTA) ran into further trouble over complementarity in the newsprint, textile and garment industries, protectionist demands by respective domestic interests, and competing pressures for access to Australia's markets by its Asian trade partners. Bluntly, New Zealand was warned to abide by Australian terms or face collapse of the arrangement.

Even more controversial was the diplomatic affray New Zealand staged with Japan over access to that market—especially beef exports—in return for Japanese demands that its vessels fish in New Zealand's extended maritime economic zone. Mr Muldoon claimed there was evidence of Japan's 'commercial imperialism' in the Pacific and indicated that it was attempting to achieve 'by peaceful means what it failed to do during the war'. After shutting out Japanese vessels and confiscating and fining intruders, the Government in June invited Japanese Agricultural Minister Nakagawa to New Zealand in an attempt to break the impasse. Although it was agreed that the Japanese would return to fish in New Zealand waters, it was by no means clear what reciprocal trade concessions, if any, had been gained. Mr Muldoon subsequently admitted that the unpublished agreements fell short of what New Zealand had sought.

A recurring headache for the Government, at home and abroad, centred around claims that it was failing to fulfil its obligations under the 1977 Commonwealth Gleneagles agreement concerning the ban on sporting relations with South Africa. Accusations that local anti-apartheid groups had spread misinformation abroad intensified following Nigeria's boycott of the Edmonton Commonwealth Games, ostensibly because of New Zealand participation.

Industrial relations generated continuing controversy. In March, at the height of a serious drought, the Government took the extreme step of authorizing more than $3 million of public money to help effect a wage settlement in the strife-torn stock slaughter or freezing industry. Farmer discontent was compounded when the Government, facing further threats of industrial action, failed to present prosecuting evidence in a criminal action it had brought against striking freezing workers. The Government's policy of attempting to enforce industrial harmony through the criminal law was thus seriously weakened, though Cabinet Ministers claimed that the decision not to offer evidence had been made 'autonomously' by their own officials.

Prosecutions were also lifted against a majority (170) of those apprehended in a May mass arrest at Bastion Point, Auckland. Almost all were Maori squatters and their supporters, variously involved in a 17-month occupation of a promontory zoned for development as Crown land, but claimed as original tribal property by Maori protest leaders. That the combined police and troop operation concerned was the largest of its kind for many years undoubtedly contributed to the mass disruption of court proceedings which, in turn, influenced the Government to call the partial stay of prosecutions.

Environmental issues were salient, and protest action ended logging of scenic, central North Island forests. Energy schemes for flooding the Clutha valley produced a highly critical environmental impact report which was all but ignored in a Government decision to proceed with the project.

In yet another poorly managed, acrimonious year, Parliament passed 149 Acts, much of this effort telescoped into the final weeks of the session. (The new Government saw the tactful Mr David Thompson replace Mr Muldoon as Leader of the House.) Legislation was passed for tougher penalties on drug offences (including special detection provisions permitting the use of listening devices); for industrial relations, substituting civil for criminal procedures for breaches of the Act and requiring unions to hold a triennial ballot on compulsory unionism; for airways, validating the Government's controversial decision to merge the National Airways Corporation with Air New Zealand; and for transport, including more stringent penalties and criteria for blood–alcohol offences. Amid continuing public disquiet as to the workings of December 1977 legislation (see AR 1977, p. 311), Parliament amended the Crimes Act extending the grounds for abortion by removing the proviso that serious danger to the mother could not be averted by any other means, and by providing for foetal abnormality as a specific ground—this in the face of one of the largest petitions presented to Parliament in recent years, calling for complete repeal of the existing laws on abortion.

In the field of energy, plans were announced to utilize some of the Maui field off-shore natural gas resources, now coming on-stream, for methanol conversion and end-use in transport. Throughout the South Island, there was discontent that national energy development and pricing policies were unduly discriminatory against Southern contributions and distances. This, added to unemployment, perceptions of 'bureaucratic dominance' from Wellington, and weakening yet increasingly expensive transport links to markets in the North, caused some of the Government's heaviest election reversals to occur in the South Island. Potentially offsetting developments included active investigation of the commercial viability of extensive lignite coal deposits in Southland, and agricultural diversification into deer farming and horticulture. In fact an increase in foreign sales of horticultural products (e.g. kiwi fruit) was one of the few bright spots in what was officially designated 'export year'.

New Zealand's 1978 also saw the first official visit by a West European head of state, Federal Germany's Walter Scheel, in October; protracted industrial trouble preventing newspaper publication; century-worst spring floods in Otago and Southland; and the television filming of unidentified flying objects near the Clarence river in the South Island.

Chapter 3

THE SOUTH PACIFIC

FURTHER decisive steps in its protracted decolonization, and the most substantial difficulties to date in its Forum's eight-year history, were key South Pacific developments for the year.

In July, the almost 200,000 people of the Solomon Islands, largest remaining British dependency in the South Pacific, gained their political independence. Mr Kenilorea's Government was to receive $43 million of assistance from the United Kingdom over the first four years after independence. Unresolved were autonomist demands from the Western district as well as health, education and communications needs. Priority was accorded to marine resource and fisheries development, timber extraction, and the decentralization of economic activity, to include agricultural diversification beyond established copra exporting. The Solomons joined the United Nations and the South Pacific Forum.

Early in October, the tiny country of Tuvalu (eight small occupied islands, a total resident population of only eight thousand) gained its independence. Formerly the Ellice Islands, Tuvalu's Chief Minister Lauti negotiated an assistance agreement earlier in the year at a London conference. This included a $4·7 million development grant, a $4·9 million general development grant for a three-year period, and $1·7 million budgetary aid for 1979–80. In 1980 there would be further talks on aid levels from 1981.

In the New Hebrides, the joint colonial powers, the United Kingdom and France, made it plain they wanted a timetable of political development culminating with independence in 1980. For the first months of 1978, the country's best organized political movement, the Vanuaaku Party, refused to countenance any such arrangement, including the establishment of a provisional Government, just as it boycotted the November 1977 elections. While mistrust between Vanuaaku Party representatives and Vila-based mainly French-speaking political interests remained intense, the former moved closer during the year to the idea of participating in the Government.

Easily the most spectacular, even lurid political upheaval occurred in the Cook Islands. In March, Sir Albert Henry's ruling Cook Islands Party retained office in a general election. His victory was achieved by repatriating Cook Islanders from New Zealand with extremely cheap air fares. Subject to police investigation and then court action, Chief Justice Donne found in July that these special flights had been financed with $350,000 of public money. Describing this as 'a perversion of democracy' the Chief Justice then invalidated the votes of passengers on Sir Albert's charter flights, this costing his party nine seats and political power. The new Premier was Dr Tom Davis who faced an uphill struggle of economic and administrative rehabilitation for his country.

In September, on the island of Niue, the twelve-member South Pacific Forum experienced sharp division over possible American involvement in its planned regional fisheries agency. For Fiji and Papua New Guinea, US participation (mainly the profitable harvest of migratory skipjack tuna) spelled dangers of commercial dominance in the industry by American companies, likely political dominance by Washington, and a reduction in the efficacy of a potentially competitive regional producers' cartel.

Smaller states, on the other hand, such as Western Samoa and the

Cook Islands, backed by Australia and New Zealand, sought American participation. They did so for its technological input, capacity to assist in the surveillance of such a vast maritime zone and, not least, direct revenue benefits accruing from licence payments and royalties.

After walk-out threats by Fiji's Prime Minister, Ratu Sir Kamisese Mara, and Papua New Guinea's Mr Somare, a compromise was struck allowing the agency's establishment, with the issue of membership deferred for no more than six months pending official studies. The same meeting also made an urgent financial call upon members to support the seriously under-capitalized, newly established (May) South Pacific Forum shipping line. Recommendations were also made calling for increased industrial development and better market access for island products in Australian and New Zealand markets.

XI INTERNATIONAL ORGANIZATIONS

Chapter 1

THE UNITED NATIONS AND ITS AGENCIES

INTRODUCTION

In 1978 the membership of the United Nations increased to 151, a hundred more than the original number, upon the admission of the Solomon Islands and Dominica. The same Charter defined its principles and proved flexible, but the procedures did not take into account the enormous challenges in absorbing over eighty newly independent states and coping with multiplying world problems. A glimpse at some of those the UN tried to tackle in 1978 shows how much was expected of it.

Who in 1945 thought the UN would deal with primary health care, pollution in the Mediterranean and Persian Gulf, the technical cooperation of developing countries, racism, discrimination, oil tanker safety and a law to govern the watery two-thirds of the earth's surface? These were not all; disarmament was a legacy of the past, while peace-keeping forces currently involving 27 nations in six operations were never envisaged in the Charter. No wonder the General Assembly had over 130 items on its agenda.

The Secretary-General, in his 1978 report, fully recognized the importance of the issues, but emphasized that the procedures were much the same as in 1919 (when the League of Nations was launched). He wrote 'we have too many gatherings, conferences and sessions of one sort or another', and invited suggestions, modern expertise and techniques to deal with this. As economic problems proliferated, changes became vital. Indalecio Liévano, President of the 33rd General Assembly, warned the press that world economic problems were as important as dangerous political situations.

The General Assembly of 1977 spilled over into 1978. There was a special session to finance the UN Force in Lebanon, a special session on the problem of independence for Namibia, and the 10th special session on disarmament.

The 33rd General Assembly opened on 19 September and was suspended from 21 December until 15 January 1979. It spent a great deal of time on the Middle East and adopted scores of resolutions reflecting the special disarmament session. It elected five new members to the Security Council for two-year terms from 1 January 1979—Bangladesh, Jamaica, Norway, Portugal and Zambia, which joined Bolivia, Czechoslovakia, Gabon, Kuwait and Nigeria with a year to run, and the five permanent members of the Council. The Assembly raised the gross interim budget to $996·4 million for 1978-79.

POLITICAL

MIDDLE EAST. Throughout the year the Secretary-General, Dr Kurt Waldheim, was kept informed of—but not involved in—the diplomatic efforts to reach a settlement between Egypt and Israel. In March the Palestine Liberation Organization (PLO) attacked buses on the Tel Aviv road, and Israel retaliated by advancing into southern Lebanon. On 19 March the Security Council adopted a resolution for immediate withdrawal by the Israeli forces and the formation of the UN Interim Force in Lebanon (UNIFIL) to assist the return of Lebanese authority. Israel accepted the cease-fire, and UNIFIL troops, under Major-General Emmanuel Erskine, were immediately sent in; but Israel was slow to withdraw. Dr Waldheim wrote to Prime Minister Menachem Begin urging him to comply, and Israel presented a plan for withdrawal by stages.

A special session of the General Assembly on 20-21 April approved the financing of UNIFIL for six months, and after a visit to the Middle East Dr Waldheim asked the Council to increase UNIFIL from 4,000 to 6,000 men. At their eventual withdrawal on 13 June the Israelis handed over a strip about 65 miles long by six miles wide to Christian irregulars who, with Israel's backing, opposed UNIFIL's access to the area, and fired on the Lebanese force of 600 men when it went to reassert the Government's authority. The Security Council renewed UNIFIL's mandate until 19 January 1979, while criticizing Israel for not cooperating with the force. On 8 December it expressed deep concern and called on all those not cooperating—particularly Israel—to stop interfering with UNIFIL's operation.

The problem of helping to care for people displaced from southern Lebanon taxed several UN agencies. Conditions in Beirut forced UNRWA, which faced a budget deficit of $11·3 million, to move its offices to Amman and Vienna.

The fighting around Beirut, between the Christians and the Arab Deterrent Force (mostly Syrians), escalated in the autumn. The Security Council met on 6 October, called for an 'effective cease-fire' and respect for the territorial integrity of Lebanon, and asked Dr Waldheim to continue his efforts to stop the fighting. He had already arranged to send Prince Sadruddin Aga Khan (formerly UN High Commissioner for Refugees) on a peace mission to Lebanon.

Although the UN was not involved in the Camp David negotiations, the General Assembly debated the Middle East at length. On 7 December it approved a comprehensive resolution covering all aspects of the conflict, especially the withdrawal of Israel from occupied territories and the rights of the Palestinians. It favoured a peace conference chaired by the US and USSR under UN auspices with the PLO participating. Subsequently it recommended that the Security Council adopt a mandatory embargo on arms to Israel. The Council renewed the mandate of the UN Force in Sinai until 24 July 1979 and of the Observer Force on the Golan Heights until 31 May 1979.

NAMIBIA. To reach a negotiated settlement and forestall demands for economic sanctions against South Africa, the five Western countries of the Security Council (Canada, France, UK, US and West Germany) continued their efforts for an acceptable solution. From 24 April to 3 May the General Assembly held a special session on Namibia, which condemned South Africa for its illegal occupation, held Walvis Bay to be a part of Namibia, asserted that the South West People's Organization (Swapo) must be involved in any settlement, and urged the Security Council to adopt measures such as sanctions against South Africa, but took no account of the Western plan. During the session South Africa declared it would accept that plan.

More consultations followed, punctuated by a South African attack on Swapo camps inside Angola. In July Swapo agreed that the Western plan should be submitted to the Security Council. On 27 July the Council asked the Secretary-General to appoint a special representative to report on measures for the early independence of Namibia, and a second resolution gave its full support to the reintegration of Walvis Bay into Namibia. Dr Waldheim sent the Finnish UN Commissioner for Namibia—Martti Ahtisaari—to Namibia with a team of experts. On the basis of his report Dr Waldheim submitted a plan on 31 August, which envisaged a UN Transition Assistance Group (UNTAG) with a military component of 7,500 men, a civilian component of 360 police and about 1,200 administrators to assure a cease-fire and fair elections.

The Prime Minister of South Africa, who resigned on 20 September, announced Namibian elections in November (without the UN). The Security Council then supported Dr Waldheim's report. But the new Prime Minister—Pieter Botha—took the same line as his predecessor. Four Western Foreign Ministers and a deputy Foreign Minister went to South Africa to dissuade Mr Botha from unilateral elections. They did not succeed, but he insisted that UN-supervised elections could also be held.

The Security Council condemned South Africa for proceeding with elections (postponed to 4-8 December), declared them null and void, demanded that South Africa cooperate with the UN plan, otherwise the Council would take action (possibly sanctions). The unilateral elections, which were boycotted by Swapo and another important political party, gave the pro-South African Democratic Turnhalle Alliance 41 of the 50 seats. On 21 December the General Assembly urged the Security Council to impose sanctions and condemned South Africa for the internal elections. The South African Foreign Minister wrote to Dr Waldheim that his

Government had decided to cooperate in the UN plan, subject to certain conditions.

RHODESIA/ZIMBABWE. The UN played a secondary role in the efforts to get majority rule in Rhodesia. Its representative—Major-General D. Prem Chand—attended the Malta talks of 30 January between Foreign Secretary Dr David Owen and the Patriotic Front leaders, when the latter accepted a UN role as part of the Anglo-American plan. After the internal settlement of 3 March the Security Council heard representatives of the Patriotic Front, but not of the Salisbury regime. It declared the internal settlement illegal and unacceptable, and later condemned the Rhodesian raids into Zambia.

The Bingham report, published on 19 September (see pp. 31–3 and 249–50), revealed how two British firms had broken oil sanctions, with the apparent knowledge of certain government officials. On 10 October the Security Council criticized the US for breaking sanctions by allowing Mr Ian Smith to visit the US. Later the General Assembly censured UK Governments for their part in violating the oil embargo and recommended that the Council extend sanctions to South Africa in order that no oil should reach Rhodesia. Also the Assembly declared the internal settlement null and void, held that the Patriotic Front must be a party to the settlement and condemned South Africa and others for supporting a racist regime.

CYPRUS. The year opened with a promising meeting arranged by Dr Waldheim with President Spyros Kyprianou and the Turkish Cypriot leader, Rauf Denktash, but closed with the communities as estranged as ever. Turkey's proposals for a settlement were later presented to Dr Waldheim who handed them to Mr Kyprianou on 19 April. The Cyprus President thought they were 'entirely unacceptable', providing virtually two separate states, not a federation. On 1 May Dr Waldheim's new representative, Reinaldo Galindo-Pohl, assumed his duties in Cyprus.

At the 10th special session on disarmament Mr Kyprianou proposed demilitarization of the island, with an integrated police force under the UN. At the 33rd General Assembly Cyprus tried to mobilize international support. On 9 November the Assembly passed a resolution demanding immediate withdrawal of foreign forces and resumption of intercommunal talks, and reaffirming the territorial integrity of Cyprus. It called on the Security Council to consider the implementation of its resolutions. During Council meetings the US presented a 12-point plan and on 27 November the Council urged the communities to negotiate under the Secretary-General's auspices and to implement its previous resolutions, subject to the Council's review of the situation in June 1979. The Council also renewed the mandate of the UN force in Cyprus to mid-June.

DISARMAMENT. The tenth special session of the General Assembly, 23 May to 1 July, was the first world disarmament conference since 1933. It was designed to provide a programme for action and machinery for negotiations, but not to serve as a negotiating forum. While accepting the ultimate goal of general and complete disarmament, it gave first priority to nuclear weapons, then other weapons of mass destruction including chemical weapons, followed by conventional arms.

The session agreed to set up a Disarmament Commission of all UN members to act as a deliberative body, and a negotiating Committee on Disarmament replacing the Conference of the Committee on Disarmament (CCD). The new committee was open to 32-35 members and the five nuclear powers, and the chairmanship was to rotate monthly among all members. Neither France nor China had taken part in the former CCD and the Assembly hoped both would join the new Committee. France submitted a variety of proposals to the session. US Vice-President Mondale and UK Prime Minister Callaghan called for consideration of a UN peacekeeping reserve. The Secretary-General suggested that for every $1,000 million spent on arms (the estimated daily world expenditure), $1 million should be set aside for disarmament and that an expert advisory board on disarmament should be established.

The General Assembly was overwhelmed by 45 disarmament resolutions, which mirrored the proposals of the tenth special session, from the banning of nuclear weapons to such confidence-building proposals as nuclear-weapon-free zones in Africa, the Middle East and South Asia. Lip-service was again paid to the principles of disarmament and practical negotiations were left to the Disarmament Committee, due to convene in 1979.

CONFERENCES

The Secretary-General's annual report questioned the use of old procedures for complex present problems—in particular over-crowded agendas and conferences. 'We seem to be wedded', he wrote, 'to the proposition that if there is a problem there should be a conference, and if there is a conference there will be documents, lengthy speeches and a plan of action, and after that, as night follows day, there will be an organization with a secretariat, which in turn will organize another follow-up conference, and so on.'

RACISM. The World Conference to Combat Racism and Racial Discrimination, held from 14 to 26 August, was designed to highlight the Decade of Action against Racism and timed to coincide with Anti-Apartheid Year which opened on 21 March 1978. But the focus of the conference on ways to eradicate racism through action against South

L

Africa was initially befogged by the General Assembly's resolution of 1975 which equated zionism with racism. Consequently the US and Israel were not among the 123 governments represented. The final document also referred to Israel; though modified, it still did not satisfy the representatives of the Common Market countries and five others, who walked out. The Declaration recommended comprehensive and mandatory sanctions against southern African racist regimes and also supported the rights of migrant workers.

TECHNICAL COOPERATION AMONG DEVELOPING COUNTRIES. In Buenos Aires 138 states met from 30 August to 12 September to map a plan for promoting cooperation among developing countries. This was not a substitute for the technical cooperation from developed countries, but a new dimension intended to pool suitable experience amongst themselves, to encourage self-reliance and to reduce dependence on the north–south relationship. The Plan of Action presupposed close collaboration with the UN Development Programme, whose administrator—Bradford Morse— was secretary-general of the conference.

THE THIRD LAW OF THE SEA CONFERENCE. The seventh session of the conference met from 28 March to 19 May and resumed from 21 August to 15 September. Instead of ranging over 373 articles (including annexes) in the composite negotiating text, the 142 countries concentrated on seven 'hard-core' issues, and reports were substituted for revisions of the text. The principal problems concerned the international seabed area, marine pollution and maritime boundaries. Pressure mounted because industrialized states, including the US, Japan, UK and West Germany, were considering deap-sea mining legislation, to which the 'Group of 77' (119 countries) strenuously objected. The conference's president warned it that to retain credibility it should set itself a deadline.

POLLUTION

TANKERS AND OIL SPILLS. Oil slicks captured the limelight. On 20 January amendments to the 1954 International Convention for the Prevention of Pollution of the Sea by Oil took effect, restricting the amounts of oily mixtures and the areas where ships could discharge them. Tanker accidents prompted the Inter-Governmental Maritime Consultative Organization (IMCO) to hold a conference in February on tanker safety and pollution prevention. It was concerned with the installation of inert gas systems and with pollution caused by oily water used in tanks for ballast. A compromise of alternatives was reached between the American desire for segregated ballast tanks and the British for crude oil washing equipment. The conference also agreed on regulations for duplicate steering gear and the inspection and certification of ships.

In July 72 nations of IMCO agreed to an international convention on standards of training, certification and watchkeeping of seafarers, including standards of age, experience and qualifications. It required ratification by 25 countries owning 50 per cent of the world's gross tonnage before coming into force.

On 16 October the IMCO convention on an international oil pollution compensation fund came into force, increasing amounts payable for maritime accidents beyond the level of the shipowner's liability. Ten of the 15 nations which ratified the convention met from 13 to 17 November to establish the administration of the fund, which was to be located in London and directed by Reinhard Ganten of West Germany.

THE MEDITERRANEAN AND PERSIAN GULF. In February three agreements of the Barcelona Convention of 1975 came into force, committing Mediterranean countries to protect the sea from pollution, prevent dumping of dangerous wastes and cooperate in emergencies. In January a UN Environment Programme (UNEP) meeting of 17 Mediterranean countries in Monaco failed to agree on a treaty on land-based pollution drafted by UNEP and WHO. Developed countries wanted more time to control their industrial wastes, while developing countries feared that controls might restrict their development. There were also differences on the question of which industrial wastes should be prohibited and the problem of pollution from up-river states.

More successful was the UNEP-instigated meeting of eight states in the oil-producing area of the Persian Gulf with its rapid industrial and population growth. The states approved two treaties—to combat pollution and to cooperate in emergencies—and agreed to establish an emergency centre against oil spills, a regional trust fund and an organization for the protection of the marine environment.

ECONOMIC, SOCIAL AND HUMANITARIAN

ECONOMIC COOPERATION. Little progress was made on economic interdependence. The General Assembly's Committee of the Whole to consider world economic issues floundered on whether its mandate was only to monitor or also to negotiate. The 33rd Assembly called on the Committee for a determined effort to achieve real progress on the issues brought before it. The new Secretariat post of Director-General for Development and International Economic Cooperation was filled by Kenneth Dadzie, erstwhile chairman of the committee on the restructuring of the UN's economic and social affairs.

Some advance was made on the problem of debts of developing countries. A special session of the UN Conference on Trade and Development (UNCTAD) Board in March generally agreed to apply the current norm retroactively, so that loans to the 29 least developed countries would become grants and repayments by the 45 countries most seriously affected by the economic situation would be softened.

By November eleven major creditor states including the UK had announced plans to cancel $6,200 million owed by the poorest countries. In 1977 most Western donors had fallen far short of the target of 0·7 per cent of gross national product for official aid, the UK providing only 0·38 per cent of gnp, France 0·63 per cent and West Germany 0·26 per cent.

In preparation for UNCTAD V in 1979, negotiations on commodity agreements multiplied, but without major breakthroughs, despite lengthy talks on copper, jute, tea and rubber, and efforts to draft a new international wheat agreement. The Director of UNCTAD was increasingly concerned over growing protectionism.

Representatives of over a hundred countries, meeting from 14 to 30 November, made limited progress towards establishing a Common Fund for stabilizing commodity prices and a 'second window' to finance productivity and diversification schemes. Industrialized countries accepted the principle of both funds, but disagreed with the 'Group of 77' on their size and function.

THE ECONOMIC AND SOCIAL COUNCIL. The all-embracing ECOSOC held meetings in April and July (resumed in October). Human rights and the advancement of women dominated the spring session. Subjects debated ranged from restructuring the economic and social sectors of the UN to narcotics, and the Council also asked the General Assembly to call on members to prevent their nationals from operating enterprises in southern Africa.

The session in July surveyed the global position with special emphasis on economic development in the Third World. It recommended help to 15 African states suffering from drought or desert problems, and to African liberation movements. The Council called for cooperation in disaster prevention and endorsed the World Food Council's Mexico declaration of June on eradicating hunger and malnutrition. The resumed session in October urged implementation of the recent plan on technical cooperation among developing countries.

LABOUR. The re-elected Director-General of the International Labour Organization (ILO), Francis Blanchard, described the body as 'stimulated by difficulties'. Among these was the loss of its major contributor, the USA, under charges of politicizing, in November 1977. The organization slashed expenditure by 21·7 per cent by cuts in staff, salaries and some programmes. By June it had received extra voluntary contributions of $6·7 million and was showing greater balance in consideration of issues. The annual conference from 7 to 28 June tackled standards to protect dock workers and reduce road transport accidents, adopted recommendations on public service labour relations, and admitted Namibia as its 137th member.

On 15 November the governing body decided to publicize its dossier alleging that the Czech Government discriminated against workers who signed Charter 77. Two other controversial complaints were under consideration, against the USSR for suppressing efforts of workers to form a union and against West Germany for denying public employment to communists.

MONEY MATTERS. The World Bank and its associates held their annual meetings at the end of September, at which the Bank's president Robert McNamara warned against protectionism. The Bank issued the first of an annual series on world development which analysed progress in developing countries and reported the importance of rural poverty and community participation.

An amendment to the International Monetary Fund Charter took effect in April, diminishing the role of gold and making possible greater use of Special Drawing Rights. The managing director of the Fund, H. Witteveen, retired and was succeeded by Jacques de Larosière de Champfeu. Saudi Arabia, the second largest lender to the Fund, became one of the Big Six, with the right to name its own director to the executive board.

UNESCO AND THE MEDIA. The highlight of the general conference of UNESCO in November was the adoption of a declaration on mass media after eight years of controversy. Third World countries were anxious to secure coverage of their affairs as seen through their eyes, and the West wanted to ensure freedom of communication not controlled by governments. The declaration was a compromise; it said that a free flow and better balanced dissemination of information are essential for strengthening peace, understanding and human rights.

HUMAN RIGHTS. As a counter-blast to the General Assembly's resolution of 1977 condemning Chile's violation of human rights, General Pinochet held a referendum on 4 January for support of his government against 'international aggression' (i.e. the resolution). He claimed a 75 per cent backing. Subsequently he agreed that a UN working group should look into the situation. It visited Chile in July, and reported to its parent organization—the Human Rights Commission—an improvement in the situation, but concluded that violations continued in certain areas.

Members of the Human Rights Commission differed on the relative importance of individual political rights and collective economic and social ones. It considered Chile, Israel and Southern Africa and invited Cambodia (Kampuchea) to comment on the records of human rights violations there.

Another UN body—the Human Rights Committee of experts—considered reports from a number of states on how their laws conformed to the Covenant on Civil and Political Rights. The UK was questioned on its policies in Northern Ireland, race relations and restrictions on passport-holders, and Russian officials spoke on freedom to leave their country and collective farms, enforced hospitalization and how the Soviet Constitution conformed to the Covenant.

HEALTH. Throughout the year the strategy for primary health care developed in WHO, UNICEF and the World Bank. The World Health Assembly of 151 member states, meeting in May, emphasized that progress in health was indivisible from progress in social, economic and political fields. The Assembly favoured taxation and restrictions on advertising to combat smoking and asked the Director-General to identify the most essential drugs and vaccines; in January WHO's Executive Board had considered only 210 drugs essential for the developing countries out of the numberless brands sapping their budgets. The Assembly elected Dr H. Mahler as Director-General for another five-year term.

Together with UNICEF, WHO prepared a report on 'a world-wide strategy of primary health care which would ensure health for the world's peoples by the year 2000'. This report was put to a meeting at Alma Ata, Kazakstan, in September. It warned that probably 80 per cent of people had no access to permanent health care. Representatives of 140 countries considered problems of sanitation, prevention of food deficiencies, traditional medicines and the training of paramedics, with the aim of ending unfair distribution of health resources throughout the world.

The UN Commission on Narcotics held its fifth special session in February. It considered the 1977 report of the International Narcotics Control Board that found cannabis to be a major threat to health, harmless neither for the individual nor for society. It adopted plans to combat the illicit production and use of heroin, a major cause of concern.

HUMANITARIAN. Urgent demands were made on the resources of UN agencies, on the World Food Programme for food to the Sahel, on the UN Disaster Relief Office for coordinating relief in flood-stricken Sudan and India, and particularly on the UN High Commissioner for Refugees (UNHCR) for aid to refugees in Africa, South-East Asia, Lebanon and Latin America.

At the end of May seventeen countries in Africa had suffered shortages due to drought and war. They were also threatened by plagues of locusts which could not be effectively controlled because of war in the Horn of Africa. The fighting was estimated to have uprooted a million people, so UNHCR's help was required in Somalia, Ethiopia and Djibouti.

Elsewhere in Africa UNHCR gave assistance to refugees from South

Africa and Rhodesia, and to those from the conflict in Zaïre, while in the Far East it took part in helping the 115,000 refugees in Thailand, some 150,000 from Cambodia (Kampuchea) in Vietnam, the 200,000 Burmese in Bangladesh and the Vietnamese boat-people.

The plight of the 2,500 refugees on the *Hai Hong* (see p. 279), refused entry by Malaysia, focused world attention on an escalating problem. The UNHCR representative approached the Malaysian authorities, already burdened by some 45,000 of these refugees, and with the help of representatives of Canada, France and the US found places for them to resettle. The UNHCR then called a meeting on 11 and 12 December and mustered 37 countries to consider the problem, but elicited only an additional promise of 5,000 more places and $12 million.

Chapter 2

THE COMMONWEALTH

THE COMMONWEALTH broke new ground when heads of government from twelve member states in the Asia-Pacific region met in Sydney, Australia, from 13 to 16 February at the invitation of the Australian Prime Minister, Mr Malcolm Fraser. The meeting got off to a somewhat inauspicious start when a bomb exploded outside the hotel where four Presidents and eight Prime Ministers were staying. In addition, the idea of a regional summit meeting of Commonwealth leaders gave rise to some misgivings in the planning stages. There were fears that the meeting constituted a self-selected caucus which would have a divisive influence upon the Commonwealth as a whole. These reservations were rapidly dispelled at the actual meeting, which produced agreement on the establishment of regional co-ordinating groups in the fields of trade, energy and the combating of international terrorism and drug trafficking. Meetings conformed to the tradition of informality and frankness now firmly established at full gatherings of the Commonwealth.

One advantage of the regional approach was that member states did not spend the bulk of their time discussing the politics of Africa, although Africa was not excluded from the agenda. Instead, they were able to spend most of it on economic and trade problems affecting the Asia-Pacific area. The leaders agreed on the need to improve communication and transport arrangements in the region and gave their support to the establishment of a Common Fund for trade in commodities. They also decided that the Commonwealth's Asia-Pacific group should continue to meet at summit level once every two years.

Another expanding concern of Commonwealth member states during the year was the encouragement of contacts between the 'official' and 'unofficial' Commonwealth. In January a group from twelve Commonwealth countries met in London to consider ways of strengthening links between governmental bodies and the myriad organizations representing professional, cultural, sporting and other interests. Sir Geoffrey Wilson, chairman of Oxfam and a former deputy Commonwealth Secretary-General, headed a 15-member committee which reported in November. It proposed a vigorous programme of encouraging the activities of the Commonwealth's non-governmental organizations (NGOs). The committee recommended appointment of a desk officer within the Commonwealth Secretariat to promote and coordinate contacts between NGOs and the official Commonwealth.

An NGO of potential future importance was created when the Commonwealth Journalists Association was formed during a meeting of the Commonwealth Press Union, an association of publishers of newspapers, periodicals and news agencies, in Ottawa in September. The CJA was brought into existence to meet the needs of working journalists interested in international affairs and economic development. A steering committee met in London in December and began work on a programme to attract the interest and participation of journalists in all Commonwealth countries. As well as providing a network of contacts, the CJA planned to promote training of journalists and work for the availability of high-quality information by providing opportunities for briefings, seminars and conferences.

At Ottawa the CPU made important changes in its organization with the object of drawing developing Commonwealth countries more fully into CPU activities. An executive committee of 20-25 members was established, including the chairmen of the twelve autonomous CPU sections outside Britain, to meet in a different country each year.

At their annual meeting in Montreal in September Commonwealth Finance Ministers reaffirmed their support for an increase of US$40,000 million in the capital resources of the World Bank. Such an increase, the Ministers decided, was essential for sustaining an annual 5 per cent growth in World Bank commitments over the next four years. The Ministers expressed 'grave concern over the trend towards protectionism' in international trade and urged a 50 per cent increase in IMF quotas.

A vigorous programme of technical cooperation continued in numerous fields throughout the year. The Commonwealth Science Council met in Cyprus from 22 to 28 February and established an action programme for the promotion of rural technology, science education, metrication and natural product utilization in developing countries. The aim of the programme was to make science directly relevant to the developmental needs of Commonwealth member states. At Dacca, scientists from Asian and Pacific countries held a 'workshop' to exchange ideas on small water-treatment plants, the medicinal use of herbs, light engineering using traditional skills, and the development of rural energy supplies. Sri Lanka's scheme for manufacturing small tools using the traditional skills of the blacksmith found favour as a useful model for other countries.

The Commonwealth Fund for Technical Cooperation opened its eighth year of activities in July with a budget of £12 million (£1 million higher than in 1977) and a new managing director, Mr David Anderson, a Briton with long administrative experience in Commonwealth African countries. The CFTC, one of the Commonwealth's most conspicuous successes of recent years, was formed in 1971 with an initial capital of £400,000. Over the last five years it had trained over 200 people from 18 countries in farm management. Another of its specialities had been help to small island states. During the year the CFTC's technical assistance group advised South Pacific countries on monitoring fishing and other activities inside recently-declared 200-mile exclusive economic zones.

The Commonwealth Secretariat's export marketing development division helped with the organization of trade fairs in New York and Toronto to promote the exports of Jamaica, Kenya and Sri Lanka. The aim was to bring buyers and sellers together, and millions of dollars worth of business resulted.

The 24th annual conference of the Commonwealth Parliamentary Association was held in Kingston, Jamaica, in September. Over 200 parliamentarians attended.

From 3 to 12 August 2,000 participants attended the eleventh Commonwealth Games in Edmonton, Alberta (see Pt. XVI, SPORT). The games were boycotted by Nigeria which continued to object to New Zealand's policy on sporting contacts with South Africa.

Three new Commonwealth members were welcomed during the year: the Solomon Islands (7 July); Tuvalu, the former Ellice Islands (1 October); and Dominica (3 November). This brought total membership of the Commonwealth to 39 nations.

Chapter 3

DEFENCE NEGOTIATIONS AND ORGANIZATIONS

THE NORTH ATLANTIC TREATY ORGANIZATION

FOR the North Atlantic Alliance, 1978 was a year of real, though unspectacular, progress. As a result of initiatives taken at the London summit of 1977 (see AR 1977, p. 328), numerous measures to adapt Nato defences to conditions likely to prevail in the 1980s were set in motion. In May the 3 per cent increase in real terms for defence expenditure which had been recommended in 1977 was generally approved. What is more, as

L*

the year progressed, the short-term programme to improve the alliance's anti-armour capability, its war reserve stocks and its reinforcement capacity went smoothly ahead. Even the ambitious Long-Term Development Programme (LTDP) forged ahead. This programme had been broken into ten main areas which lent themselves to cooperative action: readiness, reinforcement, reserve mobilization, maritime posture, air defence, communications, command and control, electronic warfare, logistics, rationalization and theatre nuclear forces.

Not all the members agreed to everything, but after the Nato heads of state gathering which took place in Washington at the end of May there was evidently a considerable degree of agreement about what needed to be done. The clashes of opinion which had divided the alliance in recent years were muted, and a new spirit of determination, cooperation and accord was evident. At the spring summit President Carter reassured the allies about the continuing American commitment to European defence. He emphasized that 'an attack on Europe would have the full consequences of a strike on the United States'.

In December, at the ministerial meeting held in Brussels, Ministers discussed a wide variety of topics. Some, like the need for greater standardization, were hardy perennials in Nato forums; others, like the continuing upheavals in Iran, were more topical. Formal approval was given to the long-awaited new airborne radar defence system (AWACS), designed to reduce the dangers of a surprise attack from the Warsaw Pact. The cost of this system was estimated at $1,900 million.

THE WARSAW TREATY ORGANIZATION

Throughout the year the military power of the Warsaw Pact continued to improve. The International Institute for Strategic Studies, in its survey *The Military Balance 1978-79*, drew attention to the fact that the Soviet Union had widened the gap between Nato and Pact armies by raising the number of its tanks from 43,000 to 50,000. The Institute pointed out that the new Soviet T72 tank was being produced at the rate of over 2,000 per year and that other equally important weapons, including new 'mirved' intermediate range nuclear missiles, were also being introduced into service at an impressive rate. However, in spite of the momentum of Warsaw Pact rearmament, informed commentators in the West continued to argue that the overall balance of power in Europe was sufficiently even to make Soviet aggression unprofitable and unlikely.

In November the seven countries of the Warsaw Pact held a two-day summit in Moscow. At this meeting of the political Consultative Committee, discussions ranged over the SALT talks, the problem of nuclear proliferation, the deadlocked MBFR negotiations, the growing power of China and the neutron bomb. The Pact countries called for a world treaty renouncing the use of force in international relations, and in a 9,000-word declaration issued at the end of the meeting suggested that military exercises in Europe should be limited to between 50,000 and 60,000 men and that confidence-building measures agreed at Helsinki should be extended to the Mediterranean. There was also a suggestion that the nuclear powers should agree immediately on the reduction of their military budgets. The ambitious proposal to disband both Nato and the Warsaw Pact was again aired, and there were some fairly hard words on the human rights issue. Western states were sharply warned of the dangers of using the human rights issue as an excuse to interfere in the internal affairs of socialist states.

Within days of the end of the Moscow meeting, it became clear that the Warsaw countries were not quite so united as the official pronouncements suggested. President Ceauşescu of Romania revealed that he had defied the Soviet Union by refusing to agree either to increased Warsaw Pact defence spending or to the increased integration of Pact forces (see p. 110). This leak from Romania prompted the entire Soviet leadership to reiterate the need to maintain and improve Warsaw Pact defences against what it called 'the arms race launched by Nato and encouraged by China'.

THE CENTRAL TREATY ORGANIZATION

The value of the Central Treaty Organization was questioned on a number of occasions during the year. Pakistan, in particular, expressed dissatisfaction with the alliance. Mr Agha Shahi, the foreign affairs advisor, reflected this disillusionment when he commented: 'People in Pakistan increasingly wonder if CENTO is relevant to their security needs, and feel . . . there could be a new look at non-alignment.' In July Mr Okum, the Turkish Foreign Minister, also suggested that CENTO should be re-evaluated in the context of detente. 'I believe our age is not an age of confrontation but an age of cooperation and detente', he said.

However, suggestions that the alliance had outlived its usefulness were firmly rejected at the twenty-fifth session of CENTO's Ministerial Council, meeting in April. The British Foreign Secretary, Dr David Owen, speaking at the end of the session, reminded his listeners of CENTO's achievements in maintaining stability in parts of central Asia, in limiting the deterioration in US-Turkish relations and in stopping Pakistan from splitting further apart from the West. Dr Owen pointed out that CENTO did not maintain a great bureaucracy and was probably a much under-rated organization. Mr Kamuran Gurun, the new secretary-general of CENTO, confirmed that despite recent statements Pakistan had no intention of leaving the alliance. Among the points covered in the communique issued at the end of the ministerial meeting was the need for a solution to the Middle East problem which recognized the legitimate rights of the Palestinians, and the need to restore the Lebanese Government's authority in Southern Lebanon.

THE HELSINKI REVIEW CONFERENCE

The diplomacy of East–West relations continued to be dominated by the arms control negotiations in Vienna and Geneva, but for the first part of the year the final stages of the Helsinki review conference in Belgrade continued to agitate East–West relationships.

On 17 January the 35-nation conference to review the 1975 Helsinki Declaration on Security and Cooperation in Europe resumed its work after the Christmas adjournment. The acrimony which had characterized the earlier meetings in the autumn of 1977 continued as the participating states tried to draw up a concluding document on which they could all agree.

Western states were particularly concerned about the way in which individual Soviet citizens seemed to be persecuted for trying to make their Government comply with the Helsinki agreement. One of the proposals rejected by the USSR would have insisted on respect for the right of individuals to point out violations of the Helsinki promises. The Russians refused to discuss the drafts by Nato and neutral countries for the concluding document, and the Western states regarded the Soviet draft as unsatisfactory because it glossed over the failure of the communist states to fulfil the Helsinki proposals, particularly on the question of improving human contacts.

Since unanimity was required for all decisions the meetings dragged on until 9 March, three weeks later than the intended closing date. In the end the best that could be achieved by way of a final document was a very short statement to the effect that 'different views were expressed' about the implementation of the agreed Helsinki proposals, and that 'consensus was not reached' on most of the new proposals. However, the members did renew their commitment to meet all the Helsinki promises and it was agreed that a second review conference would begin in Madrid on 11 November 1980.

MUTUAL FORCE REDUCTIONS

The talks on mutual force reductions were resumed in Vienna on 31 January after a six-week recess and some five years after the initial meetings. Progress was slow but in March it was announced that an agreement had been reached on the exchange of information about the two alliances' respective troop strengths in the region. In April the Nato allies modified their ideas and presented a new set of proposals to the conference. The allies accepted the idea of equal percentage cuts once an appropriate parity of forces had been achieved, and they then offered to exchange 29,000 American soldiers and 1,000 US nuclear warheads for 1,700 Russian tanks and five Soviet divisions.

In June further progress was made when the Russians, who had resisted the idea of asymmetrical reductions from the outset of the talks, accepted the idea of a common ceiling for each side. It was suggested that a manpower ceiling of 900,000 men for each side's combined ground and air forces should be adopted. For ground troops alone a figure of 700,000 was thought to be appropriate. The Russians also showed flexibility by dropping their demands for country-by-country ceilings in troop levels in favour of an assurance that no country with forces in Central Europe would be allowed to reinforce above present manpower levels. Unfortunately, this concession did not meet the Nato requirement that each alliance should enjoy complete freedom to decide what combination of national forces should be adopted to meet the overall manpower ceiling.

Another fundamental disagreement between the two sides was over the size of Warsaw Pact ground forces in Europe. The Pact claimed to have 805,000 troops in the central region whereas Nato insisted that 955,000 was a more realistic figure. This discrepancy of 155,000 soldiers—ten divisions—was too much for Nato to swallow, and the fifteenth round of talks ended without agreement. In September discussions were resumed but the year ended without any significant breakthrough.

THE STRATEGIC ARMS LIMITATION TALKS

The SALT talks were resumed in Geneva on 9 January in a mood of qualified optimism. It was hoped that a new SALT treaty lasting until 1985 would be speedily concluded, but even at the end of the year a number of significant sticking-points remained. Throughout the year familiar issues occupied the negotiations. There was disagreement about the Soviet 5 SS-20 missile and the 'Backfire' bomber and there was a great deal of argument about the American cruise missile and its strategic/tactical missions. In an attempt to break the deadlocks Mr Cyrus Vance visited Moscow in April and talked with Mr Gromyko. At the end of the talks a guarded statement announced that the two sides had held a 'useful and detailed discussion', and that 'the positions of the sides on some of the remaining uncoordinated matters drew somewhat closer together'.

But progress was painfully slow and it was evident that the atmosphere of the negotiations was sometimes soured by wider political disagreements between the two countries. Soviet intervention in Africa, the supply of Mig 23 aircraft to Cuba, the harsh treatment of dissidents in the USSR, the American decision to order neutron warhead components—all these issues made themselves felt around the negotiating table in Geneva. In July Mr Gromyko and Mr Vance again met, this time in Geneva, to give a new fillip to the protracted discussions, but again no significant breakthrough was made.

On 22 October a new round of talks opened in Moscow and it was reported that the issues had been reduced to a few, admittedly important, details in a draft of more than sixty pages. The outstanding issues concerned details of restrictions on cruise missiles and the 'Backfire' bomber, and details about the degree of freedom each side would have to modernize existing ICBMs and bombers. In November it seemed that a treaty might be signed by the end of the year, but in the event this proved impossible.

Chapter 4

THE EUROPEAN COMMUNITY

FROM the spring onwards, and especially under the German presidency of the second half of the year, all other EEC business was overshadowed by the proposal for a new European monetary system (EMS), the brain-child of Herr Helmut Schmidt, the German Chancellor, assisted by the intellectual midwifery of President Valéry Giscard d'Estaing of France (see Pt. XVII, Ch. 1). The seeds of the idea, however, had been sown during the autumn of the previous year by Mr Roy Jenkins, the President of the European Commission (see AR 1977, p. 332).

Beside the EMS discussions most other items on the EEC's agenda had a distinctly jejune air and evoked all-too-familiar responses from member governments. However, one hardy annual—the need to curb the budgetary extravagance of the Common Agricultural Policy (CAP)—acquired a new political momentum, in large part as a by-product of the EMS debate. At the end of the year the European Commission indicated its intention of proposing a farm price 'freeze' in 1979-80 in a bid to reduce costly food surpluses.

The European Parliament also caused some surprises (see p. 337), serving notice on member governments that it was likely to be a much less malleable body once its democratic credentials had been enhanced by direct elections. Heads of government agreed in April that the first such elections should be held between 7 and 10 June 1979.

The French and the British both made clear they would tolerate no extension of the powers of a directly elected parliament, and heads of government also agreed, largely at British insistence, that Euro-MPs should not be paid more than national MPs. This meant that British Euro-MPs would get less than a third of the salary of their highest-paid Continental colleagues. On the left wing of the Labour Party a campaign was mounted to put up anti-marketeers for election.

Economic and monetary policy. Herr Schmidt gave his colleagues their first inkling of his plans for a new monetary system at a highly confidential dinner-table discussion during their summit meeting in Copenhagen on 7 and 8 April. General interest was expressed in the idea, and it became apparent that President Giscard had been squared in advance. However,

Mr James Callaghan, the British Prime Minister, who was nettled at the way he felt the Franco-German initiative had been sprung on him, made clear his reservations from the outset. These hardened in May and June, when Mr Denis Healey, the Chancellor of the Exchequer, argued the impracticality of fixed exchange rates when rates of inflation and other indices differed so widely from one member state to another.

There was thus some surprise when Mr Callaghan, evidently under considerable pressure, went along with other EEC leaders in putting his name to an ambitious blueprint for the EMS at the summit meeting in Bremen on 6 and 7 July. Broadly, the Bremen paper envisaged the linking of all EEC currencies within a narrowly defined margin of fluctuation, the creation of a $50,000 million support fund by the pooling of member states' gold and foreign currency holdings, and the introduction of a new reserve asset, the European Currency Unit (ECU).

Mr Callaghan made clear that he would want to see the results of preparatory work on the EMS blueprint before finally committing Britain to the scheme. With the backing of his Italian colleague, Signor Guilio Andreotti, Mr Callaghan also secured agreement that there should be 'concurrent studies' on how the EEC's 'less prosperous' member states could be strengthened financially, and thus better equipped to withstand the rigours of the new monetary system. In this context, Mr Callaghan stressed the 'perverse' influence of the CAP on wealth distribution.

Discussion of the details of the EMS was pursued during the summer and autumn by EEC Finance Ministers, by the Community's economic policy and monetary committees, and by central bank governors. Broadly, the argument was between those, led by the Germans, who wanted a system modelled on the existing 'snake' mechanism, a so-called 'parity grid' linking the Deutschemark with several other strong EEC currencies, and those, led by the British, who wanted a currency's permissible margin of fluctuation to be defined in terms of its divergence from the average value of all EEC currencies, arguing that this would place a less one-sided intervention burden on weaker currencies, like the pound and the lira.

As the December summit in Brussels approached, it became clear that the British were losing this argument, and were also not having notable success in persuading their partners that there was any necessary link between the EMS and reform of the CAP and the budget. It came as no surprise, then, on 5 December, when Mr Callaghan announced that, while not opposing the establishment of the EMS, Britain could not participate fully for the time being. (For full details of the final agreement see DOCUMENTS.) Much less expected was the initial decision of both Italy and Ireland also to opt out of full EMS membership. However, these difficulties, apparently caused by misunderstandings about the amount of financial help promised by the French and the Germans, were resolved two weeks later, leaving Britain once again the odd man out.

But this was not quite the end of the story. In the closing days of the year last-minute objections were raised by the French, who claimed that the phasing-out of monetary compensatory amounts (MCAs), the special subsidies and levies applied to intra-EEC farm trade to offset the effects of currency fluctuations, was part-and-parcel of the establishment of the EMS. This was denied by the Germans, whose farmers would suffer loss of income if MCAs were abolished (while French farmers would gain). This dispute led to the postponement of the originally intended starting-date for the EMS—1 January 1979—and there was no clear indication as to how serious the delay might be.

During the early part of the year the Germans had been under persistent pressure, especially from the British, to reflate their economy and thus play a 'locomotive' role in leading the rest of the EEC out of the prolonged post-oil-crisis recession. This the Germans steadfastly refused to do—apart from a token gesture at the world summit in Bonn in June. Currency stability, Herr Schmidt argued, would provide a sounder basis for economic growth than inflationary pump-priming of national economies, and the EMS initiative was clearly designed to shift the focus of economic debate within the Community decisively towards the German way of thinking.

Whatever the causes, real growth in the EEC remained stubbornly low, amounting (according to provisional estimates) to no more than 2·6 per cent over the year as a whole—a slight improvement on 1977 but still way below the Community's targets. The number of jobless continued to grow, reaching a little over 6 million or 5·7 per cent of the total EEC labour force, and was not expected to decline significantly in 1979. On the brighter side, the EEC's overall balance of payments on current account improved substantially, thanks mainly to an increase in the West German trade surplus and a marked reduction of the Danish and French deficits, while the average inflation rate dropped from 10·5 to 7·5 per cent.

The budget. As a direct consequence of the EMS discussions the size of Britain's net contribution to the EEC budget—that is, the excess of its gross contribution over receipts from such Community instruments as the agricultural, regional and social funds—became the object of a fiercely politicized debate. The controversy was intensified by a report from the economic policy committee in November containing figures which showed that Britain was likely to become the biggest net contributor, ahead of Germany, by 1980. Other statistics in the report, however, showed Britain's budgetary balance in a much more favourable light.

This discrepancy concealed a furious dispute over which member states should be regarded as deriving most benefit from budgetary expenditure on the MCA subsidies—food importers like Britain or food exporting countries like Germany with appreciating currencies. The majority view was that MCAs should be regarded in effect as payments to the importer. In addition, it was argued that, if Britain was still operating its pre-membership system of deficiency payments, it would be paying British farmers £1,100 million out of taxation—much more than the net British contribution to the CAP.

For their part, the British argued that because more than 70 per cent of the Community budget was spent on agriculture, and because they had few farmers and were large net importers of food and other commodities, they got strikingly less return on their budgetary contributions than several much richer member states with large farming populations. In addition, it was argued, the British were penalized by the budget's dependence for its revenue on the agricultural import levies and industrial customs duties collected by member states. The Treasury estimated that the net British contribution in 1978 amounted to £730 million and could rise to more than £890 million by 1980.

The most sympathetic response to the British case came from the European Commission—a fact thought by some to be not unconnected with the presence of a Briton, Mr Christopher Tugendhat, in charge of the budget portfolio. In a 'green paper' on the budget released in November the Commission proposed a new revenue-raising system that would tax countries, like individual citizens, in accordance with the size of their income. Current sources of budgetary revenue were likely to be exhausted by 1982, the Commission pointed out, so some reform of the system would be required anyway.

The final weeks of the year were enlivened by an unprecedented dispute between national governments and the European Parliament, which adopted a £9,890 million budget for 1979, including an appropriation for the regional fund nearly 80 per cent higher than that approved by EEC heads of government and the Council of Budget Ministers. The Parliament contended that decisions taken at summit meetings had no legal status under the Rome Treaty, and that the Budget Ministers had failed to muster the majority needed to overturn the Parliament's proposals within the required time. The legal implications were not entirely clear, but there was thought to be a possibility that national governments might refuse to fund the expenditure approved by the Parliament.

Enlargement and external affairs. The expansion of the Community towards the Mediterranean became an increasingly pressing preoccupation as the year progressed. Entry negotiations with Greece, which had begun two years earlier, were substantially concluded (though not without difficulty) a few days before Christmas, leaving only relatively minor matters still to be settled (see p. 162). An accession treaty was expected to be signed by mid-1979, enabling parliamentary ratification procedures to be completed in time for Greece to become the EEC's 10th member on

1 January 1981. It was agreed that in general Greece should have a transitional period of five years after entry, with seven years for 'sensitive' agricultural products and the free movement of workers.

In October EEC Foreign Ministers opened negotiations on Portugal's entry application, which had been submitted in March of the previous year. The Ministers also decided to open negotiations on Spain's application, dating from July 1977, in the first quarter of 1979, probably in February. At the insistence of the French, however, it was stipulated that the substance of the negotiations could not be tackled until a 'common basis' for them had been agreed with the Spanish. This was widely interpreted as a delaying tactic dictated by domestic pressure on the French Government from the Gaullists and the Communists, who both opposed Spanish and Portuguese entry.

Another major preoccupation of the EEC throughout the year concerned the final stages of the Tokyo round of multilateral trade negotiations, which took place in Geneva under the aegis of the General Agreement on Tariffs and Trade (Gatt). By the end of the year, the EEC had reached broad agreement with the USA and Japan on a range of important non-tariff questions, but developing countries still strongly opposed the EEC's demand that Gatt members should be allowed to impose temporary 'selective' controls against imports damaging domestic industries. The amount by which tariffs should be reduced was also unresolved.

In July EEC Foreign Ministers formally opened negotiations with 54 developing countries in Africa, the Caribbean and the Pacific (ACP) on the terms of the successor agreement to the Lomé Convention, which was signed on 28 February 1975 (see AR 1975, p. 328) and would expire on 1 March 1980. Regarded by the EEC as the showpiece of its relations with the developing world, the Convention was sharply criticized by the ACPs as inadequate in relation to their needs and Europe's capacity. The question of whether in future aid should be withheld from countries which failed to respect basic human rights—a case strongly argued by Dr David Owen, the British Foreign Secretary—also emerged as a highly contentious issue.

In February the EEC negotiated a five-year trade agreement with China, the first such agreement between the EEC and any communist country apart from Yugoslavia. The large trading surplus of China's neighbour Japan continued to cause concern to EEC governments, which remained dissatisfied with Japanese efforts to reduce it, and negotiations with Comecon made little if any progress, mainly because of the EEC's refusal to recognize the Soviet-led body's competence to sign trade agreements on behalf of its member states (see Ch. 5 below).

Agriculture and fisheries. Agricultural Ministers finally approved the annual farm review on 12 May, a month and a half behind schedule, with an agreement to hold the increase in the common support prices paid to the EEC's 8½ million farmers to no more than 2·1 per cent, the lowest rise in some years. (However, the average rise when expressed in national currencies was about 8 per cent, because of the operation of the so-called 'green' exchange rates). Mr John Silkin, the British Minister, had held out for a price freeze, but yielded after winning an assurance that Britain's milk marketing boards would be allowed to continue in their traditional form (see p. 34). Mr Silkin claimed that the boards, whose monopoly powers had been challenged as illegal by some member states, were essential for the maintenance of the daily doorstep delivery of fresh milk in Britain.

The Agricultural Ministers also approved a substantial package of aids to hitherto neglected Mediterranean farmers, partly to assuage their fears about future Spanish competition. This involved the spending over the next five years of some £470 million on irrigation in Italy's Mezzogiorno, the improvement or conversion of vineyards in southern France, the modernization of processing and marketing techniques, and the provision of roads, electricity supplies and drinking water. A further £550 million was to be spent over the same period on market aids to Italian and French olive oil, wine, fruit and vegetable producers.

During the year the European Commission produced plans for reducing the output and improving the quality of the EEC's vineyards, for reform of the surplus-ridden dairy sector, which was estimated to be consuming more than 40 per cent of all price support expenditure, and for establishing a common market for trade in lamb and mutton. This last gave rise to fears among New Zealand sheep farmers that prices in Britain, by far their largest export market, would be pushed up, thereby reducing lamb consumption.

Fisheries Ministers argued fruitlessly throughout the year about the terms of a new common fisheries policy to take account of the world-wide move to 200-mile fishing limits. At a meeting in Berlin at the end of January broad agreement was reached by eight member states but rejected by Mr Silkin, who had boycotted the meeting because of an unrelated dispute over the 'green pound' (see p. 34). Little progress was made during the spring and early summer, but a sudden flurry of optimism was provoked by the declaration of Mr Callaghan and Herr Schmidt at their summit in Bonn on 18 and 19 October that they were determined to end the fish dispute by the end of the year.

These hopes were dashed when Mr Silkin and his EEC colleagues met in Brussels in late November. Mr Silkin restated familiar British demands for the phasing-out of the 'historic rights' claimed by other member states within 12 miles of the British coast, and for preferential access for British fishermen to waters lying between 12 and 50-80 miles from the coast. These claims were angrily rejected by other member states as discriminatory and contrary to the principles of the Treaty of Rome. A month earlier the

European Commission had initiated legal proceedings against Britain for taking allegedly discriminatory fish conservation measures.

Industry and the internal market. Despite the recession and growing competition from the developing world in such sectors as textiles, steel and shipbuilding, Germany and the Benelux countries continued for the most part to champion free trade (though not of course in agriculture) and to oppose state support of uncompetitive industry. The British and the French were the most open advocates of the right of national governments to use state subsidies to save jobs and achieve social and regional ends, while the European Commission argued in favour of interventionism, but only as a part of a centrally planned and coordinated restructuring of European industry. After much internal agonizing the Commission decided against proposing a modification of the Rome Treaty that would have permitted industries in crisis to form temporary protective cartels. It also refused to approve a cartel formed by the EEC's 11 biggest synthetics fibres producers.

The 'anti-crisis' plan for the EEC's ailing steel industry, the brain-child of Vicomte Davignon, the Commissioner for industrial affairs, went into operation on 1 January 1978. This involved the setting of internal guideline prices for a wide range of laminated steel products, and the fixing of mandatory minimum prices for certain products. Foreign suppliers were asked to accept 'voluntary' price and volume limits on their exports to the Community, and those which failed to do so were liable to automatic anti-dumping duties. EEC Trade Ministers agreed to pursue the Davignon scheme in 1979 despite inconclusive evidence of its efficacy. The Commission failed, however, to persuade member states to observe a new code limiting national aids to the steel industry.

In April the Commission took Britain to the European Court of Justice for failing to install tachographs in lorries above a certain size. Of various anti-trust rulings by the Court, the decision against United Brands, the world's biggest grower and supplier of bananas, attracted the most attention; the American multinational was convicted of 'abuse of a dominant market position', even though its share of the markets in question—about 40 per cent—was much less than the norm in previous convictions of the same type.

A common energy policy proved as elusive as ever, and many in the Community were inclined to see the determined opposition of Mr Tony Benn, the British Energy Secretary, to any surrender, however formal, of national control over Britain's energy resources as the chief obstacle to progress. A Commission proposal for subsidizing the burning of EEC-produced coal, in order to make it competitive with imported varieties, offered substantial benefits to Britain, but the scheme was blocked by other member states, partly because of Mr Benn's refusal to endorse a plan for rationalizing over-capacity in the oil refining industry, which he saw as a device for bailing out countries that had over-invested in this sector.

Britain was also at odds with most of its EEC partners, but most of all with France (supported by the Commission), in its reluctance to commit the Community to large-scale development of plutonium-fuelled fast-breeder reactors. In July, in addition, Britain was prevented by the Commission from signing a bilateral agreement for the import of Australian uranium. The Commission argued that the agreement would impose 'safeguard' conditions on British use of the Australian supplies that would violate Community rules on the free flow of materials among its members.

In the closing weeks of the year EEC Environment Ministers struck a more harmonious note by adopting a long-awaited directive on bird protection, which had been held up mainly by France's insistence that two small songbirds, the skylark and the ortolan bunting, should be retained in the list of species allowed to be shot as game. It was eventually agreed that French and Italian huntsmen could shoot the skylark but that the ortolan bunting should be protected.

Chapter 5

COUNCIL OF EUROPE—WESTERN EUROPEAN UNION—NORTH ATLANTIC ASSEMBLY—EUROPEAN FREE TRADE ASSOCIATION—ORGANIZATION FOR ECONOMIC COOPERATION AND DEVELOPMENT—NORDIC COUNCIL—COMECON

COUNCIL OF EUROPE

THE Council of Europe welcomed Liechtenstein as the 21st member of the organization on 23 November 1978, when its head of government presented his country's instrument of accession and signed the European Convention on Human Rights. With 21 member states, a British Minister described the Council of Europe as 'the authentic voice of Europe'.

Another year of successful activities saw the signature of the hundredth European Convention. It celebrated the 25th anniversary of the coming into force of the European Convention on Human Rights; the European Court of Human Rights gave its first judgment in an inter-state case (Ireland *v.* the UK) and was now meeting quite frequently to hear and give rulings in other cases.

The extension of the European Youth Centre should enable the activities to be doubled and offer enormous scope for improved educational work. (A new centre had been created in Venice for training craftsmen in the conservation of the architectural heritage.) In a new series of prizes for museums, the European Museum of the Year award was presented to the Ironbridge Gorge Museum, United Kingdom; the Council of Europe museum prize was awarded to the Bryggens Museum, Bergen, Norway.

The Resettlement Fund now embraced seventeen of the Council's member states and had made loans totalling almost $500 million.

Some notable scientific conferences took place on the Council's initiative, or under its auspices, and led to the strengthening of cooperation within the European scientific community and to a better assessment of the social, economic, cultural and political impact of scientific and technological research through the organization of public European parliamentary hearings. The Council considered holding a high-level conference on migration and a tripartite (governments, employers, trade unions) meeting on unemployment. These examples illustrate the variety of Council of Europe activities.

In approving a declaration on human rights at their meeting on 27 April, and a declaration on terrorism on 23 November, the Foreign Ministers of the member states drew attention to two major aspects of contemporary political life. With regard to the organization's commitment to respect for human rights and fundamental freedoms, the Committee of Ministers decided to give priority to the Council's work in exploring the possibility of extending the lists of rights of the individual, notably in the social, economic and cultural fields, which could be protected by European Conventions or other appropriate means. With regard to the prevention and suppression of acts of terrorism, the Committee emphasized the importance of the work being undertaken by the Council with the aim of intensifying European cooperation in the fight against terrorism. The danger of overlapping in European cooperation was raised by the agreement in principle on a text concerning terrorism between the Ministers of Justice of the nine members of the EEC within the framework of political cooperation. It was believed, however, that European cooperation in the fight against crime and, therefore, also against terrorism would be best promoted by speeding up the ratification of the Council of Europe conventions and their protocols.

A major part of the Committee of Ministers' activities was also devoted to considering the follow-up to be given to the Helsinki agreements and the need to keep the CSCE process intact and consolidate it as a vital factor in East–West relations. In this context, it was important to develop bilateral and multilateral preparations among all CSCE member states; the Council of Europe continued to contribute to coordination among governments of member states.

The Council's Parliamentary Assembly also persisted in its attempt to offer a parliamentary platform for discussion of the implementation of the Final Act of the CSCE. A major debate was held in April on the results of the Belgrade follow-up conference, with contributions from various Assembly committees and with the participation of parliamentary observers from Finland and Canada. The Assembly also devoted a considerable part of its work to the protection of human rights. A fundamental discussion on the state of human rights in the world opened the debate in January. More specific debates on widening the scope of the European Convention on Human Rights and on the revision of the European Social Charter followed, both expressing the conviction that the development of human rights must take greater account of the economic, social and cultural aspects. Debates on the plight of political prisoners in Chile, the situation in Czechoslovakia ten years after the Soviet invasion and the condition of the Jewish community in the Soviet Union covered some of the present human rights violations throughout the world.

Among the technical subjects dealt with by the Assembly were the crucial issue of energy and the environment, and recommendations on the pollution of coastal zones by hydrocarbons. Representatives of European regions emphasized the need to develop a 'North–South dialogue' within the Council of Europe itself which should find concrete expression in a summit meeting of heads of governments of the 21 member states.

WESTERN EUROPEAN UNION

At the June session of the Assembly of WEU Herr Kai-Uwe von Hassel of West Germany, former President of the Bundestag and Minister of Defence, was re-elected President. In his opening speech, Herr von Hassel referred to the political and military threats overhanging Europe, and stressed that WEU, as the sole European body charged with cooperation and mutual assistance in defence matters, must not be weakened; the modified Brussels Treaty, he said, must remain a basis for the Europe of tomorrow. The organization's key importance in European defence was likewise emphasized by other speakers at both the June and November sessions, including Mr Mulley, the UK Secretary of State for Defence, and M Bernard-Reymond, Minister of State for Foreign Affairs of France. Resolutions on defence, disarmament and strategic arms limitations were carried against the votes of only a few Communist members, though a French Communist successfully moved amendments to a text on strategic arms, including one adding to the recommended programme of arms control 'the creation of demilitarized zones and zones free of military bases in various parts of the world'.

The Assembly, in June, gave special attention to security in the Mediterranean, where the Greco-Turkish dispute aroused its anxiety: the resolution, generally recommending the strengthening of Nato in the area, called on the US 'to eliminate its discrimination against Turkey'. Presenting a committee report on China and European security, the British rapporteur disclosed that, as a result of a leak, the Soviet Government had approached WEU member governments with the object of having it withdrawn. He hoped that the Assembly would unanimously oppose the pressure. Eventually, the resolution, 'considering that total resistance to extreme aggression from any source is a fundamental element in Chinese political thinking as it is in Western Europe', 'reciprocating the Chinese Government's continuing efforts to develop good relations with Europe', and consequently recommending the Council to encourage member governments to develop bilateral trade relations with China and favourably consider China's request for increased industrial technology, but deliberately omitting reference to the supply of arms, was passed by 44 votes to 8 with two abstentions.

Besides its work on security, disarmament and Europe's external relations, including those with the USA and the Third World, especially Africa, the Assembly at its two sessions made important recommendations to the Council, and through the latter to member governments, on international terrorism, application satellites, technological and aerospace development and weather forecasting.

NORTH ATLANTIC ASSEMBLY

The annual conference of the North Atlantic Assembly, held in Lisbon in November 1978, was attended by delegates from all the Parliaments of the countries of the alliance.

The purpose of these meetings is to provide a forum in which parliamentarians from both sides of the Atlantic can discuss the achievements and problems of the alliance. Because of a new procedure suggested by the President, Sir Geoffrey de Freitas (UK), there was less reading of resolutions and reports and more debate in Lisbon than at previous conferences. Not only did this debate proceed between Europeans and Americans but also among the nine US Senators, including Senators Jackson and Javits, who differed strongly on President Carter's defence policy.

The speakers from outside the Assembly were the President of the Assembly of the Portugese Republic, Dr Luns, Chairman of the North Atlantic Council, and General Haig, Supreme Allied Commander. Both Dr Luns and General Haig answered questions for over half an hour and their lively interventions helped to stimulate the debates which followed.

During the year there were visits by members of the Assembly to military installations on both sides of the Atlantic and committee meetings on such matters as energy and the standardization of weapons. Dr Luns assured the Assembly of the importance which the Governments attached to the reports of these committees.

Sir Geoffrey de Freitas, who was one of the three founders of the Assembly in 1955, retired from the Presidency and Mr Paul Thyness (Norway) was elected in his place. The Vice-Presidents come from West Germany, the USA and the UK, and the Treasurer from Canada.

EUROPEAN FREE TRADE ASSOCIATION

The signature of a multilateral trade agreement between the seven Efta members and Spain was among the most important developments in the Association in 1978. The pact provided that, upon its ratification, Efta countries would cut their tariffs on almost all Spanish industrial products by 60 per cent, and Spain would cut its tariffs on imports from Efta countries by 25 per cent on some products and 60 per cent on others. These percentages accorded with those already applied between Spain and the European Community, and it was further agreed that Efta would follow the Community in any future measure of liberalization of trade with Spain.

The agreement thus followed the pattern framed in 1977 (see AR 1977, p. 343) of establishing an area of free trade in manufactured goods comprising both Efta and the Community. Cooperation between the two institutions developed further during the year.

Efta participated in setting up a joint committee to consider the expansion of economic relations with Yugoslavia, which already enjoyed free-trade or low-tariff terms for industrial exports to Efta countries under the UNCTAD generalized system of preferences for developing countries.

Through its Economic Committee, representing finance ministries and central banks, and its Consultative Committee representing not governments but different sectors of economic life, as well as its Council, Efta gave increasing attention during 1978 to general, longer-term economic problems—industrial recession and lack of growth, inflation and exchange instability—common to its members, besides continuing to work against protectionism and for the reduction of non-tariff barriers to trade both within and beyond its own membership.

ORGANIZATION FOR ECONOMIC COOPERATION AND DEVELOPMENT

The Ministers of Agriculture of the OECD countries met on 9 and 10 February and carried out a broad review of the outlook for agricultural policies and markets, including relations with developing countries in the field of food and agriculture.

Senior officials from governments, national agencies and regulatory bodies were among those who attended a ceremony at the beginning of February to mark the 20th anniversary of the OECD Nuclear Energy Agency. The implications of the projected growth of nuclear power as a form of energy over the next 15 years were examined, as well as the shape of international cooperation in the years ahead.

The Economic Policy Committee, under its newly-elected chairman, Mr Charles Schultze, chairman of the Council of Economic Advisers to the President of the United States, met in Paris on 27 and 28 February. The Committee agreed that the time had come to adopt a more widely based and concerted approach in implementation of the medium-term strategy of non-inflationary economic growth. Mr Schultze stressed that, together with the enactment of effective energy plans, particularly in the US, the new policy stance would help to stabilize and strengthen foreign exchange markets and assist in the reduction of both inflation and unemployment.

Foreign and Finance Ministers attended the meeting of the OECD Council at ministerial level on 14-15 June. The major result of this meeting was agreement on a broad programme of internationally concerted action aimed at stepping up economic growth, reducing unemployment, assuring price stability and improving the present balance of payments situation. Respective responsibilities of individual member countries in achieving these objectives were agreed upon by Ministers. Reaffirming their commitment to an open-market-oriented economic system as an essential part of this programme, Ministers renewed the OECD Declaration of 30 May 1974, widely known as the Trade Pledge, in an up-dated version adapted to the present economic environment.

At a conference in Washington in July, experts from OECD member countries sought to explore the relationships between collective bargaining on the one hand and national economic, employment and related social policies on the other, in the perspective of the need for sustained non-inflationary growth.

The OECD Education Committee met for the first time at ministerial level in Paris on 19 and 20 October. Two major issues were discussed: how to raise the overall quality of education and to continue to widen access to educational opportunities against a background of economic uncertainty and structural change; and how to reinforce the role of education in preparing the young for working life and facilitating their entry into employment.

The OECD Council on 26 October set up a Steel Committee, designed to enable governments to examine together, in a general economic context, the critical problems—both long-term and short-term—facing the industry, and to develop common approaches in dealing with them. The Committee would be initially composed of 20 OECD member countries, plus the Commission of the European Communities. The Council decision also provided for possible invitations to non-OECD countries with substantial steel interests to participate in the Committee.

The OECD Development Assistance Committee held its annual high-level meeting on 14-15 November. Ministers and heads of aid agencies reviewed their development cooperation policies and discussed future trends in the light of an emerging new international development strategy. The design of a new strategy was seen as important in setting the broad framework for international cooperation in support of the developing countries over the next decade and for the mobilization of public and national support.

The Club du Sahel, an informal association of aid donors, which included members of OECD's Development Assistance Committee and the eight countries in the drought-prone West African Sahel region, held its third ministerial meeting in November in Amsterdam. A communique indicated that donors had already firmly committed financing for 30 per cent of the development projects in the First Generation Programme (1978-82) of the Sahel Long-Term Development Strategy.

A symposium on development cooperation was organized by the OECD and the Parliamentary Assembly of the Council of Europe on 6 and 7 December, bringing together some 80 parliamentarians from their member states. The main aim was to promote a wide exchange of views among parliamentarians and between them and the OECD secretariat in order to further public and parliamentary understanding and support for development cooperation policies.

To mark its fifteen years of activity the Development Centre of the OECD held a seminar on 'Interdependence and Development' on 12 and 13 December; the seminar focused on two main sub-themes in relations between developed countries and the Third World: 'mutual requirements' and 'prerequisites for a fruitful dialogue'.

NORDIC COUNCIL

At the Nordic Council's annual session, held in Oslo on 18-22 February, 15 recommendations were approved by members for action by the Ministerial Council or the respective national Governments. The three which looked beyond their own frontiers called for a European convention for the protection of the environment, an ILO convention on hours of labour, and a Nordic project for providing the developing countries with fishery techniques and appropriate products. Approval was also given to a 56-paragraph document in which the various committees of the Council expressed their views on the programme presented by the Ministerial Council; sections on policies for the environment, sex equality and tourism were combined with a more ambitious general survey, entitled 'The people and resources of the North'. The tourism programme aimed to improve cooperation on tourist facilities; that for the environment revised and extended the Nordic Convention on the Environment which came into force in 1976. On promoting equality between the sexes the Council of Ministers proposed a coordination of national measures, including the more even distribution of appointments to public bodies.

Speakers in the general debate seemed to share the view expressed by an Icelander, who called the survey 'superficial and verbose'. It had indeed said very little about the parlous state of the national economies, inhibiting the dynamic growth which, it was maintained, was essential for the success of any form of international cooperation. According to the Danish Prime Minister, Anker Jørgensen, only changed attitudes on the part of both employers and unions offered a solution. Dynamism in the internal activities of the Council had been easy during the long period of widespread prosperity, but Mr Olof Palme of Sweden posed the awkward question, 'Might Nordic cooperation be one of the victims of the crisis'? Another Social Democrat of long experience, the Norwegian Guttorm Hansen, argued that the Nordic economy was so unified that direct and indirect protectionist trends in the separate states risked cutting off the branch on which they were all seated. Closer cooperation on currency questions, energy and raw materials was called for. The Council of Ministers decided to order a study of the economic situation in the region and seek means of strengthening the coordination of national economic policies.

The other main subject of debate was the proposed Nordic television satellite, which might promote both linguistic and cultural understanding among all five nations. The cost would be very high, special provision would be needed for the many Finns who did not (and would not) learn Swedish, and there was the risk that business interests would exert undue influence. The matter was referred to the Ministerial Council, which in turn set up four sub-committees, charged to prepare a basic document by 15 June 1979, so that a decision could be taken early in the following year.

At their half-yearly meetings in March and September, the five Nordic Foreign Ministers agreed on a four-point programme against apartheid, imposed a visa requirement upon South Africans, and expressed their approval for a voluntary sports boycott of the Republic. They also gave their support to Norway's successful candidature for a seat on the UN Security Council.

COMECON

The political relations of its members with China dominated Comecon's year. In Europe the visit of Chairman Hua Kuo-feng to Romania strengthened Bucharest's hand in its call for more favourable terms in Comecon collaboration, while in the Far East Vietnam was made a member a few days before China terminated its aid in a welter of recrimination. The notable deterioration in Sino-Albanian relations the previous year (see AR 1977, pp. 120-2) culminated in an open break: after economic assistance from China had been stopped, the Albanian press moderated its tone towards the USSR in a manner which could indicate readiness to reactivate Comecon membership. Finally, the tenure of an Executive Committee meeting in Ulan-Bator (the 87th, 27 September to 1 October), in contrast to its almost invariable convocation in Moscow, must also have been intended as a supportive gesture towards the other member with a long frontier with China.

The agenda of the 32nd session of the Council (Bucharest, 27-29 June) had the admission of Vietnam as its first substantive item in order that its representative Le Thang Nguy (a member of his Party's Politburo and a Deputy Premier) could participate throughout the session. Only a few days before (on 17 June) the Vietnamese Ministry of Foreign Affairs had made public the Chinese Note of 12 May which announced the unilateral termination of aid to Vietnam (see p. 294), and the replacement of that assistance was an unspoken theme of Nguy's speech. Collaboration between each Comecon member and Vietnam had become an accomplished fact over the preceding two years, he said, and he thanked the Executive Committee's 'working party on Vietnam' (an *ad hoc* body not hitherto publicly mentioned) for the care with which it had resolved the first stages in solving the still numerous problems of collaboration. Vietnam sought both economic and technological cooperation and had 'rich natural resources and vast reserves of manpower . . . to deepen participation in the international socialist division of labour'. Help from the USSR and other socialist states would result in rapid economic growth and hence in balanced trade with them. The Vietnamese treaty of friendship with the USSR of 3 November (see DOCUMENTS) exhibited a positive bilateral response in agreeing on plan coordination and joint measures for economic development.

Albania, too, lost Chinese aid at that time: the Peking Note was dated 7 July (see p. 117) and claimed, *inter alia* that China had spent over 100 million yuan renminbi (approximately $50 million) on research and development to exploit Albanian nickel–iron ores. When on 24 November one of those projects was put into commission, the official address (by the chairman of the Albanian planning commission) criticized Chinese and Khrushchev's 'revisionism' (*Zëri i popullit*, 25 November). The absence of criticism of the USSR could suggest that Albania was toying with renewal of its Comecon membership (in suspense since 1962).

The visit of the Chairman of the Chinese Communist Party to Belgrade in August may have been relevant to Albanian reconsideration of its position vis-à-vis Comecon, but his preceding acclaim in Bucharest was a certain factor in the Romanian-Soviet tension, which permeated the Comecon session there. Of the five 'long-range special purpose programmes' launched at the 1976 session and confirmed in 1977 (see AR 1976, p. 350, and 1977, p. 349), only three were ratified (in energy and raw materials; engineering; and food and agriculture); those on transport and communications and on consumers' goods were apparently not mentioned. The formal approval, moreover, remained to be carried into effect, and the Chairman of the Soviet Council of Ministers, Alexei Kosygin, was impelled to warn the delegates to the session that they were 'not declarations, but plan documents, plans for our joint action' and to ask them 'to ascertain the interest and degree of participation of countries in the implementation of the corresponding measures by the end of 1979' (*Ekonomicheskoe sotrudnichestvo stran-chlenov SEV*, No. 4, 1978). It was to accelerate such decisions that the Bucharest agenda—according to unofficial reports—contained a proposal to apply majority voting on certain issues. Two decades of Romanian unwillingness to accept pan-Comecon decision-making persisted, and the proposal, if it was in fact tabled, seemed to have been dropped.

Romania may also have expressed reservations about Comecon's aid programme. The Bucharest session resolved 'to extend support and assistance to accelerate the development and raise the efficiency of the economies of Cuba and Mongolia' and the meeting of the Executive Committee in Ulan-Bator agreed 'to extend aid to Vietnam in the restoration of its economy and in building the material and technical bases of socialism'. Soon afterwards Romania opposed Soviet action to concert another burden, defence spending. During July and August Leonid Brezhnev had conversations in the Crimea with his fellow Party leaders from Comecon states (except Cuba and Vietnam whose military expenditure was already high), stressing the Nato decision in Washington on a further arms build-up on a large scale and the approval by the US Congress of 'the biggest military budget of all time' (CPSU Politburo commentary on the meetings, 26 August). The summit conference of the Warsaw Treaty organization was squarely told (Moscow, 22-23 November) that Romania would not increase its military budget, and immediately afterwards Romania made a deliberate gesture of reducing its 1979 appropriation (see p. 110).

Romania was also the 'odd man out' in Comecon's negotiations with the European Communities, with which it alone had a tariff agreement. How each side was to sign the long-discussed treaty was finally resolved at a meeting (Brussels, 22-25 November) between the EEC External Affairs Commissioner, Wilhelm Haferkamp, and Comecon's Secretary, Nikolai Faddeev: Comecon itself as well as each of its members would sign a treaty which mentioned, but made no provisions with respect to, trade. As agreed in September 1977 (see AR 1977, pp. 335 and 348), the two principals met in Moscow on 29-30 May: Haferkamp made the crucial gesture of accepting that the proposed treaty could mention trade, and experts from both organizations settled on procedures in Brussels on 25-28 July.

The 84th Executive Committee (Moscow, 14-16 February) approved closer relations with the International Investment Bank (IIB) in coordinating member countries' plans for 1981-85: a long-term credit plan would be jointly elaborated by Comecon and IIB with their members.

The International Bank for Economic Cooperation (which Vietnam had joined in May 1977) held two Council sessions in Moscow (11 April and 28 September): the first approved the 1977 accounts, which exhibited a record increment in credits to members (6,904 million transferable roubles, 63 per cent above the 4,224 million of 1976) and a rise of 13 per cent in operations in convertible currency. For the first time the Council distributed a dividend to its members: 6·7 million TR were handed out and the balance (22·2 million TR) of the 1977 profit was put to reserve. The much greater profit may perhaps be associated with the change of the 1963 Statutes (last amended in 1970) that was decided upon on 23 November 1977 which permitted the Bank to lend direct to the international production organizations of Comecon members. The 1977 accounts of IIB (which Vietnam had also joined), approved at a Council session on 12-13 April, also showed a substantial increase (of 22 per cent on 1976) in credit issue (826 million TR); the session made its first credit to a non-member country, for the expansion of a tool-factory at Nova Gradska, Yugoslavia. The project to which it had accorded most finance, the Soyuz gas pipeline from the Orenburg deposits across the western frontier of the USSR, was completed at the end of the year, and each of the European members would begin to receive 15,000 million cubic meters annually from 1979. The Bank Council *in corpore* had visited the sections being built by GDR and Polish teams (each member was providing equipment and labour for parts of the length within the USSR) in October 1977. As at 1 January 1978 nearly 80 per cent of IIB credits were for energy projects.

Chapter 6

AFRICAN CONFERENCES AND INSTITUTIONS—SOUTH-EAST ASIAN
ORGANIZATIONS—CARIBBEAN ORGANIZATIONS

AFRICAN CONFERENCES AND INSTITUTIONS

INTERNATIONAL preoccupations with Africa, which in 1978 centred not only on the mounting tension in Southern Africa, but also on the whole question of foreign intervention, were inevitably reflected in the activities of the Organization of African Unity (OAU). The summit of heads of state and government, held in Khartoum from 18 to 21 July, was attended by 30 Presidents and 4 Prime Ministers, from a total membership of 49, the largest-ever presidential participation in an OAU summit. This reflected the importance attached by members to the organization, as the best guarantee against super-power and other foreign involvement in African questions.

President Nimeiry of Sudan, opening the summit, said that he feared that Africa would take 'the same path that Asia has taken in 20 years of war and destruction. The flight of refugees and the flow of armies across the continent involves foreign faces new and old to Africa. Each invitation for intervention is followed by another for counter-intervention until this armed foreign presence is about to outstrip our capacity to defeat it.' Other speakers criticized the Western interventions in Zaïre and elsewhere, and Soviet–Cuban operations in Angola and Ethiopia. The head of state of Nigeria said 'To the Soviets I should like to say that, having been invited to Africa in order to assist the liberation struggle and the consolidation of national independence, they should not overstay their welcome.'

The resolution that was finally produced on foreign interventions was a compromise emerging from the earlier meeting of Foreign Ministers, which had involved acrimonious exchanges attacking either French or Cuban interventions. The resolution said:

(1) that the responsibility for defending the security and stability of Africa would always fall incontestably on Africans alone;
(2) that every state had the right to seek assistance from any other state when its security and independence were threatened;
(3) that the formation of a pan-African force must be viewed in the light of threats to Africa from certain countries and the cause of liberating Africa from colonial rule;
(4) that a committee of defence must be coordinated and asked to study the pan-African defence force in its theoretical and scientific aspects;
(5) that the committee of mediation must be coordinated to enable it 'to contain and solve all our conflicts and problems in a peaceful manner and in an African spirit';
(6) that the political committee study the Congolese proposal—which had referred to the 'reconfirmation of the expansionist policies of the Western countries in Africa', thereby reflecting a strong view by progressive countries that Soviet-Cuban activities could not be put on the same footing as Western, especially French, interventions.

Other subjects of resolutions included different aspects of the Southern Africa situation, including Namibia and South Africa's nuclear armament, Palestine and the non-aligned movement. A special resolution on the Western Sahara, abandoning the idea first put up two years before for a special summit on this issue (which it had proved diplomatically impossible to hold), set up a 'committee of wise men' comprising at least five heads of state to find a solution 'compatible with the principle of self-determination'. This committee ran into similar diplomatic headaches and had been unable to meet before the end of the year. One of the complicating factors was the recognition of the Sahraoui Republic by Tanzania, increasing to 11 the number of OAU countries to have recognized the Sahraouis.

Another controversial issue was the two resolutions put forward by the ministerial meeting on French territories in the Indian Ocean, the overseas department of Réunion and the island of Mayotte. On Réunion there was a call for self-determination and independence as 'part of Africa', and on Mayotte a condemnation of the two 1976 referenda and of the 'illegitimate' occupation by France of that Comoran island. Several states, mainly French-speakers, reserved their positions on these two resolutions, which in the end were not adopted by the summit, as was a proposed resolution on independence for the Canary Islands.

The conference also elected a new secretary-general to hold office for a four-year term. He was Edem Kodjo, former Foreign Minister of Togo, who was elected after eight ballots by 39 votes to 9. His predecessor, William Eteki Mboumoua, withdrew his candidature because soundings indicated that he had no chance of success in view of the solid support for Kodjo from the 15 other countries of ECOWAS (the Economic Community of West African States). Five new regional assistant secretaries-general were also elected.

In February a budget session of the Council of Ministers in Tripoli approved the OAU budget for 1978-79 at $11,964,391, an increase of more than six million dollars over its budget of four years ago.

The main other OAU meetings of the year were two sessions of the Liberation Committee in June and December in Dar es Salaam, the latter composed of specialized commissions concerned with Rhodesia/Zimbabwe.

Part of the controversy over foreign intervention arose from the fifth France–Africa summit, which was held in Paris in May, shortly after the Franco-Belgian intervention in Zaïre; this had been followed by the establishment of an African intervention force to replace the French and the Belgians, consisting of 1,500 Moroccans, 500 Senegalese, 300 Centrafricans, and token forces from Togo, Ivory Coast, Gabon and Egypt (see p. 234). Contacts for the establishment of the force took place during the Franco-African summit, and the meeting certainly officially discussed security questions, but there was no agreement on the force, since several of the states attending the Paris meeting refused to take part in it and criticized the intervention. Participants, mainly heads of state, were from French-speaking Africa (minus Cameroon and Madagascar) plus Mauritius and Seychelles, with observers from Guinea-Bissau and São Tome.

Mutual security was also the subject of a formal non-aggression declaration at the summit of ECOWAS held in Lagos in April. Among other decisions taken was the setting of 28 May 1979 as the effective date for a freeze in customs tariffs on goods originating in member states, in accordance with the ECOWAS Treaty, to take effect in all member states. This was regarded as the first positive step towards abolition of customs duties within ECOWAS on internally-originating goods. A multilateral agreement on the free movement of persons was also to be approved by the heads of state at their 1979 meeting. The appointment of Dr Ouattara as executive secretary of the Community was ratified, but not that of

M

Romeo Horton as head of the ECOWAS Fund, about whom there had been some controversy.

Within ECOWAS other groupings were active, such as the Senegal, Niger and Gambia River organizations and the Council of the Entente. In East Africa, while the pieces of the now defunct East African Community were still being picked up, more substance was being acquired by the Great Lakes Community of Zaïre, Rwanda and Burundi.

Among the OAU resolutions was one providing guidelines for the renegotiation of the Lomé Convention between 54 states of Africa, the Caribbean and Pacific and the European Community. It was generally assumed that the convention would be renewed before its expiry in 1980, but there was criticism of its implementation, and doubts as to whether the increase in the funds made available by the EEC would be sufficient, or would even keep pace with inflation. President Nimeiry of Sudan, on a visit to Brussels, put forward Khartoum as an alternative to Lomé for signature of the new convention.

SOUTH-EAST ASIAN ORGANIZATIONS

The Association of South-East Asian Nations (Asean) consolidated its position as the most active grouping in the region. The USSR and Vietnam were still openly hostile in February, but by June had adopted a more ingratiating approach, while concentrating on efforts to bring the Cambodian regime to heel or to substitute more compliant men. China made no secret of its view that this attempt to control all Indo-China from Hanoi was a first step in a scheme to extend a Soviet-backed Vietnamese hegemony more widely in South-East Asia, with the USSR filling the vacuum left by American withdrawal. China saw Asean as an obstacle to this design and therefore encouraged it to become more cohesive. The USSR and Vietnam tried to stimulate Asean concern over Peking's policy towards the Overseas Chinese and the Chinese tried to allay these fears.

There was in consequence an improvement in formal relations between the Asean countries and Vietnam and its Laotian satellite and great diplomatic activity both by Vietnam and the USSR and by China and the Chinese-supported regime in Cambodia. Vietnamese Ministers made tours of South-East Asia, culminating in September and October in visits by the Prime Minister, Pham Van Dong, to all five Asean states, hastily arranged to precede the arrival in November of the Chinese senior Vice-Premier, Teng Hsiao-p'ing, in Thailand, Malaysia and Singapore. A Soviet deputy Foreign Minister visited all five capitals during March and October, while a Cambodian Vice-Premier was in Thailand in July and the Philippines and Indonesia in October.

These visits demonstrated the extent to which the Asean countries were coordinating their foreign policies. Dong was everywhere received politely, but no enthusiasm was shown for his proposals for agreements. His under-takings 'to refrain from using force . . . from interfering in . . . other's internal affairs, and from carrying out subversive activities, directly or indirectly' were given publicity, but such trust as may have been reposed in them was dissipated by the defence treaty with the USSR of 3 November (see DOCUMENTS) and the Vietnamese establishment of a Front for National Salvation clearly designed to replace the existing Cambodian regime. Teng's approval of Asean carried greater conviction, although his inability to dis-own support for local communist movements was cited by Indonesia as a reason for postponing resumption of diplomatic relations.

Cooperation within Asean proceeded more slowly in the economic field. Inter-Asean tariff preferences on 71 items came into force on 1 January; a further 755 were to be added in September and 500 in March 1979, but these were mostly of limited significance. No use was made of the Asean swap arrangement, and, although it was decided in September to double the sums available, these remained limited. Progress was made with tele-communication links and with power supply links between Singapore, Malaysia and Thailand, while the first two Asean joint industrial projects, urea/ammonia plants in Indonesia and Malaysia, were formally approved. Interest in the Thai soda ash project was revived, but the Singapore Government had to treat its proposal for a diesel engine plant as a national, rather than Asean, project and so reduced its equity participation in other projects to the level of 1 per cent needed to attract Japanese aid.

Japanese promises of aid, partly because of Asean's own failure to present sufficiently organized projects, proved disappointing, and greater attention was directed to economic relations with the USA, Canada, Australia, New Zealand and the EEC. From 20 to 23 November Asean and EEC Foreign Ministers and the EEC Commission met in Brussels to discuss trade, investment, technical and financial aid, and formal arrange-ments for inter-group cooperation. This meeting also considered problems caused by the rising flow of refugees from Indo-China, which imposed an especially heavy burden on Thailand and Malaysia. The numbers fleeing Vietnam were inflated further by an exodus of Vietnamese of Chinese origin, as a result of worsening relations between Vietnam and China and of Vietnamese measures to abolish private commerce and industry.

The annual meeting of Escap held from 7 to 17 March voted to support 'a new international economic order'. There was emphasis on rural develop-ment, including farm-based industries and the design of tools and machinery suitable for peasant use. In July a regional meeting in preparation for the UN conference on science and technology for development stressed 'labour-intensive, smaller-scale, energy-saving and less sophisticated technology'. The widely-supported typhoon committee agreed in October to carry out research in the Western Pacific on the mechanism of typhoons. The com-mittee for joint prospecting for mineral resources in Asian offshore areas

(CCOP) extended its capacity to help member states, the first use of new equipment to be in searching for tin in Thai waters in the Andaman Sea. The International Natural Rubber Council held its first meeting on 10 January, but rising price levels led it to postpone any attempt to create a buffer stock.

Following a meeting in Vientiane in January, Laos, Thailand and Vietnam undertook to revive Mekong Committee projects, and the first session of an interim Mekong Committee opened in Hanoi on 23 February; Cambodia was invited, but did not attend. The second phase of the Nam Ngum hydro-electric project in Laos was completed, raising generating capacity to 110 mw, mostly for export to Thailand. Future priority was to be given to irrigation, allied with fish production and water transport. These discussions reflected an improvement in Thai relations with Vietnam and Laos, which also permitted agreement on the reopening, on 23 March, of the main civil air corridor from Bangkok to Hong Kong over Laos and Vietnam.

CARIBBEAN ORGANIZATIONS

The Caribbean Common Market (Caricom) reversed expectations concerning its collapse. Jamaica eased its restrictions on Caricom imports and permitted entry of goods to the value of J$45 million. Problems of intra-regional payments were resolved through the region's central banks. The Caribbean Council of Trade Ministers had a very successful meeting in July. Dr Kurleigh King, a Barbadian, was selected as the Secretary-General of Caricom, a post vacated in 1977 by the previous incumbent.

The most important matters resolved were the updating of the common external tariff, final agreement to implement the new Caricom rules of origin in January 1979, and approval of a 10 per cent rise in the price of copra. A negotiating position for renegotiation of the 1975 Lomé Convention was adopted.

The most promising development was a meeting of the Caribbean Group for Cooperation in Economic Development, which held its first meeting in Washington from 17 to 24 June. That meeting established a Caribbean Development Facility (CDF) through which extended and increased bilateral aid would be secured. It was determined that the Caribbean would need nearly US$2,000 million in development assistance to stabilize the various economies. Ten donor countries and development agencies contributed US$112 million initially, but the intention was to secure up to US$650 million annually over the next three to five years.

Concern had been expressed that this form of assistance would further strengthen United States penetration in the region, especially since the allocations of aid to the various countries from the CDF would be determined by American-controlled institutions. Their operating procedures did not offer the sort of flexibility which would yield maximum returns to the respective territories. The Caribbean territories would be required to control welfare expenditure, to submit their medium and long-term programmes for approval, to restimulate private enterprise and so on. However, because of their serious balance of payments problems, high levels of unemployment, unfavourable terms of trade and limited scope for development, these territories had very restricted options.

The Caribbean Development Bank, apart from approving loans to the various member territories, successfully floated its first public bond issue, a twenty-year loan of TT$12 million, in Trinidad and Tobago. There was strong support for Belize from its Caricom partners in its quest for self-determination, independence, territorial integrity and secure borders. Venezuela stepped up its interest in the Caribbean and a Caribbean basin tour by President Perez was a diplomatic success. Many countries, Trinidad and Tobago in particular, remained suspicious of Venezuela's motives.

XII RELIGION

THREE POPES. Pope Paul VI died of a heart attack on 6 August, aged 80, after a pontificate of 15 years (see OBITUARY and AR 1963, p. 382). Among his last acts was a handwritten letter pleading for the release of the kidnapped Aldo Moro, and later the Pope attended his funeral mass. Pope Paul presided over the last three sessions of the Second Vatican Council, 1963-65, was the most travelled Pope, and had issued the controversial encyclical *Humanae Vitae* (see AR 1968, p. 499) condemning artificial birth control.

The secret conclave of 111 cardinals which met in the Sistine Chapel to choose a successor included 55 from the Third World, compared with 23 in 1963. It was governed by rules issued in 1975 which limited its number to 120, all under the age of 80, and required a majority of two-thirds plus one vote for a valid election. On 26 August, at the fourth ballot, Cardinal Albino Luciani, aged 65, Patriarch of Venice, was elected and took the name of John Paul after his two predecessors, whose work he promised to continue. The new Pope's smile and simplicity endeared him to the crowds, and instead of coronation with the triple crown his pontificate was inaugurated by a solemn mass in St Peter's Square and investiture with a white wool pallium symbolizing his position as Patriarch of the West. He died suddenly of a heart attack on 28 September, after the shortest pontificate since Leo XI in 1605 (see OBITUARY).

On 16 October the cardinals on the eighth ballot elected Cardinal Karol Wojtyla, Archbishop of Cracow, who took the name of John Paul II. Aged 58, he was the 264th Pope, the first non-Italian to be elected since Adrian VI in 1522, and the first from Poland, a strongly Catholic country with a communist government. Pope John Paul II was born in Wadowice near Cracow of poor parents, and during the German occupation in 1939 he did forced labour in a chemical factory and later enrolled in an illegal seminary in Cracow. Ordained to the priesthood in 1946 he studied also in Rome, and held professorships in Lublin and Cracow. He was appointed auxiliary bishop of Cracow in 1958, archbishop in 1964 and created a cardinal by Paul VI in 1967.

Addressing the cardinals the Pope spoke of the Second Vatican Council as 'a milestone in the 2,000-year history of the church, and indeed in the religious and cultural history of the world'. It was a primary duty to promote 'with prudent but encouraging action' the norms and directives of the Council. He spoke of ecumenism, that 'we might arrive finally at full communion', and he desired to contribute to peace and international justice, with special concern for 'the dear land of Lebanon'. This Pope also was inducted with a solemn mass, among those present being the President of Poland and the Archbishop of Canterbury, the first Primate of England to attend the investiture of a Pope since the Reformation.

ANGLICAN ACTIVITIES. On 21 July 440 bishops representing 25 member churches of the Anglican Communion met at Canterbury for one of the ten-yearly Lambeth Conferences, established in 1867. Dame Barbara Ward, the economist, addressed the bishops on the shortage of world resources and demands for greater equality, saying 'there will be no check on the demand for human respect; there will be no quiet acceptance of massive starvation'. Bishop Desmond Tutu, first black general secretary of the South African Council of Churches, pleaded for the identification of the church with the poor; and the report of the Conference said that 'the Church should not lend unthinking support to anti-communist campaigns'.

In six Reith Lectures on BBC radio entitled *Christianity and the World Order*, Dr Edward Norman, Dean of Peterhouse, Cambridge, attacked both the Lambeth Conference and the World Council of Churches for preaching a 'political Christ', and he asked 'what will happen to Christianity as its content is drained away into the great pool of secular idealism?' The bishops at Lambeth had processed to the accompaniment of a steel band, 'apparently intended to evoke the spirit of the Third World', remarked Dr Norman, and Dame Barbara had vilified 'colonialism' and 'referred approvingly to China's economic priorities'. The lectures aroused much controversy, some agreeing with comments on ecclesiastical political silliness and others concerned that religion might become merely 'pie in the sky' and remarking that the Hebrew prophets spoke on political matters.

Before the Lambeth Conference the bishops were warned by Roman Catholic and Orthodox observers against approving the ordination of women to the priesthood. But Anglican churches in the USA, Canada, Hong Kong and New Zealand already ordained women, and the Conference was advisory and not legislative. On 8 November the General Synod of the Church of England, meeting in London, rejected a proposal from Bishop Hugh Montefiore asking for legislation to remove the barriers to ordination of women to the priesthood and consecration to the episcopate. A simple majority was needed in each house but the voting was: bishops 32-17 in favour; clergy 94-149 against; laity 120-106 in favour. One of the national campaigners, Dr Una Kroll, shouted 'we asked you for bread and you gave us a stone', and Canon Mary Simpson of New York, the first woman to preach in Westminster Abbey, said that the church should stop treating women as 'second-class Christians'.

A report of the Anglican Marriage Commission, *Marriage and the Church's Task*, recommended in May that in some circumstances a divorced person should be allowed to remarry in church while the former partner was still alive, a practice officially disapproved though performed in some dioceses, but the General Synod rejected this suggestion. The United Reformed Church reported that half its marriages involved people who had been divorced, including some Anglicans and Roman Catholics,

In June the Queen gave her consent for the marriage of Prince Michael of Kent to a Roman Catholic, Baroness Marie-Christine von Reibnitz, whose first marriage had been annulled. But when the prince emphasized that any children would be brought up in the Church of England, Pope Paul VI refused to allow a dispensation to marry in a Roman Catholic church, and since the Church of England did not recognize nullity a civil ceremony was performed. On 30 June Prince Charles, at a Salvation Army congress, criticized Christians who were 'still arguing about doctrinal matters', apparently in reference to the marriage. In December Mr Enoch Powell warned that the possibility that Prince Charles might marry a Roman Catholic would be a threat to the Constitution. In December also a document by the Bishop of Chelmsford, John Trillo, pleaded with the Roman Catholic church to sanction intercommunion at a mixed marriage ceremony.

On 25 October, in the presence of the Queen, the Anglican cathedral of Liverpool, founded in 1904, was finally dedicated. Designed by Sir Giles Gilbert Scott, it was the largest cathedral in the British Isles, in a traditional Gothic style which contrasted with the modernism of the new Roman Catholic cathedral in Liverpool. In November the Queen made her first appearance at a Methodist church for the re-dedication after extensive repairs of Wesley's Chapel, London, founded just 200 years ago.

WORLD COUNCIL GRANTS. The Executive Committee of the World Council of Churches, meeting in Helsinki from 18-22 September, authorized an eighth allocation of money totalling $434,500 from the Special Fund to Combat Racism to 29 organizations in 12 countries (see AR 1970, p. 370). The committee also endorsed a decision made on 10 August for a special grant of $85,000 to the Patriotic Front of Zimbabwe (Rhodesia) for food, health, educational and agricultural programmes run in Botswana, Mozambique and Zambia by the two wings of the Patriotic Front, ZANU and ZAPU. The grant had been designated in 1977 for the 'liberation struggle' but had been held back pending a 'review of the total situation'.

The second grant aroused a storm of protest, especially in Britain. The bishops of Chichester and Truro criticized it in diocesan letters. Dr Kenneth Slack, director of Christian Aid, formally and without qualification dissociated his organization from the action, stating that 'it gives direct church support to the Patriotic Front at a time when its individual acts of violence have deeply distressed many who are anxious to see justice established'. The Elim Pentecostal Church, which was not a member of the World Council but had lost nine missionaries and four children at a massacre in Rhodesia in June, wrote to the Council in protest. The Salvation Army newspaper *War Cry* was 'perplexed and distressed' at the grant, since two Salvationists had recently been shot dead by the guerrillas, and General Arnold Brown, the army's world leader, decided to suspend its membership of the World Council pending inquiries.

The grant was defended by Miss Pauline Webb, a leading Methodist and British representative on the executive committee of the World Council, saying that 'it is vital that a voice of support be given to the cause of freedom'. It was stressed that there had been previous agreement with the recipients that the money would be used only for humanitarian purposes. *War Cry* also noted that the Special Fund was quite separate from the general funds of the World Council and that 'those who make contributions to the former do so deliberately and the Salvation Army is not one of these'. The Special Fund had never been popular in Britain, where the total raised for the grants since they started was about £15,000, compared with nearly £500,000 in the Netherlands, £150,000 in West Germany and £120,000 in Sweden. Critics pointed out that the World Council, instead of making its grant directly to a political and violent organization, might have learnt from other agencies, forbidden by their charitable status to aid political parties, which had channelled help through the Red Cross or the United Nations High Commissioner for Refugees.

POPULAR CULTS. On 27 August, for the first time in 45 years, the reputed Holy Shroud went on public view in the cathedral of Turin and attracted thousands of visitors. The Shroud, one of several mediaeval relics said to have been imprinted with a true image of the crucified Christ, was a 14-foot length of ivory-coloured linen apparently bearing the shadowy outline of a corpse, especially clear when seen in negative. There was no documentary evidence of its existence before 1350, but a Swiss forensic expert said that pollen traces on the fabric proved it could have come from Palestine and the weave of the cloth was consistent with similar origin. Critics said that both of these could have existed elsewhere and no carbon tests had been made. On 13 May half a million pilgrims attended mass at the Shrine of Fatima in central Portugal, where the Virgin Mary was said to have appeared to three children on that day and several other occasions in 1917. Despite scepticism expressed after the fall of the Salazar regime, Fatima remained a great attraction.

The murders of a United States Congressman and his three companions in Guyana in November were the prelude to mass carnage among the cult which they had gone to investigate. The Rev. Jim Jones and his People's Temple had first come into prominence in Indianapolis and California, attracting needy and rootless people, especially blacks. Jones himself was white and became a powerful force in San Francisco politics until 1977 when newspaper stories told of slave conditions, beatings and extortion in his community and death threats to those who tried to leave. Jones, a 46-year-old father of seven, moved then to a 27,000-acre settlement in Guyana as an agricultural retreat, and black and white members followed

M*

him. After the murders of the investigators, some 900 members of the People's Temple, including Jones, were found dead by suicide or murder.

RESURGENT ISLAM. A revival of militant Islam appeared in a number of countries. In Iran (see pp. 259-61), a mixture of social, economic and religious dissent caused increasing rioting throughout the year. The exiled Ayatollah Khomeini in Paris claimed that 'Iran's problems can only be solved through an Islamic republic', based on universal suffrage. The secret police should be disbanded, corrupting films banned and alcoholic beverages prohibited. Women should be able to choose their activities and dress, 'provided they observe some guidelines'. Riots between Islamic factions caused the introduction of martial law in Turkey in December (see p. 167), and in Indonesia fundamentalist Muslim leaders, once strong supporters of President Suharto's regime, attacked it for corruption and 'irreligious' management of power. In Egypt the revived Muslim Brotherhood criticized the Government as 'damned because it denies the sovereignty of God', and in Pakistan General Zia ul Haq, after ousting Mr Bhutto, declared: 'In Islam lies our salvation—both worldly and spiritual.' Traditional Islamic punishments for smuggling or using alcohol, applied to some unwary foreigners in Saudi Arabia, were part of the same affirmation of Islamic ways.

BOOKS. Topical publications included *The Year of the Three Popes* by Peter Hebblethwaite, and *Illustrissimi*, lightweight letters of Albino Luciani, later Pope John Paul I, written first for a parish magazine in Padua and addressed to eminent dead figures. A symposium *Yes to Women Priests* was edited by Hugh Montefiore, Bishop of Birmingham, and an opposing collection, *Man, Woman, and Priesthood*, by Peter Moore, Dean of St Albans. A long historical study by Alan Stephenson gave the background and concerns of *Anglicanism and the Lambeth Conferences*, and essays on movements for church reform were edited by Derek Baker in *Renaissance and Renewal in Christian Thought*. In *The Turin Shroud* Ian Wilson sought to trace it back to Edessa in AD 30. Several books appeared on the Crusades: *The Origin of the Idea of Crusade* by Carl Erdmann, *The Albigensian Crusade* by Jonathan Sumption, and *Jerusalem Pilgrims, Before the Crusades* by John Wilkinson.

Jurgen Moltmann of Tübingen completed a trilogy with *The Church in the Power of the Spirit*, after earlier books on *The Theology of Hope* and *The Crucified God* which showed him to be a true successor to the outstanding German theologians of the past. In *The Encounter with the Divine in Mesopotamia and Israel* H. W. F. Saggs examined the evidence for the assumed uniqueness of Israelite religion and showed parallels in ancient Mesopotamia. *The Lord's Prayer and the Jewish Liturgy*, edited by Jakob Petuchowski and Michael Brocke, showed counterparts to phrases and words of the Paternoster in Jewish prayers, notably the Kaddish, the prayer of Jesus being more personal though it became the chief public Christian prayer.

XIII THE SCIENCES

Chapter 1

SCIENCE, MEDICINE AND TECHNOLOGY

At the end of the year British scientific research received an unexpected increase in financial support from the Government. Mrs Shirley Williams, Secretary of State for Education and Science, announced that the science budget was to be increased by £10 million in 1979-80, £10 million in 1980-81, £12 million in 1981-82 and £15 million in 1982-83. This represented a small but real turnabout after five years of cutbacks and restrictions which had brought morale among British research scientists to a low ebb. The fact that the extra support was allotted to the physical and biological sciences, not the social sciences, also represented the reversal of a trend. Also in December the Prime Minister announced that the Government was to invest £100 million in the development of microprocessors in British industry. Of this sum, £40 million was to be spent on encouraging the use of microprocessors, £35 million on educational schemes to show businessmen, industrial designers and others what could be done with microprocessors, and £25 million on training and retraining of personnel to ease the transformation in patterns of living which were bound to come with increased automation.

These developments suggested that the Government was becoming increasingly aware of the real long-term value of pure research to the economy, and of the need actively to encourage enterprising concerns which had already made forays into what the Prime Minister called the 'unexplored territory' of the microelectronics revolution.

MEDICINE AND BIOLOGY. A book published in June, 'In His Image', by the American author David Rorvik, purported to describe how a human baby, said to be fourteen months old at the time of publishing, had been produced from a single body cell provided by a male donor. The announcement was regarded by the scientific world with great scepticism, as it was generally agreed that cloning was not yet possible, for humans at least. Progress had been made along these lines but only in experiments on frogs and tadpoles.

'Test-tube' babies were one of the events of the year. A healthy, normal girl baby, Louise Brown, born on 25 July, had been conceived in a laboratory dish, where her father's sperm had fertilized an ovum removed surgically from the ovaries of her mother. The birth, two weeks early and by Caesarean section as a precaution, was the culmination of several years of research by gynaecologist Patrick Steptoe and physiologist Dr Robert Edwards. The success of the technique promised hope for many couples childless because of blockages in the wives' fallopian tubes, which normally carry ova from the ovaries to the womb for fertilization. At the end of the year other 'test-tube' babies were said to be on the way, though full details of the techniques used by Steptoe and Edwards had still not been published, and an Indian claim to have produced a 'test-tube' birth was widely doubted.

Far more would-be mothers than could ever be helped by the 'test tube' technique stood to benefit from improvements in prenatal screening which were perfected in 1978. One such technique, developed at California and Harvard Universities, involved actually searching for genetic abnormalities in cells from the unborn foetus. It became possible to take samples of amniotic fluid from around the foetus, to extract genetic material from foetal cells floating in the fluid, to break up the genetic material into segments using so-called 'restriction' enzymes, developed for genetic engineering, and to examine the separate segments for evidence of abnormality. This technique proved greatly superior to the much more dangerous method of taking blood samples, as a means of identifying foetuses suffering from severe anaemias due to genetic abnormalities, such as thalassaemia and sickle cell anaemia. If the condition was severe enough, the mother-to-be could then be asked if she would prefer the foetus to be aborted.

Another technique, developed at King's College Hospital, in London, in which a flexible telescope-like instrument was moved around the sac containing a foetus to search visually for deformities, allowed doctors for the first time to examine a developing foetus as though it had already been born. Previous screening methods had all studied remote changes, such as alterations in the amniotic fluid. The technique not only allowed very severe abnormalities to be observed so that abortion could be carried out if wished; it also allowed relatively small abnormalities to be seen and prepared for, so that surgery for a hare lip, for example, could be carried out as soon as possible after birth.

On one front genetic engineering made rapid progress during the year. In March an American court decided to allow the patenting of a hybrid bacterium produced artificially for the purpose of breaking down oil slicks at sea and producing protein food from waste oil. The oil-eating bacterium contained genetic material 'spliced' into its own genetic code from other micro-organisms. The main thrust of research in genetic engineering was towards inserting foreign genetic material, DNA, into bacteria to enable them to manufacture useful hormones and enzymes to the instructions of the inserted DNA. Bacteria, being much the fastest-growing and multiplying of living things, provided ideal living factories for this purpose.

The question, however, remained, would the instructions contained in human or animal type DNA be translated into reality by bacterial systems? In June Professor Walter Gibson and his colleagues at Harvard University announced their success in making bacteria manufacture insulin to the instructions of synthetic DNA, produced artificially in the laboratory. Bacterial manufacture of insulin having been one of the first targets of the genetic engineers, the success of this experiment was very encouraging. However, the DNA used in these experiments had had to be made synthetically, an expensive process, which left unanswered the question whether bacteria would transcribe animal DNA into bacterial type instructions, and translate those instructions into protein. But in October another research group published their report of experiments in which a bit of mouse DNA had been transferred into a bacterium, *Escherischia coli*, and further manipulations had shown that a chemical characteristic of the mouse was being produced by the genetically-engineered bacteria.

This still left lingering doubts in two directions; would the bacteria make foreign compounds in quantities sufficient to be useful, and would they make substances which differed markedly from those the bacteria normally made themselves—the mouse chemical made by the bacteria was very similar to one made naturally by the mouse. None the less, the future for genetically-engineered bacteria as drug factories now looked bright. This was emphasized by the award of the 1978 Nobel prize for medicine and physiology to scientists who had discovered and developed the tools which had made modern genetic engineering possible (see p. 376).

Public concern continued, however, about the possible risks inherent in genetic engineering. There were fears that viral DNA able to cause cancer might accidentally be transferred into previously harmless viruses or other organisms, and that new lethal strains of bacteria might be created and might escape even from laboratories, such as those at Porton Down in England and Atlanta, Georgia, in the USA, which were designed and believed to be able to contain them. Molecular biologists generally felt that the complex restrictions placed on their work in genetic engineering in the USA, in the UK by the Genetic Manipulation Advisory Group and in Western Europe were excessive and would lead to unnecessary delays in obtaining the potential benefits of genetic engineering. At the same time, there were doubts as to whether such restrictions would be the rule in laboratories elsewhere in the world.

The World Health Organization's announcement that as far as could be known smallpox had at last been eradicated was overshadowed, in the UK at least, by the death in August of Mrs Janet Parker, a photographer who had worked in a room above one of the world's few remaining laboratories working on smallpox, that of Professor Henry Bedson in Birmingham University. Her death was followed by the suicide of Professor Bedson. An enquiry by a team headed by an eminent virologist, Professor R. A. Shooter, was set in motion. On 3 January 1979 the Shooter report was leaked to the press, while legal action against Birmingham University by the Health and Safety Executive was pending, on the grounds of breach of safety regulations.

The enquiry found that the virus taken from Mrs Parker's body was of an identical strain to one held in stock in the smallpox laboratory where Professor Henry Bedson was researching. Work in Bedson's laboratory should have been controlled by four sets of safety rules, which, however, had not been scrupulously observed. Tests showed that air currents, which could have carried virus that had consequently escaped, flowed out of the smallpox laboratory, through the outer laboratory and up through an air duct to the floor where Mrs Parker worked: she had not been vaccinated recently enough to protect her from smallpox.

Professor Bedson's research was developing ways to distinguish between harmless smallpox-type viruses infecting animals and others which might emerge from animal reservoirs to infect people. As WHO had virtually eliminated human smallpox, the risks of the disease re-emerging from animal reservoirs to infect unprotected and unprepared populations clearly had to be taken into account. By the same token WHO was also anxious to close down all but the bare minimum of smallpox laboratories, to prevent their acting as sources of infection, and for this reason had asked Bedson to close down his smallpox work by the end of 1978. The pace of work in the Birmingham laboratory was stepped up to try to complete its research programme by the end of the year, and this sense of urgency might have led to laxity in precautions. The Shooter report criticized three inspecting bodies—a university safety committee, which had not inspected the laboratory since 1975; the official Dangerous Pathogens Advisory Group, which should have seen that precautions in the Birmingham laboratory were insufficient; and a team of inspectors from the WHO, who visited Bedson's laboratory in August 1978, and who ought to have seen that the changes they recommended were put into effect. Thus the responsibility for Mrs Parker's death was spread through the whole structure of medical research into smallpox. The report called for an immediate and comprehensive inspection and review of all laboratories handling the most dangerous pathogens. The Birmingham laboratory and another in London were closed.

Medical research workers in Cambridge and London reported the discovery of Cyclosporin A, a compound which, from tests in animal experiments, appeared to be by far the most effective drug ever used to prevent the rejection of transplanted organs. Tests by teams led by Dr Tony Allison in the Clinical Research Centre at Northwick Park and surgeon Mr Roy Calne in Addenbrooke's Hospital, Cambridge, showed that Cyclosporin A prevented the rejections of foreign kidneys grafted into rabbits and foreign hearts grafted into pigs far more effectively than any other immunosuppressive drugs. Cyclosporin A appeared to act in a different and more selective way, and, when it prevented rejection, to do so completely after the drug had been given for only a relatively short period. In December, however, the publication of the results of the first clinical trials of Cyclosporin A showed that a number of problems would have to be overcome before the drug could be used on a large scale in human transplant surgery; in particular, it had some toxic side-effects on kidney and liver.

Important evidence was obtained to link three serious diseases, leukaemia, rheumatoid arthritis and multiple sclerosis, with viruses as the basic though only partial causes. In no case was the evidence conclusive. In each case, however, the advance, in a notoriously difficult area of research, was big enough to be regarded as highly significant by experts.

Dr Abraham Karpas of the Cambridge Clinical School carried out experiments which showed that normal, healthy bone marrow cells in tissue culture could be made leukaemic by contact with culture of leukaemic cells, and that they then exhibited virus particles of the same type as those found in the leukaemic cell culture. Dr Karpas also produced some evidence that similar viruses occurred in the bodies of leukaemic patients. Although at the end of the year the work had not yet been repeated by other laboratories, doctors were already discussing the long-term prospects for preventing or treating leukaemia with a vaccine made from the (killed) virus involved.

A team led by Dr Alan Salsbury of the Brompton Hospital in West London demonstrated that bone marrow from multiple sclerosis patients had effects on cell cultures with which it was mixed strongly suggesting that an unusual virus was present. Evidence of viral particles was subsequently found in the tissue from the patients. American researchers at California University showed that artificial mutants of a common virus could cause symptoms identical to those of multiple sclerosis in experimental animals. As with the leukaemia virus, scientists hoped to use this work as a basis from which to search for environmental factors at work in activating the viruses to cause disease in some people while others, probably the majority, carried the virus infections throughout life in a dormant and harmless form.

Dr Eng Tan of the Scripps Institute in California, Dr Alan Brown of the bone and joint unit in the London Hospital and others reported evidence to suggest that infection with Epstein Barr (EB) virus might be an underlying cause of rheumatoid arthritis. Here it seemed certain that other factors were involved, as the virus commonly occurred as a harmless infection. But it was also thought to be capable of causing other diseases, including forms of cancer, once again when triggered by environmental factors.

The cause of another crippling disease, myasthenia gravis, was more firmly pinned down by researchers at University College and the National Hospital for Nervous Diseases in London. They demonstrated that the disease was caused by an auto-immune reaction. In this the patient's body produced antibodies which blocked the receptor sites on muscles that normally responded to nervous stimuli. No immediate advances in treatment resulted from this advance in understanding the disease, but the discovery did immediately provide a rationale for the remarkable success of the 'blood swap' technique employed in the USA and Scotland as a means of treating myasthenia gravis. The merit of the complete transfusion of blood plasma used was, clearly, that it washed out, temporarily at least, the harmful auto-antibodies responsible for blocking the receptor sites.

A combination of factors was identified as being responsible between them for a high risk of developing cancer of the large bowel. These factors were; a high level of metabolic breakdown products, bile acids, in the large bowel; large concentrations of a particular species of bacteria, clostridia; the presence of an enzyme, a decarboxylase; and other chemical factors. It was now theoretically possible, according to Dr Michael Hill of the Central Public Health Laboratory at Colindale, one of the authors of the research (speaking at a conference on advances in medicine held in London in July) to screen the population to identify those at special risk of large bowel cancer, who could then be put on special diets. The screening measures required would be exceedingly expensive, but cheaper tests might be developed.

Research at the Molteno Institute in Cambridge had led scientists to the point of testing new experimental drugs against sleeping sickness, one of the most intractable of tropical diseases. Dr Roger Klein had identified a fundamental difference between the metabolism of the trypanosome parasites which caused the disease and that of their cattle or human hosts. The difference involved the way in which parasite and human respectively broke down certain amino acids (protein constituents) and subsequently used the breakdown products to assemble cell wall material. During the year Dr Klein tested compounds able to block this vital metabolic pathway in trypanosomes without affecting the different pathway in human metabolism.

In medical technology EMI, who had led the world with their revolutionary X-ray computerized axial tomography (CAT) scanners for brain and body, recorded another 'world first' with the first brain scans made by nuclear magnetic resonance (NMR) scanning. In recent years scientists at Nottingham University had produced clear cross-sectional views of a human wrist and the head and abdomen of a rabbit, using NMR scanning. Working with the Nottingham group the EMI scientists produced a clear image of a cross-section of a man's head and brain. The picture showed anatomical features including the eye sockets and eyeballs and the ventricles, fluid-filled spaces in the brain. EMI published their first NMR brain scan alongside their first X-ray CAT head scan, to emphasize that NMR scanning was at now the same stage of development as X-ray scanning had then been. Some advantages of NMR over any other form of scanning were already clear. The technique worked by differentiating

Keystone Press   *Associated Press*

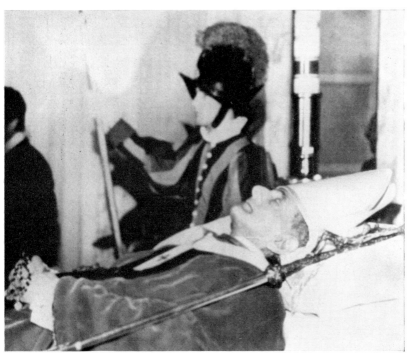

Keystone Press

1978 was the Year of the Three Popes: below, the body of Paul VI lies in state after his death on 6 August; above, left, John Paul I, elected 26 August, died 28 September; John Paul II, elected 16 October.

Camera Press   *Camera Press*

The Commonwealth lost in 1978 two very different elder statesmen: left, Sir Robert Menzies, long-serving Prime Minister of Australia; right, Jomo Kenyatta, President of Kenya.

Camera Press   *Camera Press*

Among the world's political leaders who died in 1978 were (left) Mrs Golda Meir, former Prime Minister of Israel, and (right) Houari Boumédienne, President of Algeria.

Keystone Press   *Camera Press*

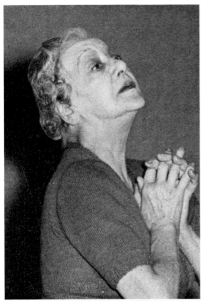 

Keystone Press   *Camera Press*

Famous names disappeared from the roll of the living in 1978: (top left) Micheál MacLiammóir, Irish actor, poet and producer; (top right) Margaret Mead, American anthropologist; (bottom left) Tamara Karsavina, Russian-born ballerina; (bottom right) Anastas I. Mikoyan, long-serving Soviet Minister and member of the Supreme Soviet.

Associated Press

On 3 March 1978 an 'internal settlement' which would bring majority rule to Rhodesia (Zimbabwe) after general elections and would immediately install an Executive Council of black and white Ministers was signed in Salisbury: the signatories were, from left to right, Bishop Abel Muzorewa, Mr Ian Smith, Chief Jeremiah Chirau and the Rev. Ndabaningi Sithole.

between tissues in different parts of the head or body on the basis of the varying amounts of radio waves absorbed by different materials at various wavelengths when the brain or body under examination was subjected to a powerful but harmless magnetic field. This allowed NMR scans, built up into cross-sectional views by computer analysis like CAT scans, to differentiate clearly between different soft structures, such as tendons, arteries and nerves—parts which could not be differentiated by X-rays, used either conventionally or in a CAT scan. The potential value of this to doctors wishing to investigate the interior of brain or body without using invasive techniques was very great, not least because repeated scanning by NMR, unlike X-rays, carried no radiation hazard.

TECHNOLOGY. The announcement of massive government support for the development of microprocessors in British industry, noted on p. 363, was described by *The Engineer* as 'a desperate shove to get the stable door shut before the last horse bolts'. As many other critics also remarked, while British scientists and engineers had been responsible for much of the progress in microprocessors, British industry had almost completely failed to introduce the new technology. Nevertheless, the world's most advanced welding robot, designed and manufactured by British concerns, and the world's most advanced computerized chemical process control system, designed by the British Government's Warren Spring technology laboratory and developed commercially by a British concern, were introduced in 1978. A British company, Ferranti, had the only European facility for making really advanced silicon 'chips'—containing complete computers, more elaborate than those which had occupied large roomfuls of electronic equipment only ten years before, on a silicon wafer one-quarter of an inch square. Britain clearly had the technological background and the inventiveness needed to exploit microprocessors.

British inventiveness in the computer field was most strikingly demonstrated by the introduction in May, at Queen Mary College, London, of the first of the British concern International Computers Ltd's new super-fast computers, distributed array processors, DAP for short, the most advanced of its kind in the world. DAPs worked faster than conventional computers by multiplying the number of processors, the parts which did the 'thinking', and their connexions with the computer's memory stores. In this way, instead of a programme of calculations having to wait in a queue for a small number of processors, they could be performed simultaneously, and so in a much shorter time. In the British home, two computer-based developments, Teletext and Prestel, were beginning to become familiar. Teletext made weather forecasts, news bulletins, sport results and other information available at the press of a button on a home TV screen, at a cost of about £600. In 1978 about ten thousand people in the UK had sets equipped to receive the service, broadcast by both the

BBC and ITV. Prestel was a similar service providing access to a larger library of news and information, provided by the Post Office and being tested in a limited area during 1978.

Another field in which technology was moving fast was offshore engineering. Visitors to the international conference and exhibition of oceanology held in March at Brighton were reminded that only nine years before, at the first such exhibition, the only hardware in the word had consisted of cautious extensions into shallow water of land-based drilling equipment, orthodox dredging gear and the like. Now there were systems for joining lengths of pipeline at depths of three or four hundred feet by remote control with the precision of spacecraft dockings. Detailed plans for underwater sea-bed oil production platforms, in which crews would live at depths down to 600 feet in luxurious quarters, breathing air at normal atmospheric pressure, were revealed and discussed at the conference. Navigation systems on sale were able to fix the position of a rig or submersible more than 300 miles from land to within a few inches.

In deeper water still, American scientists from the Woods Hole Oceanographic Institute, speaking at a meeting to discuss monitoring of the marine environment, revealed how an abandoned sandwich had changed the course of marine biology. The sandwich had been part of a lunch pack left inside the American deep submersible *Alvin* when that vessel had accidentally been released from its support ship and had sunk empty to the deep sea bottom. Ten months later, when *Alvin* had been recovered, the sandwich was found to be perfectly fresh in spite of exposure to what had previously been thought to be a voracious population of micro-organisms on and around the sea bottom. The discovery had prompted scientists to investigate further and discover that decay processes at great depth are very slow or non-existent, a finding which had upset old ideas about the safety of dumping various forms of refuse on deep sea floors.

British Rail introduced their highly successful diesel-electric high speed train on the East Coast route from London to Edinburgh and Aberdeen. By the end of the year several HST sets were running at up to 125 miles per hour on this route, where BR hoped they would bring as big an improvement in passenger traffic as the 33 per cent increase they had already achieved on the London to Bristol and Wales services. The next step, BR's first production Advanced Passenger Train (APT), with electric locomotive and tilting coaches, able to run at up to 150 mph on ordinary tracks and tight bends, was unveiled for reporters in June. It was expected to enter trial service between London and Glasgow in 1979.

The Intermediate Technology Development Group, devoted to identifying, inventing and introducing technology appropriate to the needs of village and cottage industries in the Third World, opened a new section—their Intermediate Technology Industrial Services (ITIS)—at

Rugby with the support of the Ministry of Overseas Development. Developments sponsored by ITIS which were introduced during 1978 included a simple candle-making set, an improved hand-driven wool spinning machine for North India, small-scale paper-making machinery, and cement reinforced with human hair clipping—an unusual freely-renewable resource which had proved ideal for the purpose—for use as a roofing material.

Among new developments in scientific instrumentation, the acoustic microscope began to show its true potential during the year. One of the most advanced of these instruments had been developed in the Electronics Department of University College, London. The acoustic microscope used sound waves directed upon a specimen under examination to form an image of its structure. The sound waves, focused by a lens of sapphire on the far side of the specimen, were translated into electrical signals which could either be stored in a computer for future reference or else be transformed straightaway into a picture on a TV screen. Sound waves, which could resolve detail down to about the same limits as visible light, could do so without the need to stain and so distort living material in order to differentiate between regions differing in such important things as density and elasticity. This enabled scientists to observe living processes, enormously magnified, which could not be seen at all using light or electron microscopy. Cell division, seed germination, changes in cell membranes associated with malignancy, and the fertilization of eggs by sperms were among the many events which acoustic microscopy promised to clarify.

Among the ideas at-first-sight wild but on examination attractive that were put forward during the year was one for sun-powered airships, proposed by engineers at Imperial College London and Surrey University at Guildford. Their fully-detailed plans provided a frame sufficiently large to carry the massive body of solar cells needed to produce enough power to drive the ship. The costs of solar cells were coming down dramatically.

AGRICULTURAL SCIENCE AND BOTANY. A technique, developed at the Cambridge Institute of Animal Physiology, for transplanting living oocytes—egg cells—from newly-slaughtered animals into others newly mated showed promise as a means of increasing the productivity of farm animals. The technique, developed by Dr Bob Moore, involved taking oocytes from ewes very soon after slaughter, keeping them alive by chilling while they were transferred to a laboratory, treating the oocytes with hormones to mature them and transferring them into the oviducts of very recently mated ewes. It was shown to be a reliable way of producing twin lambs and Dr Moore saw no difficulties in extending it to produce twin calves, something of great economic value.

Weeds might be in for a shock, as a result of work at the department of electronic engineering at Sheffield University, where a team led by

Professor F. A. Benson had developed an economic technique for weed control by electrocution. They had built a tractor-drawn machine able to kill weeds between rows of a crop, or growing to a different height from that of the crop, by passing a high-voltage current from one electrode touching the tops of the weeds to another touching the soil near their roots. The team announced the development at a crop protection conference in October. They claimed that the training necessary, for safety and other reasons, could cost us more than that properly required by workers using toxic chemicals.

Several events during the year pointed to the need to conserve plants and to a growing realization of the importance of plants as an irreplaceable natural resource. At an international conference held at Kew in August, botanists and the directors of botanic gardens from many parts of the world joined in lamenting the lack of public interest in plant as opposed to animal conservation.

As speakers at this conference and on other occasions pointed out, nearly half the medical prescriptions written each year contained some ingredient of plant origin. Ninety per cent of the world's food came from twenty plant species. At current rates the world was due to lose one-third of its arable land by the end of the century and nearly half the tropical rain forests had already been felled. These and other disturbing statistics showed how the world's plant and tree resources were being exhausted just when the true value of plants as resources was becoming appreciated.

At the annual meeting of the British Association for the Advancement of Science, in August, Professor A. J. Vlitos, a research director in the sugar concern Tate and Lyle, gave a presidential address in which he said that, with the exhaustion of hydrocarbons, plants and trees were bound to come more and more into their own as renewable sources of energy and providers of chemical feedstocks for industry. As he pointed out, fast-maturing trees, and crops like cane and cassava, were excellent ways to trap the energy in sunlight, hard to collect by man-made means. Legumes could provide an excellent alternative to increasingly expensive artificial nitrogenous fertilizers. Ethylene, the most important of all feedstocks in industrial chemistry, was expected to be mainly derived from ethanol made by fermentation from carbohydrate crops.

The Wolfson Foundation's grant, in October, of £120,000, to scientists in Sheffield University to develop plant single-cell cultures also showed the growing importance of plants as a natural resource. The value of plants as sources of drugs such as digoxin the heart stimulant, quinine for treating malaria, vegetable laxatives and many other compounds had long been realized. But plants and trees, subject to the unpredictability of the weather and other inconveniences, could not be treated like production lines. Now however, developments were making it possible to grow plant tissue as isolated single cells in nutrient liquids in big tanks, as bacteria and moulds were already grown to make antibiotics. The grant from the Wolfson Foundation was to assist biochemists at Sheffield in finding better ways to keep plant cells in single-cell cultures separated and to stop them sticking to the sides of the tanks, and to help to solve other technological problems. During the year, botanists demonstrated that it was possible, simply by repeatedly selecting the highest-yielding cultures, to increase the productivity of plant single-cell cultures several times over at no extra cost. In spite of the high capital cost of the equipment, cell culture systems could become economic as a means of producing not only drugs like digoxin but also the steroids used in contraceptive pills. These steroids were conventionally extracted from Mexican yams, which were beginning to prove insufficient as a source of supply.

The need to conserve plants in the wild (as well as developing cell culture techniques) was emphasized by Dr Conrad Gorinsky, a lecturer in biochemistry in St Bartholomew's Hospital, London, who had founded there a group known as the Biotechnical Research and Development Organization—BoTech—for the purpose of gathering plant-based remedies for illnesses from the traditional oral cultures of Latin American Indians and other primitive peoples, before the destruction of their cultures led to the permanent loss of the knowledge of such folk medicines. Dr Gorinsky, who publicized and extended his activities widely during the year, pointed out that nearly all man-made drugs in use were molecular copies or derivatives of a relatively few naturally-occurring compounds, and that only nature had had the time—the hundreds of millions of years of evolution—to devise a vast range of molecules active in biological systems. His researches, and expeditions organized by his group, had already shown that at least as many potent new drugs remained to be discovered as had already been exploited by modern and primitive cultures together. Gorinsky pleaded for cultural conservation on the grounds that, in his own words, 'the best way of storing genetic resources is in the security of their own habitats and in the living cultures of primitive people themselves'.

Simple fungi, yeasts, as well as plants were being prepared for use as drug factories during the year. Dr Jean Beggs of the Plant Breeding Institute at Trumpington near Cambridge reported how she had devised and tested a complete system for genetically engineering yeasts, introducing foreign genetic material into the yeasts so that they would manufacture hormones and enzymes to order, like the genetically-engineered bacteria mentioned earlier. The potential advantage of yeasts was that, as their systems for translating genetic instructions into proteins were closer to those of animals and humans than those of bacteria, it should prove easier to make yeasts form human-type enzymes and hormones. Other proposed uses for genetically engineered yeasts included better beer and high-protein food additives with protein constituents inserted to order.

SPACE RESEARCH AND ASTRONOMY. On 16 March Yuri Romanenko and Georgiy Grechko, who had been crewing the Soviet space station Salyut Six in Earth orbit, returned to Earth after a 96-day stay, at that time a record spaceflight. (The previous record had been the 84-day stay in space of the last crew of the American space station Skylab.) During their stay two other cosmonauts had paid a brief, five-day visit to the space station and had left in the Soyuz ferry ship which had carried the long-stay crew up, leaving their own ship for the long-stay crew to return in. While in space the long-stay men were also supplied with food, water, scientific equipment and other needs by an unmanned 'Progress' supply ship. This was loaded with rubbish and sent back in a trajectory towards the Earth which ensured that it would burn up harmlessly in the atmosphere. This pattern, repeated in a later flight, was made possible by the double docking hatches of the Salyut 6 space station, which enabled two ferry or supply ships to be accommodated simultaneously.

The system was exploited further in the next Soviet space mission, in which Vladimir Kovalyonok and Alexander Ivanchekov spent 140 days in orbit, returning to earth on 2 November. Previous flights had shown that the physiological problems of long-term space flight lay not so much in the relatively minor adjustments needed to live in weightless conditions as in the painful return to Earth, when the heart and other muscles had to readjust to working against the pull of gravity. The long-stay cosmonauts were released from medical care, and pronounced as healthy as when they had left the ground, after a shorter time than some of their predecessors. So it was clear that the time-limits of uninterrupted weightless spaceflight had by no means been reached. But changes in the men's bodies— shrinkage of muscles, reduction in the size of red blood cells and other continuing adaptations—suggested that a time-limit would eventually be reached, at a point where these changes had progressed so far as to make readaptation to gravity dangerous or impossible.

The third and last crew had left America's orbiting space station Skylab in 1974 and since then the station had been uninhabited. There had been talk of reactivating the station and crewing it from the Space Shuttle, the returnable, reusable, aircraft-like spacecraft being built by NASA and expected to make its first orbital flight in the autumn of 1979. But by 1976 it had become apparent that unexpected solar activity was warming up the upper atmosphere and causing it to expand outwards into space, thickening the air Skylab moved through and increasing the frictional drag on the space station so that it was moving towards the Earth much faster than had been expected. Unlike Russian Salyut space stations, Skylab had not been fitted with a rocket engine able to direct its final fall out of orbit down into uninhabited ocean. In 1978 it became apparent that Skylab was liable to come down, in pieces too big to burn up in the atmosphere and over inhabited areas, as early as 1979. Ground controllers managed to reactivate the space station's systems in order that its attitude could be controlled from the ground, and then so manoeuvred the space station as to offer the minimum resistance to the air. However, plans to accelerate the building of a 'satellite snatcher', a remotely-controlled space tug, to push Skylab up into a higher, safe orbit, or to direct it down over uninhabited ocean, had to be abandoned and NASA warned the world that, while 80 per cent of the space station would probably burn up, parts of its 78-ton structure weighing up to two tons might crash, by May 1979, over a huge area of the world's land mass, including south-western England. The risks to life were, however, estimated as no greater than those from natural meteorite showers. There was no risk from radioactivity, as Skylab drew its power not from nuclear plant but from solar cells transforming sunlight into electricity.

Venus was intensively probed by fleets of American and Russian spacecraft arriving within a few days of each other in December. America's Pioneer Venus 1 arrived on 4 December and entered orbit around the planet, sending back information about the upper atmosphere. Pioneer Venus 2 arrived on 9 December and split up into three small probes, nicknamed 'North', 'Day' and 'Night' (from their time and place of landing), a larger probe and the 'bus' that had carried all the others, all of which descended to the surface of the planet. The American probes were not designed to survive on the surface but one at least did so, for more than half an hour. Four out of five of the probes returned information all the way down to the surface. The two Russian probes which arrived two weeks later, Venera 11 and 12, were designed to send back surface information and Venera 12, which got there first, relayed data for 118 minutes. None of the data had been released by the end of the year.

But one big surprise was revealed; the atmosphere of Venus contained 100 times as much of an isotope of the inert gas Argon as did the atmosphere of Earth, and 1,000 times as much as that of Mars. This suggested that, while the inner core of Venus had formed in the same way as those of Earth and Mars, its outer layers might have been formed in some quite different way.

THE NOBEL PRIZES. The chemistry prize was awarded to a British biochemist, Dr Peter Mitchell, at the age of 58, for his discoveries concerning the way in which the Sun's energy is absorbed by chlorophyll and passed on to be used in living processes. Dr Mitchell's discovery had been that the solar energy is used to drive a molecular pump, which builds up a concentration of charged hydrogen atoms which in turn provides the energy to manufacture adenosine triphosphate, ATP, the universal energy fuel of living cells.

The prize for physics was shared by two Americans, Drs Arno Penzias and Robert Wilson, with Dr Pyotr Kapitza of the Soviet Union. The

Americans received their share for their discovery, in 1965, of the so-called 'black body' radiation which fills the universe and is thought to have been produced very shortly after the original Big Bang. The importance of the discovery lay in the evidence it offered for the Big Bang theory of the origin of the Universe. Dr Kapitza received his share for his pioneering work in low-temperature physics, especially on the effects of very low temperatures and very strong magnetic fields on matter. Much of this work had been done at the Cambridge Cavendish laboratory in the 1930s, before Kapitza was prevented by the Stalinist regime from returning to Cambridge after visiting his mother in Russia in 1934.

The prize for medicine was shared by two Americans and a Swiss, Daniel Nathans and Hamilton Smith of Johns Hopkins University and Werner Arber of Basle University, for their discovery of restriction enzymes. The importance of these enzymes had become apparent during the development of genetic engineering, in which they were used to chop up DNA in controlled ways, so that the required sequences could be inserted into bacteria or other organisms being genetically engineered.

Chapter 2

THE ENVIRONMENT

ON 16 March the supertanker *Amoco Cadiz* went aground off the Brittany coast. The wrecking, which ironically took place on the first World Maritime Day proclaimed by the Inter-Governmental Maritime Consultative Organization (IMCO), caused the world's worst-ever oil tanker pollution disaster. More than 220,000 tons of oil were spilled into the sea, twice as much as from the previous worst accident, the wrecking of the *Torrey Canyon* almost exactly eleven years before. According to one investigation—by the US Department of Commerce and the Environmental Protection Agency—about 64,000 tons of the oil came ashore along a 40-mile stretch of the Brittany coast within two and a half weeks, most of the rest evaporating or remaining in the sea. By November, compensation claims from the French Government and local authorities, the tourist and fishing industries and others were estimated to have reached $1,700 million.

The wreck was to be just the first of a series of incidents in Western Europe during 1978. Less than two months later, another tanker, the *Eleni V*, was cut in two in a collision with the French merchant vessel *Roseline* off East Anglia. One part of the tanker was safely salvaged, but the British authorities spent over three weeks trying to find a way of pumping the oil out from the other section, before finally blowing it up. Some 5,000 tons of oil were spilled.

The authorities were rather more successful with the next incident, when the Greek tanker *Christos Bitas* hit rocks off the South Wales coast in October. Some 2,400 tons of oil were lost, but another 31,600 tons were safely pumped from the hull at sea into another tanker, and the *Christos Bitas* was eventually scuttled in the Atlantic some 320 miles off the Irish coast. The year ended with two more tanker accidents. Late at night on 30 December, the *Esso Bernicia* hit a jetty at the Sullom Voe terminal, losing over 1,000 tons of oil. And on New Year's Eve there was an explosion on the supertanker *Andros Patria*, which was carrying nearly as much oil as the *Amoco Cadiz*. About 50,000 tons of oil spilled out off the Spanish coast, and many of the crew were killed.

The year's incidents focused public and political attention in Britain and France on oil pollution for the first time for many years, and 1978 saw great pressure for changes in tankers' operating practices and in clean-up procedures and technology. Ironically only a month before the wrecking of the *Amoco Cadiz*, a special international conference convened precisely to draw up new measures for preventing pollution from tankers took place in London almost unnoticed, except among a small group of experts and civil servants. IMCO's conference on tanker safety and marine pollution prevention met to consider a series of proposals from the USA, where public opinion had already been aroused by a series of tanker accidents off the east coast of the country during the previous two years. The USA suggested, among other measures, that all new tankers of more than 20,000 tons deadweight should have double bottoms to prevent spills caused by grounding and that both new and existing tankers above that weight should be fitted with segregated ballast tanks (SBT), a system of separate compartments for carrying oil and stabilizing water which was almost universally regarded as the best way to avoid routine discharges of oil from tankers (which every year released five times as much oil into the ocean as did major accidents). This was vigorously opposed by Britain, among other nations, and the eventual compromise laid down that only new tankers should be fitted with SBT—a measure that was expected to have little effect for many years since there was a considerable glut of the vessels in the world and few new ones were envisaged. Supporters of the British position could argue that the alternative methods for avoiding routine pollution laid down in the agreement for existing tankers were nearly as effective as SBT and less expensive to instal, but some pollution experts commented bitterly after the wrecking of the *Amoco Cadiz* that, if the accident had happened just a month earlier, the American proposals would have been approved.

As it was, the series of incidents exposed major deficiencies in Western Europe's—and the international community's—defences against oil pollution. After the *Torrey Canyon* disaster, the chemicals used to disperse the oil were widely acknowledged to have done more damage than the original pollution, and so new dispersants had since been developed which, it was claimed, were a thousand times less toxic. Other national authorities, and some British scientists, were far less confident of their relative harmlessness, but, in any case, the dispersants proved ineffective in dealing with the heavy type of oil spilt in both the *Eleni V* and the Sullom Voe incidents, and had patchy success, at best, in combating pollution from the *Amoco Cadiz* and the *Christos Bitas*. No comparable effort had been devoted to developing machines which could skim oil from the surface of the sea, a clean-up method much preferred in principle by many authorities; although the British Government's Warren Springs laboratory was working on such a 'skimmer' at the time of the *Eleni V* incident, it proved inadequate when it was tried out on the slick, even in ideal weather conditions. After an inquiry into the *Eleni V* accident, the House of Commons Select Committee on Science and Technology said that the British authorities were 'unprepared' for a spill of this kind of oil, and that the South Coast of England was 'virtually unprotected' against major spills. This was denied by the Government, but soon after the *Amoco Cadiz* incident it revealed that less than a third of the main shipping routes around the British coast had been surveyed to full modern standards for hazards to shipping.

Although many new rules for preventing and combating pollution had been agreed by IMCO conferences over previous years, they were taking so long to be ratified by member states that they were acknowledged to be out of date by the time they came into effect, and there were not enough inspectors to enforce them. Nevertheless 1978 did see some progress both internationally and in the two nations most affected by the year's oil spills. IMCO drew up rules for training and certifying ship's crews, a particularly important measure since at least 80 per cent of tanker accidents were attributed to human error, and reviewed salvage procedures. Britain set up a unit for coordinating action against spills and reviewed its clean-up arrangements. France insisted on a new lane for tankers at the south-western entrance to the English Channel, in order to keep them well clear of her coasts, and the two countries agreed on a new emergency coordination plan to deal with spills in the Channel.

The oil pollution incidents of 1978 overshadowed the other great energy issue which had dominated the environmental debate over previous years, nuclear power. This remained, however, the major preoccupation of many activist environmental groups. The major event of 1978 in Britain was the publication, in March, of Mr Justice Parker's report on the previous year's public inquiry into British Nuclear Fuels Ltd's application to build a new plant for reprocessing oxide nuclear fuel at Windscale (see AR 1977, pp. 377-8). The report was a lucid, sweeping and almost unequivocal endorsement of BNFL's case and dismissal of the arguments raised by objectors. After an initial welcome, the credibility of the report was quickly drawn into doubt. Leading witnesses at the inquiry wrote to Mr

Peter Shore, Minister for the Environment (to whom the report was addressed), to protest that their testimony had been seriously misrepresented. There was considerable surprise that the report should have come to such a one-sided view after what was acknowledged to be a finely balanced debate at the inquiry, and commentators particularly pointed out weaknesses in its treatment of the hazards of nuclear proliferation (it was received almost with contempt by some proliferation experts in the US Administration) and its view that reprocessing was necessary to deal safely with nuclear waste.

Shortly after the publication of the report, studies by the Swedish atomic industry were made public, showing that spent nuclear fuel could be safely stored underground without reprocessing for 5,000 years—striking support for the Windscale objectors' case that it could be kept safe for several decades while the need for reprocessing was reassessed. Indeed, other work published during the year threw grave doubts on the means Britain was developing for disposing of waste after reprocessing, a system of binding the wastes in glass which formed part of the expansion of Windscale. Experiments by Professor Ted Ringwood of the Australian National University suggested that there was a strong possibility that the glass would break up and allow radioactivity to escape, and that the wastes would be much safer if they were stored in the form of synthetic rock. In the end the Windscale report proved controversial enough to provoke the two most intensive debates on nuclear power in the House of Commons to date. The final vote to allow the Windscale expansion was a decisive 224 votes to 80, but the opponents of the scheme were able to console themselves with the fact that they had achieved much more support in Parliament than had ever been mustered on an anti-nuclear issue.

The result of the Windscale inquiry caused a split in the anti-nuclear movement. Several groups argued that the treatment of the opposition's case in the report showed that rational debate was fruitless and that environmentalists should resort to 'direct action' instead. Others, like Friends of the Earth, retorted that argument still had its part. As it happened, the divergence on tactics was not put to the test during the year, mainly because the Government continued to postpone calling a public inquiry on the issue of whether Britain should have its first commercial fast breeder reactor, repeated downward revisions of forecasts of Britain's energy needs having deprived the issue of all urgency.

Instead opposition centred on a plan to build a new reactor at Torness in Scotland (the site was occupied for a while by protesters), unease among people in the Channel Islands about pollution from the French reprocessing plant nearby at Cap de la Hague, and a somewhat narrow and irresponsible opposition by local communities to allowing the UK Atomic Energy Authority to explore for possible sites for the disposal of nuclear waste (both Northumberland county council and the Kyle and Carrick council in Ayrshire refused to let the authority carry out drilling programmes). The nuclear issue continued to achieve prominence in other nations, particularly Austria, where a Government proposal to build a nuclear power station was defeated in a referendum, and Sweden, where Mr Thorbjörn Fälldin, who became Prime Minister on an anti-nuclear platform two years before, was forced to resign after a disagreement with his coalition partners over whether to call for a referendum in that country.

Conditions in the atomic weapons research plant at Aldermaston proved the major industrial health issue of the year in Britain. All plutonium-handling areas of the plant were closed in the summer in the face of a workers' revolt, following the announcement that preliminary tests indicated that twelve workers at the plant might have levels of plutonium in their lungs ranging from about the maximum allowed by international regulations to several times the maximum. An inquiry under Sir Edward Pochin reported serious deficiencies in areas of the plant: all his recommendations were accepted by the Government.

In the United States, the Secretary for Health, Education and Welfare, Mr Joseph Califano, announced that between 21 and 38 per cent of all cancer cases were occupational in origin, and Dr Eula Bingham, the dynamic new head of the Occupational Safety and Health Administration, brought in sweeping reforms both in her bureaucracy and in working practices in industry.

There was continued concern about asbestos; in another statement Mr Califano said that up to half the people heavily exposed to asbestos during the past 40 years would die as a result. Meanwhile work in Turkish villages by Professor Y. I. Baris of Hacattepe University in Ankara implicated natural fibrous rocks, zeolites, as the cause of cancers normally associated with asbestos—a significant finding since similar, though not identical, zeolites are widely used in the petrochemical industry. Towards the end of the year the report of an inquiry by the US Institute of Medicine and the National Research Council branded saccarhin, the only permitted artificial sweetener in the US, as a cause of cancer. More hopefully, research published in January suggested that a new chemical designed to improve the efficiency of nitrogenous fertilizers might greatly reduce the release of nitrous oxides, seen by some scientists as one of the greatest dangers to the globe's protective ozone layer.

Anxiety about the effects of pollution by heavy metals continued to grow. In Britain the year saw a growing popular campaign greatly to reduce the amount of lead permitted in petrol, and some evidence suggested that one-third of the children in Western cities might be suffering mental retardation as a result of low levels of lead poisoning. And Professor Lars Friberg, the doyen of metal toxicology, told the nineteenth International Congress on Occupational Health in Dubrovnik in September that 5 per cent of the people of some industrialized countries, including Japan and the United States, could be suffering kidney damage from poisoning by cadmium.

Meetings between the Mediterranean states over cleaning up their common sea continued to experience a slowing in progress during 1978, but the states around the Persian Gulf agreed an anti-pollution 'action plan' for their sea and several other regions showed interest in following suit.

The International Union for the Conservation of Nature and Natural Resources, meeting on its 30th anniversary in Ashkebad, southern Russia, approved a World Conservation Strategy which marked a turning-point in concern over wild-life. Increasingly wild-life experts had been warning that a million species might disappear, possibly within a generation. The strategy advocated abandoning the traditional ad-hoc response of trying to save a few endangered species, in favour of a planned programme aimed at conserving great patches of the web of life. More traditionally, a protest led by the conservation group, Greenpeace, succeeded in stopping a special seal cull in the Orkneys.

XIV THE LAW

Chapter 1

INTERNATIONAL LAW—EUROPEAN COMMUNITY LAW

INTERNATIONAL LAW

The International Court of Justice continued to be underemployed. In April it issued a revised set of Rules of Court; no radical revision was possible, but a number of alterations were made, designed, in particular, to simplify the procedure and to reduce the expense for participants.

On 19 December the Court decided, by 12 votes to 2 (Judge de Castro and Judge *ad hoc* Stassinopoulos) that it lacked jurisdiction to entertain the Application of Greece concerning the Aegean Sea continental shelf. In proceedings instituted on 10 August 1976, Greece had in essence asked the Court to pronounce against Turkey's claim to exercise sovereign rights over the continental shelf adjacent to certain Greek islands in the Eastern Aegean (see AR 1976, pp. 383-84). Greece and Turkey had both acceded to the General Act for the Pacific Settlement of Disputes, 1928, and according to the Applicant Article 17, read in conjunction with Articles 36(1) and 37 of the Court's Statute, conferred jurisdiction on the Court. Turkey, conforming to a practice which had become lamentably common of late, refused to appear before the Court to present its arguments, but did make its views known in a series of communications. It argued, first, that the General Act was no longer in force; alternatively, that even if it was still in force the rule contained in the Court's Statute that it has jurisdiction only if the parties to the dispute have accepted the same obligation precluded the Applicant from relying on the General Act, because in acceding to the General Act in 1931 Greece had excluded from its acceptance of jurisdiction 'disputes concerning questions which by international law are solely within the domestic jurisdiction of States, and in particular disputes relating to the territorial status of Greece, including disputes relating to its rights of sovereignty over its ports and lines of communication'. The Court, rejecting various Greek arguments, held that the present dispute did indeed fall within the exclusion of 'disputes relating to the territorial status of Greece' and that Turkey was entitled to invoke this reservation. To the evident chagrin of some members of the tribunal, it was consequently found unnecessary to decide the much-debated question whether the General Act is still in force.

The second basis of jurisdiction relied upon by Greece was a joint communique issued directly to the press by the Prime Ministers of the two countries on 31 May 1975, following their meeting in Brussels. The relevant paragraphs stated:

They [the two Prime Ministers] decided that those problems [between the two countries] should be resolved peacefully by means of negotiations and as regards the continental shelf of the Aegean Sea by the International Court at the Hague. They defined the general lines on the basis of which the forthcoming meetings of the representatives of the two Governments would take place.

In that connection they decided to bring forward the date of the meeting of experts concerning the question of the continental shelf of the Aegean Sea and that of the experts on the question of air space.

According to the Applicant, this constituted a definitive agreement directly conferring jurisdiction on the Court; the parties were committed to concluding any implementing agreement needed and, in the event of a refusal by one of them to do so, the other was entitled to refer the dispute unilaterally to the Court. Turkey maintained that the communique did not amount to an agreement under international law at all, let alone to an undertaking to resort to the Court without the special agreement (*compromis*) usual in such cases, or to an agreement by one state to submit to the Court's jurisdiction upon the unilateral application of the other.

Having regard to the background of negotiations against which the communique was issued, to its terms and context, and to the subsequent conduct of the parties, the Court concluded that there was no immediate and unqualified commitment to accept the unilateral submission of the dispute to it. It deliberately refrained from deciding whether the communique amounted to a binding obligation to conclude a *compromis* at a future date conferring jurisdiction upon it, adding that nothing it had said should be understood as precluding the dispute from being brought before it if and when the conditions for establishing its jurisdiction were met.

Five of the twelve judges forming the majority appended separate opinions or declarations in which they put forward additional or different reasons for coming to the same conclusion as the Court. Judges Gros and Morozov were even more negative than their brethren, the latter stating, and the former hinting, that the General Act of 1928 was not in force. On the other hand, three judges were somewhat more positive than the other members of the majority: Vice-President Nagendra Singh held that the Brussels communique constituted an obligation to negotiate in good faith for the peaceful settlement of the dispute and hinted that the Greco-Turkish Treaty of Friendship, Neutrality, Conciliation and Arbitration of 1930—which had not been relied on by Greece—could afford a basis for the exercise of jurisdiction by the Court if efforts to resolve the dispute by conciliation failed. Judge Lachs specifically found that the Brussels communique committed the parties to concluding a *compromis* conferring jurisdiction on the Court; Judge Tarazi agreed with Judge Lachs on this point, and broadly shared the view of Vice-President Singh of the possibilities under the treaty of 1930.

In his dissenting opinion, Judge de Castro held that the General Act of 1928 was still in force, and that the Greek reservation did not apply to rights over the continental shelf—rights which were not even claimed by states at the time it was made. Judge *ad hoc* Stassinopoulos agreed with this, adduced further reasons why the Greek reservation did not apply to the present dispute or why Turkey was not entitled to rely on it, and finally expressed the view that, in any event, the communique did amount to an agreement conferring jurisdiction on the Court.

On 31 October the United Nations Security Council and General Assembly re-elected Platon D. Morozov (USSR), and elected Roberto Ago (Italy), Richard R. Baxter (USA), Abdullah Ali El-Erian (Egypt) and Jose Sette Camara (Brazil) to vacancies on the Court.

On 1 December Tunisia, in pursuance of a special agreement (*compromis*) submitted to the Court a dispute with Libya concerning the delimitation of the continental shelf between the two states.

There was a curious sequel to the 1977 decision on the delimitation of the continental shelf between the United Kingdom and France by a specially constituted Court of Arbitration (see AR 1977, pp. 382-85). The UK alleged that there was a discrepancy between the principles on which the Award was based and the techniques used by the Court's expert for drawing the boundaries and embodied in the *dispositif* ('operative part') of the Award and in the accompanying boundary-line chart. In the first place, whereas the Court had decided that there should be a special continental shelf enclave around the Channel Islands extending to '12 miles from the established baselines of [their] territorial sea', the *dispositif* and the boundary drawn on the Chart ignored some of the relevant basepoints, resulting in discrepancies of up to $2\frac{1}{2}$ miles in favour of France. Secondly, it was claimed, in the South-Western Approaches the boundary line decided on by the Court had been incorrectly drawn on the chart and in the coordinates set out in the *dispositif*, since a standard Mercator projection had been used without allowing for the fact that, due to the Earth's curvature, it was not accurate for measuring horizontal distances on a long boundary line (170 miles) passing through different latitudes. The western terminus of the line on the chart was some 4 miles north of where it would have been had a geodesic line been used, as it should.

After dismissing various French arguments as to the admissibility of the application, the Court decided unanimously that, in respect of the Channel Islands boundary, there was a contradiction between what it had decided and what it had done, amounting to 'a "material error" analogous to one resulting from a "slip of the pen" or from miscalculation or miscasting of arithmetical figures' which it had the inherent power to correct, over and above the competence accorded it in the agreement setting it up to resolve disputes regarding the 'meaning and scope' of its original decision.

On the other hand, it dismissed by 4 votes to 1 the British claim concerning the South-Western Approaches. Although virtually conceding that the use of a geodesic would have been more accurate, it did not consider that the technique actually employed in drawing the line was 'either inadmissible in law or as yet so outmoded in practice as to make its use open, in general, to challenge'. Moreover, the original decision to give 'half-effect' to the presence of the Scilly Isles in the region by bisecting two equidistance lines, one of which took the Isles fully into account, while the other ignored them, 'was adopted by the Court as an equitable variant of the equidistance principle expressing a necessarily approximate appreciation of diverse considerations; and . . . the method for implementing it was devised as a modified rather than as a strict application of the equidistance method'. Accordingly it had not been established that there was such a discrepancy as to constitute a material error requiring rectification. Mr Herbert W. Briggs (USA) disagreed. He frankly admitted that the Court had not appreciated that the line drawn by its expert had omitted to take into account the Earth's curvature, and thought that rectification was both necessary and permissible. Sir Humphrey Waldock, the British arbitrator, indicated that it was only reluctantly that he had concurred with the majority on this point. He thought that the wrong method had been used to implement the basic decision. However, a majority of the Court had held that, even if it was open to them to review the techniques employed, this would entail a fresh examination of a whole variety of factors and techniques, which would go beyond their jurisdiction to interpret the Award and correct material errors. While he did not necessarily consider that anything more would have been entailed than the substitution of a geodesic line, he agreed that reopening the whole question of techniques of delimitation was beyond the Court's competence.

On 22 August a UN conference adopted the Vienna Convention on the Succession of States in Respect of Treaties. The Convention is based on a draft produced by the General Assembly's International Law Commission, and is designed to codify the law concerning the circumstances in which treaties applying to a particular territory are to continue in force when that territory becomes independent or is transferred to another state, or when states unite or separate. Under Part I, state succession is not to affect boundaries or boundary regimes established by treaty, 'other territorial regimes' established for the benefit of a foreign state (except agreements for the establishment of foreign military bases), or 'the principles of international law affirming the permanent sovereignty of every people and every state over its natural wealth and resources'. Part II provides that, in cases of succession in respect of a part only of a state's territory, treaties of the predecessor cease to be in force in relation to that territory and, with certain exceptions, are replaced by treaties of the successor. For newly independent states, Part III, broadly speaking, lays down the 'clean slate' principle, which allows them to choose whether or not to be a party to a predecessor's treaty; this is in contrast to Part IV which, with certain

N

exceptions, envisages the continuance in force of treaties in cases of succession caused by the uniting or separation of states. Part V contains miscellaneous provisions dealing with such matters as state responsibility, the outbreak of hostilities and military occupation. Provision is made in Part VI for the settlement of disputes by conciliation and other means.

A further session of the UN Conference on the Law of the Sea was held, the first part in the spring and the second in the summer. An attempt was made to reach agreement on seven 'hard-core' issues: deep sea-bed mining, financial arrangements, organs of the proposed International Sea-Bed Authority, access of land-locked and other states to fisheries in the 200-mile exclusive economic zone, dispute settlement in regard to coastal states' rights in that zone, the continental shelf, and maritime boundaries. No dramatic breakthroughs occurred. It was decided to continue negotiations in 1979.

One piece of British legislation of particular interest to international lawyers was the State Immunity Act, which entered into force on 22 November. The Act would enable effect to be given to the European Convention on State Immunity, 1972, as well as to the 1926 Brussels Convention for the Unification of Certain Rules concerning the Immunity of State-owned Ships and the 1934 Protocol thereto; however, it went beyond the scope of those conventions. Though the doctrine had been challenged in some recent judicial decisions (see, e.g. AR 1976, p. 385), the British courts had long adhered to a rule according absolute immunity from their jurisdiction to foreign States and their property. Along very broadly similar lines to the US Foreign Sovereign Immunities Act 1976 (see AR 1976, pp. 384-85), the British Act radically altered this. States would lose their immunity in respect of commercial activities, as opposed to those conducted in the exercise of sovereign authority; where there was a prior submission to the jurisdiction; and in regard to obligations under a contract to be performed in the UK, contracts of employment, personal injuries and damage to property, disputes relating to immovable property in the UK, ships used for commercial purposes, and so on. Special procedures were laid down for service of process and judgment in default, and various procedural advantages were accorded, notably immunity from enforcement of judgments save in limited instances. 'Separate entities' such as state-owned corporations would be immune only if they were acting in the exercise of sovereign authority and the parent state would, if sued, have been immune. Part II of the Act provided, with specified exceptions, for recognition by UK courts of judgments against the UK itself given by courts in states parties to the European Convention. Part III contained 'miscellaneous and supplementary provisions', including one non-routine section broadly assimilating the personal immunities of heads of state, their families and retinue to those enjoyed by the head of a diplomatic mission under the Diplomatic Privileges Act 1964.

EUROPEAN COMMUNITY LAW

The pace of Community law continued to accelerate rapidly. During 1978 the legislative spurt that was already noticeable in the previous year increased in momentum, the Court of Justice produced a good crop of major decisions, and many constitutional changes of fundamental importance reached a significant stage of development.

Constitutionally, the Community spent the year laying the basis for later events. Of these, the most radical was the agreement between the heads of government to set up a European Monetary System, which, however, had still not been brought into force at the end of the year (see pp. 447–50 and DOCUMENTS). The second great constitutional non-event was the preparation for direct elections to the European Assembly in 1979. The problems and fears over ratification and national implementation, which had occupied the scene the previous year, were all resolved early in 1978, except for some dying spasms in the Debré wing of the Gaullist party in France, and the date for the elections was fixed by the Council as June 1979. The voting system was left to each member state and varied from a pure constituency arrangement (one member for each geographical area— UK) to a single constituency comprising the whole national territory returning all 81 MPs (France); suffrage varied from the Irish system (all EEC nationals resident within the country) and the French (all French nationals anywhere) to the British (only UK nationals resident and present in the UK), through various intermediate solutions.

Thirdly, negotiations about enlargement of the Community reached a penultimate stage for Greece and an opening stage for both Spain and Portugal. One effect of this was a concern for the future political structure of the Community which, together with the earlier failure of the Tindemans report, led to the appointment at French initiative of 'Three Wise Men' (Robert Marjolin, Barend Biesheuvel and Edmund Dell) to 'consider what adaptations to the mechanisms and procedures of Community institutions are necessary in respect of and having regard to the Treaties, their institutional structures, the harmonious functioning of the Communities and progress towards European Union'. In August the President of the European Court of Justice had released to the press a memorandum proposing significant changes in the working of the Court to ease the burden of its increasing case load, and that had led to counter-proposals from a meeting of the Community's Ministers of Justice shortly afterwards, in which drastic curtailment of the Court's jurisdiction was proposed, especially in private cases.

Finally, constitutional issues of great doctrinal and political import surfaced, but were not resolved during the year, in two widely differing contexts. The 'fisheries dispute' between the UK and the EEC began the 'year of the 200-mile zone' with a ruling of the European Court that Irish no-trawl areas were discriminatory and so illegal. This was followed by severe political in-fighting in the Council meetings of the Agriculture Ministers on control of fishery resources; and the year ended with threats by the Commission to bring proceedings against the UK, alleging that several of its unilateral fishery conservation measures were illegal, and with the filing of an action against the UK by France, the first instance of an action brought before the European Court by one member State against another.

Parallel with this fight for control over the maritime waters round Europe, a serious debate over judicial and legislative sovereignty opened up as a result of two events. One was the judgment of the European Court in *Simmenthal* (*No. 2*), in which the Court reaffirmed the superiority of Community law over national law and asserted its direct and immediate enforceability even against the internal (Italian) constitutional rules requiring questions of validity and enforceability of national laws to be referred to the domestic constitutional court. The second was a thoughtful report by the House of Lords scrutiny committee on the use made by the EEC of Article 100 of the EEC Treaty on harmonization legislation, in which the question of a division of legislative powers between the Community and the member states was raised virtually for the first time in serious discussion of EEC constitutional theory.

It was followed by the beginnings of far-reaching debate in law journals and the general press, starting with a lengthy correspondence in *The Times* in the spring in which many of the leading constitutional law professors took part; the debate (which might come to be called the Diplock–Ehlermann controversy) was extended later in the year with an article in the *International and Comparative Law Quarterly* by another senior Commission official, Dr Ivo Schwarz (in charge of much of the Article 100 legislation), proposing a wide interpretation of Article 235 of the Treaty, which embodied the doctrine of 'implied powers' for the EEC. Hitherto in the Community the concept of states' rights had been promoted almost entirely on the political level. Now, for the first time, a respectable body of theoretical principle was beginning to be worked out.

It was probably no mere coincidence that this constitutional development was occurring at the same time as a vast increase in important Community legislation. The jeremiads of politicians and journalists at the apparent stagnation of the Community were wholly unjustified if one considered the legal realities. During 1978 it seemed as if the Community machine had passed through a barrier, and the Council enacted a number of laws which would probably be of the very greatest importance in years to come. These included the Third and Fourth Company Law Directives (on company mergers and company accounts respectively), discussion being far advanced on several others in the series; the Co-insurance Directive, imposing sex equality on national social security systems, the third of the Community's sex equality directives, which went much further than most previous national rules on the subject; and, of greatest potential importance, the final signing by the new member states of the 1968 Convention on Jurisdiction and Enforcement of Judgments—the European equivalent of the US 'Full Faith and Credit clause'—by which court judgments (on most matters) given in any part of the Community become automatically enforceable in all other parts.

The legal unity of the Community was further emphasized during the year by the entry into force of the Lawyers' Services Directive and the invention of a 'lawyers' identity card', partly to dramatize the fact and partly to facilitate the actual application of this freedom. For a limited number of lawyers this unity was stressed still further by the entry into operation of the European Patent Office in Munich, beginning a process of centralization of patent activity which was expected to grow over the years.

As for the European Court of Justice, it saw a marked rise in the number of cases referred to it, which reached a record total of some 250 for the year. It delivered one key judgment on dominant positions (*United Brands*) which was controversial but influential, and very shortly afterwards the Federal Court of Australia specifically adopted it as the basis for its own decision in *Trade Practices Commission* v. *Ansett Transport Industries (Operations) Pty Ltd* [1978] E.C.C. 340. In the *IBG* case the Court tempered the increasingly activist attitude of the Commission's anti-trust division (DG IV) by annulling the latter's decision holding BP guilty of abuse of a dominant position in confining petrol supplies to its regular customers during the OPEC oil crisis. In the *Isoglucose* case it confirmed its earlier approach (in the *Milk Powder* case) and held in a subtle judgment that Community legislation to protect its sugar producers by laying a tax on isoglucose manufacturers was disproportionate and void; on the other hand it dismissed a claim for damages arising out of the success of the plaintiffs in the *Milk Powder* case for lack of a sufficient causal connexion. The *Pigs Marketing Board* case gave the Court an opportunity to consider the validity of this unique form of regularizing agricultural marketing, holding it to be a hindrance to inter-state trade and so illegal (but without considering the anti-trust aspects); and in *Defrenne* (*No. 3*) it spelled out the implications of its earlier decisions to the effect that Article 119 of the EEC Treaty applies only to equal pay and does not cover other conditions of work. But since that last judgment the Sex Discrimination Directive came into force (in August); and, in so far as that has direct effect, litigants will, for the future, be able to rely on that rather than try to force Article 119 into inappropriate service.

One clear factor became increasingly apparent during the year. The Court of Justice has time after time held that, even though particular conduct may be outside the scope of existing Community law, it will be struck down if it has as its aim the partitioning of the Community market into its national components. This attitude, which is still being worked out by the Court, can be expected to have very important consequences for the future development of Community law and may well turn out to be the distinguishing feature of the 'Kutscher Court'.

Chapter 2

LAW IN THE UNITED KINGDOM

AN unusually large number of criminal cases reached the House of Lords in 1978. In *Nock*[1] the defendants had been convicted of a conspiracy to produce cocaine even though it was quite impossible to do so by the method employed. Their Lordships, disagreeing with the Court of Appeal, applied the principle adopted in the case of attempts in *Haughton* v. *Smith* (1975), thus preserving consistency in the inchoate offences. A course of conduct which was incapable of resulting in the commission of an offence could not amount to a conspiracy to commit it. One of the few decisions of the House to win the unanimous approval of criminals and lawyers alike[2] decided that the fact that a defendant charged with murder was 15 years old was a matter the jury could bear in mind when considering whether the prosecution had proved beyond reasonable doubt that he was not provoked. Three earlier cases on provocation were overruled and the new doctrine fits snugly the subjective approach to *mens rea* adopted in *Morgan* (1975).

The robust principle that 'a man should not be gaoled on an ambiguity' was applied in *Goodchild*[3] where it was held that it would be irrational and unjust to construe the Misuse of Drugs Act 1971 so as to convict a man of the serious offence of unlawfully possessing a cannabinol derivative when it was merely an unseparated constituent of the leaves and stalk of the plant. In an appeal from the Court of Criminal Appeal of Northern Ireland[4] the House approved the decision that a person may properly be convicted of aiding and abetting the commission of a criminal offence without proof of prior knowledge of the actual crime intended if he contemplated the commission of a crime of the same type by the principal and intentionally assisted him.

A 1930 decision of the Court of Criminal Appeal was overruled in April when the House decided that a wife was not a compellable witness against her husband in a case of violence to her by him.[5] The contrary view

---

[1] [1978] 3 W.L.R. 57.   [2] Camplin [1978] 2 All E.R. 168.
[3] [1978] 2 All E.R. 161.
[4] *D.P.P. for Northern Ireland* v. *Maxwell* [1979] Cr.L.Rev. 40.
[5] *Hoskyn* v. *Metropolitan Police Commissioner* [1978] 2 All E.R. 136.

of the court below had been that the public interest required that evidence of personal violence should be freely available to the court. In March the Court of Appeal had upheld the convictions of the editor and publishers of *Gay News* for blasphemous libel but quashed the suspended prison sentences.[1] An appeal was heard by the Lords in December and a full review of the law was expected in the New Year.

In civil matters their Lordships were less surefooted. In one remarkable decision the House divided 3-2 in favour of the view that where a rent review clause provided that a new rent should be the sum 'as shall be assessed as a reasonable rent for the demised premises for the appropriate period' the proper method of fixing rent required the valuer to include improvements paid for by the tenant.[2] In this case the tenant, who had spent £32,000 on improvements after a fire, had to pay not only interest on the money borrowed for the purpose but an increased rent as well. The contrary view of Lord Wilberforce would have produced a fairer result. Also by 3-2 the House, following a New Zealand decision, refused to extend the doctrine that a barrister is immune from actions for professional negligence in the management of litigation to cover pre-trial matters not intimately connected with the conduct of the plaintiff's case in court.[3]

The House also adopted its own variant of the *forum non conveniens* doctrine, extending its earlier decision in *The Atlantic Star* (1973). Where a Scotsman suffered injuries in Scotland the fact that his employer was an English company was not enough to entitle him to bring an action in England even though he might do better there.[4] Scotland was the natural forum. The same doctrine was also referred to where the House held that no jurisdiction existed to entertain actions to determine title to foreign land or for damage for trespass.[5] Their Lordships found it necessary to consider the effects of inflation when they approved guidelines for the assistance of judges when awarding interest on damages under the Fatal Accidents Act and in personal injuries actions.[6] The guidelines were applied when a woman doctor was awarded £243,000 for brain damage negligently caused during a minor operation.[7] The House also overruled a Court of Appeal decision which since 1962 had prevented the courts from awarding to persons who suffer injuries or disabilities which shorten their lives damages for loss of what they might have earned during their 'lost years'.[8]

Short shrift was given to Lord Denning's view that the Court of

---

[1] *R* v. *Lemon* [1978] 3 All E.R. 175.
[2] *Ponsford* v. *HMS (Aerosols) Ltd.* [1978] 2 All E.R. 837.
[3] *Saif Ali* v. *Sydney Mitchell & Co.* [1978] 3 All E.R. 1033.
[4] *MacShannon* v. *Rockware Glass Ltd.* [1978] 2 W.L.R. 362.
[5] *Hesperides Hotels* v. *Muftizade* [1978] 2 All E.R. 1168.
[6] *Cookson* v. *Knowles* [1978] 2 All E.R. 604.
[7] *Lim Poh Choo* v. *Camden and Islington Health Authority, The Times,* 8 July 1978.
[8] *Pickett* v. *British Rail Engineering Ltd., The Times,* 4 November 1978.

Appeal should be free to depart from an earlier decision if convinced that it was wrong. The rule is that with three limited exceptions that court is bound to follow its own decisions. Nor would the Lords alter the 'well and long established rule' that Hansard may not be referred to by counsel or relied upon by the court. But they agreed that a county court could grant an injunction excluding the respondent from premises when domestic violence was alleged, irrespective of his proprietary rights, thus overruling two Court of Appeal decisions. The unmarried applicant's licence to occupy the premises, unlike that of a married woman, was revocable but only after reasonable notice.[1] Since the concept of permanence was lacking, however, a woman's lover was not a member of her family and therefore not entitled to succeed her as statutory tenant under the Rent Acts.[2] Nor was a 'platonic' friend.[3] A licence to occupy was not a protected tenancy if the contrary intention was clearly expressed.[4]

Just before Christmas the Court of Appeal held that the National Union of Journalists had acted unlawfully and unreasonably in instructing journalists to black copy provided by the Press Association. Section 13 of the Trade Union and Labour Relations Act did not grant a blanket immunity to trade unions and before the blacking could be 'in furtherance of a trade dispute' it had to be shown objectively that it was reasonably capable of advancing the trade dispute. Some important pronouncements on damages were made in a case concerning pigs which had died as the result of being fed mouldy nuts from a hopper bought from the defendants.[5] The Court of Appeal examined the extent to which remoteness of damages principles in contract and tort are the same.

Women's rights were further extended in a case where a female counterhand in a betting shop was paid less than the men. The employers' contention that men should be employed at a higher wage because they might need to cope with trouble from customers was rejected by the Court of Appeal.[6] The Employment Appeal Tribunal held that a barmaid who was dismissed for refusing to obey an order not to serve coloured customers was entitled to claim compensation from her employers even though she had not personally been discriminated against.[7] To avoid absurd or unjust situations not intended by Parliament, Section 1 of the Race Relations Act should be construed as overriding any apparent limitations in subsequent sections.

In the administrative law field the Court of Appeal refused to extend the doctrine of estoppel (as applicable to statements by officials of plan-

[1] *Davis v. Johnson* [1978] 1 All E.R. 1132.

[2] *Helby v. Rafferty, The Times,* 5 May 1978.

[3] *Joram Developments v. Sharratt, The Times,* 8 May 1978.

[4] *Somma v. Hazelhurst, The Times,* 7 March 1978.

[5] *Parsons v. Uttley, Ingham & Co.* [1978] 1 All E.R. 525.

[6] *Shields v. E. Coomes (Holdings) Ltd., The Times,* 28 April 1978.

[7] *Zarczynska v. Levy, The Times,* 21 October 1978.

ning authorities) beyond the cases where powers had been delegated to officers or where formal procedural requirements had been waived. Thus an argument that statements made by its officers estopped an authority from denying that a company had an existing use right was rejected.[1] A particularly welcome decision was *Ex parte Germain*,[2] where the Court of Appeal, allowing an appeal from the Queen's Bench Division, held that disciplinary decisions of the Hull Prison Visitors under the Prison Acts were judicial in character and therefore subject to review by the High Court. In another case Megarry V.-C., drawing a distinction between application and forfeiture cases, held that the Boxing Board was under no duty to give reasons or to grant a hearing when refusing a boxing manager a licence.[3]

A clear case of fundamental breach of contract arose where the employee of a security firm hired to guard a factory deliberately burned it down.[4] Not surprisingly a limitation clause was ineffective to reduce the firm's liability! The prize for the most readable case of the year must, however, go to *Re Brocklehurst*[5], where a gift by an elderly wealthy and eccentric baronet of valuable shooting rights to a local garage proprietor was held not to be vitiated by undue influence.

Civil liberties cases of interest included on the one hand *Jeffrey* v. *Black*[6] and *R* v. *Francoisy*,[7] where the courts were prepared to admit evidence obtained in breach of the common law and the Judges' Rules, and on the other *Wershof*,[8] where damages were awarded to a solicitor for wrongful arrest and false imprisonment by the police, and *Jones*,[9] where a woman was held to be entitled to use reasonable force to resist unauthorized attempts to take her fingerprints. The 'ABC' trial under the Official Secrets Act (see p. 37) led to further calls for repeal of the Act and criticism of the role of the Attorney General in granting his consent for the prosecution. This trial had earlier given rise to contempt proceedings when the name of a witness, 'Colonel B', was published in defiance of a court ruling.[10]

In February liability for negligently caused antenatal injuries was admitted in *Williams* v. *Luff*,[11] and the vital importance of punctuation in wills was stressed in *In re Steel's Will Trusts*.[12]

[1] *Western Fish Products* v. *Penwith District Council, The Times*, 1 June 1978.
[2] *The Times*, 4 October 1978.
[3] *McInnes* v. *Onslow-Fane* [1978] 3 All E.R. 211.
[4] *Photo Production* v. *Securicar Transport* [1978] 2 L.L. Rep 1972.
[5] [1978] 1 All E.R. 767.
[6] [1978] 1 All E.R. 555.
[7] *The Times*, 23 June 1978.
[8] [1978] 3 All E.R. 540.
[9] [1978] 3 All E.R. 1098.
[10] *Attorney-General* v. *Leveller Magazine* [1978] 3 All E.R. 731.
[11] *The Times*, 14 February 1978.
[12] [1978] 2 All E.R. 1026.

In Parliament the Scotland and Wales Acts received the Royal Assent and dates for the referendums were set. The State Immunity Act, which came into force on 22 November, codified the restrictive immunity doctrine in the United Kingdom. Thus state activities which could equally be performed by trading corporations or private individuals were generally no longer immune from the jurisdiction of courts and tribunals. The Consumer Safety Act provided a half-way house between the traditional remedies provided by the Sale of Goods Act and the 'neighbour principle' of Donoghue v. Stevenson on the one hand, and the strict liability schemes proposed by the Royal and Law Commissions on the other. It was now generally simpler for an injured party to bring an action for breach of statutory duty under the 1978 Act than an action for negligence, and better remedies were provided than under the Sale of Goods Act. Section 16(2) of the Theft Act 1968 was replaced by a new Act which dealt with dishonestly obtaining services by deception and evading liability by deception, and created the offence of dishonestly making off without payment (bilking). The Civil Liability (Contribution) Act reformed and extended Section 6 of the Law Reform (Married Women and Tortfeasors) Act 1935, while the Suppression of Terrorism Act enabled the Government to ratify without reservation the 1977 European Convention which aimed to eliminate or restrict terrorists evading extradition by claiming their crimes to be political offences. The European Assembly Elections Act contained in Section 6 the novel constitutional restriction that Parliament must approve a treaty by legislation before it was ratified by the Crown.

The Judicature (Northern Ireland) Act provided for the constitution, jurisdiction and procedure of the Supreme Court of Northern Ireland, established a Crown Court, and amended the law relating to magistrates and county courts. A Matrimonial Causes Order amended the grounds upon which divorce and judicial separations were available in the province and the grounds on which marriages were void or voidable.

Exactly 100 years after Parliament first conferred a matrimonial jurisdiction on magistrates' courts, enabling them to make separation orders when a wife had been assaulted by her husband, the Domestic Proceedings and Magistrates' Courts Act abolished such orders and replaced them with protection orders by which a husband (or wife) could be evicted from the home if he (or she) had used violence against the other spouse or a child of the family. The Act also enabled magistrates to order payment of lump sums as well as periodical maintenance, and introduced a degree of specialization by requiring magistrates who sit in domestic courts to be members of specially selected and trained domestic panels.

XV THE ARTS

Chapter 1

OPERA

THE international nature of the opera world was reflected in the new works staged during 1978. The Hungarian composer Ligeti's *Le Grand macabre*, based on writings by the Belgian Ghelderode, was first given in Stockholm on 12 April; this grotesque comedy was enthusiastically received. The Polish composer Penderecki's *Paradise Lost*, to a libretto by Christopher Fry and described as a *sacra rappresentazione*, received its first performance in Chicago on 29 November; whether this complex and demanding work would enjoy more than a *succès d'estime* would become clear after planned European stagings. The first known Vietnamese opera, *My-Chau Trong-Thuy* by Nguyen Thien Dao (a pupil of Messiaen), was performed in Paris on 7 December, and its theme of conflict between Vietnam and China seemed strangely prophetic. The Hungarian Sandor Balassa's *Az ajton kivül* (*The Man Outside*), by a factory worker turned composer and based on a German novel, made a strong impression when given in Budapest on 20 October.

There were new operas in Brazil (*The Militia Sergeant* by Francisco Mignone, 15 December), Portugal (*En nome da paz* by Alvaro Cossuto, 12 March) and three in Finland, a country in the middle of an extraordinary operatic renaissance: on 10 March *Miehen Kylkilum* (*Man's Rib*) by Ilkka Kuusisto, a robust social comedy; on 14 June *Jaakko Ilkka* by Jorma Panula, on a historical subject and performed in the open air with a cast of 400, including many horses; and most notably *Punainen Viiva* (*The Red Line*), Aulis Sallinen's second opera. This inspiring work, about a peasant family at the time of Finland's first election in 1907, enjoyed a hugely successful premiere in Helsinki on 30 November. In Germany Aribert Reimann's *Lear* was launched on what would seem to be a successful career at the Munich Festival on 9 July.

Things were quieter in the United Kingdom. There were two new operas for children: Peter Maxwell Davies's *The Two Fiddlers* (Orkney, 16 June), an enchanting piece that stretched the capabilities of its young performers to but not beyond their limits, and *Through the Looking Glass, and What Alice Found There* by Wilfred Josephs (Harrogate Festival, August). Robert Sherlaw Johnson's *The Lambton Worm*, to a libretto by Ann Ridler based on a Northumberland folk tale, a well-crafted work deserving wider performance, was commissioned and performed by the Oxford University Opera Club in February.

Rising costs encouraged production-sharing. The Paris Opéra and La Scala, Milan, shared stagings of *Simon Boccanegra* and *Madama Butterfly*; costs for a new double bill of *Dido and Aeneas* and *Savitri* were shared by Scottish Opera and the Aix Festival; and the Zurich Opera's prestigious but stylistically dubious Monteverdi cycle toured to Vienna, Milan, Hamburg and Edinburgh.

Anniversaries included those of Vivaldi, Janáček and Schubert. Four of the Venetian master's reputed 94 operas were given either on stage or in concert form to general delight. There were Janáček cycles in Brno and Düsseldorf, and on 28 December the English National Opera mounted a busy new production of *The Adventures of Mr Brouček*, brilliantly conducted by Charles Mackerras. Performances of Schubert's intractable stage works were largely confined to the concert hall. The Hamburg State Opera celebrated 300 years of activity with many guest appearances, and 200 years of opera at La Scala were marked by an expanded and star-studded season. A less happy event in Italy was the dawn arrest of many distinguished opera-house administrators for allegedly contravening a law forbidding the use of artists' agents. The machinations leading up to this coup in June would, as many commentators remarked, make an ideal plot for an *opera buffa*.

Industrial disputes at the Coliseum once more disrupted the English National Opera's season. The new production of *Aida* and a proposed new *Fidelio* were postponed, and an excellent staging of Menotti's chorus-less *The Consul* (12 August) was added. The company mounted an economic but successful version of Verdi's *Il due Foscari* (4 May), and more spectacular productions of *Gianni Schicchi* (8 February), *The Seven Deadly Sins* (22 August) and a thoughtful new *Marriage of Figaro* produced by Jonathan Miller (22 November). An excellent staging by Anthony Besch of Martinů's surrealist opera *Julietta* was given by the New Opera Company in cooperation with the English National Opera on 5 April.

It was on the whole a quiet year at Covent Garden. Götz Friedrich's severely social-realist *Idomeneo* (9 March) was enlivened by Colin Davis's conducting and Dame Janet Baker's singing as Idamante; Filippo Sanjust's traditional *Luisa Miller* (19 June) was quietly successful, with a beautiful performance of the title-role by Katia Ricciarelli. Meyerbeer's *L'Africaine* was exhumed on 13 November; no expense was spared to suggest the necessary spectacle and vocal splendour, but many felt that the lumbering work scarcely justified the effort. Other notable events were a stunning series of performances by Jon Vickers in *Tristan und Isolde* during the summer, and the first-ever Prom *Ring* cycle, which attracted capacity audiences and much publicity. In both cases, Colin Davis confirmed his ever-growing skill as a Wagner conductor.

Outside London, the Arts Council showed remarkable faith in establishing English National Opera North in Leeds, the first full-scale company to be founded for over thirty years. Its opening productions of *Samson et Dalila* (15 November) and *Dido and Aeneas* and *Les Mamelles de Tirésias* (16 November) were wholly admirable, with the new chorus and orchestra coming in for special praise.

Scottish Opera's season was one of consolidation. The Welsh National Opera added to their admirable Britten cycle new stagings of *Let's Make an Opera, A Midsummer Night's Dream* and *Peter Grimes*, and offered two new productions by guest directors from East Germany. Harry Kupfer's *Elektra* (15 March) and Joachim Herz's *Madam Butterfly* (1 November), for all their powerful stagecraft, brought ideological glosses to bear that would have surprised the creators of these works. Less controversial but equally brilliant technically was David Pountney's production for the company of *The Makropoulos Case* (6 September), with the uniquely gifted Elisabeth Söderström in the title-role.

Mr Kupfer also surprised Bayreuth audiences by producing *Der fliegende Holländer* as a schizophrenic dream (25 July). Other notable festival stagings included Jean-Pierre Ponnelle's *Die Zauberflöte* (Salzburg, 28 July) and Peter Hall's *Così fan tutte* (Glyndebourne, 9 July). The Maggio Musicale, Florence, mounted an uncut production of *Les Vêpres Siciliennes* on 13 May, excitingly conducted by Riccardo Muti.

Internationally, the trend towards reassessment of French opera continued: relatively unknown works by Rameau, Gounod, Chabrier, Massenet and Thomas were revived world-wide, and in Europe the inexhaustible treasure chest of eighteenth-century *opéra-comique* was profitably rifled. Wagner's *Ring* was once more interpreted in socio-critical terms with productions in Stuttgart, Basle, Mannheim and Nuremberg.

The year's obituary list included the singers Alexander Kipnis and Willi Domgraf-Fassbaender, the administrators Norman Tucker, Edis de Philippe and Günther Rennert, the designer Leslie Hurry, and Jani Strasser, the Viennese répétiteur who virtually single-handed established and maintained the musical standards for which Glyndebourne is famous.

BALLET

The year saw Dame Ninette de Valois' eightieth birthday duly celebrated with many performances and parties in her honour. The centenary of the birth of Adeline Genée was marked by a special exhibition at the Victoria and Albert museum, but the bicentenary of the birth of Joe Grimaldi went unnoticed despite a remarkable resurgence of interest in clowns and mimes during the year.

Kenneth MacMillan, in his new role as chief choreographer of the

Royal Ballet, created an outstanding masterpiece with *Mayerling* (music by Liszt), with Lynn Seymour and David Wall as the unhappy lovers Mary Vetsera and the Crown Prince Rudolf. A special television version of this work subsequently won the Prix Italia. The company's new director, Norman Morrice, made the statesmanlike decision not to engage any guest artists during the season but to foster the talents of some of the younger dancers. The morale of the company rose considerably as a result, but some of its strength was lost when Anthony Dowell left to join American Ballet Theatre, Ann Jenner to join the Australian Ballet and Lynn Seymour to become director of the Munich Ballet. The company toured Korea and the United States. In the Sadlers Wells Royal Ballet a young choreographer, David Bintley, showed much promise with his ballet *The Outsider* (music by Bohac) and with other small pieces. London Festival Ballet (who moved into new premises near the Albert Hall) took New York and Washington by storm with Nureyev dancing in his new *Romeo and Juliet*, and they brought Tetley's *Greening* into their repertoire. The Dutch National Ballet (with Nureyev) and the West Berlin Ballet (with the Panovs) also danced in New York, which had now established itself as the world centre of ballet activity.

For his New York City Ballet (NYCB), Balanchine choreographed two new works, *Ballo della Regina* (music by Verdi) and *Kammermusik No. 2* (music by Hindemith), thereby proving that he had lost none of his creative activity. Furthermore he invited Mikhail Baryshnikov to leave American Ballet Theatre (ABT) (where he was replaced by Anthony Dowell) and join his company. Before he left ABT Baryshnikov mounted *Don Quixote* for them. Two outstanding young dancers emerged from NYCB—Merrill Ashley and Daniel Duell. For the Paris Opéra Ballet Yuri Grigorovich (director of the Bolshoi Ballet) choreographed a version of Prokoviev's *Romeo and Juliet* in a style that was so eccentric (and in his view 'modern') that not only was it a disaster but it so displeased the Russians that they stopped the modern production there of a Tchaikovsky opera lest it should dishonour the composer's name (possibly forgetting that they had banned Prokoviev's great ballet score when it was written). During the last few years there had been a great burgeoning of young French dancers— Dominique Khalfouni, Claude de Vulpian, Florence Clerc—and in 1978 they reached their peak, becoming *étoiles*. It was Violette Verdy's first year as director of the Paris Opéra Ballet, but within a few months she had decided to retire. The ballet scene in Paris (as in London and New York) was seriously disrupted by the activities of the stage-staffs' unions. The French 'modern' company, Ballet Théâtre Contemporain (which appeared at Sadlers Wells during the year), was about to be disbanded following a municipal election in the city where it was based (Angers) but it was quickly rehoused in Nancy, replacing a very good company, the Ballets de Lorraine (headed by Gheorghe Caciuleanu), who found a new home in Rennes.

In Glasgow, the Scottish Ballet invited Poul Gnatt to mount the complete Bournonville ballet *Napoli*, which proved an enormous success.

John Neumeier in Hamburg mounted his own version of *The Sleeping Beauty*, while in West Berlin Valerie Panov created a successful *Sacre du Printemps* and José Parès put on *Fille Mal Gardée* using the later Hertel score and danced by Eva Evdokimova. The controversial work of Pina Bausch at Wuppertal was seen at the Edinburgh Festival (it included her own *Sacre du Printemps*) and was universally praised by international critics. The National Ballet of Iran, under Ali Rourrfarokh, had just achieved international status by the excellence of its dancers and its interesting repertoire when the riots against the Shah (whose personal company it was) made it cease its activities and the dancers (mostly British and American) returned home. In Italy André Prokovsky put on a well-received *Sleeping Beauty* in Rome (but resigned soon afterwards) and a new company was started in Reggio Emilia by the ballerina Liliana Cosi and the Romanian star Marinel Stefanescu. This company, mostly of non-Italian dancers, toured Italy continuously throughout the year with *Don Quixote* and enjoyed some success.

Among the modern dance companies London Contemporary Dance Theatre and the Ballet Rambert consolidated their positions and toured widely, but there was an eruption of small groups and soloists, who were brought together in London at the end of the year in an 'Umbrella Festival' (a term common in America for a concentration of similar activities in one place and at one time). Many of the performances consisted of self-indulgent soloists 'doing their own thing' (to use their jargon), often without music and sometimes without even moving from one spot. However, it seemed immensely popular with a young generation which was now turning away from classical ballet (as being elitist and in any case too difficult)—a stratification of ideas which might soon make 'ballet' and 'dance' two entirely different art forms. Two groups seemed particularly noteworthy during the year—MAAS Movers (a team of Negro dancers) and Moving Picture Mime Show (three mimes). An amusing evening's entertainment devised by Maina Gielgud, *Steps, Notes and Squeaks*, showed back-stage ballet—Gielgud herself and Jonathan Kelly being rehearsed in a classical *pas de deux* by Svetlana Beriosova with sardonic comments from a disillusioned pianist (James Slater); it caught London's imagination and was subsequently filmed, televised, performed in the provinces and then had a season at the Espace Cardin in Paris.

An American film, with a ballet theme, *The Turning Point*, directed by former dancers Herbert Ross and Nora Kaye, had a deserved success all over the world. Acted by Anne Bancroft, Shirley MacLaine and a young dancer Leslie Browne, it showed the dancer's eternal conflict between marriage and a career, and it contained many excellent ballet sequences.

Of the many books published during the year Lincoln Kirstein's *Nijinsky Dancing* and Mary Clarke's and Clement Crisp's *Ballet in Art* were noteworthy. Among the deaths were those of Tamara Karsavina (see OBITUARY), Ludmilla Schollar, Professor Derra de Moroda, Dr Julian Braunsweg (founder of Festival Ballet), Yuri Slonimsky (the Russian critic), Romola Nijinsky and Alice Nikitina.

THE THEATRE

The British theatre has become even more like the equivalent of Two Nations: on the one hand the subsidized companies, large and small, some abundantly nourished, some half-starved, all of them prodigiously hard-working; on the other, the commercial managements, trying very hard, no doubt, but made more and more cautious by the huge financial risk involved. In 1978 it cost an independent management little short of £40,000 just to put on a far from lavish production, and its takings would have to be rather more than £10,000 a week if it was to break even. Add to this the Government's refusal to lift the crippling burden of VAT from theatre tickets, and the commercial theatre had every incentive to expire, sighing, with Oscar Wilde, that this is an expensive city to die in.

So it should cause no surprise that its contribution to the year's work was unremarkable and that it nourished itself on the products of subsidized companies. To begin with the most commercial fare of all—it was a poor year for musicals. Leslie Bricusse's new creation, *Kings and Clowns* (Phoenix), starring Frank Finlay, and his medley of old songs, *The Travelling Music Show* (Her Majesty's), starring Bruce Forsyth, both died quickly, with enormous loss of blood; and so, sadly, did Jule Styne and Jack Rosenthal's *The Barmitzvah Boy* (Her Majesty's). The one success was Andrew Lloyd-Webber's and Tim Rice's *Evita* (Prince Edward), in which Lloyd-Webber's cunningly apt music and an awe-inspiringly skilful production by Hal Prince rammed home a distasteful fairy tale about Eva Peron. Audiences flocked to it with innocent pleasure; but rarely can there have been a more unpleasant dish served up with greater culinary skill.

In the straight theatre Alan Ayckbourn resumed his annual progress through the West End with *Ten Times Table* (Globe), a viciously funny tale of little provincial egos eyeball-to-eyeball in conflict. It must be borne in mind, however, that all Ayckbourn's plays were written for and first produced in his own Stephen Joseph Theatre (and formerly his Library Theatre) in Scarborough which is, of course, subsidized. His London impresario, Michael Codron, to whom the commercial theatre owes a great deal of gratitude, bravely continued to support another of his regular authors, Simon Gray, whose *The Rear Guard* (Globe) and *Molly* (Comedy), starring Billie Whitelaw, were both more muted in tone than his earlier successes; both closed after short runs. (And behold! Gray's next play was to be produced by the National Theatre.)

Elsewhere in the West End Brian Clark scored a considerable critical and popular success with *Whose Life Is It Anyway?* (Savoy), in which Tom Conti gave a virtuoso performance as a patient facing death. But this production, too, first opened at the Mermaid (subsidized). From the Nottingham Playhouse (subsidized) came Tennessee Williams's new play, *Vieux Carré*, to the Piccadilly with a raucously authentic performance by Sylvia Miles in a return to Mr Williams's earlier style—which was welcome news for those who like Mr Williams's earlier style. Michael Hastings's hilarious *Gloo Joo* (Criterion), a sharp comedy about the vagaries of racial attitudes, first saw the light at the Hampstead Theatre Club (subsidized). *Alice's Boys*, a thriller by Felicity Browne and Jonathan Hales, was a swift failure at the Savoy despite the presence of Sir Ralph Richardson and Lindsay Anderson as star and director. By contrast, Harold Pinter's icily brilliant *Homecoming*, not usually regarded as popular fare, had a run of nearly six months at the Garrick under Michael Codron's management, masterfully directed by Kevin Billington and with Gemma Jones and Timothy West turning in grippingly intelligent performances. And Tom Stoppard, who had mostly been writing for the Royal Shakespeare or the National, pitched his tent in the West End with *Night and Day* (Phoenix), a mordantly funny tale of the ethics of journalism starring Diana Rigg and John Thaw. This is not Stoppard's best play; but he has the gift of being able to write both for tired businessmen and for agile philosophers, and if the commercial theatre can still get away with such a play then perhaps there is life in it yet.

Otherwise the year in the West End was remarkable for the continuing survival of *Jesus Christ Superstar* and *Ipi Tombi* as well as *No Sex Please, We're British* and *The Mousetrap*; and for two lavishly presented plays, both about Dracula, running almost concurrently and with movie stars (George Chakiris and Terence Stamp) in the lead. Both died prematurely, bleeding heavily, presumably, from the neck.

In the subsidized theatre proper the main event of the year took place in Stratford-upon-Avon. This was the return, after an eight-year absence, of Peter Brook to the Royal Shakespeare Company with a new production of *Antony and Cleopatra*. One wishes one could say it was worth waiting for; but in truth the great man demonstrated all the evils of applying the thinking mind instead of theatrical flair to such a gaudy and tempestuous play. It may seem strange, in this day and age, to make such a criticism, and to make it of Peter Brook of all people; but nothing else can account for the bleak tedium of this production, the perversely subdued tone of most of the acting, and the grimly un-erotic central performances given by

Alan Howard and Glenda Jackson. It does not seem, however, to be just an aberration on Brook's part. He brought to the Young Vic his Paris production of Jarry's *Ubu*, which also turned out to be a pale copy of its original. Brook seemed to be putting into practice the theory expounded in his book *The Empty Space*, which says, roughly, that a director ought not to take sides but let the text speak for itself. This principle brings forth results which negate rather expand the principle of theatre. It is not that the emperor wears no clothes but that he has abdicated.

The RSC were, by and large, more successful with their classical revivals than with their new plays. At the Aldwych David Mercer had a qualified success with *Cousin Vladimir*, while Steve Gooch's *The Women Pirates Ann Bonney and Mary Reed* was an unqualified disaster. At their London studio theatre, the Warehouse, the company put on Edward Bond's *The Bundle*, which showed the playwright in his most bleakly admonitory mood in a play of intermittent theatricality and dubious political honesty. Pete Atkin's *A & R*, more limited in scope, had more life and conviction, as did Barrie Keeffe's *Frozen Assets* and Howard Barker's *The Hang of the Gaol*. Stephen Poliakoff's *Shout Across the River*, though splendidly acted, made one look forward anxiously to his next play.

Go back a few centuries, however, and this company was to be found in much better shape. At the Aldwych, Trevor Nunn's production of Ben Jonson's *The Alchemist* was one of the best Jonsonian evenings in this critic's experience, in which Ian McKellen and John Woodvine gave performances of inspired dementia. Congreve's *The Way of the World*, directed by John Barton, was a tough, unsparing comedy with first-rate acting from Michael Pennington, Judi Dench and Beryl Reid. The same director was responsible for the jewel of the company's Stratford season, a thoughtful and hilarious production of *Love's Labour's Lost*, starring Michael Hordern, Michael Pennington and Jane Lapotaire. The same actress scored a remarkable success, in Stratford's studio theatre, in Pam Gems's new play, *Piaf*. And the RSC brought the year to an exquisite close with their exhumation of Bronson Howard's American comedy of dubious manners, *Saratoga* (Aldwych), in which television star Denis Waterman returned to the stage with a sparkling comic performance.

The National Theatre made a grim start with an over-anglicized and heavy-handed version of Ferenc Molnár's *The Guardsman*; the mannered acting of Diana Rigg and Richard Johnson took away any sense of reality left by Peter Wood's flamboyant production. Chekhov's *The Cherry Orchard*, directed by Sir Peter Hall, improved the picture, Albert Finney's Lopakhin exuding more subtlety and humanity than this actor had given us for some time. It was a pity that he and Sir Peter followed this up with a *Macbeth* which was remarkable for a hideously old-fashioned sense of style and a standard of acting that would have been questionable in a regional repertory theatre.

Christopher Morahan's production of Ibsen's *Brand*, on the other hand, was a triumph of intelligent direction and acting (especially by Lynn Farleigh, and by Michael Bryant in the title role) over difficult material. It also displayed the stage machinery of the Olivier Theatre to stunning advantage. David Hare's *Plenty* marked this young writer's debut at the NT: a tough, passionate, flawed and thought-provoking play with acting by Stephen Moore which overshadowed everyone else. Edward Bond, too, made his NT debut with *The Woman*, an eloquent but heavy-handed allegory on the evils of war based on Greek legend. The year was brought to a triumphant close. Christopher Morahan's production of Galsworthy's *Strife* was a masterpiece of muscular realism; and Peter Wood's direction of Congreve's *The Double Dealer* was in the finest tradition of modern Restoration style, both tough and sparkling. Michael Bryant was the star of both these plays, taking two utterly different roles with effortless virtuosity and intelligence. Finally, Harold Pinter's new play, *Betrayal*, directed again by Sir Peter Hall, was a sombre, unsentimental and moving account of adultery, cunningly crafted, bleak and grimly funny: the master's voice.

The year saw the promising growth of Riverside Studios in Hammersmith, living on a perilous budget under the direction of Peter Gill. The best of their work was a brilliantly idiosyncratic account of *The Cherry Orchard*. The Royal Court gave London three new playwrights: Bill Morrison, author of *Flying Blind*, an unforgettably harrowing and comic play of Belfast life; Leigh Jackson, who wrote the sensitive and promising *Eclipse*, an anatomy of the British colonial mind; and Nigel Williams, whose *Class Enemy*, set in a London comprehensive school, was a blistering but deeply human picture of working-class life. The RSC set up a small touring company headed by Ian McKellen, which visited many small towns that never see first-class theatre. (National, please note.) The tiny Half Moon Theatre in Aldgate, housed in a converted synagogue, made a brilliant contribution to the Anglo-German season, '20s meet the 70s', with Brecht's *Arturo Ui* and Ernst Toller's apostolic-Expressionist play *The Machine Wreckers*. And the year saw works by a new wave of young American playwrights. Thomas Babe's *Prayers for my Daughter* (Royal Court), David Rabe's *Sticks and Stones* (New End, Hampstead) and *Streamers* (Roundhouse) and David Mamet's *American Buffalo* (National, Cottesloe) all spoke with memorable and individual voices that one would like to hear again.

The New York Theatre

Although for years the division between Broadway and Off-Broadway had been decreasing, in 1978 George Abbott, with 65 years and 118 Broadway productions behind him, directed at the active and successful

Hudson Guild Theatre. The demarcation became merely geographical, and not consistently so at that. Regrettably the production, *Winning*, was weak, but the Guild, under the artistic direction of Craig Anderson, throve and planned to move two past productions to Broadway.

Despite inflationary ticket prices, larger audiences flocked to the theatres than ever before. The fare they encountered was often meagre. Outstanding among the better works was the Irish play, moved from the Hudson Guild, *Da* by Hugh Leonard, starring Bernard Hughes who crowned a distinguished career with his Tony Award performance—other 'Tonys' went to the playwright and director Melvin Bernhardt.

Another outstanding performance was that of James Earl Jones as *Paul Robeson*, a solo performance of stunning range and power. Solo performances studded the season—Vincent Price as Oscar Wilde, Emlyn Williams as Saki, Donal Donnelley as George Bernard Shaw, and Alec McCowen delivering *The Gospel of St Mark*.

The stage also had a welcome return of stars too long absent—Henry Fonda in *First Monday in October* (the date set by law for the opening of the Supreme Court sessions), concerning the appointment of the first woman judge to that body. Other performances were set within inferior material—John Wood could not redeem Ira Levin's *Deathtrap*; Jack Lemmon, despite his redoubtable appeal and skills, could not conceal the weaknesses of Bernard Slade's tale of a professional comedian confronting his terminal illness in *Tribute*; Mary Martin's perennial charm was overwhelmed by the heavy-handed *Do You Turn Somersaults?* of Alexei Arbuzov; Shelley Winters did not manage to refresh the dated *Effect of Gamma Rays on Man in the Moon Marigolds*; nor could the combined skills of three towering professionals, Claudette Colbert, Rex Harrison and George Rose, salvage William Douglas Home's *The Kingfisher*.

Revivals of musicals continued—*Hello Dolly* with Carol Channing (the original Dolly); *Timbuktu*, an adaptation of the former *Kismet*, notable for the return of that dynamic star Miss Eartha Kitt. Musical biographies abounded—*Mahalia* (Jackson); *Sparrow* (Ethel Waters); *Eubie* (Blake, the black composer); and *Aint Misbehavin'*, a collage of the *oeuvre* of Fats Waller, which had a cast of five of such infectious delight and energy that it too earned a 'Tony'. Elizabeth Swados, known chiefly as a composer of incidental music for Peter Brook, Andrei Serban and others, wrote, composed and directed *Runaways*, a moving series of personal tales of young and old people who had fled their homes; it is gripping for one act, but the lack of development palls, as art imitates life too insistently. Betty Comden and Adolph Green adapted the Hecht-MacArthur hit of the 1920s into *On the Twentieth Century*, which was thoroughly professional, but could be the only musical on record where the audience leaves the theatre 'humming the scenery', ingeniously designed by Robin Wagner. An agreeable musical with a provocative title, *The Best Little Whorehouse in Texas*, proved durable. Some notable failures were *Platinum*, redeemed somewhat by the allure of Alexis Smith; *Ballroom*, in which Michael Bennett, using a format similar to his *Chorus Line*, dealt with some aging dancers to far less dramatic effect; *A Broadway Musical* tried to depict the mounting of such a work, but was not saved by the doctoring skill of Gower Champion; Bob Fosse's *Dancin'*, which tried to present an evening of theatrical and social dance without a book, evolved ultimately into a mere recital without focus.

The continued industriousness of both new and long-established groups which presented a few major works and large numbers of secondary but worthy ones must be commended, such as, notably, The Public Theatre's productions of *Drinks Before Dinner* by E. L. Doctorow, starring Christopher Plummer; Gretchen Cryer's (book, lyrics and leading performance, music by Nancy Ford) *I'm Getting My Act Together and Taking it on the Road*; Andrei Serban's evening of Molière farces; the same director's adaptation of Mikhail Bulgakov's novel, *The Master and Margarita* (in Moscow, or *The Gospel According to the Devil*) is a complex and perhaps over-ambitious project, but nonetheless a further example of this director's brilliance; and yet another work by the prolific David Mamet, *The Water Engine*. Bulgakov has been honoured by another distinguished production at the Collonades Theatre, an adaptation of *A Cabal of Hypocrites*, retitled *Molière in Spite of Himself*. *The Biko Inquest*, by Norman Fenton and Jon Blair about the African leader, starred Fritz Weaver heading a distinguished cast. Joe Orton's first play, *The Ruffian on the Stair*, was presented by Theatre Genesis. The San Francisco Mime Troupe, a visiting company which does speak, offered another moving social comment from its leftist viewpoint, *False Promises/Nos/Now Enganaron*. And New York had a 300-year-old world premiere, *The Country Gentleman*, by Sir Robert Howard and George Villiers, second Duke of Buckingham. It proved to be not quite a first-rate play, and, while one can admire the energy of the producers in tracking it down, it was a further reminder that New York managers were straining to find good material for the ever-increasing numbers of theatregoers.

MUSIC

In the creative sense it was an uneventful year for music, such new works as came along exerting a minority interest for the hour and then fading into the background. Peter Maxwell Davies attracted the most attention by composing a symphony in spite of having dismissed the form as obsolete several years previously. He showed the extent of his conversion by producing a work lasting just under an hour, though breaking with traditional symphonic structure in many respects. Premiered by the

Philharmonia Orchestra conducted by Simon Rattle, it certainly offered a stimulating experience, notably in the technical juggling with thematic material, the speed at which elaborate musical development was carried out, and the complexity of its mixed metres and cross-rhythms. It was disappointing, however, to find that the elaborate tuned percussion section, designed 'to carry as much of the thematic and harmonic argument as any other section', was scarcely audible. The eye might see its importance in the printed score, but the ear was denied its contribution in performance.

The curious fact that works written in the 'universal language' of music take longer to travel the world than they did a century ago was exemplified by the case of Sir Michael Tippett's Fourth Symphony. This work by Britain's senior composer was not heard in London, at a Promenade Concert, until a year after its premiere in Chicago. The playing of the Chicago Symphony Orchestra under Sir Georg Solti was breathtakingly brilliant, as indeed it needed to be in such adventurous music, so the event was well worth waiting for. It seemed odd, on the other hand, that British concertgoers had to wait at all.

Two other British composers proved that the symphony is still a valid challenge to creativity. John McCabe's Third, which was exotically coloured—unlike the themes by Haydn and Nielsen on which it was based—gripped the attention when expertly played by the Royal Philharmonic Orchestra under Charles Dutoit. Anthony Milner's Second, though more soberly scored, also made a warm lyrical appeal, especially in its settings for tenor (John Elwes) of poems by Hopkins. This was premiered by the Royal Liverpool Philharmonic Orchestra conducted by Meredith Davies. The City of Birmingham Symphony Orchestra presented a less formal new work, John Joubert's *Deplorations for Orchestra*, a tribute to the memory of Benjamin Britten, which Vernon Handley conducted with a keen sense of the sorrow expressed in tautly constructed music.

Festivals produced a crop of novelties, most of them displaying skilful craftsmanship as well as imagination, yet none made any progress as general repertoire pieces. At Cheltenham there were Peter Racine Fricker's tightly structured *Anniversary for Piano* (Colin Kingsley); Phyllis Tate's *Scenes from Kipling*, three straightforward yet atmospheric songs for baritone (Peter Knapp); and Iain Hamilton's *Cleopatra*, a dramatic scena for soprano (Lois McDonall) which effectively portrayed the Egyptian queen's grief at Antony's betrayal, her recollection of past happiness and her yearning for his return. Bath presented Hugh Wood's Third String Quartet and Robin Holloway's *Hymn for Voices*.

The tercentenary of the birth of Vivaldi made 1978 a bonus year for violinists, the Venetian contemporary of Bach and Handel having composed several hundred concertos for their instrument. The most popular collection, *The Four Seasons*, turned full cycle almost daily, while other works, some of them forgotten for centuries, were featured in concerts, on the radio and in recordings. Phonogram alone brought out ten box-sets comprising a grand total of forty-eight records. Celebrations of other anniversaries had often made it clear that works by a major composer which had fallen into neglect deserved their fate because they were below his usual standard, but in the case of Vivaldi it became evident that his creative drive operated at a consistent level. That certain of his works had become widely popular while the vast majority had been forgotten was the result of mere chance, selectivity being inevitable in the work of so prolific a composer.

The sesquicentenary of Schubert's death brought no such surprises, since the bulk of his music is so familiar, though the year saw many performances of his works prepared with more than usual care. A third composer, Anton Webern, came into the limelight by sheer accident. The massive biography by Hans Moldenhauer was published in English by Gollancz at the same time as the CBS release of the first of two sets of recordings of Webern's complete works conducted by Pierre Boulez and a series of concerts of his entire works by the London Sinfonietta. A key figure in twentieth-century music, Webern had never before made such an impact in Britain.

It was also a year for the piano and the pianist. The British company of Broadwood, ironically founded by a Swiss, celebrated its 250th anniversary and declared that it had maintained all its old traditions apart from the acceptance of its first girl apprentice. The first John Broadwood invented the sustaining pedal, the second presented Beethoven with a piano which is still maintained in playing order in a Prague museum, and the family remains in control of the business in the person of Stewart Broadwood. The house of Bösendorfer, though a century younger, enjoyed more lavish publicity because its anniversary occurred during the Vienna Festival. A gala concert was given by the Vienna Philharmonic Orchestra, with Horst Stein conducting and Paul Badura-Skoda as soloist, and there were speeches and presentations. The Bösendorfer, which was made famous by Liszt, is the Rolls Royce of pianos. Each instrument is individual in quality, so that it can be made to any pianist's exact specifications. The firm's output is accordingly limited: it produces about 600 grand pianos a year, whereas the Japanese firm of Yamaha produces 22,000 and Steinway 7,000.

Vladimir Horowitz, still without rival as a keyboard virtuoso, celebrated the fiftieth anniversary of his New York debut in sensational style, playing Rachmaninov's Third Piano Concerto at Carnegie Hall to an audience made up of the world's musical élite. The performance was recorded live for the enjoyment of lesser mortals. A recital for President Carter and guests at the White House was shown world-wide on television, but even this was not enough. Since Horowitz refuses to travel, the mountain was taken to Mahomet: a Carnegie Hall recital was given exclusively for the pianist's admirers abroad, a project involving international package deals covering round-trip air fares and hotel accommodation. The new star to appear on the musical scene, 22-year-old Andrei Gavrilov, was inevitably acclaimed as 'the new Horowitz'.

The musician who most successfully carried classical music beyond its normal frontier was the flautist James Galway, who became the idol of millions of television viewers who would not otherwise watch a programme of serious music, and whose recordings soared to the top of the popular charts. In search of a new flute concerto, he commissioned a work from Joaquín Rodrigo, whose *Concierto de Aranjuez* had long been a favourite with all classical guitarists. The Spanish composer obliged with an agreeable *Concierto Pastoral*, combining melodic fluency with opportunities for virtuoso display. Though a work of minor significance, it was enthusiastically received at its London premiere and was recorded by Galway and the Philharmonia Orchestra a few days later.

In an attempt to popularize a less romantic instrument, an international double bass competition was held in the Isle of Man. The winner, Jiri Hudek from Czechoslovakia, surprised even the panel of judges, all double bass players themselves, by the ravishingly warm tones he drew from an instrument usually regarded as the joker in the orchestral pack. He was further rewarded with a concerto composed by Richard Rodney Bennett, though this proved a disappointing work unworthy of the player's remarkable talent.

Groups performing early music on ancient instruments, either original or accurate reconstructions, continued to develop as something of a cult. Several new ensembles were formed, though the Academy of Ancient Music remained in the forefront. This group, under its director Christopher Hogwood, embarked on an ambitious project for the Decca record company. In association with the American musicologist Neal Zaslaw, it began recording the complete cycle of Mozart symphonies in accordance with the performing techniques and practices of the eighteenth century. This was yet another example of the important role played by the gramophone in extending musical horizons. Opportunities to hear Mozart symphonies in their original style in the concert hall would be limited to a few major cities of the world, whereas recordings would be readily available everywhere.

Again it would seem that the musical world looked back on the past rather than towards the future. However regrettable it might be, the fact remains that there was no narrowing of the gap between the contemporary composer and the general musical public, and with the death of Aram Khachaturian (see OBITUARY) there survived less than a handful of composers whose new works could be expected to fill a large concert hall. A detailed survey of concert-hall attendances in London, Paris, Berlin, Rome,

Moscow and New York revealed that only one living composer enjoyed a place among the ten box-office favourites. This was Hans Werner Henze, and he held his position only in Berlin.

THE CINEMA

In the difficult economic climate of the 1970s, the film industry can be said to have held its own remarkably well, integration increasing each year between the cinema and television as complementary production and exhibition outlets. As an indication of success, Hollywood received during 1978 its best collective gross for many years; speaking in September, Jack Valenti, President of the Motion Picture Association of America, said: 'The American film industry is thriving this year', with $2,400 million invested in production, of which $500 million was involved in films being made abroad, including Britain and Canada. The latter country was now established as a thriving new centre of production, not only with indigenous product but with $15 million of US production as well. Canadian tax legislation being easier than that in the USA, Canada was seen by some experts as due to become a new Hollywood.

Some 70 per cent of American films were the product of independent producers, as compared with 50 per cent five years back. The US was producing some 300 independent features a year, compared with 70 from the 'major' companies, which tended to specialize in high-budgeted spectaculars, their return representing 85 per cent of the US box-office: *Star Wars* grossed $200 million in 63 weeks, and as a result *Star Wars II* entered production at Elstree in Britain during the year. Hitherto unheard-of sums were invested in spectacular productions: $25 million for Francis Ford Coppola's Vietnam war film, *Apocalypse Now*, $50 million for *Superman I and II*, the first being made in Britain, Canada and the USA, the second based on Britain during the final months of the year. The rarer stars such as Marlon Brando, Clint Eastwood, Burt Reynolds, Robert Redford and Jack Nicolson earned as much as $2 million for each film.

British studios (led by Pinewood, EMI Elstree and Shepperton) were involved successively with around twelve productions throughout the year. Lord (Lew) Grade headed the British producers; during the summer he announced he would finance 18 films at a total cost of some $120 million, and he established in the US a new Anglo-American company, Associated Film Distribution Corporation (AFD), to distribute his product. Interest in Britain continued to centre on the future establishment of a government-initiated Film Authority, as recommended in January in an interim report of the committee of enquiry into the film industry chaired by Sir Harold Wilson. The film union (the Association of Cinematograph, Television and Allied Technicians) and the TUC strongly supported the creation of the proposed Authority, but the Minister responsible for film said in April that time for proper consultation must be allowed before any necessary Bill could be proposed. The 270-strong Independent Film-makers' Association, representing most of the new generation of producers, remained extremely critical of the Wilson proposals.

Production remained healthy in France, with a total of 190 features completed in 1977. Nevertheless, Claude Degand of the French National Film Centre declared in September that the American share in exhibition in France had increased to 30·5 per cent in 1977, a percentage virtually the same as that in Italy, while in West Germany the figure had gone as high as 41·1. Annual cinema attendance presented some interesting contrasts: 8 visits per head of population in Italy, 3·3 in France, but only 2 in Britain and West Germany, the two countries with the highest-quality television in Europe.

After the resounding success of the spectacular *Star Wars*, other similar films were *Dark Star* (John Carpenter) and *Close Encounters of the Third Kind* (Steven Spielberg), but the most marked subject innovation in America was in retrospective films about the Vietnam war—*Tracks* (Henry Jaglom), *Coming Home* (Hal Ashby), *Heroes* (J. P. Kagan), *Go Tell the Spartans* (Ted Post) and the English director Karel Reisz's *Dog Soldiers*, all expressing disillusion, while in contrast *MacArthur the Rebel General* (Joseph Sargent, with Gregory Peck) traced that officer's career with distinct admiration.

Disillusion also emerged from a further genre, the films of psychological interest: Diane Keaton's self-destructive heroine in *Looking for Mr Goodbar* (Richard Brooks), Gena Rowlands's aging actress in John Cassavetes's *Opening Night* and Jill Clayburgh's study of a deserted wife in search of independence in Paul Mazursky's impressive *An Unmarried Woman*. *Interiors*, Woody Allen's wholly serious and excellently acted family study (with Diane Keaton, Geraldine Page, E. G. Marshall, Maureen Stapleton) was thought by some very inappropriately to be 'poor man's Bergman'. Only the low-budget Canadian film, *Outrageous*, managed to make a virtue out of mental disturbance, while another low-budget American film, *Girlfriends* (Claudia Weill), offered a most sympathetic study of an unattractive girl suffering from loneliness.

Violence due to racial tension was shown in a Puerto Rican community in America in *Saturday Night Fever* (John Badham) and in a West Indian area of London's Notting Hill in *Pressure* (Horace Ové). The crime films of the year were headed by Clint Eastwood's *The Gauntlet*, portraying the rehabilitation of a demoralized policeman, and showing Eastwood to be at least as good a director as actor. Dustin Hoffman portrayed the decline into violent crime of a prisoner on parole in Ulu Grosbard's *Straight Time*, while a total dedication to the depiction of violence in a revolting manner occurred in the British film, *Midnight Express* (Alan Parker), exploiting to the full the horrors of a Turkish prison. Michael Crichton's *Coma* dealt with murder under the guise of hospital treatment, Paul Schrader's *Blue Collar* exposed embezzlement and murder through union corruption, while *F.I.S.T.* (Norman Jewison) showed the violent establishment of a union during years going back to the 1930s.

More experimental themes were portrayed in *Damien Omen II* (Don Taylor) and in Jerzy Skolimowski's *The Shout*, an improbable story of death dealt by a terror-shout of aboriginal origin. Other unusual subjects included two Australian films, *Newsfront* (Phillip Noyce), presenting the social history of Australia in the 1950s as experienced by two rival newsreel companies, and *Mad Dog* (Philippe Mora) about the legendary career of an outlaw a century ago. Phillip Noyce was also responsible for *Backroads*, while the outstanding Australian director, Peter Weir, made *The Last Wave*, another film of aboriginal magic. From Britain came an imaginative satiric fable, *Jubilee* (Derek Jarman), about contemporary England as revealed by the angel Ariel to Elizabeth I.

Good comedies were rare. Mel Brooks produced one of his frenetic burlesques in *High Anxiety*, and Robert Altman's *A Wedding* showed a *nouveau riche* Southern family assembled in wholly incongruous and damaging circumstances at a wedding. Sam Peckinpah in *Convoy* returned to ironic good humour in this fable about a group of truckers seeking freedom from authoritarian pressure. Animated cartoon features were in evidence with Martin Rosen's *Watership Down*, Ralph Bakshi's *Wizards*, René Goscinny's and Albert Uderzo's *The Twelve Tasks of Astérix*, and Richard Williams's *Raggedy Ann and Andy*. So, too, were feature documentaries, of which the more notable were, from America, the Maysles' *Running Fence*, the Mariposa Film Group's *Word is Out* (investigating homosexuality), Barbara Kopple's *Harlan County USA* (recording a miners' strike in Kentucky), and two outstanding films celebrating and evaluating rock music, Martin Scorsese's *The Last Waltz* and Bob Dylan's *Renaldo and Clara*. Yet another biographical study of Hitler (*Hitler, a Career*) came from West Germany, made by the historian, Joachim Fest, while in Britain the Arts Council sponsored their most ambitious film to date, *Europe after the Rain* (Mick Gold), an investigation of Dada and Surrealism. Peter Watkins was responsible for a monumental, obsessive, almost three-hour-long biographical study, *Edvard Munch*.

Among the foreign-language films to be shown in Britain, France produced outstanding work from well-established directors: Robert Bresson's *The Devil, Probably*, Alain Resnais's *Providence* (made in English with John Gielgud and Dirk Bogarde), François Truffaut's *The Man who Loved Women* and Claude Chabrol's *Blood Relatives* (also in English), as well as Buñuel's *That Obscure Object of Desire* and Borowczyk's *The Beast*. The exceptional productivity of Fassbinder topped the films from West Germany (*Effi Briest*, *The American Soldier*, *Gods of the Plague*, *Chinese*

Roulette, Love is Colder then Death and *Despair*—the last made in English with Dirk Bogarde—films representing work going back to 1969). Two German-sponsored films of exceptional interest were made in English, Bergman's *The Serpent's Egg* and Wim Wender's *The American Friend*, while Herzog's *Stroszek* was partly in English, with some action set in America. From Italy came the late Luchino Visconti's last film, *The Innocent*, and two remarkable historical films, Bertolucci's *1900* (made in two parts) and the Tavianis' *Allonsanfàn*. *Iphigenia*, Cacoyannis's very free adaptation of Euripides' *Iphigenia in Aulis*, was his most ambitious and spectacular rendering of Greek classical tragedy yet. From Japan came four most notable films, Kurosawa's Russian film, *Dersu Uzala*, Terayama's *Throw Away Your Books, Let's Go into the Streets*, Shindo's *The Life of Chikuzan* (a Shamisen player) and the much-debated film of obsessive sexuality, *The Empire of the Senses* (*Ai no Corrida*), made by Oshima.

Among the more distinguished film personalities who died during the year were the actors Oscar Homolka, Robert Shaw, Claude Dauphin and Charles Boyer, the producer Jack L. Warner, and the cinematographers Geoffrey Unsworth and Lee Garmes. (For Boyer and Warner, see OBITUARY.)

TELEVISION AND RADIO

In broadcasting 1978 was a year of expanding satellite communication, proliferating pirates, wavelength changes, new broadcasting constitutions, continuing concern over finance, and increasing international exchanges.

For broadcasters in Britain, the most important event was the long-awaited appearance of the Government's White Paper which, if implemented, would determine the overall pattern of television and radio in the United Kingdom for the rest of the century. When eventually published on 26 July, after rumours of Cabinet dissension, it was seen to follow fairly closely the recommendations of the 1977 Annan Report (see AR 1977, pp. 411–2). Like Annan, it advocated that the fourth TV channel should be given to a new independent body, the Open Broadcasting Authority, which would commission programmes from many sources, including educational institutions, independent producers and the individual ITV companies. Initially at least, it would probably depend on direct government grant.

The White Paper echoed Annan in stating its reasons for preferring a 'third force' in television to an extension of existing structures: 'A unique opportunity will be missed if the Fourth Channel is not used to explore the possibilities of programmes which say something new in new ways. The Government agrees with the Annan Committee that a different kind of service requires a new authority'. The new channel, by definition, would be non-competitive and aimed at minorities, catering particularly for 'tastes and interests which are not adequately catered for on the existing three services'. This included minority ethnic cultures and, in Wales, programmes in the Welsh language.

Annan was rejected in the White Paper's conclusions regarding local radio. In place of yet another supervisory body, the Government proposed to extend the existing chains of local stations administered by the BBC and the Independent Broadcasting Authority. But the Committee's proposals for an independent complaints commission and for regular public hearings to be conducted by the BBC and IBA were adopted.

Unexpectedly, the most contentious part of the White Paper concerned the organization of the BBC. While endorsing Annan's view of the Corporation as 'arguably the single most important cultural organization in the nation', and the main national instrument of broadcasting, the Government wanted to see significant changes in the BBC's top management structure. It proposed the introduction of three 'service management boards', consisting partly of BBC executives and partly of outsiders appointed by the Home Secretary, to be ultimately responsible for the administration of television, radio and external services respectively. The motive behind this proposal, it was explained, was to 'distance' the main Board of Governors from day-to-day management and restore them to their true role as 'trustees of the public interest'.

Predictably, this was widely interpreted as an attempt by Whitehall to secure a voice in internal BBC affairs. Some saw the 'service management boards' as a sop to that part of the Labour left which, like a minority on the Annan Committee, had hoped for the dismemberment of the BBC. Even more predictable was the bitter reaction of the ITV companies to the Fourth Channel proposals. Their hopes, however, were not completely dashed; for the channel's final disposition still depended on the outcome of the 1979 general election, and Conservatives remained committed to an ITV-2.

For most of the year the BBC continued to be greatly preoccupied with its financial position. In November the Government announced new licence fees of £25 a year for colour, an increase of £4, and £10 for monochrome, an increase of £1. The BBC's managers had asked for £30 and £12. Their dismay was understandable. Already £17 million in debt, they had been forced throughout 1978 to bolster the under-funded TV service with unacceptably high levels of repeats and American series. The BBC's inability to compete with the much richer ITV network was reflected in the loss of entertainment stars like Morecambe and Wise, and the constant drain (sometimes at reportedly double salaries) of crucial technical staff. By European standards British licence fees were modest, as the list overleaf shows:

Television licence fees as at 31 December 1978
(*to nearest £ sterling*)

	monochrome	colour
United Kingdom	£10	£25
Netherlands	29	29
France	24	34
Italy	16	32
West Germany	33	33
Republic of Ireland	23	38
Sweden	32	46
Norway	39	49
Switzerland	49	49
Finland	32	54
Belgium	42	61
Austria	63	63
Denmark	38	64

Poverty-stricken or not, the BBC continued—often with foreign co-production aid—to mount a number of notable new series. Most original among these was Dennis Potter's *Pennies From Heaven*, a bitter-sweet tale of love and longing punctuated by elaborate production numbers from the popular hits of the 1930s. Potter also dramatized the highly successful TV version of Hardy's *The Mayor of Casterbridge*. ITV drama seemed to be caught up in a bout of Victorian and Royal nostalgia, culminating in Thames TV's fascinating six-part reconstruction of the 1938 Abdication, *Edward and Mrs Simpson*. November saw the start, with productions of *Romeo and Juliet* and *Richard II*, of the BBC's ambitious six-year project to screen all 37 Shakespeare plays.

The various documentary departments produced a strikingly beautiful filmed account of Darwin's *Beagle* odyssey, *The Voyage Of Charles Darwin* (BBC); a 15-part series consisting entirely of internationally celebrated philosophers talking to camera, *Men Of Ideas* (BBC); and a revealing glimpse of Britain's Communist Party thrashing out policy differences in *Decisions: British Communism* (ITV). Other notable events were the ending of the BBC's veteran police series, *Z Cars*, after 16 years, and the re-broadcasting of French TV news bulletins (in French) as *Télé-journal* on BBC-2. A medium year occasionally rising to distinction culminated in an unprecedented British win in all three sections (drama, documentary and music) of the Prix Italia.

While Britain firmly rejected the idea of dismembering the BBC, the much smaller Swedish broadcasting system was being propelled in the opposite direction. Following the recommendations of their own Annan-style report, the Stockholm Government decided to split Sveriges Radio (SR), hitherto a monopoly, into four semi-autonomous corporations, responsible respectively for two TV channels, three radio channels, local radio and educational broadcasting. The new structure was due to come into being on 1 July 1979. Its targets included the expansion of TV transmission hours, a greater role for regional production, and possibly a fourth radio channel. Critics of the Government plan complained that it would multiply bureaucracy, prove inordinately expensive, and do nothing to achieve the true end of any broadcasting reform—improved programmes.

All five Scandinavian nations (Norway, Sweden,'Denmark, Finland and Iceland) were actively considering an exciting technical development for the 1980s—a Nordic regional satellite (Nordsat) which would allow viewers in each country to watch the programmes of the others (see p. 384). Meanwhile America's chain of Public (non-commercial) TV stations received an important boost in the shape of nation-wide satellite links. Previous land links were less flexible and yielded poor-quality pictures. Since the first PTV station went on air at Houston, Texas, in May 1953, the system had grown to a 1978 count of 273 stations, living precariously on a total income of some £150 million derived from federal and local grants, contributions from big business, and individual subscriptions. But legislation being considered in its 25th year could give Public TV a better deal.

Satellites for domestic communications were also planned by the Chinese Government, which hoped to launch two in 1980. They were evidently to be part of a general communications expansion in the People's Republic. Three new national TV channels were reported to be in preparation, bringing China's total to five. At the same time Western observers reported a marked turning-away from the inward-looking policies of the 'Cultural Revolution' days, with entertainment replacing 'educational' programmes.

Broadcasters in India were immensely heartened by their first prospect of complete independence from government under proposals presented by the Verghese committee. In the new structure, which bore striking resemblances to the formal organization of the BBC, control would be handed over to a National Broadcast Trust, supervising a Central Executive Board. This would have 13 members, including directors of radio, television, news and current affairs, and five regional directors. The parent body of 12 (akin to the BBC Governors) would be appointed by the Government from a list drawn up by the Chief Justice, the ombudsman and another official. While recognizing the importance of television, the report recommended that priority for the next 15 years should be given to the development of radio as the medium most relevant to India's particular needs. The over-riding stress on autonomy, which the committee wanted to see guaranteed in the Indian constitution, clearly reflected the Janata Administration's determination that broadcasting should never again become the tool of central government, as it had been under Mrs Gandhi. 'The objective of communication policy must be to awaken the people; to inform, mobilize, and educate them to be democratic citizens', the report stated. 'Dissenting opinions and minority voices must be heard.'

In Italy the proliferation of 'pirate' broadcasting stations had reached such proportions that the Government were forced to introduce a Bill designed to restore 'rational and efficient' use of the air waves. The country's troubles stemmed from a Constitutional Court decree of 1976, which effectively ended the monopoly of the state broadcasting system, RAI (Radiotelevisione Italiana), and legalized private cable stations. By June 1978 an official survey put the 'pirates' at an incredible total of 2,275 local radio stations and 506 TV stations—a world record in relation to population. Most of these were low-grade commercial operations dispensing recorded music or old cinema films. The Government's Bill sought to re-establish the primacy of RAI and to licence the freelance operators under the overall control of a National Broadcasting Committee. Where applications for licences exceeded available frequencies, attempts would be made to merge the competing interests. With so many vested interests in continuing chaos, the measure seemed destined for a rough passage.

The major technical event of 1978 was the mass switch-over in 100 countries of Europe, Asia, Africa and Australasia, at 00.01 hours on 23 November, to new radio frequencies. This was the outcome of international agreements reached at Geneva exactly three years before, and resulted in an increase in the European area from 1,450 transmitters with a combined power of 82 megawatts to 2,700 transmitters of 214 megawatts. In Britain the BBC, which had failed to obtain any significant increase in frequency allocations, decided to make the best of a bad job and re-design its entire medium and long-wave system, putting Radio 4 on to the powerful long-wave band and greatly improving the medium-wave transmission of Radio 1.

Other technical developments included growing international interest in Viewdata (or Prestel), the Post Office's elaborate information retrieval system involving domestic TV sets, telephone cables and multiple computer centres. Due to begin full public operation in Britain in 1979, it had already been sold to Germany, Holland and Hong Kong, and demonstrated in 14 other countries, including Russia.

The major world event in TV broadcasting was the World Cup, staged in Argentina. The final match (Argentina v. the Netherlands) was relayed to 63 satellite stations round the globe and broke all previous worldwide audience records. In Britain the BBC and ITV gave the 25-day event 100 hours of coverage, duplicating six matches. European broadcasting rights for the 1980 Moscow Olympics were acquired by the European Broadcasting Union for £3 million, a bargain compared with the £50 million already paid by NBC in the US for North American rights.

Two more Third World nations, Swaziland and Afghanistan, inaugurated TV services in February and March. Ireland, after many false starts, successfully launched its second TV channel on 2 November, depending largely on imported British programmes. A second radio channel was due to follow in 1979, partly to combat the estimated 12 pirate stations in Dublin. In Britain the broadcasting of Parliament became a regular feature of domestic radio from 3 April. Its mixed reception suggested that television in either House was still a long way off.

Chapter 2

ART—ARCHITECTURE—FASHION

ART

THE most visible visual spectacular of 1978 was the long-anticipated $100 million extension to the National Gallery of Art, Washington, DC, funded by the indefatigable public spirit of the Mellon family. This was but the latest addition to the impressive, even awesome museum complex of Washington. The architect, I. M. Pei, has created a secular cathedral, a temple to art. At its best, the extension is a homage to the spirit of art; its interior, however, has been compared (unfavourably) to a major railway station (Victorian railway stations were also secular temples, dedicated to the spirit of progress), and some think the galleries of art themselves have taken second place to the building as a whole. The contemporary artists included in this pantheon must have felt themselves in the process of canonization. It was more than appropriate that in the year of Henry Moore's 80th birthday a major piece by him was installed at the entrance to the National Gallery extension in Washington.

Henry Moore is indeed the most public sculptor not only of his day but, as far as can be discerned, of any day. His work is the most widely dispersed over the world of any sculptor's in history. The celebrations in England for his 80th birthday began with a sensitive, very well arranged exhibition of all aspects of his work in Bradford, the largest and most representative display there had yet been in his native country north of the Tate Gallery. The Tate itself responded with a magnificent show of Moore drawings, and a display of the Henry Moore Gift to Britain's national gallery for modern art. The Serpentine in Kensington Gardens (an Arts Council gallery) had an exhibition of major Moore bronzes in the park itself, and within the gallery an exhibition which included the small found objects from which Moore has derived inspiration. Fischer Fine Art had a choice show of Henry Moore, the carver.

Art benefactors still survived in beleagured Britain. At the University of East Anglia the Sainsbury Centre for the Visual Arts, donated by Sir Robert and Lady Sainsbury and their son David, was opened. The Centre, a building greeted by architectural critics with acclaim, was designed as a great silvery shed by Norman Foster, to house the Sainsbury collection of

O

primitive and European art, as well as the University's Department of Fine Art. How the collection, and the building, would fit into a working university and the local community was a matter of great interest to those concerned with using art, rather than putting it away and having all but the few ignore it. (See also ARCHITECTURE, p. 422).

An unusually substantial bequest to the University of London was the late Count Seilern's collection, an art collection of the highest quality (for example, drawings by Michelangelo), conservatively valued at £30 million.

As insecurity, financial and political, dogged the Western world, the commercial value of art continued to rise. London was reaffirmed as the world's art market capital, with all auction houses reporting percentage increases of more than a third. For the 1977-78 season, Sotheby Parke Bernet recorded worldwide turnover figures of £162,500,000; the 1978 autumn season figures (part of the 1978-79 season) were up 38 per cent from the year before, at £71,750,000. Christie's figures for 1977-78 October–July season were £89,106,000, and their 1978 autumn figures were £42,185,000, an increase of over 40 per cent on the same period of 1977.

The sale of the year, that most susceptible to publicity, was the von Hirsch sale conducted by Sotheby's in June. Von Hirsch was a very wealthy Jewish German who found asylum in Switzerland during the Nazi period. He was more connoisseur than collector; for the way in which he lived was described as almost as much a work of art as the art of all periods that he selectively collected. Sotheby's orchestrated viewing days at the Royal Academy, for which admission was charged; publicity was brilliant; and the ensuing high prices at the sale were described by one eminent commentator as nothing less than the outcome of group hysteria. The clubbing together of various West German public galleries, helped by the federal government, to buy back for the fatherland some highly desirable indigenous art objects was praised as a rational reaction to the sale. After all the ballyhoo, the prices were very high.

Nelson Rockefeller entered the art business by manufacturing reproductions of items in his own collection for sale to the public. Prices here were high too, and publicity flowed. A millionaire reproducing for profit items of original art in his own collection was a new concept in the art business. While many might consider the Rockefeller business sense acute, others found the enterprise distasteful. No one has satisfactorily decided whether or not art is a business like any other.

Meanwhile in Britain one aspect of care for the national heritage received European commendation: the Ironbridge Gorge Museum Trust, Telford, Shropshire, Britain's Museum of the Year in 1977, won the first-ever European Museum of the Year Award, presented under the umbrella of the European Cultural Foundation. The heritage lobbies, which had squandered much credibility in the over-reaction in 1977 to the sale of Mentmore, were faced in 1978 with something far more important to the historical past of Britain: the discreet dispersal of some of the contents of Warwick Castle, and finally the sale of the Castle itself and its remaining contents, by the self-exiled heir Lord Brooke. This last sale would safe-guard the attractions of the property, for the buyer was Madame Tussaud's. As the nation had made no concessions to Lord Brooke, Lord Brooke was under no need to make any concessions to the nation, but the episode warned us that some mutual pact should be considered if the nation wished to safeguard some things for the nation's future. By the end of the year two of the four Canaletto paintings of views of Warwick Castle had been 'saved for the nation', entering the collections of the Birmingham City Art Gallery; Birmingham also managed yet another appeal for help and extra funds, and purchased the Giovanni Bellini altarpiece of 1505, the last important Bellini still to have been in private hands in England (Cornbury Park). Meanwhile many of the controversial suggestions contained in the tenth report of the Standing Commission on Museums and Galleries, covering the period 1973-77 and published in 1978, had yet to be fully debated; the futures of the university and provincial museums were under financial threat; and in the debate over the Land Fund the rumoured Government recommendation that a substantial sum from the Treasury be administered for heritage purposes by independent trustees had not yet been publicly confirmed. Museum services still saw no adequate replace-ment for the circulating exhibitions provided by the Victoria and Albert which were axed in the cuts of 1976. And union problems, little ventilated in the newspapers, continued to bedevil the service given to the public. Yet what has been destroyed can be renewed: Arthur Lucas, the retiring head of conservation at the National Gallery, as his swan-song brilliantly rescued Poussin's Adoration of the Golden Calf, which had been cut to pieces by a mentally disturbed visitor in the spring.

And in spite of the often reiterated statement that the day of the spectacular, costly and revelatory exhibition was now over, the facts of the matter in the major cities of the West were quite different. The Metro-politan, New York, was host in the spring to a scintillating exhibition of the later Monet, in its way as superlative as the late Cezanne which drew record-breaking crowds in Paris, after its sensational showings in America in 1977.

After nearly two years of life, the Beaubourg Centre in Paris outclassed the Eiffel Tower as an attraction, put on scores of special exhibitions, and in terms of pleasing the crowds more than fulfilled the most optimistic forecasts. The Centre also managed in the summer to please art specialists with a remarkable exhibition, Paris–Berlin, which examined the new hunting-ground for twentieth-century retrospectives—the inter-war period of the 'twenties, with a foray into the 1930s. This confirmed the unpre-cedented success of the Council of Europe's 1977 show, The Trends of the Twenties (West Berlin). The Paris–Berlin exhibition had another significance for recent cultural history: a willingness of the French at least to look outside their own cultural borders. Politics, however, dictated that the original show, which included Moscow, was split into two: Paris–Moscow is now due in 1979.

The 1920s and '30s in Europe were also ruthlessly examined in two major historical exhibitions mounted by the Arts Council in London: in January, Dada and Surrealism Reviewed, and in November, Die Neue Sächlichkeit, an examination of German realism in the 1920s and early '30s. Both were real eye-openers: the former told us much of the internationalism of these movements, and their immense influence; in the latter, the Germans—and others—began to re-examine the past in an area which the evil happenings in Germany under the Nazis had obscured until recently.

In New York the more recent past was examined: the New York School (Whitney), and a much-praised show of Mark Rothko (Guggenheim). As the year drew to a close, New York surpassed all other cities in the fervent reaction to the Tutankhamun exhibition (Metropolitan): the numbers of tickets sold, and the cost of the whole enterprise, threatened to become as legendary as the Egyptian boy-king himself.

There was a minor shock-wave in Britain when in September two scholars questioned some long traditional attributions of paintings hitherto thought to be by John Constable. The Tate Gallery's 'Near Stoke-by-Nayland' was the most notable work to be reassigned to Constable's son, Lionel. Since the art market was little affected, an unusually good-humoured time was had by all involved in the debate. Another pleasing event which involved the Tate was that the Anglo-American Mitchell prize for the history of art, in its second year of existence, was won by British authors: Martin Butlin of the Tate, and Evelyn Joll of Agnew's, for *The Paintings of J. M. W. Turner*.

Not quite so good-humoured were the debates held for three days in February at the Institute of Contemporary Arts in London (an institution recently revivified under new direction). This collective examination of 'The State of British Art' looked at the contemporary scene. Everyone had a good time listing various symptoms of decline, decay and decadence, and a bad time pointing to any solutions. The debates involved much mutual recrimination, and offered a repetitive theme for art publications. Much enjoyed in America—in Kansas City—were the 'Wrapped Walk Ways' by the artist Christo, another of his huge environmental pieces which are temporary works of art. They involve a good deal of local labour, which is not only good for the local economy but also genuinely involves hundreds of people in a way that many of the talkers in the world of art fail to understand.

The end of several eras was painfully felt on both sides of the Atlantic. Harold Rosenberg, poet, teacher and art critic for *The New Yorker*, died in July; in that same month, Thomas Hess, an influential critic newly installed as consultative chairman of the Department of 20th Century Art. Duncan Grant, much-loved painter and one of the last survivors of first-generation Bloomsbury, died earlier in the year (see OBITUARY); and in the spring Benedict Nicolson, editor of the *Burlington Magazine* for over thirty years, also died. Giorgio de Chirico died in November (see OBITUARY), and Gluck, the English lady painter of stylish portraits and landscapes, in January.

In life, little that was new appeared: the anger, energy, imagination, inventiveness and ferocity exhibited in so much of the now admired art on view from the 1920s and '30s was not being echoed in the West in the 1970s. Reforms were not wanted. The mood was very much one of artists keeping their heads below the parapet and just trying to get on with it. Disturbance was not the order of the day. Tom Wolfe, the American journalist, christened the 1970s the 'Me-Decade'. Certainly this was felt in Venice, where the Biennale did not repeat the great success of 1976. Art in Nature, Nature into Art was the theme, and, as might be imagined, ecology in various ways informed the exhibits. But an unhealthy self-indulgence on the one hand, and inept biological experiments on the other, were the dominant characteristics of the jamboree.

Those major exhibitions did well which dealt with the past, both recent and far, were researched with care, and seemed to have either glamour or some relevance to the concerns of today. The appeal of today's art— more and more 'doing your own thing'—became more and more uncertain, while some elderly survivors, such as the Polish–French Balthus and Joan Miró—whose delightful, witty and disturbing costumes for the Spanish theatrical troupe La Claca were acclaimed in London and Paris—had now achieved the status of Old Masters, whose work is not questioned, only admired.

Books of the year included:

Life in the English Country House by Mark Girouard (Yale); a new approach in understanding not only the material survivors from the past but also what houses and their objects meant then, and how they were used.

The New Sobriety by John Willett (Thames and Hudson); a thrilling, scholarly, examination of arts and politics in the Weimar Republic.

Jackson Pollock by Francis Valentine O'Connor and Eugene Victor Thaw (Yale); new standards are set in these four volumes for the catalogue raisonné of a modern artist.

Rembrandt's House by Anthony Bailey (Dent); a book filled with charm and information, an informed exploration of Amsterdam in Rembrandt's time.

Sport and the Countryside by David Coombs (Phaidon); art, sport and the countryside, the first recording the interaction of the latter two.

The Painters of Ireland by Anne Crookshank and The Knight of Glin (Barrie and Jenkins); the first modern survey of the subject, witty and thoughtful.

Paris 1900–1914 by Nigel Gosling (Weidenfeld); a blow by blow, painting by painting account of the years of experiment and change.

Romantic Art by William Vaughan (Thames and Hudson); an excellent survey, intelligent and unusual, of a difficult period.

ARCHITECTURE

British architects were encouraged by the slight uplift in commissions during 1978 after the depressing position in 1977, the worst year since 1964. The prospects for the whole building industry looked brighter in December when the Department of the Environment reported that orders in the third quarter of the year were 8 per cent higher than those of the second, and 11 per cent above the corresponding period in 1977. Nonetheless the profession had faced a dull year on the whole. Architects were no better off financially, since the increase in their earnings rate was still below that of the country's inflation rate.

The year started for completed buildings with publicity for Wheeler and Sprosan's new L-shaped wing for Edinburgh's College of Art. Built in red sandstone to match the College's original buildings, the new wing contained a library and students' living accommodation. The entrance facade facing the road had small widely-spaced windows to reduce traffic noise, but facing the gardens on the inner sides the windows were virtually continuous between bands of sandstone. Trinity College Dublin was also building a new arts centre by Ahrends, Burton and Koralek, commissioned in 1973 and virtually completed in 1978. The reinforced concrete structure was deeply modelled and set back in long steps with glass between structural supports, except for the flat white granite-clad facade facing the city.

The Sainsbury Centre for the University of East Anglia, certainly the most unusual architectural work of the year, was opened in April. The architects, Foster Associates, had produced a perfectly rectangular building over 100 feet across, roofed in a single span with a tubular space frame. The ends of the box were filled with glass. The long sides and roof were covered with the same kind of cladding, a system of interchangeable aluminium or glass panels. The importance of the building, after the compelling Pompidou Centre in Paris, was the suggestion it gave of a new post-modern approach to architecture, already noted in a gymnasium (C. F. Murphy Associates) in the USA and a house in England by Michael and Patricia Hopkins. The space inside the Sainsbury Centre was taken up by a gallery-lounge for an art collection, donated by Sir Robert and Lady Sainsbury, an art school, restaurant, senior common room and exhibition space. There were no internal walls. The activities were separated by screens. (See also ART, p. 417).

In February, Peterborough's brick-walled new magistrates' court by Cambridge Architect's Department (Ken Matthew, Roger Allin and Stuart Denham being the responsible architects) was in use, adding a distinguished traditional-looking building to the town's development. In another expanded town, Swindon, the final phase of the £10 million Brunel Centre by the architects for the whole of the Centre, Douglas Stephen and

Partners in association with Building Design Partnership, was nearing completion. The tower block containing flats and offices dominated the surroundings but demonstrated a commendable post-modern feeling in the glass and aluminium cladding with rounded corners, and in the curved profiles of the roof.

In London, Coutts's new bank in the Strand (Frederick Gibberd and Partners), opened in December, was designed with a spectacular glass and metal front. Passers-by were able to see business going on in the banking hall, and also the interior planting. Flanking the modern addition were Nash facades, most of which had been precisely restored by the architects. Another bank, the Bank Nationale de Paris (Fitzroy Robinson & Partners), was also completed in the City of London. The building's finish in Portland stone and granite followed the traditions of other offices on King William Street. In the City not far away the reconstructed London Bridge railway station (Nigel Wikeley, British Rail regional architect) was reopened, after bomb damage to the old Victorian buildings in World War II had been repaired.

Historical architecture was prominent among notable events of the year. In October Sir Giles Gilbert Scott's Anglican Liverpool Cathedral, a competition winner in 1901, was completed at last. The exterior exhibited Scott's Gothic, but many changes had been made to the original design, including a new west front, still to be finished, by Frederick Thomas, who took over when Scott died in 1960. Earlier in the year a proposal by the Department of the Environment (DOE) to build an extension to Lord Burlington's eighteenth-century villa, Chiswick House, on the foundations of the nineteenth-century Wyatt extensions removed in 1950, was approved by the Royal Fine Art Commission, but displeased many people. It was true that Chiswick House had no lavatory or catering facilities, which were needed by the people visiting probably the best example of Palladian architecture in the country; but critics considered the additions would be an affront to the original building, and were too expensive. The same department of DOE, the ancient monuments and historic buildings branch, caused further controversy by threatening the fine ironwork railings of Sir Robert Smirke's nineteenth-century Greek Revival British Museum in order to build a porter's lodge and gates. The entrance doors of the Museum were to be changed as well, to a more modern kind.

A fight to save Liverpool's neo-classical Lyceum seemed ended in May when redevelopment with a shopping centre was approved. Fortunately a temporary ban on demolition was placed on the building in August, and hopes were raised that it might be rescued. Another popular decision in August was that Richmond Terrace off Whitehall was to be incorporated in a new scheme for government offices (architect William Whitfield), making it safer from demolition.

Town planning events were less memorable perhaps than those of recent years. An important announcement, made by the Secretary of State for the Environment in April, named dates for winding up the development corporations of the following new towns: in 1980, Corby, Stevenage, Harlow; in 1981, Runcorn; in 1982, Bracknell, Redditch, Washington; in 1983, Basildon. Dates for Aycliffe, Peterlee and Skelmersdale were to be announced later. The redevelopment of the sites between the new National Theatre (see AR 1976, p. 415) and the King's Reach development came into the news in September when a proposal for flats, offices, theatres, a sports complex and an hotel (Derek Stephenson and Partners) was backed by the Greater London Council but opposed by Lambeth Borough Council. The controversy centred on Lambeth's claim that the sites should be used for housing. Lambeth already had a scheme for 250 houses on part of the area. No final decision had been reached by year's end. A large scheme for offices, a roofed-over bus garage and space for sports facilities (architects, Foster Associates) in the centre of Hammersmith was exhibited to the public in October. It came in for no serious criticism from local people, and was expected to go forward.

In March Colin St John Wilson's proposed first phase for the new British Library building next to St Pancras station, London, was given the green light. Much of the scheme was in brickwork with pitched roofs, not to the liking of some critics. Brighton Marina, with roads and harbour completed, could move no further towards completion until decisions about the proposed buildings had been taken. In October the Property Services Agency were expected to design new offices for the Post Office on a site near St Paul's Cathedral, on which a scheme by Ahrends, Burton and Koralek had never gone ahead in 1975, because of the need to economize, though it had received high praise from the Royal Fine Art Commission. Also in October the Government promised another £15 million towards cleaning up and repairing derelict sites in specific inner city areas, to be spent during the next three and a half years.

The 1978 Royal Gold Medal for Architecture was awarded to Jørn Utzon, designer of the Sydney Opera House (see AR 1973, p. 442), the first Danish architect to receive the award. The R. S. Reynolds Memorial Award for an outstanding work in aluminium was won by Johnson/Burgee and S. I. Maris Associates for their office towers in Houston, Texas. At the beginning of the year Philip Johnson of Johnson/Burgee had been awarded the American Institute of Architects Gold Medal, presented annually. Philip Johnson built his famous Glass House, Connecticut, in 1949, and was co-author with the late Mies van der Rohe of the Seagram Building, New York, in 1958. The *Financial Times* Industrial Architecture Award for 1978 went to the Solid Wastes Rail Transfer Station, Brentford, designed by the GLC Architects' Department. Even the judges remarked that it was a singular achievement to turn the receiving-end of the borough's dust-carts into an award-winning piece of architecture.

In the USA, Washington's National Gallery east building (I. M. Pei & Partners), lying between the White House and the Capitol, offended neither of those neo-classical buildings when it was opened in the summer. The building's clean cubist lines were emphasized by the fine Tennessee pink marble sheathing, liberal glass surfaces on some facades, and cavernous entranceways surrounded by solid wall in others (see also p. 417). The building was a private venture for the Gallery, financed by the Mellon family. The centre was to house facilities for advanced study in the visual arts, library and offices. The entrance courtyard was lit from above through an enormous glazed space frame. In November it was announced that the old State House, Hartford, Connecticut (Charles Bulfinch 1796), was to be saved in a restoration programme, beginning with strengthening the structure and then restoring the interior. Fears had been felt earlier for a less historic but important piece of architecture, the soaring-roofed Dulles International Airport building, Washington, D.C., by Eero Saarinen (1962). Some people thought the design might be affected significantly by proposals for enlarging the airport, to be undertaken by architects Hellmuth, Obata & Kassabaum. The late Frank Lloyd Wright's 140-feet freestanding bell tower for the First Christian Church in Phoenix, Arizona, designed by the master in 1957, was completed during the year.

In Teheran a proposal for a new city centre (Llewelyn Davies International) included a long central spinal avenue, like the Champs Elysées, Paris, leading from both sides to a great square; it was considered a model of its kind.

Charles Eames, born 1907, world-renowned architect and designer, died in August at his birthplace St Louis. He won the 25-year American Institute of Architects Award for his 1949 Eames House, near Los Angeles. Edward Durrell Stone, born 1902, died in August. He had been architect for the Kennedy Centre, Washington, D.C., the US embassy, New Delhi, and the Museum of Modern Art, New York.

FASHION

The most significant change in fashion during the year was the consolidation of a square-shouldered, slimmer silhouette, first suggested by leading designers in Paris and London at the end of 1977. During the first months of 1978 the look was introduced with variations of a wide-shouldered dress worn over straight trousers or narrow skirts, thus emphasizing the new line. This led the way to a neat, more tailored look for winter clothes, which was seen in all price ranges from high fashion to chain store. With the return of the tailored look, skirts became shorter and waists were accentuated with wide belts. Legs were given an illusion of more length by the wearing of high-heeled shoes.

o*

The full, blouson garment continued over from the previous year, but became much less bulky and was mostly worn with trousers, which had already come back strongly into daily use, for both pleasurable and practical reasons. Day skirts fell straight and were either pleated or tube-shaped. During the summer months, lace-trimmed petticoats, worn to show some inches below coloured, patterned skirts, introduced a frivolous note into an otherwise sombre summer scene.

The blazer jacket, made popular two years earlier, proved itself to be still the most useful garment for women of all ages, and waistcoats retained their wide use, being made in fabrics for all seasons, from fur to pure silk. Shirt blouses were the universal choice when sweaters were not worn, and the introduction of lace as a trimming for shirts was in violent contrast to an intentionally crushed linen used as a passing fashion for suits and trousers; this introduced a feminine note into a rather masculine and casual style of dress.

On economic considerations, and also because of a summer of bad weather, most women stayed safely within the bounds of classic dressing. More fashion-conscious people adopted a form of casual sportswear, which consisted of putting full skirts and long shirts over trousers, or teamed short, culotte skirts with square, lightweight jackets.

In the autumn the effects of the growing number of discos opening all over the country was felt in fashion. 'Disco dresses' became a breakaway fashion on their own. Young people with uninhibited taste wore shiny satin, plunging necklines and skinny pants when patronizing the disco, while wealthy customers of trend-setting nightclubs wore short dresses with low decolletage bought from top fashion houses like Christian Dior and Yves Saint Laurent.

Knitwear continued to be a mainstay of the wardrobe, and shapes and patterns remained close to the classic, high roll collars and V-necklines proving most successful at all budget levels. Thanks to a swing throughout the year towards the soft look of silk and lace for leisure clothes, a number of knitted sweaters were given a lacey stitch and had softly frilled collars and cuffs.

Fabrics continued to be soft and light in weight, with wool and silky jersey widely used for day and evening clothes. Corduroy continued from the previous year as a top choice for trousers and skirts and proved to be hard-wearing and satisfactory for continuous daily wear. For evening, pure silk dominated the scene and the price of evening clothes consequently rose quite dramatically. Evening dress, however, had become a still more informal affair generally and women tended to go their own way, rather than adhere to the current dictum of fashion. Skirts and trousers were equally acceptable at night and the fabrics in which they were made were interesting, unusual and often extremely luxurious. A tendency to over-do dressing up at night after wearing practical and durable clothes during the day was clearly recognizable as a feminine form of escape from difficult and frustrating economic conditions.

A large number of women who went out to work were from the group who dressed up in the evening, and this brought about the adoption of an evening suit, made in a fine fabric, that could be worn equally well during the day and evening, when a slight change of accessories was all that was necessary. For the same reason, the idea of velvet jackets and glamorous blouses caught on in the mass markets as well.

Boots and shoes continued to be expensive. Heels were mostly two to three inches high, except for sports wear and country boots. The steep rise in the cost of footwear, which reached a peak in 1977, continued to make people economize on this particular accessory, and strappy sandals using little leather were an indication of how fashion responds to economic need.

Shawls still proved the best value as a light wrap during summer. Many women took to wearing a little round hat when autumn arrived. This 'beanie' followed the big popularity of the flat cap that entered fashion in winter 1977, and proved that milliners were still fighting to regain favour with a public who had been hatless for too long. The cocktail hat, too, became popular at the end of the year, the chief trend-setter being pillbox-shaped and worn with a veil.

On 27 November, Biba reopened at 22 Conduit Street, London. This shop, founded by Barbara Hulanici in the 1960s, gained world-wide fame with swinging young people in the decade that produced the Beatles and the mini-skirt. It closed its doors in 1975, but on its return brought back the same moody style of fashion as that for which it had always been renowned.

Chapter 3

LITERATURE

In a year when more books were produced in Britain than ever before, the only category of books that showed a decline was fiction. The total number of new books and new editions issued was 38,766, an increase of 6·7 per cent over the previous year. The number of new editions was 9,236, forming a smaller proportion of the total than in recent years. In 1970 new editions had formed 30 per cent of the total output; the ratio was now down to 24 per cent. In general the book trade was buoyant, selling well besides producing more titles. In the early months of the year there had been considerable customer resistance to rise in the prices of paperback editions, but by its end the public had become accustomed to the idea that it might be necessary to pay over £1 for a paperback novel and that most novels in hardback would cost around £5.

In particular, publishers were happy that the Consent Decree, ratified in the United States two years earlier, ending the unofficial agreement between British and American publishers dividing the world into separate spheres of interest, had had less effect than the more timorous had expected. A number of British companies set up American subsidiaries to market their books in the United States, while American publishers sold their titles in the British Commonwealth. The only real effect was that the new situation tended to make the best-selling author and his agent become even more powerful, in that publishers were invited to bid for 'world rights' rather than for a section of the globe. For instance, Frederick Forsyth, the writer of a number of successful thrillers, was involved in a deal which would bring him, before publication, something in the region of £2$\frac{1}{4}$ million for the world rights in a book that was no more, at the time of the contract, than an idea in his head.

Novelists in less commanding positions were not so fortunate—at the year's end they did not even have the satisfaction of knowing that the Public Lending Right, under which they would get payment for the borrowing of their books from public libraries, was on the statute books, though at the Christmas recess it had got further through Parliament than ever before in the history of this unlucky measure. Even if the number of works of fiction issued in Britain was smaller—at 4,379 down by 2$\frac{1}{2}$ per cent from the previous year's total—the year, in the field of literature, was dominated by the novel.

The high point was a new book by Graham Greene, *The Human Factor*. This was yet another of this outstanding writer's examinations of the conscience of the individual, this time in terms of his loyalty to his country. For high moral motives the central figure had become involved with the Russians and in return for a favour had been forced to betray his country while working for British Intelligence. Another traitor is suspected and eliminated by the British authorities, who act with peculiar cynicism before the real culprit defects to Russia and learns to live the isolated and lonely life of the agent no longer of any use to his masters. Much of this novel showed Mr Greene at his best, the master of narrative, the deft hand at portraits, the man supremely able to present moral problems in human terms; but there were moments that showed Mr Greene was getting old— the book was published in his 74th year—and the tension flagged. Almost certainly a younger Mr Greene would have hidden the identity of the traitor with greater skill. Its revelation could have come as a surprise to very few readers.

It had been hoped by many that the Nobel prize for literature would go during 1978 to Mr Greene but in fact it went to the Yiddish writer, born in Poland but living for most of his life in New York, Isaac Bashevis Singer, who, by chance, was exactly the same age as Mr Greene. Unusual among Nobel laureates Mr Singer was still a practising writer, but as with most of his predecessors it was considered that the award was more for the *corpus* of his work than for any particular recent novel, though few would deny that Mr Singer was an outstanding writer both of short stories and of long novels presenting in glowing prose his Polish Jewish inheritance.

Indeed the question whether literary prizes should be given for current work or for long service was under discussion during the year over the choices both for the Prix Goncourt and for the Booker Prize. The first of these went to Patrick Modiano, who though young had published a number of novels; the one that won the Goncourt, *Rue des boutiques obscures*, was thought to be his weakest so far. Iris Murdoch's name appeared on the Booker Prize short list for the fourth time. Was the award of the prize for her latest novel, *The Sea, the Sea*, yet another acknowledgment of an *oeuvre* of standing? There were divided opinions on this, though the majority thought the award more than justified. *The Sea, the Sea* was Miss Murdoch's longest novel to date and in many ways her most ambitious, modelled to some degree on *The Tempest*, with an actor manager withdrawn from the world to a place by the sea, remembering ancient glory and old loves while trying to manipulate the lives of those around him.

Kingsley Amis's *Jake's Thing*, also on the Booker short list, showed him at his most jokily outrageous. The central character, finding that he is impotent, tries modern remedies to recover his sex drive, at the same time, in his capacity as an Oxford don, repelling plans to allow women to enter his college. This double framework allowed the author to hit out at the things in contemporary life that he abhorred in a way that made even those who disagreed with him laugh. Anthony Burgess, in *1985*, made a rather different sort of protest against the way he suspected Western society was evolving. He divided his book into two: the first half consisted of a critique of George Orwell's *1984* and the second presented his own fictional forecast of a trade-union-controlled society in Britain only a year after Orwell's chosen date.

The tendency towards short novels continued. Two others on the Booker short list, Penelope Fitzgerald's *The Bookshop* and Jane Gardham's *God on the Rocks*, were barely more than *novella* size, a fact which might have appealed to judges faced with a pile of books to get through. Certainly there was more critical praise for larger efforts, notably A. S. Byatt's *The Virgin in the Garden*, a long complicated novel of human relationships entangled while most of the characters rehearsed and performed a pageant for the coronation of Queen Elizabeth II, and a further instalment of Olivia Manning's multiple sequel to her earlier *Balkan Trilogy*, *A Battle Lost and Won*, which cleverly contrasted the inner turmoil of the heroine's life with the actual Battle of Alamein. Not a great year for American fiction, though a negro family saga, *Song of Solomon* by Toni Morrison, attracted much notice, as did an accomplished first novel, *Final Payments* by Mary Gordon. The Whitbread award went to an American-born writer, Paul Theroux, but one who had lived in Britain for a number of years. His

Picture Palace, an ironic study of a fashionable photographer, was more British than American in its humour.

That the long novel with ample plots and subplots was not dead was demonstrated by the success of M. M. Kaye's superior romantic story of India, *The Far Pavilions*, and by Nicholas Monsarrat's first instalment of the adventures over four centuries of a sea-going version of the Wandering Jew, *Master Mariner*. The most promising British first novel, *The Cement Garden* by Ian McEwan, someone already known as a short story writer, did not get the praise it deserved because reviewers were distracted by the fact that the main plot line (children concealing the death of their mother in order that they should not be separated by welfare officers) had been used in another novel 14 years earlier. The most impressive translation into English was Günter Grass's *The Flounder*, a heavyweight study of rapacious womanhood based on the Grimm folk tale of the magic fish who gave his captor three wishes which were misused by the fisherman's wife.

The year produced no outstanding work of non-fiction. A number of notable works of scholarship were continued: among them were Leslie A. Marchand's masterly editing of Byron's Diaries and Letters, the 8th volume of which was entitled *Born for Opposition*, and the Pilgrim edition of *The Letters of Charles Dickens*, the fourth volume of which was edited by Kathleen Tillotson. There was also the second volume of Robert Gittings's study of the novelist and poet, *The Older Hardy*. Another much praised work was John Bayley's *Essay on Thomas Hardy*. The second Lord Birkenhead completed his biography, *Rudyard Kipling*, in 1948 but was refused permission to publish it by the poet's daughter, who disapproved of its tone. Her death removed the barriers to publication and three years after its author's death *Rudyard Kipling* appeared, a work of great competence but so innocuous in presentation that it was difficult to see any rational reason for opposing publication.

The more interesting literary biographies were concerned with relatively minor figures: John Pearson's joint biographies of the three Sitwells, Edith, Osbert and Sacheverell, *Façades*; Constance Babington Smith's *John Masefield* (published in his centenary year), and Gladys Mary Coles's biography of the novelist Mary Webb, *The Flowering Light*. Among the autobiographies two by literary figures were of particular interest, by chance written by men who were contemporaries at Balliol College, Oxford, Anthony Powell and Philip Mason. Mr Powell told of life as a young publisher in the London of the late 1920s in the second instalment of his memoirs, to which he gave the general title, *To Keep the Ball Rolling* and for this volume the subtitle *Messengers of Day*. Mr Mason's account, confined to a single volume, described how he joined the Indian Civil Service and prospered there before retiring to this country to expand his literary activities from part-time novelist to full-time writer.

Two outstanding theatrical biographies were published: John Lahr described with almost brutal frankness in *Prick Up Your Ears* the growing talent and messy life of the playwright Joe Orton, who just as he was reaching maturity was murdered by a jealous boyfriend, and Irving Wardle did justice to one of the seminal figures of the modern stage in *The Theatres of George Devine*. Dirk Bogarde provided something very different from the normal film-star autobiography in his second instalment, *Snakes and Ladders*: here was a sensitive and observant man describing his 30 years before the camera.

The tendency to instant history continued: the former President's side of the Watergate scandal was given in *The Memoirs of Richard Nixon*; a vastly documented account of the activities of the heir apparent to the Kennedy presidency, murdered like his brother, was presented by Arthur M. Schlesinger in *The Life and Times of Robert Kennedy*. Of slightly more mature vintage was David Caute's analysis of the McCarthy anti-communist purges in the United States in the 1950s, *The Great Fear*. The prize for instant history must have gone to *The Pencourt File*, an investigation by Barrie Penrose and Roger Courtious of allegations concerning the former leader of the Liberal Party, Mr Jeremy Thorpe.

Among the books about World War II, outstanding was R. V. Jones's *Most Secret War*, a model to all writers on how to explain technical matters—the author's part in defeating German plans in the use of radar as an aid to bombers and the development of flying bombs—in a way that was readable yet made no concessions to popularization. The work of the allied code-breakers was well described by Ronald Lewin in *The Ultra Secret*.

The Whitbread award for biography went to a political work of some authority, John Grigg's *Lloyd George, the People's Champion, 1902-11*, a second volume of a large-scale work. This was in essence a straightforward work of history but other works more surprising in their approach gained wide attention. Chief among these was Emmanuel Le Roy Ladurie's *Montaillou*. The author had discovered the records of a visit by the Inquisition to a village in the south-west of France in the late 13th/early 14th century which were so detailed as to give unrivalled picture of what medieval life was like. Richard Cobb, known for his investigations into the by-ways of French history, added to the sum of knowledge of life during the French Revolution with *Death in Paris*, basing his examination on the records of suicide and other sudden deaths in a part of Paris during those years and drawing his conclusions about social conditions there.

How the techniques of modern book production, with the use of colour plates and plentiful photographs, could be used with advantage in scholarly works was shown in two very well-researched works of social history: Mark Girouard's *Life in the English Country House: a Social and*

Architectural History and Robert Altick's learned investigation of popular entertainment, *The Shows of London*.

Among those who died during the year was the most controversial figure in English literary criticism, F. R. Leavis (see OBITUARY), revered by his disciples, feared by his opponents, sound on what he knew but over-dismissive of writers whom he did not perhaps fully understand. The novelists dying during the year included the Italian Ignazio Silone (see OBITUARY), the American James G. Cozzens and the British Paul Scott (see OBITUARY) and Robert Shaw. Among others who died during the year were the Spanish historian and scholar, Salvador de Madariaga (see OBITUARY), the poets John Pudney and Ruthven Todd, the publisher who did so much to promote D. H. Lawrence and others, Martin Secker, the literary agent David Higham, the American historian Bruce Catton and the writer on criminal matters, Edgar Lustgarten.

Among the interesting new books published in Britain were:

FICTION: *Momo* by Emile Agir (Collins and Harvill); *A Rude Awakening* by Brian W. Aldiss (Weidenfeld); *Jake's Thing* by Kingsley Amis (Hutchinson); *Success* by Martin Amis (Cape); *Young Adolf* by Beryl Bainbridge (Duckworth); *Family Business* by Anthony Blond (Deutsch); *Autumn Manoeuvres* by Melvyn Bragg (Secker); *Palace without Chairs* by Brigid Brophy (Hamish Hamilton); *1985* by Anthony Burgess (Hutchinson); *The Virgin in the Garden* by A. S. Byatt (Chatto); *Walter* by David Cook (Secker); *SS-GB* by Len Deighton (Cape); *Madder Music* by Peter de Vries (Gollancz); *The Destinies of Darcy Dancer, Gentleman* by J. P. Donleavy (Allen Lane); *Housespy* by Maureen Duffy (Hamish Hamilton); *Livia or Buried Alive* by Lawrence Durrell (Faber); *The Singapore Grip* by J. G. Farrell (Weidenfeld); *The Bookshop* by Penelope Fitzgerald (Duckworth); *God on the Rocks* by Jane Gardham (Hamish Hamilton); *Final Payment* by Mary Graham (Hamish Hamilton); *The Flounder* by Günter Grass (Secker); *The Human Factor* by Graham Greene (Bodley Head); *Men on White Horses* by Pamela Haines (Collins); *A Kingdom* by James Hanley (Deutsch); *The Good Husband* by Pamela Hansford Johnson (Macmillan); *The World according to Garp* by John Irving (Gollancz); *The Far Pavilions* by M. M. Kaye (Allen Lane); *The Action* by Francis King (Hutchinson); *Nothing Missing from the Samovar and Other Stories* by Penelope Lively (Heinemann); *In Between the Sheets* by Ian McEwan (Cape); *The Cement Garden* by Ian McEwan (Cape); *The Battle Lost and Won* by Olivia Manning (Weidenfeld); *Rues des boutiques obscures* by Patrick Modiano (not published in Britain); *You Must Be Sisters* by Deborah Moggach (Collins); *The Master Mariner. Book I: Running Proud* by Nicholas Monsarrat (Cassell); *Song of Solomon* by Toni Morrison (Chatto); *The Sea, the Sea* by Iris Murdoch (Chatto); *Mrs Reinhardt and Other Stories* by Edna O'Brien (Weidenfeld); *Selected Stories* by V. S. Prichett (Chatto); *Sweet Dove Died* by Barbara Pym (Macmillan); *Five Year Sentence* by Bernice Rubens (W. H. Allen); *Girl in a Blue Shawl* by Sylvia Sherry (Hamish Hamilton); *Victims of Love* by Colin Spencer (Quartet); *Picture Palace* by Paul Theroux (Hamish Hamilton); *Ormerod's Landing* by Leslie Thomas (Eyre Methuen); *Live Bait* by Frank Tuohy (Macmillan); *Kalki* by Gore Vidal (Heinemann); *The Ivankiad* by Vladimir Voinich (Cape); *The Pardoner's Tale* by John Wain (Macmillan); *The Little Sisters* by Fay Weldon (Hodder); *Unguarded Hours* by A. N. Wilson (Secker).

POETRY: *The New Oxford Book of Light Verse* chosen and edited by Kingsley Amis (Oxford); *The Faber Popular Reciter* edited by Kingsley Amis (Faber); *Collected Poems* by Basil Bunting (Oxford); *The Complete Poems of Keith Douglas* edited by Desmond Graham (Oxford); *In the Egg and Other Poems* by Günter Grass (Secker); *Selected Poems* by John Masefield (Heinemann); *The Cost of Seriousness* by Peter Porter (Oxford); *Allen Tate: Collected Poems, 1919-76* (Faber); *Collected Poems of Edward Thomas* edited and introduced by R. George Thomas (Oxford).

LITERARY CRITICISM: *Samuel Johnson* by W. Jackson Bate (Chatto); *An Essay on Hardy* by John Bayley (Cambridge); *Wordsworth and the Human Heart* by John Beer (Cambridge); *Women and Children First: the Fiction of Two World Wars* by Mary Cadogan and Patricia Craig (Gollancz); *Tennyson* by Philip Henderson (Routledge); *Gerard Manley Hopkins* by Paddy Kitchen (Hamish Hamilton); *The Case for Walter Pater* by Michael Levey (Thames & Hudson); *Edward Thomas: a Poet for his Country* by Jan Marsh (Elek); *Fiction and the Fiction Industry* by J. A. Sutherland (University of London: Athlone Press); *Arnold Bennett; a Last Word* by Frank Swinnerton (Hamish Hamilton); *The Tell-tale Heart: the Life and Works of Edgar Allan Poe* by Julian Symons (Faber).

BIOGRAPHY: *Samuel Beckett: a Biography* by Deirdre Barr (Cape); *John Masefield: a Life* by Constance Babington Smith (Oxford); *Rudyard Kipling* by Lord Birkenhead (Weidenfeld); *A Portrait of Jane Austen* by David Cecil (Constable); *The Flower of Light: a Biography of Mary Webb* by Gladys Mary Coles (Duckworth); *Gilbert Cannan: a Georgian Prodigy* by Diana Farr (Chatto); *William Makepeace Thackeray: Memoirs of a Victorian Gentleman* edited by Margaret Forster (Secker); *E. M. Forster: a Life. Vol II: Polycrates' Ring* by P. N. Furbank (Macmillan); *Lewis Carroll: Fragments in a Looking Glass* by Jean Gattengo (Allen & Unwin); *The Older Hardy* by Robert Gittings (Heinemann); *The Minister's Wife* by Huntley Gordon (Routledge); *Lloyd George: the People's Champion 1901-11* by John Grigg (Eyre Methuen); *Lady Unknown: the Life of Angela Burdett Coutts* by Edna Healey (Sidgwick & Jackson); *Charles Dickens: His Tragedy and Triumph* by Edgar Johnson (Allen Lane); *Prick Up Your Ears: the Biography of Joe Orten* by John Lahr (Allen Lane); *The Magic Years of Beatrix Potter* by Margaret Lane (Warne); *Façades: Edith, Osbert and Sacheverell Sitwell* by John Pearson (Macmillan); *Robert Kennedy and His Times* by Arthur M. Schlesinger (Deutsch); *A Pre-Raphaelite Circle* by Raleigh Trevelyan (Chatto); *The Theatres of George Devine* by Irving Wardle (Cape); *Gertrude Bell* by H. V. F. Winstone (Cape).

AUTOBIOGRAPHY AND LETTERS: *Snakes and Ladders* by Dirk Bogarde (Chatto); *Boothby: Recollections of a Rebel* by Lord Boothby (Hutchinson); *To Build a Castle: My Life as a Dissenter* by Vladimir Bukovsky (Deutsch); *Born for Opposition: Byron's Letters and Journals, Vol. 8. 1821* edited by Leslie A. Marchand (Murray); *The Letters of Charles Dickens: Pilgrim Edition. Vol. IV* edited by Kathleen Tillotson (Oxford: Clarendon Press); *Double Harness: Memoirs* by Lord Drogheda (Weidenfeld); *You Can't Find Me* by Christopher Fry (Oxford); *The Gladstone Diaries. Vol. V, 1855-60; Vol. VI, 1861-68* edited by H. C. G. Matthew (Oxford: Clarendon Press); *The Goebbels Diaries: the Last Days* edited by Hugh Trevor-Roper (Secker); *Collected Letters of Thomas Hardy: Vol. I, 1840-1892* edited by Richard Little Purdy and Michael Millgate (Oxford: Clarendon Press); *Literary Gent* by David Higham (Cape); *Most Secret War* by R. V. Jones (Hamish Hamilton); *Janus: a Summing-up* by Arthur Koestler (Hutchinson); *Suez, 1956: a Personal Account* by Selwyn Lloyd (Cape); *March Past* by Lord Lovat (Weidenfeld); *The Lyttelton Hart-Davis Letters* edited by Rupert Hart-Davis (Murray); *In the Office of Constable* by Sir Robert Mark (Collins); *A Shaft of Sunlight: the Memories of a Varied Life* by Philip Mason (Deutsch); *The Memoirs of Reginald Maudling* (Sidgwick & Jackson); *North of South* by Shiva Naipaul (Deutsch); *Nuremberg: a Personal Record of the Trial of the Nazi War Criminals* by Airey Neave (Hodder); *A Pacifist's War* by Frances Partridge (Hogarth); *Infernal Child* by Erin Pizzey (Gollancz); *To Keep the Ball Rolling: the Memoirs of Anthony Powell, Vol. II: Messengers of Day* (Heinemann); *The Brendan Voyage* by Tim Severin (Hutchinson); *The Letters of Sidney and Beatrice Webb* edited by Norman Mackenzie (Cambridge); *From Apes to Warlords: the Autobiography (1904-46) of Solly Zuckerman* (Hamish Hamilton).

HISTORY: *The Shows of London* by Robert Altick (Harvard: Belknap Press); *In for a Penny* by Wilfrid Blunt (Hamish Hamilton); *The Ballad and the Plough* by David Kerr Cameron (Gollancz); *The Great Fear: the Anti-communist Purge under Truman and Eisenhower* by David Caute (Secker); *Death in Paris* by Richard Cobb (Oxford); *Kohyma: the Arctic Death Camps* by Robert Conquest (Macmillan); *Life in the English Country House: a Social and Architectural History* by Robert Girouard (Yale); *The Third World War, August 1985* by General Sir John Hackett and others (Sidgwick & Jackson); *Danton* by Norman Hampson (Duckworth); *Red Gold: the Conquest of the Brazilian Indians* by John Hemming (Macmillan); *The Great Mutiny: India, 1857* by Christopher Hibbert (Allen Lane); *Gollancz: the Story of a Publishing House, 1928-78* by Sheila Hodges (Gollancz); *Stuart England* by J. P. Kenyon (Allen Lane); *Montaillou: Cathars and Catholics in a French Village, 1290-1324* by Emmanuel Le Roy Ladurie (Scolar); *Ultra Goes to War* by Ronald Lewin (Hutchinson); *A Place Apart* by Dervla Murphy (Murray); *First Lady of Versailles* by Lucy Norton (Hamish Hamilton); *The Gulag Archipelago III, 1918-53* by Alexander Solzhenitsyn (Collins and Harvill); *And When Did You Last See Your Father: the Victorian Painter and History* by Roy Strong (Thames & Hudson); *The Oxford University Press: an Informal History* by Peter Sutcliffe (Oxford: Clarendon Press).

XVI SPORT

RUGBY UNION FOOTBALL

Although Wales is steeped in the history and tradition of numerous great rugby teams it has produced in the past, the one which added its contribution during the 1977-78 international championship is likely to remain long in the memory. It won the title and achieved the Grand Slam for the country for the second time in three seasons, ending with a memorable victory over the reigning champions, France—who had swept all before them in the previous season—by 16 points to 7 at Cardiff Arms Park. But that, alas, was the last time this magnificent side was to appear intact. Shortly afterwards, the scrum half, Gareth Edwards, and the fly half, Phil Bennett, announced their retirements. Edwards closed his international career with a record 53rd consecutive appearance for Wales, and Bennett with two points-scoring records—168 in the international championship and a world top mark of 210, beating by three the previous best by New Zealander Don Clarke.

Both players declined to make a short tour of Australia, where their absence was keenly felt in defeat for Wales in two Test matches. It was after this tour that wing Gerald Davies joined Edwards and Bennett in retirement after making 46 appearances in 12 years. Before the 1978-79 season was properly under way they were joined by their captain Terry Cobner—'a born leader' said one sad Welsh RFU official. Thus, in the space of 44 days, the team lost four of its greatest players.

So it was with considerable pride that Welsh supporters watched the depleted team come closest of all to beating in an international the most successful New Zealand All Blacks side to visit Britain and Ireland. They led for 70 minutes and were 12-10 ahead when in the last minute New Zealand were awarded a penalty for a debatable line-put infringement and won the game when McKechnie converted. Having already beaten Ireland 10-6, the All Blacks went on to overwhelm England 16-6 and, in the last minutes, Scotland 18-9 to become the first-ever New Zealand touring team to beat all four home countries. Although their tour record was not quite immaculate (they were beaten by Munster in an early game) the All Blacks completed an historic visit by beating The Barbarians 18-16 at Cardiff with a drop goal by Dunn, again with almost the last kick of the match.

But accompanying many of these exciting events was the spectre of unduly rough play. Wales returned home from Australia with one man in a wheelchair and another nursing a broken jaw. An English international, Chris Ralston, had his scalp split open in a club game against a Welsh side, and the new captain of Wales, J. P. R. Williams, had to have several stitches in his face after emerging from a ruck when his club, Bridgend, played the New Zealanders.

Even before this last incident, the English RFU had announced that any player sent off the field in a game under its jurisdiction would be automatically suspended for 30 days. The President, Mr Stanley Couchman, had already made a pledge 'to clean up the game' during his year of office.

SWIMMING

As in the European athletics championships, success for the Soviet Union in the world swimming championships held in West Berlin in August was marred by a scandal over drugs, when their 17-year-old backstroker Vladimir Kuznetsov, a bronze medallist in the 100 metres event, was found to have taken anabolic steroids.

In the pool, the championships were most notable for a reversal of their form of two years earlier in the Montreal Olympics by the United States women competitors. They won nine of the 14 world titles in such devastating times that they produced eight world records and did most to put the US above the Soviet Union in the final medals table. Backstroker Jesse Vassallo and butterfly specialist Tracy Caulkins, both Americans, were voted respectively male and female swimmers of the year—the first time since 1970 that the two titles had gone to swimmers from the same country—and the 15-year-old Miss Caulkins, who in one period of four months set 14 national records and one world record in butterfly, breast-stroke and medley events, also won a world-wide poll for the International Sportswoman of the Year.

For British swimmers, the world championships were a disappointment, probably because they followed too quickly on the Commonwealth Games. Only two bronze medals were won in Berlin. Their problems were typified by the performances of the outstanding girl, Sharron Davies. After a winter of hard preparation she collected a record seven titles at the national championships, won individual gold medals in two medley events at the Commonwealth Games and silver and bronze in relay races, but at 15 years of age had not the strength to repeat those triumphs in the world championships.

In long-distance swimming, youth seemed to be at an advantage in the strength-sapping endurance of crossing the Channel. Only a year after David Morgan, of Yorkshire, had become the youngest-ever to swim the crossing, at 13 years and ten months, a schoolboy from Blackpool, Lancashire, Karl Beniston, took $12\frac{1}{2}$ hours to claim the record at 13 years and seven months. His feat followed by only a few weeks the death of Edward Temme, who in 1934 took nearly 16 hours for the England–France swim when he became the first to cross in both directions.

Another British swimmer, Miss Stella Taylor, made two courageous attempts to swim the 100 miles from the Bahamas to the Florida coast of the USA but had to give up on each occasion, the second after being in the water for 51 hours, surviving shark attacks and jellyfish stings. Although she failed, Miss Taylor's feat ranked with any in still or tidal waters throughout the world during the year because she was 46 years old and learned to swim only eight years ago.

ATHLETICS

The continuing battle against the use of drugs and revelations about the payment of illegal expenses provided stories which rather overshadowed events in the stadiums. The drug problem was exposed once again at the European championships in Prague and resulted in the banning for life of five athletes—four Russians and a Bulgarian, including Nadia Tkacenko, winner of the women's pentathlon and world record holder. All the athletes were involved in field events and failed the tests for anabolic steroids, the drug which appears to be most useful in their branch of the sport because it encourages excessive body-weight.

The British shot-putter Geoffrey Capes had at first refused to compete in Prague against Eastern European rivals who, he claimed, used the steroids unfairly. The barb appeared to strike home because when Capes was eventually persuaded to change his mind and compete in the championships he was prevented from entering the arena for the final for the somewhat flimsy reason that he was wearing only one number instead of two. The frustrated Capes lost his temper with officials and was eventually disqualified for 'serious misconduct and unsporting behaviour'.

The Soviet Union and East Germany dominated the championships, finishing with 36 and 31 medals respectively. The British team managed only seven medals—one gold—a disappointment after striking a rich vein of athletic success in the Commonwealth Games in Edmonton a few weeks earlier (see below, p. 446).

The disclosure of illegal expenses paid to athletes was made in Edinburgh after local council officials had examined the financial accounts of the city's Highland Games meeting held on 19 August. The subsequent public revelation that some £11,000 had been paid in cash to competitors and coaches from Britain and overseas for non-existent air-fares and the like forced the British Amateur Athletic Board (BAAB) to start an official enquiry. In addition it seemed likely that a court action might ensue and the Inland Revenue expressed interest in the matter. One way or another the practice—which had been fairly widespread but often ignored by the ruling bodies, including the international federation, 'for lack of evidence'— might now be fully disclosed for the first time. According to a report in

The Observer on 17 December, Mr David Shaw, secretary of the British Board, admitted that the BAAB itself had been guilty of failing to disclose an expenses fraud involving an East European runner in Britain.

On the track, the man who dominated affairs was the Kenyan, Henry Rono, a 26-year-old student at Washington State University, USA, who in the space of 80 days set four world records, two in the United States, one in Oslo and one in Vienna. He became the first man to hold world records for the 5,000 metres and 3,000 metres steeplechase at the same time and also ran the fastest times for the 10,000 metres and 3,000 metres flat races.

British star Steve Ovett beat Rono in a two-mile race in a world-best time, and also won the European championships 'classic' 1,500 metres after narrowly failing in the 800 metres.

TENNIS

For a few weeks during an otherwise undistinguished 12 months, it looked as if British tennis might end the year on its highest note for many decades. On 7 October at the indoor courts at London's Crystal Palace the men's Davis Cup team reached the final by taking a winning 3-0 lead over Australia. On 4 November at the Royal Albert Hall, the women's Wightman Cup team beat the United States 4-3 to take the trophy for only the 10th time in 50 years.

An historic—possibly unique—'double' was in sight as the Davis Cup squad prepared to meet the USA in Palm Springs, California, early in December, in Britain's first appearance in the final since 1937—when the USA won 4-1 at Wimbledon. It was the first meeting between the two countries in this competition in the United States since 1903, when Britain won 4-1. That part of history did not repeat itself. The modern Lloyd brothers, David and John, could not match the performances of their Edwardian compatriots, the Doherty brothers, and Britain's only crumb of comfort in a 4-1 defeat was a fine singles victory by 'Buster' Mottram over Brian Gottfried on the first day. The outstanding player for the United States was young John McEnroe, quickly fulfilling the promise he showed at Wimbledon in both 1977 and 1978.

However, nothing McEnroe or anyone else could do could take Wimbledon away from the remarkable Swede, Bjorn Borg, who beat his perennial American rival Jimmy Connors in straight sets to become the first since Fred Perry in 1936 to win the men's singles title three years in succession. But it was Connors who equalled an even older record—held by Bill Tilden in the 1920s—in the 'new' US Open championships, held for the first time at the specially built £4 million stadium at Flushing Meadow, New York. Connors made his fifth consecutive appearance in the men's final, reversed his Wimbledon defeat by Borg, and was the first to become US champion on the three different surfaces, grass, clay and hard courts, on which the championships have been staged in recent years.

Virginia Wade could not repeat her Wimbledon triumph of 1977 and the title went to Martina Navratilova, who beat Chris Evert by two sets to one in the final. Miss Navratilova had been a stateless person for three years since leaving her homeland, Czechoslovakia, to live in the United States. Her family, still living near Prague, were refused permission to travel to Wimbledon to see her become the first Czech-born woman to take the title.

A 16-year-old American Pam Shriver became the youngest to reach the last four of the women's singles in the US championships by beating Miss Navratilova, but the title went to Chris Evert, equalling a 40-year-old record in becoming champion for the fourth successive year.

BOXING

At the age of 36, Muhammad Ali continued to dominate boxing from his throne as world heavyweight champion. He seemed to be indestructible, and there was nothing much left for him to do except to pick his moment to retire. Ali's activities this year finally deprived the boxing pundits of any logical discussion of their next favourite subject after speculation on his retirement—finding a successor capable of beating him and keeping him beaten.

In February, the latest challenger was produced who seemed to fit the bill. Like Ali, Leon Spinks, a fellow-American negro, came into the professional ranks with an Olympic title to his credit, won in good style in Montreal in 1976. After only seven professional fights he lacked experience, but he had age on his side, being 12 years younger than the champion. That seemed to tip the scales, for Ali was soundly beaten on points—and admitted it. Once more he was urged to retire.

Instead, the defeat only seemed to spur Ali on to even more record-breaking feats. In September, the new young champion and the old challenger met again, and Ali completely reversed the roles of their previous fight, winning one of the most decisive points victories of his long career. He thus became the first man to win the title three times; and he also left Spinks with a record—a reign as champion of 214 days, the shortest in world heavyweight championship history.

Still, Ali was not recognized by the less prestigious of the two bodies controlling world boxing—the World Boxing Council—which staged its own heavyweight title fight in November, won by a knockout in seven rounds by another American, Larry Holmes, over a Uruguayan-born contender, Alfredo Evangelista. A match between Ali and Holmes seemed the only meaningful prospect on the horizon, but it was unlikely while the World Boxing Association and the WBC remained at odds.

Across the Atlantic also there was disaffection between the British Boxing Board of Control and the European Boxing Union, which reduced European championship fights from 15 to 12 rounds following the death of the Italian Angelo Jacopucci in August, some hours after losing a middleweight title contest to Britain's Alan Minter. It was later revealed that Minter was in no way to blame for his opponent's sudden collapse at a reception after the fight. Another leading British boxer, John Conteh, lost the chance of a world light-heavyweight title crown when a very debatable points decision was given against him in Belgrade in a fight with the Yugoslav Mate Parlov. But the domestic scene in Britain was not much happier; the British heavyweight title, vacant for two years, was at last acquired by John L. Gardner when his opponent, Billy Aird, retired after only five rounds—an event believed to be unprecedented in a British heavyweight title fight.

Finally, the year was saddened by the death in November at the age of 80 of one of the truly great world heavyweight champions of the past, the American Gene Tunney, conqueror of Jack Dempsey, who in 1927 collected the first million-dollar cheque paid to a fighter in boxing history— and used it to become a successful businessman (see OBITUARY).

GOLF

It is axiomatic in sport that youth must win in the end because the body, alas, is not ageless like the spirit. But veterans everywhere in all sports who have had to give way to the relentless march of youth have, in golf, two of their greatest champions—the American Jack Nicklaus and the South African Gary Player. Once more they resolutely refused to give way to the generation of young golfers who have been pursuing them for many years.

Nicklaus started his 17th season in top golf by winning the US tournament players championship for the third time in five years, then won his third British Open title at St Andrews in July and his sixth Australian Open—by six strokes—in November. The only record left open to him in the last tournament was to equal Gary Player's seven Australian titles. But Player, now 42, was the only man matching Nicklaus in the 'big ones'. In April he became the oldest player in nearly 25 years to win the US Masters, making up a five-stroke deficit with nine holes to play on the last round, and tying the tournament record with a 64. He made a similar masterful comeback to snatch the US Tournament of Champions title in the same month.

The next threat, it seemed, might come from Japan, two of whose players made commendable efforts to win the British Open and one of whom, Isao Aoki, a former caddie, became the first from his country to win the World Matchplay Championship at Wentworth. But Aoki was already 36 years old.

A new tournament, the European Open, was won by the American Bobby Wadkins at Walton Heath only a few hours after his brother, Lanny, had won the Garden State PGA title in Melbourne, Australia. Neither tournament was entered by Player or Nicklaus.

The European women's championship was won by the 21-year-old Mexican-American Nancy Lopez, who thus completed a remarkable first year on the circuit in which she won five US tournaments in succession and easily beat the record earnings ever won in a year by any woman golfer.

MOTOR SPORT

The American driver Mario Andretti won the world championship, with several races in hand, at the Italian Grand Prix at Monza in September but under tragic circumstances for his all-conquering John Player Lotus team led by Colin Chapman. After finishing first and second respectively in the Dutch Grand Prix at Zandvoort two weeks earlier, Andretti and his Swedish team-mate Ronnie Peterson were so far ahead of their rivals that they could not be overhauled. But the first start to the Italian race resulted in a disastrous nine-car accident in which Peterson's car caught fire. Peterson was rescued from the blazing wreck by the British driver James Hunt but was found to have both legs severely fractured. These injuries caused blood clots which brought about his death several hours later in hospital. At 34, Peterson was one of the most experienced drivers on the circuit and had won the Italian race three times.

The Monza event was restarted after the accident, and although Andretti was first across the finishing line he was penalized and put down to sixth place for 'jumping the gun' at the start. However, he ended the race as undisputed world champion for the first time. In the aftermath of the fatal accident, a committee of the Formula 1 drivers banned a novice Italian, Riccardo Patrese, from the following US Grand Prix at Watkins Glen, although Patrese had been cleared of blame by an Italian magistrate investigating the Monza crash.

Andretti had held the world championship lead from as early as May and the Chapman Lotus team shortly established what seemed to be an unbreakable grip on the constructors' championship. Their only challenge in this field came at the Swedish Grand Prix in the middle of June when the Alfa-Romeo team led by the Australian former world champion Jack Brabham (later knighted in the New Year Honours List) suddenly produced a technical development which threatened to revolutionize the championship form. In searching for a new method of cooling their Alfa-Romeo engines, the Brabham team designer had produced a fan operating on top of a horizontally-placed radiator. The unexpected result of this was to force down the rear of the car, thus enabling it to corner at far higher speeds than normally. One expert estimated that 60 mph could be added to the car's speed, and driven by former world champion Niki Lauda at its first appearance in the Swedish Grand Prix it won easily. However, rival teams complained to the controlling body of the sport that the new development made the car illegal. Their protest was quickly upheld on safety as much as technical grounds until new regulations could be drafted.

THE TURF

Jockeys rather than horses dominated the scene on both sides of the Atlantic, resulting in two historic 'Classic' achievements. At Epsom and The Curragh, 38-year-old Greville Starkey won both the English and Irish Derbys on Shirley Heights and the English and Irish Oaks on Fair Salinia. He was the first jockey to achieve these feats in the same season.

Starkey's late run at Epsom on Shirley Heights to win in the last few strides robbed an even older veteran of the saddle, the 46-year-old American Willie Shoemaker, of victory in the Derby at his first attempt. Riding the same horse, Hawaiian Sound, Shoemaker was also beaten into third place in the Irish Derby. However much the English (and Irish) racing fraternity enjoyed watching one of America's greatest jockeys at work among his British rivals, there was a certain disappointment that only the closeness of the climaxes of both the English and American Classics prevented them from seeing the possible achievement of a unique feat of jockeyship in the whole history of horse racing in England or the United States.

The ride on Hawaiian Sound at Epsom was originally offered to the young American genius Steve Cauthen, who again dominated the American scene in only his second full season at the age of 18. Riding Affirmed, Cauthen won the Kentucky Derby at his first attempt, and with the Preakness Stakes already under his belt needed only victory in the Belmont Stakes to become the youngest-ever to complete America's Classic Triple Crown. Unfortunately, for him to ride both at Epsom and Belmont would have meant flying between the US and Britain twice in four days. He elected to stay at home and duly rode Affirmed to victory again.

A British veteran, Lester Piggott, won the Prix de l'Arc de Triomphe on Alleged for the second year in succession, but finished only fifth in the race for champion jockey in England. This was won by Willie Carson with 182 victories; but a virus infection which closed Peter Walwyn's stable for two months in August and September probably deprived its leading jockey, Pat Eddery, of his fifth successive championship on the flat.

Irishman Jonjo O'Neill beat the previous record number of wins in a National Hunt season with a total of 149, but the unluckiest combination over the sticks was Tommy Stack and Red Rum. After receiving a severe pelvis injury early in the 1977-78 season, the courageous Stack suffered months of painful treatment with only one major object in mind—to get fit to ride Red Rum to yet another Grant National triumph. The jockey was ready in time—just—but on the very eve of the race, which nearly everyone tipped him to win for the fourth time in six years, Red Rum was declared unfit and withdrawn. Later the great horse was retired from racing and a few weeks later Stack followed suit.

ASSOCIATION FOOTBALL

THE XIth World Cup finals were held in Argentina for the first time and resulted in a win for the host country, also for the first time. Sustained by enormous public support, Argentina's flamboyant footballers, brilliantly led by their enigmatic manager–coach Cesar Menotti, overcame a somewhat shaky start in the tournament to emerge the best, on results, of the 16 finalists.

In the final itself, Argentina were given a very hard fight by the Netherlands and the match went to extra time (for the first time since England's victory in 1966) before the South American team won, 3-1. For the Dutch, it was their second successive disappointment at the last gasp. In the 1974 final they had been beaten by the host country, West Germany. In the match for third place, Brazil, winners a record three times between 1958 and 1970, beat Italy 2-1 in a 'replay' of the 1970 final in Mexico. The holders, West Germany, reached the last eight, but without the majority of their best players of four years earlier could make no further progress.

The tournament as a whole was notable more for extraordinary results than for outstanding football. Argentina contributed perhaps the mos startling performance in the last match of the second round, against Peru. To be sure of qualifying for the final, Menotti's men needed to win by at least four clear goals against opponents who had already caused the biggest upset of the tournament by eliminating Scotland. They won by six.

For Scotland, the only British representatives in the finals for the second time in succession, the tournament was an absolute disaster. Dispatched on a wave of euphoria by pipe bands and thousands of cheering supporters, they returned a few weeks later disillusioned, defeated and disgraced. Faced successively by Peru, Iran and the Netherlands in their first-round group, Scotland were clear favourites to be one of the two teams to qualify from this group for the next round. But they were beaten by Peru, held to a draw by Iran and only began to approach their best form too late when they beat the Netherlands, but not by sufficient margin to prevent their early elimination. In addition, one player, Willie Johnston, was sent home after failing a drug test, and he and two others, Don Masson and Lou Macari—accused of talking too freely to the press about dissension in the Scottish camp—were banned for life from further selection for the international team. On his return, the manager, Ally MacLeod, survived (only narrowly, it was reported) a vote of confidence by the Scottish FA, but later resigned to return to club management.

For England, a long-awaited run of success came just too late to secure a place in the World Cup finals. Under new manager Ron Greenwood, the team was beaten only by West Germany in Munich during the year, won all its home international championship matches and defeated the current European champions, Czechoslovakia. In December, the former manager, Don Revie, faced an FA enquiry into the circumstances under which he resigned in 1977 (see AR 1977, p. 442) and as a result was banned from taking any post in English football until 1987.

There was success, also, for England in European club competition. By beating FC Bruges (Belgium) in the final at Wembley by a single goal, Liverpool became the first British club to retain the European Champions Cup. But they could not retain their supremacy in the League against the upsurge by Nottingham Forest, inspired by their controversial manager, Brian Clough. Forest beat Liverpool after a replay in the League Cup final and also won the League championship. Ironically, Liverpool—who qualified as holders—and Forest were drawn in opposition in the first round of the 1978-79 European Champions Cup competition and again the Nottingham side proved superior. And it was an England international, Kevin Keegan, formerly of Liverpool now playing for Hamburg, who was voted by the European football writers their Footballer of the Year.

The start of the 1978-80 European Nations championship also saw a unique sporting event take place in Dublin on 20 September when Eire and Northern Ireland met for the first time ever on the football field. They had been drawn together in the same qualifying group and the European Football Union insisted that the matches—a return game was due in Belfast in 1979—take place. The match ended in a goalless draw and was conducted both on the pitch and on the terraces without untoward incident.

CRICKET

Few players in the whole history of the game can have experienced such a traumatic year as 1978 was for the Yorkshire and England opening batsman Geoffrey Boycott. In January, towards the end of a tour of Pakistan and New Zealand, he finally achieved a lifetime's ambition by being made captain of England when Mike Brearley had to return home with an injury. But it was under Boycott's leadership that England lost a Test to New Zealand for the first time in 47 years. New Zealand and Pakistan both made return short tours of England in the summer and were beaten handsomely in Test series by teams captained by Brearley. In August, when the England tour party to Australia in 1978-79 was announced, Boycott was deprived of even his vice-captaincy. Shortly afterwards, in September, he was dismissed as Yorkshire captain after eight years and then became the subject of an unprecedented public row; his supporters forced the issue to a vote among Yorkshire CCC members at a special general meeting, which decided nearly two to one in favour of Boycott's dismissal from the captaincy.

By this time, the unhappy player was in Australia and having difficulty on the field in justifying the mantle of 'the world's No 1 batsman' cast upon him in the summer of 1977 after his stupendous performances on his return to Test cricket for England (see AR 1977, p. 445). He was the subject of one official protest because of his apparent reluctance to accept an umpire's decision and the unfortunate object of barracking and missile-throwing from the crowd while fielding in Sydney.

But it was a year in which activities off the field tended to dominate, particularly in the repercussions of the establishment of the Australian entrepreneur Kerry Packer's cricket 'circus' in 1977. In January, one of Packer's leading recruits, Tony Greig, was sacked as captain of Sussex shortly after being reappointed, following a public attack he made on Boycott for the latter's alleged anti-Packer views. In February, the International Cricket Conference decided to accept without appeal a High Court ruling that its action in banning Packer players from Test and county cricket was illegal, and in July Australian players contracted to Packer won a similar action in the Australian Supreme Court. But later the ICC rejected a move for 'co-existence' between themselves and Packer. The reactions of the counties varied. Nottinghamshire sacked their captain, Clive Rice, after he had joined Packer, but the decision of the Kent CCC committee to offer new contracts to three of their Packer players resulted in the resignation of one member, David Clark, who had been 30 years on the committee, president of MCC and chairman of the ICC.

Some benefits for those who had rejected Packer began to come through, however. The Test and County Cricket Board recommended an increase in basic wage to £4,000 a year for capped county players. It also established new rules for yet another innovation in the game—the use of protective helmets by batsmen and close fielders. The TCCB ruled that batsmen could be caught out if the ball rebounded off their helmets direct into a fielder's hands, but not if the 'catch' had also rebounded off a fielder's helmet or if the ball lodged in his helmet visor. By contrast, the ramifications of the Packer business seemed comparatively simple.

COMMONWEALTH GAMES

The XIth Commonwealth Games were held in Edmonton, Canada, from 4-12 August and were attended by 1,450 competitors from 46 countries—both record figures for the Games. They were opened officially by the Queen, speaking in both French and English, and comprised for the first time ten instead of nine sports, with gymnastics added to the usual programme.

Apart from a boycott by Nigeria—unsupported by other African nations—in protest against New Zealand's continuing rugby links with South Africa, there were no untoward political incidents before or during the events, which maintained their reputation as 'The Friendly Games' throughout. Canada headed the medals table with a total of 109 awards (45 gold, 31 silver and 33 bronze), England (87 medals) being second and Australia (84) third. Altogether 17 of the participating countries won medals.

Among many notable individual achievements were those of Precious McKenzie in weightlifting and David Bryant in bowls. McKenzie, an emigrant from England to New Zealand after the 1974 Games in Christchurch, became the first man to win a gold medal at four consecutive Games, dating back to 1966. Bryant, of England, won his fifth gold medal since 1962 and his fourth successive singles title—a sequence broken only in 1966 when bowls was not on the programme. In the swimming, Graham Smith, of Canada, won a total of six gold medals.

XVII ECONOMIC AND SOCIAL AFFAIRS

Chapter 1

MONETARY STABILITY IN EUROPE

THE currency instability which had been so pronounced a feature of markets between 1976 and 1978 led to a marked reaction during 1978 in the form of the proposals for a European Monetary System (EMS). (The full text of the EMS plan, with official UK comment, is printed in DOCUMENTS.) The attempt to create what was described as a 'zone of monetary stability' within the nine countries of the European Economic Community (EEC) had important economic and political implications. The proposals represented a further stage in the search for closer economic and monetary ties which dated back to the principles embodied in the Treaty of Rome in 1957. The first major initiative had been an agreement, at a summit in 1969, by the leaders of the (then) six EEC members as to the creation of economic and monetary union; in the following year the Werner report proposed the establishment of this in stages by 1980.

The initial step was the creation in April and May 1972 of the 'snake', which involved the close linking within narrow margins of the currencies of EEC members, and one or two others. However, this system did not last long; for Britain and Ireland were forced out within six weeks, Italy dropped out in February 1973 and France was in and out of the snake twice. The hopes for closer monetary union were blighted by the currency upsets, accelerating inflation and widely divergent economic performances of 1974-78, so that even the objective of currency stability seemed a remote possibility.

The idea of economic and monetary union was, however, revived by Mr Roy Jenkins, the President of the EEC Commission, in a speech in Florence in October 1977, when he argued for a big leap forward to provide the opportunity for both economic and political gains (see AR 1977, p. 332). Although the speech provoked much sceptical comment it was the catalyst for practical discussions about closer convergence of member countries' policies.

The main initiative came in April 1978 at a meeting of EEC heads of government in Copenhagen when, to most participants' surprise, Chancellor Helmut Schmidt of West Germany suggested that the EEC should consider the desirability of moves to achieve greater currency stability. This was set out in a Franco-German paper to a further summit of leaders of the chief industrialized countries in Bremen on 6 and 7 July 1978, and these proposals formed the basis of discussions among the nine EEC members during the rest of 1978.

The motives and aims of Chancellor Schmidt and the other EEC leaders were widely debated and hotly disputed throughout the year. The starting-point was the view, expressed by many bankers and financial officials in Europe, that the breakdown of the Bretton Woods system of fixed exchange rates had imposed substantial costs on the international monetary framework and had aggravated inflationary problems. Consequently several EEC leaders called, during the first half of 1978, for greater exchange rate stability in order to curb inflation and provide the pre-conditions for sustained growth.

The immediate trigger for the German initiative was the continuing sharp fall in the dollar during the early months of 1978 (see p. 456). This led both to heavy inflows in currencies like the Deutschemark and the Swiss franc, through a switching of investments of reserve assets, and to a large appreciation in their exchange values.

West Germany was thus faced with the dilemma of whether to allow its exchange rate to rise and accept the effect upon the export competitiveness and profitability of much of its industry, or to intervene to hold down the rate, and thus boost the growth of the domestic money supply. The priorities naturally differed among bankers, industrialists and politicians, but the general response was conditioned by the German reluctance to allow the Deutschemark to assume the formal role of an international reserve currency. The result was a compromise whereby West Germany sought to spread the burden of the dollar problem throughout the EEC while attempting to achieve currency stability within the nine.

The Franco-German proposals subsequently put forward at Bremen fell far short of any specific move towards economic and monetary union and referred solely to a scheme for the 'creation of closer monetary co-operation leading to a zone of monetary stability in Europe'. The EMS project essentially revived the idea of fixed but adjustable parities which had broken down in 1973. In detail, the Bremen plan envisaged exchange rate margins 'at least as strict as the snake', though with provision for wider fluctuations for new entrants. The main new features related to the credit facilities; it was proposed that a European Monetary Fund should be established consisting of one-fifth of member states' gold dollar holdings and a similar amount of their own currencies. But it was recognized in the communique that 'a system of closer monetary cooperation will only be successful if participating countries pursue policies conducive to greater stability at home and abroad; this applies to deficit and surplus countries alike'.

The debate on the EMS proposals in the summer and early autumn turned on this latter point—were the chances of a successful linking of EEC currencies any better now than when several of the original snake members left in 1972-73? On the EEC's own figures, the disparity in inflation rates in 1978, although less than in 1975, was still much higher than before 1973-74, and a much greater convergence of inflation rates would be required to achieve a durable and smoothly functioning EMS.

Discussing this point in early 1979, Mr Gordon Richardson, the Governor of the Bank of England, commented: 'a static snapshot taken in 1978 would compare unfavourably in most respects with the same photograph in the album of 1969. Viewed dynamically, on the other hand, the conjuncture in 1978 was generally pointing in a better direction for the EEC countries than at any time since before 1973.' In particular, Mr Richardson pointed to narrower inflation differentials between the EEC countries, signs of renewed growth, a somewhat more balanced distribution of balance of payments surpluses and deficits, and a convergence of ideas and aims, notably on the desirability of more stable exchange rates.

The convergence of ideas, however, proved to be insufficient in the technical debates of the second half of 1978. The discussions at the Council of Finance Ministers focused especially on the nature of the intervention mechanism and the supporting credit facilities. The UK, whose Ministers had been irritated at the way the Franco-German plans had been put forward, took the lead in trying to make the system more accommodating for some of the less prosperous EEC members. Britain sought to place the burden of adjustment more equally on debtor and creditor countries by using the new idea of the European Currency Unit (ECU) as a means of urging an inducement to adjust upon strong countries whose currencies were manifestly diverging most from the Community average represented by the ECU. In the event, there was a compromise whereby the working of the ECU established a presumption, but not an obligation, that a country whose currency diverged too sharply would take prompt action. Nevertheless the essence of the system was similar to that of the snake, under which the day-to-day rules of intervention were that each currency was linked to the others in a parity-grid.

This arrangement was seen as unsatisfactory by the UK, which also had reservations about the absence of a clear-cut policy on the dollar; this defect might place special strains on sterling in view of the UK's substantial trading and other relationships outside the EEC. There was also pressure from the UK and other less prosperous EEC members like Italy and Ireland for a greater transfer of resources to improve the redistributive impact of the EEC budget.

In the end, the decisions were determined less by technical reservations than by underlying political attitudes towards the EEC. Thus a Labour Administration in the UK was not keen to reopen fundamental arguments about European relationships, even though Ministers stressed Britain's commitment to pursue parallel economic policies, especially by maintaining exchange rate stability. Italy and Ireland eventually felt able to join, after initially holding back at the Brussels summit on 4 and 5 December (see p. 335). Although both countries were offered more regional

P

and other financial assistance, and Italy took advantage of the option of a wider exchange rate margin, the key point seemed to be the greater commitment of both states than that of the UK to the ideals of the EEC.

So, after various alarms and diversions, it looked as though EMS would start at the beginning of 1979 with eight out of the nine as full participants. What they would be joining was a watered-down version of the original Bremen plan in that the main emphasis was on the intervention mechanism, backed up by more extensive short-term and medium-term credit facilities, but with no signs of real progress towards the goal of establishing within two years a fully-fledged European Monetary Fund with pooled reserves.

At the last minute, however, the French Government prevented the start of the system as planned on 1 January. Just before Christmas the French indicated that their approval was dependent on agreement on the phasing-out of Monetary Compensatory Amounts (MCAs) which penalized French farmers but subsidized German ones (see p. 336). This dispute went to the heart of one of the EEC's most deep-rooted issues. Meanwhile, at the end of 1978, the currencies of the EEC were effectively being linked informally and were under no great pressure.

Chapter 2

INTERNATIONAL ECONOMIC DEVELOPMENTS

IN the international economic conclaves of 1978 the main effort was concentrated on securing a better balance in the development of the major economies, and by the end of the year there were some signs that this process was beginning. Yet this was happening against the background of continued slow growth in overall output, with high unemployment and only a marginal reduction in the rate of price inflation. In many respects the general picture in 1978 was very much the same as in the previous year. But because of a rise in the price of manufactured goods relative to oil and other commodities the current account deficit of industrialized countries fell sharply, at the expense of both the oil producing states and non-oil developing countries.

Total output in the 24 countries of the area of the Organization for Economic Cooperation and Development (OECD) rose by roughly $3\frac{1}{2}$ per cent in 1978, slightly less than in the previous year. But there was an uneven pattern during the year, production being held back in the first few months by severe weather in many countries and by the coal strike in the USA. This was followed by a sharp rebound, as private consumption remained strong and the rate of growth of public spending picked up. The strengthening of demand in the second half partly reflected the impact of earlier expansionary measures taken, for example, in Japan and West Germany, where low interest rates and ample credit fuelled a construction boom.

The relatively modest overall growth in output was matched by a surprisingly strong expansion of employment, notably in the USA but also in Japan and Canada. This in turn was reflected in a very poor productivity performance. Although unemployment fell in a number of countries there was little change in the OECD area as a whole, the rates standing at 5¼ to 5½ per cent.

The rate of consumer price inflation also showed little change over 1978, only coming down from 7¾ per cent to 6¾ per cent in the OECD area. Food prices rose in the early months of the year but fell later, and, in general, the trend in world commodity and raw material prices was favourable to consumers. However, there were few signs of any significant deceleration in labour costs; rather there was a slight acceleration in the USA and Britain. Indeed, rising commodity prices at the end of the year meant that the forward indicators for inflation in most countries were not pointing downwards.

Within this overall picture there remained marked differences in the relative expansion of demand among the main industrialized countries. In particular, the growth of real Gross National Product in the USA stayed well above that of its main competitors in Europe. Total output in the USA increased by nearly 5 per cent in 1977 and by about 4 per cent in 1978 compared with increases of 2½ and 2¾ per cent for those years respectively in the four major European countries (West Germany, France, Britain and Italy).

I. Percentage increase in real Gross National Product from
previous year

	1965-66 to 1975-76 (average)	1977	1978 (estimates)	1979 (forecast)
USA	2·7	4·9	3·8	2
Japan	8·2	5·2	5·8	4·8
Germany	3·3	2·6	3	4
France	4·7	3	3	3·5
Britain	2·1	1·6	3	2·25
Canada	4·7	2·7	3·5	4
Italy	4·1	1·7	2	3·5
Other OECD	4·4	1·8	2·25	3
Total OECD	4·1	3·7	3·5	3

Source: *OECD, Economic Outlook*, December 1978.

The results were summarized by M Jacques de Larosière, a senior French Treasury official who had taken over in the middle of the year as managing director of the International Monetary Fund from Dr Johannes Witteveen. M de Larosière noted that 'the divergences tended to narrow in 1978 but not before demand had closed in on productive capacity in the USA, where as a result the deficit on current account continued at a high level and inflation accelerated'. M de Larosière added that 'at the same time rates of inflation remained low or had even decelerated in Switzerland, West Germany and Japan. In consequence, the spread of nominal interest rates in favour of the USA was overwhelmed by a change in inflationary expectations, and destabilizing capital movements set in. Finally, intervention in exchange markets designed to moderate exchange rate movements gave rise to a massive increase in international liquidity'.

The major industrial countries and organizations such as the IMF and OECD had been pressing for action designed to reduce this divergence from early 1977 onwards—in particular at the seven-nation economic summit in London in May 1977 and at the IMF annual meeting in the following autumn. The results had been disappointing and the pressures were renewed ahead of the Bonn economic summit in mid-July 1978. There, the goals of a programme of concerted action were in general reaffirmed, together with commitments to maintain demand or reduce inflation according to the particular conditions of participating countries. There was, however, a noticeable shift away from agreement on ambitious overall growth targets, previously unattained, towards greater emphasis on improving the balance of performance.

By late September, when the annual meeting of the IMF was held in Washington, there were signs at least of cautious optimism, for the first time in many years. In part, this could be seen as an attempt to talk up the dollar, but some positive real indicators could be identified, notably the delayed impact both of the various expansionary measures taken in Europe in the previous 18 months and of the significant changes that had occurred in exchange rates.

Consequently, M Emile van Lennep, the secretary-general of the OECD, felt able to say that the outlook for the industrialized countries as a whole was, if not one of much faster growth, then at least one of much better balanced growth. He pointed out that over the 18 months to the middle of 1978 domestic demand in the USA rose at an average annual rate of 5 per cent, while in the rest of the OECD area it rose at an annual rate of only $2\frac{1}{4}$ per cent. However, over the next 18 months, to the end of 1979, he expected a growth of domestic demand of around 3 to $3\frac{1}{2}$ per cent in the USA as against 4 to 5 per cent in the rest of the OECD area.

This slightly more encouraging view of the prospects was in general maintained at the end of the year, though there were few indications of any early slowdown in the US economy. Overall, the OECD annual report noted that 'many factors seem to be running in favour of less turbulent conditions in exchange markets and better business confidence'. This followed a sharp appreciation in the Japanese yen, Swiss franc and Deutschemark during 1978.

Apart from the generally improved balance between the USA and the rest of the industrialized world there was evidence also that in a number of countries firm stabilization policies over the previous two years had led to greatly reduced inflation and swollen external deficits—notably in France, Italy and Britain. Efforts to limit domestic demand and inflation resulted in particularly big swings in the current account balances of Sweden, Norway, Austria, Spain and Turkey. This happened in spite of a further large rise in the current account surpluses of West Germany and Japan; these, however, were expected to lessen substantially during 1979 as a result of earlier exchange rate adjustments and expansionary moves.

The changes in current account balances within the industrialized world were matched by notable shifts in the position of this group relative to the oil producers and developing countries. While the deficit of the OECD area dropped from $27,500 million in 1977 to around $750 million in 1978, the surplus of the oil producing countries shrank from $31,500 million to $11,000 million between the two years, and the deficit of the non-oil developing countries increased from $24,000 million to $34,000 million.

II. Current Account Balances

	1973	*1974*	*1975*	*1976*	*1977*	*1978*	*1979 (forecast)*
				$000 million			
OECD	9½	−27½	¼	−18¾	−27½	−¾	−1¼
Oil producers	8	59¼	27¼	37	31½	11	7½
Non-oil developing	−7	−24½	−38½	−26	−24	−34	−38
Other	−3¼	−9¾	−18½	−12¾	−10	−10¾	−9¾

Source: *OECD Economic Outlook*, December 1978. Figures do not sum to zero because of statistical anomalies and asymmetries.

These shifts in turn reflected a major change in the terms of trade in favour of industrialized countries; the dollar price of exports of manufactured goods rose by 14½ per cent during the year while the price of oil rose by only 1½ per cent and the average value of non-oil commodities exported by developing countries increased by only 5 per cent. The gap, however, did not look like lasting and by the end of the year there were indications of a rise in the price of many commodities. This applied, in particular, to oil in view of the troubles in Iran and the larger-than-expected 14·5 per cent increase in the official oil price recommended in December by the producing states for implementation in stages in 1979.

Chapter 3

ECONOMY OF THE UNITED STATES

IN 1978, for the second year in a row, the US economy remained among the most buoyant of those of the major industrialized countries. Both consumer spending and housing and industrial investment were strong, with the result that total output rose by about 4 per cent in real terms during the year. This compared with an average growth rate of about $3\frac{1}{2}$ per cent in 1978 in the 24 countries within the area of the Organization for Economic Cooperation and Development (OECD).

The continued, albeit narrower, gap between the rate of expansion in the USA and that in Europe was the main reason why the former had a large deficit on the current account of its balance of payments. At the same time, the pressures on the dollar intensified and the US currency fell sharply against the Japanese yen, the Deutschemark and the Swiss franc. The fall in the dollar, together with strong growth in domestic demand, also led to an acceleration in the internal rate of inflation.

Output and Investment. Demand and output had been strong during the second half of 1977 but there was a setback during the first quarter of 1978 as a result of the coal miners' strike and unfavourable weather conditions; the effects, however, proved to be short-lived and the economy rebounded strongly during the spring and early summer. Private consumption continued to provide much of the impetus throughout 1978 and public spending also rose sharply in the second half of the year, to offset a decline in residential investment. The result was that the rate of growth of industrial production accelerated from an annual rate of $4\frac{3}{4}$ per cent in the first half to $7\frac{3}{4}$ per cent in the second half of the year.

The strong growth of output was, however, accompanied by a poor productivity performance. The rate of output growth per head had halved to an annual rate of 1·6 per cent in the ten years to 1978 from a rate of 3·2 per cent in the previous 20 years, and during 1978 the gain was less than 1 per cent. This was reflected in a big rise in total employment—up about 3 million during 1978 alone and 7 million higher than in early 1977. A large part of this increase came from new entrants to the work-force, notably women and members of minority groups.

Consequently there was a disproportionately small decline in unemployment, which fell from around $6\frac{3}{4}$ per cent of the work-force at the end of 1977 to roughly $5\frac{3}{4}$ per cent by December 1978. Indeed, as the expansion of activity was maintained at the year's end, there were signs of shortages of labour in many areas. This indicated that the economy might be near—and in some areas beyond—the limits of its productive capacity, the remaining unemployment being of a structural rather than a cyclical kind.

Inflation. The poor productivity performance and the pressures caused by sustained buoyant domestic demand were major contributors to a significant worsening of inflation during 1978. The surge in prices became evident early in the year, and the blame was at first laid on a sharp rise in food prices caused by the exceptionally bad winter weather and by the initial impact of higher social security charges and minimum wages legislation. Consumer price inflation accelerated from an annual rate of 5·1 per cent in the second half of 1977 to 7·7 per cent in the first half of 1978. There was some deceleration, notably of food prices, during the summer, but then underlying inflationary pressures reasserted themselves and the annual rate of consumer price inflation was around 7 per cent in the second half of 1978. The pick-up of labour costs, and of import costs as a result of the depreciation of the dollar, were important influences. In addition, the cost of land and building materials was pushed up by a housing boom.

Government Policies. The acceleration of inflation clearly replaced unemployment as the top priority problem for both the public and politicians. This was reflected in the widespread taxpayers' revolts and in attempts to curb public spending, as well as in a change in the Federal Government's policies. These became markedly less expansionary, and a comprehensive counter-inflation programme was introduced in October. The Administration's proposals for tax reductions were reshaped by Congress and spending cuts were the main feature of the tighter budgetary stance. The estimated size of the budgetary deficit in the fiscal year 1978-79 was reduced during the course of 1978 from $60,500 million to $38,800 million.

A pledge by the Federal Government to limit its spending and reduce the deficit to below $30,000 million in fiscal 1980 formed a major part of the counter-inflation programme announced in October. Other elements were a voluntary standard of 7 per cent for annual increases in wages, price standards to limit rises, and a programme of real wage insurance. Under the last proposal, groups of workers meeting the pay standard would receive a tax rebate if the rate of inflation over the next year were to exceed 7 per cent, though at the end of 1978 this notion was facing opposition in Congress.

In addition, monetary policy became markedly more restrictive during the course of 1978, and this, coupled with buoyant credit demand, led to a sharp rise in interest rates. The federal funds rate rose from 6¾ per cent at the beginning of 1978 to 10¼ per cent by the year's end, while the prime rate of the main banks was raised from 7¾ per cent to 11¾ per cent.

External Finance. For the outside world, the most important US development in 1978 concerned the current account of the balance of payments and the dollar. The current deficit increased significantly in the first few months of 1978 in response to a decline in export volume, a surge in imports and the initial effect of the decline in the dollar in raising import prices in dollar terms. The deficit widened from $16,500 million in the second half of 1977 to $11,250 million in the first quarter of 1978 alone.

A strong recovery in the trade performance occurred during the rest of 1978, thanks to buoyant agricultural exports and some improvement in the volume of manufactured exports as well as a more favourable export/import price ratio. The result was that a trade deficit of $19,000 million in the first half of 1978 was cut to $16,000 million in the second half.

The trade deficit was, however, only one influence, though a crucially important one, upon the foreign exchange markets, where attitudes and investment decisions were also affected by concern about the rate of expansion of domestic credit and the signs of accelerating inflation. But as the December 1978 report by the OECD pointed out 'none of these factors, alone, could reasonably have justified the position of the dollar at the end of October', when it had fallen by nearly one-fifth in 12 months against other major currencies.

But, the report added, 'together they may provide a rough indication why—without external help—a further decline of the dollar may have been required to convince enough investors to move into dollar assets, thereby providing the necessary financing for the continuing current account deficit, some structural capital outflows (US investment overseas) and possibly some diversification of official reserves from dollars into other currencies'.

These pressures were reflected in figures showing that total intervention in support of the dollar up to the end of October was nearly 80 per cent larger than the current account deficit over the same period. The problems appear to have been aggravated by the diversification of reserves by oil-producing states and developing countries. Indeed in the second quarter of 1978 the oil producing countries reduced their financial investment in the USA, for the first time since the increase in oil prices in late 1973.

The combination of these influences and the apparent ineffectiveness of the Carter Administration's response explained the continued slide in the dollar, even after the late 1977 policy of benign neglect had been replaced by what the market saw as half-hearted measures. The selling became so intense by late October that the US Government was forced to introduce a wide-ranging package of remedies. The measures consisted not only of a tightening in the domestic credit squeeze but also of external financial support. This amounted to $30,000 million from central banks and the IMF, from the issue of foreign currency securities outside the USA and from sales of gold. This package reassured the market and was followed by a sharp recovery in the dollar in November.

The hope clearly was that these measures would be a successful holding operation until the US current account started to improve and the rate of inflation stopped rising. But there were doubts about the speed of the turn-round and by the end of 1978 the dollar was again weak, partly in response to the troubles in Iran. There were reliable market estimates of official support of as much as $10,000 million since early November.

Chapter 4

ECONOMY OF THE UNITED KINGDOM

THE UK economy was stronger in 1978 than at any time since the rise in oil prices of 1973 and the subsequent recession. Yet, in many respects, it was a year of only temporary advances and overall disappointment; for many of the long-standing British problems of weak trade performance and chronic inflationary pressures resurfaced by the autumn.

The starting-point was a mood of considerable confidence at the end of 1977. The UK's external and internal financial position had improved dramatically in the preceding 12 months, the prospects for the current account of the balance of payments looked reasonably good, the pound was strong, the rate of price inflation was falling and the stage seemed set for the long-awaited recovery in output and living standards. But the performance, as so often in the past, did not live up to expectations.

The results were best summarized, just after the end of 1978, by Mr Gordon Richardson, the Governor of the Bank of England. He noted that 'the contribution of some £5,000 million made by North Sea oil to our Gross Domestic Product over the past four years has been very largely matched by the strong growth in personal consumption recorded last year—a growth satisfied importantly by imports. This reflected the combination of the very rapid growth of nominal earnings, the reduction in taxation and the relatively strong sterling exchange rate (itself partly a consequence of North Sea oil) that has helped significantly to moderate the rise in prices over the last two years.

'Even though personal consumption had been depressed for the three preceding years or more', the Governor continued, 'and though we could not expect to see output and activity start to revive except on the basis of some rise in consumer spending, we cannot in my view regard the pattern of demand in 1978, and only a marginal surplus on the current account of our balance of payments, with much satisfaction'.

Inflation. The key to both Britain's performance and its prospects was inflation. The combination of continued, reasonably successful pay restraint, a firm exchange rate and weak world commodity prices kept the rate of price inflation down during 1978. There was a good start to the year as the 12-month rate of increase in retail prices moved into single

P*

figures in January for the first time since 1973, and continued down to a low point of 7·4 per cent in June. This was less than the average for industrialized countries generally.

However, during the 1977-78 pay round the rate of increase of average earnings accelerated from 8·5 per cent to 14·2 per cent. This ensured a rapid growth of real earnings, which was augmented by sizeable income tax cuts effective in autumn 1977 and from spring 1978. The result was that by autumn 1978 living standards, as measured by real personal disposable incomes, were 8½ per cent higher than a year earlier; about a quarter of the rise was due to lower personal taxes. This more than offset the previous sharp decline in disposable incomes. But the gap between prices and earnings could not last indefinitely. Eventually the rise in labour costs started to work through to retail prices and the annual rate edged up to 8·4 per cent by the end of 1978. There was some surprise that the pick-up in the inflation rate had not been greater, but higher wages were partially offset by stable import costs and by competitive pressures, notably from imports, which squeezed profit margins.

The underlying trend was clearly moving upwards, however. In the absence of any agreement between the Government and the trade unions about pay policy any reduction in the rate of wage increases appeared hard to achieve. The difficulties were underlined at the start of the pay round by a nine-week strike at the Ford Motor Company which ended with a 17 per cent settlement (see pp. 24-5). The Government had been attempting to discipline the private sector through the use of sanctions, such as the withholding of contracts or discretionary industrial assistance, but this policy was rejected by the House of Commons (see p. 19), leaving the official pay policy looking rather threadbare at the end of the year.

Output and Employment. The sharp rise in living standards during 1978 led to a major recovery in consumer spending, back to the levels of 1973 after several years of restraint. For 1978 as a whole, the volume of spending was roughly 6 per cent higher than in the previous year, sales of durable goods and motor cars being particularly buoyant. This was the main reason for the rise in output and sharp increase in imports.

The rise in industrial production was slightly disappointing compared with earlier expectations, especially when account was taken of the build-up of North Sea oil production. Industrial output rose by around 3¾ per cent in real terms during the year, and total production, as measured by real Gross Domestic Product, increased by about 3 per cent, the highest rate of growth since 1973.

The upturn in the economy also affected the labour market, which showed a sharp rise in notified vacancies and a slight increase in total employment. The result was a steady decline during the year in the total number of adults registered as unemployed—down 102,000 to 1·32 million by mid-December 1978. However, the fall in the number out of work was larger than might have been expected, given both the small rise in employment and the projected increase in the work-force from school-leavers and others. The disparity may have been due to a rise in self-employment and to earlier retirement.

Domestic finance. The financial side of the economy developed less favourably during 1978 than in the previous year: interest rates increased sharply and a tight squeeze was imposed on the growth of the banking system's operations. The essential problem was the difficulty of reconciling the Government's budgetary stance with monetary restraint at a time when the economy was expanding and increasing its demand for bank loans.

The potential conflict first became apparent at about the time of the main Budget in April, when official figures indicated that the rate of growth in sterling M3, the broadly-defined money stock, might be above the upper end of the 9 to 13 per cent range set as the target for 1977-78; a rise of just under 14 per cent was predicted by Mr Denis Healey, the Chancellor of the Exchequer, in his Budget speech, and the increase turned out to be $16\frac{1}{4}$ per cent.

The City's faith was shaken by the Budget strategy whereby Mr Healey sought to reconcile a rise in the estimated public sector borrowing requirement from £5,700 million to £8,500 million in 1978-79 (reflecting higher public spending and tax cuts), and a slight tightening in the monetary target to a range of 8 to 12 per cent, with hopes of meeting industry's demand for funds. The markets and institutional investors believed the fiscal and monetary policies were incompatible, and confidence was further undermined by a successful amendment to the Finance Bill which cut the standard rate of income tax (see p. 7).

The result was that the Bank of England was unable to sell sufficient gilt-edged stock to investors outside the banking system to meet its funding target, and the Government was forced to introduce a package of measures in early June. This consisted of a rise in Minimum Lending Rate (MLR), a reactivation of the so-called 'corset' controls on the banks' interest-bearing deposits (thus squeezing their lending) and an increase in the employers' national insurance contributions to recoup the revenue lost through the income tax cut. The package worked in the sense that the rate of growth of the money supply had slackened by the early autumn. But the respite proved to be only temporary, and money market interest rates rose during October, while there was growing domestic concern about the prospects for inflation. The Government tried to take the initiative by raising MLR by $2\frac{1}{2}$ points to $12\frac{1}{2}$ per cent on 9 November, compared with $6\frac{1}{2}$ per cent in early January. In consequence, by the end of 1978 even top-quality borrowers from the clearing banks were paying $13\frac{1}{2}$ per cent on their overdrafts, against $7\frac{1}{2}$ per cent at the start of the year.

But the dilemma of fiscal and monetary policy was unresolved, and the City and monetarist economists remained convinced that the Government had been too expansionary. Figures in the January 1979 expenditure White Paper (Cmnd. 7439) showed that the volume of public spending was likely to have risen by 6·2 per cent during 1978-79. This partly reflected a substantial unforeseen shortfall in the previous year, when expenditure dropped by 7·2 per cent; if various financial transfers were excluded the underlying rise was about 2 to 3 per cent.

External finance. The improvement in Britain's external standing during 1977 was generally maintained in 1978, even though the current account was not as strong as had been hoped. In particular, the exchange rate held up well for most of the year, notably against the dollar, and for the first time since March 1976 the pound was above $2.00 during late October and in December. Sterling was less strong against the main Continental currencies and came under particular pressure during the spring, when some of the speculative inflows of 1977 were withdrawn. Between early February and the end of April, sterling's trade-weighted index against a basket of other currencies dropped by $7\frac{1}{2}$ per cent, though over 1978 as a whole the index fell by only 2 per cent.

The relative stability of sterling for most of the year could be explained not only by the problems of the dollar but also by the continued favourable balance on the current account of the balance of payments. This ended the year in surplus by £109 million, after a surplus of £406 million in 1977. However, this was a much smaller balance than the April Budget projection of a £750 million surplus, let alone an earlier forecast (in autumn 1977) of a surplus of £1,500 million for the year.

The difference was principally explained by a disappointing import performance, the volume of purchases being $6\frac{1}{2}$ per cent up over the year and the volume of exports $3\frac{1}{2}$ per cent higher. This implied a further significant increase in the penetration of imported manufactured goods at a time of buoyant domestic demand. Favourable relative price movements for exports and imports were required to produce a surplus.

NOTES ON ECONOMIC AND SOCIAL DATA

The statistical data on the following pages record developments from 1973 to the latest year, usually 1978, for which reasonably stable figures were available at the time of going to press. Year headings 1973 to 1978 are printed only at the head of each page and are not repeated over individual tables unless the sequence is broken by the insertion of series of figures recording developments over a shorter (or longer) period than is shown on the remainder of the page. Shorter-term or longer-term data are separated by fine rules from the main tables which they follow.

Pages to which the point is relevant include a comparative price index, allowing the current-price figures to be reassessed against the background of inflation. This year, the index has been rebased on 1975 = 100, in common with other economic indicators.

Unless figures are stated as indicating the position at the *end* of years or quarters, they should be taken as annual or quarterly *totals* or *averages*, according to context.

Tables 2, 3, 4 and 21. Statistics which are normally reported or collected separately in the three UK home jurisdictions (England and Wales, Scotland, and Northern Ireland) have been consolidated into UK series only to show general trends. As the component returns were made at varying times of year and in accordance with differing definitions and regulatory requirements, the series thus consolidated may therefore be subject to error, may not be strictly comparable from year, to year, and may be less reliable than the remainder of the data.

Symbols. — = Nil or not applicable . . = not available at time of compilation.

Sources

A. THE UNITED KINGDOM
Government Sources
Annual Abstract of Statistics: Tables 1, 2, 3, 4, 13, 14, 18, 20, 21, 25, 26.
Monthly Digest of Statistics: Tables 1, 5, 6, 7, 8, 9, 16, 17, 18, 19, 20, 23, 25, 26, 27, 28, 30.
Financial Statistics: Tables 5, 6, 9, 10, 22, 24.
Economic Trends: 6, 11, 12, 15, 22, 24.
Social Trends: Tables 2, 3, 4, 21.
Department of Employment Gazette: Tables 27, 28, 29, 30.
Housing and Construction Statistics: Tables 13, 21.
Additional Sources
National Institute of Economic and Social Research, *National Institute Economic Review:* Tables 11, 12, 15.
Bank of England Quarterly Bulletin: Tables 5, 7.
Midland Bank: Tables 8, 9.
United Nations, *Monthly Bulletin of Statistics:* Tables 1, 6.
The Financial Times: Tables 5, 8.
British Insurance Association: Table 14.

B. THE UNITED STATES
Government and other Public Sources
Department of Commerce, *Survey of Current Business:* Tables 31, 32, 33, 34, 35, 36, 41, 42, 44.
Council of Economic Advisers, Joint Economic Committee, *Economic Indicators:* Tables 35, 40.
Federal Reserve Bulletin: Tables 37, 38, 39.
Additional Sources
A. M. Best Co.: Table 39.
Insurance Information Institute, New York: Table 39.
Bureau of Economic Statistics, *Basic Economic Statistics:* Tables 42, 43.

C. INTERNATIONAL COMPARISONS
United Nations, *Annual Abstract of Statistics:* Tables 45, 46, 47, 55, 56, 57, 58.
UN *Monthly Bulletin of Statistics:* Tables 45, 46, 55, 56, 58.
IMF, *International Financial Statistics:* Tables 46, 48, 49, 50, 51, 52, 58, 59.
OECD, *Main Economic Indicators:* Tables 46, 52.
Institute of Strategic Studies, *The Military Balance:* Table 54.

Chapter 5

ECONOMIC AND SOCIAL DATA
A. THE UNITED KINGDOM

1. Population

	1973	1974	1975	1976	1977	1978
Population, mid-year est. ('000)	55,913	55,922	55,900	55,886	55,852	55,822
Density (persons per sq. km.) (1)	232	232	232	232	232	232
Live births registered ('000)	779·5	737·1	697·5	675·5	657·0	687·2
Crude birth rate (per 1,000 pop.)	13·9	13·2	12·5	12·1	11·8	..
Deaths registered ('000)	669·7	667·4	662·5	680·0	655·1	668·1
Crude death rate (per 1,000 pop.)	12·0	11·8	11·2	12·1	11·7	..

(1) Based on land area of 241,042 square kilometres.

2. Health

	1973	1974	1975	1976	1977	1978
Public expenditure on National Health Service (£ million)(1)	2,524	3,572	4,903	5,788	6,477	7,354
Hospitals:						
staffed beds, end-year ('000)	516·7	506·0	497·0	488·8	480·0	..
ave. daily bed occupancy ('000)	415·1	410·4	396·3	393·0	390·0	..
waiting list, end-yr. ('000)	624·0	629·0	704·0	722·0	700·0	..
Certifications of death ('000) by:						
ischaemic heart disease	175·5	177·0	177·4	180·8	179·5	..
malignant neoplasm, lungs and bronchus	36·4	37·4	37·2	38·0	38·3	..
road fatality	8·2	7·6	7·0	7·2	7·0	..
accidents at work (number)(2)	874	786	730	684	619	..

(1) Central government and local authority, capital and current. (2) Great Britain.

3. Education

	1973	1974	1975	1976	1977	1978
Public expenditure (£ million)(1)	4,081	5,253	6,643	7,438	7,907	..
Schools ('000)	38·1	38·3	38·1	38·2	37·7	..
Pupils enrolled ('000) in schools	10,635	11,030	11,222	11,300	11,321	..
maintained primary(2)	6,072	6,077	6,035	5,998	5,909	..
maintained and aided secondary(3)(4)	3,944	4,205	4,332	4,448	4,559	..
direct grant(5)	121	122	122	122	119	..
independent(5)	414	419	422	426	423	..
middle schools(5)	205·6	347·7	407·5	443·0	473·7	..
Pupils per full-time teacher at:						
maintained primary schools	25·6	24·9	24·2	23·9	23·8	..
maintained secondary schools(4)	16·9	17·3	17·0	16·9	16·8	..
independent schools(5)	15·6	15·6	15·1	15·2	..	..
middle schools(5)	22·3	22·2	21·7	21·7	21·7	..
Further education: institutions(6)	8,192	8,562	8,299	8,046	7,073	..
full-time students ('000)	348	352	392	392	404	..
Universities(7)	51	51	52	52	52	..
University students ('000),	270	276	283	295	294	..
in mainly arts faculties(8)	118·3	122·5	127·5	135·3	135·1	..
in mainly science faculties(9)	128·4	128·7	130·1	133·4	144·3	..
First degrees awarded (number)	52,472	54 813	55,650	55,920	57,047	..
Open University graduates ('000)	3·6	5·2	5·5	6·0	..	..

(1) Central government and local authority, capital and current. Figures are for financial year: 1973 = year ending March 1974, etc. (2) Including nursery schools. (3) Including special schools. (4) 1976 estimate excludes some voluntary maintained or aided grammar schools which became independent. (5) England and Wales. (6) Great Britain. (7) University College, Buckingham, added 1975. (8) Including economics, social sciences, law. (9) Including medicine.

4. Law and Order

	1973	1974	1975	1976	1977	1978
Public expenditure (£ million)(1)	1,065	1,365	1,786	1,823	2,025	..
Police	558	695	909	1,137	1,187	..
central government grants	226	258	..	..	..	..
Prisons	107	148	193	234	270	..
Administration of justice(2)	162	217	284	332	485	..
local authority expenditure	57	66	79	..	..	..
Police establishment ('000)(3)	124·4	127·7	129·2	130·0	130·0	..
Full-time strength(3)	112·5	114·3	120·0	122·2	119·4	..
Ulster, full-time strength	4·4	4·6	4·9	5·3	5·7	..
Offences known to police ('000) (4)(5)	1,858	2,189	2,375	2,450	2,810	..
Persons convicted ('000)(4)(6)	2,179	2,201	2,245	2,320	2,222	..
Burglary or robbery	64	75	81	81	86	..
Fraud, forgery	18	20	22	25	24	..
Handling stolen goods/receiving, theft	184	207	222	229	254	..
Violence against the person	49	49	52	55	51	..
Murders (number)	132	173	217	266	224	..
Intoxicating liquor laws	121	127	139	148	125	..
Criminal/malicious damage	35	38	42	45	50	..
Traffic (excl. drunken driving)	1,331	1,306	1,316	1,357	1,250	..
Prisons: average population ('000)	44	44	45	47	51	..

(1) Gross expenditure, capital and current, by central government (direct and by grant to local authorities) and by local and police authorities. Figures are for financial year: 1973 = year ending March 1974, etc. (2) Includes expenditure on parliament and courts. (3) Police establishment and full-time strength: Great Britain only. (4) Because of differences in juridical and penal systems in the three UK jurisdictions (England and Wales; Scotland; Northern Ireland), totals of offences and convictions are not strictly comparable from year to year: they should be read only as indicating broad trends. Crimes and offences are in general described by the terms applicable in England from 1972 onwards. (5) Series revised to cover indictable offences and (Scotland) crimes only. (6) Series revised to include non-indictable and (Scotland) miscellaneous offences.

5. Interest Rates and Security Yields(1)

(% per annum, end of year)

Bank rate/minimum lending rate(2)	13·00	11·50	11·25	14·25	7·00	12·50
Treasury bill yield	12·82	11·30	10·93	13·98	6·39	11·91
London clearing banks base rate	13·00	12·00	11·00	14·00	7·12	12·50
Finance houses base rate	14·00	12·00	12·00	15·00	5·50	11·50
2½% consols, gross flat yield (3)	10·85	14·95	14·66	14·25	10·47	12·34
10-year government securities (3)	10·65	14·21	13·18	13·61	12·02	13·19
Ordinary shares, dividend yield (3)	4·12	8·23	6·81	5·96	5·42	5·70
Local authority bonds, 2 years	14·30	14·50	12·25	14·75	8·63	12·50
Local authority 3-month deposits	16·63	13·25	11·31	14·88	6·75	12·44
Interbank 3-month deposits	16·19	12·44	11·16	14·38	6·64	12·52
US $ 3-month deposits in London	10·19	10·06	5·87	5·06	7·19	11·69
Clearing bank 7-day deposits	9·50	9·50	7·00	11·00	4·00	10·00

(1) Gross redemption yields, unless stated otherwise. For building society rates see Table 13. (2) Bank of England MLR replaced bank rate on 13 October 1972. (3) Revised series.

6. Prices and Costs (index 1975 = 100)

Total home costs per unit of output(1)	66·8	78·2	100·0	114·3	126·9	140·0
Labour costs per unit of output	62·1	76·7	100·0	111·3	120·3	132·1
Mfg. wages, salaries/unit of output	61·2	75·6	100·0	113·7	125·3	142·0
Import unit values	59·6	87·4	100·0	121·8	141·3	146·5
Wholesale prices, manufactures	66·7	81·8	100·0	117·3	140·5	153·3
Consumer prices	69·4	80·5	100·0	116·5	135·0	146·2

(1) Used as 'Overall price index' on remaining pages of UK statistics.

7. Banking(1)	1973	1974	1975	1976	1977	1978
(£ million, at end of period)						
Current and deposit accounts	71,490	84,615	129,073	163,476	178,097	204,051
Advances: to	64,285	76,134	115,978	149,964	169,324	195,698
local authorities	2,335	2,094	3,932	4,026	4,376	4,688
public corporations(7)	1,207	1.442	1,918	2,693	3,301	2,880
financial institutions	2,648	2,640	3,781	4,329	4,465	5,238
property companies(6)	1,669	2,716	2,956	2,789	2,521	2,219
companies	14,219	18,026	19,993	23,335	26,357	29,248
manufacturing(6)	5,923	8,426	7,126	8,545	9,366	10,646
construction(6)	1,320	2,207	1,715	1,560	1,578	1,707
personal sector	7,056	7,165	7,101	7,723	8,983	10,860
for house purchase(2)(6)	1,011	1,233	1,291	1,364	1,471	1,713
overseas residents(3)(7)	38,134	46,222	62,126	85,529	88,127	106,083
Eligible liabilities (4)	26,574	30,584	32.686	36,876	40,850	45,003
Special deposits(5), cumulative(%)	5	4	3	6	3	3
Overall price index (1975 = 100)	*66·8*	*78·2*	*100·0*	*114·3*	*126·9*	*140·0*

Shorter-term data	1976	1977	1978:I	II	III	IV
Current and deposit accounts	163,476	178,097	180,156	190,389	190,488	204,051
Advances	149,964	169,324	171,548	181,903	182,846	195,698
Overall price index (1975 = 100)	*114·3*	*126·9*	*136·1*	*137·9*	*141·5*	*144·7*

(*1*) *Unless otherwise stated, this table covers all banks in the UK observing the common 12·5 per cent reserve ratio introduced on 16 Sept. 1971 and includes the accepting houses (merchant banks), discount houses and, for deposits, the National Giro and the banking department of the Bank of England. Except in the case of overseas advances, inter-bank transactions have been omitted.* (*2*) *1971-75: excluding Northern Ireland banks.* (*3*) *Individuals, corporations, financial institutions; revised series to give gross advances outstanding, in sterling and other currencies, at current prices and allowing for effects of exchange rate changes.* (*4*) *Sterling deposit liabilities excluding those having original maturity of over two years, and sterling resources obtained by switching out of foreign currency holdings: special deposits called in by the Bank of England are expressed as a percentage of banks' eligible liabilities.* (*5*) *Including supplementary deposits from July 1974.* (*6*) *1977 figure: November.* (*7*) *From 1976, public utilities and national government.*

8. The Stock Market	1973	1974	1975	1976	1977	1978
(£ million, unless otherwise stated)						
Turnover(1) (£000 mn.)	55·7	56·8	94·0	106·4	173·3	138·8
ordinary shares (£000 mn.)	13·7	12·6	17·6	14·2	20·2	19·2
New issues, less redemptions (value)	168·7	78·2	1,551·0	1,114·3	926·2	819·7
Government securities	1,778	1,127	5,706	5,927	10,004	4,888
Local authority issues (2)	−15·6	27·2	186·0	107·8	239·0	48·0
UK companies (gross)	214·1	102·0	1,402·3	1,080·3	730·1	833·7
by ordinary shares	136·8	120·4	1,270·4	1,053·7	789·2	924·5
preference shares	21·7	15·6	40·1	31·0	15·7	22·3
convertible loan stock	34·4	1·7	84·0	8·0	−4·8	−20·5
other debt	21·2	−35·7	7·8	−12·4	−70·0	−92·6
FT ordinary share index (1935 = 100)(3)	435·6	251·2	311·0	368·0	452·3	479·4
FT-Actuaries index (1962 = 100)(3)	184·61	106·75	133·11	153·04	191·91	216·68
Industrial, 500 shares	185·26	108·84	135·97	162·91	208·79	237·80
Financial, 100 shares	188·85	102·45	122·85	124·18	145·68	165·99

(*1*) *London and Scottish Stock Exchanges to March 1973; thereafter The Stock Exchange.* (*2*) *Includes public corporation issues.* (*3*) *Average during year.*

Overall price index (1975 = 100)	*66·8*	*78·2*	*100·0*	*114·3*	*126·9*	*140·0*

9. Companies	*1973*	*1974*	*1975*	*1976*	*1977*	*1978*
(£ million)						
Total income	17,877	20,875	21,030	26,632	29,952	32,888
Gross trading profit in UK	8,932	9,508	9,762	12,499	15,508	16,782
Investment income in UK	4,267	5,933	5,803	6,962	6,427	7,399
Total overseas income	2,432	2,686	2,345	3,401	3,419	3,647
Dividends on ord. and pref. shares	1,638	1,469	1,608	1,825	2,242	2,706
Net payments of UK tax	1,895	2,819	2,255	2,088	2,991	3,848
Net profit	7,890	8,099	8,679	12,812	13,934	14,708
Companies taken over (number)	1,313	576	388	402	523	599
Total take-over consideration	1,742	640	460	578	1,126	1,280
of which in cash (%)	51	66	51	68	56	55
Liquidations (number)(1)	2,575	3,720	5,398	5,939	5,831	5,080
Receiverships (number)(1)	3,917	5,718	7,271	7,207	4,485	3,895

(*1*) *England and Wales.*

10. Money and Savings
(£ million, amounts outstanding at end of period, unless otherwise stated)

Money stock M_1(1)	13,120	14,550	17,340	19,150	23,330	27,190
Money stock M_3(2)	33,040	37,230	40,170	44,540	48,940	56,330
Sterling M_3	31,610	34,840	37,200	40,570	44,660	51,370
Notes and coins in circulation	5,042	5,638	6,473	7,265	8,062	9,276
Domestic credit expansion	8,055	6,934	4,528	7,464	1,084	7,917

Shorter-term data	*1976*	*1977*	*1978:I*	*II*	*III*	*IV*
Money stock M_3	44,540	48,940	51,220	53,230	54,100	56,330
Domestic credit expansion	7,464	1,084	765	2,841	1,184	3,127

	1973	*1974*	*1975*	*1976*	*1977*	*1978*
Personal savings ratio (%)(3)	11·9	14·4	15·0	14·6	14·2	
National savings		7,555	7,978	8,418	9,707	11,270
Trustee savings bank	3,365	3,534	3,849	4,217	4,534	5,002
National savings bank	2,065	2,087	2,141	2,200	3,051	3,001
National savings certificates	2,567	2,467	2,630	2,978	4,021	5,134
Premium bonds	1,016	1,049	1,110	1,186	1,259	1,372
Save as You Earn	147	190	221	290	351	421

(*1*) M_1 = *Notes and coins in circulation with the public plus resident private sector sterling current accounts with the banks minus 60 per cent of transit items.* (*2*) M_3 = *notes and coins in circulation plus total deposits of the domestic sector.* (*3*) *Personal savings as a percentage of personal disposable income.*

11. Personal Income and Expenditure
(£ million, seasonally adjusted, current prices unless otherwise stated)

Wages and salaries	38,018	45,916	58,974	66,932	73,523	83,372
Current grants	6,420	7,875	10,283	12,763	15,100	..
Forces' pay	925	1,071	1,283	1,473	1,500	..
Other personal income	13,136	15,507	17,885	21,220	24,239	..
Personal disposable income(1)	51,303	60,614	74,361	86,155	97,347	111,881
Real personal disposable income (2)	74,362	74,881	74,361	74,184	73,109	77,593
Consumers' expenditure	45,182	51,863	63,192	73,538	83,530	95,738

Overall price index (1975=100)	*66·8*	*78·2*	*100·0*	*114·3*	*126·9*	*140·0*

Shorter-term data	*1976*	*1977*	*1978:I*	*II*	*III*	*IV*
Real personal disposable income (2)	74,184	73,109	18,663	19,446	19,645	19,918
Consumers' expenditure (2)	63,540	62,954	16,296	16,487	16,858	16,756

Overall price index (1975 = 100)	*114·3*	*126·9*	*136·1*	*137·9*	*141·5*	*144·7*

(*1*) *From rent, self-employment (before depreciation or stock appreciation provisions), dividend and interest receipts and charitable receipts from companies.* (*2*) *At 1975 prices.*

12. Fixed Investment
(£ million, 1975 prices, seasonally adjusted)

	1973	1974	1975	1976	1977	1978
Total, all fixed investment(1)	21,609	21,173	20,536	20,395	19,961	20,514
Dwellings	4,281	3,979	4,160	4,152	3,841	3,917
public	1,790	1,938	1,964	2,040	1,849	1,621
private	2,491	2,041	2,196	2,112	1,992	2,296
Mainly private industries & services(2)	4,281	3,979	4,163	4,144	3,656	..
manufacturing	1,790	1,938	1,967	2,039	1,828	..
other(2)	2,491	2,041	2,196	2,105	1,828	..
Mainly public industries & services(3)	3,504	3,822	3,522	3,345	3,573	..

Shorter-term data

(Quarterly average rates)	1976	1977	1978:I	II	III	IV
Total, all fixed investment(1)	20,395	19,961	5,151	5,161	5,147	5,055
Public dwellings	2,040	1,849	420	384	443	374
Private dwellings	2,112	1,992	614	586	551	545
Mainly private manufacturing	3,345	3,573	921	959	968	..
Mainly public industries	6,612	5,624	1,288	1,316	1,249	..

Overall price index (1975 = 100)	*114·3*	*126·9*	*136·1*	*137·9*	*141·5*	*144·7*

(1) Includes investment in North Sea oil platforms and equipment (from 1975 onward) and in mining and quarrying (all years), not allocated to sectors. (2) Includes distribution, agriculture, shipping. (3) Excludes the nationalized steel industry, which is included in manufacturing.

13. Building Societies
(Condition at end of financial year ended in year indicated, unless otherwise stated)

	1973	1974	1975	1976	1977	1978
Societies on register (number)	447	416	382	364	339	316
Interest rates (%):						
Paid on shares, ave. actual	6·51	7·33	7·21	7·02	6·98	..
BSA(1) recommended, end-year	7·50	7·50	7·00	7·80	6·00	8·00
Paid on deposits, ave. actual	6·04	6·88	6·74	6·61	6·13	..
BSA recommended, end-year	7·25	7·25	6·75	7·55	5·75	7·75
Mortgages, ave. charged	9·59	11·05	11·08	11·06	11·05	..
BSA recommended, end-year	11·00	11·00	11·00	12·25	9·50	11·75
Shares and deposits, net (£ mn.)	2,162	1,993	4,172	3,405	6,099	4,879
Government advances (£ mn.)(2)	32	358	23	20	13	..
Mortgage advances, net (£ mn.)	1,999	1,490	2,768	3,618	4,100	5,096

(1) BSA: Building Societies Association. (2) Excludes 3-month bridging grant in 1973.

14. Insurance(1)
(£ million)

	1973	1974	1975	1976	1977	1978
Life assurance(1)(2), net premiums	2,464	2,758	3,111	3,825	4,280	..
investment income	1,340	1,580	1,830	2,230	2,560	..
benefits paid to policyholders	1,620	1,970	2,180	2,560	2,320	..
life funds, end-year	18,286	18,293	21,877	23,342	30,700	..
Non-life(1)(2), net premiums	3,360	3,858	4,641	6,043	6,460	..
underwriting profit/(−)loss(3)	19·0	−107·0	−183·0	−151·0	..	..
Lloyd's (4), premiums	1,191	1,539	1,661	690	..	..
balance(5)	110	82	1,229	531	..	..

(1) Companies only; excludes Lloyd's. (2) World-wide business of UK companies and authorized UK affiliates of foreign companies. (3) Including net transfers of marine, aviation and transit branch revenues to/from profit and loss accounts. (4) 1975 and 1976; years 2 and 1 only of three-year open account. (5) Including net interest on underwriting funds, less claims, expenses and other outgo.

Overall price index (1975 = 100)	*66·8*	*78·2*	*100·0*	*114·3*	*126·9*	*140·0*

15. National Income and Expenditure(1)

(£ million, 1975 prices, quarterly figures seasonally adjusted)

	1976	1977	1978	1978:I	II	III	IV
GDP(2), expenditure basis	23,959	24,313	25,118	24,709	25,131	25,411	25,222
income basis(3)	26,547	30,567	34,885	33,000	34,499	35,644	36,396
output basis (1970 = 100)	102·1	104·7	107·7	105·9	108·0	108·8	108·3
average estimate (1970 = 100)	102·9	104·9	108·1	105·9	108·4	109·2	108·8

Components of gross domestic product:

Consumers' expenditure	15,830	15,738	16,599	16,296	16,487	16,858	16,756
General government consumption	5,854	5,829	5,906	5,923	5,887	5,873	5,943
Gross fixed investment	5,122	4,934	5,128	5,151	5,161	5,147	5,055
Exports, goods and services	7,341	7,872	8,053	7,916	7,960	8,200	8,135
Total final expenditure, excluding stocks	34,212	34,581	35,927	35,577	35,775	36,380	35,978
Stockbuilding	65	262	240	291	280	302	89
Imports of goods and services	7,546	7,569	7,948	8,003	7,796	8,088	7,906
Adjustment to factor cost	2,657	2,699	2,861	2,865	2,848	2,881	2,850

(1) The longer-term development of the UK gross domestic product is recorded in Table 46 of the international comparative data, page 476. (2) At factor cost. (3) Current prices.

16. Industrial Production

(Index, average 1975 = 100, seasonally adjusted)

All industries	102·0	105·8	109·7	106·9	110·9	111.2	109·9
Mining and quarrying	125·7	187·6	233·4	208·7	230·6	237.5	256·8
Coal mining	92·8	90·1	89·4	90·2	88·8	89·8	88·8
Manufacturing industries	101·4	102·8	103·6	102·1	104·7	104·9	102·7
Food, drink and tobacco	102·7	103·9	106·3	106·7	107·7	104·0	106·8
Chemicals	111·3	114·4	115·3	111·1	115·0	117·3	117·8
Oil and coal products	105·7	102·7	101·0	98·6	98·3	105·3	102·1
Metal manufacture	106·9	102·0	100·5	95·0	107·8	101·6	97·5
Engineering and allied	97·0	98·9	99·3	100·0	100·0	101·0	96·0
Mechanical	95·1	93·2	93·3	91·9	92·6	94·9	93·7
Electrical	98·5	102·7	108·4	107·4	108·6	110·0	107·6
Shipbuilding and marine	96·5	93·2	89·0	93·4	92·9	89·6	80·0
Vehicles and aircraft	97·0	100·9	98·4	104·1	101·2	100·5	88·0
Textiles	100·9	101·6	100·6	97·8	101·0	102·8	100·6
Bricks, pottery, glass	101·0	99·8	101·7	96·1	103·2	103·7	103·7
Timber, furniture, etc.	103·9	97·6	102·7	96·7	103·6	104·8	105·7
Paper, printing, publishing	102·5	106·9	110·2	105·7	109·1	111·4	114·4
Construction	98·6	98·2	105·0	101·7	107·2	106·7	106·0
Gas, electricity, water	102·9	107·0	109·5	108·2	112·2	111·3	106·3

17. Productivity

(Index of output per head 1970 = 100)

All production industries	102·0	105·8	109·7	106·9	110·9	111·2	109·9
Manufacturing	101·4	102·9	103·6	102·1	105·0	104·9	102·7
Mining and quarrying	125·7	187·7	233·4	208·7	230·6	237·5	256·8
Metal manufacture	106·9	102·0	100·5	95·0	108·4	101·6	97·5
Engineering	96·5	97·3	100·0	98·4	99·7	101·6	100·1
Vehicles	97·2	101·6	98·4	105·2	102·2	100·5	88·5
Textiles	103·0	100·9	99·1	97·1	99·8	101·7	97·8
Gas, electricity, water	102·9	107·0	109·5	108·2	112·2	111·3	106·3

Overall price index (1975 = 100)	*114·3*	*126·9*	*140·0*	*136·1*	*137·9*	*141·5*	*144·7*

18. Energy	1973	1974	1975	1976	1977	1978
Coal, production (mn. tonnes)	132·0	110·4	128·7	123·8	122·1	123·6
Stocks, end-year (mn. tonnes)(1)	27·9	21·8	31·2	33·1	31·5	34·7
Power station consumption (mn. tons)	76·9	67·0	74·6	77·8	79·9	80·7
Power stations' demand for oil						
(million tonnes coal equivalent)	28·4	29·1	21·3	17·2	18·2	19·2
Electricity generated ('000 mn. kwh.)	258·8	250·4	251·2	254·8	262·1	266·8
by nuclear plant ('000 mn. kwh.)	23·7	29·4	27·1	32·2	40·0	33·3
Natural gas sent out (mn. therms)	9,188	13,104	13,692	14,217	15,252	15,855
Town gas sent out (million therms)	2,433	1,602	754	229	73	42
Crude oil output ('000 tonnes)(2)	372	408	1,560	11,678	37,884	53,376
Oil refinery output (mn. tonnes)(3)	105·9	103·1	86·6	90·3	86·3	89·2
Inland deliveries (mn. tonnes) of:						
Petrochemical feedstock	7·2	7·2	4·9	5·7	5·7	5·9
Motor spirit(4)	16·9	16·5	16·1	16·9	14·8	16·0
Other vehicle/engine fuels(5)	25·0	22·8	22·3	22·6	23·8	24·0
Vehicle miles travelled (1970 = 100)(1)	100	97	99	103	107	..
Other fuel oils	42·0	39·4	30·0	27·8	27·8	28·2

(1) Excluding Northern Ireland. (2) Including natural gas liquids. (3) All fuels and other petroleum products. (4) Including aviation spirit (for piston-engined aircraft). (5) Including diesel-engined road vehicle fuel (Derv) and other gas/diesel oils, and jet (aviation turbine) kerosene.

19. Industrial products and manufactures, output

Crude steel (million tonnes)	26·7	22·3	19·8	22·3	20·4	18·4
Aluminium, UK smelted ('000 tonnes)	462	499	498	541	549	539
Sulphuric acid (million tonnes)	3·89	3·85	3·17	3·27	3·40	3·45
Synthetic resins (million tonnes)	2.39	2.28	1·95	2·45	2·49	..
Man-made fibres (million tonnes)	0·73	0·63	0·56	0·62	0·55	0·51
Cars ('000)	1,747	1,534	1,268	1,334	1,316	1,223
Motor vehicles, cars imported ('000)(1)	414	401	423	488	1,347	..
Commercial vehicles ('000)	417	402	381	372	398	384
Merchant ships(2) completed ('000 gr.t)	1,069	1,189	1,203	1,460	1,007	1,135
Tankers(3) completed ('000 gr.t)	221	457	592	720	426	649
Aircraft delivered (number)	293	364	353	342	353	261

(1) Including imported chassis. (2) 100 gross tons and over. (3) 300 gross tons and over.

20. Agriculture
(Production, 1973–76, '000 tonnes 1977–78, unless otherwise stated)

Wheat	4,951	6,130	4,488	4,740	5,274	6,588
Barley	8,954	9,133	8,513	7,648	10,531	10,023
Sugar, refined from UK beet	835	770	666	605	900	984
Beef and veal	865	1,061	1,202	1,074	1,002	1,027
Mutton and lamb	230	248	254	247	223	228
Pork	677	687	566	601	650	631
Milk, disposals (million Litres)			13,092	13,128	13,620	14,400	15,084

Prices(1), farm years ended June (index 1968/69–71/72 average = 100)

Wheat	141·8	241·0	236·8	266·3	347·0	328·9
Barley	125·6	219·4	244·4	254·0	349·3	310·7
Cattle, clean	159·8	172·8	162·1	203·2	276·5	297·2
Pigs, clean(2)	125·2	163·2	192·4	248·9	251·2	283·3
Milk	114·3	136·4	173·7	212·4	243·1	254·7
Chemical fertilizers(3)	139·9	161·4	251·5	266·1	300·9	346·3
Compound feedingstuffs(3)	124·6	191·9	203·9	216·8	291·1	291·0
Farm net income (£ million)(4)	866	1,275	1,263	1,357	1,566	..

(1) Based on producer prices after subsidy or intervention; barley, market prices. (2) 1972–June 75, at bacon factory. July 1975 onwards all clean pigs, excluding subsidy in 1977. (3) Based on manufacturers' average prices. (4) Years to 31 May.

Overall price index (1975 = 100)	66·8	78·2	100·0	114·3	126·9	140·0

21. Housing	1973	1974	1975	1976	1977	1978
Public expenditure (£ million)(1)	2,620	4,405	4,609	5,170	5,029	..
by local housing authorities(2)	1,818	2,966	2,890	2,665	2,366	..
Dwellings completed ('000)	305	280	322	325	313	289
by and for public sector(3)	114	134	167	170	170	136
by private sector	191	145	155	155	143	153
Dwellings: sold by local housing authorities(2)(4)('000)	41·8	5·4	2·7	6·1	13·0	..
Housing land, private sector, weighted ave. price (£/hectare)	61,194	60,897	42,054	42,260	44,432	..
Dwelling prices, average (£)(5)	10,690	11,340	12,406	13,164	14,478	..

(1) Capital and current, net of rents, etc., received, and adjusted to eliminate double counting of grants and subsidies paid by central government and expended by local authorities. Figures are for financial year: 1973 = year ending March 1974. (2) Including new town development corporations. (3) Including government departments (police houses, military married quarters, etc.) and approved housing associations and trusts. (4) England and Wales. (5) Of properties newly mortgaged by building societies. See also Table 13 above.

22. Government Finance
(£ million)

	1973	1974	1975	1976	1977	1978
Revenue(1)	26,235	32,723	42,015	49,011	56,282	62,464
taxes on income	9,295	12,548	16,537	18,704	20,295	22,449
corporation tax(2)	1,533	2,262	2,859	1,996	2,665	3,343
taxes on expenditure	10,122	11,470	14,162	16,549	20,446	23,452
purchase/value added tax(2)(3)	1,388	1,848	2,507	3,452	3,766	4,230
taxes on capital(4)	878	987	879	853	866	899
National Insurance surcharge(5)	283	16	1	0	829	1,573
Expenditure(2)(6)	27,507	31,944	42,702	53,710	59,404	63,617
social services(7)	13,704	16,245	21,996	27,900	32,145	35,631
defence	3,399	4,012	5,097	6,163	6,780	7,492
net lending(8)	1,826	1,284	3,131	3,485	1,857	−114
Deficit(−) or surplus	−2,331	13,523	−8,345	−6,786	−4,465	−8,376
Domestic borrowing, net						

(1) Total current receipts, taxes on capital and other capital receipts. (2) Financial years ended 5 April of year indicated. (3) 1973/74 figure includes first net receipts of VAT, introduced April 1973 (£1,469 million), plus outstanding receipts of purchase tax, abolished at that date. (4) Capital gains tax and estate/death duties. (5) 1973–75, selective employment tax (abolished 1973). (6) Total government expenditure, gross domestic capital formation and grants. (7) Including expenditure by public authorities other than central government. (8) To private sector, local authorities, public corporations, and overseas. For external reserve and official borrowing overseas, see Table 24.

23. Terms of Trade
(Index 1975 = 100)

Volume of exports(1)	97·4	102·4	100·0	109·7	118·9	122·9
manufactures	98·4	103·8	100·0	109·0	118·0	121·0
machinery/transport equip't.	87·9	94·0	100·0	101·0	105·0	105·0
Volume of imports(1)	105·6	106·0	100·0	105·6	107·3	112·8
food	104·0	101·0	100·0	106·4	108·8	117·2
fuels	125·1	119·1	100·0	102·0	102·0	101·0
Unit value of exports(2)	63·4	81·8	100·0	120·9	142·6	155·4
manufactures	64·2	81·0	100·0	121·0	143·0	157·0
machinery/transport equip't.	65·3	79·0	100·0	123·0	148·0	165·0
Unit value of imports(2)	59·1	89·1	100·0	121·8	141·3	146·5
food(3)	68·1	87·4	100·0	113·0	132·0	142·0
fuels(3)	30·6	87·3	100·0	131·0	148·0	139·0
Terms of trade(4)	111·4	92·7	100·0	99·2	100·8	105·6

(1) Seasonally adjusted; f.o.b. (2) Not seasonally adjusted. (3) c.i.f. (4) Export unit value index as percentage of import unit value index, expressed as an index on the same base.

Overall price index (1975 = 100)	66·8	78·2	100·0	114·3	126·9	140·0

24. Balance of Payments
(£ million: current transactions seasonally adjusted; remaining data unadjusted)

	1976	1977	1978	1978:I	II	III	IV
Exports (f.o.b.)	25,424	32,184	35,217	8,380	8,752	9,053	9,032
Imports (f.o.b.)	29,013	33,891	36,512	9,022	8,925	9,418	9,147
Visible balance	−3,589	−1,709	−1,295	−642	−173	−365	−115
Gov't services/transfers (net)	251	292	454	89	81	119	165
Private(1) services/transfers (net)	456	500	547	130	140	139	138
Public sector interest etc (net)	−648	−685	..	−108	−112	−118	..
Private sector interest etc (net)	1,963	1,169	..	230	301	304	..
Invisible balance	2,452	2,115	1,213	229	308	316	360
Current balance	−1,137	406	327	−413	135	−49	200
Current balance (unadjusted)	−1,137	406	327	−554	213	3	665
Capital transfers(2)	—	—	—	—	—	—	—
Official long-term capital	−158	−291	−348	−57	−14	−42	−235
Overseas investment in							
UK public sector	203	2,182	−81	−3	−15	−13	−50
UK private sector	2,063	3,096	2,835	1,023	464	432	916
UK private investment overseas	−2,156	−2,167	−3,288	−685	−535	−774	−1,294
Overseas borrowing/lending (net) by UK banks to finance:							
UK investment overseas	165	520	865	150	360	175	180
other loans/credits (net)	−271	−136	−1,464	−35	−1,315	153	−267
Exchange reserves in sterling(3):							
British government stocks	14	5	−115	−34	−20	−38	−23
Bank/money market liabilities	−1,421	−24	−4	194	−211	43	−30
Other external stg. liabilities	255	1,471	304	−59	−156	159	360
Import credit(4)	165	179	165	142	101	−88	10
Export credit(4)	−1,145	−408	−655	−318	−345	13	−5
Other short-term flows	−608	175	−441	−226	−118	54	−151
Total investment/capital flows	−2,894	4,602	−2,267	92	−1,804	74	−589
Balancing item	404	2,596	847	664	106	−37	114
Total official financing(6)	3,629	−7,361	1,126	−173	1,494	−210	15
Foreign liabilities(5) net	8,320	9,404	7,765	9,457	8,970	8,309	7,765
Overall price index (1975 = 100)	*114·3*	*126·9*	*140·0*	*136·1*	*137·9*	*141·5*	*144·7*

(1) Including transfers made by and to public corporations. (2) Payments under the sterling guarantee agreements. (3) Sterling reserves of overseas countries and international organizations, other than the IMF, as reported by banks, etc., in the UK. (4) Excluding trade credit between 'related' firms, after deducting advance and progress payments to suppliers. (5) Includes eurodollar facility (1974-75) and public sector exchange cover scheme. (6) From 1972, transactions with the IMF were included as changes in the official reserves. Total official financing is the reverse counterpart of the item 'Total currency flow' or overall current/capital balance omitted from this table for space reasons (see table below). Total official financing less foreign borrowing produces amount by which official reserves were added to or drawn down.

Longer-term data (£ million)(1)	1973	1974	1975	1976	1977	1978
Current surplus (+)/deficit (−)	−999	−3,591	−1,843	−1,137	+298	+254
Overall surplus (+)/deficit (−)	−771	−1,646	−1,465	−3,629	+7,361	−1,126
Official reserves, end of year	2,787	2,890	2,683	2,426	10,715	7,689
Foreign liabilities(2), net, do.	1,283	3,018	4,409	8,320	9,404	7,765
Overall price index (1975 = 100)	*66·8*	*78·2*	*100·0*	*114·3*	*126·9*	*140·0*

(1) Reserves and borrowings calculated at $2.40 = £1.00, December 1967–September 1971; $2.60571 ('Smithsonian' parity) October 1971–May 1972, and at closing market rate from June, 1972; gold and SDRs at closing dollar parity throughout $2.6057 from January 1972. (2) To IMF and foreign monetary authorities and institutions; includes foreign currency borrowing by government and, under exchange cover scheme, by public sector.

25. Trade by Areas and Main Trading Partners

(£ million; exports f.o.b.; imports c.i.f.)	1973	1974	1975	1976	1977	1978
All countries: *exports*	12,454	16,494	19,761	25,909	33,331	37,363
imports	15,840	23,117	24,037	31,170	36,978	40,969
E.E.C.: *exports*	4,030	5,508	6,349	9,197	12,152	14,103
imports	5,197	7,222	8,686	11,386	14,171	16,584
Other Western Europe: *exports*	2,225	2,877	3,268	4,287	5,606	5,710
imports	2,694	3,420	3,518	4,579	5,576	6,991
North America: *exports*	1,936	2,258	2,319	3,137	3,821	4,245
imports	2,358	3,237	3,203	4,225	4,948	5,341
Other developed countries: *exports*	1,218	1,700	1,890	1,967	2,110	2,334
imports	1,460	1,594	1,784	2,119	2,698	2,834
Oil exporting countries: *exports*	800	1,209	2,280	3,144	4,374	4,767
imports	1,494	3,785	3,324	4,207	3,800	3,470
Other developing countries: *exports*	1,809	2,368	2,934	3,381	4,261	5,033
imports	2,042	2,591	2,665	3,514	4,362	4,385
Centrally planned economies: *exports*	409	514	680	730	911	1,070
imports	598	748	741	1,110	1,371	1,300
United States: *exports*	1,219	1,522	1,770	2,478	3,095	3,447
imports	1,180	1,622	2,254	3,048	3,695	4,233
West Germany: *exports*	590	785	1,016	1,843	2,526	3,105
imports	841	1,351	1,892	2,757	3,608	4,513
France: *exports*	511	678	914	1,712	2,166	2,530
imports	604	979	1,349	2,090	2,694	3,212
Netherlands: *exports*	451	604	983	1,501	2,178	2,256
imports	615	912	1,637	2,426	2,524	2,525
Belgium-Luxembourg: *exports*	394	620	838	1,402	1,843	2,202
imports	316	442	730	1,300	1,685	1,831
Ireland: *exports*	469	625	821	2,255	1,648	2,045
imports	445	527	810	1,004	1,299	1,606
Switzerland: *exports*	521	601	805	1,003	1,435	1,914
imports	592	717	736	932	1,372	2,156
Italy: *exports*	284	386	510	827	986	1,124
imports	353	504	724	1,104	1,564	1,935
Sweden: *exports*	405	515	724	1,048	1,201	1,171
imports	513	740	929	1,187	1,268	1,374
Canada: *exports*	380	414	488	638	702	740
imports	605	736	983	1,162	1,214	1,089
Saudi Arabia: *exports*	59	120	200	400	601	786
imports	318	1,176	857	978	1,132	870
Denmark: *exports*	330	429	444	657	804	841
imports	477	577	621	705	816	962
Norway: *exports*	241	334	390	476	777	650
imports	326	428	605	623	853	1,445

26. Trade by Selected Product Groups
(£ million)

	1973	1974	1975	1976	1977	1978
Exports: transport equipment	1,555	1,839	2,455	3,065	4,356	4,540
chemicals	1,296	2,146	2,153	3,045	3,817	4,201
textiles	929	1,176	1,147	1,606	1,193	1,238
beverages	305	384	437	525	629	805
oil and petroleum products	341	696	721	1,162	2,092	2,375
Imports: food and livestock	2,714	3,372	3,931	4,495	5,375	5,329
oil and petroleum products	1,682	4,533	4,169	5,512	5,088	4,529
wood, paper and products	1,307	1,866	1,654	2,165	2,355	2,387
transport equipment	919	933	1,179	1,749	3,489	4,343
mineral ores	390	675	632	683	749	635
Overall price index (1975 = 100)	66·8	78·2	100·0	114·3	126·9	140·0

27. Employment
(millions of persons, in June each year)

	1973	1974	1975	1976	1977	1978
Working population(1)	25·54	25·60	25·83	26·09	26·33	..
Employed labour force(2)	24·43	24·51	24·41	24·76	24·88	..
Employees: production industries	9·92	9·81	9·53	9·26	9·14	9·08
Including mining	0·36	0·35	0·36	0·35	0·34	0·33
manufacturing	7·83	7·77	7·55	7·25	7·23	7·17
construction	1·38	1·34	1·28	1·31	1·23	1·24
Transport and communication(3)	1·50	1·49	1·47	1·44		
Distributive trades	2·74	2·76	2·76	2·72		
Financial, professional, scientific	4·30	4·49	4·66	4·76	11·72	11·63
Catering and other services	2·15	2·13	2·20	2·30		
Public service(3)	1·58	1·60	1·66	1·63	1·63	1·64
Total employees	22·66	22·79	22·71	22·54	22·66	22·72
of whom, females	8·89	9·13	9·17	9·15	9·28	9·36

(1) Including registered unemployed and members of the armed services. (2) Including employers and self-employed. (3) Excludes employees of nationalized industries but includes British Rail and Post Office.

28. Demand for Labour

Average weekly hours worked, manufacturing industry, men over 21(1)	44·7	44·0	42·7	43·5	43·6	43·5
Manufacturing employees:						
Total overtime hours worked ('000)(2)	15,504	14,655	12,947	13,459	15,447	15,105
Short time, total hours lost ('000)(2)	215	348	2,449	968	592	446
Unemployed, excl. school-leavers, adult students (monthly ave., '000)(3)	611·0	615·1	977·6	1,358·8	1,378·2	1,375·0
Percentage of all employees	2·6	2·6	4·2	5·7	6·2	6·2
Unfilled vacancies, end-year ('000)	462·1	496·8(4)	153·8	163·1(5)	171·5	219·4

(1) October. (2) Great Britain, June. (3) Seasonally adjusted. (4) End-November. (5) 8 October.

29. Industrial Disputes

Stoppages (number)(1)(2)	2,873	2,922	2,262	2,016	2,703	2,349
Known official stoppages (number)	132	125	139	69	79	82
Workers involved ('000)(3)	1,513	1,622	789	666	1,155	939
in official stoppages ('000)	396	467	80	46	205	..
Work days lost ('000), all inds., services	7,197	14,750	6,012	3,284	10,142	9,306
Mining and quarrying	91	5,628	56	78	97	181
Metals, engg., shipbdg., vehicles	4,799	5,837	3,932	1,977	6,133	6,066
Textiles and clothing	193	255	350	65	266	173
Construction	176	252	247	570	297	412
Transport and communications	331	705	422	132	301	343
All other industries/services	1,608	2,072	1,006	461	3,050	2,131

(1) Excluding protest action of a political nature, and stoppages involving fewer than 10 workers and/or lasting less than one day except where the working days lost exceeded 100. (2) Stoppages beginning in year stated. (3) Directly and indirectly, where stoppages occurred; lay-offs elsewhere in consequence are excluded.

30. Wages and Earnings

Basic hourly rates (31 July 1972 = 100), all manual employees(1)	115.6	138·7	179·8	214·5	228·4	260·2
women(1)	116·5	145·9	198·8	243·0	265·2	299·4
Ave. weekly earnings (£)(2): mfg.	41·52	49·12	59·74	66·97	72·89	83·50
food industries(3)	40·24	47·97	60·29	66·81	72·46	83·91
coal and oil products(3)	42·41	57·01	69·74	76·75	82·36	95·65
mechanical engineering(3)	40·51	48·49	58·86	66·11	73·38	83·39
construction(3)	41·41	48·75	60·38	65·80	72·91	81·77

(1) In all industries and services. (2) Of male manual workers, aged 21 and over. (3) October.

Overall price index (1975 = 100)	*66·8*	*78·2*	*100·0*	*114·3*	*126·9*	*140·0*

B. THE UNITED STATES

31. Population	1973	1974	1975	1976	1977	1978
Population, mid-year est. (mn.)	210·41	211·90	213·54	214·12	216·82	
Density (persons per sq. km.)(1)	22·47	22·63	22·81	22·87	23·16	
Crude birth rate (per 1,000 pop.)	15·0	15·0	14·8	14·7	15·3	
Crude death rate (per 1,000 pop.)	9·4	9·2	8·9	9·0	8·8	

(1) Based on land area of 9,363,345 sq. km.

32. Gross National Product
('000 million current dollars)

Gross national product	1,306·6	1,412·9	1,528·8	1,700·1	1,887·2	2,106·6
Personal consumption	809·9	889·6	979·1	1,090·2	1,206·5	1,339·7
Gross private domestic investment	202·1	205·7	201·6	232·8	292·3	328·8
Net exports, goods and services	7·1	6·0	20·4	7·4	−11·1	−11·8
Government purchases	269·5	302·7	338·4	359·5	394·0	434·2

33. Government Finance
('000 million dollars, seasonally adjusted)

Federal government receipts	265·0	288·2	286·5	331·4	374·4	431·6
from personal taxes(1)	114·5	131·2	125·7	146·8	169·4	193·2
Federal government expenditure	264·0	299·7	357·8	385·2	422·6	460·9
Defence purchases	73·9	77.3	84·3	86·8	94·3	99·5
Grants to state/local govts.	40·9	43·9	54·4	61·1	67·4	76·6
Federal surplus or (−) deficit	1·0	−11·5	−71·2	−53·8	−48·1	−29·3
State and local govt. receipts	194·5	210·4	235·7	264·7	296·2	327·7
from indirect business tax(1)	96·8	106·9	114·7	127·1	140·0	150·3
State and local govt. expenditure	184·0	202·8	229·8	246·2	266·6	299·8
State/local surplus/(−) deficit	10·5	7·6	5·9			

(1) Includes related non-tax receipts on national income account.

34. Balance of Payments (millions of dollars)	1973	1974	1975	1976	1977	1978
Merchandise trade balance	911	−5,338	9,049	−9,353	−31,125	
Balance on current account(1)	22	−5,028	18,445	−4,339	15,292	
Change in US private assets abroad(2)	−13,998	−32,323	−35,368	−43,865	−30,740	
Change in foreign private assets in US(2)	12,220	21,452	8,643	18,897	13,746	
Official reserves transactions(3)	−5,304	−7,960	−2,037	−3,976	−4,708	

(1) Includes balance on services and remittances and US government grants other than military. (2) Includes reinvested earnings of incorporated affiliates. (3) Includes net liquid private capital flows.

35. Merchandise Trade by Main Areas (millions of dollars)	1973	1974	1975	1976	1977	1978
All countries: exports (f.o.b.)	70,223	97,144	106,157	113,323	119,042	
imports (c.i.f.)	68,656	107,112	192,984	128,872	156,758	
Western Europe: exports	21,339	29,439	30,874	35,901	36,296	
imports	22,109	24,048	21,200	23,640	28,331	
Canada: exports	15,577	19,936	21,744	24,106	25,748	
imports	17,442	21,924	21,747	26,238	29,356	
Latin America/other western hemisphere:						
exports	9,948	14,501	15,670	15,487	16,347	
imports	9,021	13,667	16,840	13,228	16,335	
Japan: exports	8,356	10,679	9,563	10,144	10,522	
imports	9,645	12,338	11,268	15,504	18,623	
Dollar purchasing power (1967 = 100)	73·2	65·2	62·1	58·7	55·1	

36. Merchandise Trade by Main Commodity Groups

(millions of dollars)	1973	1974	1975	1976	1977	1978
Exports:						
Machinery and transport equipt.	27,842	38,189	45,668	49,501	50,248	
Motor vehicles and parts	5,989	7,878	10,028	10,949	11,796	
Electrical machinery	5,031	7,019	7,582	9,278	10,285	
Food and live animals	11,931	13,986	15,484	15,710	14,116	
Grains and cereal products	8,495	10,331	11,642	10,911	8,755	
Chemicals and pharmaceuticals	5,749	8,819	8,691	9,959	10,812	
Imports:						
Machinery and transport equipt.	20,970	24,060	23,465	29,824	36,407	
Motor vehicles and parts	9,216	10,264	9,921	13,104	15,842	
Food and live animals	7,986	9,386	8,509	10,267	12,538	
Meat and preparations	1,668	1,353	1,141	1,447	1,273	
Coffee	1,565	1,505	1,561	2,632	3,861	
Petroleum and products	7,549	24,270	24,814	31,798	41,526	
Iron and steel	3,009	5,149	4,595	4,347	5,804	

37. Interest Rates

(Per cent per annum, annual averages, unless otherwise stated)

Discount rate(1), end-year	7·50	7·75	6·00	5·25	6·00	9·50
Treasury bill rate	7·03	7·87	5·82	4·99	5·27	8·57
Government bond yields: 3-5 years	6·92	7·81	7·55	6·94	6·85	8·30
Long-term (10 years or more)	6·30	6·99	6·98	6·78	7·06	7·89
Banks' prime lending rate(2)	9·75	12·00	7·86	6·84	6·84	9·06

(*1*) *Of Federal Reserve Bank of New York.* (2) *Predominant rate charged by commercial banks on short-term loans to large business borrowers with the highest credit rating.*

38. Banking, money and credit

('000 million dollars, outstanding at end of year, seasonally adjusted)

Money supply M₃(1)	919·5	981·5	1,092·6	1,235·6	1,374·3	1,500·9
Currency	61·5	67·8	73·7	80·8	88·6	97·5
Deposits of commercial banks	681·9	741·7	789·5	838·2	939·4	993·1
Advances of commercial banks	494·9	549·2	542·1	576·0	617·0	709·0
Consumer credit	180·5	190·1	225·1	249·0	..	..
Instalment credit	148·3	158·1	165·0	194·0	230·8	275·6
Motor vehicle contracts	51·3	52·2	55·9	66·1	75·6	88·9
Non-instalment credit : retail charge accounts	7·8	7·7	7·5	7·3	..	..
Credit cards	2·1	2·1	2·2	2·5	..	..

(*1*) *Demand deposits at banks, currency in circulation, deposits at mutual savings banks and savings capital of savings and loan associations.*

39. Insurance

	1973	1974	1975	1976	1977	1978
($million, unless otherwise stated)						
Property-liability, net premiums written	42,019	44,631	49,550	60,380	72,730	
Automobile(1)	18,811	19,069	20,932	25,255	30,700	
Underwriting gain/(−) loss(2)	−3	−2,643	−4,257	−2,210	1,034	
Combined ratio(2)	99·2	105·4	107·9	102·4	97·1	
Automobile(1)	98·6	102·0	110·4	103·9	95·6	
General liability(3)	117·1	125·9	116·2	107·9	95·1	
Life insurance, total assets, end-year	252,436	263,349	289,304	321,552	350,506	

(*1*) *Physical damage and liability, private and commercial.* (2) *After stockholder and policy-holder dividends and premium rebates.* (3) *Sum of ratios of losses and loss expenses to earned premiums, and underwriting expenses to written premiums.*

Dollar purchasing power (1967 = 100)	73·2	65·2	62·1	58·7	55·1	

40. Companies(1)	*1973*	*1974*	*1975*	*1976*	*1977*	*1978*
('000 million dollars)						
Net profit after taxes	67·1	74·5	70·6	91·7	102·1	118·3
Cash dividends paid	27·8	31·0	31·9	37·9	43·7	49·3

(*1*) *Manufacturing corporations, all industries.*

41. The Stock Market
(millions of dollars, unless otherwise stated)

Turnover (sales), all exchanges	186,173	124,891	166,606	194,969	187,203	
New York Stock Exchange	8,012	105,372	142,754	164,545	157,250	
Securities issued, gross proceeds	100,417	105,372	114,430	113,297	120,027	
Bonds and notes: non-corporate	67,025	51,862	58,299	55,750	66,409	67,544
corporate	21,049	32,066	41,756	41,182	37,532	
Corporate common stock	7,642	3,994	7,413	8,304	8,034	

Stock prices (Standard and Poor's indices, 1941-43 = 10, end of year):

Combined index (500 stocks)	107·43	82.85	85·17	102·01	98·20	96·02
Industrials (400 stocks)	120.44	92.91	96·56	114·35	108·44	106·92

42. Employment
('000 persons)

Civilian labour force(1)	88,714	91,011	92,613	94,773	97,401	100,420
in non-agricultural industry	80,957	82,443	81,403	84,188	87,302	91,031
in manufacturing industry	20,068	20,046	18,347	18,958	19,560	20,329
in agriculture	3,452	3,492	3,380	3,297	3,244	3,342
unemployed	4,304	5,076	7,830	7,288	6,855	6,047
Industrial stoppages(2) (number)	5,353	6.074	5,031	5,600	5,590	..
Workers involved ('000)	2,251	2,778	1,746	2,508	2,296	..

(*1*) *Aged 16 years and over.* (*2*) *Beginning in the year.*

43. Earnings and Prices

Average weekly earnings per worker

(current dollars): mining	201·03	220·90	249·57	274·78	302·88	
contract construction	235·69	249·08	265·35	284·56	295·73	
manufacturing	166·06	176·40	189·51	208·12	226·90	

Average weekly hours per worker

in manufacturing	40·7	40·0	39·4	40·0	40·3	
Farm prices received (1967 = 100)	179	192	186	186	183	210
Wholesale prices (1967 = 100)	134·7	160·1	174·9	182·9	194·2	
Petroleum products	126·7	223·4	257·5	276·6	307·9	
Consumer prices (1967 = 100)	133·1	147·7	161·2	170·5	181·5	195·4
Food	141·4	161·7	175·4	180·8	192·2	211·4
Dollar purchasing power (1967 = 100)(1)	73.2	65·2	62·1	58·7	55·1	

(*1*) *Based on changes in retail price indexes.*

44. Production

Farm production (1967 = 100)	112	108	111	113	116	
Industrial production (1967 = 100)	129·8	129·3	117·8	129·8	137·1	145·1
Manufacturing	129·8	129·4	116·3	129·5	137·1	145·5

Output of main products and manufactures

Coal (million tons)	523·6	544·5	635·4	665·0	670·1	
Oil, indigenous (million tons)	517·9	492·0	469·0	443·7	472·9	
Oil refinery throughput (mn. tons)	624	580	615	656	618	
Natural gas (million cubic metres)	635·9	586·8	558·0	559·9	630·0	
Electricity generated ('000 mn. kwh	1,947	1,863	1,903	2,108	1,926	
Steel, crude (million tonnes)	136·5	132·0	116·5	116·3	124·9	
Aluminium ('000 tonnes)	4.968	5,306	4,360	4,984	5,166	
Cotton yarn ('000 tonnes)	1,356	1,512	1,368	1,676	..	
Man-made fibres (million lbs.)	8,329	8,085	7,167	7,317	8,201	
Plastics/resins ('000 tonnes)	11,880	10,068	8,213	9,785	..	
Motor cars, factory sales ('000)	9,658	7,331	6,713	8,497	11,040	

C. INTERNATIONAL COMPARISONS

45. Population of Selected Countries	Area '000 sq. km.	Population (millions), mid-year estimate			Annual Growth %	Persons per sq. km.
		1967	1977	1978		
Argentina	2,777	22·49	26·06	26·39	1·3	9
Australia	7,695	11·60	14·03	14·26	1·6	1·8
Belgium	31	9·53	9·83	..	0·3	317
Canada	9,976	20·05	23·32	23·50	1·3	2
China	9,561	722·22	877·96	..	1·9	92
Denmark	34	4·80	5·09	5·11	0·3	150
France	552	49·16	53·12	..	0·4	96
Germany, Western (incl. W. Berlin)	248	59·68	61·40	61·31	−0·2	248
India (incl. Indian-admin. Kashmir)	3,268	493·39	627·15	..	2·4	192
Ireland	69	2·88	3·15	..	1·1	46
Israel (excl. occupied areas)	21	2·63	3·51	3·69	5·0	167
Italy	301	52·33	56·45	..	0·6	188
Japan	370	99·79	113·86	114·90	0·9	308
Netherlands	34	12·45	13·85	13·94	0·7	407
New Zealand	104	2·68	3·12	..	1·0	30
Norway	324	3·75	4·04	..	0·4	13
South Africa (incl. S.W. Africa)	1,221	20·84	27·73	..	3·5	23
Spain	505	32·39	36·35	37·11	2·3	72
Sweden	450	7·81	8·26	..	0·4	18
Switzerland	41	5·92	6·50	..	0·7	159
Turkey	781	32·02	41·17	43·21	4·9	53
USSR	22,402	233·53	258·70	..	0·8	12
UK	244	54·50	55·85	..	−0·1	229
USA	9,363	196·56	216·67	..	0·8	23

46. Gross Domestic Product, Expenditure Basis, Selected Countries
(current prices, '000 million national currency units)

	1973	1974	1975	1976	1977	1978
Argentina (new pesos)	364·6	497·1	1,345·0	..	..	..
Australia (Australian dollars)(1)	46·49	55·73	66·05	77·49	86·38	..
Belgium (Belgian francs)	1,781	2,092	2,306	2,622	2,839	..
Canada (Canadian dollars)	125·38	149·78	168·09	194·80	214·58	..
Denmark (kroner)	164.93	183·85	203·78	232·89	276·24	..
France (francs)	1,114·2	1,273·8	1,437·1	1,669·3	1,870·3	..
Germany, W. (Deutschemarks)	918·6	987·1	1,031·8	1,125·6	1,198·5	..
India (rupees)	591·86	700·34	729·53	771·92	..	..
Italy (lire)	82,503	101,723	115,012	143,849	172,988	..
Japan (yen)	113,085	135,345	148,982	167,267	..	..
Kuwait (dinars)(2)	2·11	3·51	3·23	3·67	..	..
Netherlands (guilders)	168·11	190·29	209·69	237·99	261·12	..
Norway (kroner)	111.85	129·73	148·70	169·42	189·47	..
Portugal (escudos)	281·1	338·0	376·7	479·4	632·9	..
Saudi Arabia (riyals)	40,551	99,315	134,211	155,053	193,100	..
South Africa (rand)	19,557	23,973	27,088	30,566	34,620	..
Spain (pesetas)	4,129	5,022	5,910	6,999	8,797	..
Sweden (kronor)	219.25	249·04	287·43	323·56	351·32	..
Switzerland (francs)	130·1	141·1	140·2	142·0	145·6	151·6
USSR (roubles)	337·2	353·7	362·8	385·7	403·0	..
UK(£)	72·6	82·2	102·9	122·6	140·5	157·5
USA (dollars)	1,297·3	1,399·8	1,518·3	1,685·7	1,869·9	2,087·1

(*1*) *Years beginning 1 July.* (*2*) *Years beginning 1 April.* (*3*) *Years ended 30 June.*

World trade prices (1970 = 100)(1)   *137·5*   *184·0*   *202·0*   *203·5*   *212·6*

(*1*) *Unweighted average of IMF series for US dollar import and export prices in developed countries.*

47. Disposable Income per head

(US dollars)	1973	1974	1975	1976	1977	1978
Sweden	5,545	6,100	7,036	8,044	..	..
USA	5,523	5,918	6,299	7,339	..	..
Canada	4,818	5,673	6,262	6,974	..	..
Denmark	4,989	5,412	6,251	6,803	..	..
Germany, West	4,878	5,363	6,007	6,451	..	..
Australia	4,994	5,856	6,311	..	..	..
Norway	4,146	4,886	5,977	6,511	..	..
France	4,204	4,423	5,658	5,860	..	..
Switzerland	5,760	6,687	7,806	8,248	..	..
Belgium	4,271	4,889	5,851	..	..	..
Netherlands	4,044	4,670	5,442	5,890	..	..
Iceland	4,280	4,457	4,682	5,503	..	..
New Zealand	3,703	4,058	3,969	..	..	..
Japan	3,283	3,559	4,026	4,478	..	..
UK	2,831	3,036	3,690	3,530	..	..
Spain	1,901	2,276	2,651	2,663	..	..
Portugal	1,402	1,442	1,484	..	..	..
Saudi Arabia	814	2,514	3,538	4,147	..	..
South Africa	969	1,151	1,178	..	..	..
India	123	136	..	..	..	..

48. World Trade(1)

(millions of US dollars. Exports fob; imports cif)

	1973	1974	1975	1976	1977	1978
World(1): exports	524,700	773,400	796,600	907,000	1,030,500	..
imports	535,300	782,400	814,400	923,200	1,059,000	..
Industrial Countries: exports	376,280	504,129	537,805	598,040	678,639	813,871
imports	386,030	543,610	545,994	633,182	720,501	839,224
USA: exports	71,339	98,507	107,652	114,997	121,212	143,659
imports	73,575	107,996	103,414	129,565	157,560	183,137
Germany, West: exports	67,502	89,055	90,107	101,977	118,091	142,295
imports	54,552	68,897	74,255	88,209	101,475	121,820
Japan: exports	36,982	55,596	55,817	67,167	81,126	98,415
imports	38,347	62,075	57,853	64,748	71,328	79,900
France: exports	36,659	46,473	52,951	57,162	64,997	79,205
imports	37,727	52,914	53,964	64,391	70,497	80,909
UK: exports	30,657	38,885	44,127	46,300	58,165	71,711
imports	38,841	54,530	53,522	55,981	64,551	78,592
Other Europe: exports	22,810	30,360	31,940	35,160	41,987	48,718
imports	34,260	52,750	56,480	56,890	66,744	70,331
Australia, NZ, S. Afr: exports	15,710	18,440	19,910	23,800	26,537	30,946
imports	15,030	23,920	22,920	22,830	23,305	26,828
Less Developed Areas: exports	109,900	225,900	267,200	246,370	137,374	..
imports	100,000	162,100	185,900	210,870	165,319	140,264
Oil exporters: exports	44,900	135,900	116,700	130,500	145,304	..
imports	22,000	37,700	41,700	66,600	83,105	37,834
Saudi Arabia: exports	9,071	35,654	29,602	35,622	41,164	..
imports	1,944	3,473	6,701	11,759	14,656	..
Other W. Hemisphere: exports	21,610	30,610	32,920	38,290	45,068	..
imports	25,250	48,115	49,273	50,312	52,392	..
Other Middle East(2): exports	3,780	5,310	6,002	8,030	9,022	9,877
imports	8,060	12,370	16,760	17,660	20,516	..
Other Asia: exports	28,810	39,170	38,570	52 550	62,891	76,240
imports	33,240	51,940	53,070	57,660	69,561	87,907
Other Africa: exports	10,870	14,960	15,660	15,180	20,078	..
imports	11,410	16,520	19,830	18,500	24,608	..

(1) Excluding trade of centrally planned countries (see Table 49). (2) Including Egypt.

World trade prices (1970 = 100)	137·5	184·0	202·0	203·5	212·6

49. World Trade of Centrally Planned Countries

(millions of US dollars)	1973	1974	1975	1976	1977	1978
European(1): *exports*	53,200	65,500	78,300	85,200	99,600	
imports	56,300	70,900	92,100	96,700	106,100	
USSR: *exports*	21,463	27,405	33,316	37,168	45,161	
imports	21,112	24,890	36,971	38,109	40,817	
China: *exports*	4,900	6,300	7,025	6,915		
imports	5,000	7,400	7,360	5,975		
Cuba: *exports*	1,393	1,691	3,551	3,246		
imports	1,701	1,674	3,751	3,093		

(*1*)*Except Yugoslavia* (*included in Other Europe in Table 48*), *and Albania.*

50. International official reserves(1)

(millions of Special Drawing Rights, end-year)						
World	152,069	179,522	193,780	221,548	261,668	227,007
Industrial countries	95,748	97,935	104,112	113,483	139,420	160,392
USA	11,919	13,115	13,567	15,768	15,965	15,032
UK	5,368	5,667	4,663	3,641	17,335	13,100
Industrial Europe	68,896	69,020	75,149	78,394	100,513	116,133
Germany, West	27,947	26,461	26,510	29,954	32,713	41,360
France	7,070	7,230	10,757	8,373	8,392	10,692
Canada	4,782	4,758	4,549	5,029	3,793	3,507
Japan	10,151	11,042	10,947	14,292	19,149	25,714
Less developed areas	24,389	25,884	26,047	36,135	44,188	50,725
Middle East	12,073	38,384	48,292	56,149	62,152	45,915

(*1*) *Excluding convertible reserves held by centrally-planned countries.*

World trade prices (*US* $ *1970* = *100*)	*137·5*	*184·0*	*202·0*	*203·5*	*212·6*	
SOR value in US $	*1·20635*	*1·22435*	*1·17066*	*1·16183*	*1·12471*	*1·30279*

51. Exchange Rates

(middle rates for overseas settlements end of year, unless stated)

	Currency units per US dollar					per £
	1974	1975	1976	1977	1978	1978
Australia (Australian dollar)	0·7576	0·7955	0·9205	0·8761	0·8692	1·7740
Austria (schilling)	17·50	18·51	16·77	15·14	13·37	27·15
Belgium-Luxembourg (franc)	36·87	39·53	35·98	32·94	28·80	58·80
Canada (Canadian dollar)	0·9980	1·0164	1·0092	1·0944	1·1860	2·4175
China (yuan)(1)	2·04	2·04	2·04	2·04		
Denmark (krone)	5·788	6·178	5·788	5·788	5·085	10·38
Finland (markka)	3·55	3·85	3·77	4·02	3·93	8·005
France (franc)	4,537	4·486	4·970	4·705	4·180	8·505
Germany, W. (Deutschemark)	2·458	2·622	2·363	2·105	1·828	3·715
Israel (Israel £)	6·00	8·31	8·90	15·39	19·01	38·85
Italy (lira)	658·89	683·55	875·00	871·60	829·75	1688
Japan (yen)	300·4	305·2	292·8	240·00	194·60	396·5
Netherlands (guilder)	2·535	2·688	2·457	2·280	1·969	4·025
New Zealand (NZ dollar)	0·7692	0·9581	1·0530	0·981	0·938	1·913
Norway (krone)	5·40	5·59	5·19	5·14	5·02	10·23
Portugal (escudo)	24·87	27·47	31·55	39·86	45·80	93·75
South Africa (rand)	0·6897	0·8696	0·8696	0·8696	0·8696	1·7652
Spain (peseta)	57·20	59·77	68·2	80·91	70·11	142·95
Sweden (krona)	4·199	4·386	4·127	4·670	4·296	8·74
Switzerland (franc)	2·619	2·620	2·504	2·000	1·615	3·305
USSR (rouble)(1)	0·746	0·746	0·746	0·734	—	1·30
UK (£)(2)	2·349	2·024	1·702	1·919	2·042	—
Yugoslavia (dinar)	17·05	17·99	18·23	18·30	18·611	37·33

(*1*) *Official fixed or basic parity rate.* (*2*) *US dollars per £.*

52. Money Supply(1), selected countries
'000 million national currency units, end of year)

	1973	1974	1975	1976	1977	1978
France (francs)	332·1	382·6	431·2	465·2	506·51	
Germany, West (Deutschemarks)	132·9	149·1	169·9	176·6	197·6	
Japan (yen)	40,311	44,950	49,948	56,179	60,786	68,928
Saudi Arabia (riyals)	5·29	7·48	14·18	24·65	36·98	
Switzerland (francs)	56·6	56·0	58·4	62·9	63·3	
UK (£ sterling)	13·30	14·74	17·48	19·47	23·66	27·19
USA (dollars)	277·4	286·7	301·6	318·7	342·5	358·4

(1) Currency in circulation and demand deposits of the private sector only: figures for the UK and USA are therefore not compatible with those in Tables 10 and 38.

53. Central Bank Discount Rates
(per cent per annum, end of year)

Belgium	7·75	8·75	6·00	9·00	9·00	6·00
Canada	7·25	8·75	9·00	8·50	7·50	10·75
France	11·00	13·00	8·00	10·50	9·50	9·50
Germany, West	7·00	4·00	3·50	3.50	3·00	3·00
Italy	6·50	8·00	6·00	15·00	11·50	10·50
Japan	9·00	9·00	6·50	6·50	4·25	3·50
Sweden	5·00	7·00	6·00	8·00	8·00	6·50
Switzerland	4·50	5·50	3·00	2·00	1·50	1·00
UK(1)	13·00	11·50	11·25	14·25	7·00	12·50
USA(2)	7·50	7·75	6·00	5·25	6·00	9·50

(1) Minimum lending rate from 1971. (2) Federal Reserve Bank of New York.

54. Defence Expenditure

	Expenditure or budget (US $ mn.)				$ per caput	% of GNP
	1975	1976	1977	1978	1978	1977
Egypt	6,103	4,859	4,365	..	..	..
France	13,984	12,857	13,666	17,518	325	3·6
Germany, East	2,550	2,729	2,900	..	..	5·9
Germany, West (incl. W. Berlin)	19,540	18,758	17,130	21,355	337	3·4
Greece	1,435	1,249	1,328	1,523	164	5·0
Iran	8,800	9,500	7,894	9,942	273	10·9
Israel	3,552	4,214	4,259	3,310	887	29·9
Japan	4,620	5,058	6,135	8,567	74	0·9
Portugal	1,088	748	545	568	62	3·3
Saudi Arabia	6,771	9,038	7,539	13,170	1,704	13·6
South Africa	1,332	1,494	2,231	2,622	95	5·1
Sweden	2,483	2,418	2,833	2,946	355	3·4
Turkey	2,200	2,800	2,652	2,286	54	5·7
USSR(1)	124,000	124,000	133,000	..	..	11·13
UK	11,118	10,734	12,103	13,579	239	5·0
USA	88,983	102,691	104,250	113,000	517	6·0

(1) Data, at dollar purchasing power (not official exchange) rates, based on reconciliation of CIA, W. T. Lee's figures.

55. Industrial Ordinary Share Prices
(Index 1975 = 100, daily average, unless otherwise stated)

	1973	1974	1975	1976	1977	1978
Amsterdam	130	101	100	95	86	87
Australia, all exchanges	144	107	100	124	119	136
Canada, all exchanges(1)	129	107	100	104	93	99
Germany, West, all exchanges(2)	106	89	100	106	105	110
Hong Kong (31 July 1968 = 100)(3)	438	118	338	444	387	..
Johannesburg	126	100	100	100	93	106
New York	70	88	100	117	122	111
Paris	124	92	100	99	79	..
Switzerland, all exchanges(4)	147	111	100	110	116	111
Tokyo	116	99	100	112	121	133
UK(5)	136	80	100	120	153	174

(1) Average of Thursday quotations. (2) Average of four bank returns each month. (3) Hang Seng index for Hong Kong Stock Exchange only: last trading day of year. (4) Average of Friday quotations. (5) Average of closing prices on last Tuesday of each month.

56. World Production

(Index 1970 = 100)	1973	1974	1975	1976	1977	1978
Food (1)	108	110	112	116	118	..
Industrial production (2)	122	126	125	136	143	..
OECD	119	120	110	120	125	..
EEC (3)	115	115	108	115	118	..
France	120	123	113	123	126	..
Germany, West	114	111	105	113	116	119
Italy	114	119	108	121	121	..
UK	110	109	103	104	106	..
Japan	129	123	110	125	130	..
Sweden	111	117	115	114	111	..
USSR (4)	123	133	143	150	160	..

(1) Excluding China. (2) Excluding China, USSR, Eastern Europe. (3) Community of nine.

57. Energy Surpluses and (−) Deficits
(million tons coal equivalent)

World	615	668	605	633	..	..
Africa	376	349	310	373	..	..
America, North	−266	−267	−263	−408	..	..
America, Central	228	288	149	144	..	..
America, South	−41	−45	−52	−57	..	..
Asia: Middle East	1,506	1,548	1,379	1,545	..	..
Asia, Other	−377	−368	−343	−353	..	..
Europe, Western	−948	−914	−818	−897	..	..
Oceania	12	15	16	20	..	..
Centrally planned economies	143	167	235	262	..	..

58. Prices of Selected Commod'ties

Aluminium, Canadian (US$/lb.)	27·2	34·7	39·4	40·4	51·9	60·1
Beef, Irish (London) (pence/lb.)	79·9	81·7	89·8	92·0	96·3	125·3
Copper, wirebars (London)(£/tonne)	727	878	537	781	751	711
Cotton, Egyptian (L'pool) (US cents/lb.)	98·44	153·61	129·39	136·53	149·24	..
Gold(London) (US $/fine oz.)	100·00	162·02	160·47	124·03	148·79	197·14
Newsprint, S. Quebec (US $/short ton)	153·1	202·4	245·0	262·8	279·73	290·80
Petroleum, Ras Tanura (US $/barrel)	3·27	11·58	11·53	12·38	12·70	12·70
Rice, Thai (Bangkok) ($/tonne)	—	545·6	363·0	254·6	272·3	367·5
Rubber, Malay (Singapore) (cents/lb.)	30·67	33·81	25·82	35·52	37·36	44·83
Steel bars (Oberhausen) (DM/tonne)	550	646	737	828	746	..
Soya beans, US (R'dam) (US$/tonne)	291	277	220	231	279	268
Sugar, f.o.b. Carib/Brazil (US cents/lb.)	9·63	29·96	20·50	11·57	8·10	7·81
Tin, spot (London) (£/tonne)	1,967	3,495	3,090	4,242	6,113	6,739
Wheat, Manitoba, No. 2 N. (£/ton)	71·3	103·8	94·7	97·0	82·5	..
Wool, greasy (Sydney) (cents/lb.)	96	62	59		91	84	..

(1) Irish.

59. Consumer Prices, Selected Countries
(index 1975 = 100)

Argentina	28·7	35·4	100·0	543·2	1,499·6	..
Australia	75·5	86·9	100·0	113·5	127·4	137·6
France	78·7	81·5	100·0	109·2	119·6	130·6
Germany, West	88·2	94·4	100·0	104·5	108·6	111·4
India	74·1	94·7	100·0	92·2	100·0	..
Japan	71·9	89·4	100·0	109·3	118·1	122·6
South Africa	78·9	88·1	100·0	111·3	123·6	136·2
Sweden	82·9	91·1	100·0	110·3	122·9	135·1
UK	69·4	80·5	100·0	116·5	135·0	146·2
US	82·6	91·6	100·0	105·8	112·7	121·2

| *World trade prices (1970 = 100)* | *137·5* | *184·0* | *202·0* | *203·5* | *212·6* | |

XVIII DOCUMENTS AND REFERENCES

THE CAMP DAVID AGREEMENTS

Signed by President Anwar Sadat and Mr Menachem Begin
on 17 September 1978

I. THE FRAMEWORK OF PEACE IN THE MIDDLE EAST

Muhammad Anwar al-Sadat, President of the Arab Republic of Egypt, and Menachem Begin, Prime Minister of Israel, met with Jimmy Carter, President of the USA, at Camp David from 5 to 17 September 1978, and have agreed on the following framework for peace in the Middle East. They invite other parties to the Arab-Israeli conflict to adhere to it.

PREAMBLE

The search for peace in the Middle East must be guided by the following:
The agreed basis for a peaceful settlement of the conflict between Israel and its neighbours is UN Security Council Resolution 242* in all its parts.

After four wars during 30 years, despite intensive humane efforts, the Middle East, which is the cradle of civilization and the birthplace of three great religions, does not yet enjoy the blessings of peace. The people of the Middle East yearn for peace, so that the vast human and natural resources of the region can be turned to the pursuits of peace and so that this area can become a model for coexistence and cooperation among nations.

The historic initiative by President Sadat in visiting Jerusalem and the reception accorded to him by the Parliament, Government and people of Israel, and the reciprocal visit of Prime Minister Begin to Ismailia, the peace proposals made by both leaders, as well as the warm reception of these missions by the peoples of both countries, have created an unprecedented opportunity for peace which must not be lost if this generation and future generations are to be spared the tragedies of war.

The provisions of the Charter of the UN and the other accepted norms of international law and legitimacy now provide accepted standards for the conduct of relations between all states.

To achieve a relationship of peace, in the spirit of Article 2 of the UN Charter, future negotiations between Israel and any neighbour prepared to negotiate peace and security with it are necessary for the purpose of carrying out all the provisions and principles of Resolutions 242 and 338.†

Peace requires respect for the sovereignty, territorial integrity and political independence of every state in the area and their right to live in peace within secure and recognized boundaries free from threats or acts of force. Progress toward that goal can accelerate movement toward a new era of reconciliation in the Middle East marked by cooperation in promoting economic development, in maintaining stability and in assuring security.

Security is enhanced by a relationship of peace and by cooperation between nations which enjoy normal relations. In addition, under the terms of peace treaties, the parties can, on the basis of reciprocity, agree to special security arrangements such as demilitarized zones, limited armaments areas, early warning stations, the presence of international forces, liaison, agreed measures for monitoring, and other arrangements that they agree are useful.

FRAMEWORK

Taking these factors into account, the parties are determined to reach a just, comprehensive and durable settlement of the Middle East conflict through the conclusion of peace treaties based on Security C⌐   Resolutions 242 and 338 in all their parts. Their purpose is to achieve peace and good neighbourly relations. They recognize that, for peace to endure, it must involve all those who have been most deeply affected by the conflict. They therefore agree that this framework as appropriate is intended by them to constitute a basis for peace not only between Egypt and Israel, but also between Israel and each of its other neighbours which is prepared to negotiate peace with Israel on this basis. With that objective in mind, they have agreed to proceed as follows:

* Text in AR 1973, p. 524.
† Text in AR 1973, p. 525.

Q

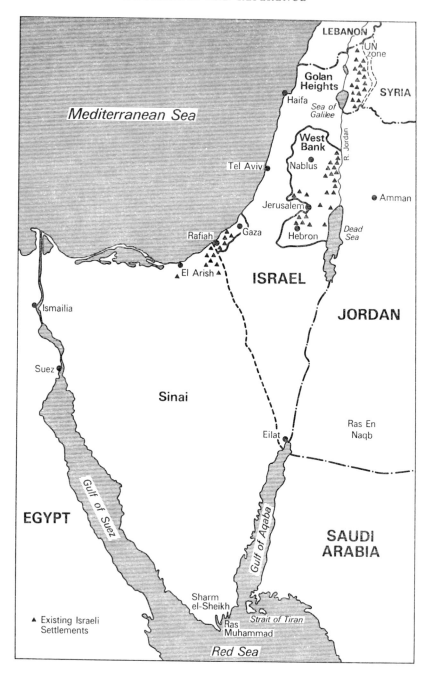

Map to illustrate the Camp David agreements.

A. West Bank and Gaza

1. Egypt, Israel, Jordan and the representatives of the Palestinian people should participate in negotiations on the resolution of the Palestinian problem in all its aspects. To achieve that objective, negotiations relating to the West Bank and Gaza should proceed in three stages.

(A) Egypt and Israel agree that, in order to ensure a peaceful and orderly transfer of authority, and taking into account the security concerns of all the parties, there should be transitional arrangements for the West Bank and Gaza for a period not exceeding five years. In order to provide full autonomy to the inhabitants, under these arrangements the Israeli military government and its civilian administration will be withdrawn as soon as a self-governing authority has been freely elected by the inhabitants of these areas to replace the existing military government.

To negotiate the details of a transitional arrangement, the Government of Jordan will be invited to join the negotiations on the basis of this framework. These new arrangements should give due consideration both to the principle of self-government by the inhabitants of these territories and to the legitimate security concerns of the parties involved.

(B) Egypt, Israel and Jordan will agree on the modalities for establishing the elected self-governing authority in the West Bank and Gaza. The delegations of Egypt and Jordan may include Palestinians from the West Bank and Gaza or other Palestinians as mutually agreed. The parties will negotiate an agreement which will define the powers and responsibilities of the self-governing authority to be exercised in the West Bank and Gaza. A withdrawal of Israeli armed forces will take place and there will be a redeployment of the remaining Israeli forces into specified security locations.

The agreement will also include arrangements for assuring internal and external security and public order. A strong local police force will be established, which may include Jordanian citizens. In addition, Israeli and Jordanian forces will participate in joint patrols and in the manning of control posts to assure the security of the borders.

(C) When the self-governing authority (administrative council) in the West Bank and Gaza is established and inaugurated, the transitional period of five years will begin. As soon as possible, but not later than the third year after the beginning of the transitional period, negotiations will take place to determine the final status of the West Bank and Gaza and its relationship with its neighbours, and to conclude a peace treaty between Israel and Jordan by the end of the transitional period. These negotiations will be conducted among Egypt, Israel, Jordan and the elected representatives of the inhabitants of the West Bank and Gaza.

Two separate but related committees will be convened, one committee, consisting of representatives of the four parties which will negotiate and agree on the final status of the West Bank and Gaza, and its relationship with its neighbours, and the second committee, consisting of representatives of Israel and representatives of Jordan to be joined by the elected representatives of the inhabitants of the West Bank and Gaza, to negotiate the peace treaty between Israel and Jordan, taking into account the agreement reached on the final status of the West Bank and Gaza.

The negotiations shall be based on all the provisions and principles of UN Security Council Resolution 242. The negotiations will resolve, among other matters, the location of the boundaries and the nature of the security arrangements. The solution from the negotiations must also recognize the legitimate rights of the Palestinian people and their just requirements. In this way, the Palestinians will participate in the determination of their own future through:

(i) The negotiations among Egypt, Israel, Jordan and the representatives of the inhabitants of the West Bank and Gaza to agree on the final status of the West Bank and Gaza and other outstanding issues by the end of the transitional period.

(ii) Submitting their agreement to a vote by the elected representatives of the inhabitants of the West Bank and Gaza.

(iii) Providing for the elected representatives of the inhabitants of the West Bank and Gaza to decide how they shall govern themselves consistent with the provisions of their agreement.

(iv) Participating as stated above in the work of the committee negotiating the peace treaty between Israel and Jordan.

2. All necessary measures will be taken and provisions made to assure the security of Israel and its neighbours during the transitional period and beyond. To assist in providing such security, a strong local police force will be constituted by the self-governing authority. It will be composed of inhabitants of the West Bank and Gaza. The police will maintain continuing liaison on internal security matters with the designated Israeli, Jordanian and Egyptian officers.

3. During the transitional period, the representatives of Egypt, Israel, Jordan and the self-governing authority will constitute a continuing committee to decide by agreement on the modalities of admission of persons displaced from the West Bank and Gaza in 1967, together with necessary measures to prevent disruption and disorder. Other matters of common concern may also be dealt with by this committee.

4. Egypt and Israel will work with each other and with other interested parties to establish agreed procedures for a prompt, just and permanent implementation of the resolution of the refugee problem.

B. Egypt-Israel

1. Egypt and Israel undertake not to resort to the threat or the use of force to settle disputes. Any disputes shall be settled by peaceful means in accordance with the provisions of Article 33 of the Charter of the UN.

2. In order to achieve peace between them, the parties agree to negotiate in good faith with a goal of concluding within three months from the signing of this framework a peace treaty between them, while inviting the other parties to the conflict to proceed simultaneously to negotiate and conclude similar peace treaties with a view to achieving a comprehensive peace in the area. The framework for the conclusion of a peace treaty between Egypt and Israel will govern the peace negotiations between them. The parties will agree on the modalities and the timetable for the implementation of their obligations under the treaty.

ASSOCIATED PRINCIPLES

1. Egypt and Israel state that the principles and provisions described below should apply to peace treaties between Israel and each of its neighbours—Egypt, Jordan, Syria and Lebanon.

2. Signatories shall establish among themselves relationships normal to states at peace with one another. To this end, they should undertake to abide by all the provisions of the Charter of the UN. Steps to be taken in this respect include:
 (A) Full recognition.
 (B) Abolishing economic boycotts.
 (C) Guaranteeing that under their jurisdiction the citizens of the other parties shall enjoy the protection of the due process of law.

3. Signatories should explore possibilities for economic development in the context of final peace treaties, with the objective of contributing to the atmosphere of peace, cooperation and friendship which is their common goal.

4. Claims commissions may be established for the mutual settlement of all financial claims.

5. The United States shall be invited to participate in the talks on matters related to the modalities of the implementation of the agreements and working out the timetable for the carrying out of the obligations of the parties.

6. The UN Security Council shall be requested to endorse the peace treaties and ensure that their provisions shall not be violated. The permanent members of the Security Council shall be requested to underwrite the peace treaties and ensure respect for their provisions. They shall also be requested to conform their policies and actions with the undertakings contained in this framework.

II FRAMEWORK FOR THE CONCLUSION OF A PEACE TREATY BETWEEN EGYPT AND ISRAEL

In order to achieve peace between them, Israel and Egypt agree to negotiate in good faith with a goal of concluding within three months of the signing of this framework a peace treaty between them. It is agreed that:
 The site of the negotiations will be under a UN flag at a location or locations to be mutually agreed.
 All of the principles of UN Resolution 242 will apply in this resolution of the dispute between Israel and Egypt.
 Unless otherwise mutually agreed, terms of the peace treaty will be implemented between two and three years after the peace treaty is signed.
 The following matters are agreed between the parties:
 (A) The full exercise of Egyptian sovereignty up to the internationally recognized border between Egypt and mandated Palestine;
 (B) The withdrawal of Israeli armed forces from the Sinai;
 (C) The use of airfields left by the Israelis near El Arish, Rafah, Ras en Naqb, and Sharm el-Sheikh for civilian purposes only, including possible commercial use by all nations;

(D) The right of free passage by ships of Israel through the Gulf of Suez and the Suez Canal on the basis of the Constantinople Convention of 1888 applying to all nations; the Strait of Tiran and the Gulf of Aqaba are international waterways to be open to all nations for unimpeded and non-suspendable freedom of navigation and overflight;

(E) The construction of a highway between the Sinai and Jordan near Eilat with guaranteed free and peaceful passage by Egypt and Jordan; and

(F) The stationing of military forces listed below.

Stationing of forces

(A) No more than one division (mechanized or infantry) of Egyptian armed forces will be stationed within an area lying approximately 50 kilometres (30 miles) east of the Gulf of Suez and the Suez Canal.

(B) Only UN forces and civil police equipped with light weapons to perform normal police functions will be stationed within an area lying west of the international border and the Gulf of Aqaba, varying in width from 20 kilometres (12 miles) to 40 kilometres (25 miles).

(C) In the area within three kilometres (1·8 miles) east of the international border there will be Israeli limited military forces not to exceed four infantry battalions and UN observers.

(D) Border patrol units, not to exceed three battalions, will supplement the civil police in maintaining order in the area not included above.

The exact demarcation of the above areas will be as decided during the peace negotiations.

Early warning stations may exist to ensure compliance with the terms of the agreement.

UN forces will be stationed: (a) in part of the area in the Sinai lying within about 20 kilometres of the Mediterranean Sea and adjacent to the international border, and (b) in the Sharm el-Sheikh area to ensure freedom of passage through the Strait of Tiran; and these forces will not be removed unless such removal is approved by the Security Council of the UN with a unanimous vote of the five permanent members.

After a peace treaty is signed, and after the interim withdrawal is complete, normal relations will be established between Egypt and Israel, including: Full recognition, including diplomatic, economic and cultural relations; termination of economic boycotts and barriers to the free movement of goods and people; and mutual protection of citizens by the due process of law.

Interim withdrawal

Between three months and nine months after the signing of the peace treaty, all Israeli forces will withdraw east of a line extending from a point east of El Arish to Ras Muhammad, the exact location of this line to be determined by mutual agreement.

RHODESIAN INTERNAL SETTLEMENT AGREEMENT

Signed at Salisbury on 3 March 1978 by Mr Ian Smith, Bishop Abel Muzorewa, the Rev. Ndabaningi Sithole and Chief Jeremiah Chirau.

Whereas the present constitutional situation in Rhodesia has led to the imposition of economic and other sanctions by the international community against Rhodesia and to armed conflict within Rhodesia and from neighbouring territories;

And whereas it is necessary in the interests of our country that an agreement should be reached that would lead to the termination of such sanctions and the cessation of the armed conflict;

And whereas, in an endeavour to reach such an agreement, delegates from the Rhodesian Government, African National Council (Sithole), United African National Council and Zimbabwe United People's Organization have met during the last two months in Salisbury and, having discussed fully the proposals put forward by the various delegations, have reached agreement on certain fundamental principles to be embodied in a new constitution that will lead to the termination of the aforementioned sanctions and the cessation of the armed conflict;

Now, therefore:

A. It is hereby agreed that a constitution will be drafted and enacted which will provide for majority rule on the basis of universal adult suffrage on the following terms:

1. There will be a legislative assembly consisting of 100 members and the following provisions will apply thereto:

(a) There will be a common voters roll with all citizens of 18 years and over being eligible for registration as voters, subject to certain recognized disqualifications.

(b) 72 of the seats in the legislative assembly will be reserved for blacks who will be elected by voters who are enrolled on the common roll.

(c) 28 of the seats in the legislative assembly will be reserved for whites (i.e. Europeans as defined in the 1969 constitution) who will be elected as follows:

(i) 20 will be elected on a preferential voting system by white voters who are enrolled on the common roll;

(ii) Eight will be elected by voters who are enrolled on the common roll from 16 candidates who will be nominated, in the case of the first parliament, by an electoral college composed of the white members of the present House of Assembly and, in the case of any subsequent parliament, by an electoral college composed of the 28 whites who are members of the Parliament dissolved immediately prior to the general election.

(d) The reserved seats referred to in (c) above shall be retained for a period of at least 10 years or of two parliaments, whichever is the longer, and shall be reviewed at the expiration of that period, at which time a commission shall be appointed, the chairman of which shall be a judge of the High Court, to undertake this review. If that commission recommends that the arrangements regarding the said reserved seats should be changed,

(i) An amendment to the constitution to effect such change may be made by a Bill which receives the affirmative votes of not less than 51 members;

(ii) The said Bill shall also provide that the 72 seats referred to in (b) above shall not be reserved for blacks.

(e) The members filling the seats referred to in (c) above will be prohibited from forming a coalition with any single minority party for the purpose of forming a government.

2. There will be a just declaration of rights which will protect the rights and freedoms of individuals and, *inter alia*, will provide for protection from deprivation of property unless adequate compensation is paid promptly, and for protection of pension rights of persons who are members of pension funds.

3. The independence and qualifications of the judiciary will be entrenched and judges will have security of tenure.

4. There will be an independent public services board, the members of which will have security of tenure. The board will be responsible for appointments to, promotions in, and discharges from, the public service.

5. The public service, police force, defence forces and prison service will be maintained in a high state of efficiency and free from political interference.

6. Pensions which are payable from the Consolidated Revenue Fund will be guaranteed and charged on the Consolidated Revenue Fund and will be remittable outside the country.

7. Citizens who at present are entitled to dual citizenship will not be deprived of their present entitlement.

8. The above-mentioned provisions will be set out or provided for in the constitution and will be regarded as specially entrenched provisions which may only be amended by a Bill which receives the affirmative votes of not less than 78 members.

B. It is hereby also agreed that, following the agreement set out above, the next step will be the setting up of a transitional government. The prime function of the transitional government will be: (a) To bring about a ceasefire, and (b) To deal with related matters such as:

(i) The composition of the future military forces, including those members of the nationalist forces who wish to take up a military career, and the rehabilitation of others;

(ii) The rehabilitation of those affected by the war.

C. It is also hereby agreed that it will be the duty of the transitional government to determine and deal with the following matters:

(a) The release of detainees;

(b) The review of sentences for offences of a political character;

(c) The further removal of discrimination;

(d) The creation of a climate conducive to the holding of free and democratic elections;

(e) The drafting of the new constitution in terms of this agreement;

(f) Procedures for registration of voters with a view to the holding of a general election at the earliest possible date.

D. It is also hereby agreed that the transitional government will comprise an Executive Council and a Ministerial Council and the following provisions will apply thereto:

1. Executive Council

(a) *Composition:* The Executive Council will be composed of the Prime Minister and three black Ministers, being the heads of those delegations engaged in the negotiations. The members will take turns in presiding as chairman of the Executive Council in such sequence and for such period as that council may determine. Decisions of the Executive Council will be by consensus.

(b) *Functions:* (i) The Executive Council will be responsible for ensuring that the functions given to, and the duties imposed on, the transitional government by the constitutional agreement are dealt with as expeditiously as possible. It will take policy decisions in connexion with the preparation and drafting of the new constitution and the other matters set out in sections B and C of this agreement and with any other matters which may arise.

(ii) The Executive Council may refer the matters set out in sections B and C of this agreement, or any other matter, to the Ministerial Council for examination and recommendation.

(iii) The Executive Council will review decisions or recommendations of the Ministerial Council and may confirm such decisions or recommendations or refer them back to the Ministerial Council for further consideration.

2. Ministerial Council

(a) *Composition:* The Ministerial Council will be composed of equal numbers of black and white Ministers. The black Ministers will be nominated in equal proportions by the heads of those delegations engaged in the negotiations. The white Ministers will be nominated by the Prime Minister. The chairmanship of the Ministerial Council will alternate between black and white Ministers. The Prime Minister will nominate which white Minister shall take the chair and the heads of those delegations engaged in the negotiations will nominate which of the black Ministers shall take the chair in the sequence and for the period determined by the Ministerial Council.

(b) *Functions:* (i) The Ministerial Council will operate on the Cabinet system. For each portfolio, or group of portfolios, there will be a black and a white Minister who will share responsibility.

(ii) The Ministerial Council will be responsible for initiating legislation and for supervising the preparation of such legislation as may be directed by the Executive Council.

(iii) The Ministerial Council will make recommendations to the Executive Council on all matters referred to it by the Executive Council and on any other matter it thinks fit.

(iv) Decisions of the Ministerial Council will be by majority vote and subject to review by the Executive Council.

3. Parliament

(a) Parliament will continue to function during the life of the transitional government and will meet for the following purposes as and when the Executive Council considers it should be summoned:

(i) To pass a Constitution Amendment Act enabling Ministers who have not been elected to Parliament to serve for periods in excess of four months;

(ii) To pass legislation for the registration of voters;

(iii) To pass the 1978-79 budget;

(iv) To enact any legislation or deal with any other matter brought forward by the transitional government (*e.g.* for the further removal of discrimination);

(v) To enact the new constitution;

(vi) To nominate 16 whites for election by voters on the common roll to eight of the seats reserved for whites.

(b) The work of the various select committees and of the Senate legal committee will proceed as normal.

E. It is also hereby agreed that independence day shall be 31 December 1978.

TREATY OF PEACE AND FRIENDSHIP BETWEEN THE PEOPLE'S REPUBLIC OF CHINA AND JAPAN

Signed in Peking on 12 August 1978
(*English text from the Peking Review No. 33 of 18 August 1978*)

The People's Republic of China and Japan,

Recalling with satisfaction that since the Government of the People's Republic of China and the Government of Japan issued a Joint Statement in Peking on 29 September 1972 the friendly relations between the two Governments and the peoples of the two countries have developed greatly on a new basis,

Confirming that the above-mentioned Joint Statement constitutes the basis of the relations of peace and friendship between the two countries and that the principles enunciated in the Joint Statement should be strictly observed,

Confirming that the principles of the Charter of the United Nations should be fully respected,

Hoping to contribute to peace and stability in Asia and in the world,

For the purpose of solidifying and developing the relations of peace and friendship between the two countries,

Have resolved to conclude a Treaty of Peace and Friendship and for that purpose have appointed as their Plenipotentiaries:

The People's Republic of China: Huang Hua, Minister of Foreign Affairs

Japan: Sunao Sonoda, Minister for Foreign Affairs

Who, having communicated to each other their full powers, found to be in good and due form, have agreed as follows:

Article I. 1. The Contracting Parties shall develop durable relations of peace and friendship between the two countries on the basis of the principles of mutual respect for sovereignty and territorial integrity, mutual non-aggression, non-interference in each other's internal affairs, equality and mutual benefit and peaceful coexistence.

2. In keeping with the foregoing principles and the principles of the United Nations Charter, the Contracting Parties affirm that in their mutual relations all disputes shall be settled by peaceful means without resorting to the use or threat of force.

Article II. The Contracting Parties declare that neither of them should seek hegemony in the Asia-Pacific region or in any other region and that each is opposed to efforts by any other country or group of countries to establish such hegemony.

Article III. The Contracting Parties shall, in a goodneighbourly and friendly spirit and in conformity with the principles of equality and mutual benefit and non-interference in each other's internal affairs, endeavour to further develop economic and cultural relations between the two countries and to promote exchanges between the peoples of the two countries.

Article IV. The present Treaty shall not affect the position of either Contracting Party regarding its relations with third countries.

Article V. 1. The present Treaty shall be ratified and shall enter into force on the date of the exchange of instruments of ratification which shall take place at Tokyo. The present Treaty shall remain in force for ten years and thereafter shall continue to be in force until terminated in accordance with the provisions of Paragraph 2 of this Article.

2. Either Contracting Party may, by giving one year's written notice to the other Contracting Party, terminate the present Treaty at the end of the initial ten-year period or at any time thereafter.

In witness whereof the respective Plenipotentiaries have signed the present Treaty and have affixed thereto their seals.

Done in duplicate in the Chinese and Japanese languages, both texts being equally authentic, at Peking, this twelfth day of August 1978.

For the People's Republic of China: Huang Hua   For Japan: Sunao Sonoda
                    (*Signed*)   (*Signed*)

TREATY OF FRIENDSHIP AND COOPERATION BETWEEN THE SOCIALIST REPUBLIC OF VIET NAM AND THE USSR

Signed in Moscow on 3 November 1978
(*English text supplied by the Vietnamese embassy in London*)

The Socialist Republic of Viet Nam and the Union of Soviet Socialist Republics,

Proceeding from the close cooperation in all fields in a fraternal spirit, from the unshakeable friendship and solidarity between the two countries on the basis of the principles of marxism–leninism and socialist internationalism,

Firmly convinced that the endeavour to consolidate the solidarity and friendship between the Socialist Republic of Viet Nam and the Union of Soviet Socialist Republics is in conformity with the basic interests of the two peoples and in the interests of the consolidation of the fraternal friendship and one-mindedness among the countries in the socialist community,

In keeping with the principles and objectives of the socialist foreign policy and the desire to ensure the most favourable international conditions for the building of socialism and communism,

Confirming that the signatories to the treaty acknowledge their international obligation to assist each other in the consolidation and preservation of the socialist achievements recorded by the two peoples through their heroic efforts and selfless labour,

Determined to work for the unity of all forces struggling for peace, national independence, democracy and social progress,

Expressing their iron-like determination to contribute to the consolidation of peace in Asia and throughout the world, and to the development of good relations and mutually beneficial cooperation among countries with different social systems,

Hoping to further develop and perfect the all-round cooperation between the two countries,

Attaching importance to the continued development and consolidation of the juridical basis of the bilateral relations,

In keeping with the objectives and principles of the United Nations charter,

Have resolved to sign this treaty of friendship and cooperation and have agreed as follows:

Article 1. In keeping with the principles of socialist internationalism, the two parties signatory to the present treaty shall continue to consolidate their unshakeable friendship and solidarity and assist each other in a fraternal spirit. The two parties shall unceasingly develop political relations and cooperation in all fields and endeavour to assist each other on the basis of respect for each other's national independence and sovereignty, equality and non-interference in each other's internal affairs.

Article 2. The two parties signatory to the present treaty shall join efforts to consolidate and broaden the mutually beneficial cooperation in the economic and scientific-technological fields in order to push forward the building of socialism and communism and to constantly raise the material and cultural standards of the two peoples. The two parties shall continue to coordinate their long-term national economic plans, agree upon long-term measures aimed at developing the most important sectors of the economy, science and technology, and exchange knowledge and experience accumulated in the building of socialism and communism.

Article 3. The two parties signatory to the treaty shall promote cooperation between their state bodies and mass organizations, and develop broad relations in the fields of science and culture, education, literature and art, press, broadcasting and television, health service, environmental protection, tourism, sports and physical training, and others. The two parties shall encourage the development of contacts between working people of the two countries.

Article 4. The two parties signatory to the treaty shall consistently strive to further consolidate their fraternal relations, and to strengthen the solidarity and one-mindedness among the socialist countries on the basis of marxism–leninism and socialist internationalism.

The two parties shall do their utmost to consolidate the world socialist system and actively contribute to the development and defence of the socialist gains.

Article 5. The two parties signatory to the treaty shall continue doing their utmost to contribute to defending world peace and the security of all nations. They shall actively oppose all schemes and manoeuvres of imperialism and reactionary forces, support the just struggle for the complete eradication of all forms and colours of colonialism and racism, support the struggle waged by non-aligned countries and the peoples of Asian, African and Latin American countries against imperialism, colonialism and neo-colonialism, for the consolidation of independence and the defence of sovereignty, for mastery over their natural resources, and for the establishment of a new world economic relationship with no inequity, oppression and exploitation, and support the aspirations of the South-East Asian peoples for peace, independence and cooperation among countries in this region.

The two parties shall strive to develop the relations between countries with different social systems on the basis of the principles of peaceful coexistence, for the purpose of broadening and consolidating the process of easing tension in international relations and radically eliminating aggressions and wars of aggression from the life of all nations, for the sake of peace, national independence, democracy and socialism.

Article 6. The two parties signatory to the treaty shall exchange views on all important international questions relating to the interests of the two countries. In case either party is attacked or threatened with attack, the two parties signatory to the treaty shall immediately consult each other with a view to eliminating that threat, and shall take appropriate and effective measures to safeguard peace and the security of the two countries.

Article 7. The present treaty does not concern the two parties' rights and obligations stemming from the bilateral or multilateral agreements to which they are signatories and is not intended to oppose any third country.

Article 8. The present treaty shall be ratified and shall enter into force on the date of the exchange of instruments of ratification, which shall take place in Hanoi as early as possible.

Article 9. The present treaty shall remain in force for 25 years and thereafter shall be automatically extended for periods of ten years if neither signatory party declares its desire to terminate the present treaty by informing the other party twelve months before the treaty expires.

Q*

Done in duplicate in the Vietnamese and Russian languages, both texts being equally authentic.

For the SRVN:	For the USSR:
LE DUAN	L. I. BREZHNEV
PHAM VAN DONG	A. N. KOSYGIN
(*signed*)	(*signed*)

THE ESTABLISHMENT OF DIPLOMATIC RELATIONS BETWEEN THE USA AND THE PEOPLE'S REPUBLIC OF CHINA

Joint communique issued in Washington and Peking on 15 December 1978

The United States of America and the People's Republic of China have agreed to recognize each other and to establish diplomatic relations as of 1 January 1979.

The United States recognizes the Government of the People's Republic of China as the sole legal Government of China. Within this context, the people of the United States will maintain cultural, commercial and other unofficial relations with the people of Taiwan.

The United States of America and the People's Republic of China reaffirm the principles agreed on by the two sides in the Shanghai communique of 1972* and emphasize once again that:

—Both wish to reduce the danger of international military conflict;

—Neither should seek hegemony—the dominance of one nation over others—in the Asia-Pacific region or in any other region of the world and each is opposed to efforts by any other country or group of countries to establish such hegemony;

—Neither is prepared to negotiate on behalf of any third party or to enter into agreements or understandings with the other directed at other states;

—The Government of the United States of America acknowledges the Chinese position that there is but one China and Taiwan is part of China;

—Both believe that normalization of Sino-American relations is not only in the interest of the Chinese and American peoples but also contributes to the cause of peace in Asia and in the world.

The United States of America and the People's Republic of China will exchange ambassadors and establish embassies on 1 March 1979.

United States Statement issued simultaneously from the White House

As of 1 January 1979, the United States of America recognizes the People's Republic of China as the sole legal Government of China. On the same date, the People's Republic of China accords similar recognition to the United States of America. The United States thereby establishes diplomatic relations with the People's Republic of China.

On that same date, 1 January 1979, the United States of America will notify Taiwan that it is terminating diplomatic relations and that the mutual defense treaty between the US and the Republic of China is being terminated in accordance with the provisions of the treaty. The United States also states that it will be withdrawing its remaining military personnel from Taiwan within four months.

In the future, the American people and the people of Taiwan will maintain commercial, cultural, and other relations without official government representation and without diplomatic relations.

The Administration will seek adjustments to our laws and regulations to permit the maintenance of commercial, cultural, and other non-governmental relationships in the new circumstances that will exist after normalization.

The United States is confident that the people of Taiwan face a peaceful and prosperous future. The United States continues to have an interest in the peaceful resolution of the Taiwan issue and expects that the Taiwan issue will be settled peacefully by the Chinese themselves.

The United States believes that the establishment of diplomatic relations with the People's Republic will contribute to the welfare of the American people, to the stability of Asia where the United States has major security and economic interests, and to the peace of the entire world.

* See the Annual Register 1972, pp. 59-60 and 305-6.

THE CONSTITUTION OF THE PEOPLE'S REPUBLIC OF CHINA

Adopted on 5 March 1978 by the Fifth National People's Congress

(*Text from the Peking Review, No. 11, 17 March 1978*)

PREAMBLE (*slightly abbreviated*)

After more than a century of heroic struggle the Chinese people, led by the Communist Party of China headed by our great leader and teacher Chairman Mao Tsetung, finally overthrew the reactionary rule of imperialism, feudalism and bureaucrat-capitalism by means of people's revolutionary war, winning complete victory in the new-democratic revolution, and in 1949 founded the People's Republic of China.

The founding of the People's Republic of China marked the beginning of the historical period of socialism in our country. Since then . . . the dictatorship of the proletariat in our country has been consolidated and strengthened, and China has become a socialist country with the beginnings of prosperity.

All our victories in revolution and construction have been won under the guidance of marxism–leninism–Mao Tsetung Thought. The fundamental guarantee that the people of all our nationalities will struggle in unity and carry the proletarian revolution through to the end is always to hold high and staunchly to defend the great banner of Chairman Mao.

The triumphant conclusion of the first Great Proletarian Cultural Revolution has ushered in a new period of development in China's socialist revolution and socialist construction. In accordance with the basic line of the Chinese Communist Party for the entire historical period of socialism, the general task for the people of the whole country in this new period is: To persevere in continuing the revolution under the dictatorship of the proletariat, carry forward the three great revolutionary movements of class struggle, the struggle for production and scientific experiment, and make China a great and powerful socialist country with modern agriculture, industry, national defence and science and technology by the end of the century.

We must persevere in the struggle of the proletariat against the bourgeoisie and in the struggle for the socialist road against the capitalist road. We must oppose revisionism and prevent the restoration of capitalism. We must be prepared to deal with subversion and aggression against our country by social-imperialism and imperialism.

We should consolidate and expand the revolutionary united front which is led by the working class and based on the worker-peasant alliance, and which unites the large numbers of intellectuals and other working people, patriotic democratic parties, patriotic personages, our compatriots in Taiwan, Hongkong and Macao, and our countrymen residing abroad. We should enhance the great unity of all the nationalities in our country. We should correctly distinguish and handle the contradictions among the people and those between ourselves and the enemy. We should endeavour to create among the people of the whole country a political situation in which there are both centralism and democracy, both discipline and freedom, both unity of will and personal ease of mind and liveliness, so as to help bring all positive factors into play, overcome all difficulties, better consolidate the proletarian dictatorship and build up our country more rapidly.

Taiwan is China's sacred territory. We are determined to liberate Taiwan and accomplish the great cause of unifying our motherland.

In international affairs, we should establish and develop relations with other countries on the basis of the Five Principles of mutual respect for sovereignty and territorial integrity, mutual non-aggression, non-interference in each other's internal affairs, equality and mutual benefit, and peaceful coexistence. Our country will never seek hegemony, or strive to be a superpower. We should uphold proletarian internationalism. In accordance with the theory of the three worlds, we should strengthen our unity with the proletariat and the oppressed people and nations throughout the world, the socialist countries, and the third world countries, and we should unite with all countries subjected to aggression, subversion, interference, control and bullying by the social-imperialist and imperialist superpowers to form the broadest possible international united front against the hegemonism of the superpowers and against a new world war, and strive for the progress and emancipation of humanity.

Ch. ONE. GENERAL PRINCIPLES

Article 1. The People's Republic of China (PRC) is a socialist state of the dictatorship of the proletariat led by the working class and based on the alliance of workers and peasants.

Article 2. The Communist Party of China (CPC) is the core of leadership of the whole

Chinese people. The working class exercises leadership over the state through its vanguard, the CPC. The guiding ideology of the PRC is marxism–leninism–Mao Tsetung Thought.

Article 3. All power in the PRC belongs to the people. The organs through which the people exercise state power are the National People's Congress and the local people's congresses at various levels. The National People's Congress, the local people's congresses at various levels and all other organs of state practise democratic centralism.

Article 4. The PRC is a unitary multinational state. All the nationalities are equal. There should be unity and fraternal love among the nationalities and they should help and learn from each other. Discrimination against, or oppression of, any nationality, and acts which undermine the unity of the nationalities are prohibited. Big-nationality chauvinism and local-nationality chauvinism must be opposed. All the nationalities have the freedom to use and develop their own spoken and written languages, and to preserve or reform their own customs and ways.

Regional autonomy applies in an area where a minority nationality lives in a compact community. All the national autonomous areas are inalienable parts of the PRC.

Article 5. There are mainly two kinds of ownership of the means of production in the PRC at the present stage: socialist ownership by the whole people and socialist collective ownership by the working people. The state allows non-agricultural individual labourers to engage in individual labour involving no exploitation of others, within the limits permitted by law and under unified arrangement and management by organizations at the basic level in cities and towns or in rural areas. At the same time, it guides these individual labourers step by step on to the road of socialist collectivization.

Article 6. The state sector of the economy, that is, the socialist sector owned by the whole people, is the leading force in the national economy. Mineral resources, waters and those forests, undeveloped lands and other marine and land resources owned by the state are the property of the whole people. The state may requisition by purchase, take over for use, or nationalize land under conditions prescribed by law.

Article 7. The rural people's commune sector of the economy is a socialist sector collectively owned by the masses of working people. At present, it generally takes the form of three-level ownership, that is, ownership by the commune, the production brigade and the production team, with the production team as the basic accounting unit. A production brigade may become the basic accounting unit when its conditions are ripe. Provided that the absolute predominance of the collective economy of the people's commune is ensured, commune members may farm small plots of land for personal needs, engage in limited household sideline production, and in pastoral areas they may also keep a limited number of livestock for personal needs.

Article 8. Socialist public property shall be inviolable. The state ensures the consolidation and development of the socialist sector of the economy owned by the whole people and of the socialist sector collectively owned by the masses of working people. The state prohibits any person from using any means whatsoever to disrupt the economic order of the society, undermine the economic plans of the state, encroach upon or squander state and collective property, or injure the public interest.

Article 9. The state protects the right of citizens to own lawfully earned income, savings, houses and other means of livelihood.

Article 10. The state applies the socialist principles: 'He who does not work, neither shall he eat' and 'from each according to his ability, to each according to his work'. Work is an honourable duty for every citizen able to work. The state promotes socialist labour emulation, and, putting proletarian politics in command, it applies the policy of combining moral encouragement with material reward, with the stress on the former, in order to heighten the citizens' socialist enthusiasm and creativeness in work.

Article 11. The state adheres to the general line of going all out, aiming high and achieving greater, faster, better and more economical results in building socialism, it undertakes the planned, proportionate and high-speed development of the national economy, and it continuously develops the productive forces, so as to consolidate the country's independence and security and improve the people's material and cultural life step by step.

In developing the national economy, the state adheres to the principle of building our country independently, with the initiative in our own hands and through self-reliance, hard struggle, diligence and thrift, it adheres to the principle of taking agriculture as the foundation and industry as the leading factor, and it adheres to the principle of bringing the initiative of both the central and local authorities into full play under the unified leadership of the central authorities.

The state protects the environment and natural resources and prevents and eliminates pollution and other hazards to the public.

Article 12. The state devotes major efforts to developing science, expands scientific research, promotes technical innovation and technical revolution and adopts advanced techniques wherever possible in all departments of the national economy. In scientific and technological work we must follow the practice of combining professional contingents with the masses, and combining learning from others with our own creative efforts.

Article 13. The state devotes major efforts to developing education in order to raise the cultural and scientific level of the whole nation. Education must serve proletarian politics and be combined with productive labour and must enable everyone who receives an education to develop morally, intellectually and physically and become a worker with both socialist consciousness and culture.

Article 14. The state upholds the leading position of marxism–leninism–Mao Tsetung Thought in all spheres of ideology and culture. All cultural undertakings must serve the workers, peasants and soldiers and serve socialism. The state applies the policy of 'letting a hundred flowers blossom and a hundred schools of thought contend' so as to promote the development of the arts and sciences and bring about a flourishing socialist culture.

Article 15. All organs of state must constantly maintain close contact with the masses of the people, rely on them, heed their opinions, be concerned for their weal and woe, streamline administration, practise economy, raise efficiency and combat bureaucracy.

The leading personnel of state organs at all levels must conform to the requirements for successors in the proletarian revolutionary cause and their composition must conform to the principle of the three-in-one combination of the old, the middle-aged and the young.

Article 16. The personnel of organs of state must earnestly study marxism–leninism–Mao Tsetung Thought, wholeheartedly serve the people, endeavour to perfect their professional competence, take an active part in collective productive labour, accept supervision by the masses, be models in observing the Constitution and the law, correctly implement the policies of the state, seek the truth from facts, and must not have recourse to deception or exploit their position and power to seek personal gain.

Article 17. The state adheres to the principle of socialist democracy, and ensures to the people the right to participate in the management of state affairs and of all economic and cultural undertakings, and the right to supervise the organs of state and their personnel.

Article 18. The state safeguards the socialist system, suppresses all treasonable and counter-revolutionary activities, punishes all traitors and counter-revolutionaries, and punishes new-born bourgeois elements and other bad elements. The state deprives of political rights, as prescribed by law, those landlords, rich peasants and reactionary capitalists who have not yet been reformed, and at the same time it provides them with the opportunity to earn a living so that they may be reformed through labour and become law-abiding citizens supporting themselves by their own labour.

Article 19. The Chairman of the Central Committee of the CPC commands the armed forces of the People's Republic of China. The Chinese People's Liberation Army is the workers' and peasants' own armed force led by the CPC; it is the pillar of the dictatorship of the proletariat. The state devotes major efforts to the revolutionization and modernization of the Chinese People's Liberation Army, strengthens the building of the militia and adopts a system under which our armed forces are a combination of the field armies, the regional forces and the militia.

The fundamental task of the armed forces of the PRC is: to safeguard the socialist revolution and socialist construction, to defend the sovereignty, territorial integrity and security of the state, and to guard against subversion and aggression by social-imperialism, imperialism and their lackeys.

Ch. TWO. THE STRUCTURE OF THE STATE

S. I. The National People's Congress

Article 20. The National People's Congress (NPC) is the highest organ of state power.

Article 21. The NPC is composed of deputies elected by the people's congresses of the provinces, autonomous regions, and municipalities directly under the Central Government, and by the People's Liberation Army. The deputies should be elected by secret ballot after democratic consultation.

The NPC is elected for a term of five years. Under special circumstances, its term of office may be extended or the succeeding NPC may be convened before its due date. The NPC holds one session each year. When necessary, the session may be advanced or postponed.

Article 22. The NPC exercises the following functions and powers:

(1) to amend the Constitution;

(2) to make laws;

(3) to supervise the enforcement of the Constitution and the law;

(4) to decide on the choice of the Premier of the State Council upon the recommendation of the Central Committee of the CPC;

(5) to decide on the choice of other members of the State Council upon the recommendation of the Premier of the State Council;

(6) to elect the President of the Supreme People's Court and the Chief Procurator of the Supreme People's Procuratorate;

(7) to examine and approve the national economic plan, the state budget and the final state accounts;

(8) to confirm the following administrative divisions: provinces, autonomous regions, and municipalities directly under the Central Government;

(9) to decide on questions of war and peace; and

(10) to exercise such other functions and powers as the NPC deems necessary.

Article 23. The NPC has the power to remove from office the members of the State Council, the President of the Supreme People's Court and the Chief Procurator of the Supreme People's Procuratorate.

Article 24. The Standing Committee of the NPC is the permanent organ of the NPC. It is responsible and accountable to the NPC.

The Standing Committee of the NPC is composed of the following members: the Chairman; the Vice-Chairmen; the Secretary-General; and other members.

The NPC elects the Standing Committee of the NPC and has the power to recall its members.

Article 25. The Standing Committee of the NPC exercises the following functions and powers:

(1) to conduct the election of deputies to the NPC;

(2) to convene the sessions of the NPC;

(3) to interpret the Constitution and laws and to enact decrees;

(4) to supervise the work of the State Council, the Supreme People's Court and the Supreme People's Procuratorate;

(5) to change and annul inappropriate decisions adopted by the organs of state power of provinces, autonomous regions, and municipalities directly under the Central Government;

(6) to decide on the appointment and removal of individual members of the State Council upon the recommendation of the Premier of the State Council when the NPC is not in session;

(7) to appoint and remove Vice-Presidents of the Supreme People's Court and Deputy Chief Procurators of the Supreme People's Procuratorate;

(8) to decide on the appointment and removal of plenipotentiary representatives abroad;

(9) to decide on the ratification and abrogation of treaties concluded with foreign states;

(10) to institute state titles of honour and decide on their conferment;

(11) to decide on the granting of pardons;

(12) to decide on the proclamation of a state of war in the event of armed attack on the country when the NPC is not in session; and

(13) to exercise such other functions and powers as are vested in it by the NPC.

Article 26. The Chairman of the Standing Committee of the NPC presides over the work of the Standing Committee; receives foreign diplomatic envoys; and in accordance with the decisions of the NPC or its Standing Committee promulgates laws and decrees, dispatches and recalls plenipotentiary representatives abroad, ratifies treaties concluded with foreign states and confers state titles of honour.

The Vice-Chairmen of the Standing Committee of the NPC assist the Chairman in his work and may exercise part of the Chairman's functions and powers on his behalf.

Article 27. The NPC and its Standing Committee may establish special committees as deemed necessary.

Article 28. Deputies to the NPC have the right to address inquiries to the State Council, the Supreme People's Court, the Supreme People's Procuratorate, and the ministries and commissions of the State Council, which are all under obligation to answer.

Article 29. Deputies to the NPC are subject to supervision by the units which elect them. These electoral units have the power to replace at any time the deputies they elect, as prescribed by law.

S. II. The State Council

Article 30. The State Council (SC) is the Central People's Government and the executive organ of the highest organ of state power; it is the highest organ of state administration.

The SC is responsible and accountable to the NPC, or, when the NPC is not in session, to its Standing Committee.

Article 31. The SC is composed of the following members: the Premier; the Vice-Premiers; the Ministers; and the Ministers heading the commissions.

The Premier presides over the work of the State Council and the Vice-Premiers assist the Premier in his work.

Article 32. The SC exercises the following functions and powers:

(1) to formulate administrative measures, issue decisions and orders and verify their execution, in accordance with the Constitution, laws and decrees;

(2) to submit proposals on laws and other matters to the NPC or its Standing Committee;

(3) to exercise unified leadership over the work of the ministries and commissions and other organizations under it;

(4) to exercise unified leadership over the work of local organs of state administration at various levels throughout the country;

(5) to draw up and put into effect the national economic plan and the state budget;

(6) to protect the interests of the state, maintain public order and safeguard the rights of citizens;

(7) to confirm the following administrative divisions: autonomous prefectures, counties, autonomous counties, and cities;

(8) to appoint and remove administrative personnel according to the provisions of the law; and

(9) to exercise such other functions and powers as are vested in it by the NPC or its Standing Committee.

S. III. The Local People's Congresses and Local Revolutionary Committees

Article 33. The administrative division of the PRC is as follows:

(1) The country is divided into provinces, autonomous regions, and municipalities directly under the Central Government;

(2) Provinces and autonomous regions are divided into autonomous prefectures, counties, autonomous counties, and cities; and

(3) Counties and autonomous counties are divided into people's communes and towns.

Municipalities directly under the Central Government and other large cities are divided into districts and counties. Autonomous prefectures are divided into counties, autonomous counties, and cities. Autonomous regions, autonomous prefectures and autonomous counties are all national autonomous areas.

Article 34. People's congresses and revolutionary committees are established in provinces, municipalities directly under the Central Government, counties, cities, municipal districts, people's communes and towns. People's congresses and revolutionary committees of the people's communes are organizations of political power at the grass-roots level, and are also leading organs of collective economy. Revolutionary committees at the provincial level may establish administrative offices as their agencies in prefectures.

Organs of self-government are established in autonomous regions, autonomous prefectures and autonomous counties.

Article 35. Local people's congresses at various levels are local organs of state power. Deputies to the people's congresses of provinces, municipalities directly under the Central Government, counties, and cities divided into districts are elected by people's congresses at the next lower level by secret ballot after democratic consultation; deputies to the people's congresses of cities not divided into districts, and of municipal districts, people's communes and towns are directly elected by the voters by secret ballot after democratic consultation.

The people's congresses of provinces and municipalities directly under the Central Government are elected for a term of five years. The people's congresses of counties, cities and municipal districts are elected for a term of three years. The people's congresses of people's communes and towns are elected for a term of two years. Local people's congresses at various levels hold at least one session each year, which is to be convened by revolutionary committees at the corresponding levels.

The units and electorates which elect the deputies to the local people's congresses at various levels have the power to supervise, remove and replace their deputies at any time according to the provisions of the law.

Article 36. Local people's congresses at various levels, in their respective administrative areas, ensure the observance and enforcement of the Constitution, laws and decrees; ensure the implementation of the state plan; make plans for local economic and cultural development and for public utilities; examine and approve local economic plans, budgets and final accounts; protect public property; maintain public order; safeguard the rights of citizens and the equal rights of minority nationalities; and promote the development of socialist revolution and socialist construction. Local people's congresses may adopt and issue decisions within the limits of their authority as prescribed by law.

Local people's congresses elect, and have the power to recall, members of revolutionary committees at the corresponding levels. People's congresses at county level and above elect, and have the power to recall, the presidents of the people's courts and the chief procurators of the people's procuratorates at the corresponding levels.

Deputies to local people's congresses at various levels have the right to address inquiries to the revolutionary committees, people's courts, people's procuratorates and organs under the revolutionary committees at the corresponding levels, which are all under obligation to answer.

Article 37. Local revolutionary committees at various levels, that is, local people's governments, are the executive organs of local people's congresses at the corresponding levels and they are also local organs of state administration. A local revolutionary committee is composed of a chairman, vice-chairmen and other members.

Local revolutionary committees carry out the decisions of people's congresses at the corresponding levels as well as the decisions and orders of the organs of state administration at higher levels, direct the administrative work of their respective areas, and issue decisions and orders within the limits of their authority as prescribed by law. Revolutionary committees at county level and above appoint or remove the personnel of organs of state according to the provisions of the law.

Local revolutionary committees are responsible and accountable to people's congresses at the corresponding levels and to the organs of state administration at the next higher level, and work under the unified leadership of the State Council.

S. IV. The Organs of Self-Government of National Autonomous Areas

Article 38. The organs of self-government of autonomous regions, autonomous prefectures and autonomous counties are people's congresses and revolutionary committees.

The election of the people's congresses and revolutionary committees of national autonomous areas, their terms of office, their functions and powers and also the establishment of their agencies should conform to the basic principles governing the organization of local organs of state as specified in S. III, Ch. Two, of the Constitution.

In autonomous areas where a number of nationalities live together, each nationality is entitled to appropriate representation in the organs of self-government.

Article 39. The organs of self-government of national autonomous areas exercise autonomy within the limits of their authority as prescribed by law, in addition to exercising the functions and powers of local organs of state as specified by the Constitution.

The organs of self-government of national autonomous areas may, in the light of the political, economic and cultural characteristic of the nationality or nationalities in a given area, make regulations on the exercise of autonomy and also specific regulations and submit them to the Standing Committee of the NPC for approval.

In performing their functions, the organs of self-government of national autonomous areas employ the spoken and written language or languages commonly used by the nationality or nationalities in the locality.

Article 40. The higher organs of state shall fully safeguard the exercise of autonomy by the organs of self-government of national autonomous areas, take into full consideration the characteristics and needs of the various minority nationalities, make a major effort to train cadres of the minority nationalities, and actively support and assist all the minority nationalities in their socialist revolution and construction and thus advance their socialist economic and cultural development.

S. V. The People's Courts and the People's Procuratorates

Article 41. The Supreme People's Court (SPC), local people's courts at various levels and special people's courts exercise judicial authority. The people's courts are formed as prescribed by law. In accordance with law, the people's courts apply the system whereby representatives of the masses participate as assessors in administering justice. With regard to major counter-revolutionary or criminal cases, the masses should be drawn in for discussion and suggestions.

All cases in the people's courts are heard in public except those involving special circumstances, as prescribed by law. The accused has the right to defence.

Article 42. The SPC is the highest judicial organ.

The SPC supervises the administration of justice by local people's courts at various levels and by special people's courts; people's courts at the higher levels supervise the administration of justice by people's courts at the lower levels.

The SPC is responsible and accountable to the NPC and its Standing Committee. Local people's courts at various levels are responsible and accountable to local people's congresses at the corresponding levels.

Article 43. The Supreme People's Procuratorate (SPP) exercises procuratorial authority to ensure observance of the Constitution and the law by all the departments under the State Council, the local organs of state at various levels, the personnel of organs of state and the citizens. Local people's procuratorates and special people's procuratorates exercise procuratorial authority within the limits prescribed by law. The people's procuratorates are formed as prescribed by law.

The SPP supervises the work of local people's procuratorates at various levels and of special people's procuratorates; people's procuratorates at the higher levels supervise the work of those at the lower levels.

The SPP is responsible and accountable to the NPC and its Standing Committee. Local people's procuratorates at various levels are responsible and accountable to people's congresses at the corresponding levels.

Ch. THREE. THE FUNDAMENTAL RIGHTS AND DUTIES OF CITIZENS

Article 44. All citizens who have reached the age of 18 have the right to vote and to stand for election, with the exception of persons deprived of these rights by law.

Article 45. Citizens enjoy freedom of speech, correspondence, the press, assembly, association, procession, demonstration and the freedom to strike, and have the right to 'speak out freely, air their views fully, hold great debates and write big-character posters'.

Article 46. Citizens enjoy freedom to believe in religion and freedom not be believe in religion and to propagate atheism.

Article 47. The citizens' freedom of person and their homes are inviolable.

No citizen may be arrested except by decision of a people's court or with the sanction of a people's procuratorate, and the arrest must be made by a public security organ.

Article 48. Citizens have the right to work. To ensure that citizens enjoy this right, the state provides employment in accordance with the principle of overall consideration, and, on the basis of increased production, the state gradually increases payment for labour, improves working conditions, strengthens labour protection and expands collective welfare.

Article 49. Working people have the right to rest. To ensure that working people enjoy this right, the state prescribes working hours and systems of vacations and gradually expands material facilities for the working people to rest and recuperate.

Article 50. Working people have the right to material assistance in old age, and in case of illness or disability. To ensure that working people enjoy this right, the state gradually expands social insurance, social assistance, public health services, cooperative medical services, and other services. The state cares for and ensures the livelihood of disabled revolutionary armymen and the families of revolutionary martyrs.

Article 51. Citizens have the right to education. To ensure that citizens enjoy this right, the state gradually increases the number of schools of various types and of other cultural and educational institutions and popularizes education. The state pays special attention to the healthy development of young people and children.

Article 52. Citizens have the freedom to engage in scientific research, literary and artistic creation and other cultural activities. The state encourages and assists the creative endeavours of citizens engaged in science, education, literature, art, journalism, publishing, public health, sports and other cultural work.

Article 53. Women enjoy equal rights with men in all spheres of political, economic, cultural, social and family life. Men and women enjoy equal pay for equal work.

Men and women shall marry of their own free will. The state protects marriage, the family, and the mother and child. The state advocates and encourages family planning.

Article 54. The state protects the just rights and interests of overseas Chinese and their relatives.

Article 55. Citizens have the right to lodge complaints with organs of state at any level against any person working in an organ of state, enterprise or institution for transgression of law or neglect of duty. Citizens have the right to appeal to organs of state at any level against any infringement of their rights. No one shall suppress such complaints and appeals or retaliate against persons making them.

Article 56. Citizens must support the leadership of the Communist Party of China, support the socialist system, safeguard the unification of the motherland and the unity of all nationalities in our country and abide by the Constitution and the law.

Article 57. Citizens must take care of and protect public property, observe labour discipline, observe public order, respect social ethics and safeguard state secrets.

Article 58. It is the lofty duty of every citizen to defend the motherland and resist aggression.

It is the honourable obligation of citizens to perform military service and to join the militia according to the law.

Article 59. The PRC grants the right of residence to any foreign national persecuted for supporting a just cause, for taking part in revolutionary movements or for engaging in scientific work.

Ch. FOUR. THE NATIONAL FLAG, NATIONAL EMBLEM AND CAPITAL

Article 60. The national flag of the PRC has five stars on a field of red. The national emblem of the PRC is: Tien An Men in the centre, illuminated by five stars and encircled by ears of grain and a cogwheel. The capital of the PRC is Peking.

THE EUROPEAN MONETARY SYSTEM

Resolution of the European Council agreed in Brussels on 5 December 1978

A. THE EUROPEAN MONETARY SYSTEM

1. Introduction

1.1 In Bremen we discussed a 'scheme for the creation of closer monetary cooperation leading to a zone of monetary stability in Europe'. We regarded such a zone 'as a highly desirable objective' and envisaged 'a durable and effective scheme'.

1.2 Today, after careful examination of the preparatory work done by the Council and other Community bodies, we are agreed as follows: *A European Monetary System* (EMS) *will be set up on 1 January 1979.*

1.3 We are firmly resolved to ensure the lasting success of the EMS by policies conducive to greater stability at home and abroad for both deficit and surplus countries.

1.4 The following chapters deal primarily with the initial phase of the EMS.

We remain firmly resolved to consolidate, not later than two years after the start of the scheme, into a final system the provisions and procedures thus created. This system will entail the creation of the European Monetary Fund as announced in the conclusions of the European Council meeting at Bremen on 6/7 July 1978, as well as the full utilization of the ECU as a reserve asset and a means of settlement. It will be based on adequate legislation at the Community as well as the national level.

2. The ECU and its Functions

2.1 A *European Currency Unit* (ECU) will be at the centre of the EMS. The value and the composition of the ECU will be identical with the value of the EUA at the outset of the system.

2.2 The ECU will be used

(a) as the denominator (*numéraire*) for the exchange rate mechanism,

(b) as the basis for a divergence indicator,

(c) as the denominator for operations in both the intervention and the credit mechanism,

(d) as a means of settlement between monetary authorities of the EC.

2.3 The weights of currencies in the ECU will be re-examined and if necessary revised within six months of the entry into force of the system and thereafter every five years or, on request, if the weight of any currency has changed by 25 per cent.

Revisions have to be mutually accepted; they will, by themselves, not modify the external value of the ECU. They will be made in line with underlying economic criteria.

3. The Exchange Rate and the Intervention Mechanism

3.1 Each currency will have an ECU-related central rate. These central rates will be used to establish a grid of bilateral exchange rates.

Around these exchange rates fluctuation margins of $\pm 2 \cdot 25$ per cent will be established. EC countries with presently floating currencies may opt for wider margins up to ± 6 per cent at the outset of EMS; these margins should be gradually reduced as soon as economic conditions permit to do so.

A Member State which does not participate in the exchange rate mechanism at the outset may participate at a later date.

3.2 Adjustments of central rates will be subject to mutual agreement by a common procedure which will comprise all countries participating in the exchange rate mechanism and the Commission. There will be reciprocal consultation in the Community framework about important decisions concerning exchange rate policy between countries participating and any country not participating in the system.

3.3 In principle, interventions will be made in participating currencies.

3.4 Intervention in participating currencies is compulsory when the intervention points defined by the fluctuation margins are reached.

3.5 An ECU basket formula will be used as an indicator to detect divergences between Community currencies. A 'threshold of divergence' will be fixed at 75 per cent of the maximum spread of divergence for each currency. It will be calculated in such a way as to eliminate the influence of weight on the probability to reach the threshold.

3.6 When a currency crosses its 'threshold of divergence', this results in a presumption that the authorities concerned will correct this situation by adequate measures, namely:
(a) Diversified intervention;
(b) Measures of domestic monetary policy;
(c) Changes in central rates;
(d) Other measures of economic policy.

In case such measures, on account of special circumstances, are not taken, the reasons for this shall be given to the other authorities, especially in the 'concertation between Central Banks'. Consultations will, if necessary, then take place in the appropriate Community bodies, including the Council of Ministers.

After six months these provisions shall be reviewed in the light of experience. At that date the questions regarding imbalances accumulated by divergent creditor or debtor countries will be studied as well.

3.7 A Very Short-Term Facility of an unlimited amount will be established. Settlements will be made 45 days after the end of the month of intervention with the possibility of pro-longation for another 3 months for amounts limited to the size of debtor quotas in the Short-Term Monetary Support.

3.8 To serve as a means of settlement, an initial supply of ECUs will be provided by FECOM against the deposit of 20 per cent of gold and 20 per cent of dollar reserves currently held by Central Banks. This operation will take the form of specified, revolving swap arrangements. By periodical review and by an appropriate procedure it will be ensured that each Central Bank will maintain a deposit of at least 20 per cent of these reserves with FECOM. A Member State not participating in the exchange rate mechanism may participate in this initial operation on the basis described above.

4. The Credit Mechanisms

4.1 The existing credit mechanisms with their present rules of application will be maintained for the initial phase of the EMS. They will be consolidated into a single fund in the final phase of the EMS.

4.2 The credit mechanisms will be extended to an amount of 25 billion ECU of effectively available credit. The distribution of this amount will be as follows:

Short-Term Monetary Support = 14 bn ECU
Medium-Term Financial Assistance = 11 bn ECU

4.3 The duration of the Short-Term Monetary Support will be extended for another 3 months on the same conditions as the first extension.

4.4 The increase of the Medium-Term Financial Assistance will be completed by 30 June 1979. In the meantime, countries which still need national legislation are expected to make their extended medium-term quotas available by an interim financing agreement of the Central Banks concerned.

5. Third Countries and International Organizations

5.1 The durability of EMS and its international implications require coordination of exchange rate policies *vis-à-vis* third countries and, as far as possible, a concertation with the monetary authorities of those countries.

5.2 European countries with particularly close economic and financial ties with the European Community may participate in the exchange rate and intervention mechanism. Participation will be based upon agreements between Central Banks; these agreements will be communicated to the Council and the Commission of the EC.

5.3 EMS is and will remain fully compatible with the relevant articles of the IMF agreement.

6. Further Procedure

6.1 To implement the decisions taken under A, the European Council requests the Council to consider and to take a decision on 18 December 1978 on the following proposals of the Commission:

(a) Council Regulation modifying the unit of account used by the European Fund of Monetary Cooperation, which introduces the ECU in the operations of the EMCF and defines its composition;

(b) Council Regulation permitting the EMCF to receive monetary reserves and to issue ECUs to the monetary authorities of the Member States which may use them as a means of settlement;

(c) Council Regulation on the impact of the European Monetary System on the Common Agricultural Policy. The European Council considers that the introduction of the EMS should not of itself result in any change in the situation obtaining prior to 1 January 1979 regarding the expression in national currencies of agricultural prices, monetary compensatory amounts (MCAs) and all other amounts fixed for the purposes of the CAP.

The European Council stresses the importance of henceforth avoiding the creation of permanent MCAs and progressively reducing present MCAs in order to re-establish the unity of prices of the CAP, giving also due consideration to price policy.

B. MEASURES DESIGNED TO STRENGTHEN THE ECONOMIES OF THE LESS PROSPEROUS MEMBER STATES OF THE EUROPEAN MONETARY SYSTEM

1 We stress that, within the context of a broadly-based strategy aimed at improving the prospects of economic development and based on symmetrical rights and obligations of all participants, the most important concern should be to enhance the convergence of economic policies towards greater stability. We request the Council (Economics and Finance Ministers) to strengthen its procedures for coordination in order to improve that convergence.

2 We are aware that the convergence of economic policies and of economic performance will not be easy to achieve. Therefore, steps must be taken to strengthen the economic potential of the less prosperous countries of the Community. This is primarily the responsibility of the Member States concerned. Community measures can and should serve a supporting role.

3 The European Council agrees that, in the context of the EMS, the following measures in favour of the less prosperous Member States effectively and fully participating in the exchange rate and intervention mechanisms will be taken.

3.1 The European Council requests the Community Institutions, by the utilization of the new financial instrument and the European Investment Bank, to make available for a period of 5 years loans of up to 1,000 million EUA per year to these countries on special conditions.

3.2 The European Council requests the Commission to submit a proposal to provide interest rate subsidies of 3 per cent for these loans, with the following elements: The total cost of this measure, divided into annual tranches of 200 million EUA each over a period of 5 years, shall not exceed 1,000 million EUA.

3.3 Any less prosperous Member country which subsequently effectively and fully participates in the mechanisms would have the right of access to this facility within the financial limits mentioned above. Member States not participating effectively and fully in the mechanisms will not contribute to the financing of the scheme.

3.4 The funds thus provided are to be concentrated on the financing of selected infrastructure projects and programmes, with the understanding that any direct or indirect distortion of the competitive position of specific industries within Member States will have to be avoided.

3.5   The European Council requests the Council (Economics and Finance Ministers) to take a decision on the above-mentioned proposals in time so that the relevant measures can become effective on 1 April 1979 at the latest. There should be a review at the end of the initial phase of the EMS.

4   The European Council requests the Commission to study the relationship between greater convergence in economic performance of the Member States and the utilization of Community instruments, in particular the funds which aim at reducing structural imbalances. The results of these studies will be discussed at the next European Council.

NOTES ON PARTICIPATION BY THE UK*

A2.1   The statement that the value and composition of the ECU will be identical with the value of the EUA at the outset of the system means that sterling will be included with other Community currencies in the ECU.

A3.1–A3.6   The UK is not participating in the exchange rate mechanism. Subject to the following, these paragraphs will not therefore apply to sterling. *3.1* contains a provision which would permit the UK to participate at a later date if it wished. *3.2* provides for reciprocal consultation about important decisions concerning exchange rate policy between countries inside and outside the exchange rate mechanism. At the end of *3.6* there is provision for a review of certain aspects of the exchange rate mechanism which would be a matter for the appropriate Community bodies, including the Council of Finance Ministers. The UK would therefore participate in that review.

A3.8 contains in its final sentence a provision which enables the UK to choose whether or not to deposit 20 per cent of gold and dollar reserves with the European Monetary Co-operation Fund against issue to us of a corresponding value of ECUs.

B3.1 and *3.2* describe a scheme of loans at subsidized interest rates which, within specified limits, would be made available to less prosperous member states of the Community participating fully in the EMS exchange rate mechanism. The loans would be those made by the European Investment Bank or as part of the so-called Ortoli facility. This facility will consist of loans raised in the market by the Community itself, but managed as regards appraisal of projects, administration etc. by the European Investment Bank. The total of loans made available at subsidized rates would be up to 1,000 million EUA (about £670 million) a year for each of 5 years, with an interest rate subsidy of 3 per cent. The interest rate subsidy would however be limited to a maximum of 200 million EUA (about £135 million) a year for 5 years. These loans would be concentrated on infrastructure projects and programmes and should not involve any distortion, direct or indirect, of the competitive position of specific industries.

B3.3 provides that a less prosperous member country which joins the exchange rate mechanism later can then have access to these subsidized loans. It also provides that a state not participating in the exchange rate mechanism will not contribute to the financing of the scheme. In the case of the UK the effect would be that it would neither qualify for loans with an interest subsidy, nor contribute towards interest subsidies for others, so long as it was not participating in the exchange rate mechanism.

THE UNITED KINGDOM LABOUR ADMINISTRATION

(as at 31 December 1978)

Prime Minister, First Lord of the Treasury and Minister for the Civil Service .	Rt. Hon. James Callaghan, MP
Lord President of the Council and Leader of the House of Commons . .	Rt. Hon. Michael Foot, MP
Lord Chancellor	Rt. Hon. The Lord Elwyn-Jones, CH
Chancellor of the Exchequer . .	Rt. Hon. Denis Healey, MBE, MP
Secretary of State for the Home Department	Rt. Hon. Merlyn Rees, MP
Secretary of State for Foreign and Commonwealth Affairs . . .	Rt. Hon. Dr David Owen, MP
Secretary of State for Education and Science and Paymaster General .	Rt. Hon. Shirley Williams, MP
Secretary of State for Energy . .	Rt. Hon. Anthony Wedgwood Benn, MP
Secretary of State for Industry . .	Rt. Hon. Eric Varley, MP

* Cmnd. 7419.

502 DOCUMENTS AND REFERENCE

Secretary of State for the Environment .	Rt. Hon. Peter Shore, MP
Secretary of State for Northern Ireland .	Rt. Hon. Roy Mason, MP
Secretary of State for Scotland . .	Rt. Hon. Bruce Millan, MP
Secretary of State for Wales . .	Rt. Hon. John Morris, QC, MP
Secretary of State for Defence . .	Rt. Hon. Frederick Mulley, MP
Secretary of State for Employment .	Rt. Hon. Albert Booth, MP
Secretary of State for Social Services .	Rt. Hon. David Ennals, MP
Secretary of State for Trade . .	Rt. Hon. John Smith, MP[1]
Lord Privy Seal and Leader of the House of Lords	Rt. Hon. The Lord Peart
Chief Secretary to the Treasury . .	Rt. Hon. Joel Barnett, MP
Minister of Agriculture, Fisheries and Food	Rt. Hon. John Silkin, MP
Secretary of State for Prices and Consumer Protection	Rt. Hon. Roy Hattersley, MP
Secretary of State for Transport . .	Rt. Hon. William Rodgers, MP
Minister for Social Security . .	Rt. Hon. Stanley Orme, MP
Chancellor of the Duchy of Lancaster .	Rt. Hon. Harold Lever, MP

MINISTERS NOT IN THE CABINET

Minister of State, Ministry of Agriculture, Fisheries and Food . .	Rt. Hon. Edward Bishop, MP
Minister of State, Civil Service Department	Rt. Hon. Charles R. Morris, MP
Minister of State, Ministry of Defence .	Rt. Hon. Dr John Gilbert, MP
Ministers of State, Department of Education and Science (Arts) . . .	Gordon Oakes, MP The Lord Donaldson of Kingsbridge, OBE
Minister of State, Department of Employment	Harold Walker, MP
Minister of State, Department of Energy	Rt. Hon. Dr J. Dickson Mabon, MP
Minister of State, Department of the Environment	Rt. Hon. Denis Howell, MP
Ministers of State, Foreign and Commonwealth Office	Frank Judd, MP Rt. Hon. The Lord Goronwy-Roberts Edward Rowlands, MP
(Overseas Development) .	Rt. Hon. Judith Hart, MP
Minister of State, Department of Health and Social Security . . .	Roland Moyle, MP
Ministers of State, Home Office . .	The Lord Harris of Greenwich Brynmor John, MP
Ministers of State, Department of Industry	Rt. Hon. Alan Williams, MP Gerald Kaufman, MP
Ministers of State, Northern Ireland Office	Rt. Hon. John Concannon, MP The Lord Melchett
Minister of State, Department of Prices and Consumer Protection . .	John Fraser, MP
Minister of State, Scottish Office .	Rt. Hon. Gregor MacKenzie, MP
Parliamentary Secretary to the Treasury	Rt. Hon. Michael Cocks, MP
Financial Secretary to the Treasury .	Rt. Hon. Robert Sheldon, MP
Minister of State, Treasury . . .	Rt. Hon. Denzil Davies, MP
Minister for Housing and Construction .	Rt. Hon. Reginald Freeson, MP

LAW OFFICERS

Attorney General	Rt. Hon. Samuel Silkin, QC, MP
Solicitor General	Rt. Hon. Peter Archer, QC, MP
Lord Advocate	Rt. Hon. Ronald King Murray, QC, MP
Solicitor-General for Scotland . .	The Lord McCluskey, QC

[1] Succeeded Rt. Hon. Edward Dell, MP, on 12 November.

OBITUARY

Adoula, Cyrille (b. 1921), Prime Minister of Congo-Kinshasa (Zaïre) from August 1961 to June 1964, was much respected for his intelligence and integrity. From the trade union movement he entered politics as a supporter of Patrice Lumumba, with whom however he broke because of Lumumba's heavy authoritarianism. Established at the head of a Government of national union at a moment of crisis, he defeated three rebellions, led by Antoine Gizenga (with communist military support), Albert Kalonji and Moise Tshombe, then a Katangan secessionist, and restored both internal order and good external relations with the UN and the West, not least with Belgium. After giving way to Tshombe as Prime Minister he became Zaïre's ambassador in Brussels and later in Washington, and was for a brief while its Foreign Minister. Died 24 May

al-Ghashmi, Ahmed Hussain (b. 1940), President of North Yemen from October 1977, had been chief of staff of the army under his predecessor President Ibrahim al-Hamdi. Assassinated 24 June

Alam, Assadollah, hon. GCMG (b. 1919), was Prime Minister of Iran 1962-64, later Minister of the Imperial Court. In and out of office he was the Shah's intimate and often his diplomatic voice. Died 14 April

Best, Professor Charles Herbert, CH (b. 1899), Canadian physiologist, joined with Fredrick Banting in the researches that led to the discovery of insulin while still an indigent medical student (after war service), and when Banting was awarded the Nobel prize the older man attributed to him an equal share in the work and split the prize money with him. From 1929 to 1965 he was professor of physiology at Toronto University, where he headed the Banting–Best department of medical research and founded the C. H. Best Research Institute, largely for the study of diabetic metabolism. By 1971, half a century after the Banting–Best discovery, it was reckoned that insulin had saved 30 million lives. Died 31 March

Boumédienne, Houari (b. Mohammed Boukharuba 1932), became President of Algeria after the coup which overthrew Ben Bella in 1965 and died in office. Fleeing from his native land as a young man to escape French conscription he became a fervent revolutionary and guerrilla warrior. By 1958 he was in command of the national liberation army and a member of the revolutionary council. At independence in 1962 he sided with Ben Bella against Ben Khedda in the struggle for power, but in Cabinet as Minister of Defence he clashed with the President, whose cult of personality contrasted with his own military pragmatism. In presidential office he nationalized the mines and oil companies, applied a sequence of 4-year economic plans and was prominent in rallying Arab reaction to the Six-Day War in 1967; but he was no ideologue and his stature as a popular and effective national leader grew both in Arab countries and in the world at large. Died 27 December

Boyer, Charles (b. in France 1898), film actor, began his professional career on the Paris stage, then acted in a number of French silent films in the 1920s. With the coming of sound films he migrated to Hollywood, eventually taking US citizenship, and from his first American film, *The Trial of Mary Dugan*, onwards he became one of the great international stars of the cinema; but he repeatedly returned to his native land to act in French films. His aristocratic good looks and his rich voice made him an idolized screen lover, but later in life he played many other roles which revealed no less his talent as an actor. Among the actresses opposite whom he played were Marlene Dietrich, Michele Morgan, Irene Dunne, Ingrid Bergman and Sophia Loren. He also acted, in middle and older age, on television and the stage. Died 26 August

Bradshaw, Robert Llewellyn (b. 1916), Prime Minister of St Kitts-Nevis–Anguilla, was founder-president of the St Kitts-Nevis labour union and of the Labour Party in St Kitts, both based on the British trade-union and social-democratic pattern, to which, along with other British political and social traditions, he passionately adhered. Before independence he warred with authority, but he became a Minister in the St Kitts Government in 1956 and then, for the whole life of the West Indies Federation, 1958-62, Federal Minister of Finance. A member of the Southwell Cabinet in St Kitts, 1962-66, he succeeded as Chief Minister 1966-67 and, upon Associated Status, as Prime Minister. The virtual secession of Anguilla in 1969, which provoked British intervention, marred an otherwise successful Premiership, marked by economic reform (including nationalization of the sugar industry) and the stern upholding of law, order and racial tolerance. Died 24 May

Brugnon, Jacques (b. 1895), French lawn tennis player, partnered Henri Cochet and Jean Borotra in doubles, and with them and René Lacoste gained and held the Davis Cup for France from 1927 to 1932. Died 20 March

Busia, Dr Kofi (b. 1913), was Prime Minister of Ghana from 1969 to 1972, when he was overthrown by a military coup d'etat. Though an able academic and a confirmed democrat, he was not successful in government. Educated at Achimota College, London and Oxford Universities, in 1954 he was appointed professor of sociology at Ghana University College. A member of the Gold Coast legislature from 1951, he became leader of the anti-Nkrumah United Party in 1957. He left Ghana to become professor of sociology at The Hague (1959-61) and Leyden (1960-61), then continued his academic career at St Antony's College, Oxford. After the coup against Nkrumah in 1966 he went back to Ghana, to become chairman of the National Liberation Advisory Council, and to form the Progress Party which swept him to office in the elections of 1969. After the coup, he returned to academic life in Oxford. Died 28 August

Clay, General Lucius D. (b. 1897), was US Military Governor in Germany after World War II, and from 1947-49 C-in-C

European Command; in the latter role he organized the Berlin airlift which saved the city from the Soviet blockade at the height of the cold war. The Federal Republic owed him a great debt for his powerful part in its economic rehabilitation, in the currency reform, in the framing of the federal constitution, and in the strengthening of morale and security in Berlin as head of a special US mission 1961-62. Professionally an army engineer, he was a superb organizer, a powerful public figure, and after his retirement from the army a successful business man. His book *Decision in Germany* (1950) recounted his experiences from 1945-49. Died 16 April

Conant, James Bryant (b. 1893), American chemist and educator, was President of Harvard from 1933 to 1953. Successively undergraduate, research student, instructor, assistant and associate professor at Harvard (with a 1917-19 break in the chemical warfare service), he became full professor in 1927 and Sheldon Emery Professor of Organic Chemistry in 1929. His publications and research, notably on chlorophyll, earned him international fame in his field. Elected president of the university at the age of 40, he championed academic freedom and the interplay of disciplines, creating the Harvard Council of the Faculty of Arts and Sciences. From 1953 to 1957 he served the US in West Germany, first as high commissioner and eventually as ambassador. In 1959 he published a trenchant study of American high schools. Died 11 February

Daoud, Muhammad (b. 1909), President of Afghanistan, began life as a soldier, becoming commander-in-chief of the central forces and military school in 1937. In 1953 he turned to politics, becoming Prime Minister and Minister of Defence under his royal cousin and brother-in-law Muhammad Zahir Shah, whom however he overthrew and exiled twenty years later when he seized power as President of a Republic. An enigmatic non-alignment policy and ineffective reforms left many Afghans disgruntled, and after five years he was in turn murderously ousted. Died 27 April

De Chirico, Giorgio (b. 1888), Italian artist, who was to become the 'great solitary' of twentieth-century painting, was born and spent his boyhood in Greece and studied at the Art School in Athens. His Italian family, however, returned in 1905 to Italy, where most of his life was spent; but some years in Germany (Munich 1905-8), where he was not only influenced by the believable fantasy and romanticism of painters like Bocklin and Klinger, but also immersed himself in the philosophical writings of such thinkers as Schopenhauer and Nietzche, influenced the development of his own so-called 'meta-physical' style. Architecture was particularly important to de Chirico, and here his formative years in Greece must be recalled. The exquisite architecture of Florence, Turin, Ferraro, as well as Rome, provided the classical settings rendered in brilliantly exaggerated perspective (influenced here by early Renaissance artists such as Uccello) with a dream-like intensity characteristic of the most inventive period of his artistic career (1910-25). This period coincided with a time of rapid innovation in European art generally, and de Chirico then had much contact with the European *avant garde*, spending some years in Paris. His paintings, usually small in size, were nevertheless vast in the spatial complexities they tackled and the scenes they depicted. They depended in part for their value on surprising the spectator by the convincing, authoritative manner in which the impossible was painted, thus anticipating surrealism. Headless bodies, like tailor's dummies, peopling fragments of Italian city architecture, were recreated in a world without shadows, lit quite often by a lurid greenish sky. Ordinary objects were blown up to giant size; collections of mathematical and geometrical instruments were treated like animate objects. A frozen melancholy, a sad nostalgia for a dream world that never was, became the dominant emotional charge of his remarkable and eventually influential paintings.

De Chirico's life, spent in the major cities of Europe, was outwardly without dramatic incident, and his career became a puzzle. For as his earlier paintings exhibited a mood of icy, disquieting calm, even when describing the absurd or im-

possible, so his later work was frozen into an ultimately unhappy and soulless repetition of his earlier innovations, or else a return to more conventional subject matter—still lifes, horses on a beach—which was curiously lifeless. Died 21 November   M.V.

Diederichs, Dr Nicolaas (b. 1903), State President of the Republic of South Africa from 1975, was one of the leading ideologues of Afrikaner nationalism. Educated at Bloemfontein, Munich, Cologne and Leyden, from 1930 he was lecturer and later professor of political science at the Free State University, Bloemfontein. He entered parliament in 1948 and became successively Minister for Economic Affairs and Mines 1961-64, of Economic Affairs 1966-67, and of Finance 1967-75, when he became known as 'Mr Gold' for his unswerving faith in the metal. Died 21 August

Duke-Elder, Sir Stewart, GCVO, FRS (b. 1895), British ophthalmologist, was the most famous oculist of his time. A brilliant academic career at St Andrew's University was followed by one equally scintillating as a researcher, at St Andrew's, University College (London) and Harvard. He was largely responsible for the merger of three major London eye hospitals into Moorfields, of which he was director from 1944 to 1965, maintaining its repute as one of the finest ophthalmological clinical and research institutions in any country. As a consultant physician and private practitioner he had a huge band of devoted and grateful patients all over the world. His wife, also an oculist, was associated with him in much of his work. His written output included the standard 7-volume *Text-Book of Ophthalmology* (1932-54), which he almost wholly re-wrote or re-edited as the 15-volume *System of Ophthalmology* (1958-76). Died 27 March

Dupont, Clifford (b. 1905), was the usurping head of state of Rhodesia after the unilateral declaration of independence in 1965 and its President 1970-75. Born in England, he bought an estate in Rhodesia in 1948 and entered politics ten years later. He was Minister of Justice in Mr Winston Field's Rhodesian Front Government in 1962, but conspired to replace Field with

Ian Smith, who appointed him Deputy Prime Minister in 1964, and whose doctrine of white supremacy he faithfully supported. Died 28 June

Foot, Sir Dingle (b. 1905), British barrister and politician, left the Liberal Party in 1956 to join Labour, which he believed had become the effective standard-bearer of radicalism. From 1931 to 1945 he had been Liberal MP for Dundee, from 1957 to 1970 he was Labour member for Ipswich. From 1964 to his resignation in 1967 he was Solicitor General in Mr Wilson's Government. Meanwhile he had conducted a large legal practice, gaining a specially high reputation in constitutional issues in the 'new' Commonwealth. This and his devotion to human rights led him to the defence of many political offenders, and the conduct of constitutional cases, in the courts of Commonwealth countries in Africa and Asia. Died 18 June

François-Poncet, André (b. 1887), French politician and diplomatist, was ambassador in Berlin 1931-38 and in Rome 1938-40, and was thus closely involved in France's critical relations with the European dictatorships in the age of Laval, whose Vichy Administration he very briefly joined. His arrest and imprisonment by the Gestapo in 1943 restored his post-war credibility, enhanced by his brilliant memoirs of his Berlin embassy (published 1947), and he became successively diplomatic adviser on German affairs 1948-49, high commissioner in Germany 1949-55 and for six months in that year again ambassador. A member of the Académie Française from 1952, he had been a professor of modern literature at the Ecole Polytechnique before World War I, in which he was wounded and awarded the Croix de Guerre, and his first experience of political office, after his election to the Chamber in 1924 as a moderate conservative, was as under-secretary for the fine arts 1928-30. For the next two years he was under-secretary for foreign affairs. From 1955 to 1964 he was president of the French Red Cross. Died 8 January

Glass, Professor David Victor (b. 1911), British sociologist, was a world authority

on demography and social biology. After serving on committees of the Royal Commission on Population he directed the family census of the UK in 1946, and in 1959 became chairman of the Population Investigation Committee, of which he had been originally (1936) research secretary. His academic career was spent entirely at the London School of Economics and Political Science, as research assistant (1932-40), reader in demography (1946-48), professor of sociology (1948-59) and Martin White professor of sociology from 1959. His books included *Population Policies and Movement in Europe* (1940), *Social Mobility in Britain* (1954) and *The Trend and Pattern of Fertility in Britain* (1954). Died 23 September

Gödel, Professor Kurt (b. 1906), Austrian mathematician, was the most seminal and constructive mathematical logician of his time. From the University of Vienna, where he was Privat-Dozent 1933-38, he moved to the Institute of Advanced Studies at Princeton, which awarded him a professorial chair in 1953. He was only 24 when he published his famous completeness proof for the first-order functional calculus. This was soon followed by an equally celebrated critique of the *Principia Mathematica* of Whitehead and Russell. His publications included *The Consistency of the Continuum Hypothesis* (1940) and *Rotating Universes in General Relativity Theory* (1950). The development of computer science owes much to his work. Died 14 January

Goodhart, Professor Arthur Lehman, KBE (Hon.), QC (b. 1891), came from a rich and distinguished American Jewish family, never broke his academic and personal connexions with the United States and retained its citizenship, but spent most of his life in England. After graduating at Yale he took a degree at Cambridge, returning to practise law in New York in World War I until upon America's entry he joined the army. After the war he became a Fellow of Corpus Christi College, Cambridge, and university lecturer in law, and in 1931 Professor of Jurisprudence at Oxford, a chair he held, with a fellowship at University College, until his election to the Mastership of that college (1951-63). He founded and edited the *Cambridge Law Journal* and for many years edited the *Law Quarterly Review*. His constructive and practical sense, displayed alike in his editorship and his teaching, allied with his profound knowledge of English law, led to his appointment in 1935 to the Law Revision Committee and in 1952 to the Law Reform Committee, which he served for 11 highly formative years. He was a member of the Royal Commission on the Police and the Monopolies Commission, of government committees on a number of legal issues, and of many national and international academic and legal bodies, and president of the American Society and of the Pedestrians Association. His warmth and humanity equalled his learning, and he was a generous benefactor especially of the Oxford college of which he became Master. His publications included *Essays in Jurisprudence and the Common Law* (1931), *The Government of Great Britain* (1946), *English Contributions to the Philosophy of Law* (1949) and *English Law and the Moral Law* (1953). Died 10 November

Goonetileke, Sir Oliver (b. 1892), was Governor General of Sri Lanka 1954-62, the first native Ceylonese to hold that office. During World War II, before independence, he was commissioner for civil defence and food; from 1951 to 1954 he was successively Minister of Home Affairs, Agriculture and Food, and Finance. Died 17 December

Grant, Duncan (b. 1885), British artist, was a leading member and last survivor of the Bloomsbury circle of artists and writers that included Lytton Strachey, Virginia and Leonard Woolf, Roger Fry, Clive and Vanessa Bell (with whom he lived for many years and collaborated as an artist). An early admirer of Matisse and Picasso, he was a pioneer of abstract art before World War I, in which he was a conscientious objector, but after the war he turned to careful and subdued representational painting of landscapes and natural objects. In both roles, and as a highly inventive designer and decorator, he was influential among British artists of his time. Died 8 May

Gronchi, Giovanni (b. 1887), was President of Italy 1955-62. As a member of the Popular Party he spent most of the Mussolini years in opposition or out of politics, but returned as a Christian Democrat, serving as Secretary of State for Commerce, Industry and Labour from 1944 to 1946. In 1948 he was elected Speaker of the Chamber of Deputies and in 1955 President of the Republic. He favoured a centre-left coalition but his manoeuvring had a contrary effect. Died 17 October

Harrod, Sir Roy (b. 1900), British economist, taught at Christ Church, Oxford, for the whole of his academic working life, from his election as Student (Fellow) in 1924 to his retirement in 1967. As a friend and correspondent of Maynard Keynes he contributed much to the emergence of Keynesian economics, of which he became one of the leading expositors; but he also added to it the dynamic element which from the start he felt it lacked. His 'Essay in Dynamic Theory' in the *Economic Journal* in 1939 and his book *Towards a Dynamic Economics* (1948) were the origin of much of the subsequent vast output of growth economics in the whole Western world. Before World War II his *International Economics* (1933) and *Trade Cycle* (1936) had already extended his influence on economic thought far beyond Oxford. From the shadow of Keynes he fell under that of Professor Lindemann (Lord Cherwell), Winston Churchill's academic adviser, on whose specialist staff he served in World War II, and he composed greatly admired biographies of both those mentors—*The Life of J. M. Keynes* (1951) and *The Prof* (1959). From 1945 to 1961 he was joint editor, with Austin Robinson, of the *Economic Journal*, in which, and elsewhere, his fertility of ideas nourished economic thought throughout his long career. Died 8 March

Humphrey, Senator Hubert Horatio (b. 1911), American Democratic politician, was narrowly defeated for the Presidency of the United States by Richard Nixon in 1968, after serving as Vice-President under Lyndon Johnson in the previous term. He tried but failed to get his party's nomination in 1960 (beaten by Kennedy) and 1972 (beaten by McGovern). Had he not been tarred with Johnson's Vietnam brush—fairly, in the light of his fervent anti-communism and his loyal commitment to Administration policy—he might well have succeeded in 1968 and become a famous liberal President; for he was a progressive passionately devoted to democracy, identified—among other activities—with the Peace Corps and Americans for Democratic Action, and a tireless and triumphant champion of civil rights. Adlai Stevenson was his hero. His intelligence, humour, charm and liberalism, however, were not enough to obliterate his image as an establishment politician in face of a Kennedy, a McGovern or a Carter. Born in South Dakota but educated at the University of Minnesota (from which poverty obliged him to withdraw after two years) he became, after war service in civil posts, a professor of political science in Minneapolis in 1943. Mayor of that city from 1945, he was elected to the US Senate in 1948. After his presidential adventures, which had saddened and impoverished him, he was re-elected to the Senate in 1970 and again in 1976. From 1973 he knew that he suffered from cancer, which he bore with indomitable courage. Died 13 January

John Paul I, Pope (Albino Luciani, b. 1912), had one of the shortest reigns in the history of the Papacy. Born of poor parents in the Venetian region, he was ordained priest in 1935 after theological training in Venetian seminaries and at the Gregorian University. Teacher as well as pastor, in 1948 he became Vicar General of the diocese of Venice, and in 1958 Bishop of Vittorio Veneto. In 1969 Pope Paul made him Archbishop and Patriarch of Venice, and in 1973 he became a Cardinal. High office did not weaken his simplicity, his humanity, his pastoral benevolence or his warm humour, traits which became evident to the whole Christian world upon his surprising election to the See of Rome on 3 September 1978. Among his first acts as Pope were to hold a press conference and to decline coronation with the traditional tiara. Although conservative in theology, and combining

the names of his two predecessors as a signal that he meant to continue their policies, in the 33 days of his Papacy he not only impressed his personality upon people of all faiths but also gave a new face to the Catholic Church. Died 28 September

Karsavina, Tamara (b. 1885), ranked with Anna Pavlova and Olga Spessivtseva as one of the greatest Russian ballerinas of the century. She made her debut—exceptionally, as a soloist in a specially composed *pas de deux*—at the Merinsky Theatre in St Petersburg in 1902. There, in 1909, a protegée of Fokine, she danced the leading role in *Swan Lake*, and in the same year she partnered Nijinsky in the first Paris season of the Diaghilev Ballet, whose most famous female star she long remained. At the end of World War I she married the British diplomatist H. J. Bruce and thereafter lived in England. Not only a superb dancer but also a woman of great beauty and intelligence, she left an indelible mark upon both classical and contemporary ballet, by her performance, her example, her teaching (Fonteyn was among her pupils) and the inspiration she gave to such choreographers as Fokine, Massine, Nijinsky and Ashton, who created or adapted famous roles for her. Died 26 May

Keldysh, Professor Mstislav (b. 1911), Russian scientist, was responsible, as President of the Academy of Sciences of the USSR 1961-75, for the Soviet Union's scientific programme, including space research and operations. His work in aerodynamics and applied mathematics began at Moscow University (professor 1937) and continued at the Steklov Institute of Mathematics and the Aerohydrodynamics Institute. He became the youngest Soviet academician when elected to the Academy of Sciences in 1946. In presidential office he helped to protect the status of some distinguished scientific dissidents like Andrei Sakharov while himself toeing the official political line. Died 24 June

Kenyatta, Jomo (b. Kaman Ngengi 1892?), President of Kenya from 1963 to his death, was of mixed Kikuyu and Masai stock, but tribally and culturally a Kikuyu.

The name by which he was known to his people and the world was adopted in his youth. Taught English by the Church of Scotland mission, he helped to translate the Bible into Kikuyu and became an interpreter at the Supreme Court. In 1928, as secretary of the Kenya Central Association, he first visited England, where he lived from 1932 to 1946, studying anthropology at the London School of Economics, publishing an afterwards famous book, *Facing Mount Kenya*, and marrying an English wife polygamously (he had four wives in all). When he returned to Kenya the KCA had become the Kenya African Union, deeply committed to African nationalism and tribal customs such as female circumcision and the taking of oaths. These Kenyatta condoned, but the degree of his involvement in the Mau Mau revolt of 1952 remained uncertain, despite his conviction in 1953, on doubtful evidence, of managing the secret society that had perpetrated many outrages. After his prison sentence he was detained in a remote part of the colony, where nevertheless his prestige as a national leader steadily grew among both Africans and whites. Released in 1961 he immediately entered Parliament and led the Kenya African National Union to a decisive victory over its non-Kikuyu rival the Kenya African Democratic Union in the elections of May 1963. Seven months later he became, upon independence, President of Kenya. In office he displayed a statesmanlike moderation both in internal policies and relations between the races, welcoming whites and Asians who adopted Kenyan citizenship, and in pan-African affairs. He believed in maintaining close relations with the West and with the Commonwealth, and his rejection of communist intervention in Africa brought him into conflict with Tanzania and with post-revolutionary Ethiopia. Though working a Cabinet system he brooked no rivals at the top. Died 22 August

Kenyon, Dame Kathleen (b. 1906), British archaeologist, educated at St Paul's and Somerville College, Oxford, began her career on the Caton-Thompson expedition to the ruins of Zimbabwe in 1929. Next came work on Verulamium (St Albans), Samaria and a sequence of British sites. During World War II she was acting director of the Institute of Archaeology of London University, in which she later became a lecturer. Then as honorary director of the British School of Archaeology in the Near East she revived the School and led its epoch-making excavation of Jericho in the 1950s. This was followed by an important exploration of Jerusalem. In 1962 she became Principal of St Hugh's College, Oxford, but she continued working and publishing in the archaeological field. Died 24 August

Khachaturian, Aram (b. 1903), Russian composer, was internationally famous chiefly for his D flat piano concerto (1936), his violin concerto (1940) and his music for ballets (especially *Gayaneh* and *Spartacus*). He was a patriotic Soviet citizen who composed popular and officially approved music, including Red Army songs and the national anthem of Soviet Armenia, though in one highly philistine phase of official policy he was criticized for 'formalism'. Died 2 May

Krag, Jens Otto (b. 1914), Danish Social Democratic politician, was his country's Foreign Minister (1958-62) and Prime Minister (1962-68 and 1971-72). A staunch internationalist, he worked for Danish membership of Nato, the Nordic Council and the EEC and was president of the North Atlantic Council 1966-67. Before becoming Foreign Minister he had held several economic portfolios and been economic counsellor at the Washington embassy 1950-52. Immediately after the 1972 referendum had endorsed Denmark's entry into the European Community he resigned from politics for personal reasons. Died 22 June

Leavis, Dr Frank Raymond, CH (b. 1895), exerted unique influence as a critic of English literature, while arousing, and indulging in, the most intense and often bitter controversy. His critical method was sharply analytical and idiosyncratic. Among the sacred cows of traditional judgment whom he herded into minor pens were Spenser, Milton and the Romantic poets; writers whom he elevated included the Augustan poets, George Eliot, Dickens and D. H. Lawrence. Born and educated in Cambridge, from 1925 to his retirement he taught at Emmanuel and Downing Colleges (Fellow of Downing 1936-62), thereafter becoming visiting professor at the University of York. His published output was immense, from *New Bearings in English Poetry* (1932) to *The Living Principle* (1975), but his most influential written work was in the quarterly *Scrutiny*, which (with his wife Queenie Roth, who shared much else of his effort) he founded in 1932 and edited until its demise in 1953, in the interest of what he called 'the literature of growth'. His influence, however, rested primarily upon his oral teaching of innumerable pupils who were drawn from the whole English-speaking world. Died 14 April

Luciani, Albino, *see* John Paul I

MacDiarmid, Hugh (b. Christopher Murray Grieve 1892), Scottish poet and nationalist, entered left-wing politics while a journalist before World War I, in which he served in the RAMC. He adopted the pseudonym Hugh MacDiarmid when he began writing Scots poetry in the 1920s, and quickly became a powerful literary force, weakened by his polemical character and extremism. He joined the Communist Party in 1934, was expelled in 1938 and rejoined in 1957, dates which express his rebellious nature. His Scottish and Celtic nationalism was intense and combative. In World War II he worked as a factory labourer and merchant seaman. Critics held his poetic masterpiece to be *A Drunk Man Looks at the Thistle* (1926). His *Collected Poems* were published in 1962 and *The Hugh MacDiarmid Anthology* to celebrate his 80th birthday in 1972. Died 9 September

MacLiammóir, Micheál (b. 1899), Irish actor and man of many parts, was one of the founders of the Gate Theatre in Dublin in 1928 and was the doyen of the Irish stage. He and Noel Coward made their London debuts in the same play in 1911. Returning to his native land in 1927, for half a century he acted in or directed countless pays, mainly in Dublin though also in London and Edinburgh, acting most of the great Shakespearean parts, and invented and delivered enthralling one-man performances such as *The Importance of Being Oscar* (Wilde of course). Playwright too—*Ill Met by Moonlight* was the best remembered of his plays—he also wrote several autobiographical books and was famous as talker and wit in the great Dublin tradition. Died 6 March

Mackintosh, John, MP (b. 1929), despite his comparative youth was one of the nationally most influential back-benchers in Parliament. He taught history and politics at the universities of Glasgow, Edinburgh, Ibadan and Strathclyde, holding chairs of politics at Strathclyde 1965-66 and Edinburgh from 1977. He became Labour MP for Berwick and East Lothian in 1966 and again in October 1974 in the only Labour gain at that general election. On the right wing of his party, he was an ardent European and equally ardent champion of devolution of power to Scotland. His many books included *The British Cabinet* (1962) and *British Government and Politics* (1970). Died 30 July

Madariaga, Salvador de (b. 1886), Spanish statesman and man of letters, spent the years of General Franco's regime in exile, becoming an honoured spokesman of liberal internationalism throughout the democratic world. He had been director of the disarmament section of the League of Nations 1922-28, professor of Spanish studies at Oxford 1928-31, Spanish ambassador to Washington 1931 and to Paris 1932-34 and Minister of Education and Industry 1934 under the republican regime, and chief Spanish delegate to the League of Nations 1931-36. He spent most of his years out of Spain in Britain, and broadcast for the BBC during World War II; but, as a fluent linguist, he lectured in many countries and after the war was one of the founders of the College of Europe at Bruges and the European Centre for Culture at Geneva. His many books included *Shelley and Calderon* (1920), *Englishmen, Frenchmen and Spaniards* (1929), *Theory and Practice in International Relations* (1928), *Christopher Columbus* (1939), *Herman Cortes* (1941), *The Rise of the Spanish American Empire* (1946) and its *Fall* (1947), and *Portraits of Europe* (1952). Died 15 December

Mallowan, Professor Sir Max (b. 1904), British archaeologist, was director of the British School of Archaeology in Iraq 1947-61 and its chairman 1966-70 and president from 1970. He began his archaeological career as assistant to Sir Leonard Woolley in the famous excavations at Ur of the Chaldees, 1925-30. War service interrupted his field work, but it was resumed with great success, notably at Imrud, from 1947 onwards. Mallowan was also professor of western Asiatic archaeology in the University of London 1947-62, president of the British Institute of Persian Studies from 1961, editor of Penguin Books on the Near East and western Asia 1948-65, Fellow of All Souls College, Oxford, 1962-71, and author of a number of books. He was married from 1930 until her death in 1976 to the novelist Agatha Christie (see OBITUARY, AR 1976). Died 19 August

Marples, (Ernest) Lord (b. 1907), British business man and politician, was responsible for major reforms of the transport system as Minister of Transport 1959-64, authorizing the construction of motorways, applying city traffic plans, instituting the system of parking meters, traffic wardens and statutory fines, sponsoring the Buchanan report (1963) on the nation's road policy, reorganizing the ports, providing long-term credits for shipbuilding, appointing Dr Beeching as chairman of the British Transport Commission and vigorously backing the Beeching report on drastic reduction and reform of the railway system. His administrative and business genius had already been demonstrated as Harold Macmillan's parliamentary secretary (1951-54) in the Ministry of Housing and Local Government, which achieved the previously remote target of 300,000 houses a year, and as Postmaster General (1957-59), when among other reforms he initiated STD (subscriber trunk dialling). The son of an engineer foreman in Manchester, he left grammar school early to train as an accountant, but on moving to London took up the building and contracting business, in which he made a fortune. Died 6 July

Mead, Dr Margaret (b. 1901), American anthropologist, was famed among non-professional readers all over the world for her application of comparative anthropology to contemporary society in the West as well as more primitive communities, as in her books *Male and Female* (1949), *Continuities in Cultural Evolution* (1964) and *Culture and Commitment: a Study of the Generation Gap* (1970). Her field studies in the South Pacific and Indonesia, however, had given rise to a number of important anthropological works, including *Coming of Age in Samoa* (1928), *Growing up in New Guinea* (1930) and (with Gregory Bateson, her third husband) *Growth and Culture: a study of Balinese Childhood* (1951). She also wrote several biographical and autobiographical books. She was on the staff of the American Museum of Natural History 1926-69 and of Columbia University from 1949, and was visiting professor at other universities. Died 15 November

Meir, Mrs Golda (b. Goldie Mabovitch in Kiev in 1898), Prime Minister of Israel 1969-74, hebraicized her married name from Meyerson in 1956. Her family migrated to the USA, where she grew up and became passionately dedicated to zionism while working as a librarian and teacher. In 1921 the Meyersons joined a kibbutz near Nazareth, then from 1923 worked in humbler employment in Tel Aviv and Jerusalem. Golda became secretary of the Women's Labour Council of Histadruth in 1928 and from 1939-46 was a member of the executive of the Federation of Labour. She was head of the Jewish Agency's political department during the post-war struggle, was a signatory of the proclamation of independence in 1948 and became the only woman member of the Council of State. After a short spell as minister to the USSR she was Israel's Minister of Labour 1949-56 and Foreign Minister 1956-66, a period which covered the Suez crisis and its aftermath. She resigned office to become secretary-general of the Mapai Party but in 1969 was drafted as Prime Minister to resolve a political deadlock. Popular and energetic, she nevertheless shared in the opprobrium incurred by her Government over the Arab-Israeli war of 1973, and resigned in May 1974 after concluding armistice agreements with Egypt and Syria. Died 8 December

Menzies, Sir Robert, KT, CH, QC (b. 1894), Prime Minister of Australia 1939-41 and 1949-66, was acknowledged in his latter years as a leading statesman not only of the Commonwealth but indeed of the world. His political mastery of his own country was unrivalled, though like others in such a position he was accused of 'cutting down the tall poppies'. He was a natural orator in a deliberate, sometimes histrionic, sometimes sarcastic, often humorous style. Outside politics and diplomacy, he left his mark upon the burgeoning of Canberra and the great expansion of university education in Australia. Educated in Ballarat and Melbourne schools and at Melbourne University, he was a brilliant law student and after World War I practised success-fully at the Victoria bar. Following a spell in state politics (attorney-general and deputy premier 1932-34) he was elected in 1934 to the federal House and was im-mediately appointed Attorney-General. Resigning in 1939, he was narrowly elected leader of the United Australia Party and was able to form a Government which instantly entered the war alongside Britain. This fell in 1941 and Menzies was in opposition (with a brief interval as Minister for Defence Coordination in the Fadden Government) until 1949, when his new Liberal Party won a notable victory in alliance with the Country Party. His majority was cut in 1954 but he won decisively a year later, and by a small margin in 1961; in January 1966 he retired. He was thus in office at the time of the Suez crisis, when at the invitation of Sir Anthony Eden he led the abortive delegation to Cairo to win acceptance of the 17-nation plan for internationaliza-tion of the canal; also at the time of the UK Government's first attempt to join the European Common Market, a move which he thought unwise and injurious to Australia but which he held to be a matter for Britain to decide in its own interests. He acted decisively in sending Australian troops to Malaya in 1955, and to Sarawak and South Vietnam ten years later, and he did much to strengthen Australia's defensive strength. He was a devoted patriot and a royalist, as he movingly displayed when the Queen and the Duke of Edinburgh visited his country in 1963. He was also a passionate lover of cricket. From 1963 he was Warden of the Cinque Ports. His autobiography appeared in two volumes, *Afternoon Light* (1967) and *The Measure of the Years* (1970). Died 15 May

Mercader, Ramon (b. 1914), Spanish communist, assassinated Leon Trotsky in Mexico and served 20 years in prison for the crime. He had had close connexions with the Soviet secret police after the Spanish civil war but never admitted for whom he had carefully plotted the murder. Released, he worked in Cuba, Czecho-slovakia and the USSR, where he was made a Hero of the Soviet Union. Died 18 October

Messel, Oliver (b. 1904), British artist, shared with Gordon Craig, Charles Ricketts and Claud Lovat Fraser the distinction of revolutionizing stage design in Britain and elevating it to an art in itself. His early opportunities were given him by C. B. Cochran in his famous revues of the 1920s and '30s. Among the shows which earned him dazzling fame were *Helen, The Miracle,* the Sadler's Wells Ballet's *Sleeping Beauty, Ring Round the Moon, The Lady's Not for Burning,* Mozart operas and a number of admired films. His use of white was particularly brilliant, and his baroque settings, how-ever sumptuous, always had a poetic eloquence. Died 13 July

Messerschmitt, Willy (b. 1898), German aircraft designer, gave his name to some of the most famous aircraft of World War II and after, his Me 262 fighter being the world's first operational jet aircraft. His most creative plane was the Me 263, which introduced the swept-back wing and rocket propulsion. In 1958, after turning his abilities to the manufacture of less lethal products, he resumed his building of air-craft and headed a major industrial com-bine making, among other things, space satellites, missiles and helicopters. Died 15 September

Mikoyan, Anastas Ivanovitch (b. 1895), was First Deputy Chairman of the Soviet

Council of Ministers 1955-64 and President of the USSR 1964-65. He was thus one of the few 'old Bolsheviks' linked with Stalin who survived in high office in the regimes of Khrushchev and Brezhnev. His shrewdness in backing the right side was exemplified in his leading the attack on Stalin at the 20th Party Congress in 1956 and his rallying to Khrushchev in the party crisis of June 1957. But this quality was supported by great administrative talent, knowledge of industry and technology, and skill in international diplomacy. An Armenian, Mikoyan joined the Bolshevik party in 1915 and became one of its leading organizers in Transcaucasia after the 1917 revolution, charged with recovering and stabilizing that multinational area. Called to Moscow in 1926, he became, as candidate member of the Politburo and full member from 1935, successively Commissar for Foreign Trade 1926-30, for Supplies 1930-34 and for Food Industry 1933-38. In 1937 he was elected a Vice-President of the Council of Ministers and in 1938 he returned to the Ministry of Foreign Trade, resigning that ministry only in 1949. During the war he was a member of the state committee for defence and the committee for economic rehabilitation of liberated areas. He was a Vice-Chairman of the Council of Ministers 1953-55, before becoming First Deputy Chairman (Deputy Prime Minister) in 1955. Died 21 October

Milverton, Lord, PC, GCMG (Arthur Frederick Richards, b. 1885) was the outstanding British colonial administrator of his day. He entered the Malayan civil service in 1908, and rose to be Governor of North Borneo (1930-33). Selected on merit for wider responsibility, he became successively Governor of the Gambia (1933-36) and of Fiji (1936-38), Captain-General and Governor-in-Chief of Jamaica (1938-43) and Governor of Nigeria (1943-47). On his retirement he was made a life peer as a Labour supporter, but later changed his political allegiance and generally voted with the Conservatives. He held many distinguished public and business posts into his old age. Died 27 October

Montini, Giovanni Batista, *see* Paul VI

Moro, Aldo (b. 1916), Italian Christian Democratic politician, was Prime Minister five times between 1963 and 1976. In 1948 he had been elected to Italy's first republican parliament and became leader of the Christian Democrats in the Chamber 1953-55. After holding Ministerial office he was appointed the party's secretary in 1959 and three years later swung it into alliance with the Socialists. His first coalition Government was formed in December 1963, and he remained Prime Minister for nearly five years. From 1968 to 1971 he was Foreign Minister but then declined to join Andreotti in a Christian Democrat-Liberal Government. From 1974 to 1976 he headed a coalition with the Republicans, and for part of 1976 a minority regime. After the election of that year, which brought Sr Andreotti back to the Prime Ministership, he became chairman of the Christian Democratic Party and guided its thought towards a parliamentary alliance with the Communists. He was kidnapped by terrorists, who slew his bodyguards, was held captive while forced to make political 'confessions', and eventually murdered. A man more of ideas and manoeuvre than of action, he failed in office to conduct the reforms that his political stance indicated and required. Died on or before 9 May, when his body was deposited by his captors.

Nikodim, Metropolitan (b. Boris Rotov 1930), ranked, as Metropolitan of Leningrad, second in the hierarchy of the Russian Orthodox Church. An ardent ecumenist, he led his Church into the World Council of Churches and became one of its six presidents. Died in the Vatican 5 September

Nobile, General Umberto (b. 1885), Italian airship designer, rose to the headship of the department of aeronautical construction of the Italian War Ministry in World War I. In 1925 he piloted one of his airships, the *Norge*, which had been sold to the Norwegian Government, on a pioneer Arctic expedition by Amundsen and Lincoln Ellsworth, with whom he quarrelled and who thought little of him as a pilot. In May 1928 he commanded another of his airships, the *Italia*, on a flight intended to cross the North Pole

R

which ended in early disaster costing ten lives, including that of Amundsen as volunteer pilot of a relief plane. An official inquiry blamed Nobile, and he was disgraced, though hotly defending himself. He joined the service of the USSR and became deputy chief of Soviet airship construction. Died 29 July

Norrish, Professor R. G. W., FRS (b. 1897), British scientist, shared with Sir George Porter the Nobel prize for chemistry in 1967 for their work on flash photolysis. From 1937 to 1965 he was director of the department of physical chemistry at Cambridge University. Died 7 June

O Dalaigh, Cearbhail (b. 1911), President of the Irish Republic 1974-76, was a profound Gaelic scholar and an intense nationalist. A lawyer by profession, he was elevated to the Bench in 1953 and was Chief Justice from 1961 to 1973, when he became a judge of the European Court. Died 21 March

Paul VI, Pope (Giovanni Batista Montini, b. 1897) succeeded Pope John XXIII in 1963. The ascetic son of a pious professional-class family, he was ordained priest in 1920, and shortly afterwards joined the papal secretariat, working under and emulating Cardinal Secretary of State Pacelli, later Pope Pius XII, and becoming pro-secretary of state 1952-54. His first and only pastoral experience was as Archbishop of Milan 1954-63. When in 1958 Pope John made him a cardinal (an honour he had refused five years earlier) he was already talked of as the next Pope. He fell under the spell of Pope John, whose Second Vatican Ecumenical Council he immediately called into its second session after his election to the papacy. To the non-Catholic world and reformists in the Roman Church he appeared as the adamant doctrinal conservative, not least in his encyclical *Humanae Vitae* which reaffirmed the Church's prohibition of all artificial birth control, but his ecclesiastic reforms were many and far-reaching. He carried through the substitution of the vernacular for the Latin Mass with unflinching determination, radically reformed the Curia, re-

organized the Vatican's finances, established the international synod of bishops, thus extending to the episcopacy the collegiate theme which he also applied to the Roman Curia, reduced the pomp and circumstance of the papacy, and imposed age-limits not only for parish priests and bishops (at 75) but also for the tenure by cardinals of active posts in the Church's central government and their voting in the Sacred Conclave. Above all, his pontificate was marked by a zeal for ecumenism and international understanding, demonstrated by the personal relations that he cultivated with the heads of other churches, including the Archbishop of Canterbury and the Ecumenical Patriarch, and by unprecedented journeys abroad, which took him, among other places, to the Holy Land, India, the United States and the Far East and totalled 69,000 miles, a greater distance than all his predecessors together had travelled. Theologically, Pope Paul resisted innovation which he feared would undermine the integrity and authority of the Church's teaching, and constantly stressed the mystery and other-worldiness of the faith as against the prevailing scientific naturalism. Died 6 August

Platt, (Robert) Lord (b. 1900), British physician, was President of the Royal College of Physicians from 1957 to 1962, a period of decisive reform. A successful consultant and researcher, he became Professor of Medicine in Manchester University in 1946, his speciality being renal and metabolic disorders and hypertension. He was present of the Eugenics Society 1965-68 and of the Family Planning Association 1968-71, and in 1972 published his philosophy of life in *Private and Controversial.* Died 30 June

Rothermere, second Viscount (Esmond Cecil Harmsworth, b. 1898), British newspaper proprietor, was a nephew of Lord Northcliffe and inheritor from 1940 of his father's control of a group that included the London *Daily Mail* and *Evening News* and a chain of provincial newspapers. From 1934 to 1961 he was a forceful chairman of the Newspaper Proprietors Association, its dogged general in the newspaper strike of 1955. He retired from the chairmanship of Associated News-papers in 1971. His most successful business achievement was the absorption of the rival, traditionally Liberal, London papers the *News-Chronicle* and *Star*, his least the venture of Associated into television, which was abandoned shortly before the big profits began to roll in. Died 11 July

Rueff, Jacques (b. 1896), French economist and philosopher, was a man of extraordinary versatility. After World War I, in which he won the Croix de Guerre, he studied at the Ecole Poly-technique and developed the application of mathematical techniques to the social sciences; his first book, *Des Sciences physiques aux Sciences morales*, later translated into English, was published when he was only 26. In 1923 he became an Inspecteur des Finances, and thereafter he swung between the academic and the practical political spheres. On the one hand he was professor of economics at the Ecole Libre des Sciences Politiques (1931-50), author of many books on monetary economics (on which subject he was a severe rationalist) and eventually a member of the Académie Française. On the other he was Vice-Governor of the Bank of France (1939-40), the leading French official expert on post-war repara-tions and president of the reparations conference in Paris in 1945, a judge of the Court of Justice of the European Steel and Coal Community (1952-58) and of the Court of Justice of the European Com-munities (1958-62) and chairman of governmental committees on economic problems, in which capacity he directed the chill open-market monetary and fiscal reforms of 1958, which raised France from near-bankruptcy to prosperity. Died 23 April

Scott, Paul (b. 1920), British novelist, achieved fame above all for his stories about British and Indian people in the transition from empire to independence, published between 1966 and 1975, which together were known as *The Raj Quartet*. Late in 1977 he was awarded the Booker Prize for an epilogue, *Staying On*, but this honour was generally regarded as a tribute to his previous work. His experience in—

indeed his obsession with—India began with his service in the Indian Army from 1943 to 1946. Besides *The Raj Quartet* he published a number of other novels and a volume of poems. Died 1 March

Selwyn-Lloyd, Lord, PC, CH, CBE (John Selwyn Brooke Lloyd, b. 1904), Speaker of the House of Commons 1971-76, had been a more controversial political figure than his temperate nature, tenacity, in-dustry, loyalty and negotiating skill seemed to deserve. As Foreign Secretary 1956-60 he was responsible for Middle Eastern policy under Sir Anthony Eden and for the retreat from Suez under Mr Harold Macmillan, but his role was secondary to theirs. As Chancellor of the Exchequer 1960-62 he imposed austerity measures in the balance of payments crisis of 1961, and attempted an incomes policy which he continued to champion after it had lost reality, a factor, no doubt, in his abrupt dismissal in July 1962 along with several other Cabinet Ministers. But aside from these heated issues he recorded in office much solid achievement, including the creation of the National Economic Development Council and (as Minister of State at the Foreign Office 1951-54) much of the donkey work behind Eden's diplomacy at the United Nations and towards the Far East. He was a firm Speaker of the House, respected and liked on all sides. Before World War II, in which he rose to the rank of brigadier, with a CBE for distinguished service, he had built a considerable reputation as a barrister on the northern circuit, and con-tinued to practise (QC, 1947) after he had been elected as Conservative MP for the Wirral in 1945—a constituency he repre-sented without a break until his elevation to the House of Lords in 1976. He was Minister of Supply 1954-55 and of Defence (in the Cabinet) 1955-56. Died 17 May

Silone, Ignazio (b. 1900), Italian author, left the Italian Communist Party, which he had helped to found, in 1930, and spent the next 14 years of the fascist regime in Switzerland. He called himself 'a socialist without a party, a Christian without a church'. Among his many works, *Fonta-mara* (1930) and *Bread and Wine* (1937) were the best-known of his novels, and

R*

Emergency Exit (1965) and *The Story of a Humble Christian* (1968) the best-known of his other books. Died 22 August

Strang, (William) Lord, GCB, GCMG (b. 1893), was Permanent Under-Secretary of State for Foreign Affairs 1949-53. With none of the traditional background of British diplomats, he joined the foreign service after fighting in the infantry in World War I. As Counsellor in the Moscow embassy (1930-33) and head of the League of Nations department in the Foreign Office (1933-37) and of the Central department (1937-39) he engaged in the most vital developments in foreign policy leading up to World War II, including the Ethiopian whitewash, Munich and the futile attempt in 1939 to negotiate a mutual assistance treaty with Russia, while himself profoundly opposed to the appeasement policies of his political masters. In the second war, now an Under-Secretary of State, Strang was British representative on the Anglo-American-Soviet European Advisory Commission which drafted the conditions to be applied after Germany's surrender. After attending the Potsdam conference he became political adviser to Field Marshal Montgomery in Germany and then head of the German section of the F.O. In retirement he was chairman of the National Parks Commission (1954-66) and of the Royal Institute of International Affairs (1958-65) and a Deputy Chairman of Committees in the House of Lords (from 1962). Died 27 May

Sutcliffe, Herbert (b. 1894), was famed throughout the cricketing world as batting partner to the equally great Jack Hobbs, with whom he notched 26 stands of over 100 runs, including 15 in Tests against Australia. But his century partnerships with Percy Holmes for Yorkshire were still more numerous—74, including one of 555 in 1932. In all he scored over 50,000 runs in 21 seasons, including 149 centuries, and three times scored 3,000 runs in a season. Died 22 January

Tsiranana, Philbert (b. 1912), President of the Malagasy Republic from its inception in 1960 to 1972, had been Prime Minister or Cabinet President from 1958 until independence. Born to a poor peasant family in Madagascar, he studied education in France and returned to teach educational theory in Tananarive. Turning to politics he formed the Social Democratic Party, of which he became secretary-general in 1957, and swiftly moved into national leadership. Died 16 April

Tunney, Gene (b. 1898), American boxer, became heavyweight champion of the world by beating Jack Dempsey on points in 1926. After successfully defending his title against Dempsey's challenge in the following year, and in 1928 against Tom Heeney, whom he knocked out, he retired from the ring, and, rich from his boxing earnings and marriage to an heiress, pursued a successful business career. Of literary bent, he was a friend of Bernard Shaw and Thornton Wilder and a lecturer and author. Died 7 November

Warner, Jack L. (b. 1892), American film magnate, was the youngest and last survivor of four brothers who founded Warner Brothers Pictures in 1923. Their fortune was made as pioneers of the sound film with *The Jazz Singer*, starring Al Jolson. Warner Brothers enlisted many of the most famous stars of the 1920s and later years, including Edward G. Robinson, George Raft, Humphrey Bogart and Bette Davis. Their last great success was *My Fair Lady* (1964). Died 9 September

Wills, Philip (b. 1907), British gliding expert, became world single-seater champion in 1952. Before then he had repeatedly broken British distance and height records, rising above 30,000 feet of absolute altitude in 1954. In 1960, at the age of 53, he glided over 500 km in Texas. In World War II he became director of operations, air transport command, and from 1946 to 1948 was general manager (technical) of BOAC. He wrote many books on gliding. Died 16 March

Wrathall, John (b. in England 1913), was President of Rhodesia from 1976 and died in office. A chartered accountant, he entered Rhodesian politics in 1954 and became a Minister in 1962. He was a signatory of the unilateral declaration of independence and a close ally of Mr Ian Smith as Deputy Prime Minister 1966-74. Died 31 August

CHRONICLE OF PRINCIPAL EVENTS IN 1978

JANUARY

1 In India, 213 killed when Air India jumbo jet exploded in mid-air off Bombay.
US President Carter in India on two-day visit.
In Cambodia, 8,000 reported killed in border clashes with Vietnam.
In Turkey, Bülent Ecevit asked to form Government.

3 In India, former PM, Indira Gandhi, expelled from Congress Party following split in which she was elected president of new faction; the latter recognized as official opposition on 12 April.

4 British PM James Callaghan arrived in Bangladesh on ten-day tour including visits to India and Pakistan.
In Chile, in a national referendum 75 per cent of voters supported policies of President Pinochet.
UK representative of PLO, Said Hammami, assassinated in London.

5 In Brazil, Gen. Joao Baptista Figueiredo chosen to succeed President Geisel in March 1979.

6 In Hungary, Crown of St Stephen, thousand-year symbol of Hungarian nationhood, returned by Cyrus Vance, US Secretary of State.

11 In UK, Lady Spencer-Churchill's executors revealed that Graham Sutherland portrait of Sir Winston Churchill presented to him by Parliament on his 80th birthday had been destroyed by her.

12 In UK, firemen's strike, which began on 14 Nov., ended.
In Finland, Dr Urho Kekkonen re-elected President for six years.
In Italy, PM Giulio Andreotti resigned after 18 months in office (see 8 Mar.).

17 Britain told EEC partners that it would not be ready to take part in direct elections to European Parliament until 1979.
Foreign Ministers from Israel and Egypt began session of joint political committee in Jerusalem. On 18th President Sadat ordered delegation to return home and accused Israel of making unreasonable demands.

18 Britain cleared by European Court of Human Rights of Irish allegations of torture in N. Ireland, but convicted of cases of 'inhuman and degrading treatment'.

22 Representatives of USA, UK, France, Italy and West Germany met in Washington to discuss situation in Horn of Africa.

23 Baron Edouard-Jean Empain, one of the most powerful industrialists in Europe, kidnapped in Paris; freed on 26 March.
Sweden became first country to ban aerosol sprays.

24 Soviet satellite, Cosmos 954, used for ocean surveillance, disintegrated in remote North-West Territories of Canada.

25 Greek PM Karamanlis in London.

26 In Cyprus, President Kyprianou re-elected for five years.
In USSR, group of Soviet workers announced formation of independent trade union for defence of workers.
In Tunisia, state of emergency after riots in the first serious challenge to President Bourguiba in 22 years.
In China, Einstein's theory of relativity officially reinstated.

30 In Java, 41 killed in floods.
In Portugal, new Government under Dr Mario Soares sworn in (see 27 July).

FEBRUARY

2 Two Soviet cosmonauts carried out unprecedented outer space refuelling of Salyut engines.

3 EEC and China initialled first trade agreement.
In Liechtenstein, Patriotic Union Party won election for new Diet; Hans Brunhart, 32, became Europe's youngest Premier.

4 In Sri Lanka, Junius Jayawardene assumed presidential office.
5 In Egypt, the first freely-created political party since Nasser era, New Wafd Party, registered.
6 In Costa Rica, Rodrigo Carazo Odio, opposition candidate, won presidential election, ousting Daniel Oduber; May, took office.
7 In Guatemala, political killings over past decade reported to have reached 20,000.
  In Pakistan, 1,750 officials lost positions in purge.
9 In Tanzania, 300 killed by cholera outbreak.
  In Syria, President Assad re-elected for seven-year term.
12 In Paraguay, ruling Colorado Party of President Stroessner won general election.
   Three anti-pollution agreements, negotiated under aegis of UN Environment Programme, came into force.
13 Leaders from 11 Asian and South Pacific Commonwealth countries met in Australia for four-day summit for first time in CW history.
14 President Carter proposed selling Egypt 50 jet fighter planes, the first time since 1950s that US had offered to arm Egypt.
15 In UK, two Government defeats in Commons on important amendments to Scotland Bill.
16 In Finland, Finnmark devalued by 8 per cent; the following day, Government of Kalevi Sorsa resigned.
19 15 Egyptian soldiers killed and 17 wounded in Cyprus airport gun battle when Egyptians tried to storm hijacked airliner in which Arab terrorists were holding hostages. 22 Feb., Egypt severed diplomatic and trade relations with Cyprus.
20 In USSR, President Brezhnev decorated with Order of Victory, highest Soviet military honour, becoming most decorated leader since Stalin.
22 Sahara summit of four North African leaders began to try to end 12-year war in Chad.
26 China opened first parliament in three years; 1 March, draft of revised constitution presented to fifth National People's Congress.

MARCH

3 In Rhodesia, Ian Smith and three black leaders signed internal settlement pact, intended to bring black majority rule by 31 Dec.
5 Sri Lanka became Democratic Socialist Republic of Sri Lanka.
  Iran broke off trade links with East Germany.
  In Guatemala, presidential poll won by Gen. Romeo Lucas Garcia.
6 In UK, Parker report on Windscale inquiry recommended proceeding with £600 million nuclear waste plant.
  In Czechoslovakia, Cardinal Frantisek Tomásek installed as first Archbishop for nearly 30 years.
7 38 black nationalists killed during Rhodesian raid on guerrilla base in Zambia.
  President Tito in USA.
  In Burma, President Ne Win re-elected for second term.
8 In Italy, 54-day political crisis ended with five-party agreement, including the Communists; 13 March, new Government headed by Giulio Andreotti sworn in.
  In Belgium, millionaire Charles Bracht kidnapped; 10 Apr. body found.
  Prince of Wales on 16-day visit to South America.
  In Romania, sweeping reshuffle of top posts.
  In China, Vice-Chairman Teng Hsiao-p'ing elected head of Chinese People's Political Consultative Conference, which had not functioned for 13 years.
  Five-month Helsinki follow-up conference in Belgrade ended.
9 In Italy, trial of Red Brigade terrorists opened.
10 President Tito in Britain on two-day visit.
   Former Gen. Pyotr Grigorenko, leading Soviet dissident, deprived of citizenship.

11 In Chile, stage of siege imposed during 1973 coup ended.
West Germany and USA signed pact on measures to aid dollar.
Flt.-Lt. David Cyster of RAF landed in Darwin after 32-day, 9,000 mile flight from England in an open-cockpit Tiger Moth.

12 In France, in first round of parliamentary elections left claimed absolute majority for the first time in French history (see also 19 March).

14 In the Netherlands, Dutch marines stormed in to release 71 hostages held by South Moluccan terrorists for 29 hours; 30 June, terrorists gaoled for 15 years.
In Argentina, 46 died when troops stormed riot prison.

15 China exploded nuclear device at Lop Nor.

16 In Italy, Aldo Moro, former PM, kidnapped by Red Brigade terrorists demanding release of all communist prisoners; 9 May, Moro found dead.
Amoco Cadiz supertanker went aground off Brittany coast causing world's worst-ever pollution disaster.

17 In Zaïre, 13 opponents of President Mobutu executed.

18 In Pakistan, Punjab High Court passed death sentence on former PM, Zulfiqar Ali Bhutto, on charges of political murder.

19 In France, at second ballot ruling coalition of Gaullists and their allies won parliamentary elections with strong majority.
UN Security Council voted to send interim force to Lebanon after massive Israeli raid on 14th.

21 In Rhodesia, three black leaders sworn in as members of a new Executive Council after 88 years of white rule.

23 In Indonesia, President Suharto re-elected for third five-year term.
British PM, James Callaghan, in USA.

24 A painting by Hitler sold for $4,500 at a New York auction.

30 In Syria, new Government formed with Mohammed Ali al-Halabi as PM.

APRIL

3 In UK, first regular radio broadcasts of Parliament's proceedings began.

6 Rhodesia's transitional Government announced release of several hundred political detainees.

7 In Philippines, general election won by President Marcos' New Society Movement.
Gutenberg Bible sold by Christie's in New York for $2 million.
Summit meeting of EEC heads of government at Copenhagen.

9 In Somalia, coup attempt crushed; 26 Oct., 17 publicly executed for complicity in plot.

10 Transkei broke diplomatic relations with South Africa.

11 In UK, Budget Day: income tax thresholds raised; initial rate reduced to 25 per cent on first £750 taxable.

15 50 killed in Bologna, Italy, in the worst rail disaster in 16 years.

16 In India, 173 died and 600 injured after tornado struck eastern state of Orissa.

18 In Chile, President Pinochet announced new Cabinet composed for the first time since 1973 coup principally of civilians.
In USA, the Senate ratified new Panama Canal Treaty.

19 France exploded neutron device at Pacific test site.
In Namibia, emergency measures imposed gave Administrator dictatorial powers.

20 Brooch containing two emeralds believed to have been acquired by Clive of India from Nawab of Murshidabad fetched £250,000 at Sotheby's.

23 West German Chancellor Schmidt in London.
Foreign Ministers from Canada, France, UK, USA and West Germany met in London for talks on Namibia.

24 In USA, Miss Patricia Hearst's appeal rejected by Supreme Court (see also 3 Oct.).
Centre and centre-right parties from UK, Denmark, West Germany, Austria, Nordic countries and Portugal formed European Democratic Union.

25 South Africa accepted Western plans for Namibia independence by 31 Dec.

European Court of Human Rights found birching as practised in the Isle of Man to be degrading and in breach of European Convention on Human Rights.

26 In Somalia, sole surviving woman hijacker in Mogadishu airport incident in Oct. 1977 gaoled for 20 years (see AR 1977, p. 525).

27 In Afghanistan, armed forces seized power and established government based on Islamic principles; President Daoud killed, new President Nur Mohammed Taraki proclaimed Democratic Republic of Afghanistan, the first country in South Asia to be ruled by communists.

28 10,000 refugees, mostly Muslim, reported to have fled to Bangladesh from Burma.

MAY

1 Naomi Uemura, Japanese explorer, became the first to reach North Pole alone.

In South Africa, new black political party, Azanian People's Organization, formed.

2 In Rhodesia, transitional Executive Council lifted 16-year-ban on Zanu and Zapu black political organizations.

3 In Argentina, Gen. Jorge Videla confirmed as President for next three years.

4 Hua Kuo-feng, Chairman of Chinese Communist Party, left for North Korea on first visit abroad.

5 Hungary and Austria reached agreement to abolish visas.

Portugal and Spain signed ten-year-treaty of friendship and cooperation.

8 Reinhold Messner (Italian) and Peter Habeler (Austrian) climbed Everest without oxygen.

13 In Comoro Islands, alliance of military officers and politicians overthrew pro-Chinese regime of President Ali Soilih; he was shot dead escaping house arrest on 29 May.

14 In Rhodesia, collapse of interim government averted when Bishop Muzorewa's United African National Council decided against withdrawing from Government, despite dismissal of black Minister.

15 In USSR, trial began of Dr Yuri Orlov, founder of Soviet group formed to monitor country's violation of human rights; 18th, sentenced to seven years in labour camp and five more in exile (see also 13 and 14 June).

President Kaunda of Zambia in London.

Turkish PM, Bülent Ecevit, in London.

President Ceauşescu of Romania in Peking.

In Nauru, Head Chief Hammer de Roburt became new President.

16 In Rhodesia, 94 black tribesmen killed when security forces opened fire on guerrillas' political meeting in the worst incident in six years.

President of Botswana, Sir Seretse Khama, in London.

19 In Dominican Republic presidential election, left-wing candidate, Silvestre Antonio Guzmán Fernández, defeated President Joaquín Balaguer after army had halted ballot count for two days.

In Zaïre, bodies of 44 Europeans found in cellars in Kolwezi; 400 French paratroops dropped into battle zone; 100 Europeans massacred.

21 In Japan, new international airport at Narita opened after 11 unsuccessful attempts to do so since 1971.

In Egypt, overwhelming victory in referendum for President Sadat's proposed curbs on political opponents.

22 HM the Queen and Duke of Edinburgh on five-day state visit to West Germany.

23 UN General Assembly began five-week special session on world disarmament.

25 In UK, Liberal leader David Steel announced end of the Lib-Lab pact after end of present parliamentary session.

29 In Israel, Yitzhak Navon inaugurated as new President.

31 Two-day Nato summit meeting in Washington.

JUNE

4 In Colombia, presidential poll won by Julio César Turbay Ayala.
5 In Bangladesh, sweeping electoral victory for President Zia ur-Rahman.
6 Indian PM, Morarji Desai, on three-day visit to London.
7 King Carl XVI Gustaf and Queen Sylvia of Sweden in Moscow, the first state visit by a Swedish monarch to the Soviet Union.
8 In UK, Government's new economic package increased minimum lending rate, restricted bank lending and raised employers' national insurance contributions.
   Five priceless statues stolen from Casa dei Vetti, outstanding villa of Pompeii.
12 'Son of Sam' multiple killer gaoled for 315 years in New York.
13 President Ceauşescu of Romania on state visit to Britain, the first such visit by a Romanian communist leader.
15 In Italy, President Leone resigned after allegations of fiscal misconduct; 8 July, Alessandro Pertini sworn in as seventh President.
   In Belgium, PM Leo Tindemans resigned; 18th, agreement reached among four coalition parties and Tindemans stayed on.
18 In Peru, in the first polls in 15 years victory for Popular Revolutionary Alliance led by Victor Haya de la Torre.
19 13 OPEC Ministers ended meeting in Geneva with agreement not to raise oil prices till Dec.
20 50 died in severe earthquake which struck northern Greece.
23 President Kyprianou of Cyprus in London on four-day visit.
   In Italy, Red Brigade's founders gaoled for 15 years.
24 In N. Yemen, President Ahmad Hussain al Ghashmi assassinated; 17 July, Lt.-Col. Ali Abdullah Saleh elected as new President.
25 In Iceland, in elections no group won parliamentary majority; Geir Hallgrímsson continued as caretaker PM (see 31 Aug.).
   12 British missionaries and children murdered in Umtali, Rhodesia.
   British PM, Callaghan, in Washington.
26 Bomb blast destroyed priceless works of art at Versailles, France.
   In S. Yemen, President Salim Rubai Ali overthrown and executed; Ali Nasir Muhammad new President.
   West German Chancellor, Helmut Schmidt, on first official visit to Africa.
   Angola and Portugal signed treaty of friendship and aid.
28 President Giscard d'Estaing on first official visit by French head of state to Spain since the Civil War.
29 In Malawi, first elections since 1961.
   Vietnam became Comecon's tenth member.

JULY

1 In Guatemala, Gen. Romeo Lucas Garcia took office as President.
2 Arab League imposed political and economic boycott on S. Yemen.
   Australia agreed to pay £4 million for purchase of Cocos Islands.
3 China cut off economic and technical aid to Vietnam.
4 Austrian Chancellor, Dr Kreisky, in London.
   Brazil, Bolivia, Colombia, Ecuador, Guyana, Peru, Surinam and Venezuela signed Amazon Pact.
5 In Ghana, in bloodless palace coup Gen. Acheampong resigned and handed over power to Lt.-Gen. F. W. K. Akuffo.
6 In S. Korea, President Park Chung Hee re-elected for fourth six-year term.
7 Solomon Islands became independent.
   Two-day summit meeting of EEC heads of government at Bremen.
   China cut off all aid to Albania and recalled experts.

9 In Bolivia, elections; 20th, results scrapped (see 21 July).
   In Malaysia, ruling National Front won decisive victory in election.
   In Afghanistan, 110 died in floods.
10 In Mauritania, coup ousted President Moktar Ould Daddah; new ruler, Lt.-Col.
   Mustapha Ould Salek.
11 About 200 died in gas tanker explosion at Los Alfaque camping site, Spain.
12 In Guyana's referendum on constitutional changes Government had landslide victory.
13 In USSR, Alexander Ginzburg, Soviet dissident sentenced to 8 years in labour camp;
   14th, Anatoly Shcharansky, member of Helsinki human rights group, gaoled for
   13 years.
14 In Italy, 46 1970 coup plotters gaoled for 18 months to 10 years.
16 Start of two-day summit meeting of leaders of the seven most important Western
   industrial nations in Bonn.
17 In San Marino, coalition of communists and socialists took office in W. Europe's
   only communist-led Government.
   In Cyprus, anti-Government plot foiled.
18 Talks at Leeds Castle, Kent, between US, Israeli and Egyptian Foreign Ministers.
   Five-day 15th summit meeting of OAU opens in Khartoum.
21 In Bolivia, President Banzer deposed after coup; new President, Gen. Juan Pereda
   Asbún (see 24 Nov.).
25 86 non-aligned nations meeting in Belgrade.
   World's first 'test-tube baby' born at Oldham, England.
   US Senate agreed to lift arms ban on Turkey.
   In Cook Islands, Government toppled by court ruling on election bribery.
27 In Portugal, PM Soares dismissed; 29 Aug. new PM, industrialist Alfredo Nobre da
   Costa (see 14 Sept.).
   HM the Queen and Duke of Edinburgh on 12-day tour of Canada (see 14 Sept.).
28 In the Maldives, Maumoon Abdul Gayoom had sweeping victory in presidential
   referendum.
30 Two Soviet cosmonauts manning orbiting Salyut 6 had two-hour space walk.
31 In China, Shakespeare permitted for first time since Cultural Revolution.

AUGUST

1 In Argentina, government demilitarized—President Gen. Videla retired from army.
4 In UK, former Liberal leader Jeremy Thorpe, MP, and three others accused of murder
   plot (see 13 Dec.).
6 Pope Paul VI died; 3 Sept. Cardinal Albino Luciani installed as Pope John Paul I
   (see 28 Sept.).
   In Honduras, Gen. Juan Alberto Melgar Castro, President, deposed in bloodless
   coup.
   UNESCO International Congress on Aristotle opened in Salonika to mark his
   2,300th death anniversary.
9 Libya and China established diplomatic relations.
12 China and Japan signed treaty of peace and friendship.
13 100 killed in bomb attack in Palestinian area of Beirut.
14 In Congo, coup crushed and leaders arrested.
15 In Egypt, President Sadat formed new party—National Democratic Party—making
   four political parties in the country.
16 Three Americans completed the first crossing of the Atlantic by balloon.
   Chairman Hua Kuo-feng arrived in Bucharest, the first European visit by a Chinese
   head of state since Mao Tsetung went to Moscow in 1951.
17 In Afghanistan, counter-coup attempt reported foiled.
19 In Iran, 43 killed by fire in cinema at Abadan.

22 In Nicaragua, 20 leftist guerrillas invaded National Palace and seized 50 Congressmen and others as hostages.

In Kenya, President Kenyatta died; 10 Oct., Daniel arap Moi elected new President.

23 In Pakistan Gen. Zia ul Haq formed civilian Cabinet.

24 Zambia claimed 12 died in attack by South Africa.

26 Soyuz 31 launched with first East German cosmonauts to link with Salyut 6 in orbit.

27 In Iran, one-party system replaced as ban on additional parties lifted; Government of
Amouzegar dismissed; new PM, Jaafar Sharif-Emami.

29 In Nigeria, new civilian constitution adopted.

In Chad, provisional military government dissolved and Hissène Habré, former
guerrilla leader, appointed PM.

30 In Denmark, Anker Jørgensen's coalition Cabinet of Social Democrats and Liberals
sworn in.

31 In Iceland, Olafun Johannesson, head of Progressive Party, formed centre-left
coalition, ending six-week political crisis.

SEPTEMBER

3 38 killed when Air Rhodesia Viscount crashed in northern Rhodesia; the following
day, 10 of the 18 survivors murdered by guerrillas.

5 Camp David summit meeting between President Carter, President Sadat and Mr
Begin began; 17th, ended with agreements on framework of peace treaty between
Egypt and Israel, to be signed within three months, and on military dis-
engagement.

7 In Sri Lanka, new constitution promulgated, enlarging powers of President.

1,291 died in floods in northern India over the past few months.

8 In Iran, 95 killed in anti-Shah demonstrations (see also 11 and 26 Dec.).

10 In Rhodesia, martial law introduced in some areas.

13 President Réné of Seychelles in London on three-day visit.

14 In Portugal, government of Alfredo Nobre da Costa voted out of office; 25 Oct.,
Carlos Alberto da Mota Pinto, became new PM.

In Philippines, 43 died in plane crash.

In USSR, supersonic TU 144 flights suspended.

15 UN Law of the Sea conference ended four-week session with plans for signing
agreement in 1980.

Paris-Bonn accord on new European Monetary System (see also 4 Dec.).

16 In Pakistan, Gen. Zia ul Haq became President.

In Iran, 21,000 killed in earthquake.

17 Pegasus 1, US research satellite launched in 1965, broke up over northern Angola.

19 Saudi Arabia and Jordan rejected Camp David agreements.

Cardinal Stefan Wyszynski, Polish primate, in West Germany.

In UK, report of Bingham Inquiry into sanctions-breaking supply of oil to Rhodesia
published.

20 In South Africa, PM Vorster resigned; 29th, elected country's fourth President;
PM Botha appointed new PM.

21 Greece and China signed cultural agreement, the first since the Cultural Revolution.

22 British PM, James Callaghan, met President Kaunda of Zambia in Nigeria.

25 150 killed in the worst air disaster in America's aviation history at San Diego airport
California; when a Boeing 727 collided with a two-seater Cessna.

26 World conference opened in Soviet Central Asia to consider charter or protection
of plants and animals at risk.

27 France decided to join UN disarmament committee after a 17-year absence.

28 Pope John Paul I died; 16 Oct., Cardinal Wojtyla, Archbishop of Cracow, elected
as John Paul II, the first non-Italian Pope for nearly 500 years.

In Israel, Knesset voted in favour of Camp David accords.

29 500 died in floods in West Bengal, India.

30 Tuvalu Islands became independent.

OCTOBER

1 In Comoro Islands, referendum adopted new federal-style constitution.
3 In UK, Warwick Castle sold for £1.5 million to Madame Tussauds.
  In USA, Patricia Hearst's kidnappers William and Emily Harris gaoled for 10 years (see AR 1974, p. 554).
4 In Egypt, first government in 38 years pledged to peace rather than war with Israel formed.
5 In Sweden, Government of K. T. Fälldin resigned; 18th, Ola Ullsten, Liberal, formed new Government.
  British Council decided to reopen office in Peking closed since 1950.
6 President Kaunda reopened Zambia's border with Rhodesia.
10 Chinese Foreign Minister Huang Hua on four-day visit to London.
11 In Belgium, PM, Tindemans, resigned; 27th, Government of Paul Vanden Boeynants, Social Christian, sworn in.
  In Panama, Aristides Royo elected new President.
12 Egypt-Israel treaty negotiations opened in Washington by President Carter.
  Airlink between China and Hong Kong reopened after nearly 30 years.
  President Amin of Uganda escaped eleventh assassination attempt.
15 In N. Yemen, coup attempt foiled.
16 Five Western Foreign Ministers met with South African Government in Pretoria to discuss Namibia's future.
  Unesco accepted universal declaration of animal rights.
17 Angola and Zaïre signed cooperation agreement, to end tension between the two.
18 In USA, President Carter ordered production of warheads with neutron bomb capacity.
  In Spain, pilot blamed for Tenerife air disaster that killed nearly 600 last year (see AR 1977, p. 520).
19 300 died in Rhodesian raid near Zambian capital.
  First meeting for 700 years of the Co-Princes of Andorra, President of France and Spanish Bishop of Urgell.
20 France and China signed agreement on scientific and technical exchanges.
23 Prince of Wales arrived in Yugoslavia, his first visit to a communist country.
24 British Council of Churches declared recent controversial grant by World Council of Churches to Patriotic Front of Zimbabwe raised no new issue of principle.
26 Syria and Iraq signed charter on mutual cooperation ending ten years of feuding.
  In Egypt, communist plot to seize power reported smashed.
27 President Sadat and Premier Begin shared Nobel prize for peace.
  In the Philippines, typhoon Rita struck, leaving 150 dead and 50,000 homeless.
  In Rhodesia, PM Ian Smith announced that the transfer of majority rule set for 31 Dec. would be delayed for practical reasons.
29 In China, Mao Tsetung's *Little Red Book* under attack in *People's Daily*.
31 In Canada, PM, Pierre Trudeau, offered at provincial premiers' meeting to transfer important powers from the federal government to the provinces.

NOVEMBER

1 Uganda occupied 701 square miles of Tanzanian territory.
2 In Mexico, 54 killed after pipeline blast.
  Two Soviet cosmonauts landed from Salyut 6 after breaking previous space endurance record by 44 days.
  Summit conference of Arab countries opposed to Camp David accord opened in Baghdad.
3 Caribbean island of Dominica became independent.
  Russia and Vietnam signed treaty of friendship and cooperation.
  Chinese Deputy PM, Wang Chen, in London.

 5 In Iran, anti-Shah riots culminated in worst rampage so far; the following day Shah
   appointed military government headed by Gen. Gholam Reza Azhari.
   In India, Mrs Gandhi won by-election in Chikmagalur for seat in Lok Sabha.
   In Austria, vote against nuclear energy in first referendum.
   Spain renounced 1878 extradition treaty with Britain.
   In India, 125 died in floods in Tamil Nadu and Kerala.
 7 In the Netherlands, Willem Aantjes, parliamentary leader of Christian Democrats,
   resigned over SS connexion.
 8 The General Synod of Church of England voted against ordination of women.
12 Former Indian PM, Mrs Gandhi, on week's visit to UK.
14 President Eanes of Portugal in Britain.
15 249 killed when Icelandic DC8 charter aircraft carrying Indonesian Muslim pilgrims
   returning from Mecca crashed in Sri Lanka.
   Agreement between UK and China signed on science and technology.
   Three-day state visit of Janos Kadar, First Secretary of Hungarian Socialist Workers
   Party, to Paris in the first such contact in 60 years between the two countries.
   China announced release of all 'important prisoners' from pre-communist Tibetan
   ruling group and appealed to all Tibetan exiles to return home.
16 West and East Germany signed agreement for building motorway through East
   German territory from West Berlin to Hamburg.
17 First sea link between China and Hong Kong since 1949 opened.
19 911 died in mass suicide by members of People's Temple sect in Guyana.
20 Ethiopia and USSR signed treaty of friendship and cooperation.
22 Italian PM, Sr Andreotti, in London.
23 Warsaw Pact countries ended two-day summit in Moscow calling for world treaty
   renouncing use of force in international relations.
   1,000 died in Sri Lanka when cyclone struck east coast.
24 President Giscard in London.
   In Bolivia, President Juan Pereda Asbun overthrown in military coup; Gen. David
   Padilla Arancibia, new leader.
   In Brazil, elections won by Arena, official party.
25 In New Zealand general election, PM, Robert Muldoon, returned to power with
   reduced majority.
27 In Japan, PM, Takeo Fukuda, resigned after defeat in party poll; 7 Dec., Masayoshi
   Ohira succeeded as PM.
   Amnesty International published report on human rights in China, revealing that
   political arrests and executions were frequent.
29 In Thailand, new constitution designed to restore democracy approved by National
   Assembly.
30 In UK, last edition of *The Times* appeared as management suspended its publication,
   also that of *Sunday Times* and *Times* supplements.
   In Rhodesia, Field Marshal Lord Carver resigned as Resident Commissioner-
   designate under the Anglo-American proposals.

                                  DECEMBER

 1 In El Salvador, guerrillas kidnapped two British bankers.
 3 Vietnam announced formation of a new 'Viet Cong' to fight Cambodian regime;
   350 Vietnamese refugees reported drowned over past ten days off Malaysian coast.
 4 Two-day EEC summit meeting to discuss EMS scheme; UK, Ireland and Italy
   indicated they would stay out; 12th, Italy decided to join; 15th, Ireland also.
   Elections under S. African aegis began in Namibia; boycotted by Swapo.
   In Venezuela, opposition candidate Luis Herrera Campius won presidential poll.
 5 Bulgaria and Egypt broke off diplomatic relations.
   Treaty of friendship signed between USSR and Afghanistan.

Nato Defence Ministers agreed on airborne warning system.

In South Africa, Erasmus commission report revealed misuse of public funds.

6 In Spain, constitutional referendum resulted in 87.79 per cent 'yes' vote; 27th, King Juan Carlos signed new constitution.

7 Canadian PM, Pierre Trudeau, in London.

In Nicaragua, state of siege lifted.

8 Norway and Sweden signed trade pact.

9 Four scientific probes from unmanned American Pioneer spacecraft landed on Venus.

11 In Iran, opponents of the Shah continued to demonstrate in record numbers; during riots in Isfahan, 40 killed and 60 wounded.

Rhodesia announced it had attacked guerrilla bases in Mozambique in order to destroy arms and ammunition.

12 In Rhodesia, guerrilla rocket raid destroyed main fuel storage depot.

13 In UK, former Liberal leader, Jeremy Thorpe, committed for trial at Old Bailey on charges of conspiracy and incitement to murder following magistrates' hearing at Minehead, Somerset.

In Zambia, sweeping victory for President Kaunda in presidential poll.

14 In China, more than 16,000 scientists reinstated.

UN General Assembly called for oil embargo against South Africa.

15 President Carter announced that USA was to establish diplomatic relations with People's Republic of China on 1 Jan. and to end those with Taiwan.

In Israel, Cabinet rejected Egyptian peace formula.

17 OPEC meeting in Abu Dhabi decided to raise oil prices by 14.5 per cent in four stages by end of 1979.

In Belgian elections, inconclusive results; Premier to continue as 'caretaker'.

18 International Commission of Jurists reported that in Equatorial Guinea 100,000 had fled to escape 'ruthless President'.

19 In India, Mrs Gandhi gaoled for one week and expelled from Parliament for breach of privilege and contempt of House.

20 Britain and Argentina announced pact for scientific research in the Falkland Islands.

Sri Lanka and China signed trade agreement.

Diplomatic barriers of 39 years between China and Hong Kong broken when Chinese Minister for Foreign Trade, Li Chiang, visited Hong Kong.

According to official figures, 12,039 killed in six-year Rhodesia war.

21 Broad terms for Greek entry to EEC agreed.

23 Chinese Communist Party announced enlargement of top leadership with aim of industrial expansion and modernization.

SALT talks ended without agreement.

25 Vietnamese troops began invasion of Cambodia in support of rebels opposed to Pol Pot regime; 400 killed in clashes.

26 In Turkey, 102 killed in three days of rioting.

In Iran, petrol rationing as oil production sunk very low following riots.

In South Korea, amnesty for thousands of political prisoners.

28 In Uganda, President Amin declared amnesty for all Ugandans who had fled country since 1971.

30 In USA, House of Representatives committee investigating killing of President Kennedy in 1963 concluded that he was fired at by a second gunman.

31 In UK, exceptionally heavy snow, gales and flooding disrupted much of the country.